For WKP
With many thanks for
many things over many
years

Signed by
editor
(Ronald Stroud)
Presentation
copy

150–

DTWD

SUPPLEMENTUM EPIGRAPHICUM GRAECUM

This volume has been produced under the auspices of the Union Académique Internationale.

SUPPLEMENTUM EPIGRAPHICUM GRAECUM

editors

H. W. PLEKET - R. S. STROUD

assistant-editors

W. PEETERS - S.B. ALESHIRE

advisory editors

J. BINGEN, P. HERRMANN
G. MIHAILOV, L. MORETTI

VOLUME XXVI
1976-1977

SIJTHOFF & NOORDHOFF 1979
Alphen aan den Rijn The Netherlands
Germantown, Maryland USA

ISBN 90 286 0468 5
ISBN 90 286 0739 0 pbk.

Printed in The Netherlands

PREFACE

With the appearance of the present volume Supplementum Epigraphicum Graecum resumes publication after an interval of eight years. The format is slightly altered, the language is now English, and there has been a change of editors but the basic purpose of SEG remains the same. The new editors have participated in the revival of this publication because we believe that an annual volume containing the complete texts of newly discovered Greek inscriptions and bibliography on previously known documents will continue to be useful for scholars. In our own research over the past eight years we have sorely missed the helpful volumes of SEG and many scholars throughout the world who share this lack have encouraged us in the view that a publication of this type is essential to the progress of Greek epigraphy. While preserving the basic format of volume XXV and its immediate predecessors we have tried to increase the value of SEG by attempting to provide full coverage of the entire Greek world and by expanding the indexes.

Concern over the demise of SEG was expressed publicly in 1972 after the former editor, A.G.Woodhead, and the publisher found it impossible to continue their existing agreement (G.Daux, Le sort du SEG, Akten VI Intern.Kongr. Gr. und Lat. Epigraphik München 1972 (Vestigia XVII (1973) 575 - 579)). Important progress on the way to reviving SEG was made in March 1975 when the Union Académique Internationale, mainly at the instigation of J.Bingen, G. Daux, and J.B.Ward Perkins, sponsored meetings in Rome to discuss plans for the future of this publication. Epigraphists from Belgium, Canada, England, France, Germany, Greece, Holland, Italy, Sweden, and the United States met under the chairmanship of T.Kraus, Vice President of the International Association of Classical Archaeology. Agreement was reached on the pressing need to resume the publication of SEG and to seek funds for this purpose from the Union Académique Internationale and other sources. A Commission scientifique, consisting of J.Bingen, chairman, P.Herrmann, L.Moretti, H.W.Pleket, and R.S.Stroud, was appointed and recommended that the format of any future SEG should remain essentially the same as in the past but that editorial comment on individual texts must be kept to a minimum. It was further agreed to open negotiations with the publisher, A.W.Sijthoff of Leiden, on the possibility of producing SEG in a less expensive manner, perhaps from camera-ready copy prepared on an electric typewriter. No final decision was reached at this time on the appointment of an editor but after discussing various possibilities, the participants in the Rome meetings agreed to consider a proposal from the Dutch Royal Academy and the University of Amsterdam which would be presented formally at a later date.

When negotiations with these two organizations failed to yield satisfactory results, H.W.Pleket approached the Commission scientifique in May 1977 with a proposal that the main editorial office of SEG be established at Leiden University. The Faculty of Letters of this university generously provided office space and funding for a full-time research assistant to help Pleket, as editor-in-chief, in the collection of material and the editing of texts. At the same time Pleket secured an agreement from the former publishers, A.W.Sijthoff of Leiden, that they would undertake to publish SEG from camera-ready typed copy without requiring a subsidy. At Pleket's request R.S.Stroud of the University of California at Berkeley agreed to assume responsibility for editing and preparing the typescript for inscriptions from Attica and the Peloponnesos. Pleket and his assistant were to be responsible for texts from the rest of the Greek world. Another important part of the proposed new organization of SEG was the creation of an editorial board of advisors whose main function would be to read preliminary drafts of the typescript covering certain parts of the Greek world in which they have special competence and to advise the editors.

This proposal was accepted by the Commission scientifique in June 1977 and the two editors then sought funding to support the operation of the two offices of SEG in Leiden and in Berkeley. In addition to the substantial contribution of Leiden University Pleket also received grants for the Leiden office from the Union Académique Internationale and the British Academy. Stroud was awarded funds for the Berkeley office by the American Council of Learned Societies, the American Philological Association, and the Department of Classics of the University of Cincinnati. The editors take this opportunity of expressing publicly their sincere gratitude to all these organizations for their generous assistance.

With the establishment of the two new offices the editors appointed as their assistants W.Peeters (Leiden) and Sara B. Aleshire (Berkeley). At the Seventh Congress of Greek and Latin Epigraphy in Constantza, September 1977, the board of advisory editors was established. The members are J.Bingen (Egypt, North Africa, the Levant), P.Herrmann (Asia Minor), G.Mihailov (Thrace and the region of the Black Sea), and L.Moretti (Italy and Sicily). At a meeting of the International Association of Greek and Latin Epigraphy in Constantza Pleket made a public announcement of the reorganization of SEG and in January 1978 a similar announcement was circulated to a large number of epigraphists and historians throughout the world (cf. now Epigraphica 40 (1978) 251-253).

As the editors began collecting material for SEG XXVI late in 1977 they had to decide what to include in this volume which was to be ca. 500 pages in length.Was it better to go back to 1969, the latest year partly covered in SEG XXV (published in 1971), and work forward, thus attempting to narrow slightly the gap left when the publication of SEG was halted? Or should we begin with current material in the hope that at some later date the texts published since 1969 could be incorporated into subsequent volumes? Because of the large number of inscriptions published in the period 1969 - 1977 and the danger that, if we started in 1969, we might for several volumes remain many years behind current discoveries, we decided to concentrate on the more recent finds. Volume XXVI, then, is devoted to those new texts and studies of previously known documents which were published in 1976. In the section covering Attica and the Peloponnesos it has also been possible to include most of the available material published in 1977. We have also printed some new texts from all regions published between 1969 and 1975 which have been the subject of significant studies appearing in 1976 or 1977. Occasionally if the 1976 volume of a periodical had not yet appeared we have included material from the volume which was to our knowledge the latest. In some cases the 1976 volume appeared after we had finished our 'dépouillement' of the preceding volume. In such cases our policy has been to include what we had already done and to add the material from 1976. Studies, which appeared in 1977, 1978 and in the beginning of 1979 and which pertained to material from 1976 have been utilized inasmuch as they came to our knowledge in the course of our regular reading-programm, i.e. without systematic investigation. In volume XXVII and its successors the editors will attempt to extend the coverage of current material onwards from 1976 and 1977 without a break. We plan to explore with the publisher the possibility of gradual incorporation into SEG of the large mass of material from the period 1969 - 1975, but the editors at the moment feel that this will be a very heavy task indeed and one which could interfere with our main responsibility of keeping up with developments after 1976.

In editing the present volume we have tried to keep the recommendations of the Commission scientifique clearly in mind. The organization of the lemmata and the presentation of the texts remain basically the same as in previous volumes. Use of the typewriter has not given us as much flexibility as previous editors enjoyed in rendering some abbreviations, numerals, koppa, etc., and broken letters, but we hope that our texts do not contain serious misrepresentations. Abbreviations of periodicals, academy publications, etc. are those used in Marouzeau, L'année philologique with a few additions (cf. our list of Abbreviations on p. XVIII). The geographical arrangement of the various regions of the Greek world is that of Inscriptiones Graecae as in previous volumes of SEG. Within these regions, however, we have followed an alphabetic, rather than a topographic, arrangement of ancient sites and finding-places of inscriptions. We trust that any minor inconvenience this arrangement might cause veteran epigraphists will be outweighed by the advantage that all users of SEG can more readily find the texts from a specific city or site without having to know all the details of its topography. Within the geographical arrangement we have presented the inscriptions in chronological order according to 4 categories: public documents (decrees, letters, laws, catalogues, honorary inscriptions); dedications; epitaphs; miscellaneous (graffiti, amphorae, vases vel sim.).

We have for the most part retained the rubrics of the Indexes of previous volumes of SEG except that we have expanded Nomina Sacra to include res sacrae and added sections on military and para-military matters (e.g. ephebes), important Greek words, and selected general topics. In the last category we have included month names; we have placed festivals, which were previously under Nomina Sacra, under Important Greek Words. Rather than multiply the categories in the Index we have placed most items in the Important Greek Words section. Since limitations of space have not permitted us to print a full Index verborum, omissions in this section will be inevitable, but we have tried to make a selection of words which in the alloted space will serve the widest range of users of SEG. We have the same aim in mind in introducing the new category of Selected Topics. We regret that in the present volume, for technical reasons, it has not been possible to include line numbers in the index, but we hope to solve this problem in subsequent volumes.

We have reduced editorial comment to a minimum and restricted it to the apparatus criticus where "(ed.)" clearly identifies our brief and infrequent interventions into the discussion of a particular text. On this point we here editorialize briefly in the hope that readers of SEG will in the future avoid the irresponsible use of such formulations as, "The restoration in line 10 of IG, II^2,43 (accepted by SEG) ..." or "Professor X's date for this text is followed by SEG." vel sim. We see as our prime purpose the recording of newly discovered texts and the reporting of significant bibliography on previously published documents. We are not primarily concerned to pass judgment on the soundness of the texts we publish or the validity of the interpretations we report. If we print dates in the lemmata and restorations in the texts which have been suggested by other scholars, that does not mean that we necessarily endorse them.

We are grateful to D.M.Lewis for providing us with a concordance of IG, I^2 and IG, I^3 and for permission to use the numbers of the latter in our lemmata of Attic public documents before 403 B.C. The editors wish to thank the many scholars who have sent us offprints of their publications and would like to encourage others to do so in the future. We are particularly eager to receive copies or even a notice of relevant articles in Festschriften, occasional publications, and less well-known local publications.

To the advisory editors we are indebted for their prompt and expert critical reading of the preliminary typescript and for much helpful advice. Ultimate responsibility for all remaining errors rests, of course, with Pleket and Stroud. In Berkeley we wish especially to thank Michael Sloan and Paula Perlman for invaluable assistance in the preparation of the section on Attica and the

Peloponnesos. In Leiden we thank Steven Moors, Jetty de Wal and Mrs C.S.Rikkers-Krantz who assisted us in the compiling and the typing of the Index.

We have been fortunate in finding as Assistant Editors two competent young scholars who have also cheerfully assumed the heavy task of typing a very difficult manuscript and performing many other unexciting duties. Without the contribution of W.Peeters and S.B.Aleshire the present volume would have been impossible and we are particularly grateful to them both.

H.W.Pleket, Leiden

R.S.Stroud, Berkeley

August 1979.

ABBREVIATIONS

Agora XV	= B.D.Meritt, J.S.Traill, The Athenian Agora vol. 15. The Athenian Councillors (Princeton 1974)
Agora XVII	= D.W.Bradeen, The Athenian Agora vol.17. The Funerary Monuments (Princeton 1974)
Agora XXI	= M.Lang, The Athenian Agora vol.21. Graffiti and Dipinti (Princeton 1976)
BE	= Bulletin Épigraphique
Belleten	= Belleten Turk Tarih Kurumu
Blinkenberg, Lindos II	= Lindos. Fouilles de l'Acropole 1902 - 1914. II. Inscriptions --- par Ch.Blinkenberg,I-II (Berlin - Copenhagen 1941)
Bradeen/McGregor Studies	= D.W.Bradeen, M.F.McGregor, Studies in Fifth-Century Attic Epigraphy (Norman 1973)
Buckler-Robinson, Sardis, VII	= Sardis. Publications of the American Society for the Excavation of Sardis, VII, Greek and Latin Inscriptions, 1, by W.H.Buckler and D. M.Robinson (Leiden 1932)
Cabanes, Épire	= P.Cabanes, L'Épire de la mort de Pyrrhos à la conquête romaine (272 - 167) (Annales litt. Univ. Besançon, 186; Paris 1976)
CIG	= Corpus Inscriptionum Graecarum
CIJ	= J. - B.Frey, Corpus Inscriptionum Iudaicarum, I - II
CIL	= Corpus Inscriptionum Latinarum
CIRB	= Corpus Inscriptionum Regni Bosporani
Clinton, Sacred Officials	= K.Clinton, The Sacred Officials of the Eleusinian Mysteries: Transactions of the American Philosophical Society 64.3 (1974)
Corinth 8.1	= B.D.Meritt, Corinth vol.8, part 1. Greek Inscriptions (Cambridge, Mass. 1931)
Corinth 8.3	= J.H.Kent, Corinth vol.8, part 3. The Inscriptions 1926 - 1950 (Princeton 1966)
DAA	= A.E.Raubitschek, Dedications from the Athenian Akropolis (Cambridge, Mass. 1949)
Davies, APF	= J.K.Davies, Athenian Propertied Families 600 - 300 B.C. (Oxford 1971)
EAC	= Études d'Archéologie Classique
EAH	= Τὸ Ἔργον τῆς Ἀρχαιολογικῆς Ἑταιρείας
Étienne-Knoepfler, HB	= R.Étienne - D.Knoepfler, Hyettos de Béotie

	et la chronologie des archontes fédéraux entre 250 et 171 avant J.-C. (BCH, Suppl.III; Paris, 1976)
F.Delphes	= Fouilles de Delphes
Follet, Athènes	= S.Follet, Athènes au IIe et au IIIe siècle (Paris 1976)
Ghiron - Bistagne, Acteurs	= Paulette Ghiron - Bistagne, Recherches sur les acteurs dans la Grèce antique (Paris 1976)
GIBM	= The Collection of Ancient Greek Inscriptions in the British Museum (Oxford 1874 - 1916)
Guarducci, EG	= M.Guarducci, Epigrafia Greca
Henry, Prescripts	= A.S.Henry, The Prescripts of Athenian Decrees; Mnemosyne Supplement 49 (1977)
I. Cret.	= Inscriptiones Creticae, ed. M.Guarducci
I. Délos	= Inscriptions de Délos
I. Didyma	= Didyma, II: Die Inschriften von A.Rehm (herausgegeben von R.Harder; Berlin 1958)
IG	= Inscriptiones Graecae
IGBR	= Inscriptiones Graecae in Bulgaria repertae, ed. G.Mihailov
IGLS or I. Syrie	= L.Jalabert - R.Mouterde, Inscriptions grecques et latines de la Syrie
IGR	= Inscriptiones Graecae ad res Romanas pertinentes
ILS	= H.Dessau, Inscriptiones Latinae Selectae (Berlin 1892 - 1916)
IOSPE	= V.Latyshev, Inscriptiones antiquae orae septentrionalis Pontis Euxini Graecae et Latinae
Inschr. v. Ol.	= Inschriften von Olympia, ed. W.Dittenberger - K.Purgold (1906)
Jeffery, LSAG	= L.H.Jeffery, The Local Scripts of Archaic Greece (Oxford 1961)
Kaibel, EG	= G.Kaibel, Epigrammata Graeca ex lapidibus collecta (Berlin 1878)
Knigge, Kerameikos 9	= U.Knigge, Kerameikos vol.9. Der Südhügel (Berlin 1976)
MAMA	= Monumenta Asiae Minoris Antiqua
Mette, UDA	= H.J.Mette, Urkunden Dramatischer Aufführungen in Griechenland: Texte und Kommentare 8 (Berlin 1977)
Meiggs-Lewis, GHI	= R.Meiggs - D.Lewis, A Selection of Greek Historical Inscriptions to the End of the Fifth Century B.C. (Oxford 1969)
Mélanges Collart	= Mélanges d'histoire et d'archéologie offerts à Paul Collart (Cahiers d'archéologie romande, 5; Lausanne and Paris 1976)

Mélanges Heurgon	=	L'Italie préromaine et la Rome républicaine. Mélanges offerts à Jacques Heurgon (Collection de l'École française de Rome, 27; Rome 1976)
Michel, Recueil	=	C.Michel, Recueil d'Inscriptions grecques (Paris - Brussels 1900)
MP	=	Muzei i pametnici na kulturata (Sofia)
OGIS	=	W.Dittenberger, Orientis Graeci Inscriptiones Selectae
Peek, GV	=	W.Peek, Griechische Vers-Inschriften, I (Berlin 1955)
Phoros	=	Phoros, Tribute to Benjamin Dean Meritt (Locust Valley, N.Y. 1974) ed. D.W.Bradeen, M.F.McGregor
Pritchett/Meritt, Chronology	=	W.K.Pritchett, B.D.Meritt, The Chronology of Hellenistic Athens (Cambridge,Mass., 1940)
Recueil Plassart	=	Recueil Plassart. Études sur l'antiquité grecque offertes à André Plassart par ses collègues de la Sorbonne (Paris 1976)
SB	=	Sammelbuch griechischer Urkunden aus Ägypten
SCIV	=	Studii şi Cercetări di Istorie Veche (Academia Republicii Populare Romîne: Institut de Arheologie)
SGDI	=	H.Collitz, Sammlung der griechischen Dialekt-Inschriften
Studia Pontica,III,1	=	J.G.C.Anderson - F.Cumont - H.Grégoire, Recueil d'Inscriptions grecques et latines du Pont et de l'Arménie, I (Brussels 1910)
Studies L.R.Palmer	=	Studies in Greek, Italic and Indo-European Linguistics offered to Leonard R.Palmer (Innsbruck 1976)
$Syll^3$	=	W.Dittenberger, Sylloge Inscriptionum Graecarum, third edition
TAM	=	Tituli Asiae Minoris
Tod, GHI	=	M.N.Tod, Greek Historical Inscriptions I^2 (Oxford 1946) and II^2 (Oxford 1948)

NOTE ON TRANSCRIPTIONS

[αβ]	=	letters restored by the editor as once having been inscribed but now lost
{αβ}	=	superfluous letters added in error by the inscriber of the text and excised by the editor
<αβ>	=	letters added by the editor which the inscriber of the text has either omitted or for which he has by error inscribed other letters
(αβ)	=	letters which complete words left in abbreviation in the text
[[αβ]] [[..]]	=	letters or spaces deliberately erased in antiquity
α̣β̣	=	letters of which sufficient traces remain to print them in the text but not enough to exclude other possible readings
[..5..]	=	lost or illegible letters equal to the number of dots for which no restoration is proposed
[-----]	=	lost or illegible letters of an uncertain number
v̲.	=	one uninscribed letter-space
vacat	=	the remainder of the line has been left uninscribed
ed.	=	the editors of SEG, not the editor of the inscription under discussion
ph.	=	photograph
dr.	=	drawing
|		denotes the start of a new line on the stone where we have not printed the text in the same configuration as on the stone
⇄		denotes the direction of each line in texts inscribed in boustrophedon or retrograde manner

ATTICA

1. ATHENS, HEKATOMPEDON INSCRIPTION, 485/4 B.C. IG, I², 4 (I³, 4). SEG X, 5; XXI, 2; XXIII, 2; XXV, 2. F. Preisshofen, AA (1977) 74-80, rejects the restored date of Philokrates' archonship (L. 26) in favor of a date in the 6th cent. B.C. He revives W. Dittenberger's view, HERMES 26 (1891) 472, that τὸ *h*εκατόμπ[εδ]ον (LL. 11, 18) denotes an area on the Acropolis, not a temple; ὁ νεός (LL. 9, 10) is the Old Athena Temple.

---

2. ATHENS, DECREE ON THE ELEUSINIAN MYSTERIES, ca. 460 B.C. IG, I², 6 (I³, 6). SEG X, 6; XV, 2; XVII, 2; XXI, 5. Clinton, Sacred Officials 10-13; new text of Face C, LL. 5-50. M.H. Jameson, AJA 81(1977) 249, questions Clinton's readings in L. 39, "the last visible stroke is oblique, not horizontal"; L. 40, "sigma does not agree with traces in space 2". Jameson reads [. . . . . .12. . . . . .]ο· *h*ιερ̣[. .4. .] in L. 6 and urges that L. 50 must be the last line of Face C because of the setting line on Face A.

---

3. ATHENS, DECREE: REGULATIONS FOR ERYTHRAI, 453/2 B.C.? IG, I², 10/13 (I³, 14/15). SEG X, 11; XII, 8; XXI, 8; ATL II, 54-57, D10. IGSK 1.4. A.S. Henry, JHS 97 (1977) 156-157, restores [οὔδε], not [οὔτε], L. 71, as in LL. 23-24. J.D. Smart, PHOENIX 31 (1977) 251, supports a date in 406 B.C.; discussion of πλῆθος, rather than δῆμος, LL. 21-22.

---

4. ATHENS, DECREE CONCERNING AIGINA, 457-445 B.C.? IG, I², 18 (I³, 38). SEG X, 8; XIV, 2; XXI, 7; XXIII, 4. H.B. Mattingly, HISTORIA 26 (1977) 370-373, restores L. 2 as [? αὐτ]οῖς αἲ γί[γνονται] and removes all connection with Aigina; speculation on possible connection with SEG X, 15.

---

5. ATHENS, DECREE: REGULATIONS FOR MILETOS, 450/49 B.C.? IG, I², 22 (I³, 21). SEG X, 14; XIV, 4; XIX, 4; XXI, 17; XXIII, 7. H.B. Mattingly, HISTORIA 25 (1976) 40-42, supports a date in 426/5 B.C. J.D. Smart, PHOENIX 31 (1977) 250-251, restores [Καλλίας ἔρχε], 406/5 B.C., in L. 3 and interprets the references to Euthynos (LL. 63, 88) as pertinent to earlier regulations for Miletos. A.S. Henry, JHS 97 (1977) 156; restoration of LL. 71-72.

---

6. ATHENS, DECREE ON COINAGE, WEIGHTS AND MEASURES, date? IG, I³, 32. SEG X, 25; XII, 12; XV, 4; XVIII, 3; XXI, 18;

XXII, 5; XXIII, 8; XXIV, 2. E. Ruschenbusch, ZPE 26 (1977) 211-215 argues for a terminus post quem of 438 B.C. on the basis of 5 districts in the tribute-quota lists. H.B. Mattingly, KLIO 59 (1977) 83-100, calculates that 10 lines on the Aphytis fragment = 10 lines + 20 letters on the Kos fragment. He offers an outline of the Kos text underlining words confirmed or supplied from the Aphytis fragment and elsewhere. He connects this decree with SEG X, 87 (cf. infra no. 13).

stoich. 41

[ἔδοχσεν τε̃ι βολε̃ι καὶ τõι δέμοι· . . . . .8. . . ἐπρυτάν]-
[ευε, . . .7. . . . ἐγραμμάτευε, . . .7. . . . ἐπεστάτε, Κλέαρ]-
[χος εἶπε· - - - - - - - - - - - - -34 - - - - - - - - - - - -]
[- -]
[- -]
[- ολε]
[- - - - - - - - - 30 - - - - - - - - -]αι τὰ γ[. . . 6 . . .]
[. . . .7. . . hοι ἄρχοντες hοι ἐν τε̃σι π]όλεσι ε̃ ἀρ[. . .5. .]
[- - - - - - - - - -23- - - - - - - ? hοι] δὲ hελλενοταμ[ίαι]
[- - - - - - - - - -23- - - - - - -ἀ]ναγραφόντον· ἐὰ[ν δ]-
[ἐ - - - - - - - - 20- - - - -τõν π]όλεόν τινος ἐσα[γ. .]
[- - - - - - - - - -22- - - - - -ἐς τ]ε̃ν ἐλιαίαν τε̃ν τõ[ν θ]-
[εσμοθετõν. . . . . . .13. . . . . .hο]ι δὲ θεσμοθέ[τ]αι πε[. .]
[. . . .8. . . .ντον. . . . . .12. . . . . .]ασι hέκαστον· ἐὰν δὲ [τ]-
[ίς πο πλὲν τõν ἀρχόντον ἐν τ]ε̃σι πόλεσι μὲ ποιε̃ι κα[τ]-
[ὰ τὰ ἐφσεφισμένα ε̃ τõν πολι]τõν ε̃ τõν χσένον, [ἄτ]ιμ[ος]
[ἔστο, καὶ τὰ χρέματα αὐτõ δε]μόσια [ἔσ]το καὶ τε̃ς θεõ τ[ὸ]
[ἐπιδέκατον· καὶ εἰ μέ ἐισι] ἄρχοντες Ἀθεναίον, ἐ[πι]-
[τελεσάντον hόσα ἐν τõι φσε]φίσματι hοι ἄρχοντε[ς h]-
[οι hεκάστες τε̃ς πόλεος· καὶ] ἐὰμ μὲ ποιõσι κατὰ τ[ὰ ἐφ]-
[σεφισμένα, ἔστο κατὰ τõν ἀρχ]όντον τούτον περὶ [ἀτι]-
[μίας δίοχσις Ἀθένεσι· ἐν δὲ τõ]ι ἀργυροκοπ[ίοι τὸ ἀρ]-
[γύριον. . . . . . . .16. . . . . . . .μὲ ἔλ]αττο[ν ε̃ hέμισυ καὶ]
[ἀποδõναι - - - - - - - - - -33- - - - - - - - - - - - - - -]

For the connection between this decree and IG, I^2, 84 postulated by H.B. Mattingly, AJPh 95 (1974) 280-285, infra no. 20. J.M. Balcer, HISTORIA 25 (1976) 273, note 32, follows this text of LL. 19-20 in discussing Athenian archontes in the cities.

---

7. ATHENS, DECREE OF KLEINIAS ON TRIBUTE, date? IG, I^2, 66 (I^3, 34). SEG X, 31; XII, 13; XV, 5; XIX, 8; XXI, 21; XXIII, 9. H.B. Mattingly, Mn 30 (1977) 66-69, urges that περυσινός, L. 73, would be an isolated usage as early as 448 B.C. and that the

decree belongs in the 420s.

---

8. ATHENS, DECREE: ALLIANCES WITH EGESTA AND HALIKYAI, date? IG I^2, 19/20 (I^3, 11/12). SEG X, 7; XII, 6; XIV, 1; XXI, 10; XXII, 3; XXV, 3. Bradeen/McGregor, Studies 71-81 (M.F. McGregor, PHOENIX 24 [1970] 179); text, commentary, (ph.); date of IG, I^2, 19: 458/7 B.C.; LL. 3-4 [*h*ά]β̣[ρ]ον ἔρχε, Ἀρ[. .4. .]|[. . . εἶπεν]; new readings in LL. 4-7, 9-11, 16-17. J.D. Smart, JHS 92 (1972) 128-146; texts of both decrees; date, 418/7 B.C. for IG, I^2, 19; L. 3 [Ἀντ]ι̣φο̣̃ν ἔρχε; new restoration of LL. 4-7; historical setting; date, 416/5 B.C. for IG, I^2, 20. T.E. Wick, JHS 95 (1975) 186-190, (ph.); date of IG, I^2, 19: 418/7 B.C. [Ἀντι]φο̃ν ἔρχε; HISTORIA 25 (1976) 288. H.B. Mattingly, ibid. 25 (1976) 42-44, dates IG, I^2, 19 after 429/8 B.C. on the basis of ἐς τὸν νομιζόμενον χρόνον, L. 15. B.D. Meritt, PAPhS 121.6 (1977) 437-447, (ph.); date of IG, I^2, 19: 458/7 B.C. [*h*]ά̣β̣ρον ἔρχε. R. Vattuone, EPIGRAPHICA 39 (1977) 43, follows Wick's dating.

---

9. ATHENS, DECREE CONCERNING KOLOPHON, ca. 446 B.C.? IG, I^2, 14/15 (I^3, 37). SEG X, 17; XXI, 22; XXIII, 10; XXV, 13. Bradeen/McGregor, Studies 94-99 (M.F. McGregor, PHOENIX 24 [1970] 181); new text, (ph.). H.B. Mattingly, EPIGRAPHICA 36 (1974) 44-45, dates the decree in 427 B.C. and restores ὀφε[λόντον Νοτιε̃ς καὶ Κολ|οφόνιο]ι καὶ Διοσιρῖται, LL. 25-26. A.S. Henry, JHS 97 (1977) 157, rejects οὔτ' in Bradeen/McGregor's restoration of L. 46 in favor of οὐδ'.

---

10. ATHENS, DECREE: REGULATIONS FOR CHALKIS, 446/5 B.C.? IG, I^2, 39 (I^3, 40). SEG X, 36; XXI, 24; XXII, 6; XXIII, 12. H.B. Mattingly, HISTORIA 25 (1976) 38-40, dates the decree in 424/3 B.C. D. Whitehead, ZPE 21 (1976) 251-259, discusses the xenoi in LL. 52-57. J.D. Smart, ZPE 24 (1977) 231-232; on the xenoi; date 424/3 B.C. S.R. Slings, ZPE 25 (1977) 277-279; syntax of LL. 52-57.

---

11. ATHENS, DECREE: TREATY WITH SAMOS, 439/8 B.C. IG, I^2, 50 (I^3, 48). SEG X, 39; XXI, 28. A.S. Henry, JHS 97 (1977) 156; restoration of negatives in LL. 15-19.

---

12. ATHENS, DECREES: TREATIES WITH LEONTINOI AND RHEGION, 433/2 B.C. IG, I^2, 51/52 (I^3, 53/54). SEG X, 48; XII, 20; XXI, 35; XXV, 22. D.M. Lewis, ZPE 22 (1976) 223-225; critique of E. Ruschenbusch, ZPE 19 (1975) 225-232; discrepancies in drafting

the texts and cutting the stones suggest that the original decrees were not contemporary; Rhegion, 445-443 B.C.; both reaffirmed in 433/2 B.C. T.E. Wick, HISTORIA 25 (1976) 288-304, argues that both alliances were made originally in 444/3 B.C., following the foundation of Thourioi, and renewed in 433/2 B.C.

---

13. ATHENS, DECREE CONCERNING COINAGE, ca. 440-420 B.C. IG, I^3, 90. SEG X, 87; XXI, 45; XXII, 10; XXV, 33. R.S. Stroud, CSCA 7 (1975) 283-290, (ph.), publishes a new text after study of the stone and argues that none of the published restorations are convincing enough to establish the length of line. H.B. Mattingly, KLIO 59 (1977) 83-100, reprints Stroud's text (correcting a misprint in L. 14) and argues that this decree was inscribed below and on the same stele as the famous decree on coinage, weights and measures, SEG X, 25 (supra no. 6).

stoich.

[- -].O[.]
[-]ATON
[- -]Σ
[-]ΣΤΑΘ̣
[- -]παν̣[τ]ός, *h*ος
[-]Ε[. . .]ΕΚΑΤ̣Ε[. .]ΑΙΤΟ
[-]Σ π[ρυ]τανεί[ας . .]ΝΑ
[- - - - - - - - - - - - - - - - - -] νόμι̣σμ[α] κ[α]ὶ .[. . .5. .]
[- - - - - - - - - - - - - - - - - -]τόδ̣ε τὸ φσ[έφ]ι̣σμ̣[α . . .]
[-] τõ χρυσίο πᾶ̣ν τὸ Λ[.]
[-]α̣ντίδος πρυτανείας
[- - - - - - - - - - - - - - - - - - -] ἐπὶ Λαυρείοι *h*όπος ἂν μ̣
[- - - - - - - - - - - - - - - - - -]Ο *h*όταν περ ἔ̃ι περὶ ΤΟΝΟ[.]
[- - - - - - - - - - - - - - - - -] Ἐπαίνετος, τοῖς δὲ ἐπ[. .]
[- - - - - - - - - - - - - - - - - -]Σ[.]Α̣ καὶ καταλλάττεν Α[.]
[- - - - - - - - - - - - - - - - - - - -]Λ̣ΕΙ τõι αὐτõι νομίσμ[α]
[τι - - - - - - - - - - - - - - - - - -̣] ἄλλο βόλονται νόμισ-
[μα - - - - - - - - - - - - - - - - -]Ε καὶ ἐάν τις ἄλλος [.]
[- -*h*]όπος ἂγ γίγνεται [.]
[-].Ι ἀπὸ τõν τραπ[εζ]-
[- -].Ο̣Ι τὸς δὲ ἄρχ[ον]-
[τας - - - - - - - - - - - - - - - - - - κε]ρ̣αμεῖα νũν [. . .]

---

14. ATHENS, DECREE: TREATY WITH KING PERDIKKAS, ca. 436 B.C.? IG, I^2, 71 (I^3, 89). SEG X, 86; XII, 16; XVI, 4; XIX, 11; XXI, 30; XXV, 18. J.W. Cole, PHOENIX 28 (1974) 55-72; date, 423/2 B.C., and discussion of the historical setting. R.J. Hoffman, CSCA 8 (1975) 89-104 (ph.), rejects Fr. b_1 (now lost) and argues against its placement next to Fr. e at the beginning of the text, as in IG, I^3, 89; anomalies in the stoichedon order make restorations of the exact line-length impossible; pp. 103-104,

notes 6, 16, 17, minor discrepancies between IG, I^3 text and Hoffman's readings. Idem, GRBS 16 (1975) 359-377; date, 431 B.C., and discussion of the historical setting. J.W. Cole, GRBS 18 (1977) 29-32, upholds 423/2 B.C. as the date, against Hoffman.

---

15. ATHENS, DECREES, ca. 435-430 B.C.? IG, I^2, 54 (I^3, 49); 77 (I^3, 131); 160 (I^3, 158); SEG X, 53; 60 (I^3, 58); XXI, 37 (I^3 130). M.B. Walbank, THE BULLETIN OF THE CANADIAN SOCIETY FOR ARCHAEOLOGY ABROAD 15 (1976) 16-21 (dr.), following H.T. Wade-Gery, ABSA 33 (1932/3) 101-136, assigns all of these inscriptions to the "Three-Chisel Mason", active in the 430's B.C.

---

16. ATHENS, FINANCIAL DECREES OF KALLIAS, date? IG, I^2, 91/92 (I^3, 52). SEG III, 17; X, 45; XII, 18; XIII, 5; XIV, 5; XXII, 7; XXIII, 15; XXIV, 3; XXV, 21. W.K. Pritchett, BCH 101 (1977) 9-10, note 5, reports the reading of L. 3 of IG, I^2, 92 from the stone as: [. . . . . .10. . . . . .]ινα καὶ τὰς Νί[κας· . . .5. .]ε[ι] δ̣ὲ καὶ τὰ Πρ̣[οπύλαια. . . .], and observes that Wade-Gery's restoration of the preamble (Meiggs-Lewis no. 58) is thus made difficult.

---

17. ATHENS, DECREES CONCERNING METHONE, 430-423 B.C. IG, I^2, 57 (I^3, 61). SEG X, 66; XXI, 40; XXV, 27. A.S. Henry, JHS 97 (1977) 155-156, restores LL. 19-20 χρε̃σθα[ι καὶ μ]|[εδὲ] ἔναι.

---

18. ATHENS, DECREE: TREATY WITH HALIEIS, 424/3 B.C. IG, I^2, 87 (I^3, 75). SEG X, 80; XIV, 8; XXI, 44. H.B. Mattingly, HISTORIA 26 (1977) 372, note 17, restores L. 16 Ἀθε[ναίος δὲ φυλάττεν ἐν Μεθάνοις φρορ]άν. Cf. Thucydides 5.18.7.

---

19. ATHENS, PROXENY DECREE, before 420 B.C. IG, I^2, 85 (I^3, 165). Ed. pr. of a new fragment once stored under the old museum on the Acropolis (EM 13258) W.K. Pritchett, CSCA 5 (1972) 159-164, no. 1 (ph.), who re-edits the whole. H.B. Mattingly, HISTORIA 25 (1976) 43, restores [δρ]|αχ[μ]αι̃ς ἱ[εραι̃ς] in LL. 5-6. B.D. Meritt, ZPE 25 (1977) 289-295; new readings from squeezes and photographs; new restorations (LL. 9, 13-14 by D.M. Lewis); date ca. 435 B.C. (?); commentary.

stoich. 32

[- - - - - - - - - - - - -τὸς δὲ πρυτάνες οἳ]
[ἂν] τυνχ[άνοσι πρυτανεύοντες . . . .8. . . .]
[πρ]οσαγ[αγε̃ν ἐς τὲν βολὲν καὶ τὸν δε̃μον ἒ]
[χ]ιλίας δ[ραχμὰς ὀφέλεν ἕκαστον τε̃ι Ἀθε]-
ναίαι κα[ὶ προσευθύνεσθαι μυρίαισι δρ]-

αχ[μ]αῖσι [ἕκαστον τõμ πρυτάνεον· τὸ δὲ φσ]-
έφισμα τ[όδε ἀναγρ]άφσα[ς ὁ γραμματεὺς τ]-
ε̃ς βολε̃ς [ἐν στέλε]ι λιθίνε[ι καταθέτο ἐμ]
πόλει ὸς [ἐν καλλί]στοι καὶ ἐν̣ [τõι βολευτ]-
[ε]ρίοι ἐγ̣ [σανιδί]οι ἵναπερ τὰ ἄλλ[α φσεφί]-
[σμα]τα· ο[ἱ δὲ κολα]κρέται δόντον τὸ ἀ[ργύρ]-
[ιον ἐς τὲν στέλ]εν καὶ τὲν ἀναγραφέν [*vvv*]
[. . . .8. . . . εἶπ]ε· τὰ μὲν ἄλλα καθάπερ Ṭ[. . .]
[. . . τὲν δὲ προχ]σενίαν ε̃ναι καὶ τοĩ[ς παι]-
[σί· καλέσαι δὲ αὐ]τὸς καὶ τὸν ἀδελφὸ[ν. . .]
[. . . . . .11. . . . . καὶ] ἐπὶ χσένια ἐς τὸ π̣[ρυτα]-
[νε̃ον ἐς τὸν εἰρεμέ]ν̣ον χρόνο̣ν. *vacat*
vacat

---

20. ATHENS, DECREE ON THE HEPHAISTEIA, 421/0 B.C. IG, I^2, 84 (I^3, 82). SEG X, 13; XXV, 35. H.B. Mattingly, AJPh 95 (1974) 281-282, connects the fund for Hephaistos and Athena in L. 17 with that of the same two deities in no. 6. E.B. Harrison, AJA 81 (1977) 139-141, note 15; the finding places of the fragments of this decree match those of IG, I^2, 370/1 (I^3, 472); i.e. top pieces at St. Demetrios Katephoris, bottom fragments at Kapnikareia. W.E. Thompson, AJPh 98 (1977) 249-251, rejects Mattingly's theory of a protected fund of Athena and Hephaistos; he interprets ἐχσαιρ<ε̃>ν not as "set aside" but as "take out" monies for sacrifices, cf. IG, I^2, 379, LL. 3-5, 421/0 B.C.

---

21. ATHENS, DECREES HONORING PHANOSTHENES, ANTIOCHIDES AND OTHERS, ca. 420-414 B.C. IG, I^2, 122 (I^3, 182) + SEG X, 131; IG, I^2, 156 (I^3, 182) + SEG X, 79. SEG XXIII, 20. To the 4 previously published fragments M.B. Walbank, HESPERIA 45 (1976) 289-295 (ph.), adds a fifth unpublished piece (EM 2505) of unknown provenance and re-edits the whole text.

stoich. 46

Decree I
[Ἔδοχσεν τε̃ι βολε̃ι καὶ τõι δέμοι, - - - -]ον[- - - ἐπρυτάν-
ευε, - -]
[- - - -ἐγραμμάτευε, - - - - -ἐπεστ]άτε, [- - - - εἶπε·]
[- - - - - - - - - - - - - - - - -]ικα]- - - - - - - - - - - - - - -]
[- - - - - - - - - - - - - - - - -]ονι̣[- - - - - - - - - - - - -]
[- - - - - - - - - - - - - - - - -]να̣[- - - - - - - - - - - - -]

lacuna

Decree II
[- - - - -10- - - - - -]α[- - - - - - - - - -35- - - - - - - - -]
[- - - - -10- - - - γ]ρ[α]μμα[τε- - - - - -28- - - - - - - -]
[- - - -7- - -Ἀν]τιοχίδει καὶ̣ [Φανοσθένει - - - -16- - -]

[- - - 9 - - -]ις 'Αθεναίοις καὶ [- - - - - - -23- - - - -]
[- - -10 - - -]ορας καὶ τὰ ἄλλα hότ[- - - - - - 20 - - - -]
[- - - 9 - - -] τὸν δε͂μον τὸν 'Αθεναί[ον - - - 18- - - - -]
[- - - -13- - - -] καὶ νῦν αὐτὸς καὶ [- - - - -19- - - - -]
[hόπος ἂν ho δε͂μο]ς hος περὶ πολλõ ποιõ[ν φαίνεται τὸς ἐσάγ]-
[οντας κο]πέας [κα]ὶ χάριν ἀποδόσον τὸ λ[οιπόν· ἀζεμίος δὲ τό]-
[κο hεκ]ατοστõ τ[ὸς] κοπέας hὸς ἔγαγον ο[ἴκοθεν δόντον τοῖς]
[τρι]εροποιοῖς κ[αὶ] hοι τριεροποιοὶ ε[ὐθὺς παραλαβόντες]
[τιθ]έντον ἐς τὸ να[υ]πέγιον καὶ ἐὰν δέ[ονται ἄλλο τινὸς hοι]
[στ]ρατεγοὶ χρόσθο[ν φρ]άζοντες τε͂ι β[ολε͂ι καὶ hάμα ἀποδιδ]-
[όν]τες τὲν τεταγμέν[εν] τίμε[ν]· καὶ hο[ι ναυπεγοὶ λογιζόσθο]-
[ν το]ῖς τριεροποιο[ῖς τὰ τε]ταγμέν[α· ἐπειδὲ οὖν 'Αντιοχίδε]-
[ς καὶ] Φανοσθένες τὸ[ν δε͂μον τὸν 'Αθεναίον εὖ ποιε͂τον καὶ π]-
[ερὶ αὐ]τõ ho hελλενοτ[αμίας - - - - - - - - -24- - - - - - -]
[- - - 9 - - -]ς χρε͂σθαι ἐς τ[ὸν πόλεμον - - - -20- - - - -]
[- - 4 - - αὐτ]οῖν ἀγαγόντ[οιν - - - - - - - - -27- - - - - -]
[- - - 8 - - -]οραι, ἐπαιν[έσαι μὲν 'Αντιοχίδεν καὶ Φανοσθένε]-
[ν hότι ἐδι]ακονεσάτε[ν τὰ τεταγμένα· ἐὰν δέ τινος δεέσθον]
[παρὰ τõ δέμο] προσάγ[εν αὐτὸ τὸς πρυτάνες ἐς τὸν δε͂μο]ν [ἐς τ]-
[ὲν πρότεν ἐκ]κλεσία[ν· πρόσοδον δὲ ε͂ναι αὐτοῖν ἐς τὲ]ν βολ[ὲ]-
[ν ἐὰν δεέσθον ἄ]λλο [τινὸς πρότοιν μετὰ τὰ hιερά· τὸ] δ{ὲ}
φσέ[φ]-
[ισμα τόδε ἀναγράφσαι τὸν γραμματέα τε͂ς βολ]ε͂ς ἐν στ[έ]-
[λει λιθίνει καὶ θε͂ναι ἐν ἀκροπόλει· ἀπομισθõσα]ι δὲ τὸς [π]-
[ολετάς· ἀποδõναι δὲ τὸς κολακρέτας τὸ ἀργύριον, - - -7- - -]
[- - - - - - - - - - - - - -46- - - - - - - - - - - - - - - -]
τιεπαι[- - - - - - - - - - 40 - - - - - - - - - - - - - - - -]-
ι εὐεργέτας ἐν [στέλει· ε͂ναι δὲ αὐτοῖς hευρέσθαι hõν ἂν δέ]-
ονται παρὰ 'Αθεν[αίον· γράφσαι δὲ 'Ανδρίος(?) ἐν τε͂ι αὐτε͂ι
στέ]-
λει εὐεργέτας 'Αθ[εναίον ἐν ἀκροπόλει τὸν γραμματέα τε͂ς]
βολε͂ς ⁘

22. ATHENS, DECREE CONCERNING SAMOS, 412/1 B.C. IG, I^2, 101 (I^3, 96). SEG X, 113; XIV, 9. U. Kron, MDAI(A) Beiheft 5 (1976) 101, rejects the identification of the elderly male figure in the relief as Kekrops; the three figures are seated Athena, Athenian Demos, and a corresponding figure from Samos.

23. ATHENS, DECREE HONORING EUAGORAS OF SALAMIS, 411-407 B.C. IG, I^2, 113 (I^3, 113). SEG X, 127; XII, 38. D.M. Lewis, Sparta and Persia (Leiden 1977) 129-130, prefers a date late in 408/7 B.C. and a 42-letter stoichedon line, as opposed to the 43-letter line supported by M.J. Osborne, ABSA 67 (1972) 129-156; ZPE 9 (1972) 55-56; HERMES 102 (1974) 87-90. Lewis restores LL. 32-39:

stoich. 42
Κλεο[. .]

[. εἶπε· τὰ μὲν ἄλλα καθάπερ τε͂ι βολε͂]ι, ἐπειδὲ δέ ἐστ̣[ιν]
[. . . . . . .20. . . . . .Εὐαγόρα]ς̣ ℎο Σαλα[μ]ίνιο[ς. .]
[. . . . . . .24. . . . . ℎό τ]ι δ̣ύναται ἀγαθὸ[ν τ]-
[ὸν δε͂μον τὸν 'Αθεναίον καὶ βασι]λέα καὶ τὸς ἄλλ[ος χ]-
[συμμάχος . . . . .14. . . . . ℎόπος] ἂν πλεῖστοι φ[. . . .]
[. .5. . τõι δέμοι τõι 'Αθεναίον κ]αὶ βασιλεῖ κα[ὶ τοῖ]-
[ς ἄλλοις χσυμμάχοις . . .7. . . Τισ]σαφρένεν ℎο[. .5. .]

---

24. ATHENS, DECREE FOR PROXENOS, 411/0 B.C. IG, I^2, 146 (I^3, 181). SEG XII, 36. Henry, Prescripts 3, rejects M. Walbank's restoration of LL. 4-6, ABSA 69 (1974) 295-298, on the grounds that a prescript of the form: enactment formula + proposer is without a parallel. Henry suggests:

[ἔδ]ο̣χσεν τε͂ι βολε͂ι κα[ὶ τõι δέμοι· Πρ]-
[όχσ]ενον τὸν [Χαλ - - - ἀναγράφσαι]
[ἐστ]ε̣λει ἐν πό[λει - - -

---

25. ATHENS, DECREE: TREATY, date? IG, I^2, 53 (I^3, 67). SEG X, 46; XIII 9; XVI, 7. B. Virgilio, SCO 25 (1976) 177-182, restores the text as an agreement between Athens and another city regarding protection from piracy, ca. 445-430 B.c.; αὐτὸς = αὐτοὺς L. 8; critique of L. Braccesi, ARCH CLASS 25/26 (1973/74) 68-73, and A. Papantoniou, Acta Fifth Int. Congress Gr. and Lat. Epig. (Cambridge 1967) 43-45. L. Braccesi, SCO 26 (1977) 313, reaffirms his interpretation of the text as an agreement between Athens and Artas, king of the Messapians, ca. 445 B.C. Cf. J. and L. Robert, BE (1977) no. 134.

---

26. ATHENS, DECREE: TREATY WITH CARTHAGE, 406 B.C.? IG, I^2, 47 (I^3, 123). SEG X, 136; XIV, 10; XXI, 56. R. Vattuone, EPIGRAPHICA 39 (1977) 41-50, dates the decree in 408/7 B.C.

---

27. ATHENS, NAVAL LAW, ca. 406 B.C. IG, I^3, 236. SEG X, 142. E.W. Handley, BICS 23 (1976) 58, corrects the readings in LL. 8-9 to ℎό τι ἂν τυιμέσει and περὶ τõνυυναυπεγõν respectively. The uninscribed spaces were caused by natural flaws in the stone.

---

28. ATHENS, TRIBUTE-QUOTA LIST 2, 453/2 B.C. IG, I^2, 192 (I^3, 225). SEG X, 147. J. McK. Camp II, HESPERIA 43 (1974) 314-318, no. 1 (ph.); ed. pr. of a new fragment (10a) found in the Agora Excavations (I 7398) which joins Fr. 10 and contains parts of cols. VII (obverse face) and VIII (right lateral face). M.F. McGregor, ibid. 45 (1976) 280-282 (ph.), in setting the new fragment into the lapis primus, found that cols. I-IX of List 2

contained 18 names (not 17, as in ATL II); new text of cols VII-IX. For reasons of space we have had to print col. IX below cols. VII and VIII.

VII		VIII	
- - - -	- - - - -	- - - -	[.]ε[- - - -]
[.]𐅄I	- - - - -	[HHH]	Κεβ[ρένιοι]
ΔΔΓ	- - - - -	[H]	Σκάφ[σιοι]
ΔΓͰIIII	Ναρ[ισβαρε͂ς]	[ΔΓ]ͰIIII	Παισεν̣[οί]
ΓͰͰͰII	Θασσθ[αρε͂ς]	[H]𐅄	Κλαζομεν̣[ιοι]
[𐅄]	Ἴγρες	H	Φ[ο]κ̣α̣ιε͂ς
𐅄	Καύνιοι		παρὰ [.]ε[.]κο
[𐅄]	Πασσανδ[ε͂ς]	HH𐅄	Φ[ο]καιε͂ς
ΔΔΔͰͰͰII	Κρυε͂ς	[X]H[H]	Τορον[αῖοι]
H	Στρεφσαῖ[οι]	[H]	Μυρι[ναῖοι]
𐅄 Ḥ Ḥ Ḥ	Χ̣α̣λχεδ[όνιοι]	- - - -	.[- - - - -]
- - - -	- - - - -	- - - -	- - - - - -
ΔΓͰ[IIII]	- - - - -	- - - -	[Λεφσ]ιμάνιοι
ΓͰͰ̇<Ͱ>II	Ἀ[στυρενοί]	[ΔΔΔΔͰIIII]	[Κα]σολαβε͂ς
ΔΓͰIIII	Γρυν̣[ειε͂ς]	- - - -	[Σ]τόλιοι
ΔΓͰIIII	Πιτανα̣[ῖοι]	- - - -	Πολιχνῖται
H𐅄	Ἀστακεν[οί]	- - - -	Σίγγιοι
HH	Σπαρτόλιο[ι]	[H]	Σαναῖοι

IX	
[HHH]	*h*αιραῖοι
[𐅄]	Νεοπολῖται
[HH]	Ὀλύνθιοι
[H]	[Μ]εκυβερναῖοι
- - - -	[Σε]ρμυλιε͂ς
Ḥ[𐅄]	[Γαλέ]φσιοι
𐅄	[Δικαιο̣]πολῖται
- - - -	[Κυζζικ]ε̣νοί
- - - -	[. . .6. . .]ες
- - - -	- - - - - -
- - - -	- - - - - -
- - - -	- - - - - -
- - - -	- - - - - -
- - - -	- - - - - -
- - - -	- - - - - -
- - - -	- - - - - -
- - - -	- - - - - -
- - - -	- - - - - -

VII.3 𐅄I Camp. || VII.4 Δ̣ΔΓ Camp. || VIII.2 [Ἀ]β[υδενοί] Camp. || VIII.8 παρὰ̣ [.]ε[.]κο̣ 𐅄 Camp. || VIII.9 Ḥ Ḥ 𐅄 Φ[ο]κ̣αιε͂ς Camp.

VII.7 Ἴγρες for Πίγρες (Πίκρες, Πίτρες) of Syangela, Camp, pp. 316-317. || IX.9 For rejection of the former reading

[Κλαζομ]ένιοι, Camp, p. 317. || VIII.8 Leukai? Camp, p. 318. [Λ]ε[υ]κο-? J. and L. Robert, BE (1977) no. 138.

---

29. ATHENS, TRIBUTE-QUOTA LIST 15, 440/39 B.C. IG, I^2, 205. SEG X, 160. B.D. Meritt, HESPERIA 41 (1972) 420-421 (ph.); ed. pr. of a new fragment (Fr. 181) from the Agora Excavations (I 7377) which joins Fr. 63 and 180 and contains parts of the heading and column II; new text of Island panel. M.F. McGregor, ibid. 45 (1976) 171-172 (ph.), confirms the physical joins; the new fragment necessitates the lowering of Fr. 157.

Νε[σιοτικ]ὸς [φόρος]

Η	[- - - - - - -]	Ḥ [- - -]	[- - - - - - -]
𐅅 Η	["Ανδριοι]	𐅅 Η[𐅄ΔΠͰΙΙΙΙ]	[Νάχσιοι]
ΔΔΔͰͰͰΙ[Ι]	['Αθε͂ναι Διάδες]	ΗΗ[- - -]	[- - - - - - -]
ΗΗΗ	[Χαλκιδε͂ς]	Χ𐅅Η[- - -]	[Πάριοι]
ΔΠͰΙΙΙΙ	[Γρυνχε͂ς]	[- - - -]	[- - - - - - -]
𐅄	['Ιᾶται]	[- - - -]	[- - - - - - -]
[Δ]ΠͰΙΙΙ[Ι]	[Σύριοι]	[- - - -]	[- - - - - - -]
[Η]ΗΗ	['Ερετριε͂ς]	[- - - -]	[- - - - - - -]
Π	['Ρεναιε͂ς]	[- - - -]	[- - - - - - -]
[ΔΔ]ΔͰ[ͰͰΙΙ]	[Διε͂ς ἀπὸ Κεναίο]	[ΧΧΧ]	[Αἰγινε͂ται]
[ΗΗΗ]	['Εφαιστιε͂ς]	[Η]	["Ιμβριοι]
[Η𐅄]	[Μυριναῖοι]	[*vacat*]	
[*vacat*]			

---

30. ATHENS, ACCOUNTS OF THE TREASURERS OF ATHENA, 410-406 B.C. IG, I^2, 304 A-B (I^3, 375, 377). SEG X, 234; XXI, 79; XXII, 49; XXIII, 36; XXIV, 43. New text after study of the stone by W.K. Pritchett, The Choiseul Marble: University of California Publications: Classical Studies 5 (Berkeley 1970) (ph.). We shall present an ap. cr. and summary of work on this text after the publication of IG, I^3. Cf. B.D. Meritt, PAPhS 115 (1971) 115-122; AD 25 (1970) A.5-11; Mélanges Daux (Paris 1974) 255-267; Mn 30 (1977) 230-235; W.K. Pritchett, BCH 101 (1977) 7-42; ANC SOC 8 (1977) 33-47; HISTORIA 26 (1977) 295-306; CSCA 9 (1977) 191-192; U. Kron, MDAI(A) Beiheft 5 (1976) 208-210; G. Daux, BCH 101 (1977) 470.

---

31. ATHENS, ACCOUNTS OF THE LOGISTAI, 426/5 - 423/2 B.C. IG, I^2, 324 (I^3, 369). SEG X, 227; XII, 44; XVI, 12; XXI, 75; XXII, 47; XXIII, 33; XXIV, 42; XXV, 46. W.K. Pritchett, HISTORIA 26 (1977) 303-306; the board of Hellenotamiai of 425/4 B.C., LL. 26-27, was continued in office for a second year and combined with the board of 424/3 B.C. to form a board of twenty designated as "old" and "new".

32. ATHENS, ATTIC STELAI: HERMOKOPIDAI, 414/3 B.C. IG, I^2, 325-334. SEG X, 237-242; XIII, 12-22; XV, 29; XVI, 13; XVIII, 7; XIX, 23-25; XXIII, 27; XXIV, 46; XXV, 48. C. Theodoridis, ZPE 23 (1976) 63-73, argues that Pollux consulted these stelai directly for Onomastikon 10 and was not using an intermediate literary source.

---

33. ATHENS, ACCOUNTS OF THE CHRYSELEPHANTINE STATUE OF ATHENA PARTHENOS, 447/6 - 439/8 B.C. IG, I^2, 354-362. SEG X, 257-263; XXI, 82; XXIII, 37; XXIV, 48-53. S. Eddy, AJA 81 (1977) 107-111, suggests that the gold for the statue was obtained by melting down gold and electrum coins paid as tribute.

---

34. ATHENS, ACCOUNTS FOR THE STATUES OF ATHENA AND HEPHAISTOS, 421/0 - 416/5 B.C. IG, I^2, 370/1 (I^3, 472). SEG X, 267; XVII, 8; XXII, 50; XXV, 49. E.B. Harrison, AJA 81 (1977) 139-146; the finding places of the fragments correspond to those of IG, I^2, 84 (I^3, 82; supra no. 20); commentary on the size and form of the anthemon and the two statues.

---

35. ATHENS, ACROPOLIS DEDICATION: PANATHENAIC FESTIVAL, 566 B.C. IG, I^2, 463 + 475. DAA no. 326; SEG XVII, 9. C. Gallavotti, RAL 31 (1976) 234-235, restores [ἀθλοθέ|ται] in LL. 1-2; Ἀντε[νορίδες] in L. 3; and [*h*οὶ τὸν ἀ]γõ[να etc. in L. 4. The dedication is made by 5 athlothetai.

---

36. ATHENS, ACROPOLIS DEDICATION: PANATHENAIC FESTIVAL, 562/558 B.C. IG, I^2, 465 + 476. DAA no. 327; SEG XVII, 9; XXIV, 59. C. Gallavotti, RAL 31 (1976) 235-237; new restorations. The 5 officials in LL. 3-5 are interpreted as the athlothetai, as in no. 35. LL. 1-5 are on Face A; L. 6 on Face B; LL. 7-8 on Face C.

boustrophedon

← τὸν δ[ρό]μον : ἐπ[οίεσαν :] *vacat*
→ τ[õι δέμοι : ἐπὶ τε̃]ι θεο-
← [ρίαι : Ἀλκμέον : Δεχσί]λ-
→ ε[ος : . . . . : . . . .]
← [. . : . . . . : Καλλί]ας ἐ-
→ γρα[μμάτευε]
→ [*h*ιερõν] *ḥ*οι τὸν ἀ[γ]õνα θέσαν γλ[α]-
← [υ]ϙ οπίδ[ι] ϙό[ρει]

---

37. ATHENS, ACROPOLIS DEDICATION: PANATHENAIC FESTIVAL, 558/554 B.C. IG, I^2, 392. DAA no. 328; SEG XVII, 9.

C. Gallavotti, RAL 31 (1976) 236, note 27, restores LL. 1-2 [τὸν δρόμον ἐποίεσαν ἐπὶ] τε͂ι θεο[ρίαι], as in no. 36.

---

38. ATHENS, ATHENIAN VICTORY OVER BOIOTIA AND CHALKIS, ca. 506 B.C. IG, I², 394 A + B. DAA 168, 173. SEG XV, 32; XXII, 54. J.H. Schreiner, SO 51 (1976) 25-35, dates B, the later copy of A ca. 454 B.C. (Diodoros 11.81).

---

39. ATHENS, SPEAR-BUTTS FROM THE ACROPOLIS, ca. 525-480 B.C. IG, I², 461. SEG X, 316. A. Johnston, AAA 9 (1976) 87-89 (dr.), interprets the ligatures on these four objects as δε(μόσιος) and cautiously suggests a possible connection with IG, I², 1, LL. 9-11.

---

40. ATHENS, DEDICATION: BRONZE BASE, 6th cent. B.C. IG, I², 410. SEG X, 309. P. Ghiron-Bistagne, Acteurs 115-116; text, ph., French translation; discussion of ὑποκρίνομαι, LL. 2-3.

---

41. ATHENS, ACROPOLIS DEDICATION, ca. 600 B.C. IG, I², 672. DAA no. 376. C. Gallavotti, RAL 31 (1976) 227-229 (ph.), reconstructs the text on the three fragments as follows:

→ - - - - - - - ϙ]όρ-
→ εν [δὲ] τάθ[ενᾶι ἀν]έϑ̣[εκ-
← [ε]ν αϝυτ̣[ὸς ἔργον δ]εκά̣[τεν]

---

42. ATHENS, GRAFFITO FROM THE ACROPOLIS, ca. 700 B.C. IG, I², 484. DAA no. 310. C. Gallavotti, RAL 31 (1976) 225-227 (dr.), suggests that this is a trial piece of someone learning to write and not an inscription meant for display. Discussion of readings.

---

43. ATHENS, TRIPOD DEDICATION FROM THE ACROPOLIS, ca. 500 B.C. IG, I², 673 + 850. DAA no. 323. D. Peppas-Delmouzou, MDAI(A) 86 (1971) 55-66 (ph., dr.), joins these two published fragments and adds a third unpublished piece (EM 13254, probably from the Acropolis) to form a rectangular tripod base. She suggests that the victorious poet was a foreigner; the contest was the first dithyrambic competition at the Panathenaia; the prize, a tripod; name of the victor at the beginning of L. 4. J. and L. Robert, BE (1972) no. 104; [προ͂]τον L. 1 indicates the poet's first victory at Athens, not the first competition. W. Peek, ZPE 13 (1974) 199-200, restores κατὰ φῦ[λα | ἀνδ]ρο͂ν and suggests that the name, patronymic, and ethnic were inscribed on another block; date ca. 480 B.C.; L. 2 [οἰκεί]ες σοφ[ίες]. C. Gallavotti, QUCC 20 (1975) 165-172, restores *h*ο [μέγισ]τον L. 1; [αἰνε]τ̣ε͂ς L. 2;

[μνεσ]άμενο[ς] L. 3; and interprets the monument as a dedication by Simonides to celebrate his victory in the Panathenaia of 477/6 B.C. P. Amandry, BCH 100 (1976) 15-18; illustrations of the type of tripod base.

> [Νικε̃]σας hó[δε πρõ]τον 'Αθένε̄σ[ιν χο]ρõι ἀνδρõ[ν]
> [hιμερ]τε̃ς σοφ[ίε̃ς] τόνδ' ἀνέθε̄[κ]εν hόρον
> [εὐχσ]άμενο[ς· π]λείστοις δὲ [χ]οροῖς ἔχσο̄ κατὰ φῦ[λα]
> [. . . .]ρõν νι[κε̃]σαι φε̄σὶ π[ερ]ὶ τρίποδος.

---

44. ATHENS, CHOREGIC DEDICATION, ca. 433/20 B.C. IG, I^2, 771. SEG X, 323; XXIV, 66. P. Amandry, BCH 101 (1977) 183-185 (ph.); detailed physical description of the base; rejects B.D. Meritt's restoration (SEG XXIV, 66) on the grounds: (1) that in 5th cent. B.C. dedications the text is not arranged symmetrically with regard to the vertical axis of the base, but the lines begin in the same vertical plane at the left; (2) no other choregic monument at Athens of 5th/4th cent. B.C. contains a genitive absolute. Amandry suggests that the victory may have been in the Thargelia, and he restores:

> [- name -]ος Δοροθέο 'Αλαιε[ὺς ἐχορέγε]
> [- tribe -ίδι] Παντακλε̃ς ἐδίδα[σκε]

2. [Κεκροπίδι] or [Αἰγεΐδι].

---

45. ATHENS, TRIPOD DEDICATION OF KEDEIDES, ca. 430-403 B.C. IG, I^2, 770. P. Amandry, BCH 100 (1976) 19-22 (ph., dr.); detailed description of the base and cuttings for the tripod.

---

46. ATHENS, DEDICATION TO DEMETER, ca. 450 B.C. SEG X, 321. G. Daux, ZAnt 26 (1976) 45-47, supports the interpretation of P. Maas, HESPERIA 15 (1946) 72, of στεφανώ, L. 3, as the title of one of the priestesses of Demeter and Kore, against Clinton, Sacred Officials 69.

---

47. ATHENS, DEDICATION TO ATHENA, 6th cent. B.C. National Museum, Inv. no. 16352. Bronze statuette of Athena, from the antiquities market. Ed. pr. M.L. Lazzarini, MAL 19.2 (1976) 182 no. 8b.

> [- - -] ἀνέθεκε
> τἀθεναίαι

---

48. MT. HYMETTOS, DEDICATION, 7th cent. B.C.? SEG XIII, 37. M.K. Langdon, HESPERIA, Suppl. 16 (1976) 41, no. 173 (ph.), suggests *h*έρ[οος - - -].

---

49. SOUNION, DEDICATION, ca. 550-540 B.C. IG, I^2, 830. SEG XVI, 18; XXII, 18. M.L. Lazzarini, MAL 19.2 (1976) 155, 308, no. 908 (dr.), rejects the restoration Διὶ 'Α[ρ]χ[εγέτει] in b. L. 1 (A. Papagianopoulos-Palaios, ΠΟΛΕΜΩΝ 7 [1958/62] 54) on the grounds that the epithet is not attested for Zeus. The text should be left as α[.]χ[- - -].

---

50. TRACHONES, DEDICATION TO HERAKLES, ca. 500 B.C. SEG X, 329. M.L. Lazzarini, MAL 19.2 (1976) 113-114, 183, no. 19, following Wilamowitz, reads L. 3 as [Θε]όχαρις, rejecting Peek's [έ]γὸ Χάρις (without discussing the gamma).

---

51. MARATHON, DEDICATORY EPIGRAM, 5th cent. B.C. Ed. pr. S. Marinatos, PAAH (1972) 6 (ph.); discussion of the position of the Herakleion. P.G. Themelis, AD 29 (1974) [1977] A.236, note 27 (ph.), corrects a misprint in L. 2 and suggests that τὸμ Πυλίοις may refer to Herakles' wounding of Hades in Elean Pylos, Homer, Il. 5.395-397; discussion of topography of the Herakleion.

*h*εραχλεῖ τόδ' ἄγαλμα τελεσ[- - -]
τὸμ Πυλίοις ἀνέθεκε *h*εραχ[- - -]

---

52. ATHENS, BOUNDARY STONE, 5th cent. B.C. White marble pillar, found at 1 Bourbache Street and 19 Syngrou Boulevard. Ed. pr. O. Alexandris, AD 27 (1972) [1976] B.43 (ph.). The stone was not found in situ, and the author does not suggest an identification for the sanctuary.

*h*όρος | *h*ιερõ

---

53. AGRILEZA, RUPESTRAL INSCRIPTION, 6th cent. B.C. In the Laureion mining district. Cut into the bedrock near nos. 137, 227, 266. Ed. pr. L.V. Watrous, HESPERIA 46 (1977) 173, no. 4 (dr.).

retrograde
'Αντιδίκε

---

54. ATHENS, GRAVESTONE OF KERAMO, 625-600 B.C. IG, I^2, 997. SEG XXI, 137. C. Gallavotti, RAL 31 (1976) 230-233 (dr.).

ἐνιάλου θυγατρ[ὸς Σπουδίδ]ο
Κεραμõς στέλε

"È la stele di Keramò, la giovinetta figlia di Spoudides."

---

55. ATHENS, GRAVE EPIGRAM, ca. 550 B.C. SEG XXII, 68. R. Merkelbach, ZPE 7 (1971) 183-184; W. Peek, ibid. 23 (1976) 75-76, who offers a complete restoration: "'exercise métrique' (um mit L. Robert zu sprechen)".

[᾿Αλκμαίονος ἰδὸν κυδρõ π]οτ᾿ ᾿Ολυμπιονίκο
σε̃[μα κατοίκτιρον τόνδ᾿ ἀγαθὸν φθίμενον].
[*h*υιὸς σύγκειται δὲ Φιλο]κλε̃ς, *h*õ τόδε μέτερ
[μνε̃μα κατέστεσεν Κοισύρα μυρομένε]·
[χσὺν δ᾿ αὐτε̃ι καὶ ἐγὸν ὀλο]φύρομαι, *h*όνεκ᾿ ἄ*h*ο|[ρος]
[εἰς ᾿Αίδεν κατέβε πένθεα πα̃σι λιπόν].

1. ᾿Ολυμπιόνικος ἐ[τύχθε] Merkelbach.|| 3. [?Περι]κλε̃ς Merkelbach.

---

56. ATTICA?, ARCHAIC GRAVESTONE, ca. 535-525 B.C. BOSTON: MUSEUM OF FINE ARTS. Three fragments of gray marble acquired by the Museum in 1940, of which one is now lost. They belong to the base of a monument consisting of a volute capital surmounted by a sphinx (in Boston) and a stele representing the legs of a young warrior (in the Metropolitan Museum in New York); G.M.A. Richter, The Archaic Gravestones of Attica (London 1961) nos. 38; 45. Ed. pr. C.W. Clairmont, AA(1974) 223-232, no. 2 (ph.), who does not commit himself on the final placement of Fr. B and C.

A. Σπου̃δ[ις
πιστ[ὸς
ε̃μα ([σ]|ε̃μα or [μν]|ε̃μα)
νυ̣ε̣

B. ἐπ]έροσε φίλογ [*h*υιὸν
γ]ὰρ σόφρον ἔ[φυ or ἔφυς
h]οι *h*ότε ἀπό[λετο

C.]õ *h*ὸν ἐ[
]ΟΡΛΟΙΣΑ
ἀ]ριστε[ύοντ- or -ύον

W. Peek, ZPE 23 (1976) 76-77, no. 2 (dr.), restores the whole, e.g.

Σπουδ[όκρατες Κρατ]έρο, σ̣᾿ ἐφίλογ [τρόπ]ο *h*όνε[κα πάντες]·
πιστ[ὸς ἔε̄σθα σὺ γ]ὰρ, σόφρο̄ν, ἐ[ν *h*]ό<π>λοις ἀ[δάμαστος].
ε̃ μά[λ᾿ ὀδυρόμεν]οι, *h*ότε ἀπõ[ιχεο, ἄ]ριστε, [πρὶν *h*õρας],
νυ̃γ [θάψαν σε φίλοι καὶ μνε̃μα τόδ᾿ ἐστε̃σαντο].

2. ΟΡΛΟΙΣ lapis.

---

57. ATHENS, BILINGUAL GRAVESTONE: GREEK/KARIAN, ca. 520 B.C. SEG XIII, 36; XV, 76; XVI, 29; XXI, 166; XXII, 76. O. Masson, KADMOS 16 (1977) 92-94 (ph.), discusses the value of "koppa" in L. 3; new readings from a squeeze: the hasta following the final Y of L. 1 is vertical and possibly joined by a slanting stroke at the right; L. 3, 6th letter is A.

---

58. ATHENS, GRAVE EPIGRAM, ca. 520 B.C. SEG XXII, 77. W. Peek, ZPE 23 (1976) 75-76, no. 1 (dr.), adds new readings to his earlier text (SEG XXII, 77); Φίλονο]ς [παῖδ]ες ἔθεκαν, L. 2.

---

59. ATHENS, OSTRAKA, 5th cent. B.C. Graffiti on lamp fragments found in the Kerameikos. Ed. pr. I. Scheibler, Kerameikos 11.149-150; 153-154 (dr.).

1. Κίμο[ν] Μιλτιάδο
2a. Μεγακλε͂ς
2b. Μεγακλέες *h*ιπποκράτω
2c. [Μεγ]ακλεῖ

3. Με[γακλε͂ς]
[Θε]μιθοκλε͂ς : Νεοκλέ[ος]
ostracism of 487/6 B.C.

Graffito on a sherd from the Pompeion in the Kerameikos. Ed. pr. W. Hoepfler, Kerameikos 10.210, no. K 100 (ph.); by the same hand as the ostrakon for Damon in MDAI(A) 40 (1915) 20, no. 50.

4. Δάμον | Δαμονί|δο

---

60. ATHENS, DIPYLON JUG, ca. 725 B.C. IG, I², 919. SEG III, 51; X, 399; XII, 67; XXII, 83; XXIV, 71. G. Annibaldis, O. Vox, GLOTTA 54 (1976) 223-228, read the last 12 letters as τõτο δέκγυ μιν "...this (vase) shows him". C. Gallavotti, RAL 31 (1976) 207-219 (ph.), reads τῶ τόδε κᾶ(μ)μιν "for him is this (vase) and for us".

---

61. MT. HYMETTOS, VASE INSCRIPTIONS, 7th/6th cent. B.C. Sanctuary of Zeus. M.K. Langdon, HESPERIA, Suppl. 16 (1976), publishes 172 graffiti on Attic sherds; dedications to Zeus (Semios), abecedaria, ὁ δεῖνα ἔγραψε, names, etc. "The graffiti and the beginning of writing in Attica." Drawings and photographs.

---

62. ATHENS, KADOS INSCRIPTION, 520-480 B.C. Graffito on an Attic kados found in the Kerameikos. Ed. pr. U. Knigge, Kerameikos 9.192, no. ES 35 (ph., dr.).

κάδος εἰμὶ καλός

---

63. ATHENS, VASE INSCRIPTION, late 6th cent. B.C. SEG XVI, 38. M. Lang, Agora 21.12, no. C5 (dr.). O. Vox, ZPE 26 (1977) 118, reads: τίτας Ὀλυ<μ>πιόδ[ο]ρος καταπύγον. The first word has an obscene connotation, and Olympiodoros is identified with PA 11385, 11389.

---

64. ATHENS, GRAFFITO, ca. 475-450 B.C. On a kothon found in the Kerameikos. Ed. pr. U. Knigge, Kerameikos 9.128, no. 162.4 (ph., dr.).

Χσ[υ]μμάχ[ο] εἰμί

---

65. ATHENS, GRAFFITO, ca. 470 B.C. On an amphora found in the Kerameikos. Ed. pr. U. Knigge, Kerameikos 9.121, no. 132 (ph., dr.).

Βατίων | καλός τωι δοκεῖ | κ

---

66. ATHENS, VASE INSCRIPTION, ca. 430 B.C. Graffito on a black-glazed cup found in the Kerameikos. Ed. pr. U. Knigge, Kerameikos 9.192, no. ES 33 (ph., dr.).

λέπτινα ἠμί

For Λεπτίνης as a proper name, Knigge cites AD 20 (1965) B.108; for λέπτινα as a noun in the nominative, she compares λεπτός LSJ[9] s.v. III.3.

---

67. ATHENS, GRAFFITO, ca. 425-400 B.C. Agora 21.B9. J. and L. Robert, BE (1977) no. 122, citing the letter published by A. Wilhelm, JOAI 7 (1904) 100, Μνησίεργος ἐπέστελε τοῖς οἴκοι χαίρεν καὶ ὑγιαίνεν etc., interpret the Agora text as the opening of a letter ("Ἐπιστέλλειν n'est pas ἀποστέλλειν"); L. 5 begins the text of the (short?) letter, and the rest is lost.

---

68. ATHENS, GRAFFITO, 5th cent. B.C. Black-glazed cup found at 4-6 Kokkines Street. Ed. pr. O. Alexandris, AD 28 (1973) [1977] B.32 (ph.).

Λάκων : Θεστίο

---

69. ATHENS, DEDICATION. IG, I[2], 730. Vase fragment from the Acropolis. M.L. Lazzarini, MAL 19.2 (1976) 87, note 122, regards the text as suspect because of the peculiar form of punctuation

and the omission of two letters.

---

70. ATHENS, DECREE AND CATALOGUE OF THASIANS, 402 B.C. IG, II², 33. SEG XIV, 34; XV, 87. G. Daux, BCH 101 (1977) 343-344, no. 4, after examining the stone, reads in col. I, L. 18 ΒΟ..ΑΔΟΣ, "et je n'ai rien à proposer."

---

71. ATHENS, DECREE, 400/399 B.C. IG, II², 11. A.S. Henry, *Prescripts* 11, restores LL. 1-5:

. . . μο - - - - - - - - - - - - - - - - - - -
[Ἐ]πὶ Λάχη[τος ἄρχοντος, nomen, patronymic]
.ο Ἁλαιεὺ[ς ἐγραμμάτευε].
[ἔ]δοξεν [τῆι βουλῆι καὶ τῶι δήμωι· - - - ἐπρυτάνευε - - -]
.τιμ -

---

72. ATHENS, LAW ON SILVER COINAGE, 375/4 B.C. Stele of white marble found in the Agora Excavations (I 7180). Ed. pr. R.S. Stroud, HESPERIA 43 (1974) 158-188 (ph.). L. 8 refers to imitation owls struck abroad; LL. 16-17 enforce acceptance of all silver owls (Attic and foreign) passed by the dokimastes. Brief, inconclusive discussion of the inscription before the ed. pr., *Thorikos and the Laurion in Archaic and Classical Times: Miscellanea Graeca* 1 (Ghent 1975) ed. H. Mussche, pp. 198-200. A. Giovannini, GRBS 16 (1975) 185-195, rejects Stroud's interpretation of LL. 16-17; denies the existence of official Athenian subaerates. M.H. Hansen, *Eisangelia: Odense University Classical Studies* 6 (1975) 28; restoration of L. 33. J.H. Kroll, GRBS 17 (1976) 329-341, rejects Giovannini's theory about subaerates and maintains that they were officially minted in Athens at the end of the Peloponnesian War. R. Bogaert, *Epigraphica* III (Leiden 1976) 23-25, no. 21; text; RBN 122 (1976) 20-24; French translation, commentary; he follows Giovannini in rejecting Stroud's interpretation of LL. 16-17. F. Sokolowski, BCH 100 (1976) 511-515, restores L. 9 ἐ[κ τõ νόμο]. H. Wankel, ZPE 21 (1976) 149-151; syntax of ὑπαρχέτω in LL. 30 and 35. J. and L. Robert, BE (1976) no. 190; (1977) no. 146, reject the arguments of Giovannini and Bogaert on LL. 16-17. M. Austin, P. Vidal-Naquet, *Economic and Social History of Ancient Greece* (London 1977) 328, no. 102; English translation; brief notes.

stoich. 39

ἔδοξε τοῖς νομοθέταις, ἐπὶ Ἱππο[δάμαντος]
ἄρχοντος: Νικοφῶν εἶπεν·
τὸ ἀργύριον δέχεσθαι τὸ Ἀττικὸν͵ στ[. . . . .9. . . . τ]-
αι ἀργυρõν͵ καὶ ἔχηι τὸν δημόσιον͵ χα[ρακτῆρα. ὁ δὲ]
δοκιμαστὴς ὁ δημόσιος καθήμενος με[ταξὺ τῶν τρ]-
απεζῶν δοκιμαζέτω κατὰ ταῦτα ὅσαι ἡ̣[μέραι πλὴν]

ὅταν ἦ[ι] χρημάτωγ καταβολή, τότε δὲ ἐ[ν τῶι βολευτ]-
ηρίωι. ἐὰν δέ τις προσενέγκηι ξ[.]ν[......12......]
ἔχον τὸν αὐτὸγ χαρακτῆρα τῶι Ἀττι[κῶ]ι ε[...7....]
ἀποδιδότω τῶι προσενεγκόντι. ἐὰν δὲ ὑπ[όχαλκον]
ἢ ὑπομόλυβδον ἢ κίβδηλον, διακοπτέτω πα[...6...]-
α καὶ ἔστω ἱερὸν τῆς Μητρὸς [τ]ῶν θεῶγ καὶ κ[αταβαλ]-
λέτω ἐς τὴμ βολήν. ἐὰν δὲ μὴ καθῆτ[α]ι ὁ δοκι[μαστὴς]
ἢ μὴ δοκιμάζηι κατὰ τὸν νόμον, τυπ[τ]όντων [αὐτὸν ο]-
ἱ τõ δήμο συλλογῆς πεντήκοντα πληγὰς τ[ῆι μάστι]-
γι. ἐὰν δέ τις μὴ δέχηται τὸ ἀ[ρ]γ[ύρ]ιον ὅ τ[ι ἂν ὁ δοκι]-
μαστὴς δοκιμάσηι, στερέσθω ὧν ἂμ [π]ωλῆτ[αι ἐκείν]-
ηι τῆι ἡμέραι. φαίνειν δὲ τὰ μὲν ἐν [τ]ῶι σί[τωι πρὸς]
τὸς σιτοφύλακας, τὰ δὲ ἐν τῆι ἀγορᾶι κ[α]ὶ [ἐν τῶι ἄλ]-
λωι ἄστει πρὸς τοὺς τõ δήμο συλλογέ[ας], τὰ [δὲ ἐν τῶ]-
ι ἐμπορίωι καὶ τῶι Πει[ρ]αιεῖ πρὸς τοὺ[ς ἐπιμελητ]-
ὰς τοῦ ἐμπορίο πλὴν τὰ ἐν τῶι σίτωι, τὰ δὲ [ἐν τῶι σί]-
τωι πρὸς τοὺς σιτοφύλακας. τῶν δὲ φανθέ[ντων, ὁπό]-
σα μὲν ἂν ἦι ἐντὸς δέκα δραχμῶν, κύριοι ὄ[ντων οἱ ἄ]-
ρχοντες διαγιγνώσκειν, τὰ δὲ ὑπὲρ [δ]έ[κ]α [δραχμάς],
ἐσαγόντων ἐς τὸ δικαστήριον. οἱ δὲ θε[σμ]οθ[έται π]-
αρεχόντων αὐτοῖς ἐπικληρõντες δικα[στήριον ὄ]-
ταμ παραγγέλλωσιν ἢ εὐθυνέσθω[ν .] δραχ[μαῖς. τῶι]
δὲ φήναντι μετέστω τὸ ἥμισυ, ἐ[ὰ]ν ἕληι ο[....8....]
ἐὰν δὲ δõλος ἦι ὁ πωλῶν ἢ δόλη, ὑπ<α>ρχέτω μ[ὲν αὐτῶι]
τύπτεσθαι 𐅄 πληγὰς τῆι μάστιγι ὑπὸ [τῶν ἀρχόντω]-
ν οἷς ἕκαστα προστέτακται. ἐὰν δέ τις [τῶ]ν ἀ[ρχόντ]-
ων μὴ ποιῆι κατὰ τὰ γεγραμμένα, εἰσαγ[αγέτω αὐτὸ]-
ν ἐς τὴμ βολὴν Ἀθηναίων ὁ βολόμενος οἷς [ἔξεστιν].
ἐὰν δὲ ἁλῶι, ὑπαρχέτω μὲν αὐτῶι πεπαῦσθ[αι ἄρχον]-
τι καὶ προστιμάτω αὐτῶ[ι] ἡ βολὴ μέχρι [𐅅 δραχμῶν. ὅ]-
πως δ᾽ ἂν ἦι καὶ ἐμ Πειραιεῖ δοκιμαστὴς [τοῖς ναυκ]-
λήροις καὶ τοῖς ἐμπόροις καὶ τοῖς ἄλλο[ις πᾶσιν],
καταστησάτω ἡ βολὴ ἐκ τῶν δημοσίων ἐὰ[ν ....7...]
ἢ ἐσπριάσθω, τὴν δὲ τιμὴν οἱ ἀποδέκται [μεριζόντ]-
ων. οἱ δὲ ἐπιμεληταὶ τοῦ ἐμπορίο ἐπιμελέ[σ]θω[ν ὅπ]-
ως ἂγ καθῆται πρὸς τῆι στήληι τοῦ Ποσειδῶνο[ς κα]-
ὶ χρήσθων τῶι νόμωι καθάπερ περὶ τõ ἐν ἄστ[ει δοκ]-
ιμαστõ εἴρηται κατὰ ταὐτά. ἀναγράψαι δὲ ἐν σ[τήλ]-
ηι λιθίνηι τὸν νόμον τόνδε καὶ καταθεῖναι ἐν [ἄσ]-
τει μὲμ μεταξὺ τῶν τραπεζῶν, ἐμ Πειραιεῖ δὲ πρό[σ]-
θεν τῆς στήλης τοῦ Ποσει[δ]ῶνος. ὁ δὲ γραμματε[ὺ]ς [ὁ]
τῆς βολῆς παραγγειλάτω μίσθωμα τοῖς πωλ[ηταῖς].
οἱ δὲ πωληταὶ ἐσενεγκόντων ἐς τὴμ βολήν. τ[ὴν δὲ μ]-
ισθοφορίαν εἶναι τῶι δοκιμαστῆι τῶι ἐν τῶι [ἐμπ]-
ορίωι ἐπὶ μὲν Ἱπποδάμαντος ἄρχοντος ἀφ᾽ οὗ [ἂν κα]-
ταστaθῆι, μεριζόντων οἱ <ἀ>ποδέκται ὅσομπερ τ[ῶι]
ἐν ἄστει δοκιμαστῆι, ἐς δὲ τὸν λοιπὸγ χρόν[ον ἔνα]-
ι αὐτῶι τὴμ μισθοφορίαν ὅθεμπερ τοῖς ἀργυ[ροκό]-
ποις. εἰ δέ τι ψήφισμα γέγραπταί πο ἐστήληι πα[ρὰ τ]-
όνδε τὸν νόμον, καθελέτω ὁ γραμματεὺς τῆς βολ[ῆς].

3. ὅτ[αν δεικνύητ]αι ἀργυρο̃γ Stroud. || 8. ξ̣[ε]ν[ικὸν ἀργύριον] Stroud. || 9. ἐ[ὰν καλόν] Stroud; ἐ[κ τὸ̃ νόμο] Sokolowski. || 11. πα[ραυτίκ]|α Stroud; πα[ραχρῆμ]|α Bogaert. || 29. ο̣ [ὠνόμενος] Stroud; ο̣[ντιναου̃ν] Bogaert. || 33. εἰσαγ[γελ-λέτω μὲ]|ν Hansen. || 39. ἐὰ̣[ν ὑπάρχηι] Bogaert; Stroud.

---

73. ATHENS, DECREE HONORING STRATON OF SIDON, 364 B.C.? IG, II², 141. SEG XII, 85. R.A. Moysey, AJAH 1 (1976) 182-189, argues on historical grounds that the decree and the Athenian embassy in LL. 2-3 belong to 364 B.C.

---

74. ATHENS, DECREE HONORING SPARTOKOS, PAIRISADES, AND APOLLONIOS, 347/6 B.C. IG, II², 212. SEG XVII, 22; XXII, 92. M.H. Hansen, GRBS 18 (1977) 50-51, discusses this meeting of the Ekklesia in connection with Demosthenes 19.154 and Aristotle AP 43.6; meaning of the term ἐκκλησία σύγκλητος.

---

75. ATHENS, DECREE, 333/2 B.C. IG, II², 339. SEG XVI, 54; XXI, 277. W.K. Pritchett, CSCA 9 (1977) 188-189, offers five different restorations of the calendar equation in LL. 5-7 and observes that the 6 preserved letters are too few to yield a reliable restoration. B.D. Meritt, Mn 30 (1977) 229-230, defends the restoration [Μεταγειτνιῶ]νος ἕκτ[ηι φθίνοντος] = [πέμπτηι και]ὶ δεκ̣[άτηι] and argues that together with the calendar equation in IG, II², 338, it shows that ἐνάτη φθίνοντος was the omitted day in Metageitnion 333/2 B.C.

---

76. ATHENS, DECREE HONORING AN ACTOR, 331/0 B.C. IG, II², 348. SEG XXI, 282; XXIII, 54. P. Ghiron-Bistagne, Acteurs 78-79; text, (ph.); French translation.

---

77. ATHENS, DECREE HONORING AN ACTOR, 350-300 B.C. IG, II², 429. P. Ghiron-Bistagne, Acteurs 80-81; text, (ph.); French translation; minor new readings (and misprinted dotted letters).

---

78. ATHENS, DECREE FOR [. . . . . . .]DAS OF KOS, ca. 331-324 B.C. IG, II², 416. A.S. Henry, JHS 97 (1977) 157-158, after examining the stone, offers new restorations:

L. 10	ὡς ἀφ[θονώτατος]
LL. 12-14	ν καὶ μηδεὶς μήτε κ[ακῶς πάσχηι]
	Ἀθηναίων μηδ’ ὑφ’ ἐνό[ς, ἀβιάστως]
	δὲ κατάγηται.

P. 157, note 31: M. Walbank reports that the two fragments published together as IG, II², 416 do not belong to the same stele.

---

79. ATHENS, DECREE, 325/4 B.C. IG, II², 360. SEG XIII, 40; XXIV, 101. P. Marchetti, RBN 122 (1976) 51-54, compares the benefactions of Herakleides described in LL. 5-13; 30-32 with those of Chrysippos in Demosthenes 34.38-39 to date the speech in 327/6 B.C.

---

80. ACHARNAI, EPHEBIC OATH, 4th cent. B.C. SEG XVI, 140; XIX, 167; XXI, 629; XXII, 142; XXIV, 192. P. Siewert, JHS 97 (1977) 102-111, examines possible echoes of the oath in Thucydides, Sophocles, and Aeschylus, and concludes that it goes back to an archaic original, possibly pre-Solonic.

---

81. ATHENS, HONORARY DECREE FOR TWO PHOKIANS, 323/2 B.C. IG, II², 367. SEG XXI, 295. C. Schwenk, ANT KUNST 19 (1976) 64-66 (ph.), joins to the stele a sculptured relief fragment, with part of L. 1, Θε[οί]; cf. O. Walter, JOAI 18 (1915) Beiblatt 91: EM 2811 + 7180. The original width is equivalent to stoich. 26.

---

82. ATHENS, HONORARY DECREE FOR EUPHRON OF SIKYON, 323/2 B.C. IG, II², 448, LL. 1-34. SEG XXI, 297, 317; XXII, 95; XXIII, 59. C. Schwenk, <u>ibid</u>. 19 (1976) 65, note 10, "five letters of Archias' name can be read (undotted) in line 2 . . . These letters were seen and confirmed by three experienced epigraphers." No text or further information.

---

83. ATHENS, CITIZENSHIP DECREE, 321-318 B.C. IG, II², 392 + 586. C. Karapa, AD 29 (1974) [1977] A.158-159 (ph.), joins these two fragments (EM 7233 + 7335) to produce the following text:

stoich. 28

[. . δεδόχ]θ̣αι τῶι [δήμωι ἐπαινέσαι μὲ]-
[ν . . .6. . .]ονα Πολυ̣[κλέους . . .5. . εὔν]-
[οίας ἕνε]κα τῆς πρὸ[ς τὸν δῆμον τὸν Ἀθ]-
[ηναίων κ]αὶ στεφα[νῶσαι θαλλοῦ στε]-
[φάνωι, ὅπ]ως ἂν εἰ[δῶσιν ἅπαντες ὅτι]
[ὁ δῆμος ὁ Ἀ]θην[α]ίω[ν τοῖς φ]ιλο[τιμου]-
[μένοις πρὸς αὐ]τὸ[ν ἀ]πο[δί]δω̣σ[ιν χάρ]-
[ιτας ἀξίας τῶν] εὐ[ε]ρ[γε]τημάτων· εἶ[ν]-
[αι δὲ . . .6. . . ον]α Π[ο]λυ̣[κ]λ̣έους Ἀθην[α]-
[ῖον καὶ ἐκγόνους] αὐτοῦ καὶ γράψασ̣-
[θαι φυλῆς καὶ δήμ]ου καὶ φρατρίας ἧ-
[ς ἂν βούληται κατ]ὰ τὸν νόμον, τοὺς δ-

[ὲ πρυτάνεις τῆς Ἀ]ντιοχίδος δοῦνα-
[ι περὶ αὐτοῦ τῶι δή]μωι τὴν ψῆφον εἰ-
[ς τὴν πρώτην ἐκκλη]σίαν· ἀναγράψαι δ-
[ὲ τὸ ψήφισμα τόδε] τὸν ἀναγραφέα κα-
[ὶ στῆσαι ἐν ἀκροπ]όλει, εἰς δὲ τὴν ἀν-
[αγραφὴν δοῦναι τ]ὸν ταμίαν τοῦ δήμ-
[ου . . . δραχμὰς ἐκ] τῶν κατὰ ψηφίσμα-
[τα ἀναλισκομένω]ν τῶι δήμωι.

As printed, LL. 1, 3, 15 have 29 letters. Perhaps read [.δεδόχ]θ̣αι L. 1 and [. .4. . εὐνο]|[ίας] LL. 2-3 (ed.).

---

84. ATHENS, DECREE ON THE AGORANOMOI, 320/19 B.C. IG, II^2, 380. SEG XXI, 307. C. Vatin, BCH 100 (1976) 557, restores LL. 38-39: [μήτε] κοπρῶ|[σαι μήτ' ἐ]ν τῆι ἀγορᾶι [μήτ' ἐν ταῖ[ς ὁ]δοῖς.

---

85. ATHENS, HONORARY DECREE FOR TWO MEN OF EPIDAMNOS AND APOLLONIA, 318/7 B.C. IG, II^2, 350. SEG XXI, 320; XXII, 98. B.D. Meritt, HESPERIA 45 (1976) 173, withdraws his redating of this decree to 331/0 B.C. (ibid. 43 [1974] 466) and supports a date on the 246th day of 318/7 B.C.

---

86. ATHENS, HONORARY DECREE FOR PHILIP, IOLAUS, AND [- - -], 307-301 B.C. IG, II^2, 561. C. Habicht, Akten VI Kongr. Epig. Munich 1973.374, note 35; S.M. Burstein, ZPE 24 (1977) 223-225; both identify the king in LL. 7-8 as Alexander IV (not Alexander the Great).

---

87. ATHENS, HONORARY DECREE, 307/6 B.C. IG, II^2, 358. SEG XXI, 326. A.B. Bosworth, AJAH 1 (1976) 167-168, 177, argues that the boularchos (L. 14) need not imply that the Aitolian koinon was in existence when the decree was passed; rejects restorations of the date in SEG XXI, 326.

---

88. ATHENS, DECREE IN HONOR OF ALKIMOS OF EPEIROS, 306/5 B.C. IG, II^2, 773. C. Habicht, AJAH 2 (1977) 37-39, identifies the honorand as the officer of Demetrios Poliorketes known from Diodoros 20.98.9 and Plutarch, Demetrios 21.

---

89. ATHENS, CITIZENSHIP DECREE FOR OXYTHEMIS OF LARISA, 303/2 B.C. IG, II^2, 558. S.M. Burstein, CW 71 (1977) 128-129, identifies the cavalry action of LL. 33-34 with the defeat of Pleistarchos by Demetrios Poliorketes in 303 B.C.; Pausanias

1.15.1; HESPERIA 17 (1948) 112-136, no. 114.

---

90. ATHENS, CITIZENSHIP DECREE, 303/2 B.C. IG, II^2, 734. C. Karapa, AD 29 (1974) [1977] A.159-163 (ph.), adds an unpublished fragment (EM 4614) of unknown provenance which joins the left side of IG, II^2, 734, augmenting LL. 4-11.

stoich. 41

[- - - - - - - - - - - - - - - - -]πολιτε[ία]
[- - - - - - - - - - - - - - - - -]ς
['Επι Λεωστράτου ἄρχοντος ἐπὶ τῆς Κ]εκροπίδος [ἐνάτ]-
[ης πρυτανείας, ἧι Διόφαντος] Δι[ονυ]σοδώρου <Φ>[ηγούσ]-
[ιος ἐγραμμάτευεν· 'Ελαφηβο]λιῶν[ος] ἐβδόμει ἐπ[ὶ δέκ]-
[α ....17........τῆς] πρυτα[νε]ίας· ἐκκλησ[ία κυ]-
[ρία· τῶν προέδρων ἐπεψήφι]ζεν̣ Νι[κό]μαχος Εὐβο[ύλου]
[...6... καὶ συμπρόεδροι· ἔ]δοξεν [τῆ]ι βουλῆι κα[ὶ τῶι]
[δήμωι· Μνήσαρχος Τιμοστρά]του Π[ροβ]αλίσιος ε[ἶπεν]·
[εἶναι ...6... κυρίαν τὴν πολι]τε[ίαν] αὐτῶι καὶ [ἐκγό]-
[νοις, τὴν δοθεῖσαν κατὰ τὸ ψήφ]ι̣σ[μα τοῦ] δήμου τ̣[οῦ 'Αθ]-
[ηναίων ....22...........] ΠΝΕΛΥΤΟΥΠ [....]
[...............29..............] ΗΙ γῆι Ω̣Λ [....]
[...............29..............] ΥΤΟ̣Ν ΕΧΟ̣Ρ [....]
[...............29..............] ΛΙ ἐτιμήθ[η ...]
[...............30...............] ΥΤΟΥ ΥΠΟ [....]
[...............31................] ΙΚ [....8....]

4. Lapis I; Kirchner II^2, 734 'Ικ[αριεύς]. || 6. [ὀγδόει καὶ εἰκοστεῖ] or [ἐνάτει καὶ εἰκοστεῖ τῆς] πρυτα[νε]ίας Karapa. The concurrence of Kekropis in the ninth prytany with Elaphebolion clashes with Kekropis as the eighth prytany in Anthesterion in IG, II^2, 490 of 303/2 B.C.; Karapa follows B.D. Meritt, AAA 5 (1972) 292, in considering the tribe in II^2, 490 as written in error.

---

91. ATHENS, DECREE, ca. 300 B.C. IG, II^2, 598. A.S. Henry, Prescripts 61, suggests that this may be a tribal or deme decree since the orator unexpectedly lacks both patronymic and demotic.

---

92. ATHENS, DECREE OF THE DELPHIC AMPHIKTYONES HONORING THE TECHNITAI OF ATHENS, 278 B.C. IG, II^2, 1132. FdD III.2.68. P. Ghiron-Bistagne, Acteurs 170-171; text and French translation.

---

93. ATHENS, DECREE, 3rd cent. B.C. SEG XXI, 370; XXV, 95. W.K. Pritchett, CSCA 3 (1970) 209-211, offers four possible restorations of the prescript, with discussion of the calendar equations. B.D. Meritt, AE (1973) 241-245, adding 2 letters read

from a photograph in L. 5, rejects Pritchett's restored versions and defends his restored text of SEG XXI, 370. W.K. Pritchett, ZPE 20 (1976) 185-192 (ph.), reporting readings by J.M. Camp, C.N. Edmonson, A.L. Boegehold, and T.L. Shear, Jr., prints a new text with epigraphic commentary. Cf. Pritchett, CSCA 9 (1977) 189-191.

[Θ]   ε   [ο   ί]
[Ἐπὶ - - - τ?]ράτου ἄρχοντος ἐ[πὶ τῆς - - -]
[- - - - - - -]της πρυτανεία[ς - - - - - - -]
[δεκάτ]ει ὑστέραι τρίτ[ει - - - - - - - -τῆς]
[πρυτανε]ί̣α̣ς [- - - - - - - - - - - - - - -]

B.D. Meritt, AAA 9 (1977) 193-194 (ph.) (cf. Mn 30 [1977] 227;242), after examining the stone with W. West, D. Peppas-Delmouzou, and W.B. Dinsmoor, Jr., reads [Ἐπὶ Πυθ]α̣ράτου in L. 2; [δωδεκ]άτης in L. 3; and reprints his restorations as in SEG XXI, 370.

---

94. ATHENS, DECREE AND CATALOGUE OF DONORS, 247/6 B.C.? IG, II^2, 791. J.H. Kroll, HESPERIA 46 (1977) 121-122, no. 54, restores the secretary's demotic in L. 4 as Ἀ[λωπεκῆθεν]. If the archon Diomedon is dated in 247/6 B.C., the restoration of the secretary's demotic (tribe XII) marks a break in the secretary cycle. Cf. B.D. Meritt, HISTORIA 26 (1977) 163-164, 176.

---

95. ATHENS, DECREE HONORING PRYTANEIS OF LEONTIS, 222/1 B.C. IG, II^2, 848. Agora 15.129. SEG XXI, 402. B.D. Meritt, HISTORIA 26 (1977) 177: "the calendar equation in lines 2-3 should be Boedromion 18 = Pryt. III.25 to avoid conflict with the Mysteries." Cf. Mn 30 (1977) 237.

---

96. ATHENS, CITIZENSHIP DECREE, ca. 220 B.C. Fragment of a gray marble stele found in the Agora Excavations (I 7254). Ed. pr. S.V. Tracy, HESPERIA 45 (1976) 283-285, no. 1 (ph.), who observes that infra no. 98 is by the same cutter; comparison with IG, II^2, 851 (infra no. 97).

non-stoich. ca. 37
[ἐπαι]νέσα[ι - - - - - - - - - - name 25-30 - - - - - - - εὐ]-
[νοί]ας ἕνεκα τῆς ε[ἰς τὸν δῆμον τὸν Ἀθηναίων καὶ]
[φιλ]οτιμίας· δεδόσθ[αι δὲ αὐτῶι καὶ πολιτείαν δοκι]-
[μα]σθέντι ἐν τῶι δικα̣[στηρίωι καὶ γράψασθαι φυλῆς]
[κα]ὶ δήμου καὶ φρατρίας [ἧς ἂν βούληται· τοὺς δὲ θε]-
σμοθέτας εἰσαγαγεῖ[ν αὐτῶι καὶ μὴ παρόντι τὴν]
δ̣οκιμασίαν ὅταν καὶ ὥ̣[ς πληρῶσιν δικαστήριον τῆς πο]-
λιτογραφίας· τὸν δὲ Γ̣[- - - - - ca. 16 - - - - τόδε]
τὸ ψήφισμα τοῖς δικασ[ταῖς· ἀναγράψαι δὲ τόδε τὸ ψήφι]-

σμα τὸν γραμματέα τ[ὸν κατὰ πρυτανείαν ἐν στή]-
ληι λιθίνηι καὶ στῆσαι ἐ[ν ἀκροπόλει· τὸ δὲ ἀνάλωμα]
τὸ εἰς τὴν ἀναγραφὴν κ̣[αὶ τὴν ἀνάθεσιν τῆς στή]-
λης με[ρ]ίσαι τοὺς ἐπὶ τ̣[ῆι διοικήσει]
vacat 0.032 m.

---

97. ATHENS, CITIZENSHIP DECREE, ca. 215-210 B.C.? IG, II², 851. M.J. Osborne, ABSA 67 (1972) 144; detailed discussion of date; ZPE 11 (1973) 157-159; new text after study of the stones; date 229-224 B.C.; ANC SOCIETY 7 (1976) 107-125; withdraws his earlier dating in favor of ca. 215-210 B.C. on the basis of the lettering which S.V. Tracy assigns to a mason active 212-173 B.C.

[- - - - - - - - - - - - - - - -]. .[3-4..]υθ.[....7-8....]
[- - - - - -ca. 25-30 - - - - - - κ]αὶ τῶν ἑαυτόν[...5-6...]
[- - - - - -ca. 24-29 - - - - - -].ς τοῖς ἐνδόξοι[ς ..3-4..]
[- - - - - -ca. 21-28 - - - - ε]ὐχαριστίαι τεῖ ε̣[ἰς .2-3..]
[- - - - -ca. 12-19 - - ἀγαθεῖ τύχ]ει δεδόχθαι τεῖ β[ουλεῖ]
[τοὺς λαχόντας προέδρους εἰς τ]ὴν ἐπιοῦσαν ἐκ<κ>λ[ησίαν]
[χρηματίσαι περὶ τούτων, γν]ώμην δὲ ξυμβάλλ[εσθαι]
[τῆς βουλῆς εἰς τὸν δῆμον ὅτι δ]ο̣κεῖ τεῖ βουλεῖ ἐ[παινέ]-
[σαι - - - - ca. 20-27 - - - - - -]ν καὶ στεφανῶσα̣[ι χρυ]-
[σῶι στεφάνωι ἀρετῆς ἕνεκα καὶ εὐ]νοίας ἣν ἔχων διατ[ε]-
[λεῖ πρὸς τὴν βουλὴν καὶ τὸν δῆμον τὸν] Ἀθηναίων καὶ ἀνε[ι]-
[πεῖν τὸν στέφανον Διονυσίων τε] τῶν ἐν ἄστε<ι> καιγ̣[ο]-
[ῖς τραγωιδοῖς καὶ Παναθηναίων καὶ Ἐ]λευσιν[ίω]ν τοῖς [γυ]-
[μνικοῖς ἀγῶσι· δεδόσθαι δὲ αὐτῶι καὶ] πολιτείαν καὶ γ̣[ρά]-
[ψασθαι φυλῆς καὶ δήμου καὶ φρατρία]ς ἧς ἂν θέλει, το[ὺς]
[δὲ θεσμοθέτας, ὅταν πληρῶσι δικαστήρι]α εἰς ἕνα καὶ πε[ν]-
[τακοσίους δικαστάς, εἰσαγαγεῖν αὐτῶι τ]ὴν δοκιμασίαν [*v*]
[τῆς δωρεᾶ]ς· [εἶναι δὲ αὐτῶι καὶ εἰς τὸ λο]ιπὸν ἐπαύξον[τι]
[τὴν π]ρὸς Ἀθ[ηναίους εὔνοιαν καθότι ἂν εἶ δ]υνατὸς καὶ ἄλ-
[λα]ις μείζοσ[ι τιμαῖς τιμᾶσθαι ὑπὸ τοῦ δήμου. τῆς δὲ] π̣[οιήσε]-
ως τοῦ στεφ[άνου καὶ τῆς ἀναγορεύσεως ἐπιμεληθῆναι]
τοὺς στρατη[γούς· ἀναγράψαι δὲ τόδε τὸ ψήφισμα ἐν στή]-
λει λιθίνηι τ[ὸν γραμματέα τὸν κατὰ πρυτανείαν καὶ στῆ]-
[σ]αι ἐν ἀκροπ[όλει· εἰς δὲ τὴν ἀναγραφὴν τῆς στήλης με]-
[ρ]ί̣σαι τὸν τ[αμίαν τῶν στρατιωτικῶν τὸ γενόμενον ἀνάλωμα].
vacat 0.022 m.

---

98. ATHENS, EPHEBIC DECREE AND CATALOGUE, late 3rd cent. B.C. Stele of blue marble found in the Agora Excavations (I 7181). Ed. pr. O.W. Reinmuth, HESPERIA 43 (1974) 246-259 (ph.); date 229/8 B.C., archonship of [Heliodoros]. S.V. Tracy, ibid. 45 (1976) 285, assigns this text to the same cutter as no. 96 and doubts the precision of Reinmuth's date. J.S. Traill, ibid. 296-303, after examining the stone, publishes a revised text,

which we print here; date 204/3 B.C., archonship of [Apollodoros].

non-stoich. ca. 49-61

[ἐπὶ Ἀπολλοδώρου ἄρχοντος ἐπὶ] τῆς Αἰα̣[ντίδος τρίτης πρυτανείας]
[ἧι ..4-5.. Θράσωνος Ὀῆθεν ἐγραμ]μάτευεν· Βοη[δρομιῶνος - - - ca. 7-8 - - -]
[- - - - ca. 12-13 - - - - τῆς πρυτανεί]ας· βουλὴ ἐν τῶι Παν[αθηναϊκῶι στα *v*]-
[δίωι· τῶν προέδρων ἐπεψήφιζε]ν Νικόστρατος Μενεμάχου Ἀχα[ρ *vv*]-
[νεὺς καὶ συμπρόεδροι· *vv* ἔδο]ξεν τεῖ βουλεῖ καὶ τῶι δήμωι· Σωσιγ[έ]-
[νης - - - - - 18-19 - - - - -]ς εἶπεν· *v* ἐπειδὴ οἱ ἔφηβοι οἱ ἐπὶ Διοδό [*v*]-
[του ἄρχοντος τὰς θυσίας τὰ]ς καθηκούσας ἀπὸ τῆς ἑστίας ἀρξάμενο[ι]
[ἐν τῶι πρυτανείωι καὶ τὰς] ἐγγραφὰς ἐκεῖ συνετέλεσαν κατὰ τὴν τοῦ [*v*]
[δήμου προαίρεσιν· ἐπόμπευσ]αν δὲ καὶ τὰς πομπὰς τήν τε τῶν Σεμνῶν Θ[ε]-
[ῶν καὶ τοῦ Ἰάκχου ὡς μάλισ]τ̣α τοῖς πατρίοις ἀκολούθως εὐτακτοῦντ[ες]·
[ἤραντο δὲ καὶ τεῖ θυσίαι τοὺ]ς βοῦς· ἀπεδήμησαν δὲ καὶ εἰς Ἐλευσῖνα εἰς [*v*]
[τὸ ἱερὸν ὅπως ἂν εὐσεβῶς] ἔχει πάντα τὰ πρὸς τοὺς θεούς· λελειτουρ *v* -
[γήκασιν δὲ καὶ τοῖς μυστ]ηρίοις καθάπ<ε>ρ ἠγγέλθη αὐτοῖς· διετέλεσαν
[δὲ καὶ τὸν ἐνιαυτὸν εἰς τὰ] γυμνάσια· ἔδραμον δὲ καὶ τὰς λαμπάδας *v*
[ἁπάσας καὶ τοὺς ἄλλους ἀγῶ]νας ἠγωνίσαντο καλῶς καὶ εὐσχημόνως·
[τοῖς δὲ Ἐπιταφίοις ἐν τοῖς] ὅπλοις ἀπόδειξιν ἐποιήσαντο· ἐπεμελή [*v*] -
[θησαν δὲ καὶ τῆς φυλακῆς τῶν] πόλεων πειθόμενοι τοῖς στρατηγοῖς κα[ὶ *v*]
[τῶι κοσμητεῖ· ἐλειτούργησα]ν δὲ καὶ ἐν τῶι Ἡφαιστιείωι· διετέλεσαν δὲ κα[ὶ]
[τὴν ἄσκησιν εὐτάκτως ποιοῦν]τ̣ες μετὰ τῶν ὅπλων οὐθενὸς αὐτοῖς μεριζ[ο]-
[μένου ὑπὸ τοῦ δήμου· ἐποιήσα]ντο δὲ καὶ πρὸς τεῖ μελέτει τεῖ κατὰ τὸν πλο[ῦν]
[τὴν περὶ τῆς ἐφηβείας ἀπόδει]ξιν τεῖ βουλεῖ τὴν ἐν τοῖς ὅπλοις ἀκολούθω[ς]
[τοῖς νόμοις καὶ τοῖς ψηφίσ]μασι τοῖς εἰς πολεμικὴν χρείαν καθήκουσιν· κα *v* -
[θάπερ παρεῖχον αὐτοὺς ὑπ]ὲ̣ρ πατρίδος μέλλοντας ἀγαθοὺς ἀγωνιστὰς
[τοῖς διδασκάλοις πειθόμεν]οί τε καὶ ἐπιμελεῖς· ἀκολούθως δὲ ταῖς ἐγγρα *v* -

[φαῖς ἐν ἀκροπόλει εὐδόξως τ]ὰ ἐξιτητήρια παρασκευάζονται ποιεῖν ἵνα
[τὰ ὅπλα αὐτῶν παρέχωσιν μετὰ] πάσης εὐκοσμίας καθάπερ καὶ τὰς χλαμύδας *v*
[καὶ τὰ ἄλλα ἐνδύματα αὐτῶ]ν· *v* ὅπως ἂν οὖν ἀεὶ τοῖς ἐφηβεύουσιν ἐφάμιλ-
[λον ἧι εἰδόσιν τοὺς πειθαρ]χοῦντας τοῖς χειροτονουμένοις ἐπὶ τὴν εὐ-
[ταξίαν τιμηθέντας, ἀγαθεῖ τύ]χει δεδόχθαι τεῖ βουλεῖ τοὺς λαχόντας *vv*
[προέδρους εἰς τὴν ἐπιοῦσα]ν ἐκκλησίαν χρηματίσαι περὶ τούτων· γνώμην *v*
[δὲ ξυμβάλλεσθαι τῆς βουλ]ῆς εἰς τὸν δῆμον ὅτι δοκεῖ τεῖ βουλεῖ ἐπαι *v* -
[νέσαι τοὺς ἐπὶ Διοδότου ἐφ]ηβεύσαντας καὶ στεφανῶσαι χρυσῶι στεφάνωι̣
[εὐταξίας ἕνεκα καὶ εὐσεβεί]ας καὶ φιλοτιμίας ἣν ἔχοντες διατετελέκα *v* -
[σιν εἰς τὴν βουλὴν κ]αὶ τὸ̣[ν] δῆμον καὶ ἀνειπεῖν τοὺς στεφάνους Διονυσίων
[τε τῶν ἐν ἄστει καὶ] Παναθηναίων καὶ Ἐλευσινίων τοῖς γυμνικοῖς ἀγῶσιν·
[τῆς δὲ ἀναγορεύσεω]ς καὶ ποιήσεως τῶν στεφάνων ἐπιμεληθῆναι τοὺς *vv*
[στρατηγοὺς καὶ τὸ]ν̣ ταμίαν τῶν στρατιωτικῶν· ὑπάρχειν δὲ αὐτοῖς καὶ̣ [*v*]
[προεδρίαν ἐμ πᾶ]σιν τοῖς ἀγῶσιν οἷς ἡ πόλις τίθησιν· δοῦναι δ' αὐτοῖς κα[ὶ]
[ἀνάθημα ἐν τόπωι ο]ὗ ἂν αὐτοὶ αἱρῶνται· ἐπαινέ̣[σαι δὲ] καὶ τὸν παιδοτρί̣ [*v*] -
[βην Ἑρμόδωρον Ἑορτί]ου Ἀχα̣ρ̣ν̣[έ]α̣ ὅτ̣[ι το]ῖς νό̣[μοις τοῦ δήμου] καὶ τοῖς ψη [*v*] -
[φίσμασιν - - - - - - - - ca. 39 - - - - - - - - -] δ̣ὲ καὶ τὸν
[- - - - - - - - - - - ca. 43 - - - - - - - - - - ἀκον]τ̣[ι]στὴν
[- - - - - - - - - - - ca. 50 - - - - - - - - - - - - - -]να̣
[- - - - - - - - - - - ca. 49 - - - - - - - - - - - - - -]ου̣
[- - ca. 6 - - κα]ὶ τὸν γραμμ̣[ατέα - - - ca. 23 - - στε]φα[*v*]-
[νῶσαι ἕκ]α̣στον αὐτῶν [θ]αλλο[ῦ στεφάνωι· ἀνα]γ̣ρ̣άψαι δὲ τό[δε τὸ ψήφι̣]-
[σμα καὶ] τὰ ὀνόματα αὐ̣τῶν τὸν γραμμ̣ατέα τὸν κατὰ πρ[υ]τ̣α-[ν]εῖαν
[ἐν στήλ]ει λιθίνει καὶ στῆσαι ἐν τεῖ ἀγοραῖ· τὸ δὲ γενόμενον ἀνάλω [*vv*] -
[μα δοῦ]ναι τὸν ταμίαν τῶν στρατιωτικῶν. *vacat*

vacat 0.027 m. *incised triple circles*	*vacat* 0.037 m. *incised triple circles*	*vacat* 0.027 m. *incised triple circles*
ἡ βουλὴ ὁ δῆμος	ἡ βουλὴ	οἱ ἔφη- βοι τὸν κο-

[τ]ὸν κοσμη-
[τ]ὴν Νικόβου-
λ̣ον Ἐργοχά-
ρ̣ου Ὀή-
θ̣εν

ὁ δῆμος
τοὺς ἐφή-
βους

σμητὴν Νι-
κόβουλον Ἐρ-
γοχάρου
Ὀῆθεν

[οἱ ἐφ]ηβεύσαντες ἐπὶ Διοδότου ἄρχοντος

[[['Αντιγονίδος]]]
[- - -]ος Σωφίλου Ἀγρυλῆθεν
[- - -]τος Φίλωνος Λαμπτρεύ(ς)

[[[Δημητριάδος]]]
[- - - -] Φιλωτάδου Φυλάσιος
[- - -Δη]μ̣ητρίου Ἀτηνεύς
[- - - -Δη]μητρίου Ἀτηνεύς
[- - - - -]φίλου Μελιτεύς

[Ἐρεχθεῖδος]
[- - - - - -]ο̣υ Κ̣ηφισιεύς
[- - - - - -] Κηφισιεύς

[Αἰγεῖδος]
[- - - - - -] Ἐ̣ρχιεύς
[- - - - -]ά̣του Ἐρχιε(ύς)
lacuna

Ἀκαμαντίδος

Οἰνεῖδος
Εὔκριτος Εὐκρίτου Ἐπικηφίσιος
Ἐργοχάρης Νικοβούλου Οἰῆθεν
Στησίλεως Νικοβούλου Οἰῆθεν
Ἀνθεμίων Θεοφῶντος Περιθοίδης
Οἰνόβιος Οἰνοβίου Ἐπικηφίσιος
Δημήτριος Μηνοφίλου Ἀχαρνεύ̣[ς]

Κεκροπίδος
Λυσῖνος Κηφισοφῶντος Ἀθμ[ονεύς]

Ἱπποθωντίδος
Κόνων Ξενοφάντο̣[υ Κειριάδης]
Ἄβας Κλεάνδρο̣[υ Ἀμαξαντεύς]

Αἰαντ̣[ίδος]
lacuna

---

99. ATHENS, DECREE, 204/3 B.C.? IG, II^2, 845, SEG XVI, 71. J.S. Traill, HESPERIA 45 (1976) 299-301, reads the secretary's name in L. 24 [- -4-5- - Θ]ράσ[ωνος Ὀῆθεν]; cf. IG, II^2, 973, L. 4 (infra no. 100). Traill assigns II^2, 845 to the same year.

---

100. ATHENS, DECREE, 204/3 B.C.? IG, II^2, 973. J.S. Traill, HESPERIA 45 (1976) 299-301, restores the secretary's name in L. 4 as [- - 4-5 - - Θράσω]νος Ὀῆθεν; cf. IG, II^2, 845, L. 24 (supra no. 99).

---

101. ATHENS, DECREE HONORING PRYTANEIS OF PTOLEMAIS, date? SEG XXII, 109; XXV, 189. Agora 15.259. M. Piérart, BCH 100 (1976) 443-447, contests the dating of Agora 15 (97/6 B.C.) and argues for 200-175 B.C.

---

102. ATHENS, CITIZENSHIP DECREE FOR ALEXANDER OF THESSALY, 198/7 B.C. IG, II^2, 850. M.J. Osborne, ANC SOCIETY 7 (1976)

115-125, discusses this as an example of his Type II in the development of citizenship decrees after 229 B.C.

---

103. ATHENS, DECREE HONORING EPHEBES, 197/6 or 180/79 B.C.? Fragment of gray marble found in the Agora Excavations (I 7286). Ed. pr. S.V. Tracy, HESPERIA 45 (1976) 285-287, no. 2 (ph.), who assigns this fragment to the Agora I 247 Cutter, active ca. 197/6-155/4 B.C. (cf. GRBS 14 [1973] 192-195). Tracy restores L. 1 [ἐπὶ Διοδότου ἄρχοντος τοῦ μετὰ Φαναρχίδη]ν or [ἐπὶ Διονυσίου ἄρχοντος τοῦ μετὰ Διονύσιο]ν.

non-stoich. 60-70?

[- - - ca. 33 - - -]ν ἐπι̣ [τῆς - - - - - - - - - - - - - - -]
[- - - ca. 30 - -ἐγρα]μμάτευε̣[ν - - - - - - - - - - - - - -]
[- - - ca. 30 - -ἐκκ]λησία ἐν τ[ῶι θεάτρωι?· τῶν προέδρων *etc.*]
[- - - ca. 32 - - -]η̣ς καὶ συμπρ[όεδροι. ἔδοξεν *etc.*]
[- - - ca. 34 - - -]Σημαχίδης εἶπ[εν. ἐπειδὴ οἱ ἔφηβοι - - -]
[- - - ca. 35 - - -]Ν ἔθυσάν τε τ[ὰς θυσίας? - - - - - - - -]
[- - - ca. 24 - -μετὰ τοῦ κοσ]μ̣ητοῦ καὶ τοῦ [ἱερέως? - - - -]
[- - - ca. 35 - - -]ετέλεσαν[- - - - - - - - - - - - - - - - -]
[- - - ca. 36 - - -] καὶ τῆι Α̣[- - - - - - - - - - - - - - - - -]
[- - - ca. 36 - - -]καὶ τὴν [- - - - - - - - - - - - - - - - - -]
[- - - ca. 36 - - -]Σ̣ τοῖς [- - - - - - - - - - - - - - - - - -]
[- - - ca. 39 - - - -]Ε̣[-]

---

104. ATHENS, DECREE, 195/4 B.C. Pritchett/Meritt, Chronology 111. B.D. Meritt, GRBS 17 (1976) 149-150, offers a new restoration of LL. 2-3 and discusses the calendric implications: [Πο|σιδεῶνος ἕνει καὶ νέαι] ἑβδόμει καὶ εἰ[κοστεῖ τῆς πρυτανείας].

---

105. ATHENS, DECREE HONORING PRYTANEIS, 191/0 B.C.? SEG XXI, 422; XXV, 115. Agora 15.207. B.D. Meritt, HISTORIA 26 (1977) 163, abandons his earlier dating, 173/2 B.C., TAPA 95 (1964) 239; Agora 15.207; he offers new restorations of LL. 1-4 and comments on their calendric significance. Timouchos is restored from Agora 15.163 L. 9.

[ἐπὶ Τιμούχου ἄρχοντος ἐπὶ τῆ]ς [Ἱ]ππο[θων]τ[ί]δος ἐν[δ]εκάτης πρυταν-
[είας ἧι - - - - ca. 11 - - - Πρασιε]ὺς ἐγ[ραμ]μάτευεν· Θαρ[γ]ηλιῶνος ἐνδ[ε]-
[κάτει κατ' ἄρχοντα, κατὰ θεὸν] δὲ ὀγδόει ἐπὶ δέκα, τρίτει καὶ εἰκοστ[εῖ]
[τῆς πρυτανείας· ἐκκλησία κυ]ρία ἐν τῶι θεάτρωι· τῶν προέδρω[ν ἐ]-

---

106. ATHENS, DECREE, 191/0 B.C.? SEG XXII, 102; XXIII, 68; XXV, 113. B.D. Meritt, HISTORIA 26 (1977) 162, offers a new restoration of the beginning of this decree and discusses the calendric implications.

[ἐπὶ Τιμούχου ἄρχοντ]ος ἐπ[ὶ]
[τῆς - - - - - -ἐνάτης π]ρυτα-
[νείας ἧι - - - ca. 11 - - -] Πρα[σ]ιεὺς
[ἐγραμμάτευεν· ᾽Ανθεστ]ηριῶνος
[ἕνηι καὶ νέαι κατὰ θε]όν, ἐνά[τηι]
[τῆς πρυτανείας· ἐκκλησ]ία κυ[ρία]
[τῶν προέδρων ἐπεψήφιζ]εν Ε[- - -]

---

107. ATHENS, DECREE HONORING PRYTANEIS OF KEKROPIS, 189/8 B.C. SEG XVI, 81. Agora 15.173. B.D. Meritt, GRBS 17 (1976) 151, note 16, restores [ἐνάτει] in place of [δεκάτει] in L. 32.

---

108. ATHENS, HONORARY DECREE FOR KLEARCHOS, 2nd cent. B.C. IG, II^2, 889 (EM 7450) + 904 (EM 7635). SEG XXIII, 68. C. Karapa, AD 29 (1974) [1977] A.163-164 (ph.), joins these two fragments to yield the following new beginning of the text:

Θ [ε ο ὶ]
[᾽Ε]πὶ ᾽Ιππ[ί]ου ἄρχο[ντος ἐπὶ τῆς - - -δος δωδεκάτης πρυτανεί]-
ας [ἧι Θε]οδόσιος Ξενοφά[ντου Λαμπτρεὺς ἐγραμμάτευεν· Σκιρο]-
[φ]οριῶνος ὀγδόει μετ᾽ εἰκ[άδας, πέμπτει καὶ εἰκοστεῖ τῆς πρυτανεί]-
[α]ς· ἐκκλησία κυρία ἐν τῶι θ[εάτρωι· τῶν προέδρων ἐπεψήφι-ζεν Δρα]-
[κ]οντίδης Λωνίκου ᾽Αφιδναῖ[ος καὶ συμπρόεδροι· ἔδοξεν τῆι βουλῆι]
καὶ τῶι δήμωι· Λακράτης Μέ[ντορος Περιθοίδης εἶπεν· ἐπειδὴ Κλέ]-
[α]ρχος εὔνους ἐστὶν κοιν[ῆι τε τῶι δήμωι *etc.*]

For the date of Hippias' archonship, B.D. Meritt, HISTORIA 26 (1977) 181; 181/0 B.C.

---

109. ATHENS, DECREE, 181/0 B.C. SEG XXI, 441; XXIII, 68. A.S. Henry, Prescripts 89, rejects H.A. Thompson's restoration of [βουλὴ ἐμ βουλευτηρίωι] in L. 12 "precisely where one would expect the enactment formula to occur" and reads [ἔδοξεν τεῖ βουλεῖ].

---

110. ATHENS, DECREE, 176/5 B.C. Pritchett/Meritt, Chronology 120. B.D. Meritt, GRBS 17 (1976) 150-151, offers a new restora-

tion of LL. 2-3 and discusses the calendric implications.

[μηνὸς Ἐλαφηβολιῶνος ἑνά]-
[τει] ἐσιόντος μιᾶι καὶ [εἰκοστεῖ τῆς πρυτανείας]

---

111. ATHENS, EPHEBIC DECREE, ca. 160 B.C. IG, II^2, 1027. SEG XVI, 98; XVII, 32; XXI, 457. B.D. Meritt, HISTORIA 26 (1977) 183, suggests that the archon's name to be restored in L. 19 might be Tychandros.

---

112. ATHENS, HONORARY DECREE FOR KLEOMACHIDES OF LARISA, 151/0 B.C.? IG, II^2, 933+. SEG XIX, 102. C. Habicht, ZPE 20 (1976) 193-199, combines these two fragments, restoring II^2, 933 to read [Κ]λεομαχί|δην|[Κρ]ατίγ̣ο̣υ|[Λαρισαῖο]ν *in corona*, and SEG XIX, 102 LL. 7-12 as follows:

[.... .... εἶπεν· ἐπειδ]ὴ Νικάνωρ Νικοκ[λέους Ῥαμ]-
[νούσιος? ἀποφαίνει Κλεομαχί]δην Κρατίνου Λα[ρισαῖον]
[εὔχρηστον ὄντα τῶι δήμωι τῶι] Ἀθηναίων καὶ τοῖς [εἰς Λάρι]-
[σαν ἀφικνουμένοις τῶν πολιτῶν κ]αὶ κατὰ κοινὸν καὶ κατ' [ἰδίαν]
[πᾶσαν ἐπιμέλειαν ποιησάμενον, σπο]υ̣δ̣ῆς καὶ φ̣ιλοτιμ[ίας οὐδὲν]
[ἐλλιπόντα *etc.*]

Habicht prefers [Ἐπαινέτου ἄρχοντος] 151/0 B.C. (L. 1) to [Διοκλέους] 138 B.C., cf. SEG XIX, 102. B.D. Meritt, HISTORIA 26 (1977) 191; his 15th Metonic cycle would require 151/0 B.C. to be an intercalary year whereas this text clearly belongs in an ordinary year.

---

113. ATHENS, DECREE HONORING PRYTANEIS OF ATTALIS, 131/0 B.C. IG, II^2, 921 (Agora 15.232) + 977 (Agora 15.246). SEG XXI, 168. D.M. Lewis, ZPE 20 (1976) 300, combines the lost II^2, 921 with II^2, 977 to form one decree; new text of II^2, 977 LL. 12-25.

[ἐ]πειδὴ δὲ οἱ πρυτάνεις τάς [τε θυσίας ἔθυσ]αν τὰ[ς
καθη]κ̣ού[σ]ας ἐν τῆι πρυτ[ανεί]-
αι, ἐπεμελήθησαν δὲ κα[ὶ τῆς συλλογῆς] τῆς βουλῆς [καὶ]
τοῦ δήμου κ[αὶ τῶν]
ἄλλων ἁπάντων ὧν αὐτ[οῖς προσέτατ]τογ̣ οἵ τε νόμοι κα[ὶ τὰ
ψηφίσ]ματ[α τοῦ δή]-
μου, ἐπαινέσαι τοὺς π[ρυτάνεις τῆς Ἀττ]αλίδος καὶ
στεφ[ανῶσαι αὐτοὺς]
χρυσῶι στεφάνωι κ[ατὰ τὸν νόμον εὐσεβεί]ας ἕνεκεν τῆς
[πρὸς τοὺς θε]-
οὺς κα[ὶ] φ̣ιλοτιμίας τῆ[ς εἰς τὴν βουλὴν καὶ τὸν δῆ]μον
τὸν Ἀθηναίων. [ἀναγράψαι]

δὲ τόδε τὸ ψήφισμα τὸ[ν γραμματέα τὸν κατὰ πρυ]τανείαν
εἰς στήλην λιθί[νην καὶ]
στῆσαι οὗ ἂν [εὔκαιρον ἧι· εἰς δὲ τὴν ἀναγραφὴν κ]αὶ τὴν
ποίησιν τῆς στήλης μερ[ίσαι]
[τὸν ταμ[ίαν τῶν στρατιωτικῶν τὸ γενόμενον] ἀνάλωμα.

[ἡ βουλή]	[ὁ δῆμος]	[ἡ β]ουλή	ἡ βουλή
[τὸν ταμίαν]	[τοὺς]	[τὸ]ν γραμ-	Λυσίμαχον
[᾿Απολλώνιον?]	[πρυτάνεις]	[ματ]έα Εὔ-	᾿Αλαιέα
[Σουνιέα]		[βου]λον Προ-	
		[βαλ]ίσιον	

23-24. Apollonios is restored from Agora 15.246 LL. 23-24, 29-30 (which should now be renumbered as LL. 28-29 and 35-36). Εὔβουλον should be restored in LL. 24 and 30 of that text (new LL. 29 and 35).

---

114. ATHENS, DECREE, 127/6 B.C. SEG XV, 104; XXI, 470; XXII, 108; XXV, 130. A.S. Henry, Prescripts 88, restores L. 4 ᾿Ανδρόνικος [᾿Ανδρονίκου Βουτάδης καὶ συμπρόεδροι] *vacat*, removing the anomaly of the omitted symproedroi. The enactment formula may have been omitted, as not uncommonly, or room for it could be found in the *vacat*.

---

115. ATHENS, DECREE HONORING PRYTANEIS OF ERECHTHEIS, 125/4 B.C. Agora 15.249. B.D. Meritt, HISTORIA 26 (1977) 166, now restores the date of the month in L. 3 as [τετράδι ἐπὶ δέκα].

---

116. ATHENS, DECREE HONORING PRYTANEIS OF HIPPOTHONTIS, 125/4 B.C. IG, II², 1003. SEG XXI, 473. Agora 15.250. B.D. Meritt, HISTORIA 26 (1977) 167, restores LL. 2-3 [Ποσιδεῶνος πέμπτει ἐπὶ δέκα, πέμπ]τει καὶ δεκάτει τῆς πρυτανείας.

---

117. ATHENS, DECREE, 117/6 B.C.? Fragment of a white marble stele found in the Agora Excavations (I 7156). Ed. pr. S.V. Tracy, HESPERIA 45 (1976) 287-288, no. 3 (ph.). B.D. Meritt, HESPERIA 46 (1977) 255, shows that there is no *vacat* in L. 3 after ἱσταμένου, as printed in Tracy's text.

non-stoich. ca. 48

[- - - ca. 12 - -ἐπὶ Μενοίτου ἄρχο]ντος ἐπὶ τῆς ᾿Αντιοχίδος *v*
[- - - - - - - ca. 26 - - - - - - - -]άδης ᾿Αττάλου Βερενικίδης
[ἐγραμμάτευεν- - - - ca. 13 - - -]τετράδι ἱσταμένου τετάρτηι
[τῆς πρυτανείας· βουλὴ ἐν βουλευτ]ηρίωι· τῶν προέδρων ἐπεψήφι-
[ζεν- - - ca. 14 - -καὶ συμπρό]εδροι *vac.* 3-4 τὸ κοιν[ὸν τῶν
᾿Αμφι]-

[κτιόνων Ἀθηναίων τῆι βουλῆι καὶ] τῶι δήμωι χαίρ̣ειν
[*vac. ca.* 4 - - -ca. 5- -]

1. [ἐκ τοῦ Μητρῴου] Tracy; cf. IG, II^2, 1132 LL. 1, 40.

118. ATHENS, CITIZENSHIP DECREE, ca. 100 B.C.? IG, II^2, 1055. M.J. Osborne, ANC SOCIETY 7 (1976) 120-121; the stone is apparently now lost. The procedure of granting citizenship is complex enough to justify an earlier date than ca. 100 B.C.

119. ATHENS, CITIZENSHIP DECREE, ca. 100 B.C.? SEG XIV, 73. M.J. Osborne, ANC SOCIETY 7 (1976) 118-120, suggests that this is one of the last inscribed citizenship decrees with a truncated formula.

120. ATHENS, DECREE, 1st cent. B.C. Three fragments of a white marble stele found in the Agora Excavations (I 2351, 1619); ed. pr. D.J. Geagan, HESPERIA 40 (1971) 101-108, no. 8 (ph.); date: 84/3 B.C., on Sulla's return from the east through Athens. J.H. Oliver, GRBS 13 (1972) 101-102; the decree marks a return to democratic government, in reaction to the Sullan reform, in 70/69 B.C. (secretary from Antiochis). E. Badian, Assimilation et résistance à la culture greco-romaine dans le monde ancien: Travaux du VIe congrès international d'études classiques, ed. D.M. Pippidi (Bucharest, Paris 1976) 517; AJAH 1 (1976) 115-117; date: 88/7 B.C., as part of Athenion's "democracy" before Sulla's attack on Athens.

non-stoich. ca. 46

A. [Ἀγαθῆι τύχηι τῆς βουλῆς καὶ τοῦ δήμου τοῦ Ἀθηναίων· ἐπὶ τοῦ δεῖνος]
[ἄρχ]οντ[ος ἐπὶ τῆς - - - - - - -πρυτανείας ἧι - - - Δημη]-
[τρ]ί̣ου Ἀνα[καιεὺς ἐγραμμάτευεν· - - -month and day - -]
[ἕ]κτηι καὶ εἰκ̣[οστῆι τῆς πρυτανείας· ἐκκλησία ἐν - - - -]
ἡ̣ μεταχθεῖσα̣ [ἐκ - - - - - -. τῶν προέδρων ἐπεψήφιζεν]
Ν̣έων Δωροθέο̣[υ - - - - καὶ συμπρόεδροι· ἔδοξεν τῶι δήμωι·]
Δημέας Δημέ[ου Ἀζηνιεὺς εἶπεν· ἐπειδὴ ὁ δῆμος ὁ Ἀθηναίων?]
ἐν δημοκρατίαι κ[ατά τε τοὺς νόμους πολιτευόμενος καὶ ὑπὸ?]
τῶν κλήρωι καὶ χε[ιροτονίαι αἱρεθέντων ἀρχόντων κληθεὶς ?]
καὶ χάριν διδόμεν[ος - - - - - - - - - - - - - - - - - -]
τὰς δὲ κληρωτὰς [ἐφ᾽] ο̣ἷς ησ[- - - - - - - - - - - - - - -]
τινες δὲ διὰ κακοτ̣[ρό]πων πα̣[λαιοὶ νόμοι?- - - - - - - -]
τοὺς̣ προαιρουμέν[ο]υς συνδ[ίκους - - - - - - - - - - εἰς τὸ]
ἐξ̣[ῆ]ς συνβαίνει κοινῆς καὶ εκ[- - - - - - - - - - - - - -]
να[ι ε]ὔνους κατὰ τ[ὸ] ὅ̣μοιον περὶ τ̣[- - - - - - - - ἔξεσ]-
τιν πᾶσιν Ἀθηνα[ί̣]οις ἤδη ποτὲ [- - - -τῶν νόμων τῶν προγε]-

γρ<α>μμένων π[ρ]ονοιαν. *vacat* Ἀ[γαθῆι τύχηι· δεδόχθαι τῶι δήμωι]
[τὰ] μὲν προνενομοθετημέν[α - - - - - - ὑπὸ τῆς βουλῆς τῆς]
[ἐν Ἀ]ρείωι πάγωι κύρια εἶναι. *vac.* [- - - - - - - - - - - -]
[...] δ' ἐξεῖναι το[ῖς] ἄλλοις Ἀ[θηναίοις - - - - - - - -]
[....]αι τὰς κληρ[ω]τὰς ἀρχὰ[ς - - - - - - ὅστις ἂν ζητεῖ?]
[ἀλλό] ποτε οὖν τρό[π]ον καταλ[ῦσαι τοὺς κειμένους νόμους εἶναι ?]
[ἄτιμο]ν καὶ ἐπάρατον· *vacat* ο[- - - - - - - - - - - - - -]
[......]τι κληρωτή τινα [- - - - - - - - - - - - - - - - - -]
[- - - - - - -]ρτ.[. .]Ιηεν[- - - - - - - - - - - - - - - - - -]
[-]

B.
[- - - - - - - - - -]
[- - - - -]το[- - - -]
[- - - - -]τενα[- - -]
[- - - - -]διδι[- - -]
[- - - - -]των[- - -]
[- - - - - -]ιπ[- - -]
[- - - - - - - - - -]

16. ΓΡΜΜ lapis.

121. ATHENS, DECREE ON THE RESTORATION OF SANCTUARIES IN ATTICA, ca. 10/9 - 3/2 B.C. IG, II^2, 1035. SEG XIV, 78. G.R. Culley, HESPERIA 44 (1975) 207-223 (ph.); complete new edition, retaining line numbers of IG; ibid. 46 (1977) 282-298 (map). He associates the decree with the purchase of Salamis by Gaius Julius Nikanor, IG, II^2, 1069 + HESPERIA 36 (1967) 68-71, no. 13. E.A. Kapetanopoulos, RF 104 (1976) 375-377, urges that if this decree is associated with Julius Nikanor, Neos Homeros, and the recovery of Salamis, it must belong to the mid 1st cent. A.D., where he dates IG, II^2, 1069 and other texts concerning Nikanor; cf. IG, II^2, 1723, infra no. 166

Fr. B: Decree I
[- - -]οντος ὃ καθιέρωσεν διὰ [- - - - - - - - - - - - - - - -]
[- - -]ν [κα]ὶ τῶν ταμιευσάντων π[- - - - - - - - - - - - - -]
[- - -]ηθηναι τῆς ἀποκαταστά[σεως - - - - - - - - - - - - - -]
[- - - -] θεῶν τινος ἢ ἡρώων ὑπ[- - - - - - - - - - - - - - -]
[- - - - - -]μένη καὶ εἴ τ<ι>να κατὰ τὸ τ[- - - - - - - - - -]
[- - - - - -]ι τῶν θεῶν καὶ τῶν [ἡρώων - - - - - - - - - - - -]
[- - - - - - - - -] προνοη[θ - - - - - - - - - - - - - - - - - - -]
[- - - - - - - - - -]ρον[- - - - - - - - - - - - - - - - - - - -]

Fr. A and C: Decree II
[- - - -]σι[-]
[- - -]σ. . .πρ[- - - - - - - - -]λια[- - - - - - - - - - - - -]

1 [- - - -]ιλους αὐτῶν [- - -]ηον[- - - - -]φοσθαι τοῖς ἀποδ-

2 [- - - -] ἀποδόσεως τοῦ ἐπὶ τοὺς ὁπλε[ί]τας [στρατηγ]οῦ [τ]ὰ τούτων πραττόμε-

2a [να -]

3 [τῶν ψήφων αἱ πλήρεις, αἷς ἐδόκει τὴν ἐγφερομένην γνώμην κυρίαν εἶ]ναι *v* XXXHHHH𐅄ΔΙ *v* αἱ δὲ τετρυπημέναι, αἷς οὐκ ἐδόκει *vv* H𐅄Γ *vvv*

[ἔδοξεν τῶι δήμωι· - - - - εἶπεν· ἐπειδὴ ὁ δῆμος ἐψήφισται περὶ τῶν ἱερῶν] καὶ τεμενῶν ὅπως ἀποκατασταθῆι το[ῖ]ς θεοῖς καὶ τοῖς ἥρωσιν, ὧν ἐξ ἀρχῆς ὑπῆρχε καὶ τοῦ δή-

5 [μου - - - - καὶ πρέπει ὑπὸ τῶν ἀρχόντων τὸ ἔργον] ἐπὶ τέλος ἀχθῆναι κ[αὶ τ]ὰ λοιπὰ τὰ δια[τείν]οντα πρός τε εὐσέβειαν καὶ τὴν τῶν ἱερῶν καὶ τεμε-

[νῶν θεραπείαν διαμένειν - - - -] δεδόχθαι τῶι δήμωι τὸν [μὲν] ἐπὶ τοὺς [ὁπλεί]τας στρατηγὸν Μητρόδωρον Ξένωνος Φυλάσιον

[ἔχειν ἐπιμέλειαν περὶ τῶν ἱερῶν καὶ τεμενῶν, ὅσα τε ὑπὸ τοῦ δήμου πρὸς τὰς τῶν θεῶν καὶ τῶν ἡρώων θυσία]ς καὶ τειμὰς ἀνεῖται τοῖς ὑπ' αὐτοῦ π[ροε]ψηφισμένοις ἀκολούθως καὶ ὅσα ἀποκαθίστησι πρὸς

[εὐσέβειαν· τὰ δὲ ἱερὰ καὶ τεμένη εἶναι τῶν θεῶν καὶ τῶν ἡρώων ὧν ἐξ ἀρχῆς ὑπῆρχε· καὶ μὴ ἐξεῖναι εἰς τὸν μετὰ τ]αῦτα χ[ρόνον ἀ]ποδόσθαι τι τῶν ἱερῶν τεμενῶν κατὰ μηδένα τρόπον, μηδὲ ὠνήσασθαι μη-

[δὲ ἀποτίμημα ἢ δῶρον λαβεῖν· εἰ δὲ μή, εἶναι φάσιν πρὸς τὸν βασιλέα τῶι βουλομένωι, καὶ τὸν βασιλέα γράφει]ν κ[ατ]ὰ τῶ[ν] ἀποδομένων γραφὰς ἀσεβείας [κ]αὶ ὀφίλειν τῆι Ἀθηνᾶι τὸ χρῆμα ὅσου ἀπέδοντο·

10 [- - - - - - - ἀκολούθως τοῖς] κιμ[έν]οις νόμοις· ἐπεὶ δὲ πάτριόν ἐστιν ἐν μηδενὶ τῶν τεμενῶν μήτ' ἐντίκτειν μήτ' ἐναπο-

[θνήσκειν - - - - -]ους [ἰ]διωτικῶν γεγονυῶν κτήσεων ἀπαρατήρητον αὐτῶν τὴν χρῆσιν γεγενῆσθαι, τὸν μὲν ἐξη-

[γητὴν - - - -] τὸν δ' ἐπὶ τοὺς ὁπλείτας στρατηγὸν Μητρόδωρον Ξένωνος μετὰ τοῦ βασιλέως Μαντίου

[Κλεομένους Μαραθωνίου κατὰ ἃ ὁ ἐξηγητὴς κελεύει ποιεῖσθαι ἐν πᾶσιν τοῖς ἱεροῖς καὶ τεμένεσι θυσίαν ἀρεσ]τήριον [ἑ]κάσ[τ]ωι τῶν θεῶν καὶ [τ]ῶν ἡρώων παριστάνοντος θύματα τοῦ ταμίου κατὰ τὰ

[πάτρια νόμιμα· ἀναγράψαι δὲ τὸν ταμίαν τῆς ἱερᾶς διατάξεως ἐν στήλαιν λιθίναιν δυοῖν τάδε τὰ ψηφίσματα] περὶ τῶ[ν] ἱερῶν κ]αὶ τεμενῶν [καὶ τ]ὰ ἀποκατασταθέντα ἱερὰ καὶ τεμένη καὶ εἴ τινα δημοτε-

15 [λῆ ὄρη ὑπάρχει ἃ κατὰ τάδε τὰ ψηφίσματα ἀποκατασταθῆι - - - καὶ ἀναθε]ῖναι ἣν μὲν [ἐν Ἀκρο]πόλει παρὰ τ[ῆι] Πολιάδι Ἀθηνᾶι, ἣν δ' ἐν Πιραιεῖ παρὰ τῶι Διὶ τῶι Σωτῆρι καὶ τῆ[ι]

[Ἀθηνᾶι τῆι Σωτείραι· ἀπομισθῶσαι δὲ αὐτὰ τὸν ἐπὶ τοὺς ὁπλίτας στρατηγὸν Μητρόδωρον μετὰ τοῦ βασι]λέως καὶ τοῦ ταμίου [τῆς ἱ]ερᾶς διατ[άξε]ως εἰς τετραετίαν καὶ ἀναγράψαι ἐν στήληι τά τε τῶν μεμι-

[σθωμένων ὀνόματα καὶ ὅσου ἕκαστος ἐμισθώσατο καὶ ἀναθεῖναι ἐν - - - - - · τὸ δὲ] ἀνάλ[ωμ]α̣ εἴς τε τὰ θύματα [καὶ τὰς στήλας μ]ε̣ρίσαι τῶι ταμ[ί]αι τῆς ἱερᾶς διατάξεως τοὺς καθεσταμέ-

[νους - - - - - -] ἱερὰ κ̣[αὶ π]ρ̣ονοησόμενον [ὅπως μὴ αἱ τῶ]ν ἀν̣α̣κτηθέ̣ντων ἱερῶν καὶ τεμενῶν μισθώσεις καὶ αἱ τῶν

[δημοσίων οἰκιῶν - - - - - -]ους[.]μ[..]ει δέ τινα διὰ τὴν ἀ[μέλεια]ν̣ παραλ[έλε]ι̣π̣τ̣[αι] τῶν πεπραμένων ὑπὸ στρατηγοῦ ἢ ταμίου τῆς

[ἱερᾶς διατάξεως - - - - - -]νωι[..] [[τ]] ἣν μίσ[θ]ω[σιν] γίνεσθ[αι τ]ῶν ἀν[ακτη]θησομέ[νω]ν κατὰ ταὐτά· τὰ δὲ ὅρη τὰ δημόσια καὶ τὰς δημοτελεῖ[ς]

[ἐσχατιὰς - - - - Δή]μητρος καὶ Κόρης [....]ωσ[...6...]ει σ[...]πασιν· εἰ δ̣[έ τι]νες ὑ̣περβάντες τοὺς ἱεροὺς ὅρους ἐπειργάσαν-

[το τὴν ἱερὰν γῆν - - - - - -]ν[..]τον[..]ναιτηι̣α̣[...]σθ̣[.]ον [εἰς τ]ὴν ἐπισκευὴ̣ν τοῦ [ἐν Ἐλ]ε̣υσῖνι ἱεροῦ ὁμοίως δὲ καὶ τὸν ἀνει-

[μένον - - - - - -]ς μετ̣[ὰ] τῶ̣ν [...] ἱερέα̣ [..]ενο̣[.]αὐτῆι ἀρ̣γ<υρ>ολογοῦσα ἀπαρχὴ̣ν[...6...]α̣νεν ἀπὸ τῶν καρπῶν τῆι θεῶι καὶ τ[- -]

[- - - - - - -]νηι ὄντα τ[ῆς π]όλεως δύο μ[ὲ]ν παραχρῆμα [ἀ]π̣ὸ τῶν νῦν [κατεχ]ό̣ντων ἰδιωτῶν ἐχόντων τὴν ἐξ αὐτ[αρ]-

[κείας γῆν αὐτῶν - - - - - -]ασ[....ἀναθή]ματα κα[ὶ ἀγ]ά̣[λ]ματα τὰ ἀνατεθέντα ὑπ' Ἀτ[τάλου β]α̣σιλέως εἰς τὴν ἀσφάλειαν τῆς

[πόλεως - - - - - - ὅπως τὰ ἱερὰ τῶν ἱερῶν καὶ] τεμ̣[ενῶν τὰ π]επολιτευμ̣[ένα πρ]ὸς ἀείμνηστον δό[ξ]αν τοῦ δ[ήμου ἀμετα]κίνητα διαμένηι, ὀμνύειν τὸγ ἀεὶ λ̣[α]-

[χόντα στρατηγὸν ἐπὶ τοὺς ὁπλείτας· - - - - διατ]ηρῆσ̣α̣ι [τὰ ἀπ]οκατασταθέν̣[τα ἱ]ερὰ̣ κ̣αὶ τεμ̣ένη· καὶ εἴ τι̣ν̣α [πρὸς θεῶν κ]α̣ὶ̣ ἡρώων θυσίας καὶ τιμὰς [ἀν]εῖτα[ι]

[ὕστερον τούτων, ὀμνύειν τὸν ἀεὶ λαχόντα στρατηγὸν ἐπὶ τοὺς ὁπλείτας διατηρῆσαι καὶ ταῦτα καθάπερ] Μη̣[τρόδ]ωρος Ξένωνος Φυλά[σιος ὤμνυ]εν. *vacat*

[*vacat* τάδε ὁ δῆμος ἀπο]κατ[έστη]σεν· *vacat*

[- - - - - ἐν τῶι ἐπὶ -]κ̣ομήδους ἄρχοντος ἐνιαυτ[ῶι] Μ̣ητρόδωρος Ξέν[ωνος Φυλ]άσιος τάδε ἀποκατέστησε·

[- - - - τέμενος? τοῦ δεῖνα ὃ Σόλ]ων ἀνῆκε τῆι Πολ̣[ιάδ]ι̣ καθι̣[ερ]ω̣θὲν πρότερον ὑ̣π' [αὐτοῦ το]ῦ̣ κτίσαντος τὴν νῆσον

[- - - - - - - ὅπου κεῖτ]αι ἡ ἀρχαία πόλις ἡ̣ [πρ]ο̣σων[ο]μασθεῖσα Κυχ[ρεία· τέμεν]ος Αἴαντος ὃ καθιέρωσε

[- - - - - - - ἀκρωτήριο]ν ἐφ' οὗ κεῖται τὸ Θ̣[εμισ]τ[οκ]λέους τρ[όπαι]ο̣ν κ̣α̣τ̣ὰ Π̣ερσῶν καὶ πολυανδρεῖον τῶν

[ἐν τῆι μάχηι τελευτησάντων· - - - - -]ένοις καὶ προθυσαμένο[ις] ἐ̣ν τῶι̣ πρὸς Μ[εγαρέας] πρὸ τῆς νήσου πολέμωι· *v* κῆπον ἐν κρ[- -]

[- - - - - - - ὅπου ὀρχή]σεις καὶ χορε[ῖ]αι ἐδρῶ[ντο..] ενπλευ [.....9....] πόλει τὸ λεγόμενον ὑπὸ Σόλωνο[ς]

[- - - - - - - -]ν τὸ ἐν Ἐλαφυδρίοις α̣[...6...]οντο[...5..]
γι̣α̣ν τὸ παρὰ τὸν παράπλουν τῶν ἱερῶν
[νεῶν· - - - - - - -]ο πρὸς τῆι καλουμένηι π[...]α̣ι̣α[.....11..
....]ν· *v* <Ἡε>τ<ιώ>νειαν ἐξ ἧς αἱ ἱεραὶ ναῦ[ς]
[- - - - - - -] ἥρωος ὑ̣λάζοντο[....]ν̣τ̣α̣[.....10.....]ο̣ν̣α̣σ̣[..]
ἅπασιν νέμειν καὶ ὑλάζεσθαι. *vv*
[- - - - - - -]φ̣α̣νω̣[...]ν̣ πρὸς τῆι[.......14.......] ὃ̣
π̣ρ̣ο̣σ̣[ωνό]μ̣α̣σ̣ται ἀπὸ τοῦ στεφανώματος τῆς θεο[ῦ]
[- - - - - - - -]ο θύειν[......12......]α̣[......11.....]ο̣ν καὶ
ψιλὰ τὰ προσόντα τῶι Ἀσκληπιείωι τὰ ἀνεθέν-
[τα - - - - - - - τ]ῆς π̣ό̣λ̣ε̣ω̣ς̣ [....8....]τ̣ο̣ῦ̣ ἄ̣[γο]ν̣τ̣ο̣ς̣ ἐ̣ν̣ τ̣ῶ̣ι̣
Π̣ε̣λ̣ο̣π̣ο̣ννησιακῶι πολέμωι καὶ τὸ προσόν· *v*
[- - - - - - -] Π̣[ιρ]αιέως παρ' ἱππασίας τὰς π̣[ρ]ὸ̣[ς] τ̣ὴ̣ν̣
Ἀκτήν̣· *v* ψιλὰ [τὰ π]ρ̣ο̣σ̣όντα τῶι Διονυσιείωι καὶ
τὰ προσόντα
[- - - - - - -] τὸ ἀρχαῖον βουλευτήριον· *v* ψύκτρας τὰς πρὸς
τ[ο]ῖ̣ς νεωρίοις τοῦ λιμένος τοῦ ἐν Ζέαι πρὸς τοῖς κλεί-
[θροις· - - - - - - -] σ̣τρατήγιον τὸ ἀρχαῖον· *v* τέμενος
Ἀγαθῆς Τύχης· *v* ψιλὸν τὸ ἀνειμένον τῶι ἀρχαίωι θεάτρωι·
v ψιλὰ τὰ
[προσόντα - - - - - - - ἱερὸν Ἀθηνᾶς? Ἐ]ρ̣κάνης ὃ ἱδρύσατο
Θεμιστοκλῆς πρὸ τῆς περὶ Σαλαμῖνα ναυμαχίας· *v* ψύκτρας
τὰς ἐν τῶι μεγάλωι
[λιμένι - - - - - - - ἀπὸ τοῦ μέρους] τοῦ περικλειομένου τοῖς
νεωρίοις καὶ τῶι Ἀφροδισίωι καὶ ταῖς στοαῖς μέχρι
τῶν κλείθρων· *v*
[- - - - - - -] ἀ̣πὸ τοῦ δίγματος τοῦ ἀνατεθέντος ὑπὸ Μάγνου
καὶ τὸ προσὸν ὕπαιθρον, ὅπου τύποι καὶ *v*
[μέτρα καὶ σταθμὰ κεῖνται - - - - - - τέμενος τὸ π]αρὰ τὰ
μακρὰ τίχη Ἀθηνᾶς Πολιάδος. *v* τέμενος Ἀγαθῆς Τύχης·
v τεμένη Θησέως· *v* τέμενο-
[ς - - - - - - - -] πρὸς Ὑμηττῶι καὶ τὰ προσόντα μέταλλα καὶ
τὸ διόδιον τῆς λιθοτομίας· *v*
[- - - - - - -] ἀφέσεις τὰς ἀπὸ τῶν ὑσπλήγων τοῦ Παναθηναϊκοῦ
σταδίου καὶ τὰ ὑπὸ
[- - - - - - - τ]έμενος Ἀθηνᾶς [Λ]αμπτρᾶσι τὸ λεγόμενον
Δορύκλειον· *vacat*
[- - - - - - - καθιερωθ]ὲν κατὰ χρησμὸν καὶ τὸν οἰκοδομ̣ηθέντα
τόπον πρὸς τῶι βωμῶι· *v* Ὑακίνθιον
[- - - - - - - ὅπου] πρὸ τῶν προβολῶν θύουσιν ἥρωι̣ Στρατηγῶι·
v ἱερὸν Εὐκλείας καὶ Εὐνομίας·
[- - - - - - -]παλαίστραν· *v* οἰκίαν τὴν λεγομε̣νην Κυρρήστου,
ἣν ὁ δῆμος προσκατεσκε[υ]-
[άσατο - - - - - - -]έντα ἀνεθῆναι Διὶ [Ὀλυμ]πίωι καθότι καὶ
πρότερον ἦν· *v* <ο>ἴκησιν τὴν πρὸς
[- - - - - - -] πάσας καὶ παραδρ̣ο̣μίδας· *v* τάφρους πάσας τὰς
κύκλωι τίχ[ο]υς· *v* Σαραπ-
[ιεῖον - - - - - -]α̣[...6...]ς ἀφώρισεν ἐν ἄστει. *vacat* 0.035m.
ἀκρόδρυα. *v* ζευγῶν λ̣ι[- - - -]

[- - - - - χ]α̣ρί̣ε̣[ν] τ̣έμε[νος Ἥ]βης· *v* ὅρος τὸ πρὸς
Ὑμηττῶι· *v* ἐσχατιὰν Λαμπτρᾶσι τὴν πρὸς [- -]
[- - - ὅρη δ]ημόσια ἃ καὶ [.....9.... ἅ]πασιν νέμειν κ[αὶ
ὑ]λάζεσθαι *vacat*

vacat 0.35 m.

---

122. RHAMNOUS, DECREE, 1st/2nd cent. A.D. Now EM 4220. J. Pouilloux, La forteresse de Rhamnonte (Paris 1954) 158-159, no. 49 (ph.). S. Follet, Athènes 25, reads from the stone and ph. 2 lines above Pouilloux' L. 1; ΓΑΒ̣ L. 1; Ω̣ΙΒΕ̣ΙΨ̣ΣΤΑ̣ L. 2, and interprets these as parts of the names of Roman consuls: Gabinus, Gavidius, Gavius, and Vipstantus. In L. 3 Ἰου[λίων] could also be restored.

---

123. ATHENS, PRYTANY DECREE: PANDIONIS, 209/10 A.D. IG, II², 1077. SEG XXIV, 144. Agora 15.460. S. Follet, Athènes 262, restores L. 39 as Κλ. Ἱεροφάντης Ἀχ<α>ρ(νεύς) on the basis of Fourmont's reading ΑΧΙΡ.

---

124. ATHENS, LETTER FROM THE EMPRESS PLOTINA, 121 A.D. IG, II², 1099. J.H. Oliver, AJPh 98 (1977) 164, discusses the title διάδοχος with Athenian parallels.

---

125. ATHENS, TWO LETTERS OF HADRIAN, 124/5 A.D. IG, II², 1097. SEG III, 226. S. Follet, Athènes 23-24, shifts the alignment of the two fragments to yield the following restoration (no line divisions are suggested): [ἐπειδὴ τῆι σεμνοτ?]άτηι μητ[ρὶ ἐδόκει τοῖς ἀεὶ τῆς Ἐπικούρου διαδοχῆ]ς προισταμέ[νοις ἐξεῖναι περὶ] ταύτης Ἑλληνι[κῆι διαθήκηι διατάσσεσθαι κἂν Ἕλληνα] βούλωνται κἂν Ῥω[μαῖον αἱρεῖσθαι - - - -τῶι σχολάρ]χ̣η̣ ἰδίᾳ τῶι σημήν[αντί μοι ταῦτα (?) καὶ πᾶσι τ]οῖς Ἐπικούρου κ[οινῆ (?) - - -] Μαρτίων ἐν Ἀθήναις, Ο̣[ὐαλερίωι Ἀσιατικῶ]ι̣ τὸ β′ καὶ Ἀκυλείν[ωι ὑπάτοις].

---

126. ATHENS, LETTER FROM MARCUS AURELIUS AND LUCIUS VERUS, 165 A.D. SEG XXI, 508. J.H. Oliver, ZPE 20 (1976) 179-181, associates a previously unpublished fragment (EM 8402) of unknown provenance with SEG XXI, 508 from the Agora Excavations (I 6602) and publishes a new text.

Αὐτοκρ[άτωρ Καῖσαρ Μ]ᾶρκος [Αὐρήλιος Ἀντω]-
νῖνος Σ[εβαστὸς Ἀρ]μενιακό[ς, ἀρχ̣ιερεὺς μέγι]-
στος, δημ[αρχικῆς] ἐ̣ξουσίας τ[ὸ ·ΙΘ̄·, αὐτοκράτωρ]
τὸ ·Γ̄·, ὕπατ[ος τὸ Γ̄], καὶ Αὐτο[κράτωρ Καῖσαρ Λούκι]-
ος Αὐρήλι[ος Οὐῆρο]ς Σεβ[αστὸς Ἀρμενιακὸς]

Παρθικὸς [Μέγιστος, δημαρχικῆς ἐξουσίας]
τὸ ·Ē·, αὐτο[κράτωρ τὸ Γ̄, ὕπατος τὸ Β̄, ἀνθύπατος],
θεοῦ Ἀντω[νίνου υἱοί, θεοῦ Ἀδριανοῦ υἱωνοί],
θε[οῦ Τραιανοῦ Παρθικοῦ ἔκγονοι, θεοῦ Νέρουα]
[ἀπόγονοι, - - - - - - - - - - - - - - - - - -]

---

127. ATHENS, LETTERS OF MARCUS AURELIUS AND COMMODUS, 178, 182/3 A.D. IG, II^2, 1108. SEG XXI, 509. J.H. Oliver, HESPERIA, Suppl. 13 (1970) 85-90. S. Follet, Athènes 59, note 4, restores [ἐν]δέ[κατον] in L. 66.

---

128. ATHENS, LETTER OF COMMODUS, 186 A.D.? IG, II^2, 1109 + 2771 + 3412. S. Follet, Athènes 24-25; new readings and restorations; on the date she follows J.H. Oliver, AJPh 71 (1950) 177-179; HESPERIA 36 (1967) 332-333; F. Grosso, MAT 4.7 (1964) 213-234.

[- - -]θύειν κ̣[αὶ ......13.......]ν̣ καὶ σ̣υ̣γ̣ε̣ορτ̣άζειν
[- - -]ταῦρον, ἐπ[έστειλα περὶ τ]ούτων καὶ τῶι ἐπιτρόπωι
[- - -. Εὐτυχεῖτε (?)]. Μ. Αὐρ. [[Κόμμοδος Σεβαστὸ]] ς̣ τ̣[ὸ] ϛ', Ἀκείλιος
Γλαβρίω[ν ὑπάτευον· Αὐρήλιος Κ]λέανδρος ὁ τροφεύς
μου καὶ ἐπὶ̣ [τὴν τοῦ θαλάμου καὶ τ]οῦ σώματος τοῦ ἐμοῦ
πίστιν ἐπιτε[ταγμένος, Αὐρήλιο]ς Λάριχος ὁ φίλος μου
καὶ τὴ̣ν τάξιν τῷ[ν Ἑλληνικῶν ἐπισ]τολῶν πεπιστευμένος,
Ἰούλιος Κάνδιδ[ος ὁ φίλος μου καὶ τ]ὴν τῶν καθόλου λόγω[ν]
προστασίαν ἐπι̣[τετραμμένος - - - - - - - -]ς, Αὐρήλιος [- -]
[- - - - - - - - συνεβούλευον *vel sim.*]

---

129. ELEUSIS, LETTER OF GALLIENUS TO THE ATHENIANS, Dec. 10-31, 265 A.D. Ed. pr. AE (1895) 103-104, no. 17; A. Skias, AE (1899) 206-207, no. 32; P. Graindor, Marbres et textes antiques d'époque impériale (Gand 1922) 75-80. To this text (not included in IG, II^2), K. Clinton adds 4 unpublished fragments in the epigraphical storeroom of the Eleusis Museum and re-edits the whole, AE (1971) 121-124, no. 17 (ph.). S. Follet, Athènes 142-143, suggests numerous restorations which we print in the ap. cr.

[Αὐτ]ο̣κ̣ρ̣[άτωρ Καῖσαρ Π]ο̣ύπ[λιος Λικίνιος Γαλλιηνὸς Εὐσεβὴς Εὐτυ]χ̣ὴ̣[ς Σεβαστός, ἀρχιερεὺς]
μ̣έγισ[τ]ος, [Γερμανικ]ὸς Μ̣[έγιστος, δημαρχικῆς ἐ]ξουσίας τὸ Δ̣!, ὕπατ̣[ος τὸ ϛ̄, ἀποδεδειγμένος]
τὸ Ζ, πατὴ[ρ πατρίδο]ς τῇ [ἐξ Ἀρείου πάγου βου]λῇ καὶ τ<ῇ> βουλῇ τῶν [Ψ̄Ν καὶ τῷ δήμῳ]
τῷ Ἀθηνα[ίω]ν [*vacat* χ]α̣ίρειν· *vacat*
Ἀπόχρη τοῖ̣ς [..] ΥΜ.[..]ΑΦ[- - - ca. 16 - - - ἐν] ἄ̣στει τὴν ἀγορὰν λα̣μ̣[βάν - - - ca. 10 - - -]

[- - - ca. 11 - - -] ΑΥΤΗΝΟ [- - - ca. 19 - - -]νος
ἅπαντας ἀπευ[θυν? - - - ca. 10 - - -]
[- - - ca. 10 - - -]μ̣ὴ τὸ̣ τῶ[ν - - - ca. 19 - - -τ]εταγ-
μ̣ένω[ν - - - ca. 12 - - -]
[- - - ca. 10 - - -]ος γα[- - - ca. 17 - - - ὑπομνημ]ατισμὸν
[τῆς ἐξ Ἀρείου πάγου]
[βουλῆς - - - ca. 28 - - - τ]οῖν θεοῖν κ[- - - ca. 13 - - -]
[- - - - - - ca. 35 - - - - - -].τα ἀστυπ[- - - ca. 13 - - -]
[- - - - - - ca. 35 - - - - - -]ΗΣΩ.[- - ca. 9 - -].ΜΕ.[. .]
[- - - - - - - -]ΟΝΔΑΥ.[- - - - - τὴν ἀγ]ορὰν.[- - ca. 7 - -]ν
στρατ[. .]
[- - - - - - - -]λαμβανο[- - - - - - - -]ΙΑΚΩ[- - ca. 4 - -].
ἐπιχε[ιρ]ο[το]-
[ν - - - - - -] ἅπασιν ἀνθ[- - - - - - -]. τὴν Ἑλ[- - ca. 4 - -]
νει ΗΔΥΝ [. . . .]
[- - - - - - -]απε[μ]φθεὶς ἐπὶ τὸν [- - - - - - -]ΝΑΙΟΙ.
[- ca. 2 -]να ὑφέξει δίκη[ν]
[- - - - - - Ἰού]ν̣ιος Μιγο̣υκιανός. *vv* [Εὐτυχεῖτε.] *vacat*

3. The crossbar of H was not cut. || 5. ἀπόχρη τοῖς [ἐς] ὑμᾶ̣[ς] ἀφ[ικνουμένοις? - - - ἐν] ἄστει τὴν ἀγορὰν λαμ̣[βάνειν] Follet. || 7. [ἵνα?] μὴ τὸ τῶ[ν σιτίων τίμημα ὑπὲρ τῶν? τ]εταγ-μένω[ν - - -] Follet. | [τ]εταγμένω[ι] Skias. || 12-13 [τ]ὸν δ' αὐτ̣ὸ̣[ν τρόπον? ἀγ]ορὰν π̣[αρασχεῖ?]ν στρατ[ιωτικῶν ὠνίων] or στρατ[ιώταις τοῖς - - - ἀπο]λαμβανο[- - -] Follet | ΟΝ δ' αὐτ̣ο̣[- - -] Skias. || 13. κω[λῦσαι] ἐπιχε[ιρ]ο[υ - - -] Follet. || 14. ἅπασιν ἀνθ[ρώποις] Clinton, Follet. | [- - - κατ]ὰ̣ τὴν Ἑλλ̣[άδα ἐ]νείη δύν[αμις etc.] Follet. || 15. [ἀποδόσθω̣ δὲ ? ὁ μετ?]απεμφθεὶς ἐπὶ τὸν ἔ[παρχον τοῖς Ἀθη]ναίοι[ς ἵ]να ὑφέξει δίκην Follet. || 16. [Ἐπρέσβευεν Ἰού]γ̣ιος Μινουκιανός. *vacat* ε̣[ὐτυχεῖτε] or ἔ̣[ρρωσθε] Follet.

130. ATHENS, BOIOTIAN DECREE, late 3rd/early 2nd cent. B.C. Fragment of a stele of blue marble found in the Agora Excavations (I 6420). Ed. pr. G.V. Lalonde, HESPERIA 46 (1977) 268-276 (ph.).

[- - - - - - - - - - - - - - - -].σ̣ε̣[- - - - - - ca. 15 - - - - - -]
[- - - - - - - - - - - - - - -]α̣θαφηγ̣[- - - - - - ca. 13 - - - - - - -]
[- - - - - - - - δε]δ̣ό̣χθη τῦ δά[μυ - - - ca. 10 - - - - - - -]
[- - - -τὼ]ς̣ σ̣τρατ[[α]]γὼς κη̣[- - - - - - - ca. 12 - - - - - -]
[- - - - - - -].φανιας κὴ τὰν ευ[- - - - - - ca. 10 - - - - - -]
[- - - - -]η̣ ἐ̣π̣ὶ τῦ βειλομένω[ι - - - - - - ca. 8 - - - - - -]
[- - - - -].ειας τόν τε θεὸν τιμ̣[- - - - - - ca. 7 - - - - - -]
[- - - - - - τῆ]ς τιμῆς κὴ ψαφιξαμ[έ]νω[- - - ca. 5 - - - - -]
[- - - - - - - - -].κακωθούσοντα τ̣[- - - - - - ca. 7 - - - - - -]
[- - - - - - - - - -].ο παιὰν τὸ ἀριστειο[- - - ca. 5 - - - - -]
[- - - - - - - - - - - -]τ̣ὰν θουσίαν κατὰ <ξ>ε[- - ca. 4 - - -]
[- - - - - - - - -Θεισ]πιέων οπο̣[- - 3-4 - -]σου..[- ca. 3 -]
[- - - - - - - - - - - - - - -]οτιαθ[- - ca. 7 - -]ω[- ca. 4 -]

[- - - - - - - - - - -]τια.[- - ca. 4 - - Θει]σπιε[- ca. 2 -]
[- - - - - - - - - - -]σϰ[- - - ca. 7 - - -]πα[.]ϰ[-ca. -]
[- - - - - - - - - -]σ̣ᾳ̣[- - - ca. 8 - - - -]αε[- - ca. 3 - -]
[- - - - - - - - - - -]ν.[- - - ca. 7 - - -]αν.[- - ca. 3 -]
[-].αντιμ.[- ca.2 -]
[-]τωσδεπ̣ο̣[- ca. 2 -]
[-]αιειτ.[- ca. 4 -]

vacat

2. ϰοθ' ἃ φήνετη? Lalonde. || 13. π]οτὶ 'Αθ[άνας? Lalonde.

---

131. ATHENS, TWO DECREES OF THE TRIBE AKAMANTIS, 361/0 B.C. and later? SEG XXIII, 78. S. Dow, In Memoriam Otto J. Brendel (Mainz 1976) 81-84, identifies the honorand of LL. 1-12 (possibly Autolykos) as an archon (either basileus or polemarch) and the two men in LL. 11 and 12 as his paredroi. The restoration of the demotic in L. 12 is not inevitable and the restoration of Nikophemos in L. 13 is rejected as too short for the space. Dow places the decree in LL. 13-26 ca. 334/3 B.C.

---

132. AIXONE, DEME DECREE, ca. 350 B.C. IG, II², 1186. P. Ghiron-Bistagne, Acteurs 90-91; text and French translation.

---

133. AIXONE, DEME DECREE, 313/2 B.C.? IG, II². 1202. Mette, UDA 136, no. 1. P. Ghiron-Bistagne, Acteurs 88-90 (ph.); text and French translation; she supports W. Peek's date, MDAI (A) 66 (1941) 218, against T.B.L. Webster, Monuments Illustr. Trag. Sat. Plays 34, no. AS 7, 340/39 B.C.

---

134. ELEUSIS, DEME DECREE, 332/1 B.C. S.N. Koumanoudes, AE (1976) 205, no. 3, quotes the following passage from an unpublished inscription of the archonship of Niketes found in 1970 which deals with the λατομεῖον τοῦ Ἡραϰλέους τοῦ ἐν Ἄϰριδι: LL. 24-28 τὸν δὲ μισθωσάμενον ἀποδιδόναι τὴν μίσθωσιν τὴν μὲν ἐπὶ Νιϰήτου ἄρχοντος ἐν ᾧ ἂν χρόν̣ῳ̣ τοὺς δημότας π̣ε̣[ί]θει, πρὸ τῆς θυσίας, μετὰ δὲ Νιϰήτην ἄ̣ρχο̣ντα εἰς τὸν Μεταγειτνιῶνα μῆνα ταῖς ἀρχαιρεσίαις, ὅταν οἱ δημόται ἀγοράζωσιν ἐν τῶι Θησείωι.

---

135. ATHENS, DECREE OF THE ORGEONES OF AMYNOS, ASKLEPIOS, ETC., ca. 350-300 B.C. IG, II², 1252 + 999. SEG XIV, 82. D. Peppas-Delmouzou, AD 27 (1972) [1976] B.10, no. 1, joins 999 to the bottom left corner of 1252 to yield a new text of LL. 19-22.

ὅπως ἂν ϰαὶ οἱ ἄλλοι φιλοτι-

μῶνται περὶ τὰ κοινὰ τῶν ὀργεώνων εἰδό-
τες ὅτι χάριτα[ς ἀποδώ]σουσι τοῖς εὐεργετοῦ-
σιν τι αὐτούς.

20. Final ο written above the δ for syllabic division. || 22. εἰαυτούς IG, II^2, 999.

136. THORIKOS?, SACRIFICIAL CALENDAR OF THORIKOS, ca. 400-350 B.C. Now lost? Ed. pr. E. Vanderpool, Thorikos and the Laurion in Archaic and Classical Times : Miscellanea Graeca 1 (Ghent 1975) ed. H. Mussche, pp. 33-41, from a copy made by D.F. Ogden of a copy made from the stone; text of 28 lines only. G. Dunst, ZPE 25 (1977) 243-264, publishes a full text from an independent and more complete copy. Underlined letters are known only from Ogden's copy. Line numbers in col. II approximate those in col. I. The position of col. II on the stone is not known.

stoich. 30

Col. I

[..........19......... Ἑκ]ατομβαιῶν-
[ος ....18.........]ΑΚΙΚΑΙ·Τ·ΟΙ
[...6... τῶι ἀκολοθῦντι ἄρ]ιστομ παρέ-
[χεν τὸν ἱερέα ....7... δρα]χμὴν ἑκατέ-
[ρο ....16........ κ]αὶ τὴν Προηρο-
[σίαν ....17........].ΙΝ <Ἀ>θηναί-
[αι ....18.........]ΕΙΑΙ Ἑκά{.}τη-
[ι ....22...........]ΗΝΟΣΑΤΗ
[..........19.........]τέλεομ πρατὸ-
[ν ....16........ Κατ]αιβάτηι ΕΝΟ
[..]σηκῶι [...]ΑΙΟ[....7...]ΟΝ τέλεον πρ-
ατόν. Ὁρκωμόσιον [..4..]χεν ἐς εὐθύνας.
Βοηδρομιῶνος. Πρηροσία. Δ<ιὶ> Πολιεῖ· κρ-
ιτὸν οἶν : χοῖρον κριτόν. ἐπαυ<ξ>όμενα [
χοῖρον ὠνητὸν ὁλόκαυστον, τῶι ἀκολο-
θῦντι ἄριστομ παρέχεν τὸν ἱερέα : Κεφ-
άλωι· οἶν κριτόν, Πρόκριδι· τράπεζαν, v
Θορικῶι· κριτὸν οἶν, Ἡρωΐνησι Θορικõ·
τράπεζαν. Ἐπὶ Σούνιον Ποσειδῶνι· ἀμν-
ὸν κριτόν, Ἀπόλλωνι· χίμαρον κριτόν, [Κ]-
ουροτρόφωι· χοῖρον κριτήν, Δήμητρι· <ῦ>[ν],
Δ<ιὶ> Ἑρκείωι· τέλεον, Κοροτρόφω[ι· αἶγα],
Ἀθηνᾶι· οἶν πρατόν, Ἑ<κ>ά[τηι] <Φ>ωσ[φόρωι· τ]-
έλεον, Ἀπόλλωνι· χοῖρον.
Πυανοψιῶνος α'. Καταιβάτηι Ε[....7...]
ημιδῶν. τέλεον πρατόν, ἕκτηι Ε[...6...']
Νεανίαι· τέλεον, Πυανόψι<α>, οἶ[ν] π[ρατόν]·
Μαιμακτηριῶνος· Θορικῶι· βοῦ[ν μήλατ]-
τον ἢ τετταράκοντα δραχμῶν [μέχρι πε]-
ντήκοντα, Ἡρωΐνησι Θορικõ· τ[ράπεζαν].
Ποσιδειῶνος· Διονύσια.

<Γ>αμηλιῶνος {Σ}. Ἥραι· Ἱερῶι Γάμων [...6...]
Ἀνθεστηριῶνος. Διονύσωι· δω[δεκάτηι]
αἶγα λειπεγνώμονα πυρρὸν ἢ [μέλανα. Δ]-
ιασίοις· Δ<ιὶ> Μιλιχίωι· οἶν πρα[τόν vvv].
Ἐλαφηβολιῶνος· Ἡρακλεῖ, Ἀμ[φιτρύωνι],
Ἀλκμήνηι· τέλεον, Ἀνάκοιν· τ[έλεον, Ἑλέ]-
νηι· τέλεον, Δήμητρι [Ἐλευσινίαι· ὗν κρ]-
ιτὴν κυῶσαν, Δι<ί>· ἄρνα κριτόν.
Μουνυχιῶνος. Ἀρτέμιδι Μουν[χίοι· (Numeral) ἢ πλ]-
έονες Πυθίο Ἀπόλλωνος τρί[ποδες, Κορ]-
οτρόφωι· χοῖρον, Λητοῖ, αἶγα, Ἀ[ρτέμιδι·]
αἶγα, Ἀπόλλωνι. αἶγα λειπογν[ώμονα, Δή]-
μητρι· οἶν κυῶσαν, Θεᾶι Φ[.].[....7... τρ]-
άπεζαν, Διονύσωι Ἐπιμυκήνω[ι· τράγον]
πυρρὸν ἢ μέλανα.
Θαργηλιῶνος. Διί· ἐπαυξόμενα <Ϲ> [...5..]
ἄρνα, Ὑπερπεδίωι· οἶν, Ἡρωΐνησ[ι Ὑπερ v]
πεδίο· τράπεζαν, Νίσωι· οἶν, ΟΘΡΝΕ[..4..]
οἶν, Σωσίνεφ· οἶν, Ῥο<θ>ίωι· οἶν, Πυ[λόχωι v·]
χο<ῖ>ρον, Ἡρωΐνησι Πυλοχίσι· τρά[πεζαν·]
Σκ<ι>ραφοριῶνος. Ὁρκωμόσιον Α[...5.., Π]-
λυντηρίοις Ἀθηναίαι· οἶν κρ[ιτόν Ἀγλ]-
αύρωι· οἶν, Ἀθηναίαι· ἄρνα κρι[τόν, Θορι?]-
κῶι· βοῦν μήλάττονος ἢ τεττα[ράκοντα]
δραχμῶν μέχρι πεντήκοντα. Π[....7...]·
οἶ{$\genfrac{}{}{0pt}{}{\Delta}{\Delta}$}ν. τὸν δ᾽ εὔθυνον ὀμόσαι καὶ τ[ὸς παρέδ]-
ρος· εὐθυνῶ τὴν ἀρχὴν ἣν ἔλαχ[εν εἰ ἦρχ]-
εν κατὰ τὰ ψηφίσματα ἐφ᾽ οἷς ἐ[σελήλυ v?]-
θεν ἡ ἀρχή. ὀμνύναι Δία, Ἀπόλ[λω, ἑαυτῶι]
<ἐ>ξώλειαν ἐπαρώμενον καὶ [τοῖς παρέδ]-
ροις κατὰ ταὐτά. ἀναγράψαι [....8....]
Ν ἐστήληι καὶ κατα{Α}θεῖναι <ἐ>[ς Ὁρκωμόσ]-
ιον. ὅσαι δ᾽ ἂν ἀρχαὶ αἱρεθῶ[σι ....7...]
- -

Col. II

ωνι· τέλεον [..........19......... Πυ]-
ανοψίοις [...........22...........]

[............. 28 .... Δι]-
ὶ Ἑρκείωι· οἶν [.........19.........]

[............. 27 .... Ἡρω]-
ΐνησιν Κορωνε[ιίσιν? ....13......]
[....]ΠΝ· οἶν [...........21..........]
- -

1. [τάδε θύεται Θορικίοις Ἑκα] Vanderpool. || 2. ΑΚΙΚΑΙΤΟΙ Ogden. || 4.]ΗΣΤΟΜΡΑΡΙ Ogden. || 5.]αι τὴν πρηρο|[σίαν

Vanderpool. || 6. ΙΘΗΝΑΙ Dunst; ΙΘΝΑΙ Ogden. || 7. ΕΚΑΤΗ Ogden. || 8. ΤΗΙ Ogden. || 10. [Διὶ Κατ]αιβάτηι Vanderpool. || 12. παρέ]χεν? Burkert apud Dunst. || 13. ΔΗ both copies. || 14. ΕΠΑΥΤΟΜΕΝΑΣ Dunst; ΕΠΑΝΤΟΜΕΝΑΣ Ogden. || 15. ὁλόκαυτον Ogden; τῶι ἀκολού|θωι τὸ Vanderpool. || 21-30 lacking in Ogden's copy. || 22. ΔΗ. || 23. Ἀθηναί<αι>? Burkert; ΠΡΑΤΟΙΕ.Α.Η.ΓΟΣ Dunst. || 26. Ἐ[πόχωι *v*] Graf apud Dunst. || 32-33 lacking in Ogden's copy. || 32. ΠΑΜ - - - ΙΕΡΩΙ end [πομπή] or [ἑορτή] Dunst. || 34. ΛΕΙΘΕΓΝΟΜΟΝΑ Ogden; λειπογνώμονα Vanderpool. || 35. ΔΗ Dunst. || 36. end ΔΑ[- - -] both copies. || 37-44. lacking in Ogden's copy. || 39. ΔΙ Dunst. || 42. Λ[....7...] Dunst. || 45. ἐπὶ Μυκήνην [αἶγα] Vanderpool. || 47-59 lacking in Ogden's copy. || 50. ΡΟΓΙΩΙ Dunst. || 51. .ΟΝΡΟΝ Dunst. || 60. Last line in Ogden's copy.

On the relationship between the state and deme sacrificial calendars, J. Mikalson, AJPh 98 (1977) 424-435.

---

137. AGRILEZA, CALENDAR, 4th cent. B.C. From the Laureion mining district. Cut into the bedrock near nos. 53, 227, 266. Ed. pr. L.V. Watrous, HESPERIA 46 (1977) 168-173, no. 3 (ph., dr.).

Col. I

Ἑρμῆς Ἀγαθός. Ἕρμα πρὸ Σουνίου.
Ἑρμη[.] θεοῦ [- - -]
[- - -]
Κ̣ΕΘ̣ [- - -]
[- - -]

Col. II

Ἑκατονβαιών
Μεταγειτνιών
[Βοηδρομι]ώ̣[ν]
[Πυανο]ψιών
[Μαιμακτηριών]
[Ποσ]ιδε̣[ών]
[Γαμη]λιών
[Ἀνθεστηρι]ών
[Ἐλαφ]ηβολ[ιών]
[Μουνυχι]ών
[Θα]ρ̣γ[ηλιών]
[Σκιροφορι]ώ̣[ν]
vacat
Ἀν*v*[. .]σώρος
ἐπί*v*τροπος
χ̣ωρίου

Two graffiti at the edges of the text: Ζωΐλος above Col. I and two lines which Watrous regards as nonsensical to the right of col. II LL. 18-20.

---

138. SACRIFICIAL CALENDARS OF THE ATTIC DEMES. ELEUSIS: IG, II², 1363; SEG XXII, 132; XXIII, 80; XXV, 168. ERCHIA: SEG XXI, 541; XXII, 131; XXV. 163. MARATHON: IG, II², 1358; SEG XIX, 127; XXV, 127. TEITHRAS: SEG XXI, 542; XXV, 165. THORIKOS: no. 136. J. Mikalson, AJPh 98 (1977) 424-435, general

discussion of the relationship of these calendars to the state sacrificial calendar.

---

139. ATHENS, GYMNASIUM INVENTORY, ca. 170-135 B.C. Four fragments of blue-gray marble found in the Agora Excavations (I 2309 = Fr. A; 5916 + 1007 + 1005 = Fr. B). Fr. A is inscribed on front (a) and right side (b). Ed. pr. D. Clay, HESPERIA 46 (1977) 259-267 (ph.). J.S. Traill, ibid. 397, prosopographic note on Eucheir of L. 59.

Fr. A: face a

[- - - -]Ε̣ΠΤ[...ca. 5..]
[- - -]τ̣ραγηματ[α *v*]
[- - -τ]ύπος Κεντα[ύρου *v*]
[- - -]ς Κουρῆτες *v*
vacat
[- - -]γυναῖα δύο καὶ
[- - -]πιον Χάρητος
[- - -]καὶ Κωμωιδία *v*
vacat
[- - -]Δ̣Α̣Ω̣[.... ca. 7 ...]ΕΝΟ[ ]

face b

[... ca. 6 ...] Κ[- - - - -]
[... ca. 5 ..]Ι̣ΟΝ[- - - -]
[. . . .]Τ̣ΗΣ[- - - - -]
[. . . .]ΙΟΥ[- - - - -]
[. . .] ΣΧΑ[- - - - -]
[. .] Δ̣ΑΜΠ[- - - - -]
[. .] ιον πρ[- - - - -]
[. .] Υ̣Γ̣Ν̣Ω̣ [- - - - -]

Fr. B:

[- - - - - -] πρὸς τ[..]
[- - - - - - -]ν καὶ παι
[- - - - - Ἀ]σκληπιός
[- - - - - -]ς καὶ Ὑγίεια
[- - - - - θ]εράπων
[- - - - - -] ἀπὸ τῶν
[- - - - - φ]αλακροῦ
[- - - - - -]υ Ἀσκληπιός
[- - - - - -]ικὸς καὶ
[- - - - - -]ον ἄλλος
[- - - - - ἐ]ν φαιῷ
[- - - - - - -]ιτης
[- - - - - - - -]ον παι
[- - - - - - - -]αι
[- - - - - - - - - - - -]
[- - - - - - - - - - - -]
[- - - - - - - - - - - -]
[- - - - - - - - -] καὶ
[- - - - - - - -]Ἑρμῆς
[- - - - - κα]ὶ ἐν τεῖ ἄλλει
[- - - - - -]τη βαλβῖδι

[- - - - - - - - -]υς ἀνδριάς
[- - - - - - - - ἔ]χων
[- - - - - - - - -]ὑμηττία
[- - - - - - - - - -]ὑμήττιος
[- - - - - - -πε]ντελεικόν
[- - - - - - - - - -]ωι
[- - - - - - -]ένη Ἑρμοκλέους
[- - - - - - -]ἐξέδραι
[- - - - - - -]ενος Ἄρτεμις
[- - - - - - - -]ἔχουσα
[- - - - - - - -]ποδήρη χιτῶνα
[- - - - - - - -]καθήμενον
[- - - - - - - -]ἐξέδραι
[- - - - - - -]λιθοι Μοῦσαι
[- - - - - - -]σιον Ἑρμοκλέους
[- - - - - - -]ἀλάβαστρον
[- - - - - - -]Ἑρμαφρόδιτος
[- - - - - - - -Ἄ]ρτεμις
[- - - - - - - -]πα[ρ]θένου
[- - - - - - - - Τ]ιμαρ̣χίδου
[- - - - - - - - -]του
[- - - - - - - - Εὔχ]ειρος
[- - - - - - - - -]η ὑπητ[τία]

140. ATHENS, CATALOGUE OF STATUES, 340-330 B.C. IG, II^2, 1498. E.B. Harrison, AJA 81 (1977) 149, suggests that the male statue in LL. 63-65 is a smaller reflection of the Hephaistos of Alkamenes.

---

141. ATHENS, NAVAL CATALOGUE, 323/2 B.C. IG, II^2, 1631. After examining the stone, N.G. Ashton, ABSA 72 (1977) 4, presents a new text of LL. 167-174; discussion of the date of the battle of Amorgos.

ἔργον: *v* ἀριθμὸς τριήρ[ων τῶ]ν ἐν <τοῖς>
νεωρίοις καὶ τῶν ἐμ πλῶι οὐσῶ[ν κ]αὶ
σὺν ἧι ἔφηνεν Ἀριστόνικ[ος Μ]α[ρ]αθ(ώνιος)
καὶ σὺν ταῖς διάζυ[ξι] δυοῖν τ[α]ῖς Ἁρ-
παλείοις: HHHΔΓ: τούτω[ν ἐμ] π[λ]ῶι
[. .]ΔΔΔIIII: τετρήρεις δὲ [ἐμ μ]ὲν [τ]οῖς
[νε]ωρίοις παρέδομεν: I : ἐμ πλ[ῶι] δὲ
[....]ΓIIII : σ[ὺν] τῆι Ἁρπαλείωι. [ἐ]μβο

172. [H𐅄]ΔΔΔIIII Ashton, cf. Diod. Sic. 18.15.8. || 174. [ΔΔΔΔ]ΓIIII Ashton, cf. Diod. Sic. 18.10.2.

---

142. ELEUSIS, CONTRACTS: PORTICO OF THE TELESTERION AT ELEUSIS, 356-352 B.C. IG, II^2, 1666. SEG XVII, 41. J.J. Coulton, AJA 80 (1976) 302-304, argues that ἀναγραφεύς in LL. A.34, 48, 55, and passim means "template". Cf. also IG, II^2, 244, LL. 54, 106; 1670, L. 20; 1685A. LL. 3, 6.

---

143. ATHENS, LIST OF ARCHONS, ca. 200 B.C. IG, II^2, 1706. SEG XIV, 87; XXIII, 84. J.H. Kroll, HESPERIA 46 (1977) 122, no. 55, identifies Chairephon Alopekethen on 4 Athenian cavalry tablets (infra no. 163) with the archon of 219/8 B.C., confirming S. Dow's restoration of the name in L. 101.

---

144. ATHENS, ARCHON LIST, 88/7 B.C. IG, II^2, 1714. E. Badian, Assimilation et résistance à la culture gréco-romaine dans le monde ancien: Travaux du VIe Congrès International d'Études Classiques, ed. D.M. Pippidi (Bucharest, Paris 1976) 510-514, 520, follows the suggestion of S. Dow, HESPERIA 3 (1934) 144-146, that the list was engraved after the capture of Athens by Sulla and that the omitted eponymous archon's name was damnatio memoriae of one of Athenion's men. C. Habicht, CHIRON 6 (1976) 127-135, suggests that the missing eponymous archon in this list was King Mithridates VI. Cf. the anarchia in IG, II^2, 1713.

---

145. ATHENS, PRYTANY CATALOGUE: AIANTIS, 125-150 A.D. IG, II^2, 1767. Agora 15.340. S. Follet, Athènes 186-187; detailed prosopographical study by which she establishes the date.

---

146. ATHENS, PRYTANY CATALOGUE, 136/7 - 148/9 A.D. IG, II^2, 1797. Agora 15.410. S. Follet, Athènes 310-311, suggests this date on prosopographic grounds and restores the titles of the aeisitoi in LL. 7-12 as follows: 7 [κῆρυξ βο]υλῆς, 8 [γρ. βουλ.], 9 [ἀντιγρα]φε., 10 [περὶ τὸ β.], 11 [ἱεραύλης], 12 [ἐπὶ Σκιάδ.].

---

147. ATHENS, PRYTANY CATALOGUE, 141/2 A.D. IG, II^2, 1764B. Agora 15.334. S. Follet, Athènes 194-195, offers a new text of LL. 59-64; prosopographic notes on Hordeonios Lollianos L. 60 and others; L. 69 Γ. Μάρκιος Κ̣[αλλίμαχος?].

Ἀγαθῇ τύχῃ [Ἀντωνείνου Σεβαστοῦ(?)]·
Ὁ̣ ἱ̣ε̣ρεὺς Ὁρδεώνιος Λ[ολλιανὸς τοὺς ἐπὶ ἄρχον]-
τος Πο̅. Αἰλίου Φιλέα [Μελιτέως ἀνέγραψεν· ἀπὸ τῆς]
πρώτης ἐπιδημίας θε[οῦ Ἁδριανοῦ ἔτος ιη'· τῆς]
Ἁδριανίδος ἐγραμμά̣[τευεν ......12...... Φι]-
λολόγου Θριάσιος. Βησαιε[ῖς] *etc.*

---

148. ATHENS, PRYTANY CATALOGUE, 146/7 A.D.? Agora 15.442. S. Follet, Athènes 304-305; newly restored text with ap. cr.; discussion of the date on the basis of the prosopography.

[Ἀίσε]ι̣τ̣οι
[Ἱεροφάντης] [κῆρυξ] βουλῆς καὶ δή-
[Δᾳδοῦχος] μου Ὀρφίτιος
[Ἱεροκῆρυξ] Βουρριανὸς Σφή.
[ἀντιγραφεὺς] [π]ερὶ τὸ βῆμα Θεο-
[- - - - - - - - -] [- - - - Ἀθ]μονεύς
[ἱεραύλης Ἑρμό]δωρος Καλλιστρά-
[γρ. βουλῆς καὶ δ]ήμου /του Βερενει
[- - - - - - - - - -Ἀθ]μονεύς /κίδης
[ἐπὶ Σκιάδος ἱερε]ὺ̣ς Πρωτίων
[ὑπογραμματεὺς Μ]η̣νόφιλος

---

149. ATHENS, PRYTANY LIST?, ca. 150 A.D. IG, II^2, 2472. S. Follet, Athènes 167; since all identifiable names in this list belong to the deme Cholleidai, it is probably a list of prytaneis.

---

150. ATHENS, PRYTANY CATALOGUE, 152/3 - 169/70 A.D.? SEG XXI, 615 + XXII, 140. Agora 15.455. S. Follet, Athènes 371-372, no. 1; text, ap. cr., discussion of the date; possible restoration

of LL. 1-4: [τῶν] | [Σεβασ]- | [τ]ῶν | Ἀγαθ[ῆι τύχηι].

151. ATHENS, PRYTANY CATALOGUE, 168/9 A.D. Agora 15.372 + 374. S. Follet, Athènes 216-217, associates these two texts and republishes the whole; new readings and restorations in LL. 3-6. She places Agora 15.372, LL. 9-16 in the right column above LL. 24-40

[ἐπὶ ἄρχοντ]ος Τ[ινηίου]
[Ποντικο]ῦ Βησ[αιέως]
[οἱ πρυτάνεις τ]ῆς Π[τολε]-
[μαΐδος φυλῆς τιμήσαντες]
5 [ἑαυτοὺς καὶ τοὺς ἀεισί]-
[τους ἀνέγραψαν].

Col. I

Agora 15.372,
LL. 1-8;
Follet, LL. 7-14.

Col. II

Agora 15.372,
LL. 17-22;
Follet, LL. 13-20.

Col. III

Agora 15.372,
LL. 9-16, 24-40;
Follet, LL. 21-43.

152. ATHENS, PRYTANY LIST, 168/9 A.D. SEG XXIV, 183. Agora 15.375. S. Follet, Athènes 217-218, proposes minor changes in L. 2: [του Σ]εβασ[τοῦ]; LL. 6-7: [ὅ]πλ[α] | [Βαλερί]ου; LL. 8-11: πρυτά[ν]ει[ς] | [τῆς - - -ίδος φ]υλῆ[ς τειμή] | [σαντες ἑαυτοὺς κ]αὶ τ[οὺς] | [ἀισίτους ἀνέγραψαν].

153. ATHENS, PRYTANY CATALOGUE: ATTALIS, ca. 175/6 A.D.? IG, II^2, 1763. Agora 15.329. E.A. Kapetanopoulos, HELLENIKA 29 (1976) 248-259; new reading from a squeeze, L. 1: Α. (sign) Λάρ(κιον) Παυλεῖνον Ἀ|γνούσιον. He also restores LL. 5-6: [ἐπὶ ἄ]ρχοντος Σαλλουστιαν[οῦ| Αἰο]λίωνος Φλυέως and redates the list on prosopographic grounds from ca. 132/3 A.D. to ca. 175/6 A.D.

154. ATHENS, PRYTANY CATALOGUE, 184/5 - 190/1 A.D. IG, II^2, 1792. SEG XXI, 608. Agora 15.423. S. Follet, Athènes 139-140; text of LL. 1-8; ap. cr.; possible restoration of the end of line 5: Σ[φηττίου, ἐπὶ ἄρχοντος Σαλουσ(τιανοῦ)] or σ[τρατηγοῦντος ἐπὶ τὰ ὅπλα Σαλουσ.]; cf. IG, II^2, 1763, L. 6. E.A. Kapetanopoulos, HELLENIKA 29 (1976) 248-266, restores σ[τρατηγοῦ τῆς πόλεως Σαλουσ(τιανοῦ)]; full prosopographic discussion of

Salloustianos Aiolion Phlyeus. Cf. infra no. 246.

---

155. ATHENS, PRYTANY CATALOGUE, 196/7 - 205/6 A.D. SEG, XIX, 156. Agora 15.481. S. Follet, Athènes 372-374, no. 2, offers a new restoration of the whole and a new identification of the archon in L. 2; discussion of the date.

ʼΑγαθ[ῆ̣ Τύχῃ̣].
ἐπὶ ἄρχο[ντος Κλ. Φωκᾶ Μ]αραθῳ̣-
νίου, νεω[κόρου τοῦ μεγά]λ̣ο̣[υ]
Σαρά[π]ι̣δ̣[ος, στρατηγοῦντος ἐπὶ]
τὰ ὅπλα Π̣[ομπ. ʽΗγία Φαληρέως?]
οἱ πρυτά[νεις τῆς - - - - φυλῆς]
[τειμήσαντες ἑαυτοὺς καὶ τοὺς]
[ἀεισίτους ἀνέγραψαν].

---

156. ATHENS, PRYTANY CATALOGUE, ca. 197/8 - 199/200 A.D. IG, II^2, 1804. Agora 15.444. S. Follet, Athènes 312, restores LL. 2-4:

[*vac.* τοῦ με]τὰ Ξενοκλέα
[ἐνιαυτοῦ, ἐ]πὶ τῆς Οἰνεΐ-
[δος φυλῆς] γ̣ʹ πρυτανείας.

---

157. ATHENS, PRYTANY CATALOGUE, ca. 200 A.D. Agora 15.414. S. Follet, Athènes 309-310, presents a new text after study of the stone; ap. cr. Her date depends on the activity of Aphrodeisios, 190/1 or 203/4 A.D.

[ʼΑίσειτοι] [- - -Δα]ι̣[δ]οῦ[χος (?)]
[- - -ʽΙεροφάντης (?)] ʽΕρεν. ῞Ιερ(ο)κῆρυξ Κ[λ. ἐπὶ βωμῷ (?)]
[γρ. βουλῆς - -]γόδ- κῆρυξ βουλῆς καὶ δήμ̣[ου]
[ωρος (?) ʼΑσκληπι(?)]άδου Φλα. Σωσιγένης *vacat*
[- - demotic - - -] πρ.(?) ἀντιγραφεὺς Κλ. Κορνηλιανό[ς]
[γρ. κατὰ πρυτανείαν] ʼΑφρ̣οδείσιος) Φλυεύς
[ἐπὶ Σκιάδος ʼΑριστείδης Φ]ρ̣εάρριος *vacat*
[ἱεραύλης ʼΕπαφρόδειτος ὁ κα]ὶ ʼΑφροδείσιος
[ὑπογραμματεὺς - - - - - - - - - - - - - - -]
vacat
[γραμματεὺς βουλευτῶν (?) - - - - - - - -]ρ. *vacat*

---

158. ATHENS, PRYTANY CATALOGUES, ca. 200 - 210/1 A.D. Agora 15.447-448. S. Follet, Athènes 101-102, assigns this date to these two lists of the archonship of Themision on prosopographic grounds and follows J.S. Traill, HESPERIA 40 (1971)

323-324, in restoring the name of the archon as Themision in LL. 1-2 of IG, II^2, 1803 = *Agora* 15.449.

---

159. ATHENS, PRYTANY CATALOGUE, shortly after 212 A.D. IG, II^2, 1820. *Agora* 15.440. S. Follet, *Athènes* 98-99, restores L. 1 as [Αὐρήλ]ιοι (IG [Σφήττ]ιοι); date on the basis of detailed prosopographic analysis.

---

160. ATHENS, PRYTANY CATALOGUE: ATTALIS, ca. 217 A.D. IG, II^2, 1825. SEG XII, 105; XIV, 95. *Agora* 15.476. S. Follet, *Athènes* 77-78, adopts the restoration of *Agora* 15. in LL. 70-73 (= LL. 18-21 in *Agora* 15) and reads in L. 48 [...6...]ους Χρ̣- or [...6...]ος Χρ̣-.

---

161. ATHENS AND PEIRAIEUS, BRONZE BALLOTS, 4th cent. B.C. A.L. Boegehold, CSCA 9 (1976) 7-19 (ph.). Catalogue of 25 ballots in NM from Peiraieus, Kerameikos, Acropolis slopes; 6 published for the first time. Nos. 1-20: ΨΗΦΟΣ : ΔΗΜΟΣΙΑ. Some also carry small stamped single letters and owls.

---

162. SALAMIS, BRONZE INSCRIPTION. Kamatero. "Χαλκοῦν ἐνεπίγραφον ἔλασμα." Ed. pr. A.G. Liangkouras, AD 27 (1972)[1976] B.179-180. J. and L. Robert, BE (1977) no. 171; "ce doit être une tablette civique".

Ἐπιγένης | Κολλυτεύς.

---

163. ATHENS, LEAD CAVALRY TABLETS, 4th/3rd cent. B.C. K. Braun, MDAI(A) 85 (1970) 198-269 (ph., dr.); ed. pr. of 574 folded tablets from the Kerameikos recording a personal name in the genitive on the outside, and inside a color designation, a symbol (or ἄσημος), a sum in hundreds of drachmas prefaced by τίμημα or abbreviations, sometimes the personal name repeated. All apply to color, brand, and evaluation of horses in the Athenian cavalry and belong to the evaluation and inspection mentioned in Aristotle, AP 49.1; Xenophon, *Hipparch*. 3.1 and 9; SEG XXI, 525, LL. 14-17.

J.H. Kroll, HESPERIA 46 (1977) 83-140 (ph., dr.); ed. pr. of 111 similar tablets from the Agora Excavations. Index of names in the Kerameikos tablets, *op. cit.* 205-235; in the Agora tablets, *op. cit.* 390-394. Kroll makes the following changes in the texts of Kerameikos tablets:

(1) Kerameikos no. 530. Kroll p. 91 reads 𐅅ΗΗΗΗ.
(2) Kerameikos no. 416. Kroll p. 119, no. 48a: prosopographic discussion.
(3) Kerameikos no. 302 + 303. Kroll p. 87: ΠΕΡΙ =

περι (στερά), not περί.

(4) Kerameikos no. 234. Kroll p. 91: under the first 2 letters of πυρρός are erased traces of BE, i.e. βουκέφαλος. The inscriber then neglected to write the brand in the proper position.

(5) Kerameikos no. 170. Kroll p. 88, note 20: The sum is not 1300 (Braun), but 1200. "The inscriber. . . crossed his two etas with a single horizontal, thereby making them look like three."

---

164. ATHENS, LEAD ARMOR TOKENS, ca. 250 B.C. Nine lead tokens bearing on one side a stamp depicting a piece of armor and a single letter on the other, Α, Γ, or Δ. Ed. pr. J.H. Kroll, HESPERIA 46 (1977) 141-146 (ph.), with references to previously published examples and discussion of the purpose of the tokens.

---

165. ATHENS, CATALOGUE OF DIAITETAI, 330/29 B.C. IG, II^2, 1924 + 2409. SEG XVI, 136, 145. D. Peppas-Delmouzou, AD 27 (1972) [1976] B.10, no. 2 (ph.), reports the rediscovery of the missing Fr. b (EM 5933) of IG, II^2, 1924 and the fact that it joins Fr. a and c, confirming D.M. Lewis' findings (SEG XVI, 136).

---

166. ATHENS, EPHEBIC CATALOGUE, ca. 61/2 A.D.? IG, II^2, 1723. SEG XIV, 90. M.T. Mitsos, AE (1972) 55-57, no. 1 (ph.), adds a previously unpublished joining fragment (EM 18215) and gives a text of the whole with prosopographic commentary. E. Kapetanopoulos, RF 104 (1976) 375-377, made the same join independently; he restores τ[ὸ *v* β] or T[ιβ *v* Κλ] or Τι̣[β *v* Κλ]|Θε[ογέν]ης Παιανιεύς in LL. 16-17 and identifies the herald as Tiberius Claudius Theogenes of IG, II^2, 1990, L. 2; 3185; 3449 etc., who held this office for the first time in 61/2 A.D. On Julius Nikanor, Neos Homeros, cf. supra no. 121.

[ἄρχων]
- - - - - -
[βασιλεύς]
- - - - - - - - -
[πολέμαρχος]
- - - - - - - - - - -
[θεσμοθέται]
- - - - - - - - - - - - - - - Εὐ̣[ωνυμεύς (?)]
- - - - - - - - - - - - - - - Παιαν[ιεύς]
- - - - - - - - - - - - - - - Εὐπυρίδ[ης]
- - - - - - - - - - - - - - -Βερενικίδ[ης]
Ἑ̣σ̣τ̣ί̣αρχ[ος . . . . .] του Φλυεύ[ς]
Δημοκρά[της)] Ἀθμονεύ̣[ς]
στρατηγὸς [ἐπὶ τὰ] ὅπλα Ἰούλιος

Νικάνωρ, νέος ["Ομηρο]ς καὶ νέος Θεμισ[τοκλῆς]
κῆρυξ τῆς ἐ[ξ 'Α]ρ[είου Π]άγου βουλῆς Ṭί[τος (?)]
Θε[ο . .]νης Παιανιεύς
κηρυκίσκος 'Αττ̣[ικὸ]ς Διοδότου Μαραθώ̣[νιος]
αὐλητὴς Νικίας) Φλυεὺς ΛΥ
λιτουργὸς 'Ισίδ[ο]τος 'Ισιγένους Μιλή̣σ[ιος]

19. λυ[ρῳδός?] Mitsos.

---

167. ATHENS, EPHEBIC CATALOGUE, 104/5 - 110/1 A.D. IG, II², 2037. S. Follet, Athènes 188-191; detailed discussion of prosopography, intercalary month, and date. E.A. Kapetanopoulos, HELLENIKA 29 (1976) 265, closely associates this list with IG, II², 2032.

---

168. ATHENS, EPHEBIC CATALOGUE, 138/9 - 169/70 A.D. IG, II², 2078. M.T. Mitsos, AD 25 (1970) [1971] 188-189, no. 8 (ph.), joins three unpublished fragments (EM 4167 + 4137 + 3855) to the right side of the stele and republishes the whole text. S. Follet, Athènes 305-306, suggests new restorations of LL. 1-3, 5.

[ὁ κοσμητὴς ...... ca. 11 ..... Γ]αργήττιος καὶ οἱ [[. .]]
[συνάρχοντες (?) ἀνέγραψαν] τοὺς ὑπ' αὐτ[οὺ]ς ἐφη-
[βεύσαντας, ἔτους . . ἀπ]ὸ τῆς θεοῦ 'Αδρ[ια]νοῦ
[ἐπιδημίας, - - - - - - -ίδος - - - -]ς πρυτανείας, ἧς ἐ-
[γραμμάτευε - - - - - - - - Σεκοῦ]νδος ὁ καὶ Ζώσιμος
[Παιανιεὺς - - - - - - - - - - -] ὁ κοσμητὴς τῶν ἐφή-
[βων - - - - - - - - - - - - - - - - 'Α]ντωνῖνος Σεβ[α]στὸς
[- - - - - - - - - - - - - - καθὼς προ?]σῆκεν καὶ κεκ[ό]σμη-
[κεν -]ν
[- κ?]αὶ αὐ-
[το -]λιν
[[...5..]]
[[...5..]]
[[...5..]]
[[...5..]]
[[...5..]]

1. ['Ο κοσμητὴς 'Αττικὸς Γ] Follet, cf. IG, II², 2104, LL. 3-4. || 2. [περὶ τὸ Διογένειον] Follet. || [βους ἀνέγραψαν, λθ'?] Follet. || 5. [γραμμάτευεν Σεκοῦ]νδος Follet.

---

169. ATHENS, EPHEBIC CATALOGUE, 143/4 A.D. IG, II², 2050. SEG XXIV, 191. S. Follet, Athènes 198, suggests that the restorations in IG are too short. In L. 1 there is room for the archon's demotic; in L. 2 add the title of the person named; in LL. 4-5 [- τοὺς ὑφ' αὐτοὺς] and παιδ[οτριβοῦντος διὰ βίου] respectively.

170. ATHENS, EPHEBIC CATALOGUE, ca. 144/5 A.D. IG, II^2, 2059 + 2267. S. Follet, Athènes 374-376, no. 3 (ph.), joins IG, II^2, 2267 (EM 3686 reported lost by Kirchner but now in EM) to LL. 22-27 of IG, II^2, 2059 to yield a new text; ap. cr. and prosopographic commentary.

ἀγωνοθέτη[ς] Ἁδριανίω̣ν̣ Εὐτυχι̣α̣[νὸ]ς Κω-
μάρχου Χολαργε[ύ]ς *vacat*
Ἡρακλείδης Ἀγάθωνος Ἀντινοεύς,
Φίλων) [Φ]ηγαιεύς, Μηνόδωρος) Στειριεύς,
Εὐκλείδ[ης] ὁ καὶ Δημοσθένης Εὐκλείδου [Ἰ]τέαθεν,
ἀγοραν[όμος] Μηνόφιλος Παραμόνου Πειραιεύς

---

171. ATHENS, EPHEBIC CATALOGUE, 145/6 A.D. IG, II^2, 2152 + 3395. SEG XIII, 182. M.T. Mitsos, AD 25 (1970) [1971] A.29-30, no. 1 (ph.), joined these two texts and added two previously unpublished fragments (EM 3755, 3798). Re-edited by J.H. Oliver, GRBS 11 (1970) 337-338, and S. Follet, Athènes 211-212, with ap. cr. and full commentary. We reproduce Follet's text with Mitsos' numbering of the lines.

[Αὐτοκ]ράτορος Κ̣[αίσαρος Ἁδριανοῦ]
[Ἀντω]νείνου Εὐσεβοῦς οἱ [ἔφηβ]οι *(ivy leaf)*
[Ἀγαθῆ] τύχῃ
[ἀντικοσμήτης (?) -]λης) Βερενικίδης
[νικήσας - - - - ἀγεν]είων παίδων στάδιον.
[Ἐπὶ ἄρχοντος Φλ. Ἀρρι]ανοῦ
[Παιανιέως, κοσμητ]εύον-
[τος Ἀθηναίου, ξυστάρχου] καὶ ἱερ[ο]-
[νείκου, οἱ ἔφηβοι τιμήσαντες (?)] τὸν ἑα[υ]-
[τῶν ἀντικοσμήτην (?) καὶ ἑαυτοὺς (?)]
[ἀνέγραψαν (?)].

---

172. ATHENS, EPHEBIC CATALOGUE, 145/6 A.D. IG, II^2, 2052. S. Follet, Athènes 210-211, proposes new restorations of LL. 6-26 and observes that it is impossible to tell if the year is ordinary or intercalary.

[γυμνασ]ίαρχοι
[Βοηδρομιῶνα ὁ π]ολέμαρχος
[Ἀπολλοφάνης Ε]ὐφήμου Σφήττιος
[Πυανοψιῶνα Δημή]τριος καὶ Δι-
[ονύσιος ? . . . . .]ου ἐξ Οἴου
[Μαιμακτηριῶνα . .] Πυλάδης Τρικορύ.
[Ποσειδεῶνα οἱ ἀγων]οθέται Δημήτρι-
[ος καὶ . . .6. . .]ς Δημητρίου Γαργήτ.
[. . .5. .ιῶνα ὁ ἀγω]νοθέτης Ἁδρια-
[νείων - - - - - Μ]ενεσθεὺς Φυλά.

[. . . .5-7. . . ὁ ἐπώ]νυμος ἄρχων
[. . . .7-8. . . .ιῶνα -- Δημή]τριος Φυλάσιος
[τοὺς ἑξῆς -- μ]ῆνας ὁ στρατη-
[γὸς καὶ ἀγωνοθέτη]ς Γερμανικεί-
[ων . . . . . .10-12. . . . . .]ς Ἀχαρνεύς
[- - - - - - - - - - - - - - - - -]ς Βησαιεύς
[ὁ ἱερεὺς Ἀντινόο]υ καὶ ἀγωνοθέ-
[της . . . . . .9-11. . . . .] Φλυεύς
[ὁ ἀγωνοθέτης τῶν ἐν Ἐλε]υσεῖνι Ἀντινο-
[είων . . . . . . .14. . . . . . .]σίου Ἀζηνιεύς
[. . . . . .20. . . . .]αχος Λαμπτρ.

---

173. ATHENS, EPHEBIC CATALOGUE, 162/3 - 169/70 A.D. IG, II², 2099 + 2100 + 2121 + 2154 + 2157. S. Follet, *Athènes* 376-382, no. 4 (ph.), joins the first four of these separately published fragments into one herm and associates IG, II², 2157 with them as a non-joining fragment; new text, ap. cr., full prosopographic commentary.

---

174. ATHENS, EPHEBIC CATALOGUE, 163/4 A.D. IG, II², 2086. SEG XXI, 622. J.H.Oliver, HISTORIA 26 (1977) 90-94; commentary on LL. 32-38, comparison with IG, II², 2113, LL. 142-149; significance of Marcus Aurelius and Lucius Verus as *archiereis*.

---

175. ATHENS, EPHEBIC CATALOGUE, 164/5 A.D.? IG, II², 2045 + 2069 + 2093a + 2138 + 2162 + 2166 + 2171. SEG XII, 113, 122, 125, 128. S. Follet, *Athènes* 221-224; detailed prosopographic commentary in support of the date suggested by E. Kapetanopoulos, CPh 65 (1970) 96-98.

---

176. ATHENS, EPHEBIC CATALOGUE, 170/1 - 175/6 A.D. IG, II², 2102 + 2134 + 2212. To these three fragments, published separately in IG, M.T. Mitsos added two unpublished pieces (EM 3030, 3851), ΠΟΛΕΜΩΝ 4 (1949) 24, no. 4 (ph.); AE (1972) 58, no. 2 (ph.). S. Follet, *Athènes* 382-392, no. 5 (ph.), publishes the first combined text with full ap. cr. and prosopographic commentary.

A

- -

[σωφρονισταί]

[ὑποσω]φρονισταί
. . . . . .ι̣ος) Μαραθώ.
[Ἐπίκ]τητος Φίλωνος Φηγ.
[Ἀφροδε]ίσιος)
[Ποσε]ίδιππος Παλλη.
[π]αιδοτρίβης Μᾶρκος
ὑποπαιδοτρίβης Ἡρακλέων Ἑστ.

[γυμνασί]α̣ρ̣χοι
. . . . . ο̣ς Ἄτταλος
[Πό. Αἴ. Φ]αῖδρος
Ἀπολλοφάνης Γοργίου
Καρείνας Δημάδης
Κλ. Μένιππος
Ἀντώνιος Κλαυδιανός
Ἄτταλος Ῥούφου
Ἐρεχθεΐδος
Πρόκλος Περικλέους
Ποσῆς Περικλέους
Φιλόπονος) Λαμ.
Κλ. Ἀττικὸς Ἀναγ.
Κλ. Μηνογένης Ἀναγ.
Ποσειδώνιος Φαύστου
Ἀθηνίων) Σουβρί.
Αἰγεΐδος
Ῥοῦφος Ἑρμολάου
Καρείνας Δημάδης
Ζωσιμιανὸς Τελ. . - - -
Ὑγεῖνος)
Διονύσιο̣ς)
Πωλλίων Νεικίου
Νεικόμαχος Ζωσίμου
Λεωνίδης Θεοφράστου
Πανδιονίδος
Κλαύδιος Μένιππος
Ἀπολλώνιος Ἀρτεμιδώρου
Ἀρτεμίδωρος)
Εἰσίδωρος Θεοδ̣- - -
Μόσχος Θεοδ- - -
Δωρόθεος)
Πίθανος)
Μύρων)
Εὔβουλος Ἐπ- - -
Ἀφθόνητος - - -
....ι̣ο̣ς [Καλ?]λ̣ίου
..........ς Καλλίου
[...... Ἀθ]ηνίωνος
[Λε]ωντίδος
[Σύν]τροφος)
[Δη]μήτριος Διονυσίου
[Πα]μμένης Δημητρίου
.......ο̣ς Ζωσίμου
- - - - [Ἀπο]λ̣λ̣ω̣ν̣[ίου]
........ος)

γραμματεὺς Τεῦκρος
προστάτης
ὁπλομάχος Δάφνος
διδάσκαλος Ἀπελλῆς) Φλυε.
ἡγεμὼν Δείφιλος
κεστροφύλαξ Φιλέας
θυρουρὸς Εὐρυβιάδης

Πτολεμαΐδος
Ἀντ. Κλαυδιανός
Σύντροφος Ἐπικτήτου
Αἴλ. Ἑρμείας
Νεικόστρατος Εὐαγγέλου
Χρῆστος Ζωσίμου
Ὀνήσιμος Ξενοκλέους
Ἀκαμαντίδος
Εἰσίδοτος) Σφήττιος
Τρύφω[ν Ἐ]λευθ̣[έρ]ου Κυρ.
[- - - - - - Μηνογ]ένους Κυ.
[- - - - - - - - - Χο]λαργ.
[- - - - - - - -]ονος Χολ.
- - - - - - - - - -ου
Πραξιτέλης [ὁ κα]ὶ̣ Ἀθήναις
Σωκράτης [)]
Πίστος [)] ἐκ Κερ.
Ἐπίγον[ος Δ]ιονυσίου
Φλ. [....]ι̣κ̣ράτης
Τ..... Ἐλευθέρου
......ος Ὀνησίμου
[Ἀφροδ]είσιος Ὀνησίμου
....λης)
[Σω]τ̣ὴρ Καλλίστου
[Ἀτ]τικὸς)
Ἁδριανίδος
Ἀγαθίας)
Πανβω.
Ἡρακλείδης ὁ καὶ Ἐλπιδηφόρο[ς]
Λήναις Φίλωνος Φηγ.
Οὐεντ. Ἀσκληπι[όδ]οτος
Φοῖβος Σωκράτου[ς]
Εὐτυχι̣... Νεικοστράτου
[Οἰ]νεΐδος
Ἀφ[ροδεί]σιος Φιλαδέλφου
.....ς)
....αντίδης
[Εὔ]κ̣αρπος)

.....νεὺς Καλλιστράτο[υ]
Ἀφροδείσιος ❩
vacat

Κεκροπίδος
Ἐλπίνεικος Εὐτύχου
Φιλοκράτης ❩
Τειμοκράτης Φιλοκράτου
Εὔτυχος Ἑρμείου
Ἀρίστων ❩
Πυθαγόρας Δημητρίου
Ἀπολλώνιος Ζωσίμου
Ὀνήσιμος ❩
Ζώσ[ιμος] ❩
Ἐπίκτητος Μάρκου
vacat

B

[Ἱπποθωντίδος ?]
- - - - - - - - - - -ν̣ίου
- - - - - - - - - -υ
[- - - - - Ἐ]πιτυνχάν.
[- - - - - -]πάτρου
- - - - - - - -ο̣υ̣
- - - - υ
- - - - - - - - - -σίου
........ου
....φάνης ❩
[Ζώ]σιμος Ἀλεξάνδρου
Φαῦστος ❩
Πό. Αἴ. Διονύσιος

Ἀ̣[ν]τιοχίδος
Νει[κ]ό̣στρατος Θοραιεύ[ς]
Λο[ῦ]κι̣ς Ζωσίμου
Ἐλπιδηφόρος Ἑρμείου
Ἀθηνόδωρος Ἐλευθερίω.
Ἐλπίνεικος Τρύφωνος
Ἀτταλίδος
Πό. Αἴ. Φαῖδρος
Δεῖος Ἡρακῶντος
Ἑρμείας Εὐκάρπου
Ἐλευσεῖνις ❩
Ἐπίκτητος Ἐλευσεινί.
Εὔοδος ❩
Δέκκιος Ἀγαθ - - -

ΕΠΕΝΓΡΑΦΟΙ

Καλλῆς Ὑγείνου
Θεόφραστος Νεικήτου
Εὐτυχίδης Ζοεί[λου]
Διονύσιος ❩
Ἀπολλώνιο̣[ς ❩]
Θρεπτίων [Ν]εικηράτου
Θάλλος [Ἀγ]αθία
Νείκων Πραξᾶ
Ζώσιμος Φίλωνος
Σωκράτης Σωτηρίχου
Ἐπαφρόδειτος Ἀπελλοῦ
Διόδωρος Ἐπαφροδείτου
Ἀνεμέσητος - - -
[Δ]ιονύσιος ❩̣
[Ὀ]νήσιμος Δι- - -
Γ̣λαυκίας Εὐ - - -
Φερένεικος- - -
Ἀθήναιος Χ- - -
Ἐλευσείν[ιος - - -]
Οὐαλέριο̣ς - - -

Ἐπαφρόδειτος Εὐτύχη
Ἐλπίνικος Μηνοδώρου
Συμφέρων Ἀβασκάντου
Σεραπίων Μάρωνος
Ἐπιτυγχάνων Εἰσιδώ̣[ρου]
Ἀθήναις Εἰσιδώρου
Ἀσκλήπων ❩
Πό. Αἴλ. Ῥωμανός
Ζώπυρος Ζωσίμου
Ἀριστόβουλος Ζωπύρου
Ἐπαφρόδειτος Δάφνου
Ζώσιμος ❩
.... Ζωσίμου
....ων Εἰσιδώρου
[..... Εὐ]πόρου
.........ς̣
- - - - - - - - - - - -

Οὐαλέριο[ς - - -]
Ἐράτων - - -
Ῥουφεῖν[ος - - -]
Πολυκράτης Σ̣ - - -
Τρόφ[ι]μος Θεοπ - - -
Σύντροφος Ἀλεξάνδρ[ου]
Ἀθήναις Χρύσου
Σύνφορος Ἑρμοῦ
Λούκιος Εὔπλοος
Μύρων Διοφάντου
Ἀβράστης Ἑρμεία
Λυδίας Χάρητος
Δώρητος Συμφέροντος
Ἐπαφρᾶς Ζωσίμου
Φιλήμων Κορίνθου
Εὔκαρπος Τελεσφόρου
Εἰσίδοτος Ὑγείνου
Ζώπυρος)
Μουσικὸς Μηνοφίλου
Ζώσιμος Διονυσίου
[Δ]ιονυσόδωρος Ζωσιμ.
[Μο]υνδίκιος Θάλαμος
Εὔκαρπος Εὐελπίστου
Χάρμος [)]
Ὑγεῖνος - - -
Ἑρμῆς - - -
- - - - - - - - - - -
- - - - - - - - - - -
- - - - - - - - - - -
- - - - - - - - - - -
Εὔπορος)̣
vacat

Σ̣- - -
Νει- - -
Ἱερογ- - -
Ἡρακλείδ[ης - - -]
Ζηνόβιος)̣
Ζώπυρος Μηγ- - -
Μουσαρίων Μο- - -
Πρεῖμος Εἰσίωνο[ς]
Ἐλευσείνιος)
Τολμίδης Γλαύκου
Ἱέραξ)
Σύμμαχος Μητροδώ.
Σωσίβιος Ἀφροδεισ.
Ἀντᾶς Διονυσίου
Ἰωνικὸς Εἰσίωνος
Βενύστος
Θάμυρ[ι]ς̣ [Σ]υμφόρου
- - - - - - - - - - -

---

177. ATHENS, EPHEBIC CATALOGUE, 176/7 A.D. IG, II^2, 2101 + 2105 + 2107 + 2148 + 2164 + 2174 + 2276. SEG XII, 120. Following the separate combination of II^2 2105 + 2101 and II^2 2107 + 2174 + 2164 + 2276 made by M.T. Mitsos, ΠΟΛΕΜΩΝ 4 (1949) 20, no. 2; SEG XII, 120, S. Follet, Athènes 392-401, no. 6 (ph.), combines all these fragments into one monument; text, ap. cr., full prosopographic commentary.

---

178. ATHENS, EPHEBIC CATALOGUE, ca. 176/7 - 187/8 A.D. IG, II^2, 2110 + 2133 + 2255. To IG, II^2, 2133 and 2255, which were joined by M.T. Mitsos, AE (1972) 59-60, no. 4 (ph.), S. Follet, Athènes 227-228, attributes IG, II^2, 2110 as a non-joining fragment of the same herm; discussion of the date.

---

179. ATHENS, EPHEBIC CATALOGUE, 2nd cent. A.D. IG, II^2, 2291. SEG XVIII, 59. S. Follet, Athènes 96, note 5, reads συνγυ̣[μνασίαρχος] in L. 5.

---

180. ATHENS, EPHEBIC CATALOGUE, 196/7 - 210/1 A.D. IG, II^2, 2203. SEG XVIII, 65. S. Follet, Athènes 235, discusses the date and adds new readings: L. 30 end Ε.ΓΙ; final sigmas in LL. 36 and 84 are certain, as is the mu in L. 67 where there is also the mark of abbreviation after Gaios; L. 76 ΣΥΝΣΤΡΕΝΜΑΤΑΡΧΑΙ; L. 86 for Π- - - read ΤΕ̣- - -.

---

181. ATHENS, EPHEBIC CATALOGUE, 196/7 - 215/6 A.D. IG, II^2, 2202 + 2081 + 2254. S. Follet, Athènes 402-405, no. 7, combines IG, II^2, 2202 with the two fragments previously joined by M.T. Mitsos, AE (1950/51) 20-21, no. 4 (ph.), and republishes a text of the whole with ap. cr. and full prosopographic commentary.

---

182. ATHENS, EPHEBIC CATALOGUE, 212/3 A.D. or slightly later. IG, II^2, 2208. J.H. Oliver, HISTORIA 26 (1977) 89-90, identifies Flavius Dryantianus of L. 8 as ephebic archon eponymous, cf. IG, II^2, 2113; συγκλητικός modifying him means "belonging to the senatorial order".

---

183. ATHENS, EPHEBIC CATALOGUE, ca. 220 - 230 A.D.? IG, II^2, 2229 + 2256. SEG XII, 138. M.T. Mitsos, AE (1971) 59-60, no. 3, combined IG, II^2, 2256 and EM 4160 (previously unpublished). In Phoros 117-118, no. 2, he associated an unpublished fragment found in 1964 at 17 Diogenes Street (EM 13449) with IG, II^2, 2229 Fr. E and F. S. Follet, Athènes 426-430, no. 11 (ph.), combines all the fragments of IG, II^2, 2229 + 2256 into one text and adds a non-joining, previously unpublished, fragment, EM 3715; text, ap. cr., full prosopographic commentary. The names are arranged in 4 columns; for spatial reasons we have had to print cols. III-IV below cols. I-II.

Col. I Col. II

[Διογένειον ?]
ca. 10 lines lost?
- - - - -ς̣ Εἰσιδ̣[- - - -]
- - - σ̣ι̣κράτης)
[Ζώ]σιμος Ἀγαθόπ[οδος]
Ἀγαθόπους)
Εὐέλπιστος
Ἀφροδεισιος)
Μηνόφιλος)
Ἰουλ. Εὔμουσ[ος]

vacat 0.051m.
Δρομο ....
Παλη[- - -]
vacat 0.01m.

- - -φ- - -
-ι̣π̣ίδη[ς]
[Σ]ωσίβιος
vacat 0.01m.
Σ̣ώσιππο̣[ς]
vacat ca. 0.013m.
[Κα]λλίστρα[τος - - - -]
vacat 0.028m.

Col. II

Εὐφρόσυνος Εὐοδ[- - -]
Λείβερτος Σφήτ[τιος]
Δῶρος ὁ καὶ Εὐτυ̣[- - -]
Εὐέλπιστος Κυ[ρτείδης]
Διόφαντος Κυ[ρτείδης]
Διοκλῆς Χολ[αργεύς]
vacat 0.01m
Εὐπλ *vacat*
vacat 0.08m.
Φιλήμων Χ̣[ολαργεύς]
vacat 0.022m.
Ἁδρι[ανίδος]
[Ε]ἰρην[αῖος - - -]
- - - - - - - - - - -
..κω- - - - - - - -
..νπ̣ι̣- - - - - - -
.γειφο- - - - - - -
Φλ. Καλλ- - - - - -
vacat 0.014m.
Οἰνεῖ[δος]
Κελερεῖνο[ς - - -]
Μάρκελλο[ς - - -]
Πάμφιλος [- - - - -]

Col. II

Ἀσκληπιά[δης - - -]
vacat ca. 0.028m.
Κεκροπίδο̣ς̣[ς]
- - -βιος Δ[- - - - - -]
ΛΠ
- - - - -∪- - - - - - - - -
- - - - - -λλω̣- - - - - -
[Ἐλ]πιδια[νός -]
- - - - - -νιος Μ[ελιτεύς]
[Πύ]ρρος Μελ[ιτεύς]
Ζώπυρος Μ̣[ελιτεύς]
Ζώσιμος Μ̣[ελιτεύς]
Ἀττικὸς Με̣λ̣ι̣[τεύς]
Νυμφαῖος)
Ζώσιμος Μελι[τεύς]
Ἐπαφρόδειτος - - -
Ἀγαθόπους Τρ[ινεμεεύς]
Ν̣ικίας Ἑρμογέ[νους]
[Ἀσκληπι?]άδης Νικ[ίου]
[Ἀφροδ]ε̣ίσιος Νι[κίου]
vacat 0.01m.
- - - - - - - -ος Μελ[ιτεύς]
- - - - - - - - - - - - - -

Col. III

πολέμ[αρχος]
Αὐρ. Κρητικ[ὸς - - -]
θεσμο[θέται]
Ἡρακλείδη[ς- - -]
Ζώπυρος Δ[- - -]
Μάρκελλο[ς - - -]
Ἀθηνίων [- - -]

Col. IV

- - - - - - - - - - - - - -
π̣ερ̣[ὶ τὸ]
] *vacat*
Αὐρ.
ος
σωφρ]ονιστής
vacat
[ἐπ]ε̣νγραφ[οι]
- - -σ̣τ̣[ρατ?]ο̣ς
- - - - - - - - -ιος
- - - -ους
- - - ορος
- - ρος
[Εὐτ]ύχης

Ἐπίγονος [- - -]
Ἀσκληπι[α- - -]
Ἐπέν[γραφοι]
Καλλικλῆ[ς - - -]
- - - - - - - - - - - -

- -ικράτης
[Σω?]ṭᾶς
- - - - - - - - - - -

---

184. ATHENS, EPHEBIC CATALOGUE, 221/2 - 229/30 A.D. IG, II^2, 2226 + 2253 + 2479. To the combined fragments of IG, II^2, 2226 + 2253, M.T. Mitsos, AD 25 (1970) [1971] 184-185, no. 1 (ph.), joined the previously unpublished fragments EM 4126, 4125, 4152, 4190, and assigned EM 3885, 4124 (not 2142) to the same stele; AE (1950/51) 27, no. 12. S. Follet, Athènes 422-426, no. 10, attributes to this group of fragments IG, II^2, 2479 and two other previously unpublished fragments, EM 4153, 8133. She edits the whole text with ap. cr. and brief prosopographic notes. The names are arranged in 3 columns; we have had to print col. III below cols. I-II.

Col. I Col. II

- - - - - - - - - - -
Ἐπίγον[ος Σφήττιος]
Ἀθηνίων Σφήττιος
Ἔκλεκτος Στειριεύς
Γυμνασίαρχοι
Βοηδρομιῶνα
Στάτιος Γλαῦκος
Πυανοψιῶνα
Κλα. Ἀφροδείσιος
φίλοι Μεμακτηριῶνα
Αὐτό- Μέμμιος Ἐπίκτητ[ος]
λυκο̣ς̣ Ποσειδεῶνα
Μέμ[μ]ιος Ἀττικός
[Ἀδ]ρια̣νιῶνα̣
Γ̣[- - -]ς̣ Ἀ̣[- - - -]
- - - - - - - - - - - -
[Ἀγωνοθέται]
- - - - - - - - - - - -
[Στ]άτιος Ι- - - - -
Γερμαγ̣[ικείων]
Φιλέρως Πα[ιανιεύς]
Ἀθήναιος Μι[- - - -]
Ἀδριανείων̣
Μέμμιος Ἀφρο[δείσιος]
Ἀλεξανδρείων
Στάτιος Μένανδρο̣ο̣[ς]
Σεβηρείων
Φιλεῖνος καὶ Κάρπο̣ς
Ἐπινεικίων
Πάμφιλος

vacat
Λαμίσκος Βησεεύς
Θυμόσοφος Τρινεμεεύς
Ἐλπιδηφόρος Ἀμυμωνε[εύς]
ὁπλομάχος
Διον[ύ]σιος Φαληρεύς
[ἡγ]ε̣μών
Παρ̣[ρά]σ̣ιος Φυλάσ̣ιο̣ς
[ὑπ]ογραμμα[τεύς]
Ὀγ̣[ήσιμ]ος ἐκ̣ [Κοίλης]
[διδά]σκ[αλος]
[Εὐτυχιανὸς Ἀχαρνεύς]
- - - - - - - - - - - -
- - - - - - - - - - - -
[Ἐρεχθεῖδος]
- - - - - - - - - - - -
Σ̣...ι̣ας)[- - - - - -]
Μ̣ενεσθε[ὺς - - - - -]
vacat 0.012m.
Σατοργ̣[εῖλος - - - -]
Κλ. Ἀφροδ̣[είσιος - - -]
Αἰγε̣[ῖδος]
Κτησίας [- - - - - -]
Ἐλπίνε[ικος - - - -]
Ἀττικὸς [- - - - -]
Ε̣ὔ̣καρπ̣[- - - - - - -]
- - - - - - - - - - - -
[Πανδιονίδος]
- - - - - - - - -δωρος
- - - -λ̣ιος Παιαν[ιεύς]
[Φιλ]έρως
[Ἔφη?]βος Παιανιεύς
vacat 0.037m.
- - - - -ε̣ρ
vacat 0.023m.
- - - -διππ̣ος
- - - - - - - - - - - -

- - -εύς
vacat 0.067m.
- - - - -εύς
vacat
- - - -ύς

- - - - - - - - - - - -
[Κεκροπίδος]
- - - - - - - - - - - -
[- - - - - - - - Μελιτ]εύς
[- - - - - - - - Μελι]τεύς
[- - - - - - - - Μελι]τ̣εύς
[- - - - - - - - Μελι]τ̣εύς
[- - - - - - - - - Μ]ελιτεύς
vacat 0.08m.
[Ἱπποθωντί]δος
[- - - - - - - Ἀμυ]μ̣ωνεεύς
[- - - - - - - -Ἀ]μυμωνεεύς
vacat 0.012m.

[- - - - - - Ἐλ]ευσείνιος
vacat 0.018m.
[- - - - - - - - - -])
vacat 0.015m.
[- - - - - - - -]γένης
[- - - - - - - -]κός
[Αἰαντίδ]ος
- - - - - - - - - Μαραθώνιος
vacat
- - - - - - - - - Μαραθώνιος
[- - - -Ε]ὐπόρφυ Μαρα[θώνιος]
[- - - -Ε]ὐπόρου Μαρα[θώνιος]
vacat
[- - - - - - Μά]ραθώνιος
[- - - - Μαράθ]ώνιος
[- - - Μαρα]θώνι[ος]
[Ἀντιοχίδος]
[- - - - - - - - - - - ε]ύς
[Ἀτταλίδ]ος
- - - θένους Ἁ[γ]νούσιος
- - - - -του
- - - - - - - - - - - - -

- - - - - - - - - - - -
- - - - - - - -σιεύς
[- - - - - -ο]υ Κηφεισειύς

[- - - -]είτου Κολλυτεύς
[- - - -]μ. Ὑβα.

Σ- - - - - - - -
Κ- - - - - - - -

Κτ- - - - - - - -
Λι- - - - - - - -
Α- - - - - - - -

Col. III
[ἐπέγγραφοι]
- - - - - - - - - - -
- - - - - - - - - - -
- - - - Λέοντος
[- - - - Λ]έοντος
- - - - -λης)
- - - - -κλιανός
[Λ. Σ]τατ. Σωζομενός
Ἀρτεμίδωρος Τυχικοῦ
Εὐτύχης
Μάγνες
Ἀλκιβιάδης Εὐφραντᾶ
Εὐάριστος Εὐαρίστου
Ἀλκιβιάδ[ης]
vacat 0.17m.

185. ATHENS, EPHEBIC CATALOGUE 221/2 - 230/1 A.D. IG, II^2, 2039 + 2076 + 2139 + 2140 + 2141 + 2151 + 2198. Following the separate combinations of 2139 + 2140 + 2141 + 2151 and 2039 + 2076 made by M.T. Mitsos, AE (1950/51) 19-20, no 3 (ph.); 23-24, no. 7, S. Follet, Athènes 414-422, no. 9 (ph.), combines all these fragments into one monument to which she also assigns IG, II^2, 2198; new text, ap. cr., full prosopographic commentary.

---

186. ATHENS, EPHEBIC CATALOGUE, ca. 222 A.D. IG, II^2, 2219 + + 2218 (= 2260). SEG XIII, 54. M.T. Mitsos, AE (1973) 90-92, no. 4 (ph.), joined IG, II^2, 2218 and 4 other unpublished fragments (EM no number, EM 4172 + 4133, 4198) to IG, II^2, 2219 and abandoned his earlier suggestion, AE (1950/51) 43-44, no. 22 (ph.), that IG, II^2, 2218 belonged with IG, II^2, 2243. S. Follet, Athènes 238, deciphers Φ̣λ̣. Ἀ̣σ̣κ̣λη̣π̣ιάδ̣η̣ς̣ in L. 6 and comments on his identity.

---

187. ATHENS, EPHEBIC CATALOGUE, 222/3 A.D. IG, II^2, 2145 + 2146 + 2149 + 2200 + 2206 + 2210 + 2228 + 2249. S. Follet, Athènes 406-414, no. 8 (ph.), combines all these fragments into one document which she re-edits with detailed ap. cr. and prosopographic commentary.

---

188. ATHENS, EPHEBIC CATALOGUE, 224/5 - 236/7 A.D. IG, II^2, 2232. S. Follet, Athènes 240-241 (ph.); measurements of the stone now in the Louvre and new readings: L. 5 ὑποπαιδοτρίβης; L. 6 Αὐρ. Πωλλίων; L. 7 ὑπογραμ̣[ματεύς]; L. 8 Αὐρ. Ὀνή̣[σιμος].

---

189. ATHENS, EPHEBIC CATALOGUE, ca. 225/6 A.D. IG, II^2, 2198. S. Follet, Athènes 327, reads in L. 3 not [Ἀμφι]αιρείων (IG), but [Ἀλεξ]ανδρείων. Supra no. 185.

---

190. ATHENS, EPHEBIC CATALOGUE, 225/6 - 232/3 A.D. IG, II^2, 2233 + 2236 + 2259. To the combined text of IG, II^2, 2233 + 2259, established by M.T. Mitsos, AD 25 (1970) [1971] 188, no. 7 (ph.), S. Follet, Athènes 434-437, no. 13 (ph.), joins IG, II^2, 2236 and publishes a new text with ap. cr. and prosopographic commentary.

---

191. ATHENS, EPHEBIC CATALOGUE, 228/9 -236/7 A.D. IG, II^2, 2108. SEG XII, 134; XIX, 163. To IG, II^2, 2108 and the small fragment joined to it by M.T. Mitsos, AD 25 (1970) [1971] 186, no. 3, S. Follet, Athènes 431-433, no. 12 (ph.), attributes the non-joining fragment SEG XII, 134 and re-edits the whole with detailed physical descriptions, measurements of letter heights, ap.cr.

[Ἀγαθῆι τύχηι]·
ὁ κο[σμητὴς τῶν ἐφήβων καὶ ἱερεὺς πυρ]φόρος (?)
Αὐρ. Μ[ελπομενὸς Ἀντινοεὺς (?) ἀνέγρα]ψεν τοὺς
ὑπ' αὐτ̣[ὸν ἐφήβους καὶ τοὺς περὶ τὸ Διογ]ένειον
τοὺς [ἐπὶ - - - - - - - - - - - - -ἄρχοντο]ς.
ἀντικ̣[οσμητὴς - - - - - - - - - - - - -Παλ]λ̣ηνεύς, ἔτος ε',
παιδοτ[ρίβης διὰ βίου ἱερεὺς Αὐρ.] Διονύσιος Ἀχαρν.,
γραμμα[τεὺς Σύντροφος Εὐκαρπί]δου ἐκ Κοίλης,
[προστάτης Τιβ. Κλ. Λεωσθένης Μελι]τ̣εύς.
- -

---

192. ATHENS, EPHEBIC CATALOGUE, 231/2 A.D. IG, II^2, 2230. S. Follet, *Athènes* 332, on the basis of M.T. Mitsos' new text, AE (1950/51) 47, no. 29, restores LL. 2-6 as follows:

[Αὐτοκ]ρ̣[άτορι Καίσαρι Μάρκῳ Αὐρηλίῳ]
[Σεουή]ρ̣ῳ Ἀλεξάν[δρῳ Σεβαστῷ].
[Ἐπὶ ἄρχο]ντος Κασι[ανοῦ ἱεροκήρυκος Στειριέως]
[ὁ κοσμητ]ὴς τῶν ἐφ[ήβων - - - - - -τοὺς ὑπ' αὐτῷ]
[ἐφηβεύσ]αντα̣[ς καὶ τοὺς περὶ τὸ Διογένειον ἀνέγραψε.]

---

193. ATHENS, EPHEBIC CATALOGUE, slightly before 235/6 A.D. IG, II^2, 2161 + 2231 + 2251 + 2487. SEG XII, 124, 133. To IG, II^2, 2251 + 2487 (joined by M.T. Mitsos, AE [1950/51] 28-29, no. 14), S. Follet, *Athènes* 438-443, no. 14 (ph.), adds IG, II^2, 2231 and 2161 and re-edits the whole with ap. cr. and prosopographic commentary.

---

194. ATHENS, EPHEBIC CATALOGUE, 235/6 A.D. IG, II^2, 2235. S. Follet, *Athènes* 239-240; 327; 453-454, no. 17 (ph.); discussion of the date, new readings, and restorations, and ed. pr. of a new non-joining fragment (EM 3894) which she assigns to the same stele. L. 2 Αὐρ. is restored after the name of the kosmetes; LL. 6-9 the restorations in IG are too short: read [παιδοτριβοῦντος διὰ βίου] in L. 6 and add [διὰ βίου] to LL. 7 and 8 and [καὶ γυμνασίαρχος] after ἄρχων in L. 9; L. 8 Κοίλης; L. 11 Αὐ̣ρ[- - -]; L. 35 Ἀλ̣[εξανδρείων] or Μ̣[αξιμεινείων]; L. 69 Ἀρτεμιδ[ώρου]; L. 118 Αὐ̣ρ. Ζώπυρος; bottom of Col. I [οἱ διὰ βίου] | ὑποπαιδοτρίβ[ης] | [- - -] | [- - -] | [- - -] | ὑπογραμματε[ὺς] | [Αὐρ. Ὀνήσιμος Εὐκαρπίδ]ου ἐκ Κοίλης | [- - -] | [κεστροφύλα]ξ | [- - -] | [- - -] | [ἰατρὸς Αὐρ. Ἀρτεμ]είσιος; L. 144 [- - -]θεν.

New fragment - - - - - - - - - - - - - -
EM 3894 [- - - Ἀγαθό]ποδος
[- - - - - - -]ς
[- - - - - - -]ι̣ος Ζωπύρου
vacat 0.045m.

[Παναθηναΐδι] Λ̄
vacat

---

195. ATHENS, EPHEBIC CATALOGUE, 237/8 -240/1 A.D. IG, II^2, 2242 + 2486. S. Follet, Athènes 443-450, no. 15 (ph.), assigns these two texts to the same monument and publishes a new text of the whole with ap. cr. and prosopographic commentary.

---

196. ATHENS, EPHEBIC CATALOGUE, 240/1 - 252/3 A.D. IG, II^2, 2243. M.T. Mitsos, AE (1973) 90-92, no. 4 (ph.), showed that IG, II^2, 2218 (= 2260) does not belong to this inscription, as he had suggested in AE (1950/51) 43-44, no. 22 (ph.), but it belongs with IG, II^2, 2219. S. Follet, Athènes 242; new readings and restorations: L. 9 the demotic of the paidotribes ought to be added; LL. 119bis-120 [ἄρχων] | Αὐρ. [Σωκράτης]; L. 120bis [θεσμοθέται]; L. 126 Ἀντιν[οείων ἐν ἄστει] or [ἐν Ἐλευσεῖνι]; L. 125 Μέστρ[ιος Σωκράτης] cf. his brother in LL. 136 and possibly 134; LL. 133-136 the lines marked *vac.* in IG were probably inscribed with short names; L. 121 ΔομϽ; L. 141 Ποσειδῶ̣[νιος]; L. 158 Κάλ[λ]ιστος; L. 160 the first letter is pi or gamma; L. 180 - - -ος.

---

197. ATHENS, EPHEBIC CATALOGUE, date? IG, II^2, 2263. S. Follet, Athènes 442, rejects Dittenberger's restoration (IG, III, 1210) of an archon's name in LL. 8-9 in favor of - - - τούς τε] | [συν]άρχο[ντας καὶ τοὺς ὑφ' ἑαυτοὺς ἐφήβο]υς ἀν[έγραψαν ἐπὶ ἄρχοντο]ς Τι. [- - -] *vel. sim.*

---

198. ATHENS, EPHEBIC CATALOGUE. IG, II^2, 2091/2. S. Follet, Athènes 312-313, restores the text as follows, but warns against trying to establish a precise date.

[. . . . .]δε - - - - -
[γρ. βου]λῆ[ς καὶ δήμου - - -]
[ἀντιγρ]α̣ [εὺς - -]
[γ]ραμματε[ὺς κατὰ πρυτανείαν - -]
Εἰσι[δ]οτο - - - -
ὑπογραμμα[τεὺς - - -]
Μελι[τεύς].

---

199. ATHENS, NAMES OF EPHEBES, after ca. 150 B.C. IG, II^2, Addenda 1960A; 4256. W. Hoepfner, Kerameikos 10. Das Pompeion (Berlin 1976) 68-69, 120-122 (ph., dr.), discusses these groups of philoi who wrote their names on the walls of the Pompeion; possible connection of the building with the ephebeia. F.K. Dörner,

*ibid.*144-145 (ph.), offers some new readings:

Μηνόδ[ω]ρος
Δημήτριος
Μιθρ̣[αδάτης]
Ἑρμ̣ῆς
Ἡρακλε[- - -]
Τ(ίτος) Γά<ι>ος ⌶ Η
ΛΣΩΝ

---

200. ATHENS, CATALOGUE OF PANATHENAIC PRIZES, ca. 400-350 B.C. IG, II^2, 2311. M.A. Tiberios, AD 29 (1974) [1977] A.147-149, computes the number of Panathenaic amphoras awarded each year at ca. 1200 and the amount of olive oil to fill them at ca. 43,200 kg.

---

201. ATHENS, DOCUMENTS OF DRAMATIC PERFORMANCES. H.J. Mette, *Urkunden Dramatischer Aufführungen in Griechenland: Texte und Kommentare* 8 (Berlin 1977). Corpus of texts recording victors and participants in all dramatic contests in Attica and elsewhere; brief ap. cr.; copious indexes.

---

202. ATHENS, LIST OF VICTORS IN MUSIC AND DRAMA AT THE GRAND DIONYSIA, 347/6 - 315 B.C. IG, II^2, 2318. SEG XIX, 168. P. Ghiron-Bistagne, *Acteurs* 7-26, 207 (ph., dr.); text and French translation with discussion of the date of the beginning of the list (560 B.C.); possible restoration of heading: [οἵδε νενικήκασιν ἀπὸ τοῦ δεῖνα ἄρχοντος, ἀφ᾽ οὗ πρῶτ]ο̣ν κῶμοι ἦσαν τ[ῶι Διονύ]σωι, τραγωιδοὶ δ᾽ [ἀπὸ τοῦ δεῖνα (ἀφ᾽ οὗ πρῶτον ἠγωνίζοντο), ἄνδρες δ᾽ ἀπὸ τοῦ δεῖνα, παῖδες δ᾽ ἀπὸ τοῦ δεῖνα, κωμωιδοὶ δ᾽ ἀπὸ τοῦ δεῖνα]. Mette, UDA 1-42, no. I; text with reconstruction from literary sources of all victors going back to 533 B.C.; discussion of chronology of early lost part of the list; *idem*, Gn 49 (1977) 725; numerous corrections of misprints and other errors in Ghiron-Bistagne's text.

---

203. ATHENS, DIDASKALIAI: TRAGEDIES AT THE LENAIA, 3rd/2nd cent. B.C. IG, II^2, 2319. SEG XIX, 169. P. Ghiron-Bistagne, *Acteurs* 28-36 (ph., dr.); text, French translation, commentary including discussion of the form of the building in which IG, II^2, 2319-2325 were inscribed. J.M. Camp, II, HESPERIA 40 (1971) 302-305, no. 8 (ph.), adds a new fragment found in the Agora Excavations (I 7151), not included in Ghiron-Bistagne's text. Cf. Mette, UDA 144-147; text; Gn 49 (1977) 725; numerous corrections of Ghiron-Bistagne's text.

[ὑπε:] Ἡφαι[στίων]
[Νι]κ̣όμαχος [τρί:]
Ἀμυμώνηι Τ [- -]
ὑπε
ὑπο: Ἡφαιστίω[ν ἐνίκα]
ἐπὶ Τιμοκράτου[ς - - -] 364/3 B.C.
[- -]ι Οἰνοπίωνι Ἑκα[- -]
[- -]ις ὑπε: Ἄρηξις
Θεοδωρίδης δεύ:
Μηδείαι Φαέθοντ[ι]
[- -]νος ὑπε: Ἀνδροσθέ[νης]
Κλεαίνετος τ̣[ρί:]
Ὑψιπύληι Φ[- -]
ὑπε: Ἵππαρ[χος]
[- -]στηι ὑπο: Ἄρηξ[ις ἐνίκα]
[- - -]ιαι̣ ἐπὶ Χαρικ̣[λείδου - - -] 363/2 B.C.

---

204. ATHENS, DIDASKALIAI, 3rd/2nd cent. B.C. IG, II^2, 2320. P. Ghiron-Bistagne, Acteurs 36-38 (ph.); text, French translation, commentary on actors and tragedians. Mette, UDA 90-92; text.

---

205. ATHENS, DIDASKALIAI, 3rd/2nd cent. B.C. IG, II^2, 2323. SEG XVI, 141; XXII, 144; XXV, 194. P. Ghiron-Bistagne, Acteurs 42-53 (ph.); text, French translation, commentary especially on the order and timing of dramatic performances. Mette, UDA 118-134; text and detailed commentary on the order of the fragments.

---

206. ATHENS, DIDASKALIAI, 3rd/2nd cent. B.C. IG, II^2, 2323A. SEG XXII, 143. P. Ghiron-Bistagne, Acteurs 40-42 (ph.); text, French translation, commentary on L. 10 [ἀργυρο]σκόπωι, illustrated by a terracotta figurine in the Louvre. Mette, UDA 114-116; text, new restorations.

---

207. ATHENS, DIDASKALIAI, 3rd/2nd cent. B.C. IG, II^2, 2325. SEG XIII, 56; XIX, 170. P. Ghiron-Bistagne, Acteurs 53-62; 131-132 (ph., dr.); text, French translation, extensive prosopographic commentary on actors. Mette, UDA 159-188; text, ap. cr.; Gn 49 (1977) 725-726; numerous corrections of G-B's text. D. Peppas-Delmousou, MDAI(A) 92 (1977) 229-243 (ph.); ed. pr. of two fragments of unknown provenance transferred from the Acropolis Museum to the EM in 1956. Both are of white marble and preserve part of the moulding at the top of the epistyle. EM 13273 (Fr. P) contains names from Cols. VI and VII of the comic poets at the Lenaia and joins EM 8200 + 8202 to form the following text:

Col. VI

Εὐ<θ>υκράτης II
Ἄροπος II
Ἐτεαγόρας I
Πολύκλειτος I
Φιλίσκος I
[Ν]εάνθης II
[Νη]λεύς I
[Θε]όδωρος I
[Χαρι]κλείδης I
[....σ]τρατος [-]
[......]η[ς] I
[Δι]όδωρ[ο]ς I
Εὐμήδη[ς] II
Σ̣ II Πανδαί[τ]ης I
Μενεσ[θ]εύς I
vacat 0.044m.

Col. VII

Πυθόδ[....]
Ἐρατο[σθένης -]
Καλλ[ίμαχος -]
Ἀρχίδ[ικος -]
Σωκ[- - -]
Φιλόμ[ηλος -]
Νικί[ας -]
Δεξι[κράτης -]
Π̣[ο]λυ[- - -]
Θεμίσ[ων?]
Θέω[ν -]
Θεόδ[- - -]
Διοσκ[ουρίδη]ς I
Εὔβου[λίδη]ς I
Θεόδω[ρος --]
[Ὀ]νησι[......] III

Col. VIII

8 lines missing

[Ἐμμ]ενίδης I
[Ἀρί]στων III
Νουΐος III
Διονύσιος II
Ἀγαθοκλῆς I
Ἀρχικλῆς II
Βίοττος I
Νικόδημος II
vacat 0.025m.

The names in LL. 17-18 are identified by Peppas-Delmouzou as the two famous librarians of Alexandria. Detailed prosopographic commentary on the poets in cols. VI-VIII.

EM 13247 (Fr. q) comes from the top of the last column of names of comic actors at the Lenaia.

Col. VII

[Φι]λ̣οκράτης I
[Ἀρισ]τ̣[οφά]ν[η]ς̣ II
[Ἀντιφ]άνης II
[- - -]

Discussion of the physical characteristics of the epistyle (pp. 241-243) and a cautious suggestion that it belonged to a stoa in the vicinity of the Theatre of Dionysos.

---

208. ATHENS, DIDASKALIAI: ACTORS IN OLD COMEDY, SATYR PLAYS, AND TRAGEDIES, 255/4 B.C. Two fragments of blue marble found in the Agora Excavations. (Fr. A I 2972; Fr. B. I 982). Ed. pr. B.D. Meritt, HESPERIA 7 (1938) 116-118 (ph.). Ghiron-Bistagne, Acteurs 75-78; text, French translation, ph.; Mette, UDA 149-152, text.

A [....... ca. 14 ....]ς
[.... ca. 8 ....] δ[εύτ]ε̣
[...5..]όδημος τρί
[ἐπὶ Ἀλ]κιβιάδου ἄρχον *vacat*
[ἀγων]οθέτης Νικοκλῆς
[παλ]αιᾶι κωμωιδίαι
[Καλ]λίας ἐνίκα
[Μισα]νθρώποις Διφι
[Διοσκ]ουρίδης δεύ
[Φάσμ]α̣τι Μενάνδρ

[...5..]ς τρί Πτωχε̃ Φιλ
[σατύροι]ς παλαιοι̃ς
[...6...]ος ἐνίκ 'Ερμει̃ ['Αστυ]
[....7...] δ̣εύ 'Ατλαν[τ - - -]
[...6... τρί] Μαθητ̣[αι̃ς (?) - - -]
[παλαιᾶι τρα]γ[ωιδίαι]

lacuna

B [..... ca. 9 .... τρί] Φυλ[- -]
[.... ca. 8 .... Μεν]εκρ
[παλαιᾶι τρ]α̣γωιδίαι
[.... ca. 7 ... ἐ]νίκα
[.... ca. 8 .... Σ]οφο
[..... ca. 9 .... δ]εύ 'Ιξί[ονι - - -]
[... ca. 6 ... τρί Οἰ]δίπ[οδι - - -]

---

1. [- - -]ς G-B; Mette. || 2. δ[εύ(τερος).]ε[- - -] Mette. || 3. ['Αριστ]ὀδ̣η̣μος? Mette. || 4. ['Αλ]κ̣ιβίαδου (sic) Mette. || 5. [ἀγων]ο̣θέτης G-B; Mette. || 6. [παλ]α̣ιᾶι Mette. || 9. [Διοσ]κ̣ουρίδης G-B. || 10. [Φάσμ]μ̣α̣τι G-B; [Φάσμα̣]τι Mette. || 11. [... ca. 5 ..]ς G-B. || 13. [- - -]ο̣ς Mette; 'Ερμει̃ *vac.*? G-B. || 14. [.... ca. 7 ...]δευ G-B. || 15. Μαθητ[αι̃ς] G-B. || 17. [..... ca. 9 .... τρί]φυλ[G-B; [......12......], Φυ̣λ[- - - τρί(τος)] Mette. || 19. τ]ρ̣αγωιδίαι

---

209. ATHENS, LIST OF TRAGIC ACTORS? IG, II^2, 2419.
P. Ghiron-Bistagne, Acteurs 68-72 (ph., dr), tentatively restores LL. 4-5 of col I [οἵδε παλαιὸν δρᾶμα ἀναδιδάσκ]οντες
[ἠγωνίζοντο παλαιᾶι τραγωιδι]ᾶι.
Mette, UDA 189; text; restores LL. 1-10 as follows; cf. Gn 49 (1977) 726.

οἵ[δε ἐνίκων]
Τολ[μίδης? - - -]
Εὐκ[....ς - - -]
[παλαιὰς ἀναδιδάσκ]οντες Πολυ[- - -]
[τραγικοὶ ὑποκριτ]αί 'Αρχία[ς - - -]
Πειθίδ[ημος - - -]
'Ονήτω[ρ - - -]
Φίλητο[ς - - -]
'Επικράτ̣[ης - - -]
Μνησίθεο[ς - - -]

---

210. ATHENS, LIST OF COMIC AND TRAGIC ACTORS. IG, II^2, 3111 (EM 8216) + 3075. Mette, UDA 197, no. 1, reports that these two fragments have been joined by D. Peppas-Delmouzou and that the second fragment of IG, II^2, 3111 (EM 8215) is part of a separate

inscription.

- - - - ωι]δῶν
- - - - - - - - -
- - - ὑπ]οκριταί
- - - Ἀ]ρτέμων
ἐνίκ]α· Θέων ἐν[ίκα]
- - -] Χρυσίππω<ι>
- - -] ἐνίκα
- - -]Σ̣[?
- - - Φι]λήμονος
- - - τρα]γωιδῶν
- - - Ε]ὐριπίδου

IG, II^2, 3111 (EM 8215)
[τρ]αγωιδῶν ὑποκριτ[ῶν]
Λη[ναϊκαί]
..τικ̣α̣ι[- - -]

---

211. ATHENS, LIST OF ACTORS? 4th/3rd cent. B.C. IG, II^2, 2418. P. Ghiron-Bistagne, Acteurs 72-75 (ph.), suggests that the 6 names on this fragmentary list are comic actors and that the stone may be related to a relief from the Acropolis showing comic masks; T.B.L. Webster, Monuments Illustr. Trag. Sat. Plays AS 5.

---

212. ATHENS, CATALOGUE, 1st cent. A.D. IG, III, 3899 (not in IG, II^2). E.A. Kapetanopoulos, RF 104 (1976) 377; new edition and restoration in L. 6; cf. supra no. 121. The letters of LL. 6-8 are much smaller than those in LL. 1-5.

[- - - - - - - - - -].ς
[- - - - - - - -].ιος·
[- - - - - - -]δης·
[- - - - -]ου Βερνικίδης
[- - - Με]λ̣ιτεύς
[- - Ἰού̣λι?]ος Νικάνωρ
[- - - - - -]ήττιος
[- - - - - -]εύς
vacat

---

213. ATHENS, DEDICATION OF MAGISTRATES?, ca. 150 A.D. SEG, XXI, 674. S.N. Koumanoudes, AE (1976) 211-212, no. 25, rejects Oikonomides' restoration (The Two Agoras in Ancient Athens [Chicago 1964] 88-90) of L. 4, ἐ[ν] Θησείο[υ στοᾶι], on the grounds that the Theseion in the Agora was a sekos. Koumanoudes locates the Theseion near the Royal Stoa and the Alphitopolis Stoa;

Schol. Aristoph. Ekkles. 685.

---

214. ATHENS, CHOREGIC DEDICATION: DIONYSIA, 364/3 B.C.? IG, II^2, 3038. P. Amandry, BCH 100 (1976) 27-28 (ph.), rejects the restoration of the archon's name (Timokrates) in L. 1 in favor of the unknown object of ἀνέθηκε of L. 2. Since the stone is uninscribed after Πλωθεύς in L. 2, [διδάξας] must not be restored here. The identity of the offering supported by the base remains uncertain. Mette, UDA 75, no. 10.

---

215. ATHENS, CHOREGIC DEDICATION: DIONYSIA, 327/6 B.C. SEG XXIII, 103. P. Amandry, BCH 100 (1976) 48-50 (ph., dr.), and Mette, UDA 78, no. 26, restore L. 1 (on the basis of the demotic in L. 2): [Κεκροπὶς] παίδων ἐνίκα.

---

216. ATHENS, CHOREGIC DEDICATION; THARGELIA?, ca. 400 B.C. IG, II^2, 3029. P. Amandry, BCH 100 (1976) 44-48 (ph.); description of the block and cuttings for a tripod. L. 1 is restored: Πυθόδωρος Μελανθίο [ἐχορήγε - - -15-20 letters: names of 2 tribes - - - ἀνδρῶν]. Amandry assigns the dedication to the Thargelia.

---

217. ATHENS, CHOREGIC DEDICATION: THARGELIA, ca. 365-349 B.C.? IG, II^2, 3070. P. Amandry, BCH 101 (1977) 178-179, suggests this tentative date on the basis of the cylindrical shape of the monument. In L. 4 the name of the flutist was probably omitted, and - - -]ος belongs to the poet's ethnic.

---

218. ATHENS, CHOREGIC MONUMENTS: THARGELIA, 363-348 B.C. Eight intact cylindrical marble bases, found in Hodos Ioseph ton Rogon. Ed. pr. S.N. Koumanoudes, AD 25 (1970) [1971] A.143-149 (ph.). P. Amandry, BCH 101 (1977) 168-169, 189-199; ph. of bases, squeezes; drawings and profiles of bases; architectural discussion; (no changes in the texts). We shall print all these texts in a later volume.

---

219. ATHENS, CHOREGIC DEDICATION: THARGELIA 358-356 B.C. IG, II^2, 3067. P. Amandry, BCH 101 (1977) 177-178 (ph.), argues for this date on prosopographic grounds and the order in which the poet and flutist are named. In L. 5 Εὐκλῆς is inscribed in rasura and ΔΙ was also erroneously repeated and ineffectively erased. In the repeated text on the back of the stone the name of the poet was added later in larger, less regular letters.

---

220. ATHENS, CHOREGIC DEDICATION: THARGELIA, 354/3 B.C. Cylindrical tripod base of marble found south of the Olympieion in Hodos Ioseph ton Rogon. Brief mention in AD 21 (1966) [1968] B.65; 25 (1970) [1971] A.143; BCH Suppl. 1 (1973) 33, note 9. Ed. pr. P. Amandry, BCH 101 (1977) 167-171, no. 20 (ph., dr.);

[..4-5..]ω̣ν̣ Α[..2-3.].ς̣
Εὐωνυμεὺς χορηγῶν
ἐνίκα Ἐρεχθηίδι Ἀντιοχίδι
παίδων Οἰνιάδης Προνόμο
Θηβαῖος ηὔλει Ἀντίφιλος
Μεγαρεὺς ἐδίδασκεν
Διότιμος ἦρχεν.

---

221. ATHENS, CHOREGIC DEDICATION: THARGELIA, ca. 350 B.C. Marble base found at 16-18 Hodos Diakou. Ed. pr. O. Alexandris, AD 25 (1970) [1972] B.60 (ph.). J.P. Michaud, BCH 96 (1972) 606 (ph.), whose text we print here; P. Amandry, ibid. 100 (1976) 53; 101 (1977) 179-181, 188-189 (ph., dr.); flutist's name omitted; speculation on the competition to be restored at the beginning of L. 3 παίδων/ἀνδρῶν; discussion of the cutting for the tripod.

[Στράτος Ἀτ]άρβου Θορίκιος
[χορηγῶν ἐνίκα Ἀκα]μ̣αντίδι Πανδιονίδι
[- - - - - - - -]ιος ἐδίδασκεν
[- - - -]ος ἦρχεν

2. ΚΥ]ΔΑΝΤΙΔΙ Alexandris. Stratos Atarbou: HESPERIA 11 (1942) 343, no. 2; Davies, APF no. 2679 (Michaud).

---

222. ATHENS, DEDICATION: AGONOTHETES, 307/6 B.C. IG, II^2, 3077. Mette, UDA 46, no. 1b, restores Φιλ[ήμων] in L. 4 and Κάλ[λιππος] in L. 5 on the basis of IG, II^2 3073, LL. 5-6.

---

223. ATHENS, CHOREGIC DEDICATIONS: AGONOTHETAI, 277/6 B.C.? IG, II^2, 3081 and 3082. P. Amandry, BCH 100 (1976) 58-63 (ph., dr.), demonstrates that these two texts are identical except for ἀνδρῶν, L. 3 of 3081 and παίδων, L. 3 of 3082. Both record victories of Erechtheis in the Dionysia organized by the agonothetes Theophanes in the archonship of Sosistratos. Detailed description of blocks and cuttings for the tripods they supported. Mette, UDA 80-81, nos. 3a-b.

---

224. ATHENS, CHOREGIC DEDICATION, 4th cent B.C. SEG XXI, 694. P. Amandry, BCH 100 (1976) 40-42 (ph.), argues that the incomplete

2-line inscription is not contemporary with the decree of 129/8 B.C. (SEG XXI.469) which is inscribed lower down on the same face of this triangular monument. The 2 missing lines, containing the name of the tribe(s) and the choregos, would have been inscribed above the two surviving lines either on the existing monument, where Amandry detects faint traces of letters, or on a crowning member.

---

225. VARKIZA, CHOREGIC DEDICATION OF SOKRATES AND A TRAGIC CHORUS, ca. 400 B.C. SEG XXIII, 102. P. Ghiron-Bistagne, Acteurs 119-121 (ph.), dates it before the death of Euripides (L. 2); discussion of the number of members of the chorus and their name τραγῳδοί; circumstances of the dedication, etc. Mette, UDA 73, no. 3, suggests that if Sokrates is identified as PA 13102 (strategos in 441/0 B.C.; rejected by Mitsos in ed. pr.), possible dates for the dedication are 441 and 428 B.C.; cf. Mette, 86, L. 66; 87, L. 86.

---

226. AIXONE, CHOREGIC DEDICATION, 400-375 B.C. IG, II[2], 3091. P. Ghiron-Bistagne, Acteurs 95-97 (ph.); text, French translation, brief commentary. Mette, UDA 44-45, no. 1. T.J. Sienkewicz, ZPE 20 (1976) 109-112, on the basis of IG Urb Rom 223 and 229, argues that Sophocles' Telepheia (IG, II[2], 3091, L. 8) was named after the satyr play Telephos.

---

227. AGRILEZA, LAND TRANSACTION, ca. 400-350 B.C. In the Laureion mining district. Cut into the bedrock near nos. 53, 137, 266. Ed. pr. M.K. Langdon, HESPERIA 46 (1977) 166-168, no. 2 (ph., dr.).

[Τι]μησίωι
[τõ] Ἀντιπάτρο
[Ἀρισ]τομένης
[ἔδαφος] πρὸς τὸν πύργ[ο]ν
[ἐναπετί]μησεν

---

228. ATHENS, BOUNDARY STONE OF A GRAVE, 4th cent. B.C.? Marble stele found at Hiera Hodos 89, peribolos Δ. Ed. pr. O. Alexandris, AD 27 (1972) [1976] B.111 (ph.).

ὅρος | μνη- | μείο

---

229. ATHENS, BOUNDARY STONE OF A GRAVE, 4th cent. B.C.? Fragment of gray marble found at Hiera Hodos 89, peribolos Γ. Ed. pr. O. Alexandris, AD 27 (1972) [1976] B.111 (ph.).

ὅρος | μνήμ- | ατος

There is no trace of alpha in the uninscribed space at the beginning of L. 3 on the photo (ed.).

---

230. ATHENS, DEDICATION OF THE LIBRARY OF PANTAINOS, 98-102 A.D. SEG XXI, 703; cf. XXIII, 114. J.H. Oliver, AJPh 98 (1977) 163, 171, discusses the title of διάδοχος used of Pantainos' father Menandros.

---

231. ATHENS, DEDICATION, ca. 147/8 A.D. IG, II^2, 3194. SEG XVIII, 71. S. Follet, Athènes 21, note 2, restores ἐκ τοῦ [ἰδίου] in L. 3 in preference to ἕκτου [ἐνιαυτοῦ].

---

232. ATHENS, HONORS FOR THE ARCHON FLAVIUS STRATOLAOS, after 162/3 A.D. IG, II^2, 3673. E.A. Kapetanopoulos, HELLENIKA 29 (1976) 259-261; new readings and restorations LL. 3-8: ἄρχο[ντα Φλάβ(ιον)] | Στρα[τόλαον] | Φ[υλάσιον] | [β]ασιλε[ύσαντα καὶ] | πολε[μαρχήσαντα] | Ν̣Υ̣ [- - -]; prosopographic commentary.

---

233. ELEUSIS, HONORS FOR L. VIPSANIUS AIOLION?, 2nd cent. A.D. Two fragments of a base of white marble now in the epigraphical storeroom of the Eleusis Museum. Ed. pr. K. Clinton, AE (1971) 134-135, no. 31 (ph.); LL. 3-4 [Αἰολίω] | [ν]α̣ (?). P. Herrmann, ZPE 10 (1973) 79-85, restores LL. 3-4 [.Οὐιψάνι] | [ο]ν̣ and identifies the honorand as L. Vipsanius Aiolion, an exegetes of the Eumolpidai for the Eleusinian Mysteries honored in an inscription from Samos, MDAI(A) 75 (1960) 153, no. 45; reconstructed stemma of the family using IG, II^2, 2776; MDAI(A) 75 (1960) 154, no. 46; AE (1971) 131, no. 27 (cf. E.A. Kapetanopoulos, HELLENIKA 29 [1976] 250); date on epigraphic and prosopographic grounds, late 1st/ early 2nd cent A.D. S. Follet, Athènes 139-140; 314, would restore Salloustianos Aiolion and date the text ca. 177/8 - 181/2 A.D. She points out that L. Vipsanius Aiolion belongs to the deme of Kephisia, not Phlya. Kapetanopoulos, op. cit., accepts Herrmann's identification. Cf. no. 234.

[Ἡ ἐξ Ἀρείου πάγου βουλὴ]
[καὶ ἡ βουλὴ τῶν Φ καὶ ὁ δῆ]-
[μος] ὁ̣ Ἀθ̣[ηναίων .... ca. 5-8 ....]
[.]α̣ Αἰολίω[νος Φλυέα ἐξηγη]-
τὴν Εὐμο[λπιδῶν, ἄρ]ξ̣[αντα]
τὴν ἐπών[υμον ἀρ]χήν, στρα-
τηγήσαν[τα, γυμνα]σιαρ-
χήσαντα [ἐκ τῶν ἰδί]ων,
κηρυκε[ύσαντα τῆς ἐ]ξ [Ἀ]-

ρείο[υ πάγου βουλῆς, - -]
[- - - - - - - - - - - - - -]

---

234. ELEUSIS, HONORS FOR L. VIPSANIUS AIOLION, 2nd cent. A.D, AE (1899) 212, no. 45. E.A. Kapetanopoulos, HELLENIKA 29 (1976) 251, restores this fragmentary text as follows:

[- - - - -] _ [-] | [- - - Λουκίου]
[Οὐιψα]νίου Αἰο[λίωνος Φλυ]-
[έως ἐ]ξ̣ηγη[τοῦ - - - - -]
[- - - - - - - - - - - - - - - -]

For L. Vipsanius Aiolion, see no. 233.

---

235. ATHENS, HONORS FOR A PRIEST?, 2nd cent. A.D. IG, III, 3871 (not in IG, II^2). S. Follet, Athènes 113, restores L. 1 [ἔτος κ]γ́ (or [λ]γ́ or [μ]γ́) τῆς θεοῦ [Ἁδριανοῦ (εἰς τὴν Ἑλλάδα) ἐπιδημίας], 146/7 or 156/7 or 166/7 A.D.

---

236. ATHENS, HONORS FOR T. COPONIUS MAXIMUS, 98-117 A.D. IG, II^2, 3571. J.H. Oliver, AJPh 98 (1977) 163-164; discussion of the title διάδοχος, with Athenian parallels.

---

237. ELEUSIS, HONORS, 2nd cent. A.D. IG, II^2, 3614. S. Follet, Athènes 321, restores LL. 6-7 as ἀγω|[νοθ]ετήσαντα τῶ[ν Παναθηναίων καὶ Ὀλυμ]πιείων on the grounds that the Grand Asklepieia (restored in IG) are not attested at Athens.

---

238. ATHENS, HONORS(?) FOR FURIUS MARCELLUS, late 2nd cent. A.D. IG, III, 3851 (not in IG, II^2); E.A. Kapetanopoulos, ATHENA 76 (1977) 182-186, presents a new text with full prosopographic commentary on the whole family: see no. 239.

[....... ca. 13 ......]
[.... ἀρχιερ]ξ̣(?)ως
[... ca. 5 .. ἱε]ρέως
[θεοῦ καὶ] θεᾶς
[Διός τε] Ε̣ὐβουλέ-
[ως . Φ]ουρίου
[Μαρκέλ]λου Γαρ-
[γηττίου], Πανα-
[θηναΐδι ...] *v v*

---

239. ATHENS, HONORS, late 2nd cent A.D. IG, II^2, 3663. E.A. Kapetanopoulos, ATHENA 76 (1977) 183-186, offers a new text

and new restorations; prosopographic commentary on Furius Marcellus and his family: see no. 238.

[Φούριον ...5..]-
νὸ̣ν̣ Φο̣[υρίου ..]-
χοὺ υἱὸ̣ν̣ [*v* ὁ ἀρχ]-
ι̣ερεὺς Φο[ύριος]
[Μ]άρκελλος̣ [Γαρ]-
[γή]τ̣τιος τὸν φ[ί]-
[λον] *vacat*

---

240. ELEUSIS, HONORARY EPIGRAM, early 3rd cent. A.D. IG, II^2, 3662. S. Follet, Athènes 265-267; text, ap. cr., prosopographic commentary. L. 8 [Μυρτ?]άλη.

---

241. ELEUSIS, HONORARY EPIGRAM, ca. 250 A.D. IG, II^2, 3709. J.H. Oliver, HESPERIA, Suppl. 8 (1949) 250-252, no. 2. S. Follet, Athènes 263-265; text, French translation, ap. cr.; L. 4 ἀρτ̣ί̣φ[ρων?]; L. 6 Ἀντολί[ηθεν]; L. 8 πέλεν [ἐκ Μαραθῶνος?]; L. 11 τήν γε Πλάτ̣[ωνος]; L. 14 [θεῖον ? ἀ]ν̣ε̣ψιαδῶν.

---

242. ATHENS, HONORS (?), no later than 117 A.D. IG, II^2, 7671. Marble stele with sculptured relief of a youth holding a bough. S. Follet, Athènes 174-175, interprets it as an ephebic monument and restores:

[Ἀγαθῇ Τύ]χῃ
[Καίσαρος Νέρου]α Τραιανοῦ.
[Χρύσιππος] Δαμασίου Φλυεύς
etc.

---

243. ATHENES, HONORARY EPIGRAM FOR EPHEBIC OFFICIALS, 126/7 A.D. IG, II^2, 3734. D. Peppas-Delmouzou, AAA 9 (1977) 241-252 (ph.), joins to this stele a small fragment found at St. Demetrios Kataphores and previously published as a Christian gravestone, K.M. Konstantopoulos, HARMONIA 32 (1900) 34 (ph.); EM 9983. It preserves the beginning of LL. 5-6 which now may be read μνημόχυννον - - - and Πτολεμ̣[αῖ]ον. Detailed discussion of the Panathenaic prize amphora represented on this stele in relief.

---

244. ATHENS, HONORS FOR EPHEBIC OFFICIALS, ca. 169/70 A.D. IG, II^2, 3749 + 3760. S. Follet, Athènes 123, 450-453, no. 16 (ph.), associates these 2 non-joining fragments of a herm; text, ap. cr., commentary.

ʼΑγα[θῆι τύχηι].
Κατὰ ṭ[ὸ ἑπερώ]-
τημ[α τῶν σεμνοτά]-
των [ʼΑρεοπαγιτῶν (?)]
ΜΕ.- - - - - - - - - - -
Φ.- - - - - - - - - - - -
- - - - - - - - - - - - -
- - - - - - - - - - - - -
- - - - - - - - - - ω̣ - -
[τῶν ἐφήβ?]ων τῶν ἐ̣-
[πὶ τοῦ με]τὰ Τινήιον
[Ποντικὸν] ἄρχοντα ἐνι-
[αυτοῦ, κοσμ]ητεύοντος
[τῶν ἐφήβων?] Εἰσιδότου
[τοῦ Καρποδώρ]ọυ Φυλασίου,
[τὸν ἀντικοσ]μήτην καὶ συσ-
[τρεμματάρ]χην καὶ ἀγωνο-
[θέτην τῶν] *phal-* ʼΕπινεικίων
lus *vacat* 0.10 m.
[Τρόφιμον Ζωσίμου]
[Εὐπυρίδην ἀνέστησαν (?)].

---

245. ATHENS, HONORS FOR AN EPHEBIC OFFICIAL, 2nd cent. A.D. Fragment of white marble of unknown provenance; now EM 460, unpublished. Ed. pr. S. Follet, Athènes 454-455, no. 18 (ph.); commentary on readings and prosopography.

[..3-4.. ον ʼΙ]ούḷιο[ν Ζήνωνος ? υἱὸν]
[..3-4..]ọτον Μαρ̣[αθώνιον, ..3-4..]
[...4-5..] ὑωνόν̣, ʼΟνά̣[σου τοῦ]
[Τροφί]μου κοσμη[τοῦ ἀπό?]-
[γονον], Ζ̣ήνων πατέ̣[ρα τιμήσας]
[*vacat*] ẹὐ̣[κοσμίας ἕνεκα?]

---

246. ATHENS, EPHEBIC EPIGRAM, ca. 175/6 A.D. Plaque of white marble found on Kallespera Street behind Agia Sophia church. Ed. pr. J. Threpsiades, AE (1971) Chr. 26, no. 15 (ph.); text in majuscules. W. Peek, AAA 6 (1973) 125-127 (dr.), restores the text:

[ἀγων]οθε[τ -]
[στ]έμμα κα[λὸν κροτάφοις ἡρμόσσατο ʽΗρακλείδης?]
ʽΗρακλέους [γεγονὼς αἵματος ἐκ πατέρων]
ἀλκῆς γαῦρον ἐλ[ὼν - - - - - - - - - ἀγῶνα],
ἡνίκα ʽΡοῦφος [ἔην οὔνομα πατρὸς ἔχων]
κοσμητής, ἦρχε[ν δὲ φιλοστεφάνων συνεφήβων]
Αἰολίω̣[ν, πόλεως δʼ ἀρχὸς ἔφυ - - - - -]
ἀγωνοθετή[σας ʽΑδριανεία? - - - - - - - -]

L. 4 ΤΑΥΡΟΝ Threpsiades. Peek identifies Rufus as the ephebe in IG, II^2, 2193, L. 11 and Aiolion as στρατηγὸς ἐπὶ τοὺς ὁπλίτας in IG, II^2, 1792, L. 4 (ca. 181 A.D.). Cf. S. Follet, *Athènes* 314. E.A. Kapetanopoulos, HELLENIKA 29 (1976) 252-253, identifies Aiolion in L. 7 as the archon eponymous Sallustianos Aiolion Phlyeus and restores LL. 6-7

κοσμητής, ἦρχε [κρατερὸς Σαλλουστιανός τε]
Αἰολίω̣[ν κλεινῶν ἐκ πατέρων πεφυώς].

Prosopographic notes on Rufus.

---

247. ATHENS, HONORS FOR AN EPHEBIC OFFICIAL, after 211 A.D. Fragmentary herm of white marble of unknown provenance (?); EM 4018 + 4077. Ed. pr. M.T. Mitsos, AE (1973) 90-91, no. 3 (ph.). S. Follet, *Athènes* 234, restores [ὁ ἄρχων or κῆρυξ τῶ]ν ἐφήβω̣[ν] in L. 3; [Τιβ. Κλ.] in L. 4; [κοσμητὴν] in L. 6 and establishes the date by comparison with IG, II^2, 2224.

[ἀγαθῆι τύχηι]
[........] ἄρχογ̣[τος]
[ὁ κοσμητὴς τῶ]ν ἐφήβω̣[ν]
[. Κλαύδιος] Δημόστρ-
[ατος Μελιτ]εὺς τὸν
[παιδοτρίβην] τῶν ἐφή-
βων Μ[. Αὐρ. Εὐ]καρπί-
δην) Βερε[ν]ει̣[κ]ίδην

---

248. ATHENS, HONORS, 235/6 A.D. IG, II^2, 3765. S. Follet, *Athènes* 239-240; discussion of the date; from the stone in Oxford she verifies Χρήστου in L. 5 and reads φράζει in L. 10.

---

249. ATHENS, HONORS, ca. 250 A.D.? IG, II^2, 3767. S. Follet, *Athènes* 242; minor new readings confirming the text of IG in LL. 1-2; L. 6 [Μᾶρκον Αὐρή]λ̣ι|[ον - - -]; prosopographic notes.

---

250. ATHENS, HONORS FOR KARNEADES, ca. 150 B.C. IG, II^2, 3781. B.D. Meritt, HISTORIA 26 (1977) 165-166, endorses the view of H.B. Mattingly, *ibid.* 20 (1971) 28-32, that the dedicants Attalos and Arianthes were not princes of Pergamon and Kappadokia, but ordinary Athenian Συπαλήττιοι. This means a break in the secretary cycle at 146/5 - 145/4 B.C.

---

251. ATHENS, HONORS FOR AURELIUS HERACLEIDES, ca. 150 A.D. IG, II^2, 3801. J.H. Oliver, AJPh 98 (1977) 164-165, discusses the term διάδοχος, with Athenian parallels.

---

252. ELEUSIS, HONORS, ca. 150 A.D. IG, II^2, 3802. S. Follet, Athènes 250, discusses the date and identity of Titus Flavius of LL. 4-5 and presents a new text with ap. cr.

[τὸν - - - - - - - - - - - μεγα]λω-
νύ[μων πατέρων (?), ἔκγο]νον
ὑπατικῶ[ν], ἀπὸ δᾳδούχων,
τὸν σεμνότατον Τίτον
Φλάβιο[ν ἐπ]ὶ βωμ[ῷ Παι]αν[ι]-
[έα, ἀπὸ - - - - -τρί?]τ̣ον καὶ δέ-
[κατον, πο]λιτευσάμενο[ν]
[ἀεὶ] ἐπιλ[ά]γ̣[πρως, ἀγ]ων[οθε]-
[τήσαντα τὴν -- Ὀλυμ]π̣ιάδα (?), σι-
[τωνήσαντα κα]ὶ τότε [σῖ]-
[τον ἄφθονον παρασχόντα (?) *etc.*]

---

253. ATHENS, HONORS FOR CN. CORNELIUS PULCHRUS OF CORINTH, 131/2 A.D. Fragment of a cylindrical base of white marble of uncertain provenance; now in the Roman Agora, no. 636. Ed. pr. S.N. Koumanoudes, AD 25 (1970) [1971] A.54-55, no. 1 (ph.), who identifies the honorand as PIR I.1164, etc., references and discussion of his career; date from the Panhellenion L. 2. ANN. EPIG. (1974) 593. S. Follet, Athènes 126, restores the beginning as: [- - -?] | [τὸν ἱερέα Ἁδριανοῦ Πανελληνίου] | [καὶ ἄρχοντα τῶ]ν̣ Πανε[λλήνων] |.

- ?
- - - Ν̣ Πανε[λλην - - - - - - - - - - -]
[Γναῖον Κορνήλ]ι̣ον Ποῦλχ̣[ρον ἀρχιερέα]
[τῆς Ἑλλάδος καὶ] Ἑλλαδάρχην̣ - - - -
[- - ἐπίτροπον] Ἠπείρου, δικα[ιοδότην]
[Αἰγύπτου καὶ Ἀλε]ξανδρεία[ς - - - -]
- - - - Ι Φ Ι - - -̣ - - - - - - - - - -

---

254. KEPHISIA, HONORS FOR POLYDEUKION, 173/4 or 174/5 A.D. IG, II^2, 3968. S. Follet, REG 90 (1977) 47-54, on the basis of the re-dating of the archon Dionysios by J.H. Oliver, HESPERIA, Suppl. 13 (1970) 66-72, shows the significance of this date for the history of the Odeion in the Athenian Agora (tiles stamped with ἄρχ(οντος) Διονυσίου); the text of Pausanias 1.8.6; the Life of Demonax of Loukian; Attic Nights of Aulus Gellius 19.12; and inscriptions such as IG, II^2, 3970 - 3975; 4774; 13194, and MDAI(A) 67 (1942) 136-139, no. 306. See infra nos. 255, 290.

---

255. RHAMNOUS, HONORS FOR POLYDEUKION, after 173/4 or 174/5 A.D. IG, II^2, 3969. B.C. Petrakos, PAAH (1975) [1977] A.33 (ph.), joins an unpublished fragment found in the sanctuary of

Nemesis at Rhamnous to the top of the stone; new text of LL. 1-2

Ψ[ηφίσματι τ]ῆ̣ς ἐξ 'Α-
[ρείου Πάγου βουλ]ῆ̣ς κ̣αὶ

For the date, see no. 254.

---

256. ATHENS, HONORS, 2nd/3rd cent. A.D.? IG, II^2, 3998. S. Follet, Athènes 184; new readings from the stone: L. 2 ἱερείας; L. 3 [υ]ἱ̣όν, but omitting the punctuation; L. 4 [υἱ]ὸ̣ς̣; stemma of the family. J. Bousquet, BCH 101 (1977) 451-452 (ph.); text; ap. cr.; Follet's restoration of L. 4 is unmetrical and contrary to the traces of letters on the stone. Krateros in L. 4 becomes Lysimachos' brother-in-law and son-in-law of Krateros of L. 1.

Λυσίμαχον Κρατέ[ρου καὶ 'Αλε]-
ξάνδρας ἱερείας
[υ]ἱόν ❯ ἀδελφειῆς θ[ῆκε]
[πόσ]ι̣ς Κράτερος

---

257. ATHENS, HONORS FOR TIBERIUS VARIUS CAELIANUS, ca. 98 - 117 A.D. SEG XXIII, 116. J.H. Oliver, AJPh 98 (1977) 160-178, observes that there are no traces of a fourth line (as reported in HESPERIA 36 [1967] 42); discussion of the meaning of διάδοχος L. 3; identification of Caelianus and his family; cf. infra no. 262.

---

258. ELEUSIS, HONORS, before 205 A.D. IG, II^2, 4216. S. Follet, Athènes 37, note 6, rejects the restoration ἔ[παρχο]ν in LL. 7-8 in favor of ε[ὐεργέτη]ν since a Roman title would not follow προστάτην.

---

259. ATHENS, HONORS, 2nd/3rd cent. A.D. SEG XXI, 747. E.A. Kapetanopoulos, HELLENIKA 29 (1976) 256, restores LL. 6-8: ων Γάιος ['Ιούλιος Κα]|σιανὸς ['Απολλώνι|ος τ]ῷ̣ν̣ and suggests a possible identification with the archon of 207/8 A.D.(IG, II^2, 2199, L. 7).

---

260. ATHENS, HONORS, before 212 A.D. IG, II^2, 4200/1. M.T. Mitsos, AD 25 (1970) [1971] A.30, no. 3 (ph.), joins the previously unpublished fragment EM 2860 to the right side of IG, II^2, 4200/1 Fr. b to form the following text of LL. 6-9:

[..... τῶν 'Αρ]εοπα-
[γ]ειτῶν Κη[ν]σωρεῖ-
νον Κηνσω[ρ]είνου

Πλ̣α̣τ̣[αιέα ?]

S. Follet, Athènes 124, note 5, restores LL. 9-10 Πλ̣α̣τ̣[ωνικὸν] | [φιλόσοφον].

---

261. ATHENS, HONORS FOR POMPEIA SOSIA FALCONILLA, ca. 150 A.D. Eight fragments of a base of white marble found in the Agora Excavations (I 5319). Ed. pr. J.H. Oliver, HESPERIA 10 (1941) 255-258, no. 61 (dr.), who reconstructs the text on the basis of CIL VIII.7066 from Cirta in Africa. ANN. EPIG. 1947,80. W.C. McDermott, ANC. SOCIETY 7 (1976) 238-239, shows that on prosopographic grounds Oliver's date near the end of the 2nd cent. A.D. is too late; discussion of Falconilla and her family.

Ψηφισαμ[ένης]
[τῆς ἐξ Ἀ̣ρείου Πάγου βου]-
[λῆς καὶ τῆς] βο[υλῆς τῶν]
Φ̄ κ̣[αὶ τοῦ δή]μ̣ού το[ῦ Ἀθη]-
ναί̣[ων Σοσία]ν Φα[λκω]-
νίλ[λαν Σοσ]ί̣[ο]υ Π[ρίσκου]
ὑπά[του θ]υ̣γατ[έρ]α̣ [) Πομ]-
πηίο̣[υ Φ]άλκω[νος ὑπα]-
τ̣ικο[ῦ ἔ]γγονο[ν) Σοσί]-
ου Σ[ε]ν[ἐ̣]κ̣ίωνος [δὶς ὑ]-
πάτ[ο]υ) Ἰο[υ]λ̣ίο̣υ [τε Φρον]-
τίνου τρ[ὶς ὑπάτου ἀπό]
γονον Α[- - - - - ἀνέ]
σ[τησεν]

---

262. ATHENS, HONORS FOR VARIA ARCHELAIS, ca. 150 A.D. SEG XXIII, 120. J.H. Oliver, AJPh 98 (1977) 170-178; discussion of the identity of L. Aemilius Juncus and his connection with the διάδοχος Tiberius Varius Caelianus; cf. supra no. 257.

---

263. ATHENS, STATUE BASE OF MENANDER, 2nd cent B.C. Kerameikos. IG, II^2, 4256. W. Hoepfler, Kerameikos 10. Das Pompeion (Berlin 1976) 68-69, 120, 124 (ph., dr.); discussion of the base in its setting in the Pompeion in the Kerameikos. Cf. supra no. 199.

---

264. ATHENS, STATUE BASE?, Hellenistic. Fragment of circular marble base. Found at 15 Miaouli Street. Ed. pr. O. Alexandris, AD 27 (1972) [1976] B.124 (ph.); BCH 101 (1977) 528 (ph.).

Σκόπα

---

265. ATHENS, STATUE BASE?, ca. 150 A.D. IG, II^2, 5212. D. Peppa-Delmouzou, AD 27 (1972) [1976] B.12, no. 8 (ph.), reports that EM 5835, previously unpublished, joins IG, II^2, 5212 (EM 2394) and that the latter was probably found on the Acropolis; discussion of the title epimeletes of the city and Gaius Mousonius Rufus. J.H. Oliver, GRBS 17 (1976) 369-370, adduces IG, II^2, 3405 as a later example of the epimeletes of the city under

Marcus Aurelius and Lucius Verus.

[Ἐ]πιμελητεύον[τος τῆς πόλε]-
[ω]ς ·Γ· Μουσω[νίου Ῥούφου]

---

266. AGRILEZA, INVOCATION TO ARTEMIS, 400-350 B.C. In the Laureion mining district. Cut into the bedrock near nos. 53, 137, 227. Ed. pr. M.K. Langdon, HESPERIA 46 (1977) 162-166, no. 1 (ph., dr.).

Ἄρτεμι, δὸς εὐμοιρ[ία]ν Δώρωι Τι-
μησίο Τιμησίωι τε παιδὶ τ[- - -]
Λυσιστράτ<ο>

3. lapis rho corrected to omicron. Langdon suggests reading the text as 2 iambic trimeters by restoring εὔμοιρ[ε͂]ν in L. 1 and παιδὶ τ[ῶι]|Λυσιστράτ<ο> in LL. 2-3.

---

267. MOYNICHIA, ACROPOLIS, DEDICATION TO ARTEMIS, ca. 350 - 300 B.C. Statue base of gray marble. Ed. pr. I. Papachristodoulou, AD 28 (1973) [1977] B.48.

Θεοδότη
[ἐκ τῶν ἰ]δίων Ἀρ[τέ]μιδι ἵλεωι

From the same place Papachristodoulou briefly notes a six-line sacred law relating to the worship of the Μοῖραι (no text).

---

268. RHAMNOUS, STATUE BASE, 4th cent B.C.? B. Staïs, PAAH (1891) 13; J. Pouilloux, *La forteresse de Rhamnonte* (Paris 1954) 166, no. 73. B.C. Petrakos, PAAH (1975) [1977] A.34 (ph.), reports the rediscovery of this base and briefly discusses the statue of Hermes it once supported; cf. R. Lullies, *Die Typen der griechischen Herme* (Königsberg 1931) 78; 83 (ph.).

Ἑρμο͂

---

269. ATHENS, DEDICATION TO APOLLO, 1st/2nd cent. A.D. IG, II^2, 2907 + 2908. D. Peppas-Delmouzou, AD 26 (1971) [1974] B.14 (ph.), joins these two fragments to form the following text:

Ἀπόλλω[νι]
ὑπὸ Μακραῖ[ς]

270. RHAMNOUS, DEDICATION. Fragment of a large marble base. Ed. pr. B.C. Petrakos, PAAH (1975) [1977] A.33.

[- - - -]M[- - - -]
[Νεμέσ]ει ἀνέθε[σαν]

---

271. ATHENS, DEDICATION TO ZEUS HYPSISTOS, Roman. IG, II^2, 4843. D. Peppas-Delmouzou, AD 27 (1972) [1976] B.11, no. 7 (ph.); this fragment (EM 6101) is of unknown provenance, although it probably comes from the Pnyx. The letter before A in L. 1 is T, Γ, or Σ, and the stone probably did not carry a third line as indicated in IG.

---

272. ATHENS, LABEL ON THE ELGIN THRONE, ca. 300 B.C.? IG, II^2, 5167. Now in the J. Paul Getty Museum, Malibu. J. Frel, MDAI(A) 91 (1976) 186-187 (ph.); after the last preserved letters ΙΟΣ there is uninscribed space; ἀνέθηκε is not to be restored. The interval between Διοδ and ιος leaves room for about 18-20 letters to complete the patronymic and the demotic or ethnic. For the shapes of the letters Frel compares IG, II^2, 646 (295/4 B.C.).

---

273. DAPHNI, BILINGUAL MILESTONE, ca. 397 A.D. IG, II^2, 5204, now EM 10736. G. Molisani, SCO 26 (1977) 307-312 (ph.), dates the stone after Alaric's invasion of Greece as part of the restoration undertaken by the proconsul Eusebios; commentary on prosopography, the term vir clarissimus, and the distance from Athens to Daphni.

---

274. ATHENS, RUPESTRAL INSCRIPTION, 4th/3rd cent. B.C. Cut into the bedrock on the Hill of the Muses. Ed. pr. W. Peek, MDAI(A) 67 (1942) 150, no. 324 (ph.). W. Peek, PHILOLOGUS 121 (1977) 306-307, citing parallels from Delphi (FdD II.5, p. 107; BCH 54/55 [1940/41] 87) and Edfu (JOURNAL OF JURISTIC PAPYROLOGY 3 [1949] 102) interprets the words as the beginning of an iambic trimeter, possibly of Euripides.

ἔπος δ' ἐφώνη[σεν τόδε]

---

275. ATHENS, INCERTUM. Fragment of a stele. Found at 5-7 Beïkou Street. Ed. pr. O. Alexandris, AD 27 (1972) [1976] B.38; no other information.

[- - -]ΚΟΡΟΙ
[- - -]ΙΥΣ
[- - -]ΔΟΥ

---

276. ATHENS, GRAVESTONE, ca. 350 B.C. IG, II², 5236; 5240. D. Peppas-Delmouzou, AD 28 (1973) [1977] B.12, no. 1 (ph.), recognized that the funerary stele EM 11609β has been published under these two distinct lemmata. The stele now reads - - -| [Πεδι]ῷς | [᾿Α]γγελῆθ[εν].

---

277. ATHENS, GRAVESTONE OF ARISTOMENES, SON OF ARISTOMENES. Columella. Found in Kokkine Street. Ed. pr. O. Alexandris, AD 28 (1973) [1977] B.33.

᾿Αριστομένης
᾿Αριστομένους
Αἰξωνεύς

---

278. ATHENS, GRAVESTONE OF MIKION, SON OF AIANTIDOROS, ca. 350 B.C. IG, II², 5633. A. Kaloyeropoulou, AD 29 (1974) [1977] A.210, note 48 (ph.), suggests that the original inscription was cut on the flat taenia below the pediment where slight traces of letters are preserved. The three names inscribed in the pediment were added later when the stele was reused over their graves. Below Μικίων in L. 4, ΘΡ can be read. Kaloyeropoulou prints Μαντοδώρου L. 1 for Αἰαντοδώρου IG, II² and ῾Αλαέως L. 5 for ῾Αλαιέως IG, II², without comment. (Her photograph seems to support IG, II² for the former, and K. for the latter. Ed.)

---

279. ATHENS, GRAVESTONE OF PROKLES, SON OF PYTHODOROS, AND GLYKERA, ca. 350-325 B.C. Found near the Panathenaic stadium; now in the Musée d'Art et d'Histoire Geneva. GENAVA 2 (1924) 47 (ph.). Pedimental marble stele with sculptured relief. C.W. Clairmont, Mélanges Collart 95-98 (ph.).

Προκλῆς
Πυθοδώρου

Γλυκέρα Προκλέος
᾿Αλωπεκῆθεν

---

280. ATHENS, GRAVESTONE OF TIMODOROS, SON OF ALEXON. Marble columella. Found at the intersection of the Hiera Hodos and Sp. Patses Street. Ed. pr. O. Alexandris, AD 27 (1972) [1977] B.64.

Τιμόδωρος
᾿Αλέξωνος
᾿Αναγυράσιος

---

281. ATHENS, GRAVESTONE OF CHRESIMOS, SON OF AGATHARCHOS. Marble columella. Found at the intersection of the Hiera Hodos

and Sp. Patses Street. Ed. pr. O. Alexandris, AD 27 (1972) [1976] B.64.

Χρήσιμος
Ἀγαθάρχου
Ἀναφλύστιος

---

282. PEIRAIEUS, GRAVESTONE OF HEDYLINE, ca. 350 B.C. IG, II^2, 5746. Fragment of marble stele with sculptured relief of a woman's head (NM 2053). B.K. Kallipolites, AD 27 (1972) [1976] B.3, no. 15 (ph.), joins this fragment to IG, II^2, 5746; no change in the text.

---

283. KANTZA, GRAVESTONE OF DEMOSTRATE, ca. 350-300 B.C. IG, II^2, 5789. Stele of white marble with sculptured relief of a standing woman and a child. Now in the collection of I. Theodorakopoulos of Athens (no. 14); A.K. Andreiomenou, AD 27 (1972) [1977] B.696, no. 2 (ph.).

---

284. ATHENS, SEPULCHRAL EPIGRAM FOR A PHYSICIAN, late 2nd cent. A.D. IG, II^2, 5935. SEG XXI, 847. J.H. Oliver, Rh Mus 119 (1976) 285-286, rejects the restoration of L. 1, the interpretation of the vacant area following Κράτωνα in L. 2, and the identification of K. Φοντήιος Κράτων with K. Φοντήιος Μάξιμος suggested by B.D. Meritt, HESPERIA 33 (1964) 224, no. 71. He restores the text as follows:

Νούσων εἰη[τὴν] σ[ὺν το]ῖ̣ς ἀγαθ[οῖσι]| Κράτωνα *v v*
Κυίντον Φοντήιον | Γαργήτ̣τ̣ι̣ο̣ν̣ ἥδε κέκευθε *vacat* |
χθών, φιλίους δὲ τύπους δείκνυ|σιν ὁ λάινος Ἑρμῆς *vacat*

---

285. ATHENS, GRAVESTONE OF HEDYLOS, after ca. 350 B.C. IG, II^2, 6133. *Agora* 17.128. G. Daux, BCH 100 (1976) 205, correcting an error in *Agora* 17 and a wrong accent in IG, shows that the name should be read as Ἡδύλος.

---

286. KATO CHARVATI, GRAVESTONE OF PHAINARETE, ca. 330 B.C. Marathon Museum no. 32. Ed. pr. A. Kaloyeropoulou, *Mélanges Helléniques: G. Daux* (Paris 1974) 191-198 (ph.); AD 29 (1974) [1977] A.194-225 (ph.); sculptured relief representing two female figures.

Φαιναρέτη Νι̣κίου Κεφαλῆθεν

---

287. ATHENS, SEPULCHRAL EPIGRAM, late 4th cent. B.C. IG, II², 6626. P. Ghiron-Bistagne, Acteurs 112-113, translates Makareus' epigram and comments on the meaning of σωφροσύνη in L. 5.

---

288. ATHENS, GRAVESTONE OF SOSIGENES, SON OF NIKOMACHOS. Marble columella. Found at 44 Achilleos Street. Ed. pr. O. Alexandris, AD 27 (1972) [1976] B.32 (ph.).

Σωσιγένης
Νικομάχου
Λαμπτρεύς

---

289. ATHENS, GRAVESTONE OF HEDUTION "KERKOPE", ca. 300 B.C. White marble funerary lekythos found at Sp. Patses Street 65, now in the Library of Hadrian Collection M1324. Ed. pr. P.A. Pantos, AAA 7 (1974) 406-416 (ph.); with a long, detailed commentary on formulaic parallels. G. Daux, BCH 99 (1975) 171; correction of L. 5 in Pantos' text; ibid. 100 (1976) 229-230; corrections of readings in L. 2; discussion of Hedution's nickname "Kerkope". J. Bousquet, ibid. p. 593 (ph.); correction of readings in LL. 2, 5. W. Peek, ZPE 18 (1975) 292; corrections of LL. 2, 5 in Pantos' text; W. Luppe, ibid. 22 (1976) 32 (dr.); reading of L. 2. We print Daux' text.

Κερκώπη μὲν ἔγωγ' ἐκαλούμην, | εἰμὶ δὲ πατρὸς
Σ[ω]κράτου Ἡδύτιον | Μαραθωνίου. Εὐθ[α]νάτως δὲ
στείχω | ζηλωτὴ Φερσεφόνης θάλαμον, |
γήραι ἀριθμ[ή]σασ' ἐννέα ἐτῶν | δεκάδας.
Εὐσεβίαι θυγατρὸς δὲ | ἐτάφην ὥσπερ με προσήκει.

2. Σ[ωσι]κράτου Ἡδυτίου Pantos; Σ[ωσι]κράτου Merkelbach apud Peek; Ἡδύτιο<ν> Peek. || 5. γηραιὰ 'ριθμ[ή]σασ' Pantos. || 6. δεκάθας BCH 99 (1975) 593.

---

290. KEPHISIA, EPIGRAM FOR A CHILD (?) OF HERODES ATTICUS, ca. 173 A.D.? Large block of white marble. Ed. pr. W. Peek, MDAI(A) 67 (1942) 136-139, no. 306; parallels for hair offering; identifies the dead child in L. 2 as the unnamed child of Herodes in Fronto, Ep. M. Aurelius 1.6 or the stillborn child with whom Regilla was pregnant at her death, Philostratos, Vit. Soph. 2.556; discussion of his other children. S. Follet, REG 90 (1977) 53-54, connects this poem with the death of Polydeukion; the three sons are not Herodes' own but his trophimoi; on the date see no. 254.

Ἡρώδης οἱ τήνδε κόμην ού πάντα ἐνιαυτόν
οὔτε κόμην θρέψας οὔτε σέ, παῖδα φίλον,

μηνὶ τρίτῳ κείρας ὑπὸ κεύθεσι θήκατο γαίης,
Ἡρώδης, δεύσας ἄκρα κόμης δάκρυσι,
σῆμ' ἔτυμον παίδων ψυχαῖς τρισίν, ὥς ποτε σῶμα
δέξεσθ' ἐν θήκαις ὑμετέροιο πατρός.

---

291. ATHENS, GRAVESTONE OF ARTEMON, 1st cent B.C./A.D. IG, II^2, 6768. EM 1348 + 1686 + 1757. Three joining fragments of a marble columella. D. Peppas-Delmouzou, AD 27 (1972) [1976] B.13, no. 9 (ph.), joins these three fragments and notes that in L. 3 Δημοκρ[ίτου] is a possible restoration.

---

292. ATHENS, GRAVESTONE OF SOSINOMOS, SON OF HENIOCHOS. Columella. Found in Paraskeuopoulou Street. Ed. pr. O. Alexandris, AD 28 (1973) [1977] B.38.

Σωσίνομος
Ἡνιόχου
ἐγ Μυρρινούττης

---

293. ATHENS, GRAVESTONE OF NAMERTIOS, SON OF PHILON, 300-275 B.C. Kerameikos. Blue marble columella. Ed. pr. U. Knigge, Kerameikos 9.162, no. 374 (ph.).

Ναμέρτιος
Φίλωνος
Οἰναῖος

---

294. ATHENS, GRAVESTONE OF HEGESIAS, SON OF HEGESIAS. Marble columella. Found at 44 Achilleos Street. Ed. pr. O. Alexandris, AD 27 (1972) [1976] B.32.

Ἡγησίας
Ἡγησίου
ἐξ Οἴου

Cf. IG, II^2, 6994 (ed.).

---

295. ATHENS, GRAVESTONE OF KALLITELES, SON OF DEMOKRATES. Marble columella. Found at the intersection of the Hiera Hodos and Sp. Patses Street. Ed. pr. O. Alexandris, AD 27 (1972) [1976] B.64.

Καλλιτέλης
Δημοκράτου
ἐξ Οἴου

---

296. ATTICA, GRAVESTONE OF POLYSTRATE, 400-375 B.C. Fragment of an Attic marble stele with heads of a man and woman in relief. Purchased by J. Paul Getty Museum, Malibu in 1973 (73.AA.116). Ed. pr. A.N. Oikonomides, GETTY MJ 2 (1975) 53-54 (ph.). On the horizontal geison of the pediment identifying the man:

[ʼΟ]ψ̣ιάδης ʼΟψιάδου ἐξ Οἴου

On the epistyle:

Πολυστρα̣[- - -]

Oikonomides expands this to Πολυστρά̣[τη ʼΟψιάδου ἐξ Οἴου γυνή] and interprets it as identifying a missing seated female figure on the right. The preserved female head in the middle he identifies as Hierokleia, daughter of Opsiades of Oion; cf. IG, II^2, 7711.

Oikonomides, <u>ibid</u>. 5 (1977) 41-42 (ph.); prosopographic notes on Aristoteles, son of Opsiades and Polystrate; revised stemma; cf. IG, II^2, 1582, L. 85 (342/1 B.C.). In the mining lease, HESPERIA 19 (1950) 261, no. 19, L. 37, Oikonomides suggests [- - - ʼΑριστοτέλης ʼΟψι]ά̣δ̣ου<ς> ἐξ Οἴου.

---

297. ATHENS, GRAVESTONE OF CHARIDEMOS, SON OF KALLITELES. Marble columella. Found at the intersection of the Hiera Hodos and Sp. Patses Street. Ed. pr. O. Alexandris, AD 27 (1972) [1976] B.64.

Χαρίδημος
Καλλιτέλου
ἐξ Οἴου

---

298. DIONYSO/STAMATA, GRAVE STELE OF PANTALKLES AND CHAIRIMENES, 4th cent. B.C. IG, II^2, 7239. SEG XVI, 201. A.D. Liangkouras, AD 27 (1972) [1976] B.153 (ph.), records the rediscovery of the stele and its transfer to the Peiraieus Museum.

---

299. RHAMNOUS, GRAVESTONE, 4th cent. B.C. IG, II^2, 7341. B.C. Petrakos, PAAH (1975) [1977] A.29, joins two new fragments found at Rhamnous to the stele and republishes the following text:

[Δ]η[μ]έας
[Δημ]οστράτου
[ʽΡ]αμνούσιος
[Μ]ενεσθεὺς
[Μ]ενεσθίδου
[ʽΡ]α̣μνούσιο[ς]

---

300. RHAMNOUS, GRAVE STELE OF DIOGEITON, SON OF KALLIAS ET AL., 4th cent. B.C. Pedimental stele. Ed. pr. B.C. Petrakos, PAAH (1975) [1977] A.24 (ph.); restored drawing of whole monument, 23. Cf. no. 349.

Διογείτων Καλλίου Ῥαμνούσιος
Ἁβρῶ Ἀρχεβίου
Λυσίμαχος Διογείτονος Ῥαμνούσιος
Χορονίκη Εὐδωρίδου
Λυσίστρατος Λυσιμάχου Ῥαμνο[ύσιος]
Τελέσταγο[ς] Θεομνήσ[του]
[- - -]ΙΣΙ[- - -]

---

301. RHAMNOUS, GRAVESTONE, 4th cent. B.C. IG, II², 7344. SEG XIII, 128. B.C. Petrakos, PAAH (1975) [1977] A.28-29, joins three new fragments found at Rhamnous to this stele and republishes the following text:

[Δ]ρομοκ̣λῆς
Ἀθην[- - -]
Ῥαμνού[σιος]

No trace of ϑ̣[υγάτηρ] IG in "L. 4".

---

302. RHAMNOUS, GRAVESTONE OF EUPHRANOR, SON OF EUPHRON, ET AL., 4th cent. B.C. White marble stele with flat top; Rhamnous apotheke no. 222. B.C. Petrakos, PAAH (1975) [1977] A.9-10 (ph.); ERGON (1975) 9 (ph.). LL. 1-3; 4-6; 7; 8-12; 13-16; 17-19 were cut at different times by different hands in chronological order from top to bottom of the stele. Euthyphron and Phainarete in LL. 8-12 died at the same time. All names were cut in a single column. BCH 100 (1976) 597 (partial ph.).

Εὐφράνωρ
Εὔφρονος
Ῥαμνούσιος
rosettes
Εὔφρων
Εὐφράνορος
Ῥαμνούσιος
Ἁβρύλλα
Εὐθύφρων
Εὐφράνορος
Ῥαμνούσιος
Φαιναρέτη
Κλεοφῶντος
Φαιναρέτη
Εὐφράνορος
Ῥαμνουσίου
θυγάτηρ
Ἀρχέδημος
Εὔφρονος
Ῥαμνούσιος

Near this stele were found fragments of a base inscribed with an epigram mentioning Euphranor, son of Euphron. Petrakos, loc. cit., prints a photograph but gives no text.

303. RHAMNOUS, GRAVE MARKER OF [THEOPH]ANES, SON OF THEOPHANES, ca. 300 B.C. Fragment of a marble vase. Ed. pr. B.C. Petrakos, PAAH (1975) [1977] A.30 (ph.).

[Θεοφ]άνης Θεοφάντου Ῥαμνούσιος

---

304. RHAMNOUS, TOMB INSCRIPTIONS, 4th/3rd cent. B.C. Inscribed on the wall of the peribolos of Diogeiton. Ed. pr. B.C. Petrakos, PAAH (1975) [1977] A.19 (ph. of no. 4); restored drawing of whole monument, 23.

1. Γλαύκων
Καλλιτέλου
Ῥαμνούσιος

2. Ὄλ[β]ιος
Τιμοθέου
Ἀφιδναῖος

3. Ἀνδρωφέλης
Νικοστράτου
Ῥαμνούσιος
Φειδοστράτη
Εὐκόλου
Πιθέως

4. Λυκέας
Κηφισίου
Ῥαμνούσιος

No. 4. BCH 86 (1962) 683; AD 18 (1963) B.44; PAAH (1958) 30; AE (1961) Chr. 11-12; J. and L. Robert, BE (1964) no. 162. Ca. 250 B.C. Cf. AE (1961) Chr. 11, no. 19 = SEG XXI, 916; IG, II^2, 1534B, L. 213.

---

305. ATHENS, GRAVESTONE OF CHARINOS, SON OF PHILONIDES. Marble columella. Found at 44 Achilleos Street. Ed. pr. O. Alexandris, AD 27 (1972) [1976] B.32.

Χαρῖνος
Φιλωνίδου
Ῥαμνούσιος

---

306. ATHENS, GRAVESTONE OF DEMOSTRATE, late classical. Columella. Found at 71 Hiera Hodos. Ed. pr. O. Alexandris, AD 28 (1973) [1977] B.31.

Δημοστράτη
Δ̣ιοφάντου
Στειριέως
θυγάτηρ

---

307. ATHENS, GRAVESTONE OF KALLIKRATES, SON OF KALLIKRATES. Marble columella. Found at 7 Kolokotroni Street. Ed. pr. O. Alexandris, AD 27 (1972) [1976] B.65.

Καλλικράτης
Καλλικράτου
Στειριεύς

---

308. ATHENS, GRAVESTONE. Upper portion of a marble stele with crowning pediment. Found at the intersection of 84-86 Thermopylon Street and Thespieon Street. Ed. pr. O. Alexandris, AD 27 (1972) [1976] B.109.

[- - -]Σ Καλλιάδου
[Τει]θράσιος
[- - -]άδης 'Ανδρίου
[Τει]θράσιος

---

309. ATHENS, GRAVESTONE OF LYDE, early Roman. Marble stele with sculptured relief. Found at intersection of 84-86 Thermopylon Street and Thespieon Street. Ed. pr. O. Alexandris, AD 27 (1972) [1976] B.109 (ph.).

Λυδὴ Εὐφρονίου
Φαληρέως γυνή

---

310. ATHENS, GRAVESTONE OF ARISTOMACHOS, SON OF ARISTARCHOS, Hellenistic. Marble columella. Found at the intersection of 84-86 Thermopylon Street and Thespieon Street. Ed. pr. O. Alexandris, AD 27 (1972) [1976] B.109.

'Αριστόμαχός
'Αριστάρχου
Φλυεύς

---

311. ATHENS, GRAVESTONE OF MELANTHIOS, SON OF GLYKIOS. Marble mensa. Found at the intersection of the Hiera Hodos and Sp. Patses Street. Ed. pr. O. Alexandris, AD 27 (1972) [1976] B.64.

Μελάνθιος Γλυκίου
ἰσοτελής

Γλ<α>υκίου? ed.

---

312. ATHENS, GRAVESTONE OF NOUMENIOS. Marble columella. Found at the intersection of the Hiera Hodos and Sp. Patses Street. Ed. pr. O. Alexandris, AD 27 (1972) [1976] B.64.

Νουμήνιος
ΔΑΕ - ΑΝΘΟΥ ?
Σωτέλης

3. [ί]σ<ο>τελής ? (ed.).

---

313. ATHENS, GRAVESTONE. Columella. Found at the intersection of 23 Hodos Navarinou and Gounare Street. Ed. pr. A.G. Liangkouras, AD 27 (1972) [1976] B.171.

[- - - - -] ?
'Αγκυρανός

---

314. ATHENS, GRAVESTONE OF EPIKTETOS, SON OF APOLLONIOS, 1st cent. B.C./A.D. IG, II^2, 7942 + 11283. D. Peppas-Delmouzou, AD 28 (1973) [1977] B.12, no. 2 (ph.), joins these 2 fragments.

'Επίκ[τ]ητος 'Απολλω-
νίο[υ] 'Αδραμυτηνός

---

315. ATHENS, GRAVESTONES OF SOTION, 2nd cent. B.C.? IG, II^2, 7945 and 12754. Marble columella (IG, II^2, 7945) and marble stele (IG, II^2, 12754) found in the Kerameikos. U. Knigge, *Kerameikos* 9 (Berlin 1976), no. 358 (ph.), suggests that both gravestones belong to the same person.

---

316. ATHENS, GRAVESTONE OF EYPHROSYNOS, SON OF MENELAOS. Marble columella. Found at the intersection of the Hiera Hodos and Sp. Patses Street. Ed. pr. O. Alexandris, AD 27 (1972) [1976] B.64.

Εὐφρόσυνος
Μενελάου
'Αντιοχεύς

---

317. ATHENS, GRAVESTONE OF SOSIAS. Marble *mensa*. Found at the intersection of Spyrou Donta Street and 44 Syngrou Blvd. Ed. pr. O. Alexandris, AD 27 (1972) [1976] B.105.

Σωσίας 'Αρμένιος

---

318. ATHENS, GRAVESTONE OF ARTEMON. Marble columella. Found at the intersection of the Hiera Hodos and Sp. Patses Street. Ed. pr. O. Alexandris, AD 27 (1972) [1976] B.64.

'Αρτέμων
'Ελαιείτης

---

319. ATHENS, GRAVESTONE OF AGATHONYMOS, late Classical. Columella. Found at 71 Hiera Hodos. Ed. pr. O. Alexandris, AD 28 (1973) [1977] B.31.

Ἀγαθώ[νυ]μος
Ἐρετρ[ιε]ύς

Probably in 2 lines (ed.).

---

320. ATHENS, GRAVESTONE OF KANTHARA. Marble columella. Found at 44 Achilleos Street. Ed. pr. O. Alexandris, AD 27 (1972) [1976] B.32.

Κανθάρα
Ἐφεσία
Μενάνδρου
γυνή

---

321. ATHENS, GRAVESTONE OF ARTEMISIA. Marble columella. Found at the intersection of the Hiera Hodos and Sp. Patses Street. Ed. pr. O. Alexandris, AD 27 (1972) [1976] B.64.

Ἀρτεμισία
Ἡρακλεῶτις

---

322. ATHENS, GRAVESTONE OF NIKON, Hellenistic. Marble stele. Found in the area bounded by Vouliagmenis, Tribonianou, and Eupompou Streets. Ed. pr. O. Alexandris, AD 27 (1972) [1976]B.97.

Νίκων
Ἡρακλεώτης

---

323. ATHENS, GRAVE STELE OF KTESIKLES, late 4th cent. B.C.? Kerameikos. Ed. pr. U. Knigge, Kerameikos 9.160, no. 362 (ph.).

Κτησικλῆς
Ἱστιαιεύς

---

324. ATHENS, GRAVE STELE OF THERON, SON OF TIMOKLES, end of 4th cent. B.C.? Kerameikos. Ed. pr. U. Knigge, Kerameikos 9.158, no. 356 (ph.).

Θήρων
Τιμοκλέους
Κνίδιος

---

325. ATHENS, GRAVE EPIGRAM OF MALICHA, ca. 350 B.C. IG, II^2, 9112. H. Raffeiner, COMMENTATIONES AENIPONTANAE 23 (1977) 13-14, no. 1; text and commentary on slave status of Malicha; δικαιοτάτην L. 3.

---

326. ATHENS, GRAVESTONE OF DIONYSIOS, SON OF ARCHEMACHOS. Marble columella. Found at 44 Achilleos Street. Ed. pr. O. Alexandris, AD 27 (1972) [1976] B.32.

Διονύσιος ᾿Αρχεμάχου Λαππαῖος

Probably arranged in 3 lines; no photo or description (ed.).

---

327. ATHENS, GRAVESTONE OF STEPHANOS, ca. 350 B.C. Marble stele with sculptured relief of crown of ivy. Found at the intersection of Achilleos Street and 52 Iasonos Street. Ed. pr. O. Alexandris, AD 27 (1972) [1976] B.34.

Στέφανος Λαρισαῖος

---

328. ATHENS, GRAVESTONE OF KLEO. Marble columella. Found at the intersection of the Hiera Hodos and Sp. Patses Street. Ed. pr. O. Alexandris, AD 27 (1972) [1976] B.64.

Κλεώ
Λυκία

---

329. ATHENS, GRAVESTONE OF SEUTHES, after 4th cent. B.C. IG, II^2, 9233. To this marble columella (EM 11962) D. Peppas-Delmouzou, AD 27 (1972) [1976] B.13, no. 10 (ph.), joins the unpublished fragment EM 1725 to yield the following text:

[Σ]εύθης
[Λ]υσιμαχεύς

---

330. ATHENS, GRAVESTONE OF NOSTON, SON OF KLEOMACHOS, late Classical. Upper part of a marble stele with crowning pediment. Found at 71 Hiera Hodos. Ed. pr. O. Alexandris, AD 28 (1973) [1977] B.31 (ph.).

Νόστων
Κλεομάχω
Μαντινεύς

---

331. ATHENS, GRAVESTONE OF ARISTON, 1st cent. A.D. IG, II^2, 10807. Two joining fragments of a marble stele. D. Peppas-Delmouzou, AD 28 (1973) [1977] B.13, no. 3 (ph.), joins IG, II^2, 10807 (EM 9805) and EM 1000, thus supplying the deceased's ethnic.

Ἀρίστων [Μει]λήσιο<ς>

---

332. ATHENS, GRAVESTONE, 1st cent. B.C. IG, II^2, 9717. Two joining fragments of a marble columella, now in the Epigraphical Museum, once identified by Kirchner, Add. nov. p. 894, with a marble columella found in the Athenian Agora, *Agora* 17.586 (ph.). D. Peppas-Delmouzou, AD 27 (1972) [1976] B.13, no. 11 (ph.), establishes that IG, II^2, 9717 is EM 1756 + 1757, not *Agora* 17.586, thus confirming Bradeen's doubts about Kirchner's suggestion.

[Κ]αλλί[ας]
[Ἀ]πολλω[νίου]
[Μ]ιλήσ[ιος]

---

333. ATHENS, GRAVESTONE OF KALLITYCHE. Marble columella. Found at 44 Achilleos Street. Ed. pr. O. Alexandris, AD 27 (1972) [1976] B.32.

Καλλιτύχη
Δημητρίου
Μιλησία

---

334. ATHENS, GRAVESTONE OF PERIGENIS. Marble columella. Found at the intersection of the Hiera Hodos and Sp. Patses Street Ed. pr. O. Alexandris, AD 27 (1972) [1976] B.64.

Περιγενὶς
Θεοφίλου
Μιλησία

---

335. ATHENS, GRAVESTONE OF PYRRHA. Marble columella. Found at the intersection of the Hiera Hodos and Sp. Patses Street. Ed. pr. O. Alexandris, AD 27 (1972) [1976] B.64.

Πύρρα
Μιλησία

---

336. LAUREION, GRAVE EPIGRAM OF ATOTAS OF PAPHLAGONIA, ca. 350-300 B.C. IG, II^2, 10051. H. Raffeiner, COMMENTATIONES AENIPONTANAE 23 (1977) 14-16, no. 2; text and commentary on slave

status and profession (μεταλλεύς) of Atotas. Cf. infra no. 365.

---

337. PEIRAIEUS, GRAVE EPIGRAM OF APOLLONIOS OF SYNNADA, 2nd/3rd cent. A.D. IG, II^2, 10385. H. Raffeiner, COMMENTATIONES AENIPONTANAE 23 (1977) 46-48, no. 24; text and commentary on slave status of Apollonios.

---

338. SALAMIS, GRAVE EPIGRAM OF TECHNON THE PHRYGIAN, 2nd cent. B.C. IG, II^2, 10490. H. Raffeiner, COMMENTATIONES AENIPONTANAE 23 (1977) 26-28, no. 9; text and commentary on slave status of Technon.

---

339. ATHENS, GRAVESTONES OF ADA, 4th cent. B.C. IG, II^2, 10574 and 10575. Marble stele (IG, II^2, 10574) and marble cippus (IG, II^2, 10575) found in the Kerameikos. U. Knigge, Kerameikos 9, no. 352 (ph.), suggests that both gravestones belong to the same person and redates IG, II^2, 10575 from the 2nd cent. B.C. (IG) to the 4th cent. B.C.

---

340. ATTICA, GRAVESTONE OF ARISTAGORA, ca. 375-365 B.C. Time and place of discovery unknown. Athens NM 5221. White marble stele with female figures in sculptured relief. Ed. pr. E.G. Papastavrou, AE (1976) 141-147 (ph.).

Ἀρισταγόρα

---

341. ATHENS, GRAVESTONE OF ARISTOPOLIS. Marble columella. Found at the intersection of Meg. Alexandrou and Salaminos Streets. Ed. pr. O. Alexandris, AD 27 (1972) [1976] B.68 (ph.).

Ἀριστοπολίς
τίτθη
χρηστή

---

342. AIGALEOS, GRAVESTONE OF ARTEMISIA. Columella. Found in Thebon Street (Nekrotapheion Γ') in Aigaleos. Ed. pr. A.G. Liangkouras, AD 27 (1972) [1976] B.157.

Ἀρτεμισία χρηστή

---

343. RHAMNOUS, GRAVE LOUTROPHOROS OF ARCHIPPE, 4th cent. B.C. Rhamnous apotheke no. 96. Ed. pr. B.C. Petrakos, PAAH (1975) [1977] A.29 (ph.).

[᾿Α]ρχίππ[η]
[Φ]ιλοστράτου
θυγάτηρ

---

344. ATHENS, GRAVESTONE OF BOUBALIS. Marble columella. Found at the intersection of the Hiera Hodos and Sp. Patses Street. Ed. pr. O. Alexandris, AD 27 (1972) [1976] B.64. J. and L. Robert, BE (1977) no. 133, add that the name is not Anatolian.

Βουβαλῖς
Φιλοξενίδου
θυγάτηρ

---

345. ATHENS, GRAVESTONE OF GEISYLLA. Marble columella. Found at the intersection of the Hiera Hodos and Sp. Patses Street. Ed. pr. O. Alexandris, AD 27 (1972) [1976] B.64.

Γείσυλλα
Κλεοφῶντος
θυγάτηρ
Θεοπίστου
γυνή

---

346. ATHENS, GRAVESTONE, ca. 350 B.C. IG, II^2, 11103. G. Daux, Phoros 42-45 (ph.), argues that the stone honors one person, not two, and he restores LL. 1-2: Δημήτριο[ς] | Θεοδότης, Demetrios, son of Theodote; BCH 100 (1976) 210; Daux suggests that Erxis, LL. 6, 9, was Demetrios' stepfather, Theodote's second husband. C.W. Clairmont, Mélanges Collart 98-100 (ph.), interprets Erxis as the wife or foster mother of Demetrios, the son of Theodote.

---

347. ATHENS, GRAVE STELE, Hellenistic. Kerameikos. Ed. pr. U. Knigge, Kerameikos 9.162, no. 373 (ph.).

Δημήτριος

---

348. ATHENS, GRAVESTONE OF DEMO. Columella. Found at 65 Sp. Patses Street. Ed. pr. O. Alexandris, AD 28 (1973) [1977] B.41.

Δημώ

---

349. RHAMNOUS, GRAVE INSCRIPTION, 4th cent. B.C. Large epistyle block seen between the sanctuary and the fortress by

H.G. Lolling, MDAI(A) 4 (1879) 281; cf. J. Pouilloux, *La forteresse de Rhamnonte* (Paris 1954) 167, no. 74. B.C. Petrakos, PAAH (1975) [1977] A.21, rediscovered the block and associates it with the tomb of Diogeiton, supra no. 300.

Διογ̣[είτων]

---

350. ATTICA?, GRAVESTONE, ca. 250 B.C. Stele with relief of seated woman and servant. Ed. pr. *Kunst der klass. Antike, Austellung 22 Nov. 1975 - 10 Jan. 1976: Galerie André Emmerich: Munzen und Medaillen* no. 40 (ph.); J. and L. Robert, BE (1976) no. 217.

Διόδωρος Φιλίππα

---

351. ATHENS, GRAVESTONE OF DIOKLEIA. Marble columella. Found at the intersection of the Hiera Hodos and Sp. Patses Street. Ed. pr. O. Alexandris, AD 27 (1972) [1976] B.64.

Διόκλεια
Διοκλέους
προξένου
θυγάτηρ

Cf. no. 352.

---

352. ATHENS, TWO GRAVESTONES OF DIOKLES. Marble columella and a marble *mensa*. Both found at the intersection of the Hiera Hodos and Sp. Patses Street. Ed. pr. O. Alexandris, AD 27 (1972) [1976] B.64. Identical texts.

Διοκλῆς
Ἱεροκλέους
πρόξενος

Cf. no. 351.

---

353. ATHENS, GRAVESTONE OF DIONYSIOS; Marble columella. Found at the intersection of the Hiera Hodos and Sp. Patses Street. Ed. pr. O. Alexandris, AD 27 (1972) [1976] B.64.

Διονύσιος
Νέωνος

---

354. ATHENS, GRAVESTONE OF DIONYSODOROS. Marble columella. Found at the intersection of the Hiera Hodos and Sp. Patses Street. Ed. pr. O. Alexandris, AD 27 (1972) [1976] B.64.

Διονυσόδω[ρ]ος

---

355. ATHENS, GRAVE EPIGRAM, Roman period? IG, II^2, 11205. H. Raffeiner, COMMENTATIONES AENIPONTANAE 23 (1977) 34-35, no. 13; text and commentary on slave status of the deceased.

---

356. ATHENS, GRAVESTONE OF DOROTHEA. Marble columella. Found at the intersection of the Hiera Hodos and Sp. Patses Street. Ed. pr. O. Alexandris, AD 27 (1972) [1976] B.64.

Δωροθέα
χρηστή

---

357. ATHENS, GRAVESTONE OF HELEN, 1st cent. A.D. IG, II^2, 11249a. D. Knoepfler, Mélanges Collart 270, note 9, corrects the reading in IG to Ἑλένηι; the rarity of ἐπὶ before the name of the deceased suggests that this might be "une pierre errante".

---

358. ATHENS, GRAVESTONE OF EXEKIAS, late Classical. Marble lekythos with sculptured relief. Found at 71 Hiera Hodos. Ed. pr. O. Alexandris, AD 28 (1973) [1977] B.31 (ph.).

Ἐξηκίας Νικονίκη

---

359. ATHENS, GRAVESTONE OF HERMAIOS, late Classical. Fragment of marble stele with pediment and sculptured relief. Found at 71 Hiera Hodos. Ed. pr. O. Alexandris, AD 28 (1973) [1977] B.31.

Ἑρμαῖος

---

360. ATHENS, GRAVESTONE OF EUKLEA, ca. 350 B.C. IG, II^2, 11407. D. Peppas-Delmouzou, AD 28 (1973) [1977] B.13, no. 4 (ph.), reports the rediscovery of the missing fragment (EM 819); no change made in the text. She suggests that IG, II^2, 11408 may belong to the same burial.

---

361. ATHENS, GRAVESTONE OF EYPHROSYNE. Marble columella. Found at the intersection of the Hiera Hodos and Sp. Patses Street. Ed. pr. O. Alexandris, AD 27 (1972) [1976] B.64.

Εὐφροσύνη
Ἀπολλοδώρου
γυνή

---

362. ATHENS, GRAVESTONE, 2nd cent. A.D. IG, II^2, 11551. J.H. Oliver, AJPh 98 (1977) 164, discusses the title διάδοχος with Athenian parallels.

---

363. ATHENS, GRAVESTONE OF THEODOTE, ca. 400 B.C. Fragment of marble stele with sculptured relief; now in the Musée d'Art et d'Histoire, Geneva. GENAVA 4 (1926) 12 (ph.). C.W. Clairmont, Mélanges Collart 93-94 (ph.).

Θεοδότη

---

364. PANKRATI, GRAVESTONE, 3rd/2nd cent. B.C. Blue marble columella. Ed. pr. R.L. Pounder, AD 28 (1973) [1977] A.241 (ph.).

Θε<ο>δώρα
Θέωνος
Ἀλεξανδρ<έω>ς
θυγάτηρ

Lapis 1. ΘΕΩΔΩΡΑ. || 3. ΑΛΕΞΑΝΔΡΟΣ.

---

365. LAUREION, GRAVESTONE OF IANIBELOS, 2nd cent. A.D.? IG, II^2, 11697. SEG XIII, 207. Brauron Museum. O. Masson, SEMITICA 26 (1976) 96-98 (ph.), interprets Ianibelos' occupation, ἀρχι-καμινευτής, as "forgeron en chef" in the Laureion mines; he is a foreigner from the Near East, as is shown by the right to left direction of the first inscription, by the shape of the stele, and the form of his name. J. and L. Robert, BE (1977) no. 181, favoring a date in the Hellenistic period, suggest that he comes from a mining area such as Paphlagonia and that his occupation was rather a "Hüttenmeister", as suggested by Kordellas, MDAI(A) 19 (1894) 243. Cf. supra no. 336.

---

366. ATHENS, GRAVESTONE OF KALLIAS, ca. 350 B.C.? Marble stele. Found at the intersection of Achilleos Street and 52 Iasonos Street. Ed. pr. O. Alexandris, AD 27 (1972) [1976] B.34.

Καλλίας

---

367. PEIRAIEUS, GRAVESTONE, Hellenistic. Fragment from the left side of a pedimental stele. Ed. pr. A.G. Liangkouras, AD 27 (1972) [1976] B.171 (ph.).

Λαι[- - -]
Ξεγ̣[- - -]
Ελα[- - -]
ΑΛΥΙ̣[- - -]

2. Ξεν[- - -]; 4. Ἀλυπ[- - -], ed. from ph.

---

368. ATTICA?, GRAVE STELE OF MYNNIA, ca. 380-350 B.C. Provenance unknown; now in the J. Paul Getty Museum, Malibu (71.AA.121). Stele of white marble with two women and a small girl in relief. Ed. pr. J. Frel, GRBS 14 (1973) 173-177 (ph.); cf. C. Vermeule, N. Neuerburg, Catalogue of the Ancient Art in the J. Paul Getty Museum (Malibu, Calif. 1973) no. 11.

Ἐνθά[δε] κεῖται Μυννία μητρὶ ποθεινή
Εὐφροσύνη : Ἀρτεμισίας Μυννία Εὐτέλο

Discussion of the interpretation of L. 2 in Frel; M. Marcovich, R. Merkelbach, ZPE 15 (1974) 168; C.W. Clairmont, Mélanges Collart 101-102 (ph.); G. Daux, BCH 100 (1976) 206-209 (ph.).

---

369. ATHENS, GRAVESTONE OF MNESISTRATE, early 4th cent. B.C. IG, II^2, 12162. D. Peppas-Delmouzou, AD 28 (1973) [1977] B.14, no. 5 (ph.), suggests that Pittakys, L'ancienne Athènes 294, is the ed. pr. not of this stele but of IG, II^2, 12159a, Add. nov. p. 896. The text of IG, II^2, 12162 (EM 4274 + 806) now reads:

Μν[ησ]ιστράτη

---

370. ATHENS, GRAVESTONE OF NIKOMACHE, ca. 325 B.C. Marble lekythos with sculptured relief. Found at 66 Phalerou Street. Ed. pr. O. Alexandris, AD 27 (1972) [1976] B.84.

Νικομάχη

---

371. ATHENS, GRAVESTONE OF NIKON. Marble plaque. Found at the intersection of 6 Psaromelingou Street and Kaloyerou Samouel Street. Ed. pr. O. Alexandris, AD 27 (1972) [1976] B.146.

Νίκων
ἐνθάδε
κεῖται

---

372. ATHENS, GRAVE STELE, late 4th cent. B.C. Kerameikos. Ed. pr. U. Knigge, Kerameikos 9.158, no. 355 (ph.).

Ὀαλλὶς χρηστή

Knigge: "Der Name. . .scheint sonst nicht belegt. Vielleicht fehlt der Punkt von Θαλλίς."

---

373. ATHENS, GRAVESTONE, early Byzantine. Marble stele with engraved cross. Found at 406 Kokkine Street. Ed. pr. O. Alexandris, AD 28 (1973) [1977] B.33.

ϑήκη Ὀλύ-
ππου

---

374. ATHENS, GRAVESTONE OF SOTAIROS, late Classical. Marble stele with sculptured relief. Found at 71 Hiera Hodos. Ed. pr. O. Alexandris, AD 28 (1973) [1977] B.31.

Σόταιρος

Σώταιρος? (ed.).

---

375. ATHENS, GRAVESTONE, 2nd/3rd cent. A.D. IG, II^2, 11557. D. Knoepfler, Mélanges Collart 270, note 9, reads this text as: ἐπεὶ (= ἐπὶ)|Συνβείωσεις (= Συμβίωσις woman's name)|Ζωσίμου.

---

376. ATHENS, GRAVESTONE OF HYGINE, late Roman. Fragment of marble stele. Found at 5 Margarite Street. Ed. pr. O. Alexandris, AD 27 (1972) [1976] B.122.

Ὑγινὴ
ὧδε
κῖτε

---

377. ATHENS, GRAVESTONE, late Classical. Marble lekythos with sculptured relief. Found at 71 Hiera Hodos. Ed. pr. O. Alexandris, AD 28 (1973) [1977] B.31 (ph.).

Φιλοκλῆς Νικομάχη

---

378. ATHENS, GRAVESTONE. Fragment of a columella. Found at the intersection of Edouardo Low Street and Stadiou Street.

Ed. pr. O. Alexandris, AD 27 (1972) [1976] B.107.

[- - -]νίδου
[- - -]δο
[γυ]νή

---

379. ATHENS, GRAVESTONE, Classical. Fragment of a base. Found at 5-7 Beïkou Street. Ed. pr. O. Alexandris, AD 27 (1972) [1976] B.38 (ph.).

[- - -]ẸẠ.[- - -]
Θρασυβούλ[ου]
θυγάτη[ρ]

---

380. ATHENS, KEPHISOPHON'S KYLIX, ca. 400 B.C. CIG I.545. SEG XXIV, 72. E. Vanderpool, HESPERIA 36 (1967) 187-189 (dr.), with earlier bibliography. Graffito on an Attic skyphos once in the collection of Fauvel, now lost. Κηφισοφῶντος ἡ κύλιξ· ἐὰν δέ τις κατάξηι, δραχμὴν ἀποτείσε, δῶρον ὂν παρὰ Ξενύλ̣[ο]υ. C. Gallavotti, RAL 31 (1976) 223-224, reads the last phrase as χ̣λωρ̣ὸν ὂν παρὰ ξέν<ο>υ.

---

381. PEIRAIEUS, VASE INSCRIPTIONS. Graffiti on the bottom of a black-glazed vase. Ed. pr. A.G. Liangkouras, AD 27 (1972) [1976] B.171 (ph.).

Φιλομένεο[ς]
Φιλομένε[ος?]

---

382. ATHENS, GRAFFITO, late Roman. Agora 21.B.20. J.H. Oliver, AJPh 98 (1977) 210, reads this text: κωνοψωμίω[ν] ὀψάρει(ον) Περσ̣ι̣κ̣ὸ̣ν̣, ναύλου ὀψάρει(ον) κ̣οινόν. He interprets ναύλου as "freight" or "cargo". "This important graffito, juxtaposing the Persian delicacy of cone-bread and ordinary opsari from a (fishing) boat's load, helps to explain how ψάρι came to be the modern Greek word for 'fish'."

---

383. ATHENS, GRAFFITI, ca. 510 B.C. - 300 B.C. One or two letters on vases from the Kerameikos. U. Knigge, Kerameikos 9.22; 47; 85, no. 5 (510-500 B.C.); 92, no. 23 (500-480 B.C.); 94, no. 30 (ca. 490 B.C.); 98, no. 41.5 (ca. 490 B.C.); 105, no. 66.3 (490-480 B.C.); 118, no. 117.23 (480-470 B.C.); 128, no. 166 (475-450 B.C.); 129, no. 175 (475-450 B.C.); 130, no. 176.2 (470-460 B.C.); 130, no. 177.3 (470-450 B.C.); 131, no. 182.2 (475-450 B.C.); 132, no. 190.1 (470-460 B.C.); 137, no. 213

(475-450 B.C.); 138, no. 214 (475-450 B.C.); 142, no. 237 (ca. 450 B.C.); 147, no. 265 (ca. 450 B.C.); 150, no. 286 (ca. 450 B.C.); 153, no. 295.9 (450-425 B.C.); 154, no. 301 (450-425 B.C.); 159, no. 359, tile (ca. 300 B.C.?); 166, no. 398; 171, no. E7.2 (ca. 500 B.C.); 171, no. E8.1; 173, no. E14 (500-490 B.C.); 176, no. E32.2 (ca. 480 B.C.); 177, no. E37 (ca. 480 B.C.); 181, no. E60.2 (ca. 460 B.C.); 182, no. E67.1 (475-450 B.C.); 191, no. ES14 (ca. 460 B.C.).

---

384. ATHENS, VASE INSCRIPTIONS. M. Lang, The Athenian Agora 21: Graffiti and Dipinti (Princeton 1976) (ph., dr.). 859 inscriptions on pottery, lamps, tiles, and miscellaneous clay objects from the 8th cent. B.C. to the 6th cent. A.D. (excluding ostraka; artists' signatures, kalos and other inscriptions painted on black- and red-figured pottery; painted convivial inscriptions which are part of the decoration of a vase; stamped and moulded inscriptions). Categories included: abecedaria, messages and lists, love and hate names, names, numerical notations, owner's marks, dedications and convivial inscriptions, commercial notations, tax notations, Christian inscriptions, miscellaneous, unclassified, pictures.

---

385. ATHENS, STAMPED TILE, late 4th cent. B.C.? Kerameikos. Ed. pr. U. Knigge, Kerameikos 9.160, no. 364 (ph.).

Αἰγιπύρου

---

386. ATHENS, STAMPED AMPHORA HANDLES, Hellenistic. From the Pompeion in the Kerameikos. Ed. pr. W. Hoepfler, Kerameikos 10: Das Pompeion (Berlin 1976) 213 (ph.).

1. Παυσανίας Rhodian
2. ἐπὶ (Πολυ)κράτοες ('Αρταμιτίου) Rhodian
3. ἐπὶ Δράκονος Εὐφρόνου Κνιδίου
4. ἐπὶ ἑρμοκράτου 'Ιππολόχου
5. ἐπὶ Εὐφραγόρα Μάρονος Κνιδίων
6. ἐπὶ 'Απολλοδώρου 'Αναξάνδρου Κνιδίου
7. ἐπὶ δαμιοργοῦ Δαιδάλου
8. ἐπὶ 'Ηροφάντου

Peiraieus. Ed. pr. A.G. Liangkouras, AD 27 (1972) [1976] B.171.

9. Θάσιος 'Ηρόδοτος
10. Θάσιος ῎Αλκιμος

Mt. Hymettos. Langdon (supra no. 61) 72, no. 335.

11. ['Επὶ] 'Αριστομή|[δ]ευς Κνιδίων | 'Αγα[prow?]θ̣ι̣ν̣[ου]

---

387. ATHENS, LAMP SIGNATURES, 2nd cent. A.D. Found at Bourbachis Street 30 and Theophilopoulou Street 10. Noted by O. Alexandris, AD 27 (1972) [1976] B.97.

(1) Χιόνης
(2) Κύρα[κος]

Found in the Zappeion near Queen Olga Blvd., Alexandris, _ibid._ 107 (ph.), Corinthian lamp:

Ὀνησίμου

For other graffiti and signatures on lamps, 4th cent. B.C./ Hellenistic, I. Scheibler, _Kerameikos 11: Griechische Lampen_ (Berlin 1976) 149-172 (ph., dr.); assorted graffiti, owners' names, labels, dedications, single letters, prices, and numerous signatures from late Hellenistic workshops.

---

388. ATHENS, DECREES. A.S. Henry, _The Prescripts of Athenian Decrees: Mnemosyne_ Supplement 49 (1977); detailed analysis of the prescripts of decrees passed by the Athenian boule and demos in chronological order; tables, indexes, bibliography.

---

389. ATHENS, GRAVESTONES. D.W. Bradeen, _The Athenian Agora 17: Inscriptions: The Funerary Monuments_ (Princeton 1974). A corpus of gravestones found in the Agora Excavations from 1931 through 1968, including 238 previously unpublished texts; photographs; full indexes.

---

390. ATHENS, INSCRIPTIONS HONORING PRYTANEIS. B.D. Meritt, J.S. Traill, _The Athenian Agora 15: Inscriptions: The Athenian Councillors_ (Princeton 1974). A corpus of all records of the members and officers of the Athenian Boule; 494 texts, including 6 published for the first time; copious indexes.

---

391. ATTIC DECREES FOUND OUTSIDE ATTICA. See no. 1282, found at Erythrai.

CORINTHIA

---

392. CORINTH, ELEIAN DECREE HONORING CORINTHIAN JUDGES, after 191 B.C. SEG XXII, 231. Fragment of blue-gray marble stele. Found at Kokkinovrysi north west of the city. Ed. pr. N.D.

Robertson, HESPERIA 45 (1976) 253-266 (ph.).

[- - - - - - - - - - - - - ἔδοξε τοῖρ συνέδροιρ, ἐπαινέ?]-
[σαι μὲν τὸν δᾶμον τῶν Κορινθίων καὶ στεφανῶσαι στεφάνωι χρυσέωι ἐπὶ?]
[τ]ᾶι καλοκα[γαθίαι καὶ τᾶι εὐνοίαι ἇι ποτ ἀμὲ ἔχων διατελεῖ·? ἐπαινέσαι]
δὲ καὶ τοὶρ δικασταὶρ διοι̣κ̣[άσαντερ πάντα φιλοδόξωρ καὶ δικαίωρ καὶ?]
ἀξίωρ̣ τᾶρ ἐγχειρισθείσαρ αὐτοῖρ πίστι[ο]ρ [καὶ σπουδᾶρ· ἦμεν δὲ καὶ? προξέ]-̣ (ca. 23)
νοιρ καὶ εὐεργέταιρ τᾶρ πόλιορ Νικοκλῆ Δια[- - - τὸν δεῖνα - - - - - - ἵπ]-
πω Νικάτα[ν Χ]ιωνίδα Πολύξενον Νικάνδ[ρου *vel* ρίδα τὸν δεῖνα τοῦ δεῖνος τὸν δεῖνα (ca. 23)]
Ἀντάν[δρ]ο[υ] Ἀ̣ρχεμαχίδαν Φιλαίθω Μνασέα[ν τοῦ δεῖνος τὸν δεῖνα τοῦ δεῖνος (ca. 26)] (ca. 26)
Τιμοσθένη Ἀγαθανδρίδα Δικαίαρχον Δαμ[- - - τὸν δεῖνα - - - - - -]
[.]δα Ἀρχέμαχον Πειθιδάμω Κ[ορ]ινθίοιρ *vv* [ὑπάρχην δὲ αὐτοῖρ καὶ ἐκγόνοιρ?]
κ̣α̣ι̣ πολιτείαν καὶ ἀτέλειαν καὶ ἀσφάλε[ιαν καὶ πολέμω καὶ εἰράναρ καὶ τὰ]
λοιπὰ τίμια ὅσα κ[α]ὶ τοῖρ ἄλλοιρ προξένοιρ κ[αὶ εὐεργέταιρ ὑπάρχει·? καλέσαι δὲ]
[αὐ]τ̣οὶρ καὶ ἐπὶ τὰ[ν κοι]νὰν ἑστίαν τοὶρ ἄρχο[ντερ· δόμεν δὲ αὐτοῖρ καὶ ξένια·?]
[τὰν δὲ ἐπιμέλειαν ποιήασσαι?] Λάδρομον τὸν ἐπιμε[λητὰν ὅπωρ τὸ ψάφισμα τόδε?]
[γραφὲν ἐγ χάλκωμα ἀνατεθᾶι? ἐν τ]ὸ ἱερὸν (ἵ)ν̣α ἐ(ν) πάντα τ[ὸν χρόνον διαμένηι *vvv* ?̣]

15. Lapis HΛ̣E.

---

393. CORINTH, SACRIFICIAL CALENDAR, ca. 600 B.C.? Corinth 8.1, no. 1. H.S. Robinson, AD 26 (1971) [1974] B.100; HESPERIA 45 (1976) 230-231 (ph.); Neue Forschungen in griechischen Heiligtümern: Symposion Olympia: 1974 (Tübingen 1976) 249-251 (ph.), publishes a new non-joining fragment (I-70-4) found on Temple Hill. Boustrophedon:

- - - →ατε̣ρ|ον ←τ- - -|- - →- τ .|. ? .

Robinson believes that this block comes from the exterior wall of the early archaic temple which was destroyed ca. 580-570 B.C.

---

394. CORINTH, CATALOGUE?, 1st cent. A.D. Two joining fragments of white marble found in the Forum Southwest (I 1651 + I-74-6).

Ed. pr. T.R. Martin, HESPERIA 46 (1977) 178-179, no. 1 (ph.); victor list from the Isthmian games? Cf. Corinth 8.1, no. 14 (3 A.D.).

Κι[- - -]
[- - -]λ̣ο̣θ[- - -]

1. Κι[θαριστάς] or Κι[θαρῳδούς] Martin.

---

395. CORINTH, HONORS FOR FAUSTINA, 2nd cent. A.D. Fragment of a white marble slab found in the Forum Southwest (I 2522). Ed. pr. T.R. Martin, HESPERIA 46 (1977) 187, no. 7 (ph.); either for the elder or the younger Faustina, the former deified in 140/1 A.D., the latter in 175/6 A.D.

[θ]ε̣ὰν Φα̣[υστεῖναν Σεβαστήν]
[Αὐ]το[κ̣ράτορος Καίσαρος - - -]

Martin suggests that in L. 1 of Corinth 8.3, no. 109, which also honors Faustina, [θεὰν] might be restored in place of [Ἀννίαν].

---

396. CORINTH, HONORS, 3rd cent. A.D. Corinth 8.3, no. 486. T.R. Martin, HESPERIA 46 (1977) 189-195, no. 10 (ph.), joins an unpublished fragment found in the Forum Southwest (I-74-4) to this block (I 2118) and publishes a new text with full commentary on the titles.

[.]α̣ρ̣χη̣ν̣ τ̣αμίαν Α̣.[- - - - - - - - - - - - -]
τῆς πόλεως ·β΄· γραμμ̣[ατέα - - - - - - - - -]
σύνεδρον ·β΄· ἀγορανόμ̣[ον]. Κ̣Α̣Ι̣.[- - - - - -]
στρατηγὸν· τῆς λαμ̣π̣οτάτης̣ Κ̣[ορινθίων πόλεως]
ὑγιῶς· κα̣ὶ̣[- - - - - - - - - - - - - - - - -]

Martin per ep. adds dots under the mu in L. 2 and sigma in L. 4 and removes the superimposed numbers printed in HESPERIA over the unpreserved spaces of LL. 1-3, 5. 1. [Ἑλλα]|[δ]ά̣ρ̣χην̣? Martin. || 3. Κ̣α̣ι̣σ̣[αρείων Ἰσθμίων?] Martin.

---

397. CORINTH, ACCLAMATION?, Roman. Two joining fragments of white marble found in the Forum Southwest (I 2445). Ed. pr. T.R. Martin, HESPERIA, 46 (1977) 196, no. 12 (ph.). Acclamation or a name?

ὠκεαν̣[έ - - -]

398. CORINTH, AINETA'S VASE, ca. 625 B.C. IG, IV, 348. C. Gallavotti, RAL 31 (1976) 222, rejects the identification of Aineta as a woman and suggests that Ainetas is the leader of a group of dancers; cf. Pyrrhias' olpe, no. 399.

---

399. CORINTH, PYRRHIAS' OLPE, ca. 580 B.C. SEG XIV, 303; XVII, 137; XXII, 229; XXIV, 269. C. Gallavotti, RAL 31 (1976) 219-222, reads the text in this order:

← Πυρϝίας | προχορευόμενο-
→ ς, αὐτõ δέ ϝοι ὄ|λπα
← πολύτερ|πος

"Purrias è il capofila, e appunto per lui è la boccetta divertentissima;" G. Annibaldis, O. Vox, GLOTTA 55 (1977) 183-190, interpret πολυτέρπο̄ς as an adverb modifying προχορευόμενος. They divide the inscription into two parts: (1) πολυτέρπο̄ς -- προχορευόμενος, 5 anapaests, and (2) αὐτõ (genitive) -- ὄλπα, also anapaestic.

---

400. CORINTH, DEDICATION TO DEMETER, 5th cent. B.C. Acrocorinth Demeter Sanctuary. SEG XXV, 339. M.L. Lazzarini, MAL 19.2 (1976) 67, identifies Οἰ|νεία, LL. 3-4, as the ethnic of Οἴνη, πόλις Ἄργους, Stephanos Byz. s.v.

---

401. CORINTH, GAMING TABLE OR ABACUS, 5th cent. B.C. Forum Southwest. Two joining fragments of a slab of white marble. Ed. pr. C.K. Williams, II, HESPERIA 46 (1977) 56-57; 72-73, no. 29 (ph.).

Top: ΜΧΗ|Δ|Ο⊢

Williams interprets these as acrophonic numerals for 10,000; 1,000; 100; and 10. The vertical strokes on either side of Δ are regarded as dividers.

Front: Στρατα[- - -]

Williams: Στρατά[γιον?].

---

402. CORINTH, GAMING TABLE OR ABACUS, late Hellenistic. SEG XI, 188; XIV, 307. Corinth 8.3, no. 42. To this broken slab of white marble, C.K. Williams, II, HESPERIA 46 (1977) 56-57; 72, no. 28 (ph.), adds new fragments found in Forum Southwest and re-edits the whole. On the top surface are five lines and the following:

Διὸς Βουλέος X H Δ I δαμόσια Κο-
ρινθίων

The large single letters are not later, but they predate the texts to either side and are badly worn from much use of the board.

---

403. CORINTH, INCERTUM, Roman. White marble fragment found in the Forum Southwest (I 2533). Ed. pr. T.R. Martin, HESPERIA 46 (1977) 189, no. 9 (ph.).

[- - - - -]ο̣μεν[- - -]
[- - - -Κο]ρ̣ινθίου

---

404. CORINTH, INCERTUM, 3rd cent. A.D. Fragment of white marble found in the Forum Southwest (I-73-3). Ed. pr. T.R. Martin, HESPERIA 46 (1977) 195, no. 11 (ph.); L. 1 has larger letters.

[- - -].Ι̣Ω̣Ι[- - - - - -]
[- - -]..ĖΛΕΩΝΗ̣.[- - - -]
[- - - - -]..[- - - - - -]

---

405. CORINTH, CHRISTIAN GRAVESTONE. Kraneion basilica. Text made public by A.K. Orlandos, ERGON (1977) 95-96; no other details.

+ Σεργίου αἰνοπαθοῦς πολυήρατον υἱέα Πέτρον,
εἰκοστὸν λυκάβαντα κ(αὶ) εἰς ἑῆα μοῦνον ἐόντα
λοιμὸς ἀμείλικτος κ(αὶ) ἀνάρσιος <ἥ>ρπασ<ε> πλουτεύς,
ὃν γενέτης ἔθρεψε κ(αὶ) ἤγαγεν ἐς μέτρον ἥβης,
Καλλιόπης μύθοισι κ(α̣ὶ) Ἑρμείαο κομίσας + >—
Μη(νὶ) Μαΐῳ γι' ἰ<ν>δ(ικτιῶνος) Η'

---

406. CORINTH, CHRISTIAN GRAVESTONES. Small fragments found in the Forum Southwest. Ed. pr. T.R. Martin, HESPERIA 46 (1977) 196-197, nos. 13-16 (ph.).

(1) No. 13 (I-57-3).

[κοιμητήριον δ]ι̣αφέ[ρον τοῦ δεῖνος]
[εὐλα]β(εστάτου) φάλ̣[του - - - -]

---

2. [- - -]B^S lapis.

(2) No. 14 (I 2520 + 2521).

[- - - - - μ]ηνὶ [- - - - -]
[- - - ἡμέρα ἕ]κτη ἐπ[ινεμήσεως - - -]

(3) No. 15 (I 2525).

[- - - μ]νῆμα [- - -]

(4) No. 16 (I 2516).

ἐν[θάδε]
ἀν[επαύσατο]
.[- - - -]

---

407. ISTHMIA, DEDICATION OF A JUMPING WEIGHT, 6th cent. B.C. SEG XVIII, 140; XXII, 207. J. Ebert, AS AKAD. LEIPZIG 63.2 (1972) 31-35, no. 1 (ph., dr.), restores:

[μνᾶμά μ]ε πενταϝεθλέον νικά[σας δϝὶς name]
[καὶ δὲ παλ]αίον δϝίς, [τᾶ]ιδ᾽ εὐχόμενό[ς ποκ᾽ ἔθεκε]

W. Peek, ZPE 23 (1976) 77-78 (dr.), rejects Ebert's restoration and offers:

[χερσὶν ἔχον ἐμ]ὲ πενταϝε|θλέον νίκα[σε Κράτιππος]||
[καὶ δὲ παλ]αίον δϝίς·| [τᾶ]ιδ᾽ εὐχόμεν[ος δ᾽ ἀνέθεκεν]

---

408. ISTHMIA, DEDICATION, 6th cent. B.C. SEG XVIII, 141; XXV, 324. W. Peek, ZPE 23 (1976) 78-79, no. 4 (ph., dr.); new restoration; ποιναῖον: "nicht 'strafend' . . . sondern 'Dank erstattend', wie ja auch ποινή in hohem Stil positive Geltung hat (GEL s.v. 3)."

πᾶσι καὶ ἐσσομέ[νοις λάμψει κλέος]| *h*έπτ᾽ Ὀνομ̣[άνδρο]
[νικᾶν, *h*ᾶν]| ποιναῖον ἔ[θεκε Ποτειδάϝονι]
- -

---

409. ISTHMIA, DEDICATION TO THE MOTHER OF THE GODS AND OURANIA. Marble stele with relief sculpture of two "Cybeles in contiguous <u>naiskoi</u>" (IS 71-4). Ed. pr. P.A. Clement, AD 27 (1972) [1976] B.229 (ph.).

[Μ]ήτ̣ηρ θεῶν   Οὐρανία

---

410. ISTHMIA, INCERTUM (DEDICATION?), ca. 160-170 A.D.? Two non-joining fragments of white marble. Ed. pr. P.A. Clement, AD 27 (1972) [1976] B.230 (ph.).

[- - - - - - - - - - - - -].[- - - - - - -]
[- - - Π]ρεῖσκ[ος Ἰο]υ̣βεντ̣[ιανὸς - - -]
[- - - -]Μ̣Ι̣[. . .6. . .]. .[- - - - -]

L.1 ed. from ph. For P. Licinius Priscus Iuventianus, <u>Corinth</u> 8.3, nos. 199-201; 306.

---

411. ISTHMIA, PRAYERS FOR JUSTINIAN AND VICTORINUS. IG, IV, 204/5. SEG XI, 52. <u>Corinth</u> 8.3, no. 508. D. Feissel, BCH 101 (1977) 220-224, discusses Cyriacus of Ancona and the textual tradition of these two inscriptions.

---

412. ISTHMIA, STAMPED ROOF TILES, Roman. Ed. pr. P.A. Clement, AD 27 (1972) [1976] B.230 (ph.); <u>ibid.</u> 28 (1973) [1977] B.145; 147; 149.

(1) COL · L · IVL · COR
(some with AC added)
(2) Ποσειδῶνος
(3) [Ποσειδῶν]ος · Ἰσθ
(4) Δημόσ̣[ιον] retrograde
(5) AA ligature of MA?
(6) "undeciphered set of ligatured letters"
(7) [- - -]ΟΝΙΟΥ
[- - -]Μ̣ΑΙΟΥ
(8) [- - -]ΜΤΦΑ[- - -]
[- - -]ΕΩΣ[- - -]
(9) [- - -]CECV.[- - -]
(10) [- - -]NDI
(11) CA[- - -]
(12) Ποσ · Ἰσθ retrograde
(13) Βαλερ[ι - - -]
(14) ΑΝΤΘΕΜΣ[- - -]

---

413. ISTHMIA, LAMP SIGNATURES, 2nd - 4th cent. A.D. Ed. pr. P.A. Clement, AD 27 (1972) [1976] B.229-230 (ph.).

(1)	[Λού]κιον	IPL 71-18	2nd cent. A.D
(2)	[Ὀκτ]αβ[ίο]υ	IPL 71-42	2nd cent. A.D.
(3)	Πωσφόρου	IPL 71-69	2nd cent. A.D.
(4)	[Σεκ]ούν̣[δου]	IPL 71-51	2nd cent. A.D.
(5)	[Ἀλε]ξάν[δρου]	IPL 71-56	3rd/4th cent. A.D.
(6)	Καλλίστου	IPL 71-55	3rd/4th cent. A.D.
(7)	Εὐ (= Eutyches)	IPL 71-35	3rd/4th cent. A.D.
(8)	Λε (= Leonteus)	IPL 71-11	3rd/4th cent. A.D.
(9)	Πρειμου	IPL 71-28; 64	3rd/4th cent. A.D.
(10)	Συνφόρου	IPL 71-63	3rd/4th cent. A.D.

---

414. KENCHREAI, INCERTUM, ca. 375 A.D. R. Scranton, CPh 71 (1976) 106-108, discusses various interpretations of the letters PH inscribed on 4 plinths of columns in a navelike hall or passage at this site.

PHLIASIA

---

415. PHLIOUS, ARTISTS' SIGNATURE, ca. 500 B.C. Fragment of a poros statue base. Ed. pr. C.B. Kritzas, AD 28 (1973) [1977] B.135γ (ph.). Phliasian epichoric alphabet.

[ὁ δεῖνα καὶ ὁ δεῖνα Φλει]ϝάσιοι ἐποίϝεσα̣ν

---

416. PHLIOUS, LIST OF NAMES, 4th cent. B.C. Slab of white sandstone. Ed. pr. C.B. Kritzas, AD 28 (1973) [1977]B.135δ (ph.).

Νεανθίδος
Εὐῶπις
Χρυσίλλα
Ἀγάθων
Ἀστεῖος

---

417. PHLIOUS, GRAVESTONE, late Hellenistic. Now in the apotheke at Nemea. Limestone slab. Ed. pr. C.B. Kritzas, AD 28 (1973) [1977] B.135δ (ph.).

Ἀχαϊκὴ
χαῖρε

---

418. PHLIOUS, INCERTUM, Roman. Sandstone slab. Ed. pr. C.B. Kritzas, AD 28 (1973) [1977] B.135β. We print Kritzas' text verbatim.

ΝΟΥΛ̣[- - -] Possibly Λ. Ἰούλ̣[ιος -ία]

CLEONAEA

---

419. NEMEA?, DEDICATION, ca. 525 B.C. Found at Tourkovrysi near Nemea. Fragment of a poros base once in the private possession of the brothers Papayanni in Hagios Georgios (New Nemea); now lost? G.D. Androutsopoulos, ΠΟΕΛΜΩΝ 4 (1949) 73-75 (ph. of a squeeze); Jeffery, LSAG 173-174, no. 7; W. Peek, ZPE 23 (1976) 79-80 (dr.); M.L. Lazzarini, MAL 19.2 (1976) 278, no. 721.

Vertical boustrophedon in LL. 2-4.

[. . .4-5. .]ιάδες με ἐποίϝεσε *v* →
[Κλ]έανδρος δὲ ἀνέθεκε καὶ *h*ι[- - -] →
[- - -κ]αλὸν ἄγαλμα· ἐμὶ δέ τοι [.ca. 2.] ←
[.ca. 2.]εια καλõν Μ*h*εῖδ[ονος - - - - -] →
[- - - -κ]αὶ ἀγόν, τὸν δὶ[ς - - - -] ←

---

1. [Μικκ]ιάδες Androutsopoulos; rejected by Jeffery and Peek. || 2. [Κ]λ̣έανδρος Jeffery; *h*ί[δρυε?] Jeffery; *h*ί[στα|το] Peek. || 3. το[̣. .ca. 3.] Jeffery; τοι [μν|εμ]εῖα Peek. || 4. καλονι̣ *h*ειδομ[- - -] Jeffery. || 4-6. [ἀέ|θλον· κ]αὶ ἀγόν, τὸν δὶ[ς ἐ̣νίκα ̣| Ὀλυμπίαι ἐν Νεμέαι τε Κλεάνδρο φίλος *h*υιός, ἔεν πάλα *h*α βαρύμοχθος] Peek.

---

420. NEMEA, DEDICATIONS?, 5th cent. B.C. S.G. Miller, HESPERIA 46 (1977) 21, briefly notes two inscribed blocks found in the 1964 excavation in the Sanctuary of Zeus (Ῥοδίων and Ἐπιδαυρίον) and discusses their possible connection with the row of 9 oikoi south of the temple of Zeus.

---

421. NEMEA, LEAD TABLETS, 4th cent. B.C. Found in the Sanctuary of Zeus. Originally rolled and inscribed on the inner surface (IL 90a-c). Ed. pr. S.G. Miller, HESPERIA 46 (1977) 10-11; 13 (ph.).

(1) Μυτονο ΘΙΙ=ΙΙ⁻
Κλεοναι *vacat*

(2) Πυρϝαλίων Κυκλίας defixio?

---

422. KLEONAI, GRAVESTONE, Hellenistic. Pedimental stele found at "Βολιμωτὴ Γούβα". Ed. pr. C.B. Kritzas, AD 28 (1973) [1977] B.135 (ph.).

Ἀρισταινέτου

ARGIA

---

423. ARGIVE HERAION, DEDICATION, ca. 550-525 B.C. Bronze mirror handle. H.F. De Cou, Argive Heraeum 2.265; 332, no. 1581 (ph., dr.); Jeffery, LSAG 159; 168, no. 11; M.L. Lazzarini, MAL 19.2 (1976) 117; 215, no. 275b (dr.).

boustrophedon

Ἀρίστεια Ἐκε- ←
[θ]αίο μ' ἀνέθεκ- →
ε ←

1. Ἐκεθαίοι De Cou; Ἐκε|[θα]ίο Lazzarini ("nome finora non attestato altrove"); εκε.|..οι Jeffery; but the A is clear on De Cou's drawing (ed.).

---

424. ARGOS, DECREE REGULATING RELATIONS AMONG ARGOS, KNOSSOS, AND TYLISSOS, ca. 450 B,C. SEG XI, 316 (with Add. p. 222); XV, 200; XXII, 264; XXV, 360. K. Rigsby, TAPA 106 (1976) 326-328, discusses the religious and topographic aspects of the settlement of the border between Knossos and Tylissos (B LL. 14-16; 26-27; 35-38).

---

425. ARGOS, HELLENISTIC DECREE. Fragment from the right side of a pedimental limestone stele. Ed. pr. C.B. Kritzas, AD 28 (1973) [1977] B.126 (ph.).

stoich.?

[- - - - - - -]ΗΝΟΣΕΡΙ
[- - - - - - ἀ]ρήτευ-
[ε - - - - - - - - -]ΡΙΣ
[- - - - - - - - - -]ΕΝ
[- - - - - - - - - -]Ν[.]

1. μ]ηνὸς Ἐρι-? Kritzas.

---

426. ARGOS, LETTER TO THE CITY OF AIGEAI IN KILIKIA REGARDING PUBLIUS ANTEIUS ANTIOCHOS, ca. 200 A.D.(?) SEG I, 69. L. Robert, BCH 101 (1977) 120-132 (ph.), re-edits the text with French translation, bibliography, ap. cr., and commentary.

- -
[Αἰγεαί]ων τῶν ἐν Κιλικίαι ἀνανέωσις τᾶς
[παλαιᾶς π]ρὸς τὰν πόλιν συγγενήας.
[Ὁ δᾶμος τ]ῶν Ἀργείων καὶ ἁ βουλὰ καὶ οἱ σύνεδροι Αἰγεαίων
[τῶν ἐν Κιλι]κίαι τοῖς ἄρχουσι καὶ τᾶι βουλᾶι καὶ τῶι δάμωι *vac.*
[τοῖς συγ]γενέσι χαίρειν. Πόπλιος Ἄντειος Ἀντίοχος, *vac.*
[πολίτας ὑμέ]τερος, γενόμενος ἐν τᾶι πόλι ἁμῶν περὶ πολλοῦ ἐποι-
[ήσατο ἀνανε]ώσασθαι τὰ τᾶς ὑμετέρας πόλιος δίκαια πρὸς τὰν ἁμε-
[τέραν καὶ ἐγ]γράψας στάλαι θεῖναι ἐν τῶι τοῦ Λυκείου Ἀπόλλωνος ἱε-
[ρῶι, ὅπερ καὶ] ἀδεῶς ἐπετρέψαμεν αὐτῶι, διδαχθέντες ἐπιμελῶς
[περὶ τούτω]ν, ἅμα δὲ καὶ ὁρῶντες καλὰν ἅμιλλαν τὰν ὑπερ τᾶς *v*
[συγγενεία]ς αὐτὸν φιλοτιμούμενον, ὅθεν βουλευτάν τε

[αὐτὸν ἐποιη]σάμεθα καὶ τὰς λοιπὰς ἃς πρόσθεν ἐψηφισάμεθα
[- - -τιμὰ]ς, καλὸν ὑπόμναμα νομίζοντες εἶναι τὰν
[τῶν ἀγαθ]ῶν ἀνδρῶν τιμάν· τᾶς δὲ στάλας τὸ ἀντίγραφον ἐ-
[πέμψαμεν] ὑμῖν τὸ ὑπογεγραμμένον·
[Ἐπειδὴ Πόπλιο]ς Ἄντειος Ἀντίοχος, ἐπιδαμήσας ἀμῶν τᾶι πόλι κοσ-
[μίως καὶ φιλο]φρόνως, ἔν τε τοῖς λοιποῖς ἐπεδείξατο τὰν ἰδίαν κα-
[λοκαγαθίαν κ]αὶ τὰν ἐν παιδείαι τελειότατα, οὐκ ἥκιστα δὲ ἐν τᾶι
[περὶ τὰν πατρί]δα σπουδᾶι τε καὶ διαθέσει, φανερὰν ἀμιν ποιήσας
[τὰν ἐκ παλαιοῦ? ὑ]πάρχουσαν ποτ' Αἰγεαίους ἀμῶν συγγένειαν· Περ-
[σέα γὰρ ἔφη τὸ]ν Δανάας ἐπὶ τὰς Γοργόνας στελλόμενον ἐς
[- - ca. 9 - ἀφίκ]εσθαι Κιλικίαν, ἅτις ἐστὶν τέρμα τᾶς πρὸς *v*
[- ca. 13-14 -] κἀκεῖ τὸ τᾶς πατρίου κομίζοντα ἀφεί-
[δρυμα - - - ca. 25 - - διὰ] τ̣ὸ̣ [μ]η̣δέπω̣ τὸ̣ν ἆθλο̣ν ἐκ
- -

---

427. ARGOS, CATALOGUE OF THEARODOKOI, ca. 330 B.C. SEG XXIII, 189. P. Cabanes, REG 82 (1969) 550-551; Épire 117-120; 144-145, restores L. 13 as [Κόρκυ]ρα [Μνασαλκ]ί̣δας on the basis of IG, IV^2.1, 94, L. 28. G. Daux, REG 84 (1971) 355, regards names in -ίδας as too common to permit a certain restoration. Cabanes (locc. citt.) also identified [Φ]ορβάδας of Ambrakia in L. 10 with the thearodokos of the same city in IG, IV^2.1, 95, LL. 32, 81. Daux (loc. cit.) confirmed from the stone that this was the correct reading. See no. 447. Cabanes, Épire 173-185, discusses the geographic and political significance of this list and IG, IV^2.1, 94 for the development of Epeiros.

---

428. ARGOS, DEDICATION TO THE DIOSKOUROI, ca. 400 B.C. Hodos Ant. Chatzi 18. Base of black limestone. Ed. pr. C.B. Kritzas, AD 27 (1972) [1976] B.203-205 (ph.). J. and L. Robert, BE (1977) no. 193, suggest τ[ὸ] in L. 2.

[- - -]ιμος ἀνέθηκε
[- - -]Ο τέμενος
[- - - τοῖ]ν̣ Ϝανάκοιν

---

429. ARGOS, DEDICATION OF PHRATRY MEMBERS TO HERAKLES PANKAMES, 1st cent. A.D. Limestone base found at Hodos Zographou 9; now in the Argos Museum (E 3266). Ed. pr. C.B. Kritzas, AE (1973) 106-119 (ph.); detailed commentary and a useful appendix of epithets of Herakles; cf. AD 27 (1972) [1976] B.198 (ph.); G. Touchais, BCH 101 (1977) 546-547 (ph.).

τῶι Πανκάμε
τοὶ τᾶς πάτρας
ἀνέθηκαν
Θρασέας Δαϊκράτεος
Τεισίας Διάκτορος
Εὔδικος Σαωνίδα
Διάκτωρ Τεισία
Δαμοκρίνης Σαωνίδα
Δαϊκράτης Θρασέα
Ἀγαῖος Θρασέα

---

430. ARGOS, STATUE BASE, 1st cent. A.D. Square statue base; reused; found in the French Excavations of the Agora. Ed. pr. BCH 100 (1976) 753 (ph.); probably part of a larger, more explicit inscription.

ἐκ τῶν ἰδίων
ἀνέθηκεν

---

431. ARGOS, HELLENISTIC GRAVESTONE. Fragment of a stele found in Grave 3 at Hodos Theatrou 49. Ed. pr. C.B. Kritzas, AD 28 (1973) [1977] B.123 (ph.).

Μυρτίλε
χαῖρε

---

432. ARGOS, GRAVESTONE, early Roman. Hodos Chatzi 18. Fragment of a stele. Ed. pr. C.B. Kritzas, AD 27 (1972) [1976] B.205 (ph.).

[- - -]χρ̣[ηστὲ] or χρ̣[ηστή]
[- - -]. ʼχαῖρε̣ [- - -̣]
[- - -]ΕΙΘΗ χα̣ῖρε̣

---

433. ARGOS, GRAVESTONE?, late Hellenistic. Ed. pr. C.B. Kritzas, AD 28 (1973) [1977] B.134 (ph.).

ΘΗΡ̣Ι̣[- - -]

θή̣κ̣η? ed.

---

434. ARGOS, CHRISTIAN GRAVESTONE. Intersection of Corinth and Zaïmis Streets. Ed. pr. C.B. Kritzas, AD 27 (1972) [1976] B.207, grave 7 (ph.); G. Touchais, BCH 101 (1977) 546-547 (ph.); D. Feissel, ibid. 224-228, discussion of curse formula.

cross Κοιμητήριον Κυριακῆς
θυγατρὸς ῾Ρόδης, εἴ τις δὲ
ἀνορύξῃ αὐτὸ παρεκτὸς
τῶν κληρο<νό>μων, ἐχέτω τὸ
ἀνάθεμα τὸ τοῦ ᾿Ιόδα (sic) *cross*
fish

4. Lapis ΚΛΗΡΟΜΩΝ.

---

435. ARGOS, CHRISTIAN GRAVESTONE. Intersection of Corinth and Zaïmis Streets. Ed. pr. C.B. Kritzas, AD 27 (1972) [1976] B.207, grave 3 (ph.).

ΧΡ *ligature*
Κοιμητήριον
᾿Ελπιδίου καὶ
Εἰερῶς
τῆς γαμετῆ̣[ς]
αὐτοῦ

---

436. ARGOS, CHRISTIAN GRAVESTONE. Intersection of Corinth and Zaïmis Streets. Ed. pr. C.B. Kritzas, AD 27 (1972) [1976] B.207, grave 1 (ph.). D. Feissel, BCH 101 (1977) 224, note 105, on LL. 2-3. J. and L. Robert, BE (1977) no. 193, on LL. 2-3.

Κοιμητή-
ριον ᾿Ελπίδ-
ηφό(ρου) σελεντι-
αρίου, ἔνθα κα<τε>-
τέθη ἡ οἰκοδέσ-
ποινα <α>ὐτοῦ Βιόλα
(ΧΡ *ligature in a circle)*

2-3. ἐλπίδ|η φῶς <Σ>ελεντ- Kritzas. || 4. end ΚΑ.

---

437. ARGOS, CHRISTIAN GRAVESTONE. Found near the Church of the Panagia before 1890; now in the Byzantine Museum in Athens (Inv. no. 601). Ed. pr. D. Feissel, BCH 101 (1977) 224-228 (ph.); discussion of curse formula in LL. 3-7.

+ Κυμητήριον δια̣[φέρον - -]
νης καὶ τῆς ταύτῃ̣[ς - - - -]
λούσης· εἴ τις δὲ [ἀνορύξῃ αὐτὸ]
ἔξοθεν τῶν [κληρονόμων]
αὐτῆς, ἐχέτ[ω τὸ ἀνάθεμα]
τοῦ ᾿Ιούδα [καὶ τῶν λεγόντων]
ἆρον ἆρον σταύ[ρωσον αὐτόν].

438. ARGOS, MOSAIC INSCRIPTIONS, 5th cent. A.D. Mosaic floor in a bath excavated at Hagios Taxiarchos. Now in the Museum of Argos. Ed. pr. G. Akerström-Hougen, The Calendar and Hunting Mosaics of the Villa of the Falconer in Argos: Acta Inst. Athen. Regni Sueciae 23 (1974) 23-26; 128-129 (ph.).

(1) Ἰα|νου|ά|ριος Φεβρου|άρι|ος Μάρ|τι|ος
Ἀπ|ρήλι|ος Μα|ΐος Ἰού|νι|ος
Ἰού|λι|ος Ἄ|γ|ου|στο|ς (sic) Σεπτέ|μβρι|ος
Ὀκτώ|βρι|ο|ς Νοέν|βρι|ος Δε|κέμ|βρι|ος

(2) Χιμών Αἶαρ Θέρος Μεθό|πωρο

(3) Ὑγιέ|νων| λοῦσε

(4) Ἀπόλαυ|σις

M. Marcovich, ZPE 20 (1976) 44, interprets no. 3 as ὑγιαίνων λοῦσαι "take your bath in good health"; no. 4 is interpreted as a "new goddess" and equated with Voluptas. J. and L. Robert, BE (1977) no. 195, observe that Ἀπόλαυσις is a late personification, not a goddess; parallels in BE (1976) no. 751. M.W. Haslam, ZPE 23 (1976) 48, cites a parallel Apolausis in a bath mosaic from Antioch.

---

439. ARGOS, BILINGUAL, Roman. Found in the French Excavations of the Roman Bath A. Brief mention by P. Aupert, BCH 100 (1976) 750.

G LIB - - -
PI ΡΗΓΟ - - -

---

440. ARGOS, INCERTUM, Roman. Small fragment of porphyry stone. Ed. pr. C.B. Kritzas, AD 27 (1972) [1976] B.211 (ph.).

[- - -]Ο̣Υ[- - -]
[- - -]Ε̣Κ[- - -]
[- - -]ΤΟ̣[- - -]
[- - -]Ω.[- - -]

---

441. ARGOS, STAMPED AMPHORA HANDLE. Ed. pr. C.B. Kritzas, AD 27 (1972) [1976] B.196.

Ἐπ' Ἀπολ̣ωνίο̣υ

---

442. ARGOS, ROMAN LAMP SIGNATURES. Ed. pr. C.B. Kritzas, AD 27 (1972) [1976] B.196; ibid., 28 (1973) [1977] B.134.

ΝΑΡΟΥ (ΙΛΑΡΟΥ? A. Bovon, *Lampes d'Argos* 98)

ibid., 28 (1973) [1977] B.126 (ph.). Corinthian lamp.

Σωτηρίδα

HERMIONIA

---

443. HALIEIS, IRON KEY, ca. 475-450 B.C. Large iron key found in the temple of Apollo. Ed. pr. M.H. Jameson, AD 27 (1972) [1976] B.235.

τ᾽ Ἀπ̣ολλον[- - -]

TROEZENIA

---

444. TROIZEN, THEMISTOKLES' DECREE. SEG XVIII, 153; XIX, 319; XXII, 274; XXIII, 191; XXIV, 276; XXV, 376. M.M. Henderson, A CLASS 20 (1977) 85-103, argues that the decree is authentic and that it survived in the Athenian archives where it was discovered by Aischines; conflicts between the decree and Herodotus are more apparent than real.

EPIDAURIA

---

445. ASKLEPIEION, DECREE HONORING DRYMOS OF ARGOS, ca. 350 B.C. Fragment of marble stele with male figure sculptured in relief. Ed. pr. M.T. Mitsos, AE (1976) 83-86, no. 2 (ph.).

Θεός. Ἔδοξε τᾶι
πόλι τᾶι τῶν
Ἐπιδαυρίων
Δρῦμον Ἐπικρά-
τεος Ἀργεῖον
θεαροδόκον
εἶμεν τοῦ Ἀσκλα-
πιοῦ καὶ πρόξενον
τῶν Ἐπιδαυρίων
αὐτὸν καὶ ἐκγό-
νους, καὶ εἶμεν
αὐτοῖς ἀτέλειαν
καὶ ἀσυλίαν καὶ
ἐμ πολέμωι καὶ
ἐν εἰράναι καὶ
κατὰ γᾶν καὶ κατὰ
θάλασσαν. Κατά-
λογος βουλᾶς
Νίκαιος
Πολιτάδος

---

446. ASKLEPIEION, DECREE, 4th/3rd cent. B.C.? Now in the Epigraphical apotheke, no. 010. Right half of a pedimental stele of gray limestone. Ed. pr. W. Peek, AS AKAD. LEIPZIG 63.5 (1972) 10, no. 11. M.T. Mitsos, AE (1976) 83, no. 1; new reading from the stone in L. 3.

[ἔδοξε] βουλᾶι καὶ δά-
[μωι τῶ]ν Ἐπιδαυρί- *v*
[ων ..3-4.. μ]αχον Φιλί[ππ]ο
[....]έα πρόξενον
[εἶμεν] καὶ εὐερ[γέτ]-
[αν τᾶς] πόλιος τᾶς Ἐ-
[πιδαυρί]ων καὶ θ[ε]α[ρο]-
[δόκον τοῦ Ἀ]πόλλωṿ[ο]ς
[αὐτὸν καὶ ἐκγόνους καὶ]
[εἶμεν αὐτοῖς ἀτέλειαν]
[καὶ ἀσυλίαν καὶ ἐμ πολέ]-
[μωι καὶ ἐν εἰράναι καὶ κα]-
[τὰ γᾶν καὶ κατὰ θάλασσαν].
[καταλόγος βουλᾶς ...]
– – –

3. [ων Φίλ]αινον Peek.

447. ASKLEPIEION, CATALOGUE OF THEARODOKOI, ca. 360-355 B.C. IG, IV^2.1, 94/95. SEG XI, 410, 411. P. Cabanes, Épire 116-120; 144-145, argues that the Epeirote cities in 95, LL. 23-38 are arranged in geographic order following that of an itinerary. For the thearodokos of Ambrakia in 95, LL. 32, 81, see supra no. 427.

448. KORONI, PROHIBITION, ca. 300-250 B.C. Fragment of white limestone stele found between Ligurio and the Asklepieion. Ed. pr. M.T. Mitsos, AE (1976) 86-91, no. 3 (ph.).

Ὅπλα̣ [μ]-
ὴ ἐπιφέρ[ειν]
ἐπὶ πολέμ̣[ωι]

449. SANCTUARY OF APOLLO MALEATAS, DEDICATION, ca. 475-450 B.C. Bronze plaque in the Argive epichoric alphabet. Text made public by A.K. Orlandos, ERGON (1977) 104-105 (ph.).

Κάλλιπος ⁝ *h*ικέτας
Εὐκλέος *h*υιὸς
τὸν Ἐπιδαύριον
παρ' Ἀπόλλονος
Πυθίο Ἀργεῖος

ἀρχὸς καὶ ϝοικιάται

3. We prefer to read τὸν Ἐπιδαυρίον (ed.).

---

450. ASKLEPIEION, DEDICATION TO ASKLEPIOS BY AISCHINES, ca. 350-314 B.C.? IG, IV^2.1, 255. SEG XI, 433; XXII, 284; XXIV, 280; XXV, 415. J. Irigoin, Recueil Plassart (Paris 1976) 121-123, rejects the identification of Aischines as the famous Athenian orator; the poem (AP 6.330) is an acrostic, ΘΕΙΕ with τὸ θεῖον L. 1, and belongs, with the lettering of the preserved fragment, in the 3rd cent. B.C. or later.

---

451. OLD EPIDAUROS, DEDICATION, ca. 350 B.C. Limestone altar found ca. 50 m. north of the ancient theatre; now in the Epigraphical Collection at the Asklepieion. Ed. pr. M.T. Mitsos, Πρακτικά, Α' Διεθνοῦς Συνεδρίου Πελοποννησιακῶν Σπουδῶν 2 (Athens 1976) 20-22 (ph.).

Τιμαίνετος ἀνέ-
θηκε Ἀνάκοιν
δεκάταν αἰγῶν

For the Dioskouroi at the town of Epidauros, Mitsos compares IG, IV^2.1, 742, L. 17 and suggests that this stone, found on the island of Kyra, was taken there from Epidauros.

---

452. OLD EPIDAUROS, INSCRIBED THEATRE SEATS, ca. 350-200 B.C. Cf. IG, IV^2.1, 5-24. E. Deïlake, AD 28 (1973) [1977] B.83-87 (ph.); discovery of more than 1,000 inscriptions on the seats of the recently excavated theatre of Dionysos. Deïlake publishes three examples:

(1) Ἀγήσανδρος Ἀριστ[αῖο]ς οἱ φρουροί
(2) Ἀριστολάϊδας [Ἀρισ]τολάϊδας οἱ φρουροί
(3) Δα[μ]ιορ[γ]οὶ Διονύσῳ
Θεόφραστος Δαμίων Εὐρυφῶν Ἰλαΐκὸς
Πολυχάρης Διονύσιος Τύρ[β]ις Ἀμφίλυτος

---

453. OLD EPIDAUROS, INCERTUM, Hellenistic? Limestone block with monumental letters found on the neck of the promontory of the town. Ed. pr. C.B. Kritzas, AD 27 (1972) [1976] B.219 (ph.).

[- - -]Δ̣ΙΛΙΟ̣[- - -]

LAKONIA

454. AMYKLAI, DEDICATION. IG, V.1, 515. A.J.S. Spawforth, ABSA 71 (1976) 139-145, shows that this text is one of the Amyklaian forgeries of M. Fourmont, who adapted it from Ins. de Délos no. 1646.

455. HIPPOLA, GRAVESTONE. Pedimental stele. Ed. pr. I.G. Taïphakos, ΠΕΛΟΠΟΝΝΗΣΙΑΚΑ 12 (1976/77) 222-223, no. 4 (ph.).

[χαῖ]ρ̣ε Ἀσκυλῖνα{ι}

456. HIPPOLA, GRAVE EPIGRAMS OF DEXIPPOS AND EUAMERIDAS, 2nd/3rd cent. A.D. Reused architectural block with earlier (unpublished) inscriptions. Ed. pr. I.G. Taïphakos, ΠΕΛΟΠΟΝΝΗΣΙΑΚΑ 12 (1976/77) 214-217, no. 1 (ph.).

a

Φιλότι χαῖρε.
Οὗτος ἐγὼ Δέξιππος, ὁ δὴ πολέεσσιν ζηλωτοῖς
ἱμερτὸν δόξας κῦδος ἀειράμενος,
ὃν τέκνωσε εὔγνωστος ἐνὶ θνητοῖσιν ἅπασιν
Δεξικλέης, προγόνων ἄξιον εὐκλεῶν.
Εἰ δὲ καὶ ἐν φθιμένοις περ ἐὼν ὑπὸ σήματι τῶιδε
κεῖμαι, μηνύσει δόξαν ἐμὸς βίοτος.
Δέξιππε χαῖρε.

b

Μάτηρ μὲν Κλεοπάτρα ἐγείνατο, ἔ(τ)ρεψε δὲ παῖδα
Δέξιππος πάντων φέρτατον ἠιθέων.
Ἅιδας δ' ἀρτιγένειον ἐδέξατο, κλαῦσε δὲ πάτρα
αὐτὸν καὶ ματρὸς πατρὶς ἀποφθίμενον.
Ἦν γὰρ πρεσβυτέρους αἰδούμενος ἥλικας ἅμα,
ἤπιος εἰς παῖδας, πρὸς δὲ θεοὺς ὅσιος.
Τοιγὰρ καὶ φθίμενος ναίει παρὰ ῥεύμασιν Ἅ[ιδου],
ἔνθα μιν Ἑρμείας ἦγε πρὸς εὐσεβέας.
Τοὔνομα δ' αὐδάσεις Εὐαμερίδαν, ὅπερ αὐτοῦ
μητροπάτωρ εἶχεν, γνήσιον ἐκ προγόνω̣ν̣.
Εὐαμερίδα{ι} χαῖρε.

2. πολέεσσιν 2nd sigma suprascript; CΗΛΟΤΟΙC lapis. At the top of the stone inscribed earlier as part of another text: ΕΥΔΑΙΜΟ.

457. MENELAION, DEDICATION TO HELEN, ca. 675-650 B.C. Bronze aryballos. Ed. pr. H.W. Catling, H. Cavanagh, KADMOS 15 (1976) 145-152 (ph., dr.); cf. ARCH REPORTS (1975/76) 14; (1976/77) 36 (ph.); BCH 100 (1976) 614 (ph.). This is the earliest inscription in the Lakonian epichoric script.

boustrophedon

Δ̣εῖνι[ς]) τάδ' ἀνέθεκε' Χα- →
ρ̣ι̣[.]) Ϝ̣ε̣λ̣έν̣α̣ι̣ ←
Μενελά Ϝο̣) →

1-2. χάρι̣[ν] or Χαρί̣[α] Catling, Cavanagh.

---

458. MENELAION, DEDICATION TO HELEN: BRONZE MEATHOOK, 6th cent. B.C. Ed. pr. H.W. Catling, H. Cavanagh, KADMOS 15 (1976) 153-157 (ph., dr.); cf ARCH REPORTS (1975/76) 14; (1976/77) 36 (ph.); BCH 100 (1976) 614 (ph.). Inscribed on the handle in Lakonian epichoric alphabet.

retrograde

τᾶι Ϝελέναι

---

459. MENELAION, DEDICATION TO MENELAOS, ca. 500 B.C. Limestone stele. Ed. pr. H.W. Catling, ARCH REPORTS (1976/77) 36-37 (ph.).

Εὐθυκρένες
ἀνέθηκε
τõι Μενέλαι
(traces)

---

460. MESSAPEAI, SANCTUARY OF ZEUS MESSAPEUS, STAMPED TILE, 2nd cent. B.C. Church of Metamorphosis at Anthochorion. Ed. pr. I.G. Taiphakos, ΠΕΛΟΠΟΝΝΗΣΙΑΚΑ 12 (1976/77) 219-222, no. 3 (ph.). Cf. idem, ΑΡΓΟΝΑΥΤΗΣ 1 (1975) 57; 2 (1976) 55-57. The tile identifies the sanctuary partly excavated by C. Christou, ERGON (1962) 134-135; AD 17 (1961/62) B.84-85; 18 (1963) B.86; cf. A.H.S. Megaw, ARCH REPORTS (1962/63) 17; G. Daux, BCH 87 (1963) 764.

[Δαμό]σιοι Διὸς
[Μεσσα]πέος Φαρ[- - -]

---

461. SPARTA, SPARTAN TREATY WITH THE AITOLIANS, ca. 500-470 B.C.? Sparta Museum Inv. 6265. Fragment of a limestone stele found on the Acropolis before 1965; rediscovered in the back yard

of the Museum at Sparta by W. Peek; ed. pr., AS AKAD. LEIPZIG 65.3 (1974) (ph., dr.); detailed commentary with copious parallels. P. Cartledge, LCM 1 (1976) 87-92 (dr.); reprints Peek's text; English translation; date: summer 426 B.C. (Thuc. 3.100) or 425/4 B.C.

[συνθε̃κ]αι Αἰτõλοῖς. κ̣[αττάδε]
[φιλία]ν̣ καὶ hιράναν ἒ̣[μεν ποτ]
[Αἰτõ]λ̣ος καὶ συνμα[χίαν ..3-4..]
[..3-4̣..]νμονος μαν[τι .1-2. hεπο]-
[μ]ένõς hόπυι κα Λα[κεδαιμόνι]-
[ο]ι hαγίονται καὶ κα[τὰ γα̃ν]
[κ]αὶ καθάλαθαν, τὸ[ν αὐτὸν]
φίλον καὶ τὸνναυτ[ὸν ἐχθρὸν]
ἔχοντες hόν περ [καὶ Λακε]-
δαιμόνιοι. μεδὲ κ[ατάλυhιν]
ποιε̃θαι ἄνευ Λα[κεδαιμονίον]
μεδενίαν hιέντ[ας πρέσβες]
ἐπὶ ταὐτὸν ποθὸν [περ Λακεδαι]-
μονίος. φεύγον[τας με δεκέθõ]-
hαν κεκοινανεκ[οτ ....7-8....]-
μάτον. αἰ δέ τις κα [ἐπὶ τὰν τõν]
Ἐρξαδιέον χọ́ραν [στρατεύει]
ἐπὶ πολέμοι, ἐπικο[ρε̃ν Λακεδαιμο]-
νίος παντὶ σθένε[ι καττὸ δυνατόν]·
αἰ δέ τ̣ις κα ἐπὶ τὰ[ν Λακεδαιμο]-
νίον χọ́ραν στρ[ατεύει ἐπὶ πολέ]-
μοι, ἐπικορε̃ν Ἐ[ρξαδιε̃ς παντὶ]
[σθένει καττὸ δυνατόν. ...]
- - - - - - - - - - - - - - - -

3-4. [ἀπὸ | ..]ἀνμονος μάν[τιος] or [ἀφ' ἱα|ρο]μ̣ν<ά>μονος Μαν[τία] or [ἀπὸ | μν]ά{ν}μονος Μαν[τία] Peek. || 15-16. κεκοινανεκ[ότας ἀδικε]|μάτον Peek.

462. SPARTA, CATALOGUE, 1st cent. A.D. Removed to the Monastery of Phaneromene near Anabryte on the slopes of Taygetos. Ed. pr. I.G. Taïphakos, ΠΕΛΟΠΟΝΝΗΣΙΑΚΑ 12 (1976/77) 217-219, no. 2 (ph.).

[Φιλω]νυμίδας
Ἀρίστων Ἐ [- - -]
Καλλικρά[τ - - -]
[- - - -]τηρίδα[ς - - -]
[- - - -Ε]ὐτύ[χι]ος
[- - - -]τα[ς] Πρατ[- - -]
[- - - - -]μαχο[ς - - -]
[- - - - -]ο[- - - - -]

463. SPARTA, DAMONON' VICTORY STELE, late 5th cent. B.C. IG, V.1, 213. SEG XI, 650; XIV, 330; XV, 216. G.S. Schwartz, ZPE 22 (1976) 177-178 (ph.), restores line 39 as [καὶ hε]β̣[õ]ν in place of [καὶ ἐφη]β̣[ῶ]ν of A.M. Woodward, ABSA 13 (1907) 178, and briefly discusses the nomenclature of Spartan age classes.

---

464. SPARTA. AGONISTIC DEDICATION, ca. 530-500 B.C. SEG XI, 652. W. Peek, ZPE 23 (1976) 80-81, no. 6 (dr.); new readings and restorations.

Side a. Boustrophedon

← [Πα]λ̣λὰς 'Αθαναία, θύγα̣[τερ Διὸς αἰγιόχοιο],
→ [σοὶ ˙νικõν τόδ' ἔθεκα· ˙κα]ὶ εἴε πολὰ Μένον[α]
← [νικά]ḥα̣ντα ϝιδε̃ν ε̣[ἰσέτ' ἄεθλα πάλας]

Side b.

[hος h]όπλ[ο]|ιο ἀκο[κὰ δείξε|ι τεĩδ' h]έκοντι
κ|αὶ σὺν χα[λκõι | hέθεν] κράνος· | ἀλ' ἀνε[παύσα|το
χαρμ]ãν κ|ές χο[ρὸν - - -]

Side c.

LL. 2-3: [κα]ὶ hι[α|ρ]ὰ βὰς λ - - -
LL. 4-5: [γ]νõνα̣ι | κατ' ἀρ - - -
LL. 5-6: [- ε]τὸ τοῦτ|ο Καπρ̣ - - -

Peek believes that b and c were inscribed by a different cutter and probably composed by a different poet.

---

465. SPARTA, DEDICATION, ca. 150 A.D.? IG, V.1, 298. A.S. Bradford, Prosopography (see. no. 468) 496-497, offers 4 possible emendations of Κριτοδαμοχ in L. 3, with discussion of the kasen relationship.

---

466. SPARTA, ARCHAIC EPISTYLE. A marble epistyle block with large letters, perhaps to be associated with figured clay metopes from a sanctuary or grave monument found in Limnai. Ed. pr. G. Steinhauer, AD 27 (1972) [1976] B.246 (ph.).

HE[- - -]

ἥ[ρωος]? hε[ρμᾶνος]? etc. Steinhauer.

---

467. TAINARON, SANCTUARY OF POSEIDON, GRAVE EPIGRAM OF EUTYCHOS, 3rd cent. A.D. IG, V.1, 1235. H. Raffeiner,

COMMENTATIONES AENIPONTANAE 23 (1977) 62, no. 36; text and commentary on slave status of Eutychos.

---

468. SPARTA, PROSOPOGRAPHY. A.S. Bradford, *A Prosopography of Lacedaimonians from the Death of Alexander the Great, 323 B.C., to the Sack of Sparta by Alaric, A.D. 396*: *Vestigia* 27 (Munich 1977).

MESSENIA

---

469. ANDANIA, SACRED LAW ON THE MYSTERIES OF THE GREAT GODS, 92/1 B.C. IG, V.1, 1390. SEG XI, 978; XXV, 434. M. Guarducci, EPIGRAPHICA 39 (1977) 140-142, comments on the high value of the gold crown awarded to Mnasistratos, LL. 52-53.

ARCADIA

---

470. ALIPHEIRA, ELEIAN DECREE, ca. 244-219 B.C. SEG XXV, 448. N.D. Robertson, HESPERIA 45 (1976) 260-266, argues that this decree is not of Alipheira but was passed by Elis when Alipheira was in Eleian hands. In LL. 3-5 he reads: - - - κύρια ἦμεν τὰ δεδ[ο]γμ[έ]να τᾶρ πόλιορ τᾶρ τ[ῶν Ἀλείων· ὅπωρ δὲ παραδοθᾶι], τ̣ὸ̣[ὶρ] δαμιοργοὶρ ἐ̣π̣ι̣μέ[λε]σ̣σ̣α̣[ι ... ἐ]λομένο[ι]ρ ἄ̣ν̣δ̣[ρερ - - - κατὰ τάδε ἔκρ]ινεν τὸ δικαστή̣ρ̣ιον τὸ τᾶρ πόλιορ τῶ̣[ν Ἀλείων- -]. In LL. 12-13 he restores τᾶρ δὲ στάλαρ τ[ὰν ἀνάθεσιν τοὶ Ἀλιφειρειρ ποιηάντω ἐ]ν τῶι ἱαρῶι τᾶρ Ἀθά[ναρ]. L. 9 μναῖρ should be accented μναίρ; L. 6 ταῖρ should be ταὶρ as subject or predicate of ἦμεν.

---

471. ORCHOMENOS, SYNOIKIA OF ORCHOMENOS AND EUAIMON, ca. 369-363 B.C. IG, V.2, 343. SEG XI, 1101; XXII, 319. M. Moggi, *I sinecismi interstatali greci* 1 (Pisa 1976) 272-290, no. 43 (ph.); text, Italian translation, ap. cr., bibliography, detailed commentary on historical, constitutional, and legal aspects of the agreement.

---

472. TEGEA, DEDICATION OF AN ATHLETE, ca. 525-500 B.C. IG, V.2, 75. SEG XI, 1065; XV, 228. Jeffery, LSAG 209; 215, 408, no. 5 (dr.); W. Peek, SB AKAD. HEIDELBERG 1971.2.13-15, no. 4 (ph., dr.); J. Ebert, ZPE 9 (1972) 285-288 (dr.); M.L. Lazzarini, MAL 19.2 (1976) 302, no. 868.

Peek's restoration:

[Κλειτομάχο Χρόμ]ιος *h*αλέαι μ' ἀνέ[θεκεν ἄγαλμα],
[σεμνὰ λαβὸν τάδ' ἄ] Ϝεθλα.
καὶ τἐπιόντα δ[ὸς λαβε͂ν].

Ebert's restoration:

[- - - -]ιος *h*αλέαι μ' ἀνέ̣[θεκεν 'Αθάναι]
[νικάσας δόλιχον καλὰ θεᾶς ἄ] Ϝ εθλα
καὶ τἐπιόντα δ̣[όλιχον] or δ̣[ίαυλον], δ̣[εύτερον] etc.

2. ἄ̣ Ϝεθλ̣[ον] Jeffery. || 3. λ̣[αβε͂ν] Jeffery.

ELIS

473. ELIS, BRONZE MIRROR, after ca. 250 B.C. Found in a "Macedonian type" tomb. The names are labels for the three figures carved on the circular surface of the mirror. Ed. pr. T. Karagiorga-Stathakopoulou, AD 28 (1973) [1977] B.203 (ph.).

'Οπώρα Θίασος Κωμωιδία

474. GOUMERON, GRAVESTONE, ca. 200 B.C. Limestone pedimental stele with elaborate architectural decoration found at Skasokoli, 2 km. NE of the monastery of Nikobe. Ed. pr. T. Karagiorga-Stathakopoulou, AD 28 (1973) [1977] B.197 (ph.).

Φίλα ⁚ χαῖρε

475. OLYMPIA, VERDICT OF THE ELEIANS IN A DISPUTE, 500-450 B.C. Bronze plaque. Olympia Museum B6362. Text and French translation: P. Siewert, REG 90 (1977) 463.

"Αγαλμα Διός· Πύρρο γρ[α]φέας·
καὶ Χαρίξενος καὶ τοὶ μαστροί.
[τ]αὶρ δίκαις, ταὶρ κὰ το͂ν Βοιοτο͂ν Μέναvδρος
[κ'] 'Αριστόλοχος τοῖρ 'Αθαναίος ἐδικαξάταν,
[ἐ]πέγγ̣ον καὶ τοῖ Θεσπιέσσιν καὶ τοῖρ σὺν αὐτὸς
[σφ]ὲ δικαίος δικαστᾶμεν κ' ἀπὸ το͂ν Θεσαλο͂ν
[ἐ]πεδίκαξαν.

476. OLYMPIA, INSCRIBED SEAT, 6th cent. B.C.? Stone seat block with the inscription carved at the outer edge on three sides. Ed. pr. A. Mallwitz, AD 27 (1972) [1976] B.275 (ph.).

Εὐϝανίου ⁝ Λακεδαιμονίου ⁝ προξένου

---

477. OLYMPIA, BUBON'S LIFTING STONE, 6th cent. B.C. IvO 717. SEG XI, 1217; XIV, 353. N.B. Crowther, GREECE AND ROME 24 (1977) 112-113, discusses the technique used by Bubon to lift and throw the stone.

---

478. OLYMPIA, STATUE BASE WITH SIGNATURE OF KALON OF ELIS, ca. 420-410 B.C. IvO 271. SEG XI, 1226. J. Dörig, Mélanges Collart 125-146 (dr.), distinguishes Kalon from his Aiginetan namesake; discussion of his career; reconstruction of the Hermes statue which this base supported.

---

479. OLYMPIA, VICTORY MONUMENT OF VALERIUS ECLECTUS, ca. 261 A.D. IvO 243. SEG XVII, 203. L. Semmlinger, Weih-, Sieger- und Ehreninschriften aus Olympia und seiner Umgebung (Diss. Erlangen-Nürnberg 1974) 351-358, no. 67; text and commentary. J. and L. Robert, BE (1976) no. 279, observe that Ῥωμαῖος L. 2 does not mean "Ratsmitglied (= Senator) zu Rom" (Semmlinger) but only that Valerius had Roman citizenship, nor was he a member of the boule at Elis, only an Eleian citizen. G. Daux, REG 90 (1977) 476-479, reads from ph. [Σιν]ω̣πεύς, L. 1.

---

480. ELEIAN DECREES FOUND OUTSIDE OF ELIS. No. 392 from Corinth. No. 470 from Alipheira.

ACHAEA

---

481. DYME, LETTER FROM Q. FABIUS MAXIMUS, 115/4 B.C. SIG^3 684. Sherk, RDGE no. 43. R. Bernhardt, HISTORIA 26 (1977) 62-73, analyzes the meaning of ἐλευθερία in LL. 15-16 in the context of the status of the defeated Achaian cities after 146 B.C.

---

482. DYME, GRAVE EPIGRAM OF SYMPHORIS, 2nd/3rd cent. A.D. G. Kaibel, RhM 34 (1879) 187, no. 481 a. Peek, GV 1091. H. Raffeiner, COMMENTATIONES AENIPONTANAE 23 (1977) 40-41, no. 19; text and commentary on slave status of Symphoris and Hilaros.

Τίκτε με δ' Ἀρκαδίης Μεγάλα | πόλις, οὔνομα δ' αὐχῶ
Καρνεάδα | πατρὸς Συμφορὶς οὖσα γένους, |
ζωᾶς δ' εἴκοστον χὤγδοον ἤνυσάμαν. |
Ἵλαρος Καίσαρος δοῦλος συνβίῳ | εὐσεβεστάτῃ.

---

483. DYME, GRAVESTONE, 2nd cent. B.C. Pedimental limestone stele now in the Patras Museum. Ed. pr. I.A. Papapostolou, AAA 8 (1975) 296-299 (ph.); Πασίαμος Χίωνος | χαῖρε. G. Daux, AAA 9 (1976) 120; ZPE 24 (1977) 226; BCH 101 (1977) 341-342, no. 2 (ph.), corrects the reading in L. 1 to Ἀ̣σ̣πασία Μοσχίωνος.

---

484. PATRAI, ROMAN LAMP SIGNATURES. I.A. Papapostolou, AD 28 (1973) [1977] B.213, briefly notes the discovery of lamps with the signatures of Πρείμου; Πωσφόρου (cf. p. 226); Σωτηρίδα Ζωσίμου; Σπωσιανοῦ; Σπωσιαίου; Corinthian lamp ΕΡΙ̣[- - -].

---

485. PATRAI, INSCRIBED ROMAN BRICK. Ed. pr. I.A. Papapostolou, AD 27 (1972) [1976] B.287; Κρισπείνου.

---

486. PATRAI, CLAY DISC. Eros in relief. Ed. pr. I.A. Papapostolou, AD 28 (1973) [1977] B.213: ὁ παῖς Λ[ί]νου.

MEGARIS

---

487. MEGARA, HONORS: ANTONINUS PIUS, 138-161 A.D. In the foundations of an early Christian basilica below the Metropolitan Church in Megara. Block inscribed on two faces. Ed. pr. P.E. Lazarides, AD 28 (1973) [1977] B.60.

(1) Ἀγαθῇ τύχῃ
Αὐτοκράτορα Καίσαρα Θεοῦ Ἁδριανοῦ
εὐεργέτου υἱὸν Θεοῦ Τραϊανοῦ υἱωνὸν
Θεοῦ Νέρβα ἔκγονον Τίτον Αἴλιον Ἁδριανὸν
Ἀντωνεῖνον Σεβαστὸν Εὐσεβῆ
Ἐπίκτητος Ἐπικτήτου ἀρχιθέαρος ἐκ τῶν
ἰδίων ἀνέστησε

(2) Ὁ δᾶμος,
Γάϊον Κοΐγκτιον
Γαΐου υἱὸν Τρῶγον
Ἀντιστράτηγον

---

488. MEGARA, GRAVESTONE. SEG XXV, 480. D. Knoepfler, Mélanges Collart 269, note 4, identifies this recently discovered stone with IG, VII, 166, previously known only from Fourmont's copy.

BOIOTIA

---

489. LITERARY CONTESTS IN BOIOTIA. G.-J.-M. te Riele, *Miscellanea Tragica in honorem J.C. Kamerbeek* (Amsterdam, 1976) 285-291 gives a survey of these contests in various Boiotian cities and focusses upon the (epigraphic evidence for) Charitesia in Orchomenos. He suggests that the many tripods, recently found in Orchomenos (cf. BCH 99, 1975, 171-246) and dedicated to Dionysos, perhaps belonged to the winners in the Charitesia.

---

490. VOCABULARY. For the meaning of the word ἀγώναρχος in the Boiotian dialect, cf. no. 1899

491-492. AKRAIPHIA, EPITAPHS. Ed. pr. S. Lauffer, CHIRON 6 (1976) 11-12, nos. 1-2. Cf. also P. Roesch, TEIRESIAS, *Epigraphica* (1977) 2, nos. 1-2.

---

491. P. 11-12, no. 1; limestone stele.

Καλιώ

---

492. P. 12, no. 2; limestone stele (Roesch, l.c., no. 2: Hellenistic period).

Κόσων

---

493. CHAIRONEA, MANUMISSION OF A SLAVE. IG, VII, 3372. Cf. D.M. Schaps, ZPE 20 (1976) 63-64 who discusses this manumission in the form of a dedication. L. 8: it is possible to construe the inscription without the supplement <ἦν>, punctuating διὰ τοῦ συνεδρίου εὐαρεστοῦν|τες· τὴν ἀνιέρωσιν πεπόηται κτλ. (communication by Prof. R. Merkelbach); L. 2-6: the people named in these lines are not witnesses (Dittenberger), but people related to the owner of the slave and agreeing to the manumission.

494-497. HALIARTOS, EPITAPHS. Ed. pr. S. Lauffer, CHIRON 6 (1976) 13-14, nos. 4-7. Cf. also P. Roesch, TEIRESIAS, *Epigraphica* (1977) 10-11, nos. 21-24.

---

494. P. 13-14, no. 4; marble cippus, before 450 B.C. (ph.).

Ἐπιϙύδες

---

495. P. 14, no. 5; marble cippus (Roesch, l.c., no. 22: 5th

cent. B.C.).

Κλιοπάτρα

---

496. P. 14, no. 6; limestone grave altar.

Μνασιλαΐς

---

497. P. 14, no. 7; marble stele, Roman Imperial period.

Νικηφόρε | χρη[στ]ὲ | χ[αῖρ]ε

---

498. HYETTOS, MILITARY CATALOGUE, 250-245 B.C. Limestone block, built into the acropolis wall. Ed. pr. Etienne - Knoepfler, HB, 72-77, no. 1 (ph.). Cf. P. Roesch, TEIRESIAS, Epigraphica (1977) 11-12, no. 25.

Θιός·
Καλλισστράτω̣ ἄρχογ-
τος Βοιωτοῖς, ἐπὶ δὲ πό-
λι(ο)ς Τιμασίωνος, πολε̣-
μαρχιόντων Ἀμινίχω
Κλιωνίω, Θιοκρίτω Καλλι-
ήω, Δαμοχαρίδαο Πολυ-
χαρείω, γραμματίδδοντος
Καλονίκω Δαμοχαρίδαο,
τυῒ ἀπεγράψαντο ἐν πελτο-
φόρας· v Σίμων Ἐ̣τιάρχω,
Ἀμουνίας Ἁγεισιλάω,
Πολυχάρεις Δαμοχαρίδαο,
Μικκ̣ίνας Φιλοκράτιος,
Κρινίων Μένε̣ι̣τος,
Ἀμφ̣ικτιο<ύ>ων Τιουδεῖος,
Μικρίων Κ̣λι̣ωνύμω,
Φίλων Μέλωνος.

---

11. Roesch prefers to read Ἐπάρχω || 12. Ἀγεισιλάω Etienne - Knoepfler, corr. Roesch || 14. Roesch prefers Μικρ̣ίνας.

---

499. HYETTOS, MILITARY CATALOGUE, 210-200 B.C. Limestone block, built into the acropolis wall. Ed. pr. Etienne - Knoepfler, HB, 77-81, no. 2 (ph.). Cf. P. Roesch, TEIRESIAS, Epigraphica (1977) 12-13, no. 26.

Θιός·
Ν̣ικασαρέτω ἄρχον-
τος Βοιωτῦς, ἐπὶ
πόλιος δὲ Φρασίλλω,
πολεμαρχιόντων Κα-
λονίκω Κλισθένιος,
Θρασουλαΐδαο Καλλι-
δάμω, Διυδότω Πουθο-
δώρω, γραμματίδδον-
τος Κουδίαο Φρασαρίδαο,
τυῒ ἀπεγράψανθο ἐν πελ-
τοφόρας· Μυρίας Ἀριστο-
κρίτω, Καπίων Ἱστιήω,
Καλλίδαμος Ἱστιήω, Ἀρί-
στιχος Πιθάλλιος, Ἄρ-
χων Νικασίωνος, Ἀμινί-
ας Φίδωνος, Ἀριστο-
κλεῖς Ἡράκωνος,
Λευκίνας Λευκίναο,
Ὀνάσιμος Κεφάλ-
λιος, Καλλίξενος
Ἀ̣πολλοδώρω.

P. Roesch dates the text to the end of the 3rd cent. B.C.

500. HYETTOS, MILITARY CATALOGUE, CA. 200 B.C. Fragment of a limestone stele, broken at the left and below and inscribed on two sides; one inscription is largely illegible. Ed. pr. J.M. Fossey apud Etienne - Knoepfler, HB, 401-403 (ph.) (=P. Roesch, TEIRESIS, Epigraphica (1977) 13-14, no. 27).

[Κ]ρίτωνος ἄρ[χ]-
[ο]ντος Βοιω[τ]-
ῦς, ἐπὶ πόλ[ιος]
[δ]ὲ Νικασίω[ν]-
[ος], πολεμαρ[χι]-
[όν]των Καλλ[ι]-
[κλίδ]αο /.Ο---
-----------Δ̣Δ̣C--
-----------IC---

4. Νικασίω[νος] Etienne - Knoepfler, l.c., 403; Γ̣ΟΚΛC.C Fossey.

501-523. HYETTOS, MILITARY CATALOGUES, 245-165 B.C. IG, VII, 2809-2832. Etienne - Knoepfler, HB, 82-112 republish these texts with photos. In most cases they indicate minor differences between the texts of IG and their own; we briefly record the most important of these. We omit the differences between IG and earlier editions, on which Etienne - Knoepfler lay undue weight. Three texts (2812, 2817, 2825) have undergone considerable changes, so that we present the whole text (without app. crit.). For the date of these texts the reader should consult the discussion of the chronology of the federal archons on p. 256-353.

501. IG, VII, 2809: L. 7. Εὔρ̣ούτιμος (instead of Εὐθούτιμος); L. 10-11. Γόργουθος (and not Γοργούλος); L. 11. Χαβ̣ρίας (instead of Χαιρίας); L. 13. Τελεσίων (instead of Τελέσ̣ων).

502. IG, VII, 2810: L. 4. τυὶ̣ is missing; L. 8. Εὐβίωνος (instead of Εὐρίωνος); L. 9-10. Φι|δόλαος Περιβ̣ω̣τάδαο (instead of Φι|λόλαος Περικο[πίδ]αο); L. 11-12. Θάλλω,| Πολιούμναστος (instead of Θάλλω|[ν]ο[ς, Σ]ύμμα[χ]ος).

503. IG, VII, 2811: L. 18. Ἀριστίων (instead of Ἀρίστων).

504. IG, VII, 2812 (Cf. P. Roesch, TEIRESIAS, Epigraphica (1977) 29-30, no. 71):

Θιός·
Ἀρτιουλάω ἄρχοντος Βοιω-
τοῖς, ἐπὶ πόλιος δὲ Ἀ̣μ̣ι̣ν<ο>κλεῖος, πολεμαρ-
χ̣ι̣ό̣ν̣τ̣ω̣ν̣ Π̣ρ̣ο̣ππίδαο Τ̣ε̣λεκλίδαο, Τιμα-
σίωνος Τ̣ιμ<α>σιθίω, Εὐμείλω Δάσωνος, γραμ-

ματίδδοντος ῾Ερμαΐω ᾿Αγασίαο, τυῒ ἀπε-
γράψανθο ἐμ πελτοφόρας · Μνασῖνος Πο-
λ̣ι̣ο̣[υ]κλεῖος, Ϙ̣αφισίων ᾿Αριστογίτονος, ᾿Αριστί-
ων Θιοφάνι̣ος, Ι̣²⁻³κ̣λεῖς ᾿Ανταντρί-
δαο, Π̣ί̣θ̣[ι]ο̣υ̣λλος Δωροθίω, Εἰρόδαμος Εἰρο-
δάμω, Πασώνδας Πουθοδώρω, ᾿Αμίνιχος
᾿Ε̣π̣ι̣χ̣ά̣ρ̣ιος, Λά̣μπων Θ̣ι̣οφάνιος, ᾿Αμινίας
Δ̣ιωνιο̣υ̣σίχω, Κάλλων Δαματρίω, ᾿Αθανίας ᾿Αν-
τ̣ι̣κ̣ράτιος, [Ε]ὔ̣ο̣δ̣ος (?) ᾿Αντιγένιος, Δρωπίδας
Δ̣ρ̣ωπίδαο, ῾Ηρακλειόδωρος Εὐρουτίμω,
Καλλίτιμος Πασίωνος, Πούρριχος Τιμο-
κράτιος.

9. Roesch proposes ῾Ι̣[αρο]κ̣λεῖς

---

505. IG, VII, 2813: L. 4-5. Κλισθέ|νιος (instead of Κλισθεί|νιος); L. 6. Δαμ<ο>ξένω (and not Δαμ<ο>ξείνω).

---

506. IG, VII, 2814: L. 9. Διωνιουσόδωρος (instead of Διονιουσόδωρος).

---

507. IG, VII, 2815: L. 6. Ϝ̣ασίαο (and not (᾿Α)γασίαο).

---

508. IG, VII, 2816: L. 9. Θαυμίναο (and not Θαυμινίαο).

---

509. IG, VII, 2817 (= P. Roesch, TEIRESIAS, Epigraphica (1977) 30, no. 72):

Θιός· Διωνιουσίω ἄρχοντος Βοιωτοῖς, ἐπὶ πόλιος δὲ
Μνασίνω, πολεμαρχιόντων Νικα̣σ̣[ί]ωνος Θυνάρχω,
Τίμωνος Καπίωνο̣ς̣, Φρασίλλω Δέξ̣ω̣νος, γ̣ραμμα-
τίδδοντος [Φιλοσ]τ̣ρ̣άτω Τελεσίππω, τυῒ ἀπεγρά-
ψανθο ϜικατιϜέτιες · Ξέναρχος Σωκράτιος, Ξενό-
τιμος [²⁻³]σάνδρ̣[ω], Μέλων Φίλωνος, Θάρσων Καλλι-
κλεῖος, Φη̣νίδας ᾿Αγασάνδρω, Κλίων Μοιρίχω, Νίκων
Πασίωνος, [²⁻³]ω̣νδας Δάμωνος, Δαμάτριος ᾿Απολ-
λοδώρω, Πασίων Πασίωνος, ᾿Επίξ̣ενος ῾Ηράκωνος.

---

510. IG, VII, 2818: L. 17-18. Φηνί|δαο (and not Φ..νί| δαο).

---

511. IG, VII, 2819: above L. 1 a graffito ΝΙΚΗ̣Ο̣Σ̣ ?; L. 4. Θρασουλαΐδαο (instead of Φρασικλίδαο); L. 5. {Λ}᾿Αριστογίτων (and not Λι......); L. 7. Διων<ο>ύσιος (instead of Διωνύσιος); Φηνο-

μάχω (instead of Κηνομάχω); Κρινίωνος Τίμων (and not Κλίων Τίμων).

---

512. IG, VII, 2820: L. 8. Ξέ<νω>νος (instead of ξένος); L. 10. Πίθιουλ<λ>ος (and not Πιθιούλος).

---

513. IG, VII, 2821: L. 6. Τ̣ι̣μασ̣ίωνος (instead of Μ[ν]άσωνος); L. 7. Τιμασιθίω (instead of [Ἑ]ρμ̣[ο]σ[τ]ρ<ότ>ω); L. 9. Ἀρίστων̣ (instead of Ἀρ....).

---

514. IG, VII, 2822: L. 7. Εὐμάριος (instead of Θυμάριος); L. 10. Κλήνετος (and not Κλ<ι>ήνετος).

---

515. IG, VII, 2823: L. 12. Γόργο̣[ς] (instead of Γόργ[ος]).

---

516. IG, VII, 2824: L. 2. Ἀνδρ̣ιτίωνος (instead of Ἀνδήνωνος).

---

517. IG, VII, 2825 (= P. Roesch, TEIRESIAS, Epigraphica (1977) 30-31, no. 73):

Θι<ός>·
Δαματρίω ἄρχοντος Βοιωτ[ο]-
ῖς, ἐπὶ πόλιος δὲ Προππίδα[ο, π]-
ολεμαρχιόντων Δάμωνο[ς 2-3]-
ώνδαο, Κάλλωνος Κάλλων̣[ος],
Ξεννίαο Καφισίωνος, γρ̣α[μμα]-
τίδδοντος Δαμαγάθω Μν̣α[σίππω]·
Ξ̣ε̣νοκράτεις Τιμοξένω, Δ̣[ε]-
ξ̣ίλαος Κουδίππω, Ἀριστόδ[αμο]ς
Κελήνω, Δαμόκριτος Φίλ̣ωνος,
Τιμάριστος Τιμαρίστω, Εὔμει-
λος Κλ̣ι̣μείλω, Διόδωρος Εἰροδώρ[ω],
Ἀνδρ̣ι̣τίων Σωκρατίνω, Τελέσιππο̣[ς]
Φιλοστράτω, Μνασικλεῖς Φίλωνος,
Δαμόξενος Φερενίκω, Δαμάτ[ρι]-
ος Φιλοστράτω, Λιούσων Πτωΐωνος.

---

518. IG, VII, 2826: L. 2. Δαματρίω (instead of Δαματρίου).

---

519. IG, VII, 2827: L. 9. Θι<ο>τίμω (and not Θιτίμω); L. 10. Καφισωδώρω (instead of Καφισ[ο]δώρω).

---

520. IG, VII, 2828: L. 1. v ἄρχοντος (instead of ...... ἄρχοντος); L. 8. ...]σικλεῖς (instead of [Σω]σικλεῖς); LL. 11, 12, 13: the restorations in these lines are more uncertain than IG allows.

---

521. IG, VII, 2830: L. 8. Ἀριστίων (instead of Ἀριστίας).

---

522. IG, VII, 2831: above L. 1 [Θι]ός; L. 1. v ἄρχοντος (instead of ...... ἄρχοντος); L. 4. Θ̣ά̣ρ̣σ̣ωνος (instead of [Θάρσων]ος); L. 5. Ϝ̣α̣ρ̣μ̣ί̣χω (instead of [Ϝαρμίχω]; L. 5-6. Ξενοκλί¦δ̣α̣ο̣ Τ̣ί̣μ̣ω-νος (instead of Ξενοκλί¦[δαο Τίμων]ος); L. 7-8. Πο|λ̣ι̣ο̣υ̣κλίδαο (and not Πο|[λιουχαρ]ίδαο); L. 9-10. Θιό|[δ]ω̣ρ̣ο̣ς ? Λιούσωνος (instead of Θιό|[ξ]ενος Λούσωνος); L. 11. ΕΜΠΕ v (instead of Ἐμπέ-[δωνος]).

---

523. IG, VII, 2832: above L. 1 a vacat (and not [....ἄρχοντος Βοιωτῦς]); L. 6. Εὐ<όδω> ? (instead of Εὐ[δώρω]).

---

524. HYETTOS, REGULATION CONCERNING AN ORACLE (OF HERAKLES ?), LATER HELLENISTIC PERIOD. Limestone cippus (the inscription is complete). Ed. pr. Etienne - Knoepfler, HB, 182-185 (ph.). Cf. P. Roesch, TEIRESIAS, Epigraphica (1977) 14, no. 29; J. Bousquet, BCH 101 (1977) 453-454.

ΟvΑΝΕΙΣ
ΕΠΙΤΩ
ΜΑΝΤΕΙΩ̣

Ὁ ἀνεὶς ἐπίτω μαντείῳ (or ἐπίτω <τῷ> μαντείῳ) Etienne - Knoepfler. It is impossible to read [μ]άνεις and to suppose that the text says that "he who is possessed, should go to the oracle"(Etienne - Knoepfler). However, J. Bousquet proposes to read on the basis of a photograph of the stone: ὁ μανεὶς ἐξίτω μαντείω ("Qui est frappé d'une crise de démence doit quitter le sanctuaire oraculaire").

---

525. HYETTOS (?), LIST OF EPHEBES, 2nd CENT. A.D. SEG, III, 421. Etienne - Knoepfler, HB, 252-256 reject the view that this stone comes from Halai and suggest that it originates from Hyettos.

---

526. HYETTOS, HONORARY STATUES FOR MEMBERS OF THE SEVERAN DYNASTY, 198-209 A.D. Etienne - Knoepfler, HB, 168-175 (ph.; cf. also p. 207) show that IG, VII, 2833 (honorary base for Septimius Severus) and IG, VII, 2834 (honorary base for Caracalla) belong to

a large monument, erected by the Hyettians for various members of the Severan family. The lettering of the two inscriptions is identical (contra IG); in 2834 the words τὸν σωτῆρα καὶ εὐεργέτην τῆς ἰδίας οἰκουμένης have been added after 211 A.D.

---

527. HYETTOS, DECREE OF THE SACRED GEROUSIA, AFTER 212 A.D. IG, VII, 2808 (Syll.^{3} 1112). J.H. Oliver, HESPERIA, Suppl. 6 (1941) 143-144, no. 6 proposed to read in L. 41-44: εἴ τις τὸ [ἀ]νθρώ|[π]ιν[ό]ν τ̣ι̣ ἄνοι, [ἀ]ντ᾽ αὐτοῦ | [τ]ῶ<ν> υ̣ἱ̣ῶν αὐτοῦ γείνεσθα[ι] | [ὃ]ν [ἂ]ν ἡ γερου<σί>α ἔληται. Etienne - Knoepfler, HB, 15, note 50 suggest: εἴ τις τὸ [ἀ]νθρώ[π]ιν[ο]ν π̣ανθ̣[ά]ν<οι, ἀν>τ᾽ αὐτοῦ κτλ. (πανθάνω being a 'dérivé tardif de πάσχω'). In L. 37-38 they propose Με[νε]κράτης (Μενεκράτους) | τοῦ Χα̣ρ̣ι̣κ̣[λέους?] (instead of Oliver's | Ξουχηρ[--]; cf. also p. 28-29 on the word Ὀλμώνιος in L. 9-16.

---

528. HYETTOS, DEDICATION TO ZEUS AGORAIOS, LATE 2nd CENT. B.C. Limestone block (perhaps part of an altar ?). Ed. pr. Etienne - Knoepfler, HB, 152, no. 19 (ph.) (= P. Roesch, TEIRESIAS, Epigraphica (1977) 14, no. 28).

[Δ]ι̣ὸς | Ἀ̣γ̣οραίου

Etienne - Knoepfler point out that in 1877 P. Girard had seen a dedication to Zeus Homoloīos in Hyettos. This text has never been published and seems lost now.

---

529. HYETTOS, SIGNATURE OF AN UNKNOWN ARTIST, END 4th CENT. B.C. Limestone block. Ed. pr. Etienne - Knoepfler, HB, 175-176, no. 20. The stone is not a statue-base but probably belonged to a wall (ph.) (= P. Roesch, TEIRESIAS, Epigraphica (1977) 14-15, no. 30).

---] ἐπόεσε

---

530. HYETTOS, STATUE-BASE WITH THE SIGNATURE OF THE SCULPTOR KANACHOS III, CA. 200 B.C. IG, VII, 2835. Etienne - Knoepfler, HB, 157-163 (ph.) suggest the following tentative restoration of this text (= P. Roesch, TEIRESIAS, Epigraphica (1977) 31, no. 75):

Χητίππα Ι[τῶ δῖνος]
τὸν ουἱὸν [τὸν δῖνα]
Ἰσμεινίαο κὴ [ὁ δῖνος τὸν ἀ]-
4 δελφιὸν τῦ̣[ς θιῦς]
Κάναχος Λεο[ντήσιος ? ἐπόιησε]

Etienne - Knoepfler found the right side of this statue-base but unfortunately it has been built into the wall of a modern chapel in such a way that the letters are invisible. In their interpretation Kanachos is a citizen from Leontion in Achaia. The IG-text runs as follows: Χητίππα .... ¦ τὸν ουὶὸν .... | 'Ισμεινίαο κη[........ τὸν ἀ]|δελφιὸν τῦ[ς θιῦς]| Κάναχος Δε[ινομένεος ? ἐποίησεν] (The restoration of Deinomenes' name derives from Pliny, NH, 34, 50).

---

531. HYETTOS, SIGNATURE OF THE SCULPTOR HOMOLOÏCHOS, 2nd CENT. B.C. Ed. pr. A. Wilhelm, JÖAI 8 (1905) 276-285. Etienne - Knoepfler, HB, 163-166 show that the text of the signature should be restored as follows (= P. Roesch, TEIRESIAS, Epigraphica (1977) 31, no. 74):

[῾Ο]μολώϊχος Σωκράτ̣[ους ᾿Ανθηδόνιος ἐ]π̣οίησε

(instead of [῾Ο]μολώϊχος Σωκράτου [- ἐ]ποίησ[εν] Wilhelm). Homoloīchos comes from Anthedon (cf. ABSA 3, 1896-1897, p. 106-111 combined with AA 83, 1968, p. 98-102) rather than from Hyettos (Roesch) or Thebes (Wilhelm).

532-546. HYETTOS, EPITAPHS. Etienne - Knoepfler, HB, 113-135 discuss the funerary epigraphy of Hyettos and publish thirteen new funerary stelai (p. 118-135, nos. 6-18, all with photos). Cf. P. Roesch, TEIRESIAS, Epigraphica (1977) 15-17, nos. 31-43.

---

532. P. 116: photo of IG, VII, 2846.

---

533. P. 117, note 346: Etienne - Knoepfer point out that in IG, VII, 2845 the reading Σωμ[ένης] is most doubtful.

---

534. P. 118, no. 6; limestone cippus, 5th cent. B.C.

᾿Επὶ Τιμοδάμοι

---

535. P. 120, no. 7; two fragments of a stele (Roesch, l.c., 15, no. 32: 5th cent. B.C.).

[----]ι̣ος

---

536. P. 120-122, no. 8; limestone cippus, ca. 350 B.C.

Κ̣ρ̣ιτόδαμος, | Ν̣ομμώ, | Κλεαρέτα

---

537. P. 122-123, no. 9; limestone cippus, ca. 300 B.C.

Ἀριστοκράτια

---

538. P. 123-124, no. 10; upper part of a stele, ca. 250 B.C.

Αρμ[3-4]

---

539. P. 124-126, no. 11; limestone cippus, with relief representing a seated human being who keeps an uncertain object in his two hands (perhaps a workman; cf. also BE, 1977, no. 218), late 3rd cent. B.C.

Διωνιουσόδωρος

---

540. P. 126-127, no. 12; limestone cippus, before 175 B.C.

Διωνιουσία

---

541. P. 127-129, no. 13; limestone cippus, ca. 200 B.C.

Δάμων, | Μένανδρος

---

542. P. 129-131, no. 14; white marble stele, with anthemion and two rosettes, ca. 200-150 B.C.

[Κ]αλλιγείτων | χαῖρε

---

543. P. 131-132, no. 15; limestone stele, with anthemion and two rosettes, early 2nd cent. B.C.

Ὠφελίμα

---

544. P. 132, no. 16; limestone stele, with anthemion and two rosettes, 2nd cent. B.C.

Δη̣[μήτ?]ρ̣ιε | Ε[-----] | [χαῖρε?]

---

545. P. 134, no. 17; limestone stele with anthemion and two rosettes, 1st cent. A.D.

Μᾶρκε | χαῖρε

(The stele itself dates from the 2nd cent. B.C.; under the present inscription there are faint traces of an older inscription).

---

546. P. 134-135, no. 18; limestone stele, with fronton and acroteria, not long before the Imperial period.

Δ̣[-----] | Ὀκ̣[τάουι?]ο̣ς | χαῖρε

---

1. Perhaps Δέκμος Etienne - Knoepfler

547. HYETTOS, EPITAPH. Marble stele, broken at the bottom. Ed. pr. A. Schachter, ABSA 56 (1961) 176-177, no. 2 (SEG, XXII, 437). Cf. S. Lauffer, CHIRON 6 (1976) 40-41, no. 47 and Etienne - Knoepfler, HB, 16, note 56 (with a comment on the name Λίλεις; cf. our no. 548). Cf. also O. Masson, RPH 52 (1978) 357.

---

548. HYETTOS (LOUTSI), MINOR RECTIFICATIONS OF SIX INSCRIPTIONS. SEG, XXII, 434-439. Etienne - Knoepfler, HB, 16, note 56 briefly comment upon SEG, XXII, 434 (perhaps an honorary inscription), 435 (in L. 1 Ἑρμαίου instead of Εὐμαίου; 4th cent. A.D.; the word τόπος points to an epitaph); 436 and 439 (note on the letter forms); 437 (cf. our no. 547) and 438 (on the name Εὐέλπιστος).

---

549. TEXTS (WRONGLY) ATTRIBUTED TO HYETTOS. Etienne - Knoepfler, HB, 6-7, note 11 point out that IG, VII, 2837 and 2838 are not from Hyettos, as in IG (followed by P. Roesch, Thespies et la Confédération Béotienne, 1965, p. 59, note 4) but from Opus and accordingly should have been published in IG, IX, 1. Similarly (p. 14, note 44) IG, VII, 2839, 2841, 2842, 2844, 4165-4171 should be assigned to Larymna or Boumeliteia rather than to Hyettos. On the other hand CIG, 1755, wrongly attributed to Opus, in fact belongs to Hyettos. Similarly (p. 137-142, with photo) the stele of Agasinos (IG, IX, 1, 292) should be assigned to Hyettos and not to Cheliadou (Boumeliteia).

---

550. KOPAI, FRAGMENT OF A MILITARY CATALOGUE, 250-230 B.C. Fragment of a grey limestone stele. Ed. pr. S. Lauffer, CHIRON 6 (1976) 12-13, no. 3 (= P. Roesch, TEIRESIAS, Epigraphica (1977) 2-3, no. 3).

Θιός
ʼΑνθιππίδ̣α̣ρ̣ ἄρχογ̣[τος, πολεμαρ]-
χιόντων Νίκωνος Σπο̣[-ca. 7-, ʼΕ]-
πικούδιος Φ̣ηνομάχ̣[ω, -ca. 8-]
νος Εἰρολάω, γραμμ̣[ατίδδοντος]
ʼΑ̣γλάωγ̣ος Μ[-ca. 7-, ἀπεγράψαν]-
θο ἐμ πελτοφόρας̣·
------ΔΙ--------
------TEN-------
--------ΑΛ-------
--------Ο̣--------

---

551. KORONEIA, DEDICATION BY A WINNING MILITARY TEAM AT THE PAMBOIOTIA, 2nd HALF 3rd CENT. B.C. Two joining fragments of a marble column. On the same column also a proxeny-decree (given under no. 552). Ed. pr. S. Lauffer, CHIRON 6 (1976) 15-17, no. 8,

L. 1-18. Restorations have been suggested by P. Roesch, TEIRESIAS, Epigraphica (1977) 4-6, no. 5 (Roesch dates the text to 250-240 B.C.) and by A. Schachter, CEA 8 (1978) 105-106, no. 12 (cf. also p. 84 and 94; Schachter suggests a date ca. 230 B.C.).

[Ἄρχοντος Βοιωτῦς Ἀπολλ]ọδώρω
ca. 6 lines vac.
τος
νικάσ]αντες
εὐ?]τακτίη
ọθιοις
]ọṇος Ἀπολ-
[λ–]Κορωνεῖος
vac.
]ω Κορωνεῖος
vac.
τῶν πελταφο]ọάων
Στρ]ότωνος, Ὀφε-
[λειμος]Ἀμφισθένιος
]ω Κορωνείων
Λεβαδειήω-
[ν]Θισβεῖος
τῶν φαρετριτά?]ων
α]ọ Κορωνεῖος
vac.

P. Roesch suggests the following text: [Ἄρχοντος Βοιωτοῖς Ἀπολλ]οδώρω (?) | vacat | [ἐπὶ δὲ πόλιος --- φῶν]τος, | [τοὶ πέδδοι νικάσ]αντες | [τὰ Παμβοιώτια εὐ]τακτίη |[5][κὴ εὐοπλίη ? τοῖ]ς θιοῖς, | [βοιωταρχίο]ṇτος Ἀπολ | [λ - patronymic -] Κορωνεῖος, | [λοχαγίοντος ?] | [- name, patronymic -]ω Κορωνεῖος, |[10][ἁγιομένων] | [τῶν πελταφο]ράων | [- name - Στρ]ότωνος, Ὀφε | [λ - patronymic -], Ἀμφισθένιος | [- patronymic -]ω Κορωνείων, |[15] [- name, patronymic -] Λεβαδειήω, | [- name, patronymic] Θισβεῖος, | [τῶν ἐπιλέκτ]ων | [- name, patronymic - α]ο Κορωνεῖος. A. Schachter suggests: [Ἄρχοντος Βοιωτοῖς Ἀπολλ]ọδώρω | vacat | [N[1] N[2] βοιωταρχίον]τος |[5][(ἐγ) Κορωνείοις, νικάσ]αντες | [τοῖς Παμβοιωτίοις (εὐ)]τακτίη |[5][τοὶ *πεδδοὶ ἀνέθιαν τοῖ]ς θιοῖς, | [τῶ ἀγείματος ἁγιόμ]ẹνος Ἀπολ | [N[2] N[2]] Κορωνεῖος | [τῶν ἐπιλέκτων] | [N[3] N[3]]ω Κορωνεῖος |[10][N[4] N[4]] | [τῶν πελταφο]ọάων | [N[5] Στρ]ότωνος, Ὀφε | [N[6] N[6], N[7]]Ἀμφισθένιος | [τῶ τέλεος ἁγιόμενοι τ]ῶ Κορωνείων |[15][τῶν δὲ σ(ο)υσ(σ)τροτευμένων] Λεβαδειήω-| [ν N[3] N[8]] Θισβεῖος. | [τῶν φαρετριτά]ων | [N[9] N[9] α]ọ Κορωνεῖος.

552. KORONEIA, PROXENY-DECREE FOR A CORINTHIAN, END 3rd CENT. B.C. Two joining fragments of a marble column. On the same column also a dedication by a winning military team at the Pamboiotia (cf. no. 551). Ed. pr. S. Lauffer, CHIRON 6 (1976) 15-17, no.

8, L. 20-26 (= P. Roesch, TEIRESIAS, Epigraphica (1977), 4-6, no. 5, L. 20-26 and A. Schachter, CEA 8 (1978) 105, no. 12, L. 20-26). For the date, cf. A. Schachter, l.c., 84.

-- ἔλεξε· Πασι-
[κλεῖν vel sim. .. patr. ca.9 .. Κορ]ι̣νθιον προ-
[ξένον εἶμεν κὴ εὐερ]γέταν τᾶς πό-
[λιος Κορωνείων κὴ αὐ]τ̣ὸν κὴ ἐσγό-
[νως κὴ εἶμεν αὐτῦς γᾶς κὴ F]υ̣κίας ἔπ-
[πασιν κὴ ἀσφάλιαν κὴ ἀσου]λ̣ίαν
[κὴ ἀτέλιαν–]

---

553. KORONEIA, HONORARY INSCRIPTION, 2nd CENT. B.C. Two fragments of a marble base. Ed. pr. S. Lauffer, CHIRON 6 (1976) 17-18, no. 9 (ph.) (= P. Roesch, TEIRESIAS, Epigraphica (1977) 7, no. 7).

A B

Ὁ δῆμο[ς ---------] Κ̣οΐντου
υἱὸν Σ[--------στρα]τ̣ηγό[ν]
vac.

1-2. [Πόπλιον Μούκιον] Κοΐντου | υἱὸν Σ[καιόλαν ---] Lauffer || 3. [ὕπατον Ῥωμαίων] Lauffer.

---

554. KORONEIA, HONORARY INSCRIPTION, ROMAN PERIOD. Marble fragment. Ed. pr. S. Lauffer, CHIRON 6 (1976) 18, no. 10 (= P. Roesch, TEIRESIAS, Epigraphica (1977) 10, no. 20).

ρω vac.
\ιδα
vac.

1-2. Perhaps Κο]ρω|[νείων Lauffer.

---

555. KORONEIA, DEDICATION TO ARTEMIS ORTHOSIA, MIDDLE OR 1st HALF 3rd CENT. B.C. Marble plaque. Ed. pr. S. Lauffer, CHIRON 6 (1976) 18-19, no. 11. Cf. P. Roesch, TEIRESIAS, Epigraphica (1977) 6-7, no. 6.

[Διο]νυσόδωρος Νικοκράτιος Περίκλιαν τὰν θυγατέρ̣[α
ἀ̣ρειάξασαν ἀνέθεικε Ἀρτάμιδι Ὀρθωσίῃ.

Date: 2nd half 3rd cent. B.C. Roesch || 2. [ὶ]α̣ρειάξασαν, Ὀρθωσίη Roesch.

---

556. KORONEIA, FUNERARY EPIGRAM, ROMAN IMPERIAL PERIOD. Marble stele. Ed. pr. S. Lauffer, CHIRON 6 (1976) 19, no. 12 (= P. Roesch, TEIRESIAS, Epigraphica (1977) 7, no. 8).

---ουσα̣ [τ]ὴ̣[ν] ¦ [ο]ὐρανίαν Ἀφροδείτην |
ἥτις ἔδωκε αὐτῇ νέκταρος |4ἀμβροσίην· |
κεῖται δὲ αὐ[τ]όθι σῆμα ἵνα | εἴδωσι οἱ παροδεῖται |
ὡς οὐδὲν γλ̣[ύ]κ̣ιον εὐσεβί|8ης πέλεται.

557-566. KORONEIA, EPITAPHS. Ed. pr. S. Lauffer, CHIRON 6 (1976) 19-22, nos. 13-20 and 22-23. Cf. P. Roesch, TEIRESIAS, Epigraphica (1977) 8-9, nos. 9-18.

557. P. 19, no. 13; marble stele.

Ἀπολλό[δωρος]

Also Ἀπολλό[δοτος], Ἀπολλο[φάνεις] etc. is possible Roesch, l.c., no 9.

558. P. 19-20, no. 14; marble cippus, before 350 B.C.

Δ̣ειμάφις

Perhaps Δειμαχίς or Δειμαρίς ? Roesch, l.c., no. 16.

559. P. 20, no. 15; limestone cippus (Roesch, l.c., no. 10: 1st cent. A.D.) (ph.).

Ζώπυρε

560. P. 20, no. 16; marble stele, 3rd cent. B.C.

Θιότιμος

561. P. 20-21, no. 17; marble stele (Roesch, l.c., no. 17: 3rd cent. B.C. ?).

Μελάντιχος

562. P. 21, no. 18; marble stele.

Ὁμολωΐς

563. P. 21, no. 19; marble stele, 4th-3rd cent. B.C.

Π]άιλλο[ς

For this name, cf. also J. and L. Robert, BE (1977) no.

212, p. 347; O. Masson, RPH 52 (1978) 358, note 1.

564. P. 22, no. 20; marble stele.

Π̣αράμογος

565. P. 22, no. 22; upper right part of a marble stele, 5th cent. B.C.

-]ρ̣ας

566. P. 22, no. 23; fragment of a marble stele, 5th cent. B.C.

--]ρρος

Perhaps [Πύ]ρρος Roesch, l.c., no. 15.

567. KORONEIA, EPITAPH (?) OR DEDICATION TO CHAROPS (?). Marble fragment. Ed. pr. S. Lauffer, CHIRON 6 (1976) 22, no. 21 (ph.) Cf. P. Roesch, TEIRESIAS, Epigraphica (1977) 9-10, no. 19.

ΦΑΓ\
Μ̣ΝΟΝ/
vac.ΧΑΡΟ,

1. Φαγ[ρίς] Lauffer; the third letter is a P rather than a Γ Roesch || 2. Μ̣ΝΟΝΧ Roesch || 3. Χαρο[πίς], Χαρο[πεῖνα] or Χαρο[πεῖνος] Roesch.

568. INSCRIPTIONS FROM KORONEIA. S. Lauffer, CHIRON 6 (1976) 41-42, nos. 49, 50 and 52 reports that IG, VII, 2873, 2917 and 3003 have been seen by him. Cf. P. Roesch, TEIRESIAS, Epigraphica (1977) 28-29, no. 68 who dates IG, VII, 2917 to the first half of the 3rd cent. B.C.

569. LEBADEIA, APOLOGIA OF AN AGONOTHETES OF THE BASILEIA. SEG, III, 369. Etienne - Knoepfler, HB, 246-250 support L. Moretti's view (Iscr. Agon. Greche, 1953, p. 105-106) that this inscription dates from the reign of Ptolemy XII (80-51 B.C.); from the fact that Ptolemy is recorded as victor in a chariot-race at the Basileia in Lebadeia under Xenarchos' agonothesia they infer that Ptolemy must have been present in Boiotia and they connect his presence (and the date of the inscription) with his trip in Greece in the years 58-55 B.C. But see J. and L. Robert, BE (1977) no. 218 who point out that Ptolemy need not at all to have been present at the Basileia in order to win the chariot-race.

570-571. LEBADEIA, EPITAPHS. Ed. pr. S. Lauffer, CHIRON 6 (1976) 23, nos. 24-25. (= P. Roesch, TEIRESIAS, Epigraphica (1977) 17, nos. 44-45).

---

570. P. 23, no. 24; marble stele, 5th cent. B.C.

Πανκρατίον

571, P. 23, no. 25; marble stele with palmettes.

Νικώ

---

572. LEBADEIA, EPITAPH. Ed. pr. AD 3 (1917) 423. S. Lauffer, CHIRON 6 (1976) 42, no. 53 reports that this inscription has been seen by him. Cf. P. Roesch, TEIRESIAS, Epigraphica (1977) 32, no. 78 who dates the text to the early Imperial period.

῾Ηρακλίδης

---

573. ONCHESTOS, PROXENY-DECREE OF THE BOIOTIAN KOINON, CA. 300 B.C. Ed. pr. AE (1909) col. 55-56. D. Knoepfler, Mélanges Collart, p. 272 suggests that this decree does not come from the temple of Athena Itonia but from the sanctuary of Poseidon Onchestios (contra P. Roesch, REA 68, 1966, p. 72 and BCH 94, 1970, p. 145, note 13); for the date cf. Etienne - Knoepfler, HB, 270.

---

574. ORCHOMENOS, LIST OF NAMES, 4th-3rd CENT. B.C. Fragment of a marble stele, broken at the bottom. Ed. pr. S. Lauffer, CHIRON 6 (1976) 36-37, no. 37 (ph.). Cf. P. Roesch, TEIRESIAS, Epigraphica (1977) 26, no. 59.

	vac.		᾿Αρισταγόρα
	῾Ηρακλίδας		Κάλλις
	Χαρικλίες		῾Η]ρακλίδας
3	Μιλείσιος	7	Χ]ήριππος

Perhaps a list of fallen warriors Lauffer; Roesch rejects this because of the presence of the names of two women (L. 4 and 5) and suggests that we have an epitaph for an unknown group of people; he dates it to the end 5th/beginning 4th cent. B.C. || 2. Χαρικλίες = Χαρικλεῖς ? A patronymic in the genitive seems to be out of the question Roesch || 3. Μιλείσιος is rather the name of a man than an ethnic as Lauffer thinks Roesch || 5. Κάλλις masculine name (Lauffer) is unknown in Boiotia, so Roesch prefers Καλλίς (feminine name).

---

575. ORCHOMENOS, FRAGMENTARY CULT-REGULATION. Fragment of a

marble stele. Ed. pr. S. Lauffer, CHIRON 6 (1976) 33, no. 29 (ph.). Cf. P. Roesch, TEIRESIAS, Epigraphica (1977) 18, no. 47.

--------σων τὼς δὲ σο-
--------Σ θυέμεν τυ
--------ΥΕΝΤΥΘΕ̣Ι̣Δ̣Ο
4 --------|ἀπὸ τῶν ε-
--------|καθὰ σουν|
6 -------- ἐνομοθετε
vac.

Date: early 3rd cent. B.C. Roesch || 3-4. --------υ ἐν τῦ Θειλο[υ] | [θίυ μεινὶ ---] Roesch.

---

576. ORCHOMENOS, FRAGMENTS OF TWO MILITARY CATALOGUES, BEFORE 250 B.C. Part of a marble column inscribed on two sides. Side A: Ed. pr. A. de Ridder, BCH 18 (1894) 504, no. 37; republished by S. Lauffer, CHIRON 6 (1976) 23-25, no. 26 (ph.). Side B: Ed. pr. S. Lauffer, l.c., 24-25, no. 26 (ph.). Cf. P. Roesch, TEIRESIAS, Epigraphica (1977) 18-20, no. 48 (who dates the texts to ca. 250 B.C.).

Side A

τ̣ιος, Χαρίλ̣α̣ο̣ς̣ Α[- -]
Δαμοκλίδαο, Ἱππο[- -]
Ἀθανιῆος, Ἀντιγ[- -]
μος Ξενοτέ̣λειος, [- -]
τιος, .ΕΤ..ca.3..Δ̣Ε̣Ι̣Σ̣Δ̣[- -]
Ο̣..ca. 7..Ἀριστό̣δ[- -]
σικράτ[εις] Ἡ̣σ̣χ̣ύλιο[ς, - Ἀ]-
θύρ[ι]ο̣[ς], Δ̣α̣μ̣ά̣σ̣ιππ[ος -]
ριος, Ἀμφίνικος Πο[- Ἐπα]-
γάθιος, Ἀριστόδαμ[ος - - Καλ]-
λ̣ικράτεις Ἐπωφέ[λιος, - -]
ρίχιος, Φίλων Καλλ̣[- -]
Ἐμπεδίων Ξενά[ρχιος - -]
θώνιος̣, Ὀμφαλίω[ν - -]
Σίλλει Τιμοξένιο[ς, - - ι]-
ος, Μνασίων Χαρι̣[- -]
Ἀμινιῆος, Μνάσω̣[ν - -]
φαντος Εὐάνδρ[ιος, - -]
νιδαο, Ἱππίας Αγ[- - Ἡσ]-
χινῆος, Λάαρχος̣ [- -]
νίκιος, Τιμοκράτε̣[ις - Καφι]-
σοδώριος, Εὔνοσ[τος - -]
[1-2]ι̣γ̣ος Τιμοκράτε[ιος, -]

---

2. Ἱππο[κλεῖς, Ἱππό[νικος Lauffer || 3. Ἀντιγ[ένεις, Ἀντιγ[ενίδας, Ἀντίγ[ων Lauffer || 5. τιος, Π̣ετακλεῖς Διδ[ύμιος, Που]- Roesch || 6. Ἀριστόδ[αμος Lauffer; θοκλε[ῖς] Ἀριστοδ[άμιος, Πα]- Roesch || 6-7. Λου]|σικράτ[εις or Μνα] | σικράτ[εις] Lauffer; Πα]|σικράτ[εις] Roesch || 11-12. Θιοδω]|ρίχιος, Μοι]|ρί-

χιος Lauffer; Θιοδω]|ρίχιος is doubtful, better is [Πουρ]|ρίχιος Roesch || 13-14. Που]|θώνιος, 'Αγα]|θώνιος, Σα]|θώνιος Lauffer; Που]|θώνιος Roesch || 15. Σίλλει or [Μνα]|σίλλει Roesch || 16. Χαρι̣[κλεῖος Χαρί̣[λαος, Χαρῖ̣[νος, Χαρι̣[άδας. Or Χαρε̣[ισιάδειος ? Lauffer || 17-18. Δαμό]|φαντος Lauffer || 18-19. 'Απολλω]|νίδαο, Εὐμε]|νίδαο Lauffer || 19. 'Αγ[εισιλάω, 'Αγ[εισάνδριος, 'Αγ[ασιῆος, 'Αγ[εισινίκιος Lauffer.

Side B

[- - -]τειος vac.
[- - -]ΟΜ̣Ε̣Δ̣ιος,
[- - -]ας Καλλι-
[- - -]έξ̣ενος ΙΑ-
[- - -]ωνιος, 'Απο̣λ̣-
[- - -]κων 'Ομολωΐχ-
[ιος, -]ω, Νικασίων Γ̣Α1-2
[- -] Χαριξ̣ένιος, Θιο-
[- - Τι]μόλαος 'Αθύρω,
[- -]ρομιος, Λάσιππο̣ς,
[- - Μ]ε̣λάντ̣ιχος Καπι̣ώ̣γ̣-
[ιος, -] Φ̣ρουνώ̣νιος, Χήρι[π]-
[πος -]ν 'Αγαθαΐχιος, Τιμα̣-
[- -]νιος, Λουσίας Εὐγο-
[- -]ς 'Ασωπόδωνος, 'Ιθυ-
[- --]Μιτίων [Λ]ευκίω, Θιογί-
[των -],Νικόδ[α]μος Λανπριῆος,
[- -]ω̣νιος, [Π]ο̣[λέ]μαρχος
[- -]Π̣ου[ca.5-6.]ος vac.
[- -]ΥΔ̣[ca.3-4Δαμ]οθοΐδας
[- - 'Ολ]υνπί[[ω]] χω,
[- -]πων[ca.2]εδάμωΤ
[- - Καλ]λ̣ικράτεις Στροτώ-
[νιος, ------------------------]

2. Φιλ]ομέλιος Roesch || 3-4. Καλλι|[κράτιος Lauffer || 4. Perhaps Μεν]έξενος Lauffer || 4-5. 'Ια|[ρώνιος Lauffer || 5-6. 'Απολ̣|[λόδωρος Lauffer || 7. Νικασίων Γλα[υ]|[κ--- Roesch || 8-9. Θιο|[γίτων, Θιό|[τιμος Lauffer || 10. Εὐδ]ρόμιος, 'Επιδ]ρόμιος Lauffer || 13. 'Αγαθάρχιος Roesch || 13-14. Τιμα̣|[σίων, Τιμα̣|[σίθεος Lauffer || 14-15. Εὐγό|[μιος, Εὐγό|[στιος Lauffer || 15. 'Ασωποδώ̣ρ̣ιος Roesch || 15-16. 'Ιθυ|[κράτεις, 'Ιθύ|[δαμος Lauffer || 19. Που[θόδωρ]ος, Που[θάνγελ]ος or the corresponding adjective Lauffer || 21. 'Ολ]υνπίχιο[ς] Roesch || 22.]πων ['Α]ρχεδάμιος Roesch.

577. ORCHOMENOS, TWO MILITARY CATALOGUES, A: BEFORE 250 B.C., B: 2nd HALF 3rd CENT. B.C. Part of a marble column, inscribed on two sides. Ed. pr. S. Lauffer, CHIRON 6 (1976) 29-32, no. 27 (ph.).

Cf. P. Roesch, TEIRESIAS, <u>Epigraphica</u> (1977) 21-22, no. 49.

Side A

- - - - / \ | -
[- - - -]γ̣ίδας Φαέ[ν-
[ιος, -], Π̣ολύρειτος Ἡσχ̣-
[- - -]ηος, Ἰάρων Κλε̣-
[- - -]ς, Μελίτων Και-
[- - -Πολ]υστρότιος, Γα.-
[- - -]γιος Φιλώνιος,
[- - - Μί]κκων Μικκώ-
[νιος, -Ἀριστ]οκλεῖος, vac.
[- - - -]ος, Ἀσωπόδο-
[τος - -]ς Θιοβώλιος,
[- - - -]οδωρι [ca.3]
- - - - \ | -

Side B

Παυσανίας Θιοδώ[ρω]
Ἀριστόνικος Ἀρ[ιστίωνος]
Δαμάτριχος Α[- -]
Ἀ̣ντιγένεις Ἀρ̣[- -]
Ξ̣ενοκλίδας Εὐαρί[δαο, -]
<Λ>ανπρίαο vac.
Φίλων Ἑρμαΐσκω vac.
Ϝελιάνγελος Ἀθαν[ίαο]
Μνασικλείδας Πιτ[-]
Τιμοκράτεις Τιμοκρά̣[τιος]
Καφισίω̣ν Μικόλω vac.
Ἀρίστοχος Ἐπηνέτω vac.
vac.

A. 2. Ἀπολλω]νίδας, Εὐμε]νίδας Lauffer || 2-3. Φαε[ί]¦[νιος Roesch || 3-4. Ἡσχ̣|[ύλιος, Ἡσχ̣|[ινῆος Lauffer; Ἡσ|[χ--- Roesch || 4-5. Κλε̣|[ώνιος, Κλε̣|[ονίκιος, Κλε̣|[αρίστιος Lauffer || 5. Μελίτων Κλι | Roesch || 6-7. Γά[θ]¦[ων Lauffer; Γα[.] or Γλ[.] Roesch || 8-9. Μίκκω|[νος or Μικκώ|[νιος Lauffer || 9. Also Δαμ]οκλεῖος or Τιμ]οκλεῖος are possible Lauffer;]οκλεῖος Roesch || 12. Καφισ]οδώρι̣[ος, Ἀπολλ]οδώρι̣[ος Lauffer;]οδώριο[ς] Roesch.

B. 2. Ἀρ[--- Roesch || 5. Εὐάρι[ος,---] Roesch || 8. Although Lauffer says "F nicht zweifelhaft", Roesch reads Κλιάνγελος Ἀθανο[---] || 9. Πιτ[θιάδαο Lauffer.

---

578. ORCHOMENOS, MILITARY CATALOGUE, MIDDLE 3rd CENT. B.C. Ed. pr. N. Pappadakis, AD 8 (1923) 214-215, no. 10 (SEG, III, 373). In line 9 S. Lauffer, CHIRON 6 (1976) 43, no. 55 reads on the photo (p. 215, fig. 5) Ἀ[μφ]αρίδας instead of Ἀ[μφι]αρίδας (AD) and Ἀμ̣φ̣[ι]αρίδας (SEG). P. Roesch, TEIRESIAS, <u>Epigraphica</u> (1977) 36, no. 87 reads on the photo Ἀμφαρίδας.

---

579. ORCHOMENOS, MILITARY CATALOGUE, 2nd HALF 3rd CENT. B.C. IG, VII, 3183. S. Lauffer, CHIRON 6 (1976) 42-43, no. 54 has revised the text and offers the following corrections: L. 2. Πισίω|[ν instead of Πισία|[ς; 4. Φί¦λ̣ωνος instead of Φί|[λ]ωνος; 4-5. Κουχί|δα or Κουχή̣|δα instead of Κουχ[ρί]¦δα; 8. Ἀρχέλαος instead of Ἀρχέλας; 9. Σίλλιος instead of ΣΙΛΑΙΟΣ or Σίλ[λ]ιος.

580-582. ORCHOMENOS, FRAGMENTS OF THREE MILITARY CATALOGUES. Three fragments of a grey-bluish marble stele or base. On the fragment at the left: IG, VII, 3184 and 3185; on the fragment in the middle: SEG, III, 371; on the fragment at the right: SEG, III, 372. IG, VII, 3185 and SEG, III, 371 are fitting together and are part of one military catalogue. S. Lauffer, CHIRON 6 (1976) 43-47, no. 56 presents the results of his study of this stele.

---

580. IG, VII, 3184 (cf. J.M. Fossey, AAA 7 (1974) 123-124), ca. 200 B.C. S. Lauffer, l.c., 45-46 makes the following remarks (= P. Roesch, TEIRESIAS, Epigraphica (1977) 36, no. 88): 6. At the beginning Lauffer adopts the IG-reading Με]νεστρότω; -]εστρότω Fossey; 6-7. at the end Lauffer reads 'Αντιγ¦ωνε|ύς; 'Αντιγ|ωνε|ῦς Fossey; it seems to be a later addition; 7. Κλιάρ[εις] IG; Κλιαρ- Fossey; Κλιάρι[στος] Lauffer; 8. Νουμφ̣όδωρο̣ς Lauffer; Νουμφόδωρ[ος] Fossey.

---

581. IG, VII, 3185 + AD 8 (1923) 213, no. 8 (SEG, III, 371) (cf. J.M. Fossey, AAA 7 (1974) 119-127), ca. 220 B.C. After examining these two fragments, S. Lauffer, l.c., 43-45 presents the following text (cf. also P. Roesch, TEIRESIAS, Epigraphica (1977) 36-37, no. 89):

IG VII 3185 SEG III 371

-α]ο ἄρχοντος Βοιωτῦς
'Ερχομενίυς δ[ὲ 'Αθαν]οδώρω Νικοκλ[εῖο]ς, πολ[εμαρ]-
χιόντων 'Αμι[νίαο] Εὐαγόραο, Μέκγαο Τελεσ[ίαο],
'Αλεξ̣ιμάχω Κ[αλλι]στρότω, γραμματίδδον[τος]
5 τῦς πολεμάρχ[υς Μ]νάσιππος (sic) 'Αντιμάχω vac. [τυὶ]
5a [Κα]λλιγίτων Καλ[οκλίδαο]
6 πρᾶτον ἐστροτ[εύα]θ̣η· 'Αμιν[-
-ς̣ Χηρετ-

---

2. δ[ὲ 'Απολ]λοδώρω Fossey; "on ne voit pas de lambda devant -οδώρω" Roesch; Νικοκλ[εῖος]ς Fossey (typing error), Νικοκλ[είιο]ς Roesch || 3. 'Αμφ.ca5. Fossey || 5a. Καλ--- Fossey || 6. 'Αμιν[ίας, 'Αμιν[άδας, 'Αμιν[όδωρος Lauffer.

---

582. AD 8 (1923) 214, no. 9 (SEG, III, 372), 1st half 2nd cent. B.C. S. Lauffer, l.c., 46-47 proposes the following text (= P. Roesch, TEIRESIAS, Epigraphica (1977) 32-33, no. 79):

[- ἄρχοντος], πολεμαρχιόν[των]
[- -]ετωνος 'Εχεκρ[άτιος],
[- - γραμ]ματεύοντος τ[ῶν]
[πολεμάρχων - Κ]αφισοδώρω τυὶ π̣[ρᾶτον]
5 [ἐστροτεύαθη -]ι όλοχος Μ̣νάσωγ̣[ος]
-ΚΛΕ

---

583. ORCHOMENOS, FRAGMENTARY LIST OF NAMES. Fragment of a marble stele. Ed. pr. S. Lauffer, CHIRON 6 (1976) 32-33, no. 28 (= P. Roesch, TEIRESIAS, Epigraphica (1977) 23, no. 51).

1 \
--α̣μων ι--
--α]ο, Ἀσωποκ--
4 --λος Κλει--

"Fragment wohl eines Militärkatalogs" Lauffer || 3. Ἀσωπόκ[ριτος, Ἀσωποκ[λίδας, Ἀσωποκ[λῆς Lauffer.

---

584. ORCHOMENOS, DEDICATION, 5th CENT. B.C. Fragment of a marble column. Ed. pr. S. Lauffer, CHIRON 6 (1976) 35-36, no. 35 (ph.). Cf. P. Roesch, TEIRESIAS, Epigraphica (1977) 25, no. 57.

--OPAK--
--ε]ὐχσάμ̣[ενος--

1. Perhaps Ἀγ]οράκ[ριτος Lauffer; "ne pas restituer" Roesch.

---

585. ORCHOMENOS, DEDICATION BY A CHOREGOS, END 3rd- BEGINNING 2nd CENT. B.C. Ed. BCH 98 (1974) 219, no. 26. S. Lauffer, CHIRON 6 (1976) 47-48, no. 58 (= P. Roesch, TEIRESIAS, Epigraphica (1977) 37, no. 90) proposes to restore in line 1: Διὶ Ὁμολ]ωΐυ ἀνέθεικαν instead of Ἀπόλλωνι Πτ]ωίυ ἀνέθεικαν. Cf. J. and L. Robert, BE (1974) no. 283 who also proposed Ὁμολ]ωίυ ἀνέθεικαν.

---

586. ORCHOMENOS, DEDICATION OF A TEMPLE TO THE MOTHER OF THE GODS, 2nd CENT. B.C. Fragment of a marble block, broken at all sides except above. Ed. pr. S. Lauffer, CHIRON 6 (1976) 34-35, no. 32 (ph.). Cf. P. Roesch, TEIRESIAS, Epigraphica (1977) 23-24, no. 53.

[Ἱππ]αρέτα [Εἱροδότω]
[ἱαρ]ε̣ιτεύωσ̣[α ἀνέθεικε]
[τὸν ν]α̣ὸν κὴ τ[ὰ ----]
4 [-----]α Ματ[ρὶ Θεῶν]

Date: early 2nd cent. B.C. Roesch || 1. [Εἱροδότου] Lauffer || 3-4. κὴ τ[ὰ λοιπὰ] | [πάντ]α or τ[ὰ θυρώματ]α Lauffer; Roesch refrains from restoring these lines.

---

587. ORCHOMENOS, DEDICATION TO APOLLO. Fragment of a marble column. Ed. pr. S. Lauffer, CHIRON 6 (1976) 35, no. 33. Cf. P. Roesch, TEIRESIAS, Epigraphica (1977) 24, no. 54.

'Απο/[---ἀνέ]--
θεικε [τῦ]
'Απόλ[λωνι Δαλίυ]

Date: before 172 B.C. Roesch (who uses the dialect as argument) || 1. 'Απολ̣[λόδωρος or 'Απολ̣[ωνίδας Lauffer; 'Α πόλ[ις] Roesch || 3. Lauffer's restoration is not certain Roesch.

588. ORCHOMENOS, DEDICATION OF THE CONFEDERATION TO A HERO. Fragment of a marble base, broken at all sides. Ed. pr. S. Lauffer, CHIRON 6 (1976) 33, no. 30. Cf. P. Roesch, TEIRESIAS, Epigraphica (1977) 23, no. 52.

---ἄ]ρχοντος Βοιω[τῦς
--ἥρωει κατ τὰ[ν μαντείαν τῶ 'Απόλλωνος-
---ω, ἀφεδριατ[ευόντων
- EN -

P. Roesch proposes the following text: [- name - ἄ]ρχοντος, Βοιω[τοὶ τὸν τρίποδα ἀνέθειкαν]|[-----------]ἥρωει κὰτ τὰ[ν μαντείαν τῶ 'Απόλλωνος]¦ [τῶ Πτωί]ω, ἀφεδριατ[ευόντων -------------]|---------EN-------

589. ORCHOMENOS, DEDICATION OF A LONG-DISTANCE RUNNER IN THE PYTHIA. Fragment of a marble stele or base, broken at the left and at the bottom. Ed. pr. S. Lauffer, CHIRON 6 (1976) 35, no.34 (= P. Roesch, TEIRESIAS, Epigraphica (1977) 24, no. 55).

--να ἀνέθ̣[εικε
Π]ούθια δό[λιχον.

590. ORCHOMENOS, DEDICATION BY AN ATHLETE. Fragment of a marble stele. Ed. pr. S. Lauffer, CHIRON 6 (1976) 34, no. 31. Cf. P. Roesch, TEIRESIAS, Epigraphica (1977) 25, no. 56.

vac.
'Απολλ]ό̣δωρος 'Η̣χ̣μ̣[όνιος
---οις νικωντα |-------
δ]ί̣αυλον vac.
vac.

1. ---]ό̣δωρος 'Η̣χ̣μ̣[--- Roesch || 2. [θε]οῖς ? νικῶν τὰ J. and L. Robert, BE (1977) no. 212, p. 347.

591. ORCHOMENOS, DEDICATION (?). Limestone architrave block. Ed. pr. S. Lauffer, CHIRON 6 (1976) 36, no.36 (ph.) (= P. Roesch,

TEIRESIAS, Epigraphica (1977) 25, no. 58).

--IONK--

Perhaps Τιβέρ]ιον or Κλαύδ]ιον Κ[αίσαρα Lauffer.

592-598. ORCHOMENOS, EPITAPHS. Ed. pr. S. Lauffer, CHIRON 6 (1976) 37-39, nos. 38-44. Cf. also P. Roesch, TEIRESIAS, Epigraphica (1977) 26-28, nos. 60-66.

592. P. 37, no. 38; upper part of a stele broken at the left, 600-450 B.C. (ph.).

ℎεσίαι

Roesch, l.c., no. 60 restores ['Εφ'] ℎεσίαι though Lauffer says that there is no room for it.

593. P. 37-38, no. 39; limestone stele, ca. 450 B.C. (ph.).

Πολύτιμος Εὐ̣-- | Μℎεγαρεύς

2. Μℎεγαρύς Lauffer, corr. Roesch, l.c., no. 61.

594. P. 38, no. 40; marble grave altar. Cf. also A. Ioannidou-Karetsou, AD 27B, 2 (1972) 324 who dated the stone to ca. 200 B.C. and described it as a grave stele.

'Αριστόκλεια | "Αβρων

595. P. 38, no. 41; limestone stele.

'Α̣ριστόμαχος

596. P. 38-39, no. 42; limestone stele (Roesch, l.c., no. 64: early Imperial period).

'Επὶ | Ζωΐλῳ

597. P. 39, no. 43; fragment of a marble naïskos-stele, 250-200 B.C.

Θιόκρι[τος]

598. P. 39, no. 44; limestone cippus, 2nd cent. B.C. (ph.).

Καφισίας

Date: early 2nd cent. B.C. Roesch, l.c., no. 66.

---

599. ORCHOMENOS, EPITAPH. IG, VII, 3286. Cf. S. Lauffer, CHIRON 6 (1976) 48, no. 60 (= P. Roesch, TEIRESIAS, Epigraphica (1977) 37, no. 91). Lauffer reads the inscription as follows:

-ν | --η̣λ̣ώ

//N | -- ⅤΙΔΩ IG

---

600. OROPOS, PROXENY-DECREE FOR THE ATHENIAN ARISTEIDES, 1st HALF 3rd CENT. B.C. Ed. pr. M.Th. Mitsos, AE (1952) 172, no. 4 (SEG, XVI, 298). According to C. Habicht, CHIRON 6 (1976) 7-10 the same Aristeides is on record in an honorary decree for three Athenian ambassadors (Kallipos, Aristeides, Glaukon), from Orchomenos: BCH 38 (1914) 451-454 (= L. Moretti, Iscr. stor. ell., I, 1967, 134-136, no. 53; 265-264 B.C.). Habicht discusses these persons and their functions.

---

601. OROPOS, PROXENY-DECREE, 3rd CENT. B.C. IG, VII, 371. This inscription (published fragmentary in IG by Dittenberger) can now, after cleaning of the surface of the stone, completely be read and is republished (with app. crit.) by B.C. Petrakos, AD 28A (1973) 188:

Θεοτέλης εἶπεν· δεδόχθαι τῶι δήμωι
[Σ]τέφανον Αἰσιμίδου Ἀθηναῖον πρόξε-
νον εἶναι καὶ εὐεργέτην τῆς πόλεος
Ὠρωπίων καὶ αὐτὸν καὶ ἐκγόνους καὶ
δ[ε]δόσθαι αὐτοῖς γῆς καὶ οἰκίας ἔγκτη-
σιν καὶ ἀσφάλειαν καὶ ἀσυλίαν καὶ πο-
λέμου καὶ εἰρήνης καὶ κατὰ γῆν καὶ κα-
τὰ [θ]άλατταν καὶ ἰ[σ]οτέλειαν καὶ τἄλλα
πάντα καθάπερ τοῖς ἄλλοις προξένοις
καὶ εὐεργέταις· ἀναγράψαι δὲ τὸ ψήφισμα
τοὺς πολεμάρχους ἐν στήληι λιθίνηι καὶ
στῆσαι ἐν τῶι ἱερῶι τοῦ Ἀμφιεράου.

---

602. OROPOS, PROXENY-DECREE, 220-200 B.C. IG, VII, 370 (right half of the inscription) + 390 (left half). B.C. Petrakos, AD 28A (1973) 187-188 joins these two fragments and presents the following text:

Πλο[υταρ]χίδης [Φιλιστίδου εἶ]πεν· ἐ[πειδὴ] Ἀρίστων εὔνους ὢν διατελεῖ
τε[ῖ] π[όλει Ὠ]ρωπί[ων καὶ κοινεῖ καὶ] ἰδίαι τ[οῖ]ς αὐτοῦ χρ[ε]ίαν ἔχουσι τῶν πολι-
3 τῶν ἐν παντὶ κ[αιρῶι χρήσιμος γί]νεται, δεδό[χ]θαι τε[ῖ] βουλεῖ καὶ τῶι δήμωι
Ἀρίστωνα Ἀνδρ[-------π]ρόξενον εἶν[αι] τῆς πόλεως Ὠρωπίων

αὐτὸν
καὶ ἐγγόνους καὶ [εἶναι αὐτοῖς γῆς] καὶ οἰκίας ἔν[κ]τησιν [κ]αὶ
ἰσοτέλειαν καὶ ἀσυ-
6 λίαν καὶ ἀσφάλε[ιαν καὶ πολέμο]υ καὶ εἰρήνης [κ]αὶ κατὰ γῆν καὶ
κατὰ θάλατ-
<τ>αν καὶ τἆλλα π[άντα καθάπερ τ]οῖς ἄλλοις προξένοις καὶ εὐερ-
γέταις.

ΙΙΜΑΙΟ

---

603. OROPOS, PROXENY-DECREE, 202-199 B.C. IG, VII, 323. B.C. Petrakos, AD 28A (1973) 189 republishes this inscription of which the left half had only partly been read in IG:

Ἐχέδημος Ἀρχεβίου εἶπεν· ἐπειδὴ Δωρίων εὔνους ὢν διατελεῖ τῆι
πόλει καὶ κοινεῖ καὶ ἰδίαι ἑκάστωι τῶν
πολιτῶν χρείας παρεχόμενος ἐν παντὶ καιρῶι, δεδόχθαι τῶι δήμωι
Δωρίωνα Καλλικλέους Σολέα πρόξενον
3 εἶν<αι> καὶ εὐεργέτην τῆς πόλεως Ὠρωπίων καὶ αὐτὸν καὶ ἐκγό-
νους καὶ εἶναι αὐτοῖς γῆς ἔνκτησιν καὶ οἰκίας
καὶ ἰσοτέλειαν καὶ ἀσφάλειαν καὶ πολέμου καὶ εἰρήνης καὶ κατὰ
γῆν καὶ κατὰ θάλατταν καὶ τἆλλα πάντα
5 καθάπερ καὶ τοῖς ἄλλοις προξένοις καὶ εὐεργέταις.

---

3. ΕΙΝ lapis; omission by the cutter Petrakos.

---

604. OROPOS, PROXENY-DECREE, END 3rd - BEGINNING 2nd CENT. B.C. IG, VII, 367 (left half of the inscription) + 389 (right half). B.C. Petrakos, AD 28A (1973) 190 joins these two fragments and presents the text as follows:

Ἱερέως Ἑρμοκράτου, Γοργίων Γοργίππου εἶπεν· ἐπειδὴ Φίλων Φι-
λίσκου Κιανὸς
εὔνους ὢν διατελεῖ τεῖ πόλει Ὠρωπίων καὶ τοῖς πολίταις χρείας
παρέχεται,
3 δεδόχθαι τεῖ βουλεῖ καὶ τῶι δήμωι πρ[όξε]νον εἶναι τῆς πόλεως
Ὠρωπίων αὐτὸν
καὶ ἐκγόνους καὶ εἶναι αὐτῶι γῆ[ς καὶ ο]ἰκίας ἔνκτησιν καὶ πο-
λιτείαν καὶ ἀσυλίαν
καὶ ἀσφάλειαν καὶ κατὰ γῆν καὶ κα[τὰ] θάλατταν καὶ πολέμου καὶ
εἰρήνης
6 καὶ τἆλλα πάντα καθάπερ τοῖς ἄλ[λ]οις προξένοις καὶ εὐεργέταις.

605-607. OROPOS, PROXENY-DECREES. B.C. Petrakos, AD 28A (1973) 187-188 presents corrections of the proxeny-decrees IG, VII, 359, 360 and 361:

---

605. IG, VII, 359. B.C. Petrakos, l.c., 188 points out that in L. 3 the name of the proxenos is Πανίτας (instead of Γανίτας) and that in L. 6 one has to read καθάπερ τοῖς ἄλλοις instead of καθάπερ καὶ τοῖς ἄλλοις.

---

606. IG, VII, 360. B.C. Petrakos, l.c., 187-188 remarks that the stone has in line 2 ΦΡΥΝΡΩΝΑ (IG: Φρυνίωνα) and that one has to read in line 5 καθάπερ τοῖς ἄλλοις instead of καθάπερ καὶ τοῖς ἄλλοις.

---

607. IG, VII, 361. B.C. Petrakos, l.c., 188 reads in line 4 [ἔ]νκτησιν instead of [ἔγκ]τησιν and in line 5 καθάπερ τοῖς ἄλλοις instead of καθάπερ καὶ τοῖς ἄλλοις.

---

608. OROPOS, DEDICATION TO ARTEMIS, 338-322 B.C. White marble base. Ed. pr. B.C. Petrakos, AD 28A (1973) 190-191.

[Γ]λυκέρα, Διομέδοντος | γυνή, Ἀρτέμιδι

---

609. OROPOS, DEDICATION TO AMPHIARAOS, LATE 3rd CENT. B.C. Three fragments of a bench. Ed. pr. B.C. Leonardos, AE (1892) 53, no. 83, 84 and 88 (no. 88 = also IG, VII, 441). B.C. Petrakos, AD 28A (1973) 191 joins these three fragments and reads the inscription as follows:

[Κηφισό]δωρος Μειδ[ίου Ἀθηναῖος Ἀ]μφιαρά[ωι]

---

610. OROPOS, DEDICATION, LATE 3rd CENT. B.C. Inscription on a bench. Ed. pr. B.C. Petrakos, Ὁ Ὠρωπὸς καὶ τὸ Ἱερὸν τοῦ Ἀμφιαράου (Athens, 1968) p. 76; cf. also AD 28A (1973) 191.

Κηφισόδω[ρος -------]

For this person, cf. also no. 609.

---

611. PLATAIAI, EPITAPH OF EUROPE. IG, VII, 1714; SEG, XXV, 503. D. Knoepfler, Mélanges Collart, 274-276 (ph.) shows that the grave-stele with the epitaph for Europe (Ἐπὶ | Εὐρώπη Σιμίου) has been re-used in the 1st/2nd cent. A.D. Under the inscription of Europe he discovers traces of an older (ca. 2nd cent. B.C.) text (---ṬẸỊḌỌỤ). Also the fronton of the stele points to a pre-imperial date.

612. PLATAIAI, EPITAPH OF DIONYSIOS. Cf. AD 20B (1965) 228 and pl 274 α. D. Knoepfler, *Mélanges Collart,* 274-276 shows that the stele with the epitaph for Dionysios (Ἐπὶ Διονυσίωι) has been re-used after 150 B.C. (= date of the inscription); the stele itself dates to the 4th cent. B.C.

---

613. PLATAIAI, EPITAPH OF PARAMONOS, BEGINNING OF THE ROMAN IMPERIAL PERIOD. Stele, now Nat. Museum Athens, no. 1299. Cf. H. Möbius, *Die Ornamente der griechischen Grabstelen* (1929) p. 47 and pl. 34 b. D. Knoepfler, *Mélanges Collart,* 269-274 shows that this stele comes from Plataiai in Boiotia (and not from the Megaris as Möbius thought). He dates the inscription (Ἐπὶ | Παραμόνωι) to the beginning of the Roman Imperial period (contra Möbius: 2nd cent. B.C.). Since the stele itself is older, Knoepfler's assumption is that the stone has been re-used.

---

614. TANAGRA, EPITAPH OF EUKLEIDAS, 3rd-2nd CENT. B.C. Limestone stele with a pediment in relief at the top. Ed. pr. E. Herckenrath, MDAI (A) 31 (1906) 434-436; cf. also J.M. Fossey, AAA 4 (1971) 240-245. A. Schachter, ZPE 23 (1976) 251-254 (ph.) discusses the meaning of the Arist[i]astai. He rejects a connection with a local cult (Ariste, Artemis or Demeter) and favours a connection with ἄριστον ("breakfast" or "midday meal": "association of (former or active) messmates"). In ZPE 25 (1977) 135-136 H. Lloyd-Jones returns to this text. Cf. also P. Roesch, TEIRESIAS, *Epigraphica* (1977) 33, no. 80 and J. and L. Robert, BE (1977) no. 214. The text runs as follows:

Ε̣ὐκλίδας
οὗτον ἔθαψαν τὺ
σουνθούτη τὺ Ἀριστ[.]-
αστὴ κὴ Ἀφροδισιαστ[ὴ]
κ̣ὴ τὺ φαρατρίτη.

3-4. Ἀριστ[η]|αστή Lloyd-Jones, who interprets this as a group of worshippers of the god Aristaios; the traditional reading is Ἀριστ[ι]| αστή.

---

615. TANAGRA, EPITAPH. IG, VII, 3515. S. Lauffer, CHIRON 6 (1976) p. 21 suggests ΠΑΙΙΛΛΟΣ (Πάιιλλος) instead of ΠΑΝΑΛΟΣ (Πάναλος). Cf. P. Roesch, TEIRESIAS, *Epigraphica* (1977) 37, no. 92: "suggestion déjà faite par Dittenberger, ad loc.". Cf. no. 563.

---

616. THESPIAI, LIST OF WINNERS IN MUSICAL CONTESTS, 2nd CENT. A.D. In IG, VII, 1773, L. 30 Etienne - Knoepfler, HB, 8-9, note 19 suggest the reading M. Αἰμίλιος Ὑηίττιος (ethnicon of Hyettos)

instead of Ὑμηττός (IG: cognomen; BCH, 1895, p. 340, no. 15: ethnicon) though P. Roesch after inspection of the stone supports Ὑμηττός. Boeckh (CIG, 1585) found ΥΜΗΤΤΙΟΣ in Cyriacus' copy and corrected it into Ὑήττιος.

---

617. THESPIAI, EPITAPH FOR THE YOUNG FLUTE-PLAYER KAPION, EARLY 3rd CENT. B.C. Peek, GV, I, 1501. Cf. D.L. Page, WS 10 (1976) 172-173 who presents the text (in mixed meter) with commentary.

DELPHI

---

618. CORPUS. J. Pouilloux, F. Delphes, III, fasc. 4 (suite): Les inscriptions de la terrasse du temple et de la région Nord du sanctuaire, nos. 351 à 516 (Paris, 1976). In SEG XXVII we shall summarize the main reviews of this corpus.

---

619. PROSOPOGRAPHY. J. Pouilloux, RDAC (1976) 158-167 gives a prosopography of Cypriots, attested by inscriptions and literary texts in Delphi, and describes the different categories to which they belonged: artists, basileis, theorodokoi, athletes and philosophers succeed each other. Pl. XXV-XXVI: photos of 6 inscriptions of Delphi: the bronze inv. 1717, F. Delphes, III, 1, 396, 426, 444, 497 and 547.

---

620. THE AMPHICTYONIC COUNCIL AT DELPHI. G. Daux, La composition du conseil amphictyonique sous l' empire, Recueil Plassart, 59-79 reconstructs the (composition of the) delegations of the various tribes to this Council from the 4th cent. B.C. until Hadrian's time. He discusses F. Delphes, III, 4, no. 302.

---

621. DELPHI, DECREE OF CHIOS, 245 B.C. F. Delphes, III, 3, 215. G. Nachtergael, HISTORIA 25 (1976) 74-76 restores L. 28-30 as follows: γίνεσ[θαι δὲ είς τὸ λοιπὸν] |29τὴν ἀπόδειξιν τῶν θεωρῶν καθ᾽ ἑκάστην πενταετηρίδα, ὅταν καὶ [Αἰτωλοὶ τὴν ἐπαγγελίαν ποι] |30ῶνται (instead of a synchronism with a Panhellenic festival).

---

622. PROXENOI. J. Pouilloux, REA 76 (1974) 111-116 reviews P. Gauthier, "Symbola." Les étrangers et la justice dans les cités grecques (Nancy, 1972). On p. 113-114 he discusses Gauthier's interpretation of Syll3 548 (Delphi, ca. 211 B.C.) and disagrees with him as to the information given by the text about proxenoi in Delphi.

---

623. DELPHI, PROXENY-DECREE FOR A CITIZEN OF PHERAI, CA. 200 B.C. Ed. pr. H. Pontow, KLIO 15 (1918) 24, no. 47; cf. A. Wilhelm, AAWW (1922) 11. C. Habicht, in V. Milojcic - D. Theocharis, Demetrias I (1976) 193 points out that in L. 2 and 5 Φρίκας and Φρίκαν respectively should be read instead of Φ̣ε̣ρ̣ί̣α̣ς̣ and Φ̣ε̣ρ̣ί̣α̣ν̣: the decree concerned the homonymous great-grandson of Φρίκας 'Αριστιούνειος (SEG, XXV, 664, A 40), gymnasiarch of Pherai in 294-293 B.C.

---

624. DELPHI, LIST OF THEORODOKOI, 200-190 B.C. Ed. A. Plassart, BCH 45 (1921) 1-85. C. Habicht, in V. Milojcic - D. Theocharis, Demetrias I (1976) 190 points out that in col. III, L. 17 one should read ἐμ Φερ[αῖς Π]ερδίκκας Διονυσίου instead of ἐμ Φερ[αῖς] 'Ελικίας Διονυσίου. For the same person, cf. SEG, XXV, 664, B 50. The reading has been verified on the stone by G. Daux.

---

625. DELPHI/KNIDOS, "PIRACY LAW", 101/100 B.C. Cf. no. 1227.

---

626. DELPHI, HONORARY INSCRIPTIONS, IMPERIAL PERIOD. E. Bourguet, F. Delphes, III, 1, p. 389-391, no. 576. Cf. J.-F. Bommelaer, BCH 100 (1976) 759. E. Bourguet presented the text of these inscriptions as follows, bringing together fr. 2801 with fr. 2608 + 2607:

2608 +2607	2801
'Α πόλις τῶν Δε	[λφ]ῶ[ν]
Γάιον 'Αριστό	[δ]αμον
Ναυπάκτιον τὸν	[ἀ]ρχ[ιερέα ? ἀρετᾶς]
ἕνεκεν καὶ εὐσ	[εβείας καὶ εὐνοίας]
τᾶς είς αὐτὰν	['Απόλλωνι]
Πυθίωι	

J.-F. Bommelaer proves from new archaeological evidence that these are parts of two separate inscriptions (2608 +2607 and 2801) for two different persons (descendants of the Naupactian Aristodamos whose sons are honored in F. Delphes, III, 1, 151-152 = 150 B.C.?). So the restorations of 2801 are quite useless. In addition he remarks on 2801: L. 3.: instead of the letters P and X one reads on the stone ΓΗ.

---

627. DELPHI, DEDICATION, 170-130 B.C. SGDI, 2, 2961. A. Schachter, LCM 1 (1976) 125-126 proposes some corrections to this inscription: the restoration of Praxias in line 1 is (to some extent) open to question; in line 2, instead of reading [ἀνέθηκε] (or preferably [ἀνέθηκεν]) he suggests [τὸν υἱὸν] and in line 4 he restores [παγκράτ]ιον instead of [τὸν ἴδιον υ]ἱὸν.

628-635. DELPHI, CORRECTIONS OF EIGHT INSCRIPTIONS. G. Daux, Recueil Plassart, 78-79 presents corrections of the following texts in A. Plassart, F. Delphes, III, 4:

---

628. No. 277, col. A, L. 24: [Γομφε]ύς instead of [Σκοτο]υσ-[σαῖος].

---

629. No. 287, L. 8: ὁ πρεσ[βευτὴς ἦν]--- (instead of [ἡ̣ρέθη]).

---

630. No. 288, L. 8: ὁ πρεσ[βευτὴς ἦν]--- (instead of ἡ̣ρέθη]).

---

631. No. 298, L. 1: --ι̣ος ΚΑΙΤ (instead of --γ̣ος ΚΑΠ).

---

632. No. 302, col. I, L. 7: [ἐξαιτοῦνται]: uncertain restoration; LL. 7-16: uncertain restorations. Col. II, L. 1: [εἴ]σ[ή-νεγκαν] γνώμην: uncertain restoration; L. 11: [παρατέθειν]ται instead of [παρατέθει]ται.

---

633. No. 303: Daux doubts whether the fragments on p. 85 belong to this letter; on p. 85, L. IV: ΡΟΣΑ πρε[σβευ---]? instead of ΡΟΣΑΠΡ̣Ε̣ (?).

---

634. No. 304, LL. 27-28: πρε[σβευ]|[ταὶ ἡ̣ρέθησαν οἱ περὶ] τὸμ Φλ[άβ. Ἀρι]στότ̣ε̣ι̣μο[ν] instead of πρε[σ]|[βευταὶ -------] Πομ, Φλ. [Ἀριστ]ότ̣ε̣ιμο[ς].

---

635. No. 350, LL. 3-4: Plassart printed ουν Δία, Λικν[ί]|[την], later suggested [Σεκ]ουνδία Λικ[ι]ν[ί-]. Daux suspects the name Σεκουνδία and proposes Δ̣ικιγ|[νία] but also gives J. Bousquet's διαφ̣ικη̣|[σαι or σας, σαντες, σω]. He concludes: "Tout cela soit dit pour montrer combien la situation est fluide (pourquoi pas διὰ Δ̣ικιγ|[νίου] ? etc.) et impose la réserve."

PHOKIS

---

636. ELATEIA, EPITAPH FOR DAMOTIMOS, EARLY 3rd CENT. B.C. IG, IX, 1, 163; Peek, GV, I, 1502. Cf. D.L. Page, WS 10 (1976) 170-171 who presents the text (in mixed meter) with commentary.

637. TITHOREA, EPITAPH, BEFORE THE AUGUSTAN PERIOD. Marble stele with fronton. Ed. pr. S. Lauffer, CHIRON 6 (1976) 39-40, no. 45.

Σωτηρίς | Ζώπυρος

EASTERN LOKRIS

---

638. TEXTS WRONGLY ATTRIBUTED. For Boumeliteia, Larymna and Opus, cf. no. 549. For Halai, cf. no. 525.

WESTERN LOKRIS

---

639. CHALEION, LAW OF THE EASTERN LOKRIANS RELATIVE TO THEIR COLONY AT NAUPAKTOS, CA. 460 B.C. IG, IX, 334; SEG, XV, 353; Meiggs - Lewis, GHI, no. 20. On the meaning of Fοικιάται in lines 43-45, cf. R. v. Compernolle, ASNP (1976) 352, with note 68; cf. also H. Heinen, ANCSOC 7 (1976) 131.

---

640. CHALEION, COVENANT BETWEEN CHALEION AND OIANTHEA, CA. MIDDLE 5th CENT. B.C. IG, IX, 1^2, 717; cf. SEG, XXIV, 393. S. Cataldi, A proposito del πρόξενος di IG, IX, 1^2, 717, ASNP (1976) 401-409 discusses the meaning of πρόξενος in this text.

---

641. CHALEION, DEDICATION TO APOLLO, 550-525 B.C. ? For Jeffery, LSAG, p. 106 and 375, no. 17 (plate 15; SEG, XVI, 336) (Jeffery attributes the inscription to Opountian Lokris), cf. C. Gallavotti, HELIKON, 15-16 (1975-76) 78-79.

ITHAKE

---

642. ITHAKE, EPITAPH FOR EUTHYDAMOS, 3rd CENT. B.C. (?). IG, IX, 1, 658; Peek, GV, I, 102. Cf. D.L. Page, WS 10 (1976) 173-174 who presents the text (in mixed meter) with commentary.

THESSALY

---

643. EPITAPHS FROM THESSALY. B. Lorenz, Thessalische Grabgedichte vom 6. bis zum 4. Jahrhundert v. Chr. (Comm. Aenipontanae XXII; 1976) lavishly comments upon 29 epitaphs from Thessaly (IG, IX, 2, 251, 255, 270, 420, 427, 1209; SEG, II, 358; XVI, 380;

XXIII, 410, 433, 434, 453; XXV, 667, 668; Peek, GV, I, 77, 168, 176, 418, 942, 1230, 1252; plus 8 epigrams transmitted by literary sources).

---

644. AZOROS, MANUMISSION RECORD, 18-17 B.C. IG, IX, 2, 1296; W. Rensch, De manumissionum titulis apud Thessalos (Halle, 1908) 97 and 116; A.M. Woodward, JHS 33 (1913) 325-328; A.S. Arvanitopoulos, AE (1913) 173-174 and AE (1923) 126-132; S.B. Kougeas, AE (1945-1947) 110-111, no. 59; A. Babacos, Actes d' aliénation en commun d' après le droit thessalien ancien (Athens, 1961) 85 and 224-227. B. Helly, PHOENIX, 30 (1976) 143-158 compares the different editions of this text and proposes a new reading of lines 31-33, which he subsequently uses for the restoration of two other manumission texts (cf. no. 670 and 689). His text runs as follows:

γεγονυῖαν εὐάρεστον ἀφῆκαν ἐλευθέραν δωρεὰν
μὴ πείπτουσαν ὑπὸ τοὺ<ς> τῶν ἀπελευθέρω<ν>
[ν]όμους ἑτέρῳ μηθενὶ κατὰ μηθένα τρόπον· ἔδωκε
[δὲ καὶ] τῇ πόλει κτλ.

δο[ῦσαν]|[31][τὰ λύτρα διὰ τὴ]ν ὑπὸ τούτων ἀπελευθέρω[σιν]|[32] [προσήκουσαν μηθ]ενὶ κατὰ μηθένα τρόπον κτλ. IG, Rensch, Arvanitopoulos (with δοῦ|σαν λύτρον instead of δοῦσαν τὰ λύτρα); δωρεὰν|[31] μὴ πείπτουσαν ὑπὸ τούτων ἀπελευθέρως|[32]υμ(?) οὐδ' ἑτέρῳ μηθενὶ κατὰ μηθένα τρόπον Kougeas; μὴ πείπτουσαν <διὰ τὴν> ὑπὸ τούτων ἀπελευθέρωσ[ιν]|[32]ὁμοῦ {σ} ἑτέρῳ μηθενὶ κατὰ μηθένα τρόπον Babacos

---

645. DEMETRIAS, HONORARY EPIGRAM FOR EUSTATHIA, CA. 400 A.D. White marble slab, found in a late 4th cent. A.D. basilica. Ed. pr. C. Habicht, in V. Milojcic - D. Theocharis, Demetrias I (1976) 199-203 (ph.).

ὦ ξίνε, μὴ θαύμαζε, τίς μερόπων ἐν|θάδε κῖτε. |
ἑστὶ γὰρ Εὐσταθία μου, ἣν | πᾶς βροτῶν οἶδε, τίς ἑστιν. |
ἰ δὲ κὲ σὺ γνῶνε θέλις, τίς γένος | ἢ πόθεν ἦδε· |
ἐστὶν ἐξ 'Εακίδου, οὗ γένος ἐστὶ | τὸ πρῶτον, |
ἥντινα μοίρῃ ἐμῇ παρέδωκα | τῷδε τῷ τύμβῳ |
Θηρολέτης ἐγὼ ἓξ ἔτεσι μίνας | σὺν αὐτῇ. |
σπεύδω δὲ κἀγὼ πῆδα τὸν κοινὸν | ἐξαναθρέψας |
βένιν πρὸς αὐτὴν ἐωνίῳ οἴκῳ | συνκαταμίνας. |
ἡδύτερον γὰρ τούτου οὔκ ἐ|στίν τι, ὡς αὐτὸς οἶδας, |
ἐωνίῳ οἴκῳ συνοικῆσε κὲ | νικῆσε Μοίρην.

1. ξένε, κεῖται || 3. εἰ, καὶ, γνῶναι, θέλεις || 4. Αἰακίδου || 6. μείνας || 7. παῖδα || 8. βαίνειν, αἰωνίῳ, συγκαταμείνας || 10. αἰωνίῳ, συνοικῆσαι, καὶ, νικῆσαι. This seems to be a Christian epigram (in view of the find-spot, the name Eustathia and the con-

tents of LL. 9-10) Habicht.

---

646. DEMETRIAS (DAMOKRATIA-BASILIKA), DEDICATION OF A PRIESTESS, 3rd-4th CENT. A.D. Greyish white marble dedicatory relief to Atargatis. Ed. pr. V. von Graeve, *Demetrias I* (1976) 145-156 (with explanation of the figures in the relief) (ph.).

[..7-8...ἱ̣ερ]ητεύσασα Παρθέν[ωι]

Παρθένωι: Atargatis von Graeve.

647-665. DEMETRIAS (PALACE), AMPHORA-STAMPS. Ed. pr. F. Henniger, *Demetrias I* (1976) 128-132 (ph.). No. 647-655: stamps from Thasos; no. 656-659: from Rhodos; no. 660-663: "Parmeniskosgroup", Northern Greece; no. 664: Knidos; no. 665: Kos.

---

647. P. 128, no. 165; 4th-3rd cent. B.C.

[Θα]σίων | Δ̣Α̣Ι | Αἴσχρων

---

648. P. 128, no. 166; ca. 200 B.C.

[Ἡρακλεί]δης | [Θασ]ίων

---

649. P. 129, no. 167; 1st half 3rd cent. B.C.

[Θασί]ων | monogram | [Ναύ]πλιος

---

650. P. 129, no. 168; late 3rd cent. B.C.

Ν̣ι̣καγόρας | Θ̣α̣σ̣[ίων]

---

651. P. 129, no. 169; late 3rd/early 2nd cent. B.C.

Θ̣ασίω[ν] | Ν̣ύ̣μφι[ς]

---

652. P. 129, no. 170; 3rd/early 2nd cent. B.C.

[ ] |]̣̣[| [Σκύ]μ̣ν̣ο̣ς̣

---

653. P. 129, no. 171; 3rd/early 2nd cent. B.C.

[Θασίων] | Σι̣ | [Φι]λ̣ο̣νίδνς

---

654. P. 130, no. 172; 4th/early 3rd cent. B.C.

[Θασί]ων | [ ]

---

655. P. 130, no. 173.
Θασί̣ω̣ν̣ | traces of letters

---

656. P. 130, no. 174.

The stamp is a monogram of the name Βούθη-ρος V. Grace

---

657. P. 130-131, no. 175; 4th-3rd cent. B.C.
[Σω]τήριχος

---

658. P. 131, no. 176; late 4th-1st half 3rd cent. B.C.
Not legible

---

659. P. 131, no. 177; 3rd cent. B.C.
--]γε | --]ου

---

660. P. 131, no. 178.
Ἡγη̣|σίνο[υ]

---

661. P. 131, no. 179.
Μικί|ωνος

---

662. P. 131, no. 180; end 3rd/early 2nd cent. B.C.
Παρμε|νίσκου

---

663. P. 132, no. 181.
Παρμε|νίτου

---

664. P. 132, no. 182; 200-175 B.C.
Κνίδιον [Νι]|κασι̣β̣ο̣ύ̣λ̣ο̣υ̣

---

665. P. 132, no. 183.
ΔΑΓ[ ]

666-669. DEMETRIAS (ANAKTORON), AMPHORA-STAMPS. Ed. pr. I. Beyer - V. von Graeve - U. Sinn, Demetrias I (1976) 71 (ph.).

---

666. P. 71, no. 39.

[Θα]σίων | [Δημ]άλκης

---

667. P. 71, no. 40.

Ἡρακλείδης | Θασίων

---

668. P. 71, no. 41.

[Φιλίσκ]ος

---

669. P. 71, no. 42; forms part of the "Parmeniskosgroup", Northern Greece.

Δημο|τίμου

---

670. DOLICHE, MANUMISSION RECORD, 2nd HALF 2nd CENT. B.C. SEG, XXIII, 462. B. Helly, PHOENIX 30 (1976) 147-149 studied the squeeze of this inscription made by the first editor A.S. Arvanitopoulos, and provides a completely changed text:

[1a] [Στρατηγοῦντος τῶν Θεσσαλῶν]
[1b] [Πετραίου τοῦ Φιλ]οξενίδου, μη-
[νὸς -------------]ου εἰκάδι· Εὔτυ-
[χος ------------- ὁ πρεσ]βύτερος Ἀλέ-
[ξανδρον τὸν ἑαυτοῦ] δουλεῖον παιδά-
[ριον ἀφῆκεν ἀπελεύθε]ρον δωρεὰν κατὰ
[τὸν νόμον· παραμενέτω] δὲ Ἀλέξανδρο[ς]
[παρὰ Εὔτυχον ποιῶν] τὸ ἐπιτασσόμε-
[νον ἕως ἂν ζῇ Εὔτυχ]ος· ὅταν δὲ [τε]-
[λευτήσῃ Εὔτυχος, ἐξέστω Ἀ]λεξάνδρῳ καὶ
[...........οἰκῆσαι] καὶ κτ[η]σ[άσθ]αι
[χρήματα ....κ]αὶ μὴ ὄντι
[..................καὶ] τοῖς κληρονό-
[μοις Εὐτύχου μὴ πί]πτοντι κατὰ
[μηδένα τρόπον ὑπὸ τ]ὸν τῶν ἀπελευ-
[θέρων νόμον· κοινοξεν]οδόκοι ταγὸς Εὐ-
.....................Α, ἰδιοξενοδόκο[ι]
.....................μάχου, Ἀρναῖος
.....................ήδης Ἀρναίου·
[ἔδωκε δὲ καὶ τῇ πό]λει στα(τῆρας) ιε.

13-15. The restoration of these lines is suggested by Helly's new reading of IG, IX, 2, 1296, lines 31-33. Cf. no. 644.

---

671. GONNOI, EPITAPH, 1st-2nd CENT. A.D. B. Helly, Gonnoi, II, Les inscriptions, no. 288. G. Daux, BCH 100 (1976) 228-229 reads in L. 2-3 γυν|ὴ δὲ Γλαύκου (instead of Helly's γυν[ὴ] | ἡ Γλαύκου).

672-676. LARISSA, DOCUMENTS CONCERNING THE REGISTRATION OR ALIENATION OF LANDED PROPERTY IN LARISSA, 200-190 B.C. White marble stele, inscribed on both sides. The inscription on the front is no. A, the inscription on the back (no. B) is only partially preserved. Ed. pr. C. Habicht, in V. Milojcic - D. Theocharis, Demetrias I (1976) 157-173 (ph.). In the same article Habicht (re)publishes four fragments (with app. crit.) which are parts of the same or of another similar and contemporary stele (C, D, E and F). F is unpublished and joins E at the right. Previous ideas about the joining of D and E have to be abandoned. It is not certain that C-F belong to one and the same stele, let alone that they belong to A.

---

672. P. 157-159, A.

--------------------]ΛΞ
[-----------]Θ..6...ΑΡ.ΑΙΕΙΑ πέλε-
[θρα...9.....πελ]εθραίας πέμπε v.v. ΙΠΠΡΟΙΟΥΛΚΙΑΣ
[....ca 13.....]ικλεία πέλεθρα ἑκατόν v.v. Εὐρυδάμα
[Εὐρυκλειαί]α πέλεθρα διεικάτια πεμπείκοντα v.v. Θέρ-
[σου]ν Θερσουνίδαιος πέλεθρα πεμπείκοντα v.v. Θρασ̣[ύ]-
[βο]υλος Μελάνταιος πέλεθρα ἑκατόν v.v. Κλεαρίστα Ν[...]
[..]λεία πέλεθρα πεμπείκοντα v.v. Γόργιππος Ξανθί̣[π]-
[π]ειος πέλεθρα πεμπείκοντα v.v. Ἄρχιππος Αὐτοβού[λει]-
ος πέλεθρα ἑκατὸν τράκοντα δύα, πελεθραίας ἕττα v.
Δαμοσθένεις Δαμόταιος πέλεθρα πεμπείκοντα v.v. [Νι]-
κοκράτεις Εὐβούλειος πέλεθρα δεκαέξε, πελεθραί̣α̣[ς]
ὄττου v.v. Εὐρυδάμα Εὐρυκλειαία πέλεθρα πεμπείκο[ν]-
τα v.v. ὀργάδας Αἰσίμα Δαμοφιλ[ε]ιαία πέλεθρα πεμ[πεί]-
κοντα v.v. Ἀγείτουρ Εὐβιότειος πέλεθρα πεμπείκοντ[α v.v.]
[Σά]τυρος Θεμιστοκλέαιος πέλε[θ]ρα πεμπείκοντα [v.v. ....]
Ἀπολλ...αία πέλεθρα δέκα v.v. Μόλυκκος Ἀμέναιος
πέλεθρα ἐ[κ]ατονέξε v.v. Θε[ί]βα..3-4ρουνεία πέλεθρα
πεμ[π]εικονταέν, πελεθραίας πέμπε v.v. Τα[.......]
Βουχίλαιος πέλεθρα πεμπείκοντα v.v. Ἱπποκράτ[εις]
[Ἀ]μφίαιος πέλεθρα ἰκατιπέμπε v.v. Φ̣α̣νοδίκα Θαυ[μ]α̣ρε̣-
[τ]εία πέλεθρα ἰκατιπέμπε v.v. Φιλῖνος [Φ]ιλίππειος [πέ]-
λεθρα ἰκατιπέμπε v.v. Ἀγεῖτορ.δασ..τόρειο[ς πέ]-
λεθρα ἰκατιπέμπε v.v. Φιλῖνος Φιλίππειος πέλεθρα
πεμπείκοντα, πελεθραίας ἐννέα v.v. ..ΛΚ̣ΙΑΣ[....]
γαξ Πτολεμαίειος πέλεθρα διε[ι]κάτια̣ ἰκατιπέμπε v.
σύμπαν λυκκάβοι· πέλεθρα [τρ]ακισχίλια ἑξείκατι ἐ-
νενείκοντα ἐννέα, πελεθραίας δύας, καπβολαία[ς δύ]-
ας v. ΑΜΟΥΛΛΟΥΝΜΕΓΑΚ.ΛΤ.Σ v.v. Φειδόλαος Τιμολε̣όν-
τειος πέλεθρα πεμπείκοντα v.v. Φιλοποιμενίδας Ἀ̣ν̣-

τίσκειος πέλεθρα πετρακονταεττά, πελεθραίας ἕξε v.
Σούστρατος Πυρρίχειος πέλεθρα δέκα v.v. Βορχίδας [..]
[.]ίππειος πέλεθρα δεκαέξε, πελεθραίας ἕξε, καπβολα[ί]-
[α]ς ἕξε v.v. Γλαυκίας Ἀρχίαιος πέλεθρα ἑτξεμείκοντα v.
Ἐμπεδίουν Οἰνίχειος πέλεθρα ἑκατὸν ἐξεικονταέν v.v.
ΛΑΛΛΕΥΣ v.v. Ἀγεισίπολις Ἀντιγένειο[ς] πέλεθρα δέ[κα],
πελεθραίας ἐννέα, καπβολαίας πέμπε v.v. Ἄλκιππος
Μέννειος πέλεθρα πεμπεικονταέν, πελεθραίας ὄττο[υ v.]
Ἀστόδαμος Ἀντιπύλειος πέλεθρα δεκαεννέα, πελεθρ[αί]-
ας ἐννέα v.v. Δαμαινέτα Ἀλευαία πέλεθρα δέκ[α......],
πελεθραίας δύας v.v. Εὐστρατίδας Πυθ[....]ειος πέλε-
θρα πετρακονταπέμπε, πελεθραί[α]ς πέμπε v.v. 2-3έουν
Κροτάτειος πέλεθρα ἕξε, πελεθραίας πέτρα[ς] v.v. .Σ.Υ..
τεις Κρατίνειος πέλεθρα ἑκατονεττά, πελεθραίας ὄττο[υ v.]
Ἀνθρούπινας Σουκλέαιος πέλεθρα δεκαέξε, καπβολαία[ς]
πέμπε v.v. Ἀμφίλοχος Φιλοξενίδαιος πέλεθρα πέμ- v.
πε v.v. Μικίνας Ἀστιούνειος πέλεθρα ἰκατιέν v.v. Παρμεί-
[δ]εις Εὐφορβίδαιος πελεθραίας τρεῖς v.v. Μνασίμαχος [..]
[1-2]γθειος πέλεθρα ἐττά, πελεθραίας πέμπε v. Δαμαινέ[τα]
[Ἀλευαία] πέλεθρα δέκα v.v. Νείκουν Ἀμύνταιος πέλεθρον ἕν,
[πελεθραί]ας ἐννέα v.v. Ἄλκιππος Μέγγειος πέλεθρα ἑκατόν.
[...9-10...]ταιος Ἀλεξάνδρειος πέλεθρα δεκαδύα v. Πο[..]
[..ca.12-13...]ια πέλεθρα τρακονταεττά, πελεθραίας ἐν-
[νέα v.v. -----------------Αἰ]νεσσάδαιος πέλε[θρα]
[---------------------------] πέλεθρα [-----]
----

11. Perhaps Δαμο[ί]ταιος Habicht || 25. [ΙΟΥ]ΛΚΙΑΣ or [ΟΥ]Λ ΚΙΑΣ (cf. L. 3) Habicht || 41. Πυθ[ούν]ειος, Πυθ[οδώρ]ειος, or Πυθ[ονίκ]ειος Habicht.

673. P. 159, B.

--------------------Πυρρε--
--------------------ΠΙΚΡΛΥ--
--------------------τρατος Εὐμ--
--- πελ[------------]α πέλεθρα--
[πέλεθρ]α πέμπε [--- πέλεθρ]α ὄττου--

674. P. 159-160, C (= IG, IX, 2, 1014).

[------πέλε]θρα [------------]
[------πελ]εθραίας, πέμπ[ε---------]
[---ἐτ]τά, πελεθραίας [---------------]
[------πέλεθ]ρα ἰκατιεννέα [--------------]
[------]ε v.v. Δίκαιος Κρο[--------------]
[------] πέμπε v.v. Σ[-----------------]
[------]ΠΒΑΣΑ[-----------------]

8 [---------]Μ[--------------------]
----

5. [πέμπ]ε̣ or [ἕξ]ε̣ Habicht

675. P. 160-161, D (= SEG, XIII, 395; BCH, 98, 1974, 251, L. 21-34).

---------------------ΕΥΣ-----------------
.̣.̣²ας v. v. Δαμαινέτα Ἀλευαία πέλ[εθρα-, πελεθραίας-, καπβο- λαί]-
ας ἐννέα v.v. Δαμαινέτα Ἀλευαία πε̣[λεθρα-, πελεθραίας-, καπ- βο]-
4 λ̣αίας ἑττά v.v. Καιριμένεις Ἀστοκράτει[ος πέλεθρα-, πελεθραίας]
πέτταρας v.v. Σουίδας Πιθούνειος πέλεθρα[-v.v. ὁ δεῖνα τοῦ δεῖ- νος πέλε]-
θρα τρά, πελεθραίας τρεῖς v.v. Ἀνθρούπινας [Σουκλέαιος πε]-
λεθραίας πέμπε, καπβολαίας τρεῖς v.v. Νικ[---------πέλεθρα δε]-
8 καδύα, πελεθραίας ἑττά, καπβολαίας [------------------]
ος πέλεθρα τρά, πελεθραίας πέτταρας, [καπβολαίας-v.v. ὁ δεῖνα]
λεμος Νεόσσειος πέλεθρα τρά, πελεθρ[αίας-v.v. ὁ δεῖνα τοῦ δεῖ- νος]
πέλεθρα τρά, πελεθραίας πέτταρας, [καπβολαίας-v.v. ὁ δεῖνα Ἐ]-
12 πιγένειος πέλεθρα δέκα v.v. Εὐστρ̣[ατίδας Πυθ....ειος πέλεθρα-,]
πελεθραίας πέμπε, καπβολαίας ὅ[ττου v.v. -------------]
[-------------] Εὐστρατίδας Π[υθ....ειος ----------------]
----

7. Perhaps Νικ[οκράτεις Εὐβούλειος] (cf. A, L. 11-12) or Νί- κ[αιος Πουτάλειος] (cf. F, L. 4) Habicht.

676. P. 161, EF (E = SEG, XIII, 394 and BCH, 98, 251, L. 1-20; F =unpublished fragment, joining E at the right).

.̣.̣²πέλεθρα ἐννέα, πελεθ[ριαίας-, καπβολαίας-v.v. ὁ δεῖνα]
θουν Ἀγαθανόρειος πέλεθρα [-, πελεθριαίας-, καπβολαίας-v. ὁ δεῖνα]
νος Μνασιμάχειος φρατρικὰ πέλεθρα [ἕ]ξε, πελεθρ̣[ιαίας πέτ]-
4 ταρας, καπβολαίας πέτταρας v.v. Θέουν Ἀγαθανόρειος πέλεθρα[-,]
πελεθριαίας πέμπε v.v. Ἀντιγ[ε]γ̣εία Ἀστοφυλιδ[α]ία πέλε̣θ̣ρα πέ[τ]-
ταρα, πελεθριαῖον ἕν, καπβολα[ί]ας ἐννέα v.v. Νίκαιος Πουτάλει- [ος]
πέλεθρα ἐννέα, πελεθριαίας πε̣μπε v.v. Θεόδοτος Ἀθαναγόραιος [πέ]-
8 λεθρα πέτταρα v.v. Κρατίδας Ἀγτιμάχειος πέλεθρα ἐννέα v.v. Κρ̣[α]-
τίδας Ἀντιμάχειος πέλεθρα̣ πέτταρα, πελεθριαίας [ὅ]ττου, κα[π]-

βολαίας ἔξε v.v. Γέννaιος Σειμία[ιο]ς πέλεθρα ἐττά, πελεθριαίας τρε[ῖς].
Μελιννοῦ Λυσιππεία πέλεθρα τ[ρά v.v.].Β...ς Δαμο[φ]ιλίδαιος πέλε-
θρα τρά, πελεθριαίας π///έμπε, κα[π]βολαίας δύας v.v. Ῥάδιο[ς] Εὐνόμ[ει]-
ος πέλεθρα δεκαέν, πελεθριαίας [...], καπβολαίας έννέα v.v. Ἀ-γησ[α]-
ρέτα Κλεομαχιδαί///α πέλεθρα δέ[κα v.v. ..]ατου Ἀριστ....ν
πέλεθρα πέμπε, πελεθριαίας πέμ[πε v.v.].ιστου Ἀριστομ..α π[έ]-
λεθρα τρά v.v. Κόττις Νικοκρατεία πέ[λεθρα ...], πελεθριαίας [-, καπ]-
βολαίας ἔξε v.v. Ἀστομάχα Νικου[νεία πέ]λεθρα τρά, πε[λεθρι-αίας πέτ]-
ταρας, καπβολαίας ἔξε v.v. Θεοζοτ[----------------------]
δρεσσιδας v. Εὐρ[--------------------------καπβο]-
λαίας δύας [-----------------------------]

Date: perhaps EF is younger than A-D Habicht || 2. perhaps Θ<έ>ουν (cf. L. 4) Habicht.

677. LARISSA, DECREE OF PEPARETHOS FOR JUDGES FROM LARISSA, 2nd CENT. B.C. White marble stele, now in the Museum of Larissa. Ed. pr. A. Giovannini, Demetrias I (1976) 205-213.

Ἐπειδὴ ἀσυντελέστου γενομέν[η]ς [τ]ῆ[ς δι]κα<ιο>νομίας
ἐν τῷ παρεληλυθότι χρόνῳ ὁ δ[ῆ]μος σπεύδων ὑπὲρ
[τ]ῆς πρὸς ἀλλήλους δικαιοδοσίας, [περί] τε τῶν ἕλκο-
μένων ἐνκλημάτων ἐκ τ[οῦ] ὑπεράνω χρόνου καὶ
[τ]ῆς ἐκ τούτων ὑπαρχούσης πρὸς αὐτοὺς διαφορᾶς, ὁ-
μοίως δὲ καὶ περ[ὶ] τῶν ἀμφι[σ]βητουμένων παρ' αὐτοῖς
κατὰ τὰς ἀπογραφὰς τὰ[ς] γεγενημένας περὶ τῶν ὑπαρ-
[χ]όντων δι' ὧν ἕ[κ]αστος τὰ ἑαυτοῦ ....ΕΩΣΕΝ
.Γ ΗΙ ΟΧΙ Ι Ι ἐψηφίσατο μεταπέμψασ[θ]αι [δ]ικαστήριον [ὑπὲρ]
τοῦ γενέσθαι τῶν διασαφουμένων τὴν διεξαγωγὴν
κατὰ τὸ κάλ<λ>ιστον καὶ προκρίνας τὸν Λαρισαίων δῆμον
[ὄ]ντα ἑαυτοῦ συνγενῆ καὶ φίλον ἔπεμψεν πρὸς αὐτὸν
[ψ]ήφισμά τε καὶ πρεσβευ[τὴν] Τιμοκράτην Χρέμητος, ἄν-
δρα καλὸν κἀγαθὸν τῶν τιμωμένων παρ' ἡμῖν τόν τά τε
γράμματα ἀποδώσοντα καὶ διαλεγησόμενον ἀκολο[ύ]-
[θ]ως τοῖς ἐν τῷ ψηφίσματι κατακεχωρισμένοις, ὁ δὲ δῆμος
[ὁ] Λ[αρι]σαίων ἀκούσας τὰ ὑπὸ τοῦ πρεσβευτοῦ παρακαλού-
[μ]εν[α, π]ρὸ παντὸς [δὲ] θέμενος τὸ καλῶς ἔχον καὶ τὴν Η
.....ΑΝ συνγένειάν τε καὶ φιλίαν προτιμήσας, τόν τε
[πρ]εσβευτὴν ἀπεδέξατο φιλοφρόνως καὶ ἐξαπέστει-
[λε]ν δικαστὰς τῶν ἐν [τ]ιμ[ῇ] καὶ δόξῃ καθεστώτων Πάνδο-
[κ]ον Ἀλκότα, Διογένην [Δ]ημητρίου, καὶ γραμματέα Ἡρα-

[κ]λείδην Σωτίωνος ἄνδρας καλοὺς καὶ ἀγαθοὺς τῶν τι-
[μωμένων παρ' αὐτοῖς κ]αὶ πιστευομένων, ἀξίους τῆς τε
[ἐ]α[υτῶ]ν πατρ[ίδος καὶ τῆ]ς ἡμετέρας πόλεως, οἵτινες παρα-
[γ]ενό[με]νο[ι καὶ περὶ πλ]είστου ποιησάμενοι τήν τε πρὸς τοὺς
[..............καὶ] τὴν τῶν ἡμετέρων νόμων τήρησιν
....Λ...............Ε^{D}Ο. τὸ δίκαιον, ἀδωροδοκήτους
[δὲ ἑαυτοὺς πᾶσι π]αρεχόμενοι τοῖς εἰς τὸ δικαστήριον εἰσ-
[αχθεῖσι(ν) ἀπέδειξαν? τ]ὴν [ἑαυ]τῶν ἀρετὴν καὶ τὴν ἐν τούτοις
[δικαιοσύνην, οὔτε πόνον οὔτε κ]ακοπάθιαν ἐκκλίνοντες, ἐκτε-
[νῶς καὶ φιλοτίμως τὴν δικαστείαν? δια]καρτεροῦντες, ἕνε-
[κεν τοῦ συλλυθέντων πάντων] τῶν ἐχόντων τὰ ἐνκλήματα
[πρὸς ἑαυτοὺς ἐκ τῆς] προυπαρχούσης διαφορᾶς εἰς ὁμόνοι-
[αν τὴν πόλιν ἀποκαταστῆ]σαι· καὶ π[ερ]ὶ ὧν ἔδει διαλαβεῖν αὐ-
[τοὺς ἐνκλημάτων, περί] τε τῶν δανείων καὶ τῶν ἄλλων πάντων,
[ἔκριναν? ἐ]πί τε [τῷ συν]φέροντι κα<ὶ> τὸ βέλτιστον πρὸ ὀφθαλ-
[μῶν ποιοῦμενοι τοῖς] Πεπ[αρ]ηθίοις κατὰ κοινὸν τυχικῆι
[........· τοῖς δὲ] πάντω[ς].ΓΙ..Ι.ΟΜΕΝΟΙΣ κρίσεως ἐδίκα-
[σαν τὰς δίκας ὀρθ]ῶς καὶ δικαίως κατὰ τοὺς νόμους, τήν τε
[παρεπιδημίαν ἐποιήσαντο π]αρ' ἡμῖν μετὰ πάσης εὐταξίας
[καὶ εὐσχημοσύνης, ἀξίους] τῶ[ν] τε ἀποστειλάντων αὐτούς, ἀξί-
[ους δὲ καὶ τῆς ἡμετέρας πόλ]εως· ὅπως οὖν καὶ ὁ ἡμέτερος δῆ-
[μος πρωτεύων φαίνηται ἐν] χα[ρί]τος ἀποδόσει, τιμῶν δὲ τοὺς κα-
[λοὺς κἀγαθοὺς ἄνδρας ταῖς ἀξίαι]ς τιμαῖς· ἐπ' ἀγαθῇ τυχῇ καὶ σω-
[τηρίᾳ ἀμφοτέρων τῶν πόλεων,] δεδόχθαι τῆι βουλῇ καὶ τῷ δήμῳ
[τῶν Πεπαρηθίων· ἐπαινέσαι μ]ὲν τὸν δῆμον τὸν Λαρισαίων ἐπὶ τῇ
[προυπαρχούσῃ πρὸς τὸν ἡμ]έτερον δῆμον εὐνοίᾳ καὶ ἐπὶ τῷ
[πέμψαι δικαστὰς καὶ γραμματέ]α ἄνδρας καλοὺς καὶ ἀγαθούς, ἀ-
[ξίους ἀμφοτέρων τῶν πόλεων] καὶ τῆς ἐπ' ἀγαθῷ μνήμης ἐπιτη-
[δείους ὄντας, καὶ στεφαν]ῶ[σ]α[ι αὐ]τὸν στεφάνῳ χρυσῷ καὶ εἰ-
[κόνι χαλκῇ· γενέσθαι δὲ τὴν ἀναγόρ]ευσιν· ὁ δῆμος ὁ Πεπαρηθίων
[στεφανοῖ τὸν δῆμον τὸν Λαρισαίων στ]εφάνῳ χρυσῷ καὶ εἰκόνι χαλκῇ
[ἐπὶ τῇ προυπαρχούσῃ συνγενείᾳ καὶ φιλίᾳ,] ἐπί τε τῇ ἐξαποστολῇ τῶν
[δικαστῶν καὶ τοῦ γραμματέως· στεφανῶσαι] δὲ ἐν τῷ αὐτῷ καιρῷ καὶ
[τοὺς δικαστὰς Πάνδοκον Ἀλκό]τα, [Δι]ο[γ]ένην Δημητρίου ἑκάτερον αὐ-
[τῶν στεφάνῳ χρυσῷ ἀρετῆς ἕνεκεν] καὶ δικαιοσύνης καὶ τῆς πρὸς
[τὸν ἡμέτερον δῆμον εὐνοίας· στεφαν]ῶσαι δὲ καὶ τὸν γραμματέα Ἡρα-
[κλείδην Σωτίωνος τῷ κιττοῦ σ]τεφάνῳ τῷ πατρίῳ τοῦ θεοῦ ἐπὶ τῷ
[παρεισχῆσθαι ἑαυτὸν κατὰ τὴν χρ]είαν ἐκτενῆ καὶ φιλότιμον· δε-
[δόσθαι δὲ αὐτοῖς καὶ ἐκγόνοις] προξενίαν καὶ ἔνκτησιν γῆς καὶ
[οἰκίας καὶ πρόσοδον πρὸς τὴν βο]υλὴν καὶ τὸν δῆμον πρώτοις μετὰ
[τὰ ἱερὰ καὶ Ῥωμαίους καὶ προεδρία]ν καὶ ἀ[σφ]άλειαν καὶ πολέμου καὶ
[εἰρήνης καὶ τὰ ἄλλα ὅσα καὶ τοῖ]ς̣ ἄ̣λλο̣[ις προξένοις] κ̣α̣ὶ̣ εὐ-ε̣[ργέ]-

[ταις τῆς πόλεως ἡμῶν ἐκ τῶν νόμων ὑπαρχ]ει· τῆς δὲ ἀναγορεύσεως
[τῶν στεφάνων ἐπιμελείσθωσαν οἱ] ἄ[ρ]χοντες οἱ κατ' ἐνιαυτὸν γι-
[νόμενοι καὶ τῶν ἄλλων τιμῶν τῶν] ἐψηφισμένων τῷ τε δήμῳ τῷ
[Λαρισαίων καὶ τοῖς δικασ]τ[αῖ]ς τ[οῖ]ς ἐξαποσταλεῖσι ὑπ' αὐτῶν καὶ τῷ
[γραμματεῖ· καλεσάτωσαν] δὲ αὐτοὺς καὶ εἰς τὸ πρυτανεῖον ἐπὶ
[ξένια ἐπὶ τὴν κοινὴν ἑστίαν· ὅ]πως δὲ καὶ Λαρισαῖοι παρακολου-
[θήσωσι τὰς ἐψηφισμένας τι]μὰ[ς] τῷ τε δήμῳ αὐτῶν καὶ τοῖς δικασ-
[ταῖς καὶ τῷ γραμματεῖ, δε]δόχθαι γράψαι περὶ τούτων τοὺς πολε-
[μάρχους τοῖς ταγοῖ]ς [κ]αὶ τῇ πόλει τῇ Λαρισαίων ὑποτάξαντ<α>ς
[τοῦδε τοῦ ψηφίσματος τὸ] ἀν[τί]γραφον καὶ σφραγισαμένους τῇ δη-
[μοσίᾳ σφραγῖδι καὶ δοῦναι] τ[οῖ]ς δικασταῖς ὅπως διὰ τούτων διακο-
[μίσηται· γράψαι δὲ καὶ δι]ότ[ι] παρ[α]καλεῖ ὁ δῆμος ὁ Πεπαρηθίων
[αὐτοὺς τόν τε στέφανον καὶ τὰς] ἐψηφισμένας τιμὰς ἀποδέξασ-
[θαι καὶ ἀναγράψαι τόδε τὸ ψήφισμα ε]ἰς στηλὴν λιθίνην καὶ ἀναθεῖναι
[ἐν τῷ ἐπιφανεστάτῳ τόπῳ·] φροντίσαι δὲ καὶ τοὺς ταγοὺς μετὰ τοῦ ἀ-
[γωνοθέτου ὅπως ἐν τοῖς] πρώτοι[ς] Διονυσίοις μετὰ τὸ συντελεσθ[ῆ]-
[ναι τὰς σπονδὰς καὶ παρ' αὐτοῖς] ἀ[ν]αγορευθῶσιν ἐν τῷ θεάτρῳ αἵδε
[αἱ ἐψηφιμέναι τιμαὶ τῷ τε δήμ]ῳ αὐτῶν καὶ τοῖς δικασταῖς καὶ τῷ γραμ-
[ματεῖ· παρακαλέσαι δὲ καὶ εἰ]ς τὸν λοιπὸν χρόνον διατηρεῖν τὴν πρου-
[πάρχουσαν ταῖς πόλεσι πρ]ὸς ἑαυτὰς συνγένειάν τε καὶ φιλίαν καὶ εὔ-
[νοιαν· ἐπιμεληθῆναι δὲ τ]οὺς πολεμάρχους τῆς ἐξαποστολῆς τῶν
[ἀνδρῶν ὅπως ἀνακομισθῶσι με]τὰ πάσης ἀσφαλείας· ἀναγράψαι δὲ τόδε
[τὸ ψήφισμα τὸν γραμματέα τ]ῆς βουλῆς εἰς στηλὴν λιθίνην καὶ ἀνα-
[θεῖναι ἐν τῷ προνάῳ τῆς Ἀθηνᾶς τῆς] Πολιάδος ἐν τῷ ἐπιφανεστάτῳ τό-
[πῳ· τὸ <δὲ ἀνάλωμα τὸ> εἰς τὴν στηλὴ]ν γ[ε]γόμεγον καὶ τὴν ἀναγραφὴν δότω ὁ χει-
[ροτονηθεὶς ταμίας ἀπ]ὸ [τ]οῦ [κ]οινο[ῦ] ἀργυρίου.

1. Ι ΑΝΟΜΙΑΣ lap. || 11. ΚΑΛΙΣΤΟΝ lap. || 18-19. ἡ|[μέτεραν] ed. || 26. perhaps τήν τε πρὸς τοὺς [πολίτας εὔνοιαν] or τήν τε πρὸς τοὺς [θεοὺς εὐσέβειαν] Giovannini || 28. perhaps [τοῖς] δ[ιαφερομένοις προσέφ]ερο[ν] τὸ δίκαιον Giovannini || 37. ΚΑΤΟΒΕΛΤΙΣΤΟΝ lap. || 43-44. also possible is: ὅπως ... δῆ[μος μὴ λείπων φαίνηται ἐν]

Giovannini || 73. ΥΠΟΤΑΞΑΝΤΟΣ lap.

678-682. LARISSA, MINOR REMARKS ON FIVE INSCRIPTIONS. C. Habicht, in V. Milojcic - D. Theocharis, Demetrias I (1976) 164-166 makes some remarks on five inscriptions from Larissa:

---

678. P. 164. Habicht points out that in IG, IX, 2, 729 one can restore [Ξάνθ]ιππο[ς Γο]ργίππειος.

---

679. P. 164. Habicht restores in AE (1930) 176, no. 1, L. 9-10 Ἀμφίλοχος Φιλ[οξενίδου].

---

680. P. 165. Habicht refers to an unpublished dedication of the 4th cent. B.C.: Θείβα ἀνέθηκε.

---

681. P. 165. He restores in IG, IX, 2, 731 -ς Βου[χίλ]αιος.

---

682. P. 166. Habicht assigns the epitaph IG, IX, 2, 1252 to Larissa (and not to Phalanna).

---

683. MELITAIA, DEDICATION TO INO, NURSE OF DIONYSOS, 2nd HALF/ LATE 3rd CENT. B.C. Ed. pr. T.G. Spyropoulos, AD 25B (1970) 241 (ph.); J. Roux, Euripide, Les Bacchantes, II, Commentaire (Paris, 1972) 634 (text of J. Pouilloux). Cf. W. Peek, PHILOLOGUS 117 (1973) 66-69 (study of the inscription with the help of a photo taken by N.S. Koumanoudis); R. Merkelbach, ZPE 21 (1976) 36 (with ZPE 23, 1976, 60).

Σώφρων Λυσάνδρου, ἱερεύ-
οντος Λυκοίτα, τᾶι θεῶι.
Δημότις, ὦ Βάχχοιο τιθηνήτειρα, καλίη[ς]
Σώφρονος, ἀλλ' ἔμπης ὥς τις ἀπὸ κτεάνων
πολλῶν, λευκόζωνε, τόδε βρέτας ὤπασεν, Ἰν[ώ],
ὑὸς ὁ Λυσάνδρου, κεκλίμενον χάρισιν·
οὕνεκεν ὦ δέσποινα, τεὰς ἀνὰ χεῖρας ὕπερθ[εν]
οἴκου καὶ κτεάνων Σώφρονος ἀὲν ἔχο[ις].
Ξένων
Ἀριστομήδης
ἐποίησαν.

---

2. ΚΑΛΙΗ.. Spyropoulos; Καλίη Pouilloux; καλίη Peek; καλίη[ς] Merkelbach || 5. ΛΕΥΚΟΙΩΝΕ Spyropoulos; λευκόζωνε Pouilloux, Peek; λευκοῖφ <σ>ε Merkelbach || ΙΝ Spyropoulos; Ἰνοῖ Pouilloux, Ἰν[ώ]

Peek, Merkelbach || 6. κεκ<ρ>ιμένον Peek || 7. ΟΥΝ Ρ̣ΕΝ Spyropoulos || 8. ΕΧΘ[Η Spyropoulos. W. Peek suggests that the poet could be identified as Theoridas (Ant. Pal., VI, 155).

---

684. ORMINION ? (MAGNESIA), CONSTRUCTION OF A ROOF, CA. 550 B.C. ? Jeffery, LSAG, p. 97, no. 2; SEG, XVII, 287. C. Gallavotti, HELIKON 15-16 (1975-76) 107-111 studies this inscription: he changes the sequence of the lines to 3-2-1 instead of 1-2-3 and translates it as follows: "Passiada costrui la tettoia, e Androcide la istallo, sistemandola a regola d' arte mediante i perni."

---

685. PHALANNA, EPITAPH. For the epitaph IG, IX, 2, 1252, cf. no. 682.

---

686. PHERAI, LIST OF GYMNASIARCHS, CA. 216-187/6 B.C. SEG, XXV, 664. Republished by C. Habicht, in V. Milojcic - D. Theocharis, Demetrias I (1976) 181-197 (ph.). Habicht restores the prescript of the inscription as follows:

[Οἵδε οἱ αἱρεθέντες? ἀφ' οὗ Φερ]αῖοι μετ' Ἀλεξάνδροιο
[τοῖ βασιλεῖος διέβησαν εἰς] τὰν Ἀσίαν γυμνασίαρχοι·

(instead of [Φερα]ῖοι μετ' Ἀλεξάνδροιο | τὰν Ἀσίαν. Γυμνασίαρχοι given as lines 1-2 of col. II, in SEG, XXV, 664). He presents also the following corrections on the SEG-text: A, 11: [Σιμμίας ? Ἀ]μυντόρειος; A, 27: [Θ]έρσουν (instead of Θ̣έρσουν); B, 31 and 33: rasura of two letters; A, 31: Φρύνειος (instead of Φρούνειος); B, 34: Κλιόνικος (instead of Κλιονίκας); B, 35: Μεννείαιος (instead of Μεννίαιος); A, 46: Ἀσάνδρειος (instead of Ἄνδριος). Habicht shows that column A and B 3-33 were inscribed ca. 216 B.C. and that subsequent gymnasiarchs were added up to 187/6, when the list breaks down; he gives detailed prosopographical commentary.

---

687. PHERAI, FRAGMENT OF A PROXENY-DECREE, CA. 200 B.C. Ed. pr. N.I. Giannopoulos, AD 10 (1926) Παράρτημα, 52, no. 8. C. Habicht, in V. Milojcic - D. Theocharis, Demetrias I (1976) 192 points out that in L. 4/5 the correct reading is Ταγευόντων | [Ε]ὐβεία Μένωνος (instead of [Κ?]υβεία). He presents a stemma of this family.

---

688. PHILIA (NEAR KARDITSA; FEDERAL SANCTUARY OF ATHENA ITONIA), DECREE OF THE THESSALIAN LEAGUE CONCERNING AMBRAKIA, CA. 179-165 B.C. SEG, XXV, 653. After a new study of the stone, C. Habicht presents in V. Milojcic - D. Theocharis, Demetrias I (1976) 175-180 (ph.) a considerably improved text, which we give below:

[-------]......[------------]
[-------]Ν̣ΚΕΝΩΙ̣[------------]
[-------]ἐπελθόντ[ε]ς· [ὅπως δ' οὖν Θεσ]-
[σαλοὶ κατὰ δύ]ναμιν φαίνωντ[αι πρόνοιαν]
[ποιησάμενοι] τῶν ἐπαρκείας προ[σδεο]-
[μένων φί]λων, δοῦναι τῆι πόλει τῆ̣ι̣ Ἀ̣[μβρα]-
[κιωτ]ῶν δωρεὰν ἀργυρίου στατῆ̣[ρας., καθ]-
[ὼς κα]ὶ οἱ πρεσβευταὶ συνευδο[κοῦσιν· ἵνα]
[δὲ πα]ραχρῆμα ἀπολύωνται, ἔχον[τες τὸ]
[ἐπεψ]ηφισμένον ἀργύριον, ΕΠΕ/[.ca.7..]
[μὲν ἐ]πὶ τοῦ παρόντος ἐν τῶι κοινῶι [ca.5.]
[....] Τισαμενὸν τὸν στρατηγὸν ΔΙ[.ca.6.]
[...], ἐπαινέσαι δὲ καὶ Ἄλυπον καὶ τ[οὺς μετ']
[αὐτ]οῦ ἐπὶ τῆι αἱρέσει ἧ̣ ἔχουσι πρὸς Θε[σσα]-
[λοὺς] καὶ Ἀμβρακιώτας καὶ εἶναι αὐτοὺς [προ]-
[ξένου]ς τοῦ κοινοῦ Θεσσαλῶν καὶ ὑπάρχ[ειν]
[ὅσα καὶ] τοῖς ἄλλοις εὐεργέταις τίμια καὶ ἐ[ν]
[τῶι κ]οινῶι καὶ ἐν ἑκάστηι πόλει, καὶ τὸν στρατη-
[γὸν ξέ]νιά τε πέμψαι αὐτοῖς καὶ καλέσαι ἐπὶ
[τὴν θυ]σίαν τήν συντελουμένην τῆι Ἀθη[νᾶι]
[τῆι Ἰτωνία]ι καὶ τοῖς ἄλλοις θεοῖς· τόν δὲ τα-
[μίαν ἀναγρά]ψαι τὸ ψήφισμα εἰς κίονα λιθί-
[νην καὶ ἀναθεῖ]ναι εἰς τὸ ἱερὸν τῆς Ἀθη-
[νᾶς]. vacat

7. After στατῆ̣[ρας a number Habicht || 10. at the end an inf. aor. Habicht || 11-12. κοινῶι [συνεδ|ρίωι] ? Habicht.

---

689. PYTHION, MANUMISSION RECORD, 2nd HALF 2nd CENT. B.C. IG, IX, 2, 1290; W. Rensch, De manumissionum titulis apud Thessalos (Halle, 1908) 111-112; A.S. Arvanitopoulos, AE (1913) 167-168 and AE (1924) 176, no. 409. B. Helly, PHOENIX 30 (1976) 149-152 studied the squeeze of this inscription made by A.S. Arvanitopoulos and proposes the following text (with app. crit. on p. 152, which we do not repeat here):

Στρατηγοῦντο[ς .... Ὁμο]-
[λ]φου δευτέρᾳ· Ἀμ[ύντας .... Φι]-
λουμένην τὴν ἑα[υτοῦ οἰκέτιδα καὶ τὸ αὐ]-
τῆς παιδάριον ᾧ [ὄνομα .... ἀφῆ]-
κεν ἀπελευθέρ[ους δωρεὰν κατὰ τὸν]
νόμον· παραμενέ[τω δὲ Φιλουμένη παρὰ Ἀ]-
μύνταν ἕως ἂν ζ[ῇ Ἀμύντας, ποιοῦσα τὸ ἐ]-
[π]ιτασ<σ>όμενον καθ' [ὅντινα τρόπον· ὅ]-
[τ]αν δὲ τελευτήσ[ῃ Ἀμύντας, ἔστων]
Φιλουμένη τε καὶ Ε[......... ἐλεύθεροι]
οἷς καὶ ἐξέστω οἰκ[ίαν καὶ χρήματα κτᾶσ]-
θαι οὗ ἂν αἵρωνται [καὶ ....]
ᾧ ἂν βούλωνται, μ[ηδὲ τοῖς κληρονό]-

μοις τοῖς Ἀμύντου [μηδ' ἑτέρῳ μηδενὶ]
πείπτου<σι> κατὰ μηδ[ένα τρόπον ὑπὸ τὸν]
16 τῶν ἀπελευθέρω[ν νόμον· κοινοξενοδόκος]
ταγὸς Διονύσιος [........· καὶ ἔδω]-
κεν τῇ πόλει τοὺς [γινομένους στατῆ]-
ρες τριάκοντα.

13-16. The restoration of Helly is based on his new reading of IG, IX, 2, 1296 (cf. no. 644) || 19. στατῆρες instead of στατῆρας, cf. Arvanitopoulos, AE (1924) 181.

---

690. PHTIOTIC THEBES, TWO MANUMISSION RECORDS. Ed. pr. P. Lazaridis, PAAH (1972) 46-48 (reprinted in the "Chronique des fouilles en 1974" in BCH, 99, 1975, 647-650). G. Daux, BCH 100 (1976) 231 proposes the following corrections: No. 1, L. 11: Ἀντιόχην (also read by B. Helly, cf. no. 691) instead of Ἀνιόχην; No. 2, L. 16-17: Λε[ον]τίδος (or any other form confirmed by the stone) instead of Λέτιδος; L. 22: ξενικῇ (juridical term) (and not Ξενική = proper name).

---

691. PHTIOTIC THEBES, MANUMISSION RECORDS. Inscriptions on a marble orthostate partly broken at the left. At the right (after L. 4) begins another text which continued on another stone (for technical reasons we print this text under the other inscriptions). Ed. pr. P.H. Lazaridis, PAAH (1972) 45-46 (ph.) (reprinted in the "Chronique des fouilles en 1974" in BCH, 99, 1975, 647-648, no. 1). B. Helly, PHOENIX 30 (1976) 156-157 announces an exhaustive study of this inscription. In the meantime he has restudied the stone and presents the following text:

[Στρ(ατηγοῦντος)--]δου τὸ [.]· μη(νὸς) Ἀφροδεισίωνος ει'· Πολυ-
ξένα Πολυξένου ἀπηλευθέρω[σε---]
[---λαβοῦσα λ]ύτρον * σν', ἐφ' ᾧ προσμείνῃ τὸν τῆς ζωῆς αὐτῆς
χρόνον· μετὰ δὲ τ[ὴν τελεύτην αὐ]-
[τῆς ἐλεύθερον ἔστω ἀπ]ολελυμένον τῶν ἀπελευθερικῶν δικαίων.
vacat
4 [Στρ(ατηγοῦντος)] Εὐμένους· μη(νὸς) Ποσειδεῶνος ηι'· Ἄμμιον
Λύκου Ὀξωνὶς ἠλευθέρωσεν
----αντιον λαβοῦσα λύτρον, ἔχον ἐξουσίαν ἐνδημεῖν, ἀποδημεῖν
[καὶ μετοι]ḳεῖν, μηδενὶ μηδὲν προσῆκον.
[Στρατηγ]οῦντος Ἀνδριανοῦ· μη(νὸς) Ποσιδεῶνος δ'· Ζώσιμος (Ζω-
σίμου)
8 [ἠλευθέρω]σεν Ζώσιμον καὶ Λέωνα τὰ τέκνα αὐτοῦ, χρη-
[ματίζοντα δ]ὲ πατρὸς ἐμοῦ· στρα(τηγοῦντος) Νικοκράτους, ὁ αὐ-
τὸς Ζώσιμος
[ἠλευθέρω]σεν Διδύμην τὴν ἑαυτοῦ γυναῖκα καὶ τὸ ἐ-
[ξ αὐτῆς γεν]νηθὲν αὐτῷ κοράσιον Ἀντιόχην, μηδενὶ μη-
12 [δὲν προσήκ]ον[τα] μηδὲ ὑποπίπτοντα ἱς τοὺς κατὰ τῶν

[ἀπελευθέρ]ων νόμους.
14 [Στρ(ατηγοῦντος) Μενάνδ]ρου τοῦ Θείτου· μη(νὸς) Ἡρεῶνος· Ὑάκινθος (Ὑακίνθου) ἠλευθέρωσεν Α[---καὶ---]
[..9-10....λύτ]ρον λαβὼν ὑπὲρ τῆς ἐλευθερίας αὐτῶν παρὰ Κοίντου τοῦ Μ--------
[..9-10....κ]αθ' ἃ καὶ οἱ ἐκ γενετῆς πεφυκότες ἐλεύθεροι, μὴ προσήκοντα μ[ηδενὶ μηδὲν μηδὲ ὑποπίπ]-
[τοντα τοῖς ἀ]πελευθερικοῖς νόμοις.

The text at the right:

AC
AMANΔ-----
PETIK-----
Στρατ(ηγοῦντος) Ἑλλανο-
κατὰ τοὺς ν[όμους---]
ΜΕΥΠΑΥΤΙ-----
THC Ῥοῦφον ΑΓ---
P αὐτῶν ..HCEN----
IC οὓς ἂν βούλωντα[ι -νό]-
μους Μα[γ]νή[των -]

---

692. MUSEUM OF VOLOS, MANUMISSION RECORD, REIGN OF HADRIAN. Ed. B. Helly, BCH 99 (1975) 127-133. Cf. G. Daux, BCH 100 (1976) 229 who reads at the end of L. 1 of this inscription: Στρ(ατηγοῦντος) Οὐλπίου Νικομάχου, μη(νὸς) Θεμιστίου Λ̥ Δ (instead of Helly's Θεμιστίου λ'). Λ̥ Δ is λο(ιπῶν) Δ (= λοιπῶν τεσσάρων) = 27th Themistios.

EPEIROS

---

693. EPEIROS IN THE EARLY HELLENISTIC PERIOD. P. Cabanes, L'Épire de la mort de Pyrrhos à la conquête romaine (272-167) (Annales litt. Univ. Besancon, 186; Paris, 1976) provides a detailed study of the political, constitutional, social and economic history of Epeiros. In an appendix (p. 534-592) he presents 77 inscriptions, some of them unpublished before; for many texts he gives new readings. Below we present the inedita and the novae lectiones.

---

694. AMBRAKIA (ARTA), DEDICATION TO HESTIA AND ZEUS BY THE PRYTANEIS, CA. 150 B.C. SEG, XXIV, 412. P. Cabanes, Épire, p. 548, no. 19 (with further bibliography) gives the following text (ph.):

Ἐπ̣ὶ ..A---------
Φίλιππος [πρύτανις]

καὶ συνπρυτάνιε[ς] Ἑστίαι Διὶ
Κάλλων Νικοσθένεος,
Σιλανὸς Παυσῶνος,
Θράσων Κλεομήδεος,
Νίκαρχος Λεοντίσκου,
Λύκος μάντις.

1. Not mentioned in SEG || 2. Φίλιππος SEG || 3. καὶ συνπρυτάνι<ε>ς τ<ῶ>ι Διὶ SEG || 6. Κλεομίδεος SEG || 7. Λεοντισίου (perhaps Λεοντίσ̣κου ?) SEG.

---

695. BOUTHROTOS, MANUMISSION RECORD. Ed. pr. L.M. Ugolini, ALBANIA ANTIQUA 3 (1942) 117 (cf. J. and L. Robert, BE, 1948, no. 98). P. Cabanes, Épire, p. 568, no. 45 reads in L. 10 Ἀριστο[κ]λ[ε]ίαν and in L. 13 Ἐ..ράσνορος (instead of Εὐφράσνορος or Ἐτῳράσνοπος).

---

696. DODONA, GRANT OF CITIZENSHIP TO PHILISTE, 370-361 B.C. SEG, XIV, 384. For this text and especially for the problems of the function of the grant, cf. J.-M. Hannick, AC 45 (1976) 139-141.

---

697. DODONA, HONORARY DECREE OF THE MOLOSSIANS, 4th CENT. B.C (PRIOR TO 330 B.C.). SEG, XXIII, 471 and XXIV, 446. P. Cabanes, Épire, 536-539, no. 2 (ph.) studied the stone with the following results: L. 1: ΙΝΟΥΜΟΛ or ΙΙΝΟΥΜΟΝ; 4. SEG, XXIII, 471 is correct; 5. [Πεί]αλος (SEG, XXIV, 446) is correct; 6. after Υ "le bas d' une lettre verticale" which excludes [Ὀπούου]; 7. ---, Μ̣[.....Τ]| Cabanes; 8. at the end Ὀ[νοπέρνο]; 12. Τρ̣[ιπολίτ]|α ; 13. at the end --ΑΡ (and not ΑΡΧ); 16-18. [Ἀριστ]|οκλεῖ, Μονδαι[ῶι --- Ἀντ]|ιγένεος Ν[αυ]πα[κτίοις, εὐε]| ; 20. --αὐτο̣[ῖ]ν καὶ γ[ενεᾶι; 21. παντὶ Μολο[σσ]ῶι̣ κ̣[αὶ ἀτέλεια]|ν; 24-25. [π]|ολιτευομέν[οις ὑπάρχειν].

---

698. DODONA, HONORARY DECREE OF THE MOLOSSIANS, 4th CENT. B.C. (PRIOR TO 330 B.C.). Ed. pr. D. Evangelidis, EPEIROTICA CHRONICA 10 (1935) 245-247. P. Cabanes, Épire, 539-540, no. 3 reads in L. 11 [Ἀρ]κτᾶνος and in L. 14 Πεὶαλ[ος]; he cannot accept N.G.L. Hammond's restitution in L. 14-15: [βασιλέος Νεοπτολέμου] τοῦ Ἀλεξά|νδρου (N.G.L. Hammond, Epirus, Oxford, 1967, p. 564).

---

699. DODONA, DECREE OF THE MOLOSSIANS, 4th CENT. B.C. (PRIOR TO 330 B.C.). Ed. pr. P. Cabanes, Épire, 541-542, no. 6 (ph.). Cabanes restores this stone fragment as follows:

[Θεοί. Βασιλεύον]-
[τος Ἀλ]εξά[νδρου],
[ἐπὶ π]ροστά[τα Μο]-
[λοσ]σῶν Ἀρ[ιστο]-
[μά]χου Ὄμ[φαλος],
[ἐπὶ] δὲ γραμ[ματέος]
[Με]νεδά[μου Λαρ]-
[ρύ]ου ἔδ[ωκαν Μολοσ]-
[σοὶ] ἀτ[έλειαν - -]

---

700. DODONA, MANUMISSION RECORD, REIGN OF ALEXANDER I. Limestone block. Ed. pr. P. Cabanes, Épire, 588-589, no. 74 (ph.):

[Θεὸς], τύχα. Βασιλεύοντος
[Ἀλεξ]άνδρου, ἐπὶ προστάτα Μο-
λοσσῶν Θευδότου Κορωνειάτα,
γραματεύοντος (sic) δὲ Μενεδάμο[υ]
Λαρρύου, ἀφῆκε Φειδέτα Ἴνων[ος]
Κλεάνορα ἐλεύθερον καὶ μένο[ν]-
τα καὶ ἀποτράχοντα ὀπαῖ κ' αὐτὸ[ς]
προαιρῆται. Μάρτυρες· Μέγα[ς]
Σίνωνος, Ἀμύνανδρος Ἐρύξιο[ς],
Δόκιμος Ἐρύξιος, Ἀμύνανδρος
Ἴνωνος, Νικάνωρ Ἀλίποντος.

---

701. DODONA, THE EPIROTES AWARD CITIZENSHIP TO ANTIPATROS, CA. 205 B.C. Two bronze fragments. Ed. pr. P. Cabanes, Épire, 558-560, no. 34 (ph.).

[Στ]ραταγοῦντος τῶν Ἀπειρωτᾶν Δέρδ[α]
.ειράκιου, ἐπὶ δὲ τᾶς χειρὸς ἀπο[τε]-
[τ]αγμένου Π[ολ]έμωνος Ὀπαδείου,
μηνὸς Πανάμ[ου] ΚΔ, ποτιπορευ-
[θ]έντος Μενάνδρου τοῦ Θύτα καὶ ἀπολ[ο]-
[γιξ]αμένου Ἀντιπάτρωι -------Α-------
-------------ποτὶ πάντας εὐ----------
-------------ς τὰν ἀναστροφὰν πο[ιήσασθαι]
-----------τὰν πολιτείαν αὐτῶι -------

[ἀνέ]γκλητος γεγόναμε[ν] -----------
- καθ' αὐτὸν τέχνας εὐε--------------
καὶ δεδόσθαι πολιτεία[ν αὐτῶι]
[καὶ] ἐκγόνοις κατὰ τὸν νόμ[ον, δεδόσθαι]
[δὲ αὐ]τοῖ καὶ γᾶς καὶ οἰκίας ἔνκτ[ασιν καὶ]
[ἀτέλ]ειαν καὶ ἐντέλειαν καὶ τὰ ἄ[λλα τίμια]
[ὅσα καὶ] τοῖς ἄλλοις πρ[οξένοις].

5. Θύτα or θύτα ("sacrificateur") J. and L. Robert, BE (1977) no. 261 || 11-12. [ἄξιον or ἀξίως]|[τᾶς] καθ' αὐτὸν τέχνας J. and L. Robert, l.c.

702. DODONA, THE EPIROTES GIVE CITIZENSHIP TO THE ACHAIAN DAMARCHOS, BEGINNING OF THE 2nd CENT. B.C. SGDI, 1338. P. Cabanes, Épire, 553-554, no. 32 restores in L. 2 [Κλαθρ]ιοῦ (instead of [Κλαθιατ]οῦ) and prefers in L. 4 [ποθόδ]ωμα to [δικαί]ωμα.

---

703. DODONA, PROXENY-DECREE FOR A CITIZEN FROM BRUNDISIUM, 175-170 B.C. SGDI, 1339 (Michel, Recueil, 318). P. Cabanes, Épire, 554-557, no. 33 (ph.) reads in L. 2-3 Κλαθρι|[οῦ] τὸ β´ (instead of Κλαθι|[ατοῦ]); 4-5. Βουνείμαις ἔκτ|αι ἐφ' ἰκάδι (instead of Βουνίμαις ἔκτ<α>ι | καὶ εἰκάδι); 5. Λύσων (instead of Λύων); 6-7. Γαίωι Δάζου Πολ|φεννίωι (instead Γαίωι Δαζούπου 'Ρεννίωι); 13-14. [κα]|θὼς καὶ (instead of πάντα | ὅσα καὶ).

---

704. DODONA, MANUMISSION RECORD, 2nd CENT. B.C. Two fragments of a bronze plaque. Ed. pr. P. Cabanes, Épire, 589-591, no. 76 (ph.).

[Θεὸς, τύχα. Στραταγοῦ]ν-
[τος Ἀπειρωτᾶν ...]ουκα
................ΠΡ δὲ
[Μολοσσῶν .....]του Λυκί-
[σκου, μηνὸς] Φοινικαίου
[ἀφίεντι ἐλεύ]θερον παρὰ
Δία Ν[άον καὶ Δ]ιώναν Ἀ[ντί]-
νους Ἀντιπ[άτρου, Κλεόμη]-
τις Τιμόνα̣ [........ Δεί]-
νωνα ἐλεύθ[ερον ἀπὸ τᾶς]
σάμερον ἀμ[έρας ποιεῖν ὅ]-
παι κα αὐτὸ[ς προαιρῆται· τύ]-
χαι ταῖ ἀγ[αθαῖ. Μάρτυρες]
Ἕκτωρ Στρα[........., Με]-
νοίτας Κλ[....., ...]
Φαλακρίων[ος, ... Λα]-
μ̣ίσκου, Ἀντ[...., ...]
Μ̊ Ὀρραίτα[ι]

3. This sign is an abbreviation of προστάτης Cabanes || 18. This sign stands for Μολοσσοί Cabanes.

---

705. DODONA, MANUMISSION RECORD. SGDI, 1359 + 1362. P. Cabanes, Épire, 583-584, no. 63 points out that W. Larfeld has already shown that these two fragments belong together. Since this fact has escaped the attention of most scholars, we present the whole text here:

Θεὸς, [τύ]χα ἀγαθά. Βο[ίσκ]ος,
Φορμί[σ]κος, Ἐχενίκα, <Δ>αμ[ν]αγόρα
Φλευχὼ ἐλευθέραν ἀφίεν[τι] καὶ αὐ-
τοὶ ἀπ' αὐτῶν καὶ τῶν ἐκγό[νω]ν αὐ-
τὰν καὶ γένος ἐκ γενεᾶς, [ἅ]ς κα [Β]οί-
σκος καὶ Δαμναγόρα τελευτά[σ]-
ωντι καὶ Φορμίσκος ἡβ[ά]ση, τρ[α]-
πεῖσθαι ὅπαι κα θέλ[η]. Μ]άρτυρ-
ες Λάγορος Βατέλω[νο]ς, Κέφ[α]-
λος Ὀπλαῖνος, Πολυπέ[ρ]χων Ὀπ-
λαῖνος, Σιμίας Κέλα[ιθ]ος.

Date: Cabanes, l.c., 455-456 suggests a date before 232 B.C. || 2-3. Φορμίονος ... Ἀν[τί]|φα Εὐχῶ SGDI || 5-6. [ἐπεὶ ἂν Βοί]|σκος SGDI || 10-11. Εὔχων Ὀπ|[λαῖνος] SGDI.

706-714. DODONA, MANUMISSION RECORDS. P. Cabanes, Épire, 577-585 gives a number of new readings in old manumission records from Dodona. We summarize them here:

706. SEG, XVI, 384. Cabanes, l.c., 577-578, no. 50 proposes in L. 3 Σαβυρ[τίου] instead of Σαβύρ[ου or ωνος]; in L. 10 he reads (as the first editor C. Carapanos) ----ος Εὐρώπι[ος]--.

707. SEG, XVI, 385. Cabanes, l.c., 578-579, no. 51 supports P. Franke's views about this text (cf. SEG, XVI, 385); L. 5. Νεοπάτρα or [Κλ]εοπάτρα.

708. SGDI, 1348. Cf. Cabanes, l.c., 579-580, no. 52: L. 1. The formula [Ἀγαθῆι τύ]χηι (instead of the common formula Ἀγαθᾶι τύχαι) surprises; 2. the first letter is a kappa (and not a chi), which precludes the reading |[ἐπὶ ναιάρ]χου in SGDI.

709. SGDI, 1352. Cf. Cabanes, l.c., 581-582, no. 56: L. 1. προσστάτα (instead of προστάτα); 5. <Ἐ>τοίμαχον (instead of Ἐτοίμαχον); 9-10. Ἀγέλαος Με..|μνος (unknown ethnic) and not Ἀγέλαος Μέν[ιος]|[Ἄμυ]μνος.

710. SGDI, 1354. Cf. Cabanes, l.c., 582, no. 58: L. 4-5. Πολιτ|[3-4.] and not Πολιτ[άρχου vel sim.]|.

711. SGDI, 1358. Cabanes, l.c., 583, no. 62 proposes in L. 2 [μη]νὸς Φοιν[ικαίου] instead of ....νος Φοιν[ατοῦ]; 6. the name of the first witness starts with a Ξ (and not with a Σ).

712. SGDI, 1360. Cabanes, l.c., 584, no. 64 points out that in L. 4-5 one should read: [Τριπο]|λίσιοι Δαμοσ[θένης] instead of |[Τριπο]λίσιοι Δαμοσθένης.

713. SGDI, 1361. Cabanes, l.c., 584, no. 65 points out that in L. 4 the stone has ΣΤΟΝΑΜΑΛ (SGDI: [εἰ]ς τὸν ἄπαν[τα χρόνον]).

714. C. Carapanos, *Dodone et ses ruines* (Paris, 1878), pl. XXX, 2; cf. W. Larfeld, BERLINER PHILOLOGISCHE WOCHENSCHRIFT (1886), no. 29-30, col. 928 and BURSIAN JAHRESBERICHT (1887) III, p. 528. Cabanes, l.c., 585, no. 68 restores in L. 5-6 [Τ]έρπον|τα κ[αὶ Πο]ι-μένα, and in L. 11-12 ʼΑγέλ|[αος].

---

715. DODONA, DONATION OF A REAL ESTATE. SGDI, 1365. P. Cabanes, *Épire*, 592, no. 77 points out that in L. 12 the correct reading is [Θρ]άσωνος (and not [Μν]άσωνος) as W. Larfeld had already observed in BERLINER PHILOLOGISCHE WOCHENSCHRIFT (1886), no. 29-30, col. 927-929 and BURSIAN JAHRESBERICHT (1887) III, p. 528.

---

716. DODONA, STAMPED AMPHORA-HANDLE. Ed. pr. S.I. Dacaris, ΠΑΑΗ (1974) 76.

Νικάρχ[ο]υ ἐπὶ ʼΑρ[ισ]τοβούλου

---

717. GOUMANI (GITANA), MANUMISSION RECORD, MIDDLE 4th CENT. B.C. Ed. pr. S.I. Dacaris, *Thesprotia* (Athens, 1972) 86. Cf. P. Cabanes, *Épire*, 576-577, no. 49. We present this text here because the editio princeps is rather inaccessible.

ʼΑγαθᾶι τύχαι· ἐπὶ προ[σ]-
τάτα Θεσπρωτῶν ʼΑλε-
ξάνδρου, ἱερέος δὲ Φυ-
σταίου, μηνὸς Γαμιλί-
ου, ἀφῆκε Ξένυς Νικάν-
6 ορος ʼΙκάδωτος Φάλακ-
7 ρον ἐλεύθερον καὶ ἀν-
έθηκε τᾶι Θέμιτι, συν-
ευδοκούντων ʼΑνδρω-
10 νος τοῦ Νικάνορος, [Σω]σ-
--- ʼΑντιγον-----------

---

718. KASSOPE, DEDICATION OF THE STRATEGOI TO ZEUS SOTER, 1st CENT. B.C. Ed. pr. S.I. Dacaris, ΠΑΑΗ (1954) 201-209; cf. P.R. Franke, *Die antiken Münzen von Epirus*, I (Wiesbaden, 1961) p. 54, no. 20. P. Cabanes, *Épire*, 564-565, no. 42 republishes this text as follows:

[ʼΕ]πὶ πρυτάνιος
[ʼΑρ]ιστίππου
[σ]τραταγοὶ
Φιλώτας
5 ...μωνος
[Μενέ]δάμος
...λωνος
8 ..κύρων
[ʼΑ]λεξάνδρου,
10 [[-----------]]
[Φί]λανδρος
[ʼΑ]λκάνορος,
Διὶ Σωτῆρι.

5. [Κί]μωνος Dacaris and Franke; "trop court" Cabanes || 6. [Εὔ]-δαμος Dacaris; [Σώ]δαμος Franke; "trop courts" Cabanes || 7. [Φί]-λωνος Dacaris; "restitution trop brève" Cabanes || 8. [Σ]κύρων Dacaris; same remark as for the other restorations Cabanes.

719. PASSARON (NEAR JANNINA), TREATY BETWEEN THE ATERARGOI AND THE PERGAMIOI, 3rd CENT. B.C. (AFTER 264 B.C.). SEG, XV, 411. Cf. P. Cabanes, Épire, 561-562, no. 35: L. 1: προστατέ[οντος] or προστατε[ύοντος]; 3. λ̣αίου instead of λ.αίου; 3-4. [παραγε]|νομέ-νων instead of [παρα]|γενομένων; 4. at the end Cabanes prefers J. and L. Robert's reading [τοῦ] (instead of ἐπὶ) but adds [τε]; 7. Cabanes prefers Ἀκραλεστῶν, ..ca. 6-7.. (Robert's suggestion) to Ἀκραλέστων[ος Ἥρω]|νος; 8-9. [καὶ ἀνανε]|ουμένων (Robert's reading) instead of [ἀνανε]|ουμένων.

---

720. PHOINIKE, MANUMISSION RECORD, 3rd CENT. B.C. (AFTER 232 B.C.). SEG, XXIII, 478. P. Cabanes, Épire, 569-573, no. 47 republishes this text with many new readings as follows (ph.):

[Ἀγαθᾶι] τύχα[ι· στρα]-
[ταγοῦ]ντος Ἀπ[ειρω]-
[τᾶν] Μενάνδρο[υ]
..ρκατου, προστα-
[τεύοντος Χαόνων]
- - - - - - - - - - - - - - -
- - - - - - - - - - - - - - -
- - - - - - - - - - - - - - -
- - - - - - - - - - - - - - -
- - - - - - - - - - - - - - -
- - - - - - - - - - - - - - -
ἀνέθηκε ἱερὸν τῶι Πο-
τειδᾶνι ἀνέφαπτον
[Δ]άζον {τὸν} τὸν δοῦ-
λον. Νίκαρχος Νικομά-
χου Ἀρβαῖος καὶ Νικόμα-
χος καὶ Μνασαρέτα
καὶ Παμφίλα καὶ Ξενο-
τίμα κατὰ τὸν νόμον
μάρτυρες· τῶν ἀρ-
χόντων.

---

721. PHOINIKE, MANUMISSION RECORD, CA. 230-200 B.C. SEG, XXIII, 479. P. Cabanes, Épire, 574-576, no. 48 republishes this text as follows (ph.):

--------Μ---------[ἐπὶ]
[πρ]οστάτα δ[ὲ Ἀδμάτου τοῦ]
[Ἀ]μφίνου Αἰγι[δορίου, ἐπὶ δὲ]
[γρ]αμματέος [----------τοῦ]
[Λυ]κόφρονος Β[------καὶ ἐπὶ]
[δὲ] γραμματ[έος Ἀριστο]-
[μ]ά̣χου, ἀφῆκε Σ----------
..Ἀττάλου -------------
..ω καὶ Παρδ[άλιν -------]
..Φυσκίωνα [τὸν Παρ]-
[δά]λιος ὑὸν, τ[οὺς ἀφεω]-
[θέ]ντας ἐλε[υθέρους]
..κ' αὐτὸς κ[αὶ -------]
..τα Λύσω Ν------------
...Μάρτυ[ρες ----------]

ILLYRIA

722. ONOMASTICS. C. De Simone, STUDALB 12, 2 (1976) 95-116 presents an onomastic study mainly based on new inscriptions from the necropolis of Durazzo (cf. V. Toci, STUDALB, 1969, 2, 163-185 and id., STUDALB, 1972, 1, 77-84) and draws conclusions from it about the character of the south-eastern "regione onomastica".

723. AMANTIA, DEDICATION TO ZEUS BOULEUS, HELLENISTIC PERIOD. Ed. pr. F. Prendi, BULETIN PËR SHKENCAT SHOQËRORE (1955) 116-121; cf. J. and L. Robert, BE (1959) no. 232. P. Cabanes, <u>Épire</u>, 562, no. 38 points out that in L. 3 γραμματεύ[ς] is the only possible reading (and not γραμματεύ[ων] as J. and L. Robert suggested). The text of this inscription runs as follows:

Διὶ Βουλεῖ
2 Ἀδύλος Ἀρχελάο[υ]
3 βουλᾶι γραμματεὺ[ς]
καὶ οἱ βουλευταί.

MACEDONIA

724. AMPHIPOLIS, EPITAPH. Base of a grave monument. Ed. pr. A.K. Orlandos, EAH (1976) 31.

Σωσαρίστη | Νικίου χαῖρε.

725. AMPHIPOLIS, CHRISTIAN INSCRIPTION. Marble votive slab. Ed. pr. A.K. Orlandos, EAH (1976) 47 and 50 (ph.and dr.).

-----------† 5 Ἀμφιπόλεως
ΝΙΚΑ...... .....ΩΝΟΣ
....ΤΗΘ.. ..ΝΥ̣Α.Υ̣ΗΣ
4 ΣΑΛΟΝΙΚΕΥΣ

2. Νικᾷ J. and L. Robert, BE (1976) no. 280 || 3-4. Θ̣ε̣σ̣|σαλονικεύς J. and L. Robert, l.c.

726. BEROIA, MANUMISSION RECORD, 235 B.C. SEG, XII, 314; XX, 787. H. Heinen, ANCSOC 7 (1976) 135-138 criticizes the interpretations of this text by T.V. Blavatskaja (in T.V. Blavatskaja - E.P. Golubcova - A.I. Pavlovskaja, <u>Die Sklaverei in hellenistischen Staaten im 3-1 Jahrh. v. Chr</u>., Wiesbaden, 1972, 96-100).

727. EDESSA, EPITAPH FOR A PIG, 3rd CENT. A.D. Ed. pr. P. Pet-

sas, AAA (1969) 189-191; SEG, XXV, 711. Cf. G. Daux, Ancient Macedonia II (Thessaloniki, 1977) 320-323 and id., JS (1977) 161-163. G. Daux rejects the interpretation of F. Chamoux, Mélanges P. Boyancé (1974) 153-162 (mentioned by P. Collart, BCH, 100, 1976, p. 186 as "une interprétation convaincante du relief") who suggested that the pig had been crushed by the sacred chariot of the phallophory, mentioned in the epigram, and that the chariot is represented on the relief. G. Daux returns (cf. BCH, 94, 1970, p. 609-618) to the view that the chariot is an ordinary wagon.

---

728. KATERINI, EPITAPH. Ed. pr. J.M.R. Cormack, Essays in memory of Basil Laourdas (1975) p. 110. G. Daux, BCH 100 (1976) 227-228 presents the following text:

Αὐρήλιος Φι-
λῷ τῇ γυναικὶ
καὶ τέκνης·
χαῖρε, παροδῖτα.

1-2. Φιλώτῃ γυναικὶ Cormack.

---

729. LEUKOPETRA, DONATION OF A SLAVE TO THE MOTHER OF THE GODS BY A FREEDWOMAN OF THIS GODDESS, 195 A.D. Inscription on the marble doorpost of the temple. Ed. pr. A.K. Orlandos, EAH (1976) 53-54 (ph.); P.M. Petsas, MAKEDONIKON HEMEROLOGION (1977) 133-135 (ph.). Cf. J. and L. Robert, BE (1977) no. 268.

Ἔτους ζκσ´ σε<βα>στοῦ τοῦ
καὶ γμτ´. Εἰερωμένης
Αἰλίας Μητρῶς κὲ
ἐπιμελουμένου Αὐ-
ρηλίου Ἀσσκληπιάδου,
Κρισπίνα, Μητρὸς
Θεῶν ἀπελευθέρα,
ἐχαρισόμην Μητρὶ
Θεῶν Αὐτόχθονι
δούλην ὀνόματι
Ἐλπιδίαν π<ρ>ο-
<σ>μένουσαν τὰς ἐθί-
μους ἡμέρας, τὸν
δὲ κατάλοιπον χρό-
νον προσμένῃ ἐμοὶ
καὶ Διονυσίῳ, τὸν
ζώομεν χρόνον.
Μετὰ δὲ τὴν ἡμε-
τέραν τελευτὴν
μηδένα εἶνε
κυριώτερον
ἢ τὴν θεόν.

9. Αὐτόχθονι: "revendication locale de nationalisme" J. and L. Robert, l.c. || 12-13. ἐθί|μους ἡμέρας: "Elpidia doit au service de la déesse un certain nombre de jours fixés par l' usage, pour le service dans le sanctuaire" J. Pouilloux, apud J. and L. Robert, l.c.

---

730. PELAGONIA (DEBRESTE), FUNERARY METRICAL EPIGRAM, 2nd - 1st CENT. B.C. Ed. pr. F. Papazoglou, BCH 98 (1974) 275-283 (ph.). Cf. J. Bousquet, BCH 98 (1974) 817-818; J. Bingen, CE 49 (1974) 196-199; W. Peek, ZPE 16 (1975) 148-149; R. Merkelbach, ZPE 20

(1976) 252.

Τὸνδ᾽ ἀγανοῦ λεύσεις ἀνδρὸς τάφον, ὃς πο[...
ἑπτὰ ἐτῶν δεκάδας ἔκ τ᾽ ἐβίωσεν ἔτ[η,
Ἀττίδω, ὃς θνήσκει τέκνα τέκνων εἰσιδών.
Οὗτος ἕως ἔζη κεχαρισμένος ἦτο φίλοισ[ι,
νῦν δ᾽ ἄλοχός τε φίλη καὶ υἱέες οὓς ἀπολ[είπει
μνημῆον τεῦξαν· σὺ δ̣ὲ χαιρετίσας με πά[ρελθε].
Ἀττίδω Καλᾶ, Ματεαῒς Λυσανίου χαῖρε[τε].
Γοργίας Ἐπι[γό]νου, Παράμονος Μνα̣[σ]ε̣ου, Ἀττίδ[ω.

1. Τὸν δ᾽ Papazoglou; τὸνδ᾽ Bousquet, Peek, Merkelbach || λεύσ<σ>εις Peek || ὅς ποτ᾽ [ἀλύπως] Peek; ὅς ποτ̣[ε τῇιδε] e.g. Merkelbach || 2. ἔτη̣ Peek, Merkelbach || 3. read ἐσιδών Merkelbach || 6. σὺ δὲ χαῖρε τισασμέ[νος Papazoglou; σὺ δὲ χαῖρε, τίς ἄσμεγ̣[ος ἦλθες] Peek; σὺ δὲ χαιρετίσας με πά[ρελθε] Bousquet (who can read on the photo the first two letters of the last word) and Merkelbach (who restores [παρέρχου]) || 7. Ματεαΐς or Ματελίς.

---

731. PHILIPPI, NAME. Re-used marble block. Ed. pr. S. Pelekanides, PAAH (1974) 68.

Ἀντιγέν[ης]

---

732. PHILIPPI, CHRISTIAN MOSAIC-INSCRIPTION. Ed. pr. A.K. Orlandos, EAH (1976) 63 (ph.); AR (1977-78) 50.

Χριστὲ βοήθι τõ δούλου σου Πρίσκου σὺν παντὶ τοῦ οἴκου αὐτοῦ.

733-770. THESSALONIKA, CORPUS OF INSCRIPTIONS. IG, X, 2, 1 (ed. C. Edson, Berlin, 1972). The following two reviews of this corpus have been examined by us: G. Mihailov, CPH 70 (1975) 47-56 and G. Daux, BCH 100 (1976) 213-225, 227. For corrections and interpretations of inscriptions in this corpus, published in the period 1972-1975 we refer to J. and L. Robert, BE (1973) no. 277-283 (notes of different authors on nos. 108, 137, 255, 259, 564, 822 of the corpus), BE (1974) no. 338-346 (notes on nos. 41, 42, 43, 140, 151, 280, 368) and BE (1976) 358-455 (notes on nos. 1, 2, 11, 14, 16, 46, 55, 59, 60, 61, 63, 65, 66, 67, 68, 72, 100, 107, 109, 126, 133, 138, 150, 152, 173, 176, 180, 181, 200, 207, 209, 217, 243, 255, 256, 259, 260, 267, 269, 271, 284, 291, 296, 351, 357, 384, 390, 418, 429, 443, 451, 463, 467, 486, 490, 494, 515, 516, 539, 565, 572, 573, 607, 608, 618, 623, 640, 666, 686, 691, 711, 712, 732, 768, 774, 789, 796, 822, 839, 842, 856, 857-858, 864, 865, 866, 896, 901, 911, 920, 926, 930, 996, 1008, 1010, 1040). G. Mihailov and G. Daux deal with the following numbers:

733. No. 32, L. 11. Ἐπικ[------]δος instead of Ἐπικ[τήτου τοῦ ..4-5..]δος Mihailov.

---

734. No. 37, L. 4. τὸ̣[ν + patronymic in the genitive] (instead of τὸ̣[ν ἀρχιερέα ·.·] Mihailov.

---

735. No. 59, L. 3. Ἄγχις or Ἀγχίς (instead of Ἀγ<κ>ίς) Mihailov.

---

736. No. 64, L. 2-3. Ἥρωνα ΤΟ[.]|ΘΟΝΙΟΝ Mihailov (who thinks that these letters possibly conceal an epithet of Heron) (instead of τὸ[ν] | ΘΟΝΙΟΝ).

---

737. No. 132, L. 2. --ἱερέ]ως τῶν <ϑ>εῶν? (instead of τῶν εῶν) Mihailov.

---

738. No. 133, L. 1. one καὶ and two letters for the date; 2. [κ]αί; 3. [κα]τά; 17. Μ(άρκου); 18. under this line a vacat Daux.

---

739. No. 160, L. 1-2. [---Αὔ]|λ̣[ον Πόν] (instead of Α̣[ὔλον Πόν]|τιον); 16. ἔτε<ι> (and not ἔτι = ἔτει) Daux.

---

740. No. 191, L. 2. κατὰ τ<ὰ> δόξαντα (instead of κατὰ τὸ δόξαντα !); 12. ε<ὐ>τ<υ>χῶς (instead of ἐπτχῶς !) Mihailov.

---

741. No. 209, L. 7. G. Daux confirms the IG-reading οἱ ἀδελφοί (and not ὁ ἀδελφός as other editors thought).

---

742. No. 245, col. I, L. 2. ---ο̣ς; 6. (after N) ὁ καί; 10. (before Π) [--- ὁ κ]α̣ί; col. II, L. 6-8. Μέστριος Ἐπ---| Μ. Ἰούλιος Σε̣[κοῦνδος] | Κ. Καικίλιο[ς--- Daux.

---

743. No. 300, L. 6-8. Ἀπολλωνίς, fem. name, or Ἀπολλώνις, name of son Mihailov (Edson only mentions the last possibility).

---

744. No. 494. ..Μ]αυρίκῳ (instead of ..αυρικῷ) Mihailov.

---

745. No. 500. προσ<τί>μου (instead of ΠΡΟΣΟΜΟΥ) Mihailov.

---

746. No. 523, L. 5-6. ἐπο[ίησα τὸ μ]<ν>η|[μ]ε<ῖ>ον (instead of ἐπο[ίησα ca.3]ΜΗ|ΕΝΟ.ca.6.) Mihailov.

---

747. No. 557, B, L. 3. θανάτοιο (instead of the misprint θανάτοιοι) Mihailov.

---

748. No. 565, L. 8. μετὰ τὸ ἡμᾶς κατατιθῆνε (instead of τὸ {ΘΗΝΑΣ} κατατιθῆνε) Mihailov.

---

749. No. 572, L. 1. Πο(πλία) Ἀντία (instead of Ὀ̣πταντία) Mihailov (who follows H. Castritius, AA, 85, 1970, p. 93-98); 2. Βιταλίῳ Ῥεστιτούτῳ διασημοτάτῳ (instead of β' πάλ{Ι}ῳ Ῥεστιτούτῳ τῷ διασημοτάτῳ) Mihailov (following Castritius, l.c.). Vitalius was a governor; for his family, cf. Castritius, l.c.; 3. κακ<ῶ>ς (instead of ΚΑΚΝC) Mihailov (following Castritius, l.c.); Mihailov accepts the restoration of J. and L. Robert, BE (1971) no. 404 <ἃ> ἀφῆκες; 5. προ<σ>τείμου (instead of προτείμου !) Mihailov.

---

750. No. 582, L. 5. The fine is not *]φ̣ but *.]φ̣; a multiple of thousand has to be restored in view of the date of the text (2nd - 3rd cent. A.D.) Mihailov.

---

751. No. 583, L. 3. κατ̣[εσκεύασαν] (instead of κατ̣[εσκεύασε]) Mihailov.

---

752. No. 618, L. 2. ἐποίουν‿καί or ἐποίου<ν> καί (instead of ἐποίου! καί) Mihailov.

---

753. No. 628, L. 3. ἀκμάζω (and not ἀκμάζων) Daux.

---

754. No. 686. Δεῖα Μελάνδρῳ | τῷ τέκνωι ζῶσα{ι} (instead of Δεῖα Μελανδρῷ | τῷ τέκνωι ζώσαι!) Mihailov.

---

755. No. 692, L. 1. After ἔτων at the end an E; 2. Πρόκλανι, dative of Πρόκλα Daux.

---

756. No. 700. Χρυσίς (fem. name) or Χρῦσις (masc. name) Mihailov (Edson mentions only the first possibility).

---

757. No. 710, L. 2-3. μνήμη|ς χά{ι}ριν Ζωσᾶ (instead of μνή-μη|ς χαίριν! Ζωσᾶ ;) Mihailov and Daux.

---

758. No. 711. Δημ<έ>ας <Θ>ήρα (instead of ΔΗΜCACΕΗΡΑ) Mihailov.

---

759. No. 745, L. 6-8. εἰ δέ | [τις ἕτ]ε̣ρος κα|[ταθῇ ἕτερον πτῶ-μα vel sim.] (instead of εἰ δέ | [τις ἕτ]ε̣ρος κ̣α̣|.c.8....Ι̣Γ̣Γ̣) Mi-hailov.

---

760. No. 746, L. 6. ἐποίε<ε> or ΕΠΟΙΕ instead of ΕΠΟΕΙ = ἐπόει (and not ἔποιε!) Mihailov.

---

761. No. 763, L. 2-4. καὶ Τρύ|[φωνι vel sim. τοῖς ἰ]δ̣ίοις | [τέκνοις] (instead of καὶ ΤΡΥ|[--τοῖς ἰ]δ̣ίοις | --------) Mihailov.

---

762. No. 771, L. 1-2. [Φλ]ά̣βιος Ἀφροδί|[σιο]ς (instead of [Φλ]άβιος Ἀφροδίσ|[ιο]ς) Daux.

---

763. No. 772, L. 1-2. Αὐρήλιος Θεόδω|ρος (instead of Αὐρήλιος Θεόδωρ|ος) Daux.

---

764. No. 819, B, L. 5. ἐδίων "résultat d' un phénomène phoné-tique i>e" (instead of ε<ἰ>δίων) Mihailov.

---

765. No. 824, L. 6. ε̣ἰκ, analogous form to εἰς? (instead of ἑ{ι}κ) Mihailov.

---

766. No. 838, L. 1. εἰ θ' ἕτερος (instead of εἶθ') Mihailov.

---

767. No. 856. Daux accepts the correction of L. 2-3 made by W. Peek and F. Papazoglou and reads the text as follows: Λούκιος καὶ Ἀλέξα|ν̣δ̣ρ̣ο̣ς̣ καὶ Δελους | ἡ ἀ̣[δ]ε̣λφὴ Μεστρίῳ κτλ. (instead of Δελουσ|η ἀ̣[δ]ε̣λφή).

---

768. No. 859, L. 1. [ἐ]<αυ>τοῦ ζῶντος? (instead of ----ΝΤΟΥΖΟΝ ΤΟC) ; 8. Δόμνη<ς> (instead of Δομνηο!) Mihailov.

---

769. No. 1021, L. 3. Θεσσαλονε[ί]κης or Θεσσαλονε[ί{..}]κης

(instead of Θεσσαλονε[ί..]κης) Mihailov.

---

770. VARIA. G. Mihailov comments upon a number of phonetic and morphological phenomena in nos. 64, 471, 512, 524, 558, 565, 579, 589, 609, 694, 827, 845, 887, 897, 1008 and finally discusses (the accentuation of) the following names: Βειθᾶς (219), Δορζινθης (242), Βρυζος (243), Παραπυρος (284), Συρα (490), Σεμέλη, Τορκος (926), Σαμβω (539), Τίτους (911), Ἀμπιανός (920), Θάλλος (69, 217, 544, 875, 920, 1035), Τέρπνος (436), Ἀρέτη (392, 443, 912), Ἑόρτη (492, 805).

771-773. THESSALONIKA, MILESTONE OF THE VIA EGNATIA WITH THREE TEXTS. Milestone, now in the Louvre. IG, X, 2, 1, no. 1018. Cf. P. Collart, BCH 100 (1976) 198, no. 4 and G. Daux, JS (1977) 145-161. G. Daux republishes the inscriptions after an exhaustive inspection of the stone (ph.). We present here his texts:

---

771. P. 152, no. I (IG, X, 2, 1, no. 1018, A and Collart, l.c., no. 4, A); 124 A.D.

Imp.
Caesar divi
Traiani Parthici
fil. divi Nervae
nepos Traianus
Hadrianus Aug.
pont. max. trib. pot.
VIII cos. III, a Thessal.
m.p.
IIII

---

772. P. 152-153, no. II (IG, X, 2, 1, 1018, C and Collart, l.c., no. 4, D); between May 305 - July 306 A.D.

[Αὐτοκράτορσι] Καίσαρσιν
Φλ' Οὐαλ' Κωνσταντίῳ
καὶ Γαλ hedera Οὐαλ Μαξιμιανῷ
[Σ]εβαστοῖς hedera καὶ Φλ' Οὐαλ
Σεβήρῳ καὶ Γαλ Οὐαλ
Μαξιμίνῳ ἐπιφανε-
στάτοις Καίσαρσιν
ἡ Θεσσαλονικέων
πόλις.
Θ

1-8. Only read by Daux || 9-10. Θ = 9 (and not πόλις | Θ(εσσαλονικέων) as Collart, l.c., 188-189 suggested) Daux.

---

773. P. 155-158, no. III (IG, X, 2, 1, no. 1018 B and Collart, l.c., no. 4, B and C); Latin text: after 11 Nov. 308; Greek text:

after 1 March 317 A.D.; line 6-9 and 13: erased after 18 Sept. 324 A.D.

	Imp. Caes. Fl.	11	καὶ Κλ. Κρίσπος
	Val.		VIIII
	Constantinus		καὶ Λι. Κλ. Λικ[ίνιος] v.
	P.F. Invictus		καὶ Κλ. Κωνσταντεῖνος
5	Aug.	15	οἱ ἐπιφ. Καίσαρες
6-9	4 lines erased		Θ
10	Aug.		

6-9. In rasura the names of the two Licinii || 10. M(ilia) P(assuum) IG, Collart || 12. ṾIIII IG; IIII Collart || 16. [V]IIII Θ IG; IIII Θ Collart; IIII belongs to no. I Daux.

---

774. NEIGHBOURHOOD OF THESSALONIKA, MILESTONE USED SEVERAL TIMES. IG, X, 2, 1, 1009. Cf. P. Collart, BCH 100 (1976) 189-190, 199-200, no. 11. Collart's interpretation differs from that of C. Edson, IG, X, 2, 1, 1009 who reproduces the interpretation of C.I. Makaronas, Studies presented to D.M. Robinson (1951) I, 380-388. Collart recognizes four (against Makaronas - Edson: five) stages in the history of the text: 1) L. 1, 7, 10: before 17 Sept. 284; 2) L. 2-6 (filling up a rasura): between spring 285 and 1 April 286; 3) L. 8-13: between 1 March 293 and 1 May 305; 4) L. 14-20: between 1 May 305 and 25 July 306.

---

775. THESSALONIKA, HONORARY INSCRIPTION. IG, X, 2, 1, 140. M. Christol, LATOMUS 35 (1976) 866-874 identifies M. Aurelius Apollinaris, procurator and vice-proconsul of Macedonia with the homonymous governor of Thrace under Gallienus (IGBR, III, 1569). He dates the inscription between 260 and 267 A.D. (against C. Edson, IG, who identified M. Aur. Apollinaris with Aurelius Apollinaris, tribune of a praetorian cohors and in 217 one of the conspirators against Caracalla: PIR^2, I, p. 295, A 1452).

---

776. THESSALONIKA, EDICT OF JUSTINIANUS I (?) ABOUT THE CHURCH OF S. DEMETRIUS, 538-565 A.D. (?). R. Bonini, EPIGRAPHICA 38 (1976) 69-73 notes the differences between the editions of G. Oikonomos, AE (1918) 41-52, C. Edson, IG, X, 2, 1, no. 23 and J.M. Spieser, TRAVAUX ET MÉMOIRES. CENTRE DE RECHERCHE D' HISTOIRE ET CIVILISATION DE BYZANCE 5 (1973) 153 f. (sub no. 4), and adds this text to the corpus of M. Amelotti - G.I. Luzzato, Le Costituzione giustinianee nei papiri e nelle epigrafe (Milan, 1972). Nevertheless, he has some doubts whether the emperor in the inscription is Justinianus I (and not Justinianus II).

---

777. THESSALONIKA, FUNERARY EPIGRAM FOR MAGNUS, CA. 2nd CENT. A.D. IG, X, 2, 1, 368. After D. Lebek, ZPE 14 (1974) 12, W. Peek, ZPE 22 (1976) 92 returns to this epigram. Lebek, ZPE 22 (1976) 92 (note) accepts Peek's view.

Μοῖρα πικρή, Λήθης Ἀχερουσίδος ἔν|τροφε, λυγρὸν
  θρῆνον ἐναψαμένη | Μάγνον ἄγ' εἰς Ἀΐδεω·
παῖδα δυωδε|χέτη (!) πατρὶ μὲν γόον, ἄλγεα μητρὶ ||
  ἠδὲ κασιγνήτῳ πένθεα λυγρότατα· |
ἄρτι γὰρ ἦν γονέεσσι μέριμνα μέν, | αὐτὰρ ἀδελφῷ
  κόσμος· χὴ πικρὴ | Μοῖρ' ἀπενοσφίσατο·
ἀλλ' ὦ τὸν πάν|τεσσι βροτοῖς μόνον οἶκον ἐσοιχνῶ<ν> |
  Μάγν', ἐπιτυμβιδίοις χαῖρε καὶ εἰνὶ τάφοις.

2. ἄγεις Ἀΐδεω Lebek, Peek; Lebek (ZPE, 22, 1976, 92, note) now prefers the original IG-reading || 7-8. 'ἄλλω<ς> ...ἐσοιχνῶ'·| 'Μάγν' ἐπὶ τυμβιδίοις κτλ. IG; "ἀλλ' ὡς τὸν πάντεσσι ... ἐσοιχνῶ."| "Μάγν'...τάφοις." Lebek; at the beginning of L. 7 ΑΛΛΩΤΟΝ in lap.

---

778. THESSALONIKA, CHRISTIAN EPITAPHS FOR MARTINOS AND ANTONINOS, RESPECTIVELY 525 and 535 A.D. IG, X, 2, 1, 804. D. Feissel, BCH 100 (1976) 269-272 studied the inscription and presents it as follows:

† Κοιμητήριον δίσωμον [διαφέρον]
Μαρτίνῳ τῷ θαυμ(ασιωτάτῳ) ἐπα̣[ρχικῷ]
τῷ κατὰ τὸν τὴν ἐνδ[οξ(οτάτην) μνή]-
μην ἀπ̣[ὸ ἐπ]άρχων [.ca.6.]-
νον, ἔγ̣[θα κατά]κιτε ἡ [.ca.6.]
ΠΑϹ[.ca.7..]ΗΤΗ[.ca.6.]
ΠΑΡ[.ἀναπαυ]σαμέν[η ca.5.]
κζ' ἰν[δ(ικτιῶνος) γ' ὑπατε]ίᾳ Φλ^{ς} [Φλ^{ς} Φιλο]-
ξένο[υ καὶ Π]ρόβου [τῶν λαμ]-
προτάτων. † Ἀναπ[άη ὁ μα]-
κάριος Ἀντωνῖνος τῇ [.ca.6.]
ἰνδ(ικτιῶνος) δι' ὑπ(ατείᾳ) Βελισαρίου λ[αμ(προτάτου)· ἔνθα]
κατάκιτε. †

Date: Edson dated the two texts to 535 A.D.

---

779. THESSALONIKA, BILINGUAL (GREEK - SAMARITAN HEBREW) INSCRIPTION OF A SAMARITAN SYNAGOGUE, 4th-6th CENT. A.D. Ed. pr. B. Lifshitz - J. Schiby, RBI 75 (1968) 368-378. J.D. Purvis, BASO 221 (1976) 121-123 assigns the stone to the 4th-6th cent. A.D. (contra Lifshitz - Schiby: 4th cent. A.D.) on the basis of a study of the Samaritan script (line 1 and 15).

---

780. INSCRIPTION WRONGLY ATTRIBUTED TO THESSALONIKA. For IG, X, 2, 1, 44 cf. no. 823.

---

781. VERGINA, EPITAPH, BEFORE 300 B.C. Stele. Ed. pr. M. Andronikos, AAA 9 (1976) 124-125 (ph).

῞Αρπαλος Πευκολάου

---

782. VERGINA, EPITAPH, BEFORE 300 B.C. Stele. Ed. pr. M. Andronikos, AAA 9 (1976) 125 (ph.).

Θεόδωρος Θευφάνους

The same patronymic in BCH 79 (1955) 101.

THRACE

---

783. RELIGION. M. Tatscheva-Hitova, KLIO 58 (1976) 25-40 studies the history of the Dolichenus-cult in Moesia Inferior and in Thrace. She presents (p. 35-40) a catalogue of 22 monuments (with Latin and Greek inscriptions) concerning this cult in these places.

---

784. AUGUSTA TRAIANA, CONSTRUCTION OF PUBLIC BATHS, 162-163 A.D. Marble slab. Ed. pr. D. Nikolov, ARCH (Sofia) 10 (1968) 43-48. Cf. L. Robert, STUDCLAS 16 (1974) 53-61, who corrects the text (twice, in line 11), presents a detailed comment on it and cites numismatic evidence about these baths.

Ἀγαθῆι τύχηι.
Ὑπὲρ τῆς τῶν αὐτοκρατόρων νείκης καὶ αἰωνίου διαμονῆς Μ. Αὐρηλί-
ου Ἀντωνείνου καὶ Λ. Αὐρηλίου Οὐήρου καὶ Φαυστείνης Σεβ(αστῆς) καὶ τοῦ
σύνπαντος οἴκου αὐτῶν καὶ ἱερᾶς συνκλήτου, ἡγεμονεύοντος Τουλ-
λίου Μαξίμου πρεσβ(ευτοῦ) Σεβ(αστοῦ) ἀντιστρατήγου, Θεαῖς Νύμφαις καὶ τῇ λαμπροτά-
τῃ Τραιανέων πόλει Οὔλπιος Ἱερώνυμος Νεικομηδεὺς ἀρχιερώ-
μενος κατεσκεύασεν ἐκ τῶν ἰδίων λουτρῶνα καὶ τὰ δύο ἀποδυτή-
ρια καὶ τὸ φριγ<ι>δάριον καὶ τὸ Νυμφαῖον ἐκ θεμελίων σὺν παντὶ τῶι
κόσμωι αὐτῶν καὶ τοῖς ἀγάλμασιν καὶ τὸ ὑδρεῖον καὶ τὸ ὕδωρ τὸ
ψυχρὸν εἰσήγαγεν, συναρχιερωμένης αὐτῶι τῆς γυναικὸς Οὐαλε-
ρίας Φροντωνίλλης, καὶ παρέδωκεν συντετελεσμένα πάντα ἔτι στε-
φανηφορῶν.

9. ΦΡΙΓΔΑΡΙΟΝ lapis || 11. Φροντωνίλλης Robert et lapis (Mihailov);

Φροντωνίμης Nikolov || 11-12. ἔτι στε|φανηφορῶν Robert et lapis (Mihailov); ἐπ<ὶ> στε|φανηφόρων Nikolov.

---

785. BYZANTIUM, HONORARY INSCRIPTION FOR A PRIEST, ROMAN PERIOD. Ed. pr. H. Wiegand, MDAI(A) 36 (1911) 289, no. 3. R. Merkelbach, ZPE 21 (1976) 270 restores L. 1. The text runs as follows:

[ἱερομ]να̣μονο̣ύσης θε[ᾶς ----------]
οἱ πρεσβύτερο̣ι στεφαν[οῦντι τὸν δεῖνα]
τὸν ἱερῆ ἑαυτῶν πολυ[ωρήσαντα καὶ ἀνδρα]-
γαθήσαντα τὸ κοινὸν τ[ῶν -------- δωρε]-
ὰν * ρ'. Οἱ μύστα[ι στεφ]αν[οῦντι τὸν δεῖνα]
῾Εκαταίου ε[--------------------------]

1. ΝΛ̣ΜΟΝCΥCΗCΘΕ Wiegand, suppl. Merkelbach.

---

786. BYZANTIUM, STELE OF LYKO OR LYKON, 2nd CENT. B.C. Ed. pr. N. Firatli - L. Robert, Les stèles funéraires de Byzance Gréco-Romaine (Paris, 1964) 56 (ph. XXVI). Cf. R. Merkelbach, ZPE 21 (1976) 96. The stone shows:

ΛΥΚΩΙΦΛΙΕΝΕΚΡΑΤΗ

Firatli - Robert, l.c., p. 64 and 170 read it as follows: Λυκῶι <Μ>ενεκράτη or Λύκω<ν Μ>ενεκράτη. Merkelbach proposes Λυκῶι Φ<α>-ιενεκράτη). (Φαιενε- instead of Φαεινε- would be an archaistic error of the cutter).

---

787. BYZANTIUM, FUNERARY EPIGRAM. Ed. pr. H. Lietzmann, Die Stadtmauer von Konstantinopel (Abh. Berlin, 1929) 24, 27 (ph.) (non vidimus). W. Peek, ZPE 23 (1976) 95-96 presents the following text (with a reconstruction-sketch):

ξ[εῖνε, εἰ θαυμ]άζεις, | [τίνος ἐνθάδε ἄ]ψεα | [κεῖται],
ἴσχεο, μ[ὴ σπεύδῃς· τυν]νὸς πόνος· | [ἀλλ' ἄγε πεύθ]ου· |
Αὐτονό[μῳ δεσμοῖσιν ὑ]π' ἀρρηκτοῖσι | [δαμάσσων] |
Κοίρανον ἔ[νθα 'Αίδης μ' ἥρ]πασε μητέρι | [τε]

ξ[εῖνε .... πελ]άζεις | [πρὸς ....]ψεα | ἴσχεο μ[...... ......]νος πόνος [....]ου | αὐτόνο[μον δεσμοῖσιν ὑ]π' ἀρρηκτοῖσι [δαμάσσων] | κοίρανον ἐ[κ θαλάμου ἥρ]πασε μητέρι [μου] Lietzmann.

---

788. (BYZANTIUM-)CONSTANTINOPLE, EPITAPH. Epigram on a sarcophagus. Drawing in Melchior Lorck, Drawings from the Evelyn Collection at Stonor Park, England, and from the Department of Prints and Drawings, The Royal Museum of Fine Arts, Copenhagen, 1962 (Catalogue by Erik Fischer), drawing no. 20, p. 91 (cf. p. 34). Cf. J. and L. Robert, BE (1964) 276 ("transcription provisoire"); B.

Kramer, ZPE 18 (1975) 299-301 (drawing) and ZPE 20 (1976) 18.

Χρῆστος Σατριανὴν τὴν <ξ>υνάορον πόσ<ις>·
πέτρῃ δὲ τοὐ|μὸν τῇδε κηδεύσας δέμ<α>ς
χάρ<ιν> δεδόωκε τῶν π<ά>λ|α<ι> νυμφευμάτων·
καὶ γὰρ κόρην ἔ{ν}φυσεν ἐγ μόχθων | ἐμῶν
εἰκόν' ἀνέλενχον τῶν εἰς ἀλλήλους πό<θ>ω<ν>· |
χαίρετε. |
λάρνακα λαϊνέην ἐ<θ>έμην αὐτῷ, <ξ>ένε, Χ<ρ>ῆστος |
θάψας <σ>ωφροσύνης παῖδα, φίλην ἄλοχον·
ἀλλ' ἐ|μὸν ἣν κρύψει δ<έ>μας ἡ πέτρο{ι}ς ἥδε, κελεύω
μούν|ῃ Χρ<η>στείνῃ λοιπὸν ἔχειν εἴσοδον·
<ἄλ>λος δ' ἰσβῆναι | τόνδ' εἰς τάφον ἣν ἐ<θ>ελήσῃ,
δώσει τῷ φίσκῳ δώ|δεκα χειλι<ά>δας.

1. ΕΥΝΑΟΡΟΝ Lorck; ξυνάορον Robert; φυνάορον Kramer (1975), but cf. ZPE 20 (1976) 18 where she accepts Robert's reading || ΠΟΣ· Lorck; πόσ<ις> Kramer || 2-3. ΔΕΜΜC ΧΑΡΤΑ Lorck; δέμ<α>ς χάρ<ιν> Robert || 3. ΠΗΛΑΘ Lorck; π<ά>λα<ι> Kramer || 4. ΕΝΦΥCΕΝ Lorck; ἐν<έ>φυσεν Robert; ἔ{ν}φυσεν Kramer || 5. ΠΟΤѠΚ Lorck; πό<θ>ω<ν> Kramer || 7. ΛΑ·Ι·ΝΕΗΝ Lorck || ΕΤΕΜΗΝ Lorck; ἐτέμην Robert; ἐ<θ>έμην (or ἔτεμεν?) Kramer || ΕΕΝΕ Lorck; ξένε Kramer || ΧΔΗΣΤΟΣ Lorck; Χρῆστος Robert || 8. ΕΩΦΡΟΣΥΝΗΣ Lorck; σωφροσύνης Kramer || Α[[Ο]]ΛΟΧΟΝ Lorck || 9. ΔΣΜΑΣ Lorck; δ<έ>μας Robert || ΠΕΤΡΟΙΣ Lorck; πέτρο{ι}ς Kramer || 10. ΧΡΙΣΤΕΙΝΗ Lorck; Χρ<η>στείνῃ Robert || 11. ΗΔΛΟΣ Lorck; <ἄλ>λος Robert || ΕΑΕΛΗΣΗ Lorck; ἐ<θ>ελήσῃ Robert || 12. ΧΕΙΛΙDΑΣ Lorck; χειλι<ά>δας Robert.

---

789. (BYZANTIUM-)CONSTANTINOPLE ?, EPITAPH, 2nd HALF 6th CENT. A.D. White marble cruciform stele with the portrait of a veiled woman with a nimbus around her head in relief. On her right side a calix, and on the left side a patena. Now in the Archaeological Museum of Venice. Ed. pr. D. Feissel, AN 47 (1976) 156-168, no. 1 (ph.).

Χέρεστε
ξένυ καὶ
παροδῖτε· ἐνθάδε κατά-
4 κιτε ἡ τῖς μακαρίας μνήμης

Δόμνα θυγάτηρ Σισινίου γα-
μετὴ Ἐπιφανίου ἀπὸ χωρίου
Μορέων ὅρ[ων Ἀ]δριανοπόλε-
8 [ως ---]

---

790. (BYZANTIUM-)CONSTANTINOPLE, EPITAPH, 6th CENT. A.D. Ed. pr. M. Gédéon, Ἔγγραφοι λίθοι καὶ κεράμια (Const., 1892) p. 95, 1. D. Feissel, AN 47 (1976) 161 restores this epitaph as follows: [Χαίρετε? ξέ]<ν>οι κ(αὶ) παρο[δῖται, εὔ]ξασθε ὑπὲρ [ἐμοῦ] τοῦ προαναπα[υσα]μένου. † Ἐνθάδε [κατ]άκιτε Θεόδωρος υἱὸς Κομιτάτου (instead of [Φί]λοι καὶ παροδῖται κτλ. Gédéon). For Feissel's restoration, cf. no. 789, L. 1-3.

791. (BYZANTIUM-)CONSTANTINOPLE, EPITAPH, 6th CENT. A.D. Ed. pr. M. Gédéon, Ἔγγραφοι λίθοι καὶ κεράμια (Const., 1892) p. 95, 2. Republished by D. Feissel. AN 47 (1976) 161:

Χέρ<ε>τε παροδῖτε
καὶ καλõς ἤλθ-
ατε κὲ καλõς [ὑ]-
πάετε, εὔχεσ[θε ὑ]-
πὲρ ἐμοῦ τοῦ [προ?]-
αναπαυσαμένου.
Ἐνθάδε κατάκητε Γε-
ώργιος πιστὸς ὑγιὸς Θ-
εοδούλου τοῦ τῆς μακαρ-
ίας μνήμης ὡρμόμενο-
ς ἀπὸ χωρίου ἐπιλεγωμ-
ένου Πίβρου τῖς μηκρᾶς Ἀ[σ]-
ίας Ω Ν ἐνταῦθα κ[εῖτ]ε τ[
ΝΤΙΥΠΟΤΙΝΑ
ΕΟΝΔ

Date: before the 15th cent. A.D. Gédéon; 6th cent. A.D. Feissel || 1-4. Feissel, l.c., 166, note 37 refers to a similar epitaph from the capital, ed. pr. E. Alexandrides, Νέος Ποιμήν 5 (1923) 30-32: Χέρετε παροδῖτε, καλῶς ἤλθατε, εὔξασθε ὑπὲρ ἐ[μοῦ] τοῦ προ[αν]απαυσα[μένου]. Alexandrides dated this text between the 10th and the 12th cent. A.D.; Feissel assigns it to the 6th cent. A.D. || 1. ΧΕΡΤΕ lapis || 3-4. [ὑ]|πάετε for [ὑ]|πάγετε, cf. Feissel, l.c., 166, note 36 || 8. ὑγιός = υἱός.

792. (BYZANTIUM-)CONSTANTINOPLE ?, BIBLICAL CITATIONS, 6th CENT. A.D. ? CIG, 8939. Large marble vase, now in the museum of Torcello. D. Feissel, AN 47 (1976) 167-172 collects several parallels for this inscription.

793-800. CHERSONESOS, CORPUS OF INSCRIPTIONS. E.I. Solomonik, (New Epigraphic Monuments from the Chersonesos, in Russian), I (1964), II (1973). B.I. Nadel, EPIGRAPHICA 38 (1976) 196-203 and J. Pecirka, EIRENE 14 (1976) 153-155 review this corpus, make some corrections and suggest other possible restorations:

793. No. 1, L. 1. θλιβομ[ένας τᾶς πόλεος] instead of θλιβομ[έ-νων τῶν πολιτᾶν]; 3. [τὰς πύλας] or [τὴν πύλην] instead of [τὰ τείχη]; 4. [καλοκάγα]θίας or [ἀνδραγα]θίας instead of [εὐστ]αθίας; 5. several other participia ending in -ενος are possible instead of [παρεχόμ]ενος; 9. φρου[ράν] or some participle of φρουρέω instead of φρούρι̣[ον] Nadel.

794. No. 4. This text is not a decree; the restoration proposed by Solomonik is too long. (Nadel)

795. No. 6, L. 3. [----- καθη]κ̣ούσαις τειμα[ῖς ----] instead of [-----]ουσαις τειμά[ν? ------] Pecirka.

796. No. 8. 'Αγα[θ..] Τύ[χ..] instead of 'Αγα[θᾶι] Τύ[χαι] Nadel.

---

797. No. 26. Possibly a honorary inscription instead of a building inscription. (Nadel)

---

798. No. 45. Dedication with [Name + patronymic] | [θε]οῖς ? instead of an epitaph with Φορμίων | name ending in -οις (ἀδελφοῖς, υἱοῖς etc.) Nadel.

---

799. No. 133. The restoration of this inscription by Solomonik is very dubious. It can also be an honorary inscription. (Nadel)

---

800. VARIA. Nadel also discusses the character of the locality Νάπις and the etymology of its name (no. 1), the meaning of the titles φιλόπατρις and πατὴρ τῆς πόλεος (no. 13), the deity of no. 58 and the meaning of ἐλεύσεις ("probably a noun with the meaning 'coming'", and not a verbal form) in line 1 of this text.

---

801. CHERSONESOS (BALAKLAOS), FRAGMENT OF AN EDICT OF THE MILITARY TRIBUNE L. ARRIUS ALKIBIADES (?), 2nd CENT. A.D. Marble fragment. Ed. pr. E.I. Solomonik, NE 11 (1974) 34-35, no. 2 (ph.).

1 -----]σṭ[--------
---]'Αρρίου 'Αλκιβ̣[ιάδου -----
---]ṭαι Λ. Ἄρριος ['Αλκιβιάδης
4 ---].. [------------

---

1. e.g. πρό]στ[αγμα Solomonik || 3. perhaps [στρατιῶ]ται Solomonik || For Arrius Alkibiades, commander of a Roman vexillatio on the Chersonesos in the 2nd cent. A.D., cf. IOSPE, I^2, 404, LL. 35 and 44.

---

802. CHERSONESOS (KALOS LIMEN), LIST OF NAMES, 2nd - 3rd CENT. A.D. Limestone block. Ed. pr. E.I. Solomonik, NE 11 (1974) 37-39, no. 4 (ph.).

'Αβαχης Εὐτύης
2 Μουσικός 4 Α̣ἰ̣ζ̣ε[ι]ός

---

3. ΕΥΤΥΗΣ lapis, for Εὐτύχης, -κης, Εὐσύης, Εὐφύης Solomonik.

---

803. CHERSONESOS, DEDICATION OF AN ALTAR BY PASIADAS, 400-350

B.C. Marble block, with boukrania, guirlandes and rosettes. Ed. pr. I.R. Pitchikian, SA (1976, 3) 248-255 (ph.).

Πασιάδας Ἀρτεμιδ[ώρου ---]
βασιλεύων ἱερεὺς ἐ[-------]

1. Ἀρτεμιδ[ώρου Παρθένωι ?] Pitchikian || 2. ἐ[ὼν ἀνέθηκεν ?] Pitchikian.

804. CHERSONESOS, AMPHORA-STAMPS. V.V. Borisova, NE 11 (1974) 99-124 presents a classification of the Chersonese amphorae and of their stamps. On p. 112 ff. she gives a catalogue of the astynomoi mentioned on these stamps, with the number of the stamps found so far and the places where they have been found. Fifteen plates illustrate all the extant stamps.

805. CHERSONESOS, INSCRIPTIONS ON AMPHORAE, 4th CENT. B.C. Ed. pr. E.I. Solomonik, VDI (1976, 3) 121-122 (dr.).

a) Βάθυλλος | Νικαγόρα
b) [Β]ạ́[θυλλος] | Νικ[αγόρα]

With no. 806 these are the first ballot-ostraka to be found in Chersonesos Solomonik.

806. CHERSONESOS, INSCRIPTION ON A KYLIX, 4th CENT. B.C. Ed. pr. E.I. Solomonik, VDI (1976, 3) 122-123 (dr.).

Ἀμφίω[ν ---]|όχο(υ)

Cf. no. 805.

807. CHERSONESOS, GRAFFITO ON THE FOOT OF A POT, 4th CENT. B.C. Ed. pr. E.I. Solomonik, VDI (1976, 3) 124 (ph.).

[ὁ δεῖνα ἔ]γραψε τὸν πίν[ακα ---]

808. CHERSONESOS, GRAFFITO ON THE INNER SURFACE OF A DISH, 4th CENT. B.C. Ed. pr. E.I. Solomonik, VDI (1976, 3) 125 (dr.).

ΕΥΜΗ---- | ΤΑΝΨΥ̣---- | ΛΕΙΧ----

1. Εὐμή[της or -δης or -λος Solomonik || 3. λείχω = to lick; perhaps a 'convivial joke' Solomonik

809. CHERSONESOS, GRAFFITI ON VASES, 5th - 4th CENT. B.C. Ed. pr. E.I. Solomonik, VDI (1976, 3) 125-128 (ph.).

a) P. 126; 5th cent. B.C. [Δι]ὸς Σῳ[τῆρος]
b) P. 126; 4th cent. B.C. [Δι]ὸς Σωτῆρ[ος]
c) P. 128; 4th cent. B.C. --- ἱερὰ Ἑρ[μᾶ]

Solomonik (p. 127) proposes to restore names of the gods on sherds, published before and now in the Chersonesos Museum (Dionysos, Hermes, Asklepios, Aphrodite, Hygieia).

---

810. CHERSONESOS, GRAFFITI FOR THE MOTHER-GODDESS AND OTHER GODS, 5th - 3rd CENT. B.C. Ed. pr. E.I. Solomonik, VDI (1976, 3) 128-133 (ph., dr.).

a) Μάτηρ (twice, on a dish; 3rd cent. B.C.)
b) ΜΑΘ (on a fragment of a krater; ca. 400 B.C.; Solomonik interprets it as Μά(τηρ) ϑ(εῶν); on this fragment representation of a lion, wild boar and a tree).

Solomonik wants to assign numerous other fragments, now in the Chersonesos Museum and inscribed with M, MA, MAT to the same cult of the Meter; ATT may point to Ἄττις; other sherds with AT (Hellenistic period; cf. p. 132-133) are supposed to refer to Artemis Tauropolos.

---

811. CHERSONESOS, GRAFFITO ON A KYLIX, 4th CENT. B.C. Ed. pr. E.I. Solomonik, VDI (1976, 3) 133-135 (ph.).

Θε(οῖς) Μ(ε)γ(άλοις), or Μ(εγ)άλ(οις)
Ἀθηναΐδος

---

812. CHERSONESOS, GRAFFITI ON SHERDS, 5th - 2nd CENT. B.C. Ed. pr. E.I. Solomonik, VDI (1976, 3) 135-136 (dr.): ΑΧΙΛΛΕ, ΑΧΙ and ΑΧ (monogram). These graffiti are the first evidence that Achilles was worshipped in Chersonesos.

---

813. CHERSONESOS, GRAFFITI ON SHERDS, 3rd CENT. B.C. Ed. pr. E.I. Solomonik, VDI (1976, 3) 136-137 (dr.): ΙΣ and Σ(Α). Solomonik interprets them as a reference to the cult of Isis and Serapis.

---

814. CHERSONESOS, GRAFFITI ON POTS. E.I. Solomonik, VDI (1976, 3) 137-138 draws attention to a number of graffiti on pots containing numeral marks in combination with names of gods (e.g. ΗΡΑ ΙΙ, ΑΡ ΔΔΔ): sums of money offered to these gods ?

---

815. CHERSONESOS, INSCRIPTION OF UNKNOWN CHARACTER, 2nd - 3rd CENT. A.D. Marble fragment. Ed. pr. E.I. Solomonik, NE 11 (1974) 33-34, no. 1 (ph.).

1 ---- αὐτοκράτ]ωρ βα[σιλέυς ? ----
-------------]λα δὲ καὶ [--------
-----------σε]βαστό[ς -----------
4 -----------πό]λιν ? [------------

---

816. CHERSONESOS, FRAGMENTARY INSCRIPTION, 2nd - 3rd CENT. A.D. Marble fragment. Ed. pr. E.I. Solomonik, NE 11 (1974) 37, no. 3 (ph.).

1 ------------ΔΟ
----- χ]αίρειν
3 --------IMENE

3. A proper name: Μενε[e.g. κράτης], or the genitive of a name like Κλειμένης. At the end of the inscription probably the names of the consuls and the archontes in the genitive. Solomonik

---

817. HADRIANOUPOLIS (EDIRNE), INSCRIPTION BY (OR FOR) A SELLER OF WINE. Ed. pr. Z. Taşliklioğlu, Trakya'da epigrafya arastirmalari II (Istanbul, 1971) 38-39, no. 9 (ph.). Cf. Z. Borkowski, ZPE 21 (1976) 75-76 who restudied the inscription with the help of the photo published by Taşliklioğlu, and comments upon the word ὑδρομίκτης in line 3 ("street seller of wine which was sold by the glass mixed with water"). His text runs as follows:

Μιχαὴλ | Ἐγυπτίου | ὑδρομίκτου

3. Ὑδρομήνου Taşliklioğlu; Mihailov reads clearly on the photo of Taşliklioğlu: ὑδρομήκτου.

---

818. HILJADNICA (BETWEEN GORNA GRADESNICA AND ILIDENCI, VALLEY OF THE STRYMON), EPITAPH. IGBR, IV, 2257. Cf. G. Daux, BCH 100 (1976) 227 who suggests in L. 3 Πυρου[λᾳ τῇ μη]τρί.

---

819. JURTA (NOT FAR FROM ODESSOS), DEDICATION TO HEKATE TRIMORPHOS, AFTER 212 A.D. Statue of Hekate, with three representations of the deity; at the right side of the central deity a dog and a deer (?); two deities carry a whip, the third a knife. On the three sides of the statue-base an inscription. Ed. pr. G. Tončeva, MP 16, 2 (1976) 28-32 (ph.). G. Mihailov sent us this text per litt., we print his corrected version:

A. At the left:

Λαμπαδηφόρε
[κ]αὶ νυκταφανῆ, δει-
[νὴ .(.)]ΟΥ/.¯ΑΔ ἀφαν-
[νῆ -------]ε,

B. In the middle:

῾Εκάτη τρίμορφε
καὶ τρίοδε, μυριώνυ-
με, ἐπήκω θεά, Αὐρ.
Φλάβιος β΄

C. At the right:

Φλαβίου
Δολιχαῖος
βουλευτὴς
εὐχαριστήρι-
ον ἀνέθ(ηκε)

A. 3-4. νη--υου αβ, ἀφαν[υμη] --νε---ε Tončeva || B. 3-4. ἐπηκόω νεᾶ Αὐρ[---]ς Φλάβιος Β Tončeva || C. 1. Mihailov assumes that Φλαβίου is a repetition of β΄(= Φλαβίου) in B, 4, so: Αὐρ. Φλάβιος <β΄> | Φλαβίου || C. 2. For another citizen of Doliche, cf. IGBR, I^2, 24 bis.

---

820. LASKAREVO (VALLEY OF THE STRYMON), EPITAPH, 3rd CENT. A.D. IGBR, IV, 2289. G. Daux, BCH 100 (1976) 226-227 suggests the following text:

Ζιλης. Πυρουλα Κατου ζῶσα ἐπύι
τῷ ἀνδρί.

---

1. Πυρουσαλα IGBR, IV, 2289.

---

821. MARONEIA, ARETALOGY OF ISIS, CA. 100 B.C. Ed. pr. Y. Grandjean, Une nouvelle arétalogie d' Isis à Maronée (Ét. prél. Relig. Or., 42; Leiden, 1975) (ph.). R. Merkelbach, ZPE 23 (1976) 234-235 offers new restorations in L. 3-10. We present the whole text below:

ΑΥΤΗΣ
ἐλ]άμβανον γὰρ
]ν θεωρήσειν, ὅταν πρὸς τὸ μέγεθος
4 [τῆς σῆς εὐε]ργεσίας οἱ λόγοι τῶν ἐπαίνων μὴ ἐλλίπωσιν· ΗΙΔΕ
[...]ρωτα τὸ μὲν ἐγκωμίου, τὸ δὲ προσώπου θεῶι κείμενον
[...ἀν]θρώπωι· ὥσπερ οὖν ἐπὶ τῶν ὀμμάτων, Ἶσι, ταῖς εὐχαῖς
[ἐπήκ]ουσας, ἐλθὲ τοῖς ἐπαίνοις καὶ ἐπὶ δευτέραν εὐχήν·
8 [κα]ὶ γὰρ τὸ σὸν ἐγκώμιον τῶν ὀμμάτων ἐστὶ κρεῖσσον,
[ἅπ]αν· οἷς ἔβλεψα τὸν ἥλιον, τούτοις καὶ τὸν σὸν βλέπω κόσμον·
πείθομαι δὲ πάντως σε παρέσεσθαι· εἰ γὰρ ὑπὲρ τῆς ἐμῆς καλουμέ-
νη σωτηρίας ἦλθες, πῶς ὑπὲρ τῆς ἰδίας τιμῆς οὐκ ἂν ἔλθοις; θαρ-
12 ρῶν οὖν πορεύομαι πρὸς τὰ λοιπά, γινώσκων ὅτι τὸ ἐγκώμιον,
νοῦς μὲν θεοῦ, χεῖρες δὲ γράφουσιν ἀνθρώπου· καὶ πρῶ-
τον ἐπὶ τὸ γένος ἥξω, τῶν ἐγκωμίων ποιησάμενος ἀρχὴν
τὴν πρώτην σου τοῦ γένους ἀρχήν· Γῆν φασι πάντων μη-
16 τέρα γενηθῆναι· ταύτηι δὲ σὺ θυγάτηρ ἐσπάρης πρώτηι·
σύνοικον δ᾽ ἔλαβες Σέραπιν, καὶ τὸν κοινὸν ὑμῶν θεμένων γάμον,
τοῖς ὑμετέροις προσώποις ὁ κόσμος ἀνέλαμψεν ἐνομματισθεὶς
῾Ηλίωι καὶ Σελήνηι· δύο μὲν οὖν ἐστε, καλεῖσθε δὲ πολλοὶ παρ᾽ ἀν-

θρώποις· μόνους γὰρ ὁ βίος ὑμᾶς θεοὺς οἶδεν· πῶς οὖν τῶν
ἐγκωμίων οὐ δυσκράτητος ὁ λόγος ὅταν δέηι τὸν ἔπαινον
πολλοῖς θεοῖς προναῶσαι; Αὕτη μεθ' Ἑρμοῦ γράμμαθ' εὗρεν
καὶ τῶν γραμμάτων ἃ μὲν ἱερὰ τοῖς μύσταις, ἃ δὲ δημόσια
τοῖς πᾶσιν· αὕτη τὸ δίκαιον ἔστησεν ἵν' ἕκαστος ἡμῶν,
ὡς ἐκ τῆς φύσεως τὸν θάνατον ἴσον ἔσχεν, καὶ ζῆν ἀπὸ τῶν
ἴσων εἰδῆι· αὕτη τῶν ἀνθρώπων οἷς μὲν βάρβαρον, οἷς δ' ἑλλη-
νίδα διάλεκτον ἔστησεν ἵν' ἧι τὸ γένος διαλλάσσον μὴ μό-
νον ἀνδράσιν πρὸς γυναῖκας ἀλλὰ καὶ πᾶσι πρὸς πάντας·
[σ]ὺ νόμους ἔδωκας, θεσμοὶ δ' ἐκαλοῦντο κατὰ πρώτας· τοι-
[γα]ροῦν αἱ πόλεις εὐστάθησαν, οὐ τὴν βίαν νομικὸν ἀλλὰ
[τ]ὸν νόμον ἀβίαστον εὑροῦσαι· σὺ τιμᾶσθαι γονεῖς ὑπὸ
[τ]έκνων ἐποίησας, οὐ μόνον ὡς πατέρων, ἀλλ' ὡς καὶ θεῶν
[φ]ροντίσασα· τοιγαροῦν ἡ χάρις κρείσσων ὅτε τῆς φύσε-
ως τὴν ἀνάγκην καὶ θεὰ νόμον ἔγραψεν· σοὶ πρὸς κατοίκησιν
Αἴγυπτος ἐστέρχθη· σὺ μάλιστα τῆς Ἑλλάδος ἐτίμησας τὰς
Ἀθήνας· κεῖθι γὰρ πρῶτον τοὺς καρποὺς ἐξέφηνας· Τριπτόλε-
μος δὲ τοὺς ἱεροὺς δράκοντάς σου καταζεύξας ἁρματοφο-
ρούμενος εἰς πάντας Ἕλληνας διέδωκε τὸ σπέρμα· τοιγαροῦν
τῆς μὲν Ἑλλάδος ἰδεῖν σπεύδομεν τὰς Ἀθήνας, τῶν δ' Ἀθη-
νῶν Ἐλευσῖνα, τῆς μὲν Εὐρώπης νομίζοντες τὴν πόλιν, τῆς
δὲ πόλεως τὸ ἱερὸν κόσμον· ἔγνω τὸν βίον ἐξ ἀνδρὸς
συνεστηκότα καὶ γυναικός· ἔγνω τερον τὴν γυ-
ναῖκα· πῶς ἔδει τὸ ἧσσον
N ἐσφραγισ

3. ΝΘΕΩΡΗΣΕΙΝΟΙΑΝ Grandjean; θεωρήσειν, ὅταν Merkelbach || 4-6. ἧι δέ | [σε ἐ]ρωτᾷ τὸ μὲν ἐγκώμιον· τὸ δὲ προσώπου θεῶι κείμενον,| [οὐκ ἀν]θρώπωι Merkelbach; in L. 4-5 Grandjean had already thought of ἧι δέ, but he also proposed ηἶδε|[α δὲ π]ρῶτα; in L. 6 he suggested [οὐκ ἀν]θρώπωι || 9. [.]ΙΑΝΟΙΣ Grandjean, who suggested [π]λά-νοις and put a comma after τούτοις. However, on the photo not the slightest trace of the lambda is visible; [ἄπ]αν· οἷς ... τὸν ἥλιον, τούτοις κτλ. Merkelbach.

---

822. MARONEIA, EPITAPH. Ed. pr. Cyriacus of Ancona, apud E.W. Bodnar - C. Mitchell, Cyriacus of Ancona's journeys in the Propontis and the Northern Aegean 1444-1445 (Memoirs American Philosophical Society 112; Philadelphia, 1976) p. 42 ("unpublished").

Δημοκρίτου γυνή.

---

823. PANION, CONSTRUCTION OR REPAIR OF A CITY-WALL, 383-408 A.D. IG, X, 2, 1, 44. D. Feissel, BCH 100 (1976) 273-275 points out that the stone originates from Thrace (Panion) and suggests the following text ("pour s' en tenir à un minimum de suppléments assurés"):

[᾿Επὶ τῆς ? ---]ν βασιλίας
[τῶν -------δ]εσποτῶν
[---------Φλαβί]ου ᾿Αρκαδίου
[---------ἐκτίσθ]η τὸ τεῖχος ...

---

824. PČELAROVO (IN THE RHODOPIAN MOUNTAINS), LEAD WEIGHT, 211-222 A.D. Rectangular lead weight; at the top a circular enlargement; inside it the seal ("cachet") of the die ("cour monétaire"): a hexagonal star surrounded by wreaths (or the crescent of the moon). Weight 336 gr. (= ± 341 gr. = Oriental standard of the 2nd-3rd cent. A.D.). Inscription on the front side and on the back. Ed. pr. V. Gerasimova-Tomova, VEKOVE 3 (1976) 77-79 (ph.); cf. also id., NUMIZMATIKA 12, 1-2 (1977) 23-24 (ph.).

A. Recto: Λεί|τρα.
In the circular enlargement: Μητ[ροπόλεως Λαο]δικαίας Αὐγύσ-τ(ας).

B. Verso: Οἱ πε-
ρὶ Αὐρ(ήλιον) ᾿Ασ-
κληπιόδω-
ρον Φιλ[τ]ε-
παρ̣[η]ν[ὸν or -οὶ δο]-
ρ̣ω̣ν̣.

A. G. Mihailov, to whom we owe this text, wonders whether one should perhaps read μετ(ρονόμοι) ?? || B. 4-6. -ρον Φιλ[τ]ε|παρ[η]-ν[ὸν or -οὶ δω]|ρ̣ο̣ν̣ (or [δο]|ρ̣ω̣ν̣; without accent) Gerasimova-Tomova (Φιλτεπαρηνός is supposed to refer to a village); Mihailov has doubts about the reading. On the photo he distinguishes (L. 4 ff.): ΡΟΝΦΙΛ⁻C|ΠΛᴰ--- . Laodikeia is in Syria (nowadays Latakija).

---

825. PERINTHOS, HONORARY INSCRIPTION FOR M. ULPIUS SENECIO SATURNINUS, REIGN OF ALEXANDER SEVERUS. IGR, I, 797. Cf. L. Robert, STUDCLAS 16 (1974) 69-74 who suggests a correction in line 6-7 (διὰ τὰς περὶ αὐ|τὴν εὐεργεσίας instead of διὰ τῆς περὶ αὐ|τὴν εὐεργεσίας) and in his study of the text rejects the remarks of H. Schaefer (R.E., Suppl. IX, 1962, col. 1303, s.v. Prostates): the statue was not erected by Perinthos but by Kyzikos, M. Ulpius Senecio Saturninus was not a Greek who had received the Roman citizenship and interceded in difficulties between Perinthos and neighbouring cities, but a governor of Thrace under Severus Alexander who restored the good relations between Perinthos and Kyzikos.

---

826. PERINTHOS, DEDICATION BY THE "PHILAPAMEIS" TO HOMONOIA, LATER IMPERIAL PERIOD. Ed. pr. Z. Taşliklioğlu, Trakya'da epigrafya arastirmalari II (Istanbul, 1971) 122-124, no. 8 (ph.). L. Robert, STUDCLAS 16 (1974) 61-69 (ph.) gives a slightly corrected

text, and, showing how Perinthos and Apameia (in Bithynia) were economicly dependent on each other, explains why an association in Perinthos, named "the Philapameis" (parallels for this word), dedicated an altar to Homonoia (= Concordia). The text of the inscription runs as follows:

	Ἀγαθῆι [τύχηι]		τὸν βωμὸν
	Τὸ συνέδρ[ιον]		τῇ̣ Ὁμονοίᾳ
3	τῶν Φιλαπαμέω[ν]	6	εὐτυχῶς

3. τῶν φιλαπαμ[ειῶν] Taşliklioğlu || 5. τῆι Ὁμονοία[ι] Taşliklioğlu.

---

827. PERINTHOS, FUNERARY EPIGRAM FOR A MOSAIC-WORKER, 1st - 2nd CENT. A.D. CIG, II, 2025 (Peek, GV, 1020). After M. Vickers, CR 22 (1972) 175, who used another copy, W. Peek, ZPE 22 (1976) 184 returns to the text (especially to LL. 1 and 4). In the text below we incorporate in L. 1-2 Vickers' readings:

[-----]ο̣λίεσσι τέχνῃ̣ νε[ί]|κησα πρόπαντας |
2 ψηφοθ̣έτας δώ|ροις Παλλάδος αὐ|ξόμενος.
υἷα λι|πὼν βουλῆς σύν|εδρον Πρόκλον ἰ|σότεχνόν μοι |
4 ὀγδωκοντούτης | [-------------------].

1. [πάσαις or πολλαῖς ἐν πο]λίεσσι CIG; [πολλαῖς ἐν π]ο̣λίεσσι Peek (ZPE), who wonders whether the first line may not have been |ΠΟΛΛΑΙΣΕΝ| so that the space-problem, as implied by the drawing in CIG (six letters before ΛΙΕΣΣΙ) could be circumvented || τέχνην [ἥσ]|κησα πρὸ πάντ[ων] CIG and Peek (GV) || 2. ψηφοδ[έ]τ[η]ς CIG; ψηφοδ[έ]τας Peek (GV), Vickers; ψηφοθέτας J. and L. Robert, BE (1972) no. 286a, in accordance with Vickers' copy || [εὑρ]άμενος CIG; [ἀρ]άμενος Peek (GV) || 4. [τοῦδε τάφοιο λαχών] CIG; [ἐνθάδε νῦν ? ἔθανον] Peek (GV); Vickers' copy has TENT̄ ---; π̣έντε̣ [τ' ἔχων ἔ|θανον] Peek (ZPE), but cf. J. and L. Robert, BE (1977) no. 297.

---

828. EMPORIUM PIRETENSIUM, MEASURING TABLE. IGBR, II, 695. Cf. L. Robert, STUDCLAS 16 (1974) 67, note 34 who restores ξέστης οἰν(ηρός) instead of οἴν(ου).

---

829. SERDICA, CONSTRUCTION OF A WALL BY MARCUS AURELIUS AND COMMODUS, 27 NOVEMBER 176 - 17 MARCH 180 A.D. Two stones, both broken at the left, bearing exactly the same inscription. I) G. Mihailov, IGBR, IV, 1902; II) M. Stančeva, ARCH (Sofia) 17, 3 (1975) 30-36. G. Mihailov, EPIGRAPHICA 38 (1976) 21-24 corrects the combined version, presented by Stančeva, and presents the following text:

Ἀγαθῆι τύχηι.
2 [Οἱ μέγιστοι καὶ θ]ειότατοι αὐτοκράτορες καίσαρες Μ(ᾶρκος) Αὐ[ρή-
λιος Ἀντωνεῖ]-
[νος σεβαστὸς Γερ]μανικὸς Σαρματικὸς πατὴρ πατρίδος [ἀρχιερεὺς
μέγισ]-
4 [τος καὶ Λ(ούκιος) Αὐρήλιος Κόμμοδος] σεβαστὸς Γερμανικὸς Σαρμ[α-
τικὸς ----]
[----πρόκριτος] τῆς νεολαίας τῇ Σερδων πόλει τὰ τ[είχη ἔδοσαν vel
sim., ἡγεμο]-
6 [νεύοντος τῆς Θρᾳκῶ]ν ἐπαρχείας Ἀσελλίου Αἰμιλιανοῦ πρε[σβ(ευ-
τοῦ) σεβ(αστῶν) ἀντι]-
[στρατ(ήγου) ὑπάτου ἀ]ποδεδειγμένου, ἐπιτροπεύοντο[ς τῆς (αὐτῆς)
ἐπαρχείας]
8 [----------]ου.

5. [ἔδοσαν vel sim. ca 12 litt. τ]ῆς νεολαίας Stančeva (with a lot of suppositions about the word which precedes τ]ῆς νεολαίας); Mihailov doubts if there was really a verb in line 5 || [πρόκριτος vel sim.] τῆς νεολαίας = princeps iuventutis Mihailov || 7-8. ἐπιτροπεύοντο[ς τῆς] | [αὐτῆς ἐπαρχείας καὶ τοῦ δήμ]ου Stančeva; Mihailov rejects in line 8 [καὶ τοῦ δήμ]ου and supposes that in this line has been mentioned the name of the procurator of Finance of the province. J. and L. Robert, BE (1976) no. 476 and BE (1977) no. 306 agree with him.

---

830. TÂŽA, DEDICATION TO THE THRACIAN HERO, 1st HALF 3rd CENT. A.D. Lower left side of a marble slab with relief, representing the Thracian Hero. Ed. pr. G. Tabakova-Canova, MP 16, 3 (1976) 8, no. 3 (ph.). We owe this text to G. Mihailov (per litt.).

Αὐλουπ[ορις --------]
τοτη δ[ῶρον ἀνέθηκεν].

MOESIA

---

831. RELIGION. For the Dolichenus-cult in Moesia Inferior, cf. our no. 783.

---

832. MOESIA SUPERIOR, CORPUS OF INSCRIPTIONS. In F. Papazoglou, Inscriptions de la Mésie Supérieure, vol. I: Singidunum et le Nord-Ouest de la province (Belgrade, 1976) one finds a number of Greek inscriptions (most of them published before): no. 70 (ph.) = Peek, GV, no. 651 (cf. J. and L. Robert, BE, 1958, no. 301; BE, 1970, no. 393; BE, 1977, no. 312); no. 71 (ph.) = CIL, III, 13811 (= JÖAI 4, 1901, Beibl. 130, no. 35); no. 113 (ph.) = JÖAI 15 (1912),

Beibl. 236, no. 39 (cf. BE, 1959, no. 233); no. 114 (ph.) = ZANT 7 (1957) 248 (cf. BE, 1959, no. 233; in BE, 1977, no. 312 J. and L. Robert suggest in L. 3-4 Π[ρα]|ΰλου instead of Π[α?]|ύλου); no. 148 (ph.) = JÖAI 8 (1905) 22, no. 63; no. 149 and 150 (ph.): two inedita (cf. BE, 1977, no. 312).

---

833. HISTRIA, COMPLAINT TO THE GOVERNOR JULIUS SEVERUS, 159-161 A.D. Ed. pr. S.J. Stoian, SCIV, II, 2 (1951) 137 ff; id., DACIA 3 (1959) 369-390. B. Gerov, EIRENE 14 (1976) 53-54, note 99 restores in frag. 3, line 7-8 [αὐτο]υργούς instead of [λιτο]υργούς. Cf. also J. and L. Robert, BE (1958) no. 341 who already had doubts about the restorations of S.J. Stoian. Cf. SEG, XIX, 476.

---

834. KALLATIS, THE TEMPLE OF HOMONOIA. Starting from the inscription published in DACIA 2 (1958) 212, which mentions the temple of Homonoia, D.M. Pippidi, STUDCLAS 16 (1974) 88-99 deals with problems connected with that temple (since the article is in Roumanian, we cannot specify these problems).

---

835. NIKOPOLIS AD ISTRUM, HONORARY INSCRIPTION FOR ALEXANDER SEVERUS, 222-235 A.D. Ed. pr. T. Dremsizova-Nelčinova, BIAB 34 (1974) 326 (ph.).

Ἀγαθῆ]ι [τύχηι
............Μ(ᾶρκον) Αὐρήλιον Σευ]ῆρον Ἀ[λέξανδρον
.........................θε]οῦ Σευήρου [ἡ βουλὴ καὶ
ὁ δῆμος τῆς Νεικοπολειτῶν πρὸ]ς Ἰστρῳ πόλις.

---

836. NIKOPOLIS AD ISTRUM, DEDICATION, 1st HALF 3rd CENT. A.D. Ed. pr. T. Dremsizova-Nelčinova, BIAB 34 (1974) 327-328 (ph.).

Ἀγαθῆι τύ]χηι
.....θεᾶ or θεῷ ἐπ]ηκόω[.....
.............Μᾶρ]κος Μο[....
ἔ]στη[σε or ἀνέ]στη[σεν

---

837. NOVAE, DEDICATION TO ASKLEPIOS. Ed. pr. E. Kolendo, BIAB 34 (1974) 193 (ph.).

Ἀσκλη[πι]|ῷ θεῷ σω[τῆ]|ρη [..] Διό[δω]|ρος?

---

838. TOMIS, HONORARY INSCRIPTION FOR P. AELIUS HAMMONIUS, ± 240 A.D. IGR, I, 623; ILS, 8851. H. Chantraine, Freigelassene und Sklaven im Dienst der römischen Kaiser (Wiesbaden, 1967) 27 expres-

ses doubt as to whether the emperor's name forms part of Catullinus' status-indication (so that he was manumitted by Gordian) or is to be taken with the occupational title λιβράριος (so that he could have been manumitted by an earlier emperor). P.R.C. Weaver, EPIGRAPHISCHE STUDIEN 11 (1976) 226 excludes the second alternative. For the functions and chronology of the career of the eques P. Aelius Hammonius (with reference to this inscription), cf. I. Piso, DACIA 30 (1976) 251-257.

---

839. TOMIS, DEDICATION TO THE THEOS HYPSISTOS, 2nd - 3rd CENT. A.D. SEG, XXIV, 1065. D.M. Pippidi, STUDCLAS 16 (1974) 260-263 (in Roumanian, with a French summary on p. 265) gives some information on the documents concerning the cult of the Theos Hypsistos discovered during the last century in the Bosporean Kingdom, Thrace and Anatolia; Hypsistos is not identical with Zalmoxis-Gebeleizis (as Pârvan thinks). To derive from SEG, XXIV, 1065 a Jewish influence on the pantheon of Tomis during the first centuries A.D. has little probability.

---

840. TOPRAISAR (AREA OF CONSTANTZA), AMPHORA-STAMPS, 4th CENT. B.C. M. Irimia, PONTICA 9 (1976) 37-54 announces the discovery of a tumulus (350-325 B.C.) at Topraisar, with 22 amphorae from Heraklea Pontica. Nine of them bear on their neck a stamp Νόσσος | ἐπὶ Κερ[κίνου], eight others have Νόσσος | ἐπὶ Παυσαν[ία] (ph.).

DACIA

---

841. THE RELATIONS BETWEEN THE GRECO-ROMAN AND THE NATIVE DACIAN WORLD. Cf. no. 1861.

---

842. CORPUS OF INSCRIPTIONS. In 1976 E. Popescu's Inscripţiile greceşti şi latine din secolele IV-XIII descoperite in România (Inscriptiones intra fines Dacoromaniae repertae graecae et latinae anno CCLXXXIV recentiores) (Bucarest, 1976) appeared. Non vidimus. Cf. J. and L. Robert, BE (1977) no. 307. In Epigraphica. Travaux dédiés au VIIe Congrès d' épigraphie grecque et latine (Constantza, 1977) p. 255-283 Popescu discusses several inscriptions from his Corpus in an article about governors, generals and bishops of the provincia Scythia during the 4th - 6th cent. A.D.

---

843. ROMULA, SIGNATURE, ROMAN PERIOD. Graffito on a Roman vase. Ed. D. Tudor, AARCHSYR 21 (1971) 73. S. Sanie, SCIV 27 (1976) 402-403 comments upon the name Γαδδατης.

NORTH SHORE OF THE BLACK SEA

---

844. SLAVERY AND INSCRIPTIONS IN THE AREA OF THE BLACK SEA. B. Nadel, Slavery and related Forms of Labor on the North Shore of the Euxine in Antiquity, Actes du Colloque 1973 sur l' esclavage (Paris, 1976) p. 197-231, uses many inscriptions from the North shore of the Black Sea in his discussion of slavery and manumission both in pre-Roman and Roman times.

---

845. BEREZAN, PRIVATE LETTER. Lead lamella. Ed. pr. Ju. G. Vinogradov, VDI (1971, 4) 74-100. Cf. J. Chadwick, PCPHS 199 (1973) 35-37; B. Bravo, DHA 1 (1974) 111-187 (non vidimus); D.M. Pippidi, STUDCLAS 16 (1974) 253-255; V.P. Yailenko, VDI (1974, 1) 133-152; id., VDI (1975, 3) 133-150; A.P. Miller, ZPE 17 (1975) 157-160; R. Merkelbach, ZPE 17 (1975) 161-162; B. Bravo, DHA 3 (1977) 52-53, note 6. We present here Chadwick's text:

Ὦ Πρωταγόρη, ὁ πατήρ τοι ἐπιστέλλε̄. ἀδικε͂ται
ὑπὸ Ματάσυος, δο̄λο͂ται γάρ μιγ καὶ το͂
φορτηγεσίο̄ ἀπεστέρε̄σεν. ἐλθὼμ παρ' Ἀναξαγό|ρην ←
ἀπήγησαι, φησὶ γὰρ αὐτὸν Ἀναξαγόρεω
δο͂λον ἔ̄ναι μυθεόμενος· "Τἄ̄μ' Ἀνα<ξα>γόρης ἔ̋χε̄,
καὶ δο̄́λο̄ς καὶ δο̄́λας κοίκίας." ὁ δὲ ἀναβῶι τε
καὶ οὔ φησιν ἔ̄ναι οὐδὲν ἑωυτῶι τε καὶ Ματάσ<υι>
καί φησιν ἔ̄ναι ἐλεόθερος καὶ οὐδὲν ἔ̄ναι ἑωυτ<ῶ>ι
καὶ Ματά<συι. Μα>τάσυ̣<ι> δὲ τί αὐτῶι κἀναξαγόρη αὐτοὶ
οἴδασι κατὰ σφᾶς αὐτο̄͂ς. ταῦτ' Ἀναξαγόρη λέγε̄ν
καὶ τῆ γυναικί. ἕτερα δέ τοι ἐπιστέλλε̄. τὴμ μητέρα
καὶ το̄͂ς ἀδε<λ>φεὺς <ο>ἵ ε̄̓σ{σ}ιν ἐν Ἀρβινάτηισιν ἄγε̄ν ἐς τὴμ πόλιν,
αὐτὸς δὲ Ε̣ὔ̣νεορος ἐλθὼμ παρά μιν <ἰ>θύωρα καταβήσεται.

Reverse:

Ἀχιλλοδώρο̄ τὸ μολί-
βδιον παρὰ τὸμ παῖδα
κἀναξαγόρην

Date: 2nd half 6th cent. B.C. Vinogradov; ca. 500 B.C. Jeffery (cf. Chadwick), Yailenko, K.S. Gorbunova (Archaeological Reports for 1971-1972, Leningrad, 1972, p. 49); 1st quarter 5th cent. B.C. Bravo (DHA, 3, 1977, 52-53) || 2. δολο͂ται Vinogradov, Yailenko, Merkelbach || 3. ἀπεστέρεσεν Vinogradov, Yailenko || 5. ΑΝΑΓΟΡΗΣ lead lamella, corr. Vinogradov || 7. ΜΑΤΑΣΙΝ lead lamella; Ματάσ<υι> Vinogradov, Chadwick; Ματασ<υ>ι{ν} Yailenko; Ματασιν Merkelbach || 8. ΕΩΤΑΙ lead lamella, corr. Vinogradov || 9. ΜΑΤΑΤΑΣΥΕΔΕΤΙ lead lamella; Ματά{τα}συ<ι>. τί δέ Vinogradov; Ματά<συι. Μα>τάσυ<ι> δὲ τί Chadwick, Yailenko; Ματ{ατ}ασυ· ε̄́ (= εἰ) δέ τι Merkelbach ||

12. ΑΔΕΦΕΥΣ lead lamella; Vinogradov corrected into ἀδε<λ>φεύς, followed by Chadwick and Merkelbach; ἀδεφεῦς (elision of the lambda) Yailenko || ΙΕΣΣΙΝΕΝΑΡΒΙΝΑ̣ΤΗΙΣΙΝ lead lamella; ἵεσσιν ἐν ἄρ<τ>' ἵνα τῆισιν Vinogradov; <ο>ἵ ἔ̣σ{σ}ιν ἐν 'Αρβινάτηισιν Chadwick, Merkelbach (who gives ἵ) || 13. Ε̣ὄ̣νεορος Vinogradov, Chadwick; Γ̣ο̣νεόρο̄ς Yailenko; ἐ̣<ς> Νεορο̄̀ς Merkelbach; Bravo reads for letter 7-10 εγον || ΜΙΝΘΥ̱ΩΡΑ lead lamella; μιν θυωρά Vinogradov, Yailenko; μιν <ι>θ̣ύωρα Chadwick; Μινθυωρα Merkelbach.

---

846. KERCH, EPITAPH ?, 2nd - 3rd CENT. A.D. CIRB, no. 838. N. V. Shebalin, VDI (1976, 4) 108-112 maintains that the text is an epitaph and proposes the following reading:

Γλυκαρίων ἁλίω<ς> ὄνομ' ἑῶν | ἔτυχ[ες]

"Glykarion they named thee all in vain" Shebalin; in the ed. pr. one finds: Γλυκα[ρ]ίων ἁλι<εύω>ν ? ΟΜΕΩΝ | ἔτυχ[εν]: "a certain Glykarion while fishing (?) got omei (?)" (ὁμεύς is supposed to be a fish !!).

---

847. NOVOGYLANSKI (DONETS), GRAFFITI, 1st CENT. A.D. Two inscriptions on a bronze cauldron, found in a tomb in the area of Donets. Ed. pr. B.J. Michlin, NE 11 (1974) 29-32 (ph.).

a) ΙΗ
b) Πιδα<κ>όης μορ<ά>ζη Σπυρυά<ν>δρου ν<η>δύς

a. 18, kotyloi Michlin; b. "Full of water, Spyriandros' stomach will receive it" Michlin (?? ed.).

---

848. OLBIA, MONETARY DECREE, CA. 350-325 B.C. Syll.³, 218 (H. W. Pleket, Epigraphica I, Leiden, 1964, no. 7). Ju. G. Vinogradov - P.O. Karyszkowski, VDI (1976, 4) 20-42 date this text to 350-325 B.C. (and not to the "4th cent. B.C." in general), restore in L. 24-25 ἐ̣[νά]|το ἡμιστατῆρο instead of ἐ̣[νδεκά]|το and point out that "if their new reading and date be accepted, the exchange value indicated for these coins by the price set in the decree accords with the market rate of exchange for Cyzicenes in the Alexander period".

---

849. PANTIKAPAION, FUNERARY EPIGRAM, END 1st - 1st HALF 2nd CENT. A.D. Ed. pr. A.I. Boltunova, STUDCLAS 15 (1973) 125-130 (ph.). Cf. R. Merkelbach, ZPE 20 (1976) 82.

Οὔνομα Δινδίανος μοι ἔχων | δ' ἔτι κούριον ἄνθος
πρωθή|βης ἱερῆς ἔπλεον ἐξ 'Αλύβης |

τυτθῆς ἐνπορίης πειρώμε|νος· ἀμφὶ δὲ γαῖαν
Κιμμερί|ην Μοίρων ἐξετέλεσσα μί|τους
ἄχνοος. Οὐδέ τι σῆ|μα κατ' ἀνθήσαντος ἰούλου, |
οὔ τι δὲ γᾶ μάτηρ οὔτε θα|νόντος ἔχει.
Πλεῖτε νέοι, | πλεῖτ' ἄνδρες ὅπου μόνον | ἠελίου φῶς·
ἓν τέλος ἀν|θρώποις πᾶσι βίου θάνατος.

6. οὔ τε Boltunova; οὔτε Merkelbach || 8. ἔντελος Boltunova; ἓν τέλος Merkelbach.

DELOS

850. THE EXPRESSION ἐν Νήσῳ IN INSCRIPTIONS FROM DELOS. J. Tréheux, Recueil Plassart, 175-204 defends the view that Νῆσος "est, à Rhénée, à cheval sur l' isthme, un territoire étroit dont les limites se confondent avec celles du sanctuaire d' Artémis-Hécate".

851. ARCHITECTURAL TERMINOLOGY. R. Martin, Recueil Plassart, 125-134 in an attempt to interpret the description of Odysseus' house in the Odyssey discusses a number of architectural terms occuring in Delian inscriptions (μέλαθρον, κίων, σταθμός, ὀρσοθύρη).

852. ARCHONS IN THE DELIAN AMPHICTYONY. J. Tréheux, EAC 5 (1976) 87-95 establishes a list of Delian archons for the Amphictyony in the period 433-314 B.C.

853. THE CHRONOLOGY OF ATHENIAN PRIESTS AND ARCHONS IN IMPERIAL ATHENS. S. Follet, Athènes, 149-199 studies several inscriptions from Delos: I. Délos 2535-2539, 2542, 2543, 2545, 2691, 2852: "L' examen des stèles et des fragments de stèles conduit donc ... à une remise en question de la chronologie traditionelle" (p. 160).

854. THE INHABITANTS OF DELOS IN THE PERIOD 166-155 B.C. M.-F. Baslez, REG 89 (1976) 343-360 discusses the meaning and position of the οἰκοῦντες ἐν Δήλωι (I. Délos 1408, A, I, 38-40; 1416, B, II, 7-8; 1416, B, I, 114; 1416, B, II, 95-96) and of the Ῥηναιεῖς (I. Délos, 1497 and 1510). On p. 360, note 58 she tries to make a stemma of the various Ἡραίπποι mentioned in I. Délos 1416, B, I, 89-99; 1416, B, II, 56; 1419, 7. Some members of this family are supposed to have received Athenian citizenship (cf. M. Guarducci, I. Cret., II, p. 144).

855. DELOS, AMPHICTYONIC ACT, 360-330 B.C. J. Coupry, I. Délos, Période de l' Amphictyonie Attico-Délienne, no. 104, 8, B. M.-F. Baslez, REG 89 (1976) 355 restores L. 14 as follows: [Ἀθην]ό[δ]ωρος Ἅγ[ν]οσιος ἐμ Προβ[αλίνθωι ἐγκεκτημένος] and rejects J. Coupry's reading [Ἀθην]ό[δ]ωρος ΑΓ.ΟΣΙΟΣ ἐμ Π̣ροβ̣[αλίνθωι οἰκῶν]. Cf. also J. Tréheux, EAC 5 (1976) 92-93.

---

856. DELOS, AMPHICTYONIC ACT, 342-341 B.C. J. Coupry, I. Délos, Période de l' Amphictyonie Attico-Délienne, no. 104, 27, B. J. Tréheux, EAC 5 (1976) 93-95 proposes to read L. 8 as follows: ἐν τῶι οἴκωι ὃ ἦγο<ν> τ̣ὰ ἀναθήμα[τα τὰ ἐκ τõ νεώ]. Coupry printed: ἐν τῶι οἴκωι·ΟΗΓΟΥ.Α ἀνάθημ[α-. Homolle read: ἐν τῶι οἴκωι ο[ὐκ] ὄν̣τ̣α ἀναθήμα[τα]. Durrbach: ἐν τῶι οἴκωι ὃ [πρ]ὸς̣ τ̣ὰ ἀναθήμα[τα].

---

857. DELOS, ACCOUNT OF THE HIEROPOIOI, CA. 304 B.C. IG, XI, 2, 144. J. Tréheux, EAC 5 (1976) 93 proposes to read in A, L. 14 Ἄμνος Δεξικράτους (and not [Φί?]λαρχος Δεξικράτους). Before Ἄμνος there is a rasura. Tréheux adduces evidence for this Ἄμνος.

---

858. DELOS, ACCOUNT OF THE HIEROPOIOI, 235-234 B.C. I. Délos, 313. In A, L. 32 J. Tréheux, EAC 5 (1976) 89-91 proposes to read: [κυ]μβία δύο, τὸ μὲν ἐ[π'] Ἀριστοφά[νους ἄ]ρχοντος, τὸ δ' ἐπ̣' Ἐπινώιδα (instead of τὸ δέ [ἐ]στ̣ιν ΩΙΔΑ). He also dates the text to 235 B.C and excludes 234 B.C. (cf. note 29, p. 89).

---

859. DELOS, DEDICATION TO ZEUS KYNTHIOS AND ATHENA KYNTHIA OF A "κατάκλυστον", END 2nd - BEGINNING 1st CENT. B.C. I. Délos, 2420. Cf. E. Will, BCH 100 (1976) 589-590 who defends against P. Bruneau (BCH, 91, 1967, 423 ff. and BCH, 99, 1975, 283-286) the view that in L. 4-5 "κατάκλυστον" = κατάκλυστρον = compluvium (and not "l' offrande portant la dédicace inscrite, c' est à dire le pavement" as Bruneau thought).

---

860. DELOS, COMMEMORATION-FORMULA. Graffito. Ed. pr. G. Siebert, BCH 100 (1976) 821 (ph.).

Μνήσθη or μνησθῇ Φίλιππ<ος>

RHODES

---

861. THE ματρόξενοι IN INSCRIPTIONS FROM RHODES. Cf. J.-M. Hannick, AC 45 (1976) 137-138.

---

862. RHODES, HONORARY DECREE FOR M. COCCEIUS TIMASARCHOS, CA. 200 A.D. Base of a honorary statue, now in the museum. Ed. pr. G. Pugliese Carratelli, PP 5 (1950) 76, no. 1. H. W. Pleket, ZPE 20 (1976) 7-9 discusses the agonothesia of Timasarchos at Olympia.

---

863. RHODES (EXACT PROVENANCE UNKNOWN), GRAFFITO ON A SUBGEOMETRIC CUP, 8th CENT. B.C. ? Jeffery, LSAG, p. 347, no. 1; Guarducci, EG, I, p. 328-329, no. 1. Cf. O. Masson, ARCHCLASS 25-26 (1973-74) 428-431 who studies the name Κόρακος and C. Gallavotti, HELIKON 15-16 (1975-76) 71-73 who discusses the inscription and proposes the following text:

ϙοράϙō ἡμὶ ϙύλιξ τ[έρεινα

ϙυλιξς̣ Jeffery; ϙύλιξ τ[õ + patronymic Guarducci, Masson.

---

864. RHODES (EXACT PROVENANCE UNKNOWN), INSCRIPTION ON A VASE, CA. 450 B.C. ? Jeffery, LSAG, p. 350, no. 30; Guarducci, EG, I, p. 333-334, no. 6. Cf. C. Gallavotti, HELIKON 15-16 (1975-76) 84-85 who thinks that in the sentence κάλλιστα γᾶς *h*α Βρασία, *h*ως ἐμὶν δοκεῖ (second part of the inscription), Βρασία is a girl from Lindos, designated by the name of the Lindian deme of the Brasioi.

---

865. RHODES (KAMIROS), INSCRIPTION ON THE MONUMENT OF IDAMENEUS. 600-575 B.C. IG, XII, 1, 737; Jeffery, LSAG, p. 348, no. 5. C. Gallavotti, HELIKON 15-16 (1975-76) 73-76 studies the inscription and presents the text as follows:

→ Σᾶμα τόζ' 'Ιδα|← μενεὺς ποίη|→ σα, *h*ίνα Κλε̄õς |← εἴη·
→ Ζεὺ δέ νιν, ὅστις |← πημαίνοι, λειō|→ λη θείε.

3. κλέος IG, Jeffery.

---

866. RHODES (KAMIROS), GRAFFITO ON A CORINTHIAN VASE (REPRESENTING A SEATED KOMAST), 550 B.C. ? Jeffery, LSAG, p. 349, no. 9. C. Gallavotti, HELIKON 15-16 (1975-76) 77-78 reads the text as follows:

χετείω, κὠὐ νᾶμα ἴχεται

χεζ̣ει οϙου ναμα ιχεται Jeffery.

---

867. RHODES (KAMIROS), INSCRIPTION ON THE LESCHE OF EUTHYTIDES, 550-525 B.C. ? IG, XII, 1, 709; Jeffery, LSAG, p. 349, no. 15; Guarducci, EG, I, p. 331-332, no. 4. C. Gallavotti, HELIKON 15-16

(1975-76) 76-77 studies this inscription and presents the following text ("in grafia ammodernata"):

Εὐθυτίδα |² ἡμὶ λέσχα, |
³τωὐπραξίου δῶ |⁴ τωὐφάγου, |⁵ τωὐφυλίδα.

He translates it as follows: "Io sono il ritrovo di Euthytida, l' ostello del pacifico, del buongustaio, del compagnone".

---

3. τõ Πραξσιόδō IG, Guarducci || 4. τοὐφ[ά]γō i.e. τοῦ (Ε)ὐφάγου IG; τοὐφ<ύ>λō (= "figlio di Euphylos") Guarducci || 5. τοὐφυλίδα i.e. τοῦ (Ε)ὐφυλίδα IG, Guarducci ("figlio di Euphylidas").

---

868. RHODES (KAMIROS), INSCRIPTION ON A KANTHAROS, 2nd HALF 6th CENT. B.C. Ed. M. Segre - I. Pugliese Carratelli, Tituli Camirenses (ASAA 27-29, 1949-1951, p. 141-318) no. 170. C. Gallavotti, HELIKON 15-16 (1975-76) studies this text and reads it as follows ("in grafia normalizzata"):

ἁ Κράτητος ἔδωκε τᾶι Λυήτω γυναικί

'Αθράφητος Segre - Carratelli.

869-871. RHODES (KAMIROS), ARCHAIC INSCRIPTIONS. C. Gallavotti, HELIKON 15-16 (1975-76) 79-80 and 82-84 studies three archaic inscriptions from Kamiros:

---

869. P. 79-80: study of Jeffery, LSAG, p. 349, no. 13 (plate 67).

---

870. P. 82-83: study of IG, XII, 1, 719.

---

871. P. 83-84: study of M. Segre - I. Pugliese Carratelli, Tituli Camirenses (ASAA 27-29, 1949-1951, p. 141-318) no. 178.

---

872. RHODES (LINDOS), REAFFORESTATION OF THE ACROPOLIS BY AGLOCHARTOS, PRIEST OF ATHENA LINDIA, 3rd - 4th CENT. A.D. J. Bousquet, Recueil Plassart, 9-13 lists all the texts about the activities of Aglochartos (IG, XII, 1, 779-783 and C. Blinkenberg, Lindos II, Inscriptions t. II, no. 498; cf. no. 430), presents some new readings made by W. Peek on the spot and emphasizes the superiority of the epigraphic text of IG, XII, 1, 783 over its literary version in Anth. Pal., XV, 11. Cf. also J. and L. Robert, BE (1977) no. 325. New readings: in IG, XII, 1, 779, L. 2 εἰροπό-

λος τεός instead of ΕΡΓΟΠΟΛ...ΕΟΣ (ἐργοπό[νος τ]εός); L. 3 [κυ]δα-λίμου instead of [κυ]δάλιμο[ς]; in IG, XII, 1, 781, L. 2 ἐοῖς τίς instead of Ε///ΙΙΕ (ἔ[τερπ]ε); L. 3 [κλε]ινός τ' instead of [ἱρεύς τ']; in IG, XII, 1, 782, L. 1 μ' ἐσιδεῖν φίλον (sc. ἐστί) instead of ΜΕΣΙΛΙΚ (μ' ἐσιδ[έ]).

LESBOS

873-941. OBSERVATIONS ON LESBIAN INSCRIPTIONS. R. Hodot, EAC 5 (1976) 17-81 publishes a long series of mostly philological observations on Lesbian inscriptions in IG, XII, 2, IG, XII, Suppl. and S. Charitonidis' posthumous Αἱ ἐπιγραφαὶ τῆς Λέσβου, Συμπλήρωμα (Athens, 1968). We present a succint list of Hodot's comments, leaving out a few quisquiliae epigraphicae, which do not change the text significantly.

873-908. Observations on Lesbian inscriptions in IG, XII, 2:

---

873. No. 1 (ph.). Date: 2nd half 5th cent. B.C. - beginning 4th cent. B.C.; L. 3. perhaps εἰς ταῦ[τα ---?] instead of εἰς τὰ[ν στάλλαν].

---

874. No. 4, L. 8. |[συνέχω]ς instead of |[διάρκω]ς; 12-13. [τὸ ἔ|ργον] instead of [τῶρ|γον]; 13-15. μίλ[τινον δὲ ἔπ]|[ει κε τ]ὸ ὔδωρ ἄχθη ἐπίγρα[ψαι Ἀθανάδ]|[αν ὄππα κ]ε θέλῃ ἐπὶ τᾶι ὐ[δρ...7...] instead of Μίλ[τωμα δὲ ἔπε]|[ι κε τ]ὸ ὔδωρ ἄχθη ἐπι-γρά[ψαις τιθέτ]|[ω ὄππα κ]ε θέλῃ ἐπὶ τᾶι ὐ[δραγωγίαι].

---

875. No. 5 (ph.). A, L. 29. Δᾶμος Με[γίστω εἶπε] instead of Δᾶμος με[τέγνω]; B, L. 29. [Δ]ᾶ[μ]ο[ς Με]γίστ[ω ---] instead of [Δ]ᾶ[μ]ο[ς ἐ]πιστ---; Hodot also remarks that in A, L. 41 one should restore the name of the proposer of the decree ([.4-5.]ος Ἐρα---?)

---

876. No. 6 (ph.). L. 4. Ζέσθω instead of Ξέσθω; 44-46. τὰ δὲ ἶρα ... ἀπυδόμεναι τοῖς βασί|[ληας ----]τον instead of τὰ δὲ ἶρα ... ἀπυδόμεναι τοῖς βασί|[ληος γενεθλίοισι κατ' ἐνίαυ]τον.

---

877. No. 7, L. 1-2. [δέχεσθ]αι δὲ [τοῦτ]|ον instead of [κ]αὶ δέ[χεσθ]|ον.

---

878. No. 14, L. 1. In fine PI (and not]στε as in IG, XII,

Suppl., p. 6); 5. in fine τᾶς̣ [X]ί[ων] is not acceptable; 12. traces on the stone justify IG's suggestion ἀ λεκ̣[α]|[νό]πωλις στωία.

---

879. No. 18 (ph.). L. 19. [προθέμε]ν̣αι.

---

880. No. 19 (ph.). Inscription of ca. 300 B.C. (small omicron and theta; pi with unequal legs; sigma with divergent horizontal strokes; but with strong apices. Cf. for the latter also nos. 72 and 73 and IG, XII, Suppl., no. 76); L. 5. προτίθε[ισι] and not προτιθέν[αι].

---

881. No. 26 (ph.). After L. 2, the text is complete at the right side (contra IG, XII, Suppl., p. 10) and runs as follows:

[- - - - - - - - -]σ̣μ̣ε.[.]
[- - - - - - - -] . . νοι τῶ παι-
[- - - - - - - - -]ἐπὶ τῶν μυσ-
[τηρίων - - - - -ἐλ]θέτω πρὸς τὰν
[- - - - - - - τὰν] Ἄρτεμιν ὐπὸ
[- - - - - - - κ]αττὰ προεψαφίσ-
[μενα - - - - - -]ματα ἐντρε-
[- - - ἀ ἀμέρα ἀ γ]ενέθλιος ὀλο-
[- - - - - - τᾷ ἀ]μέρα̣ ταύτα̣
[- - - - - - - Και]σαρήων ἔαυτον
[- - - - - - τὰν] π̣όλιν ἀοίδιμον
[- - - - - - - τὰ]ν θέαν συνδρα-
[μοντ - - - - - -] ὠ̣ς τοῖς εὐεργε-
[τ - - - - - - ἀγ]ώ̣ν̣ισται συνεχεσ-
[- - τὰν Ῥώμαν τὰν Νικ]όφο̣ρον α̣ὔ̣τα̣

4. --θε τῶ πρὸς τὰν -- || 5. --Α̣ Ἄρτεμιν -- || 6. -- κὰ]τ τὰ -- || 13. ---]ος τοῖς -- || 14. -- ἀξι]ο̣πίσταις IG, XII, Suppl., p. 10

---

882. No. 30, L. 8.]ε νομίσθην instead of ἐνομίσθην.

---

883. No. 34, L. 6. O[..]Ṭ ΕΛΗ instead of -ο̣ιρ̣ε ελη-.

---

884. No. 37, L. 4. [ἀπο- or ὐπο]λήψεως instead of [ἀπολάμ]ψεως.

---

885. No. 68, L. 2. In fine perhaps Δάδα, Λεσ[βία] instead of Δάδα Λεσ[βώνακτος --].

---

886. No. 74, L. 14. After τᾶς Κιλλάω restore [μόρον] (sc. ἀμπέλων).

---

887. No. 81 (ph.). L. 9-10. π̣[αῖδι]|[--- στα ε'· ἄρχει Θ]ε̣δαισίω instead of π̣[αῖδι -- στα : ε']|[ἄρχει] Δ̣αισίω.

---

888. No. 86, L. 10. --]φ̣ίμου instead of --]οιμου.

---

889. No. 88, L. 15. Keep Ἀσκληπιάδη (IG) and not Ἀσκληπιάδης (IG, XII, Suppl., p. 15).

---

890. No. 106, L. 1. [ὀ]χ̣ετόν instead of ὑδραγώγ]ε[ι]ον.

---

891. No. 108 and 109. Hodot shows that these two fragments join and he presents the following text:

[Ζ]αθέῳ Ἀρτέμιδι Θε[ρ]-
[μ]ίᾳ Ὀμονοίᾳ Τε-
[λ]έσφορος Συμ-
[φ]όρω καὶ Φλ. Τύχα
[τ]ὰν χαλκίαν εἴκο-
[ν]α καττὰν ἐπιτά-
[γα]ν καὶ χρημάτισ-
[μ]ο̣ν αὔτας ὄντε-
[θή]κοντες καὶ τὸ
[εὐ]θ̣έμιδος (?) παν-
[θ]έ̣ω Ἀφροδείτας
ἄγαλμα ἐν τῷ εἴ-
ρῳ.
Σ̣υνκαθιέρω-
σαν οἱ τὴν σκυτι-
[κ]ὴν τέχνην ἐργα-
[ζ]ό̣μενοι.

1. [Μεγά]λᾳ || 10. [τᾶς] Θ̣έ̣μιδος (Aphrodite Euthemis - Venus Iusta) IG.

---

892. No. 143, L. 3. [σ]ώ̣τηρι instead of [σα]ότηρι.

---

893. No. 183, L. 5-6. Ὀλυμπί|<ῳ> κτίστ<η̣> instead of Ὀλυμπι|οκτίστω.

---

894. No. 210, L. 5. Θεδαίσιος (month) instead of Θελαίσιος (proper name).

---

895. No. 243 (ph.). L. 3-4. στροταγήσαν|τα instead of στρατηγήσαν|τα; 10. δὲ καὶ ἐν τᾷ instead of ΔΕΚΑΙΚΑΙΕΝΤΑ; 11-12. Περ|γαμήννων instead of Περ|γαμήνων. Cf. also L. Robert, Stele N. Kontoleon (1977) 8-9.

---

896. No. 257. Comment upon the term ματροία.

---

897. No. 273 (ph.). A new name on the seats of the theatre: Ἀρισστọ-.

---

898. No. 294 (ph.). The stonecutter corrected a mistake (ΗΡΩΙ ΔΑΟΣ) into Ἀριστίαος; this text is the same as IG, XII, Suppl., p. 24, no. 70, where Ἀγωνίαος has been printed. The name Ἀγωνίας is to be deleted in the IG-index.

---

899. No. 297. A third line [χαῖρε] is to be added.

---

900. No. 335 (ph.). Ca. 200 B.C.

---

901. No. 338. [Πλ]ọυταρχίδọ[υ] instead of -ιδο[ς].

---

902. No. 357. Πυλά̣[δ]η Λ̣ε̣ο̣δ̣ά̣|μαντος instead of Πυλά[δ]η Μά-[τρ]ιος.

---

903. No. 449 and 451 (dr.). Kiepert's drawing does not confirm the IG-readings.

---

904. No. 465 (ph.). The stone is broken above and at the left (contra IG). Hodot gives the following text:

   ˘ / ˘
1 XINONΔEKA'≐'‿|_|
καὶ μνᾶμα v̲. Καθη![--
-μ?]ένοις κ̄αὶ διὰ ταῦτ̣[α --
4 -].ην καὶ τὰν ὕπερ.[--
ε]ί̣ς τὸν δᾶμον κα.[--

---

905. No. 503 (ph.). Ca. 200 B.C.

---

906. No. 504, L. 8. IG is to be preferred to IG, XII, Suppl., p. 30.

---

907. No. 528, L. 4. ΑΛΕΚΙΑΣ lapis (and not ΑΛΙΚΙΑΣ): ἀλεκίας is a dialect form of ἀλικίας.

---

908. No. 534 (ph.). Date: 3rd - 2nd cent. B.C.; ["Ε]ρμησις rather than ["Ο]ρμησις.

909-920. Observations on Lesbian inscriptions in IG, XII, Suppl.

---

909. No. 2 (ph.). Hodot dates this text to the end of the 4th cent. B.C. (instead of the end 3rd cent. B.C.). The honorand is now supposed to be a citizen of Magnesia on the Meander (and no longer an Athenian as in IG, XII, Suppl.). LL. 1-11 are in stoichedon; the stone is broken on all sides. Hodot gives the following text (we do not repeat his app. crit. on p. 50):

A. --
[δέδοχθαι] τᾶι βό[λλαι καὶ τῶι δάμωι· ἐπα]-
[ίνεσσαι τ]ε Ἀτρόμητο[ν .... Μάγνητ]-
[α εὐνοί]ας ἕνεκε τᾶς πρὸ[ς τὸν δᾶμον τῶν]
[Μυτιλη]νάων, καὶ στεφάν[ωσαι ....]
[. τὰν π]όλιν χρυσίωι στε[φάνωι κατὰ τὸν]
[νόμον κ]αὶ ὀγκάρυξαι τοὶς [βασίληας ἐν τ]-
[οῖς Δι]ονυσίοισι, ὅτι στε[φάνοι ὁ δᾶμος]
[ὁ Μυτι]ληνάων Ἀτρόμητον [...........]
[.. αὔτ]ον πρόξενογ καὶ εὐ[εργέταν ....]
[. Μυτιλ]ηνάων ἀνδραγαθί[ας ἕνεκε καὶ ε]-
[ὐνοία]ς τᾶς πρὸς τὸν δᾶμο[ν --vacat ?---]
[ν ? Τοὶς] δὲ στροτάγοις αἴ τοὶς [κατισταμέ]-
[νοις ?] καὶ δᾶμον ἐπιμέλεσθ[αι αὔτω ὅππως]
[αἴ κὲ τ]ινος δεύηται τᾶς π[όλιος τᾶς Μυτι]-
[ληνάων] ὐπηρετήσεται α[ὔτωι πάντα κατὰ]
[τὸ δύνατ]ον· δόμεναι δὲ καὶ ξ[ένια Ἀτρομήτωι]
[ὡς προ]ξένωι τοὶς ταμίαις [ὅσα ἀ πόλις δια]-
[τέλει δί]δοισα προξένωι vacat.

B.
["Εγνω δᾶμος·] περὶ Ἀτρομήτω ΤΛ[..ca.10-12..]
[..ca.8.. Μα]γνήτων, ἄνδρων [...ca.10-12.]
[..ca.11....]ντων εἰς τὰμ π[όλιν ca.6-7.]
[..ca.11....]τρος· δέδοχθαι [τᾶι βόλλαι καὶ]
[τῶι δάμωι (?)· ἐπ]ειδὴ ἔστι εὐν[...ca.12....]
[..ca.12-13...]. τε αὔτοις ι..[...ca.12.....]
[.ca.6. Μυτιλη]νάων Ἀτρο[μητ.ca.8-10..]
[...ca.13.....]ΑΙΝΟΝ....[..ca.10...]
[πολίταις ἔμμεναι] καὶ αὔτοις [καὶ ἐκγόνοις]
[καὶ μετέχην πάντων] τῶγ καὶ οἰ ἄ[λλοι πολίται]
[μετέχοισι· ca.5.] εἰς θίασον .[..ca.8-10.]
[...ca.14......]αι ὄπποι κε [θέλωισι· ἐπι]-
[μέλεσθαι δὲ τοὶς] στροτάγ[οις .ca.8-10..]
[....ca.15......]ν καὶ δ[...ca.14......]
[--------]ι^ -[------------]

---

6. "Le iota de τοίς [--] est gravé en surnombre à la limite de deux cases du damier" Hodot.

---

910. No. 50, L. 2. [κ]α[ί] is impossible; perhaps βολλάα[ν].

---

911. No. 63 (ph.). Ca. 200 B.C.

---

912. No. 66, L. 5. In fine δ̣[υσαίων].

---

913. No. 72. Ca. 150 B.C. ?

---

914. No. 105. End 3rd cent. B.C.; Ζμίθων ῎Ιρω[νος] instead of ῎Ιρω[ς].

---

915. No. 109 (ph.). Two more lines on the stone: [---]πο[---]| [χ]ρ̣η̣στὴ̣ [χαῖρε].

---

916. No. 114, L. 28. τὸ δ' είς τὰν κλῆσ[ιν ἀνάλ]ω̣μ[α]|;29. [--- ἐκ τ]ῶν είς πόλιος [διοίκε]σιν.

---

917. No. 115 (ph.). Perhaps the lines contained more letters (2-4) than IG, XII, Suppl. assumed. This leads Hodot to a number of less important "new" readings.

---

918. No. 125 (ph.). L. 1. Πίνδασος [῎Ι]ρω̣ν̣ος instead of .ΝΙΛ̣ ΙΟΣ; 18. ἀτέλε̣ι̣αν.

---

919. No. 127 (ph.). Hodot (cf. also L. Robert, <u>Monnaies antiques en Troade</u>, 1966, p. 115-121) presents the following text (a,b, c, and d are different scripts):

Side A:

Col. III: (a) [Μαρ]σ̣ύας
[Φί]λιππος
Σ̣μιθίναιοι̣
ʼΑθάναιοι·
Σάτυρος
Εὐξένειος
ΙΣ

[Col. I] Col. II: (b) [------]ε̣λλεος

[------] Λεύκωνο[ς]
[------] Πυθίωνος Βυ̣(ζάντιος)
(c) --ξης Σκύμνω
---ανος 12
(a) [Μυ]τ̣ι[λή]ν̣αιοι· (c) Ἀπολλωνι.[?]
[Φ]αι̣ν̣ίας Ποσείδειος
[Κ]ύ̣λησις Μνασιλάειος
Πραξ̣ιφάνης Δαμοσθένει̣[ος] 16
Δίης Δ̣[αμο]σ̣θέν[ει]ο[ς]

Side B:

(a) [.4-5.]νδεῖς·
[3-4.]ων Δημετρίου (sic)
(c) [Μα]θ̣ύ̣μναιοι· 20
[ca. 3]αγόρας Εὐφρονιδ-- (b) Καλλιγ--
(a) [Αἰ]γίναται· Τιμεία (?)
[Δα]μαγόρας Θεοκόσμ[ω]
[Θε]όκοσμος Δαμαγόρα 24
[Ἀ]νδρομήδης Δαμαγόρα
Μ<α>θύμναιοι· Βάκχων
Ἀγλαοκέρτειος (c) Εὔβουλος
Καρύστιοι· Ἀπ[ο]λ̣λοδ̣ώρω 28
[Μ]άντις Ἀριστοκράτειο̣ς·
[..]όφρων Ἀριστοκράτειος
(b) [Ξά]νθιππος Πολύστ-
(c) [Ἀγ]αθάναξ Ὀνομάστο̣[υ] Δῖος 32
[ρα]τος Πολυδώ̣ρου
Χαιρέας Ἀριστομ̣ή̣δου
(a) Μ̣εγάρειες·
[Λ]εόντης Μελιδώρειος 36
[Κα]λλιτέλης Ἀριστογείτ[ω]
(d) [Σαλ]υμβριανοί·
[...σ]τρατος Μυλλίν[α]
(a) [Χερσονά]σιται· 40

Side C:

Col. I

(a) [.]λ̣εφα|[---]
[Π]λ̣ειστί[ας ---]
Ἀνδρίας Δ[---]
(c) Ἀπολλωνίδαν Εὐ̣[---] 44
Πολύστρατο[ς ----]
(c) Ἄγλ̣[αο]ν Ἀντιλέοντο[ς]
Ἰόλαος Ἀ̣ντα[---]
(c) Πόπλιον Ἀρέλλιον Κοι̣ν̣[---?] 48
Ἀνδρίας Σκυθίν̣[ειος]
Ἀρχέας Εὐξίαιο̣ς
(b) Ἀριστόδαμος Πραξίκλ[ειος]
[Ζ]αίθων Πραξίκλειος 52
(c) Ἔφορος Ἐφόρω Λυσιμάχευς
Ἱππίας Μορμώ̣ττειος
Ζ̣ώ̣ΐ̣λος Λυσίαιος : Μέλαγχ[ρος]

(c) ῎Αγησις Λυ. Col. II 56
Πύρραιοι ᾿Ανδρίαιος ,\------
Φιλύτα
Μελέδαμος ᾿Ιωνόκλειος Προ[---]
(c) [...]Δ̣[...]ος Λαντρία ῾Υ̣μεσσεύς 60
[Κ]υδίας Λαοδάμαντειος ῎Αχαι[οι·]
---Γ̣ά̣θεω̣ς Χῖος Μνησί[θεος?-----]
Κλειταγόρας Κυδρόκλειος Δράκω[ν ---]
(c) --Γρα.... ᾿Α̣ντώ̣ν̣ι̣ο̣ν ῾Ρωμαῖον, ᾿Ασκληπιάδη̣ν̣ Δι̣ο[---] 64
Λαοφάνης Κυδρόκλειος Μιλάσι̣[οι·]
(c) Π̣ό̣λεμο̣ν̣ [---]ωνος καὶ Πυθίαν Πυθία Μυτιληναίο[υς?]
[..]μίας Νεόκλειος (c) Κ̣[άμ]μης Κριτολέ̣[ως?---]
[------]ς Βάκχιος Σκ̣[ά]μωνος ῾Ιππ[---] 68
[---------]κ̣[λ]ειος Μυτιλήναιος

---

920. No. 693, L. 15. τῷ συνγένεος instead of συνγένεος.

921-940. Observations on Lesbian inscriptions in S. Charitonidis, Αἱ ἐπιγραφαὶ τῆς Λέσβου, Συμπλήρωμα (Athens, 1968).

---

921. No. 2. Date: 3rd cent. B.C.; the beginning (and not the end) of the lines have been preserved; L. 2-3. [--------᾿Αρ]|χιαίω Ν[-----] instead of ---]χιλίων|; 5. ΤΑΠΑ instead of ΤΑΓΑ; 11. α̣ὐ̣τ̣[---].

---

922. No. 3. Date: 3rd cent. B.C.; L. 2. in fine καὶ ᾿Α̣π̣[όλ-λωνος] ?

---

923. No. 4. Date: 3rd cent. B.C.; Hodot restores LL. 1-6 as follows:

[῎Εγνω βόλλα καὶ] ὁ̣ δᾶμος· περὶ ὧν
[ὀ δεῖνα ..ca.7..᾿Αντι]άνορος ἐπὶ τὰν̣ β̣ό̣λ̣-
[λαν καὶ τὸν δᾶ]μον ἦλθε ἐμφ[ανί]-
4 [ζων ὄτ(τ)ι 3-4.] λείφθεις ὐπὸ τῶ π̣[..]-
[.ca.6. καὶ π]ροπεύθεις ὐπὸ ΠΥ̣[..]
[.ca.10....]άτη ἀξίως τᾶς τῶ̣[ν Μυ]-
[τιληναίων πόλιος ----.

---

4. Also possible is: ὐπὸ τῶγ̣[κ.]- Hodot.

---

924. No. 6, L. 10 (col. B). ἐφ' ὦν ἐ̣[πιγραφήσεται ὄτι ὀ δᾶμος στεφάνοι Ποτάμωνα] instead of ΕΦΑΝΕ.

---

925. No. 13, L. 4. Ποτ]άμω̣ν̣[--.

---

926. No. 14, L. 4. τ]ὰ̣ν πά̣τ̣ρ̣ι̣ν instead of]ΝΠ[....]Ν; 6. ἄν-δ̣[ρων] ?

---

927. No. 15, L. 3. Μ]ηννίτα ?

---

928. No. 19. Ζώειος is wrong; Hodot reads Σ̣ΗΞΩΕΙΟΣ.

---

929. No. 22. Μένιππος Νικία̣<ο>ς ? instead of Μένιππος, Νικίας.

---

930. No. 30, L. 4. πάϊν (= παῖδα) τ[-- instead of παίντ[ι.

---

931. No. 84. Study of the squeeze confirms Charitonidis' suggestions: [Μεγ]ίστιον Ἀπ̣ο̣|[λλ]ω̣ν̣ίω, Ζωίτ|[τ]α δὲ μάτηρ, χαῖρε.

---

932. No. 101, L. 6-7. Νικόπολει χρη|σ[τή or -τέ].

---

933. No. 104. Θέσπεσι χρηστὲ | χαῖρε (instead of Θεεπεσι).

---

934. No. 111 (ph.). Hodot reads:

[Ὁ δεῖνα ---]
[3̣-4̣.]ο̣υ Μαγ̣γ̣[.]
3 [3̣-4̣.]ς̣ ἐνθάδε
[κεῖ]τ̣αι, ζήσας
5 [ἔτη] κα'.

---

935. No. 118. Hodot presents the following text (which he dates to the 5th cent. B.C.):

Ἐνθάδ' ἐγὼ
ἐμὶ Θεάνα-
ξ ἰερῷ ἐπὶ χ-
4 ώρῳ (?) Φιλέα
δὲ μ' εἰσ̣ε<ε>-
κάλεσσε v.
Σὺν δ' ἄγω
μοῖ γυν̣[..]
[...]ε̣νιοο
[..]υθ̣ι̣ ιντοι̣
[.]η μικρο[.]
[.]α̣ τελεω̣ (?)

2-3. Also possible is Θεῶνα|ξ Hodot.

---

936. No. 119. [--Ἀγ]αθίων instead of [--Ἀν]αξίων ?

---

937. No. 122 (ph.). Date: 2nd cent. B.C.; the right edge of the stone has been preserved; L. 1. ε̣ἰρ̣ήσε̣[ται ? instead of ε̣ἶπ̣ε̣ν̣; 2-3. οἱ πα|[ρέοντες προτίθεισι, ὅτε πρ]ύτανις; 3. in fine AX; 4-5. οἱ ἰρό|[νομοι ---]; 5. in fine οἱ ἰρόποοι οι̣-; 6-7. τῶν ἄλ|[λων πολίταν instead of ἀρχόντων; 9. Τιμασικ<ρ>έοντος (lapis: -ΚΕΟΝΤΟΣ); 10. in fine Πρωτοφάϊ, Πρ̣[.] or Πε̣[.]-; 11. Ἀριστοτ̣έ̣λ̣η̣ς instead of Ἀριστότιμ̣[ο]ς; 12. Πρωτοφ]άϊ ?, Πανκρατίδας Σαμίδα̣, Σ̣αύλαος; 21. [ἀπὸ τᾶς πρώτα]ς̣ ἀλεκίας; 24. [----]ε̣ τοῖς; in fine κα[.]ΑΤΟ.[---]; 25. [σέ]σωκεν τῶ̣ν τε̣ πολίτα̣[ν ---].

---

938. No. 125 (ph.). Hodot reads: Κα̣λ̣λ̣ιφάνης | καὶ συνίρωρ|γοι Ἀφροδί|τα instead of καὶ Σινίρωρ | τᾶι (L. 2-3).

---

939. No. 133, L. 2. [χρ]ησ̣τ̣[.] instead of [χρ]ηστή.

---

940. No. 134. Hodot reads: Φιλέταιρει Ζή|λω̣ι χρηστὲ χαῖ|ρ̣ε̣.

---

941. In an appendix Hodot groups 20, mostly very fragmentary, inscriptions, published before in various publications but not included in the corpora. In three inscriptions, published by Petrakos in AD 22 (1967) Chron., p. 461 Hodot contributes new readings: (1) p. 461 (pl. 338β): L. 4. τᾶς πόλιος; (2) ibidem (pl. 338α): L. 2. Θέω υἰῳ (instead of θεοῦ); (3) ibidem: L. 2. καὶ Ἐπινίκη Ἑρμογένη̣ (instead of Ἑρμογένο[υ]).

SYME

942. SYME, DECREE OF KLEARCHOS ON COINAGE, DATE ? Cf. no. 6.

THERA

943-945. THERA, THREE HONORARY INSCRIPTIONS FOR MEMBERS OF THE SAME FAMILY, 1st HALF 2nd CENT. A.D. Large statue-base broken into three fragments. On fragments I+II: honorary inscription for Mnasikritos, son of Diodoros, husband of Chairopoleia (CIG, 2462; IG, XII, 3, 522); on fragments II+III: honorary inscription for Chairopoleia, daughter of Tiberios Klaudios Kureina Aglaophanes (CIG, 2463; IG, XII, 3, 522); on fragment III: honorary inscription for Tiberios Klaudios Medon, brother of Chairopoleia (ed. pr. C. Sigalas, AD 26A, 1971, 194-200). G. Daux, BCH 100 (1976) 231-234 reprints the texts with a short commentary (ph.).

---

943. IG, XII, 3, 522: Honorary inscription for Mnasikritos.

Ἁ βουλὰ καὶ ὁ δᾶμος
ἐτείμασεν Μνασίκριτον
Διοδώρου υἱόν, ἱερέα διὰ
γένους τοῦ πρὸ πόλεως
Διονύ̣σου, ἀρετᾶς ἕνεκα
καὶ κ̣αλοκάγαθίας, τὰν ἀνά-
στασιν ποισαμένας τᾶς
γυναικὸς αὐτοῦ Χαιροπολεί-
ας Τι. Κλαυδίου Κυρείνα
Ἀγλαοφάνους θυγατρὸς
ἐκ τῶν ἰδίων.

7. [π]ο[η]σαμένας IG.

944. IG, XII, 3, 522: Honorary inscription for Chairopoleia.

Ἁ βουλὰ καὶ ὁ δ[ᾶμ]ος
ἐτείμασεν Χαι[ροπ]όλειαν
Τι. Κλαυδίου Κυρ[είν]α Ἀγλαο-
φάνους θυγατέρα, [ἀρ]ε̣τᾶς ἕνε-
κα καὶ σωφροσύ[νας]
τὰν ἀνάστασιν [ποι]σαμένας
αὐτᾶς ζώσας [ἐκ] τῶν ἰδίων.

6. [ποησαμένας] IG.

945. AD 26A (1971) 194-200: Honorary inscription for Tiberios Klaudios Medon.

Ἁ βουλὰ καὶ ὁ δᾶμος
ἐτείμασεν Τι. Κλαύδιον
Κυρείνα Μέδοντα, υἱὸν
Τι. Κλαυδίου Κυρείνα Ἀγλαο-
φάνους, ἀρετᾶς ἕνεκα
καὶ καλοκάγαθίας, τὰν ἀνά-
στασιν ποισαμένας
τᾶς ἀδελφᾶς αὐτοῦ Χαι-
ροπολείας, Τι. Κλαυδίου
Κυρείνα Ἀγλαοφάνους
θυγατρὸς ἐκ τῶν ἰδίων.

946. THERA, GRAFFITO ON A ROCK, 7th CENT. B.C. IG, XII, 3, 545. Cf. O. Masson, ARCHCLASS 25-26 (1973-74) 430 and C. Gallavotti, HELIKON 15-16 (1975-76) 71, note 1 who reads the graffito as follows:

ϙόραϙος [καὶ] πρόμο[ς] ἀγαθ<ό>ς

ϙόραϙς ἀγαθὸς πρόμο- (?) IG; Masson remarks: "la graphie qoppa + sigma en finale est à noter pour le xi".

947. THERA (SELLADA), DEDICATION. Painted inscription on a small bottle. Ed. pr. A.K. Orlandos, EAH (1976) 165-166. Cf. AR (1977-78) 56.

Αἰσάλῳ τάνδε Εὐμάθης

948. THERA (SELLADA), NAME, 5th CENT. B.C. Inscription on a block built into the wall of a Roman tomb. Ed. pr. N.S. Zapheirophoulos, PAAH (1974) 195.

ΛΥΣΙΘΕΟ

KOS

---

949. KOS, THE JEWISH COMMUNITY. S.M. Sherwin-White, ZPE 21 (1976) 183-188 studies the Jewish community in Kos. She mentions the relations of Kos with the Herodian dynasty and identifies members of the Jewish community in Koan inscriptions: she cites Paton-Hicks, Inscriptions of Cos (Oxford, 1891) 278 (epitaph of Εἰρήνη θεοσεβής. Cf. L. Robert, Nouv. Inscr. de Sardes, Paris, 1964, p. 44, n. 8 who has shown that Eirene is to be recognized as a Jew by her description as theosebes) and recognizes the Jewish character of Paton-Hicks, o.c., 303 (epitaph of Εὔτυχος), 323 (epitaph of Αὐρήλιος Γάϊος) and 63 (dedication by Θέανος to the Theos Hypsistos).

---

950. KOS, SACRIFICIAL CALENDAR, MIDDLE 4th CENT. B.C. - EARLY 3rd CENT. B.C. F. Sokolowski, Lois sacrées des cités grecques (Paris, 1969) 151 A. Deborah Wichtel Kaestner, CJ 71 (1975-76) 344-348 publishes, as a correction to D.R. Smith, CJ 69 (1973-74) 25, a translation of this text (with explanation of cruces in the notes).

---

951. KOS, SACRED LAW, 1st CENT. B.C. Syll.^{3}, 1000 (cf. W.A.P. Vreeken, De lege quadam sacra Coorum, 1953). H. Heinen, ANCSOC 7 (1976) 141 rightly rejects E.P. Golubcova's interpretation of ἰατρικόν as evidence for fixed prices of slave-doctors (apud T.V. Blavatskaja - E.P. Golubcova - A.I. Pavlovskaja, Die Sklaverei in hellenistischen Staaten im 3-1 Jahrhundert v. Chr., Wiesbaden, 1972, p. 129).

---

952. KOS, LETTER OF CN. DOMITIUS CORBULO, GOVERNOR OF ASIA, TO THE CITY OF KOS, REIGN OF CLAUDIUS. Ed. G. Pugliese Carratelli, PP 30 (1975) 102-104 (texts of M. Segre and R. Herzog). G.P. Burton, ZPE 21 (1976) 63-68 uses this letter to defend the accuracy of Dio Cassius' statement (53. 15. 4) that proconsuls received ἐντολαί from the emperor from the reign of Augustus onwards (against F. Millar and A.N. Sherwin-White, and with Mommsen). Cf. also P.J. Sijpesteijn, ZPE 22 (1976) 107 who proposes to read in LL. 14-15: εἰ μὲν ἐπὶ τὸν Σεβαστὸν | [ἐπί]κλησις ("appeal") γείνηται instead of [ἡ ἔκ]κλησις.

---

953. KOS, DEDICATION TO THE CHARITES, 3rd CENT. B.C. Ed. pr. G. Konstantinopoulos, AD 23B (1968) 449; AAA 3 (1970) 251. Relief with inscription, representing four Charites, Pan and in a cave the figure of a reclining man. F.T. van Straten, BVAB 51 (1976) 1 ff. shows that the reclining man is the person who dedicated the stone on the basis of a dream. The inscription runs as follows:

Δαϊκράτης Πασία Χαρίσιν.

---

954. KOS, HELLENISTIC EPIGRAM ON THE FLUTE-PLAYER ARISTON. Ed. pr. S.K. Pantelides, BCH 11 (1887) 75; W.R. Paton - E.L. Hicks, The Inscriptions of Cos (Oxford, 1891) no. 58. R. Merkelbach, GB 5 (1976) 143-146 gives some explanatory notes on verses 5-6, 7, 8, 9-10 and prefers in verse 14 αὔσαθ' (Pantelides) to <δ>ύσαθ' (Paton - Hicks).

IOS

955. IOS, DECREE FOR THE PTOLEMAIC NAVAL COMMANDER ZENON, 3rd CENT. B.C. OGIS, 773. H. Heinen, ANCSOC 7 (1976) 146 correctly points out that in LL. 5 ff. there is no question of slaves who used unguarded warships for their flight (... τῶν πλοίων τῶν ἀφράκτων), as E.P. Golubcova assumed (apud T.V. Blavatskaja - E.P. Golubcova - A.I. Pavlovskaja, Die Sklaverei in hellenistischen Staaten im 3-1 Jahrh. v. Chr., Wiesbaden, 1972, p. 161) but of slaves who either hided themselves on these ships or registered for service without mentioning their legal status. Cf. also R.S. Bagnall, The Administration of the Ptolemaic Possessions outside Egypt (Leiden, 1976) p. 147-148.

NAXOS

956. NAXOS, DEDICATION. Part of a re-used perirranterion (aspersorium) (probably from the sanctuary of Apollo at Yiroula) with a boustrophedon dedicatory inscription. Ed. pr. A.K. Orlandos, EAH (1976) 159 (ph.). Cf. AR (1977-78) 55.

→ --ν ἀνέθεκεν
← δεκάτην α--

2. Ἀ[πόλλωνι Orlandos.

PAROS

957. INSCRIPTIONS FROM PAROS. A.K. Orlandos, AE (1975) Chron., 3-36 publishes 75 new inscriptions, originating from various places in the ancient city of Paros (agora, gymnasium, temple of Serapis and necropolis) and built into the ancient Christian church of Katapoliani. We do not present below Orlandos' nos. 35, 39, 43, 44, 45, 48, 52, 54, 57, 61, 62, 67, 70, 71, 72: they are all tiny fragments.

---

958. PAROS, HONORARY INSCRIPTIONS FOR AUGUSTUS' SONS, 18 B.C. - 1 A.D. Marble block. Ed. pr. A.K. Orlandos, AE (1975) Chron., 3-5, no. 1 (ph.).

A. Γάϊον Ἰούλιον
Αὐτοκράτορος
Θεοῦ Υἱοῦ Σεβας̣[τοῦ Υἱὸν]

B. Λεύκιον Ἰούλιον Καίσαρα
Αὐτοκράτορος Καίσαρος
Θεοῦ Υ̣ἱοῦ Σεβαστοῦ Υἱὸν

C. ----------------ν-------
Αὐτοκρ-------------
Θεοῦ------------------
Θε
ου

C is restored by Orlandos as follows: [Ἀγρίππαν Ἰούλιο]ν [Καίσαρα] | Αὐτοκρ[άτορος Καίσαρος] | Θεοῦ [Υἱοῦ Σεβαστοῦ Υἱὸν] | Θε | ου.

---

959. PAROS, HONORARY INSCRIPTION FOR TRAJAN, 116-117 A.D. Rectangular marble block. Ed. pr. A.K. Orlandos, l.c., 5-6, no. 2 (ph

Αὐτοκράτορα Νέρουαν Τραϊανὸν ἄρισ̣[τον]
Καίσαρα Σεβαστὸν Γερμανικὸν Δακι[κ̣ὸν]
Παρθικὸν

---

960. PAROS, HONORARY INSCRIPTION FOR M. AURELIUS (?), 2nd CENT. A.D. Rectangular marble block. Ed. pr. A.K. Orlandos, l.c., 20, no. 29 (dr.).

A. At the left: ΣΙΒΑ | ΨΗΦΙΣΜΑ
B. At the right: Καί]σαρα Μ(ᾶρκον) Αὐρήλιον ο
ο

961. PAROS, HONORARY INSCRIPTION FOR PARMENION, ROMAN PERIOD. Mutilated marble block, with a wreath engraved on it; inside the wreath the inscription. Ed. pr. A.K. Orlandos, AE (1975) Chron., 9, no. 5 (ph.).

Παρμε̣[νίωνα]
φίλον φι[
3 ἀ]ρετῆς ἕν[εκα]
καὶ εὐνοίας τ[ῆς]
5 εἰς ἑαυτούς.

Perhaps dedicated by ephebes or neoi in the gymnasium J. and L. Robert, BE (1977) no. 340, p. 376 || 2. φί[λοι ?] ed.

962. PAROS, FRAGMENT OF A HONORARY INSCRIPTION, ROMAN PERIOD. Marble fragment, with part of a geison and kymation. Ed. pr. A.K. Orlandos, l.c., 30-31, no. 56 (ph.).

Civiṭ[as
ἡ βουλ̣[ὴ καὶ ὁ δῆμος

Cf. no. 50 in Orlandos' series: on a marble block a wreath with the words ἡ βουλή (Hellenistic Period).

963. PAROS, HONORARY INSCRIPTION FOR TIMOGENES, 3rd - 4th CENT. A.D. Marble disc surrounded by a wreath. Ed. pr. A.K. Orlandos, l.c., 9-10, no. 6.

ἡ] βουλὴ
καὶ] ὁ δῆμος
[στεφανοῖ]
4 χρυσῷ σ]τεφάνῳ
Τιμ]ογένην
Τι]μογένους
πρ]ομοίρω[ς
8 βιώσαντα̣

964. PAROS, HONORARY INSCRIPTION, 3rd - 4th CENT. A.D. Marble block with wreath; broken at the right and below. Ed. pr. A.K. Orlandos, l.c., 10, no. 7 (ph.).

ἡ βουλὴ
καὶ ὁ δῆμος
στεφανοῖ [-
Σ.⌜--------
----

965. PAROS, FRAGMENT OF A HONORARY INSCRIPTION, LATE ROMAN PERIOD. Marble fragment. Ed. pr. A.K. Orlandos, l.c., 33-34, no. 66 (dr.).

Κουάρτον
προ]μοίρως β[ιώσαντα
τεγ

---

966. PAROS, FRAGMENT OF A HONORARY INSCRIPTION. Marble fragment, with part of a wreath; inside the wreath the inscription. Ed. pr. A.K. Orlandos, l.c., 13-14, no. 11 (ph).

Μνασέου

---

967. PAROS, INSCRIPTION CONCERNING FUNCTIONARIES OF THE CULT OF SERAPIS, 3rd - 4th CENT. A.D. Circular block. Ed. pr. A.K. Orlandos, l.c., 11-12, no. 9 (ph.). Cf. J. and L. Robert, BE (1977) no. 342, for LL. 4, 9 and 11.

Ἀγαθῆ
τύχη.
Ἄρχοντος τὸ
<β'> Ἀσκληπιάδου
τρίς, ἱερεὺς Σεράπι-
δος Αὐρ(ήλιος) Ἑρμήρακλος
υἱὸν Εὐφροσύνου /
λλοισαδειρχεις ἐτε-
λείωσεν{ε} τὴν εὐσέ-
βειαν νεοκόρου
Μ(άρκου) Αὐρ(ηλίου) Χαιρονει-
κίου τοῦ Νει[κίου]

4. Φ lapis || 7-8: "... pas compréhensibles" J. and L. Robert || 8-9. ἐτε|λείωσενε Orlandos || 11. Μ(ᾶρκον) Αὐρ(ήλιον) Orlandos.

---

968. PAROS, RITUAL BANQUET IN THE CULT OF SERAPIS, 3rd - 4th CENT. A.D. Marble block, with inscription engraved within a wreath. Ed. pr. A.K. Orlandos, l.c., 12-13, no. 10 (ph.). Cf. J. and L. Robert, BE (1977) no. 342 for LL. 2, 3, 5 and 6.

Ἀγαθῆ τύχη.
Ἄρχ]οντος Αὐρ(ηλίου)
--]νοτέλους τοῦ
--]του, ἱερεὺς
[Σεράπ]ιδος Αὐρ(ήλιος) Σύμ-
[μαχος] Ζωσίμου νε[οκ]-
όρου Μ(άρκου) Αὐρ(ηλίου) Χα[ιρο]-
νεικίου τοῦ Νει[κί]-
ου. Εὐφράνθημεν.
Εὐτυχῶς.

2. Αὐρ(ηλίου) [τοῦ] Orlandos || 3. [Φα]νοτέλους Orlandos || 5. [Ἴσ]ιδος Αὐρ(ήλιον) Σύμ[μαχον] Orlandos || 9. for εὐφραίνομαι cf. J. and L. Robert, l.c.

---

969. PAROS, A PRIEST OF SERAPIS, ROMAN PERIOD. Marble fragment. Ed. pr. A.K. Orlandos, l.c., 14-15, no. 14 (ph.).

ἄρχοντος Χάρη-
τος ἱερεὺς Σαράπι

2. Σαράπι(δος) Orlandos.

970. PAROS, LIST OF EPHEBES, AFTER 212 A.D. Rectangular marble block. Ed. pr. A.K. Orlandos, EAH (1963) 139-141; republished by Orlandos in AE (1975) Chron., 6-8, no. 3 (ph.). He accepts the suggestions made in BE (1964) no. 344 (cf. BE, 1977, no. 340) for LL. 24 and 30.

Ἀγαθῇ τύχῃ.
Οἵδε ἐφήβευσαν
ἐ]πὶ γυμνασιάρχου καὶ ἄρ-
χοντος τὸ β' κατὰ τὸ αὐτὸ
τῆς λαμπρᾶς Παρίων πό-
λεως Μάρ(κου) Αὐρ(ηλίου) Ζήνωνος
τοῦ Πυρράκου, ἐφηβάρχου
δὲ Μάρ(κου) Αὐρ(ηλίου) Ζηνοδότου
τοῦ Ζωσίμου. Πρωτέφη-
βος ὁ υἱὸς αὐτοῦ τοῦ γυ-
μνασιάρχου καὶ ἄρχον-
τος Μᾶρ(κος) Αὐρ(ήλιος) Ζήνων
Αὐρ. Σαβεινιανὸς Ζωσίμου
Αὐρ. Ζηνόδοτος Ζηνοδότου
Αὐρ. Κράτερος Ζηνοδότου
Αὐρ. Στεφανηφορικὸς Στεφανηφορικοῦ
Αὐρ. Παῦλος Ὡροτύχου
Αὐρ. Ἡρᾶς Ὡροτύχου
Αὐρ. Σεραπίων Σεραπίωνος
Αὐρ. Τειμόσστρατος Τειμοσστράτου
Αὐρ. Ἰουλειανὸς Ἀρτεμεισίου
Αὐρ. Ζώσιμος β' τοῦ Στρατονείκου
Αὐρ. Ἑρμῆς Ἑρμοῦ
Αὐρ. Εὐτύχης β' τοῦ Ζωσίμου
Αὐρ. Ζώσιμος Εὐγένους
Αὐρ. Ζωσᾶς Ἀφροδεισίου
Αὐρ. Εὐάριστος Ζωσίμου
Αὐρ. Δῖος Φιλοκάλου
Αὐρ. Ὀνησᾶς Ἱπποκράτου
Αὐρ. Ζώσιμος β' τοῦ Σεραπᾶ
Αὐρ. Συνίστωρ Μενίππου
Αὐρ. Ζώσιμος Χαρίτωνος

971-972. PAROS, NAMES OF EPONYMOUS GYMNASIARCHS AND PAIDONOMOI, ROMAN PERIOD. Two mutilated marble blocks. Ed. pr. A.K. Orlandos, l.c., 14, nos. 12 and 13.

971. No. 12 (ph.).

]ίππου γυμνασιαρχοῦντος Δη̣
]ης Σ̣ [παιδο]νόμου

1. [Τελεσ?]ίππου Orlandos.

972. No. 13 (dr.).

σωι
ου πα̣
ὀ̣λαος ἐπ[ὶ ἄρχ]-
ο]ντος Καλλι̣
σιθέου γυμ̣[νασιαρ]-
[χοῦντος] Τεισάρχο̣[υ]
[π]αιδο̣[νόμου -----]

973-977. PAROS, NAMES OF VISITORS OF THE GYMNASIUM, ROMAN PERIOD. Various marble blocks (some with tabula ansata). Ed. pr. A.K. Orlandos, l.c., nos. 16, 18, 19, 20, 55. Cf. J. and L. Robert, BE (1977) no. 340.

---

973. P. 15, no. 16 (dr.).

Διο]νυσίου
καὶ
Δημητρίου
Ναστάρου
Πλάτωνος

---

974. P. 16-17, no. 18; three inscriptions (ph.).

A.
ἐπικι
αι ιστορω
ελαου
υ
Ἀλ]κιβίου
Ἀρι]σ̣τοβούλου
Ἀ]ριστοδήμου
Ἀλε]ξάνδρου
Μελά]μπου

B.
σκοπου
Διονυσοδώρου
Φήλικ[ος
καὶ
Ἀ̣λεξ[άνδρου]

C.
Σωγένης
Πρόκλου
Ε[ὐ]άνασσα
Πρόκλου

---

975. P. 17, no. 19; two inscriptions (dr.).

A.
Ἀρτεμιδώρου
ι M
Ὀνησίμου
ι α
πρωτων

B.
Ὀνησίμου καὶ
δωου
ομωλίου

---

976. P. 17, no. 20 (dr.).

Σωκράτου

καὶ Ζωΐλου
Ἐπινίκου Ζωσί[μου

---

977. P. 30, no. 55 (dr.).

καὶ
Μάρωνος Δημι
καὶ
μ̣ι̣γένου

---

978. PAROS, DEDICATION TO ZEUS ELEUTHERIOS, 5th CENT. B.C. Marble block with triglyphs. Ed. pr. A.K. Orlandos, AE (1975) Chron., 8-9, no. 4 (dr.).

Διὸς Ἐλευθερίου

---

979. PAROS, DEDICATION TO A HERO, 5th - EARLY 4th CENT. B.C. Marble relief, with a rider on horseback and a standing figure, raising his right hand in adoration. Ed. pr. A.K. Orlandos, AE (1960) Chron., 2, no. 9; id., AE (1975) Chron., 28, no. 49 (dr.).

ΙΠΟ-Ι ἥρ]ωι εὐχήν

---

980. PAROS, DEDICATION TO APHRODITE TIMOUCHOS, 2nd - 1st CENT. B.C. Marble block. Ed. pr. A.K. Orlandos, AE (1975) Chron., 15-16, no. 17 (dr.).

Ἀφροδίτ]ει Τιμούχωι

For this goddess see L. Robert, GNOMON (1971) 40-41 (cf. BE, 1977, no. 341)

---

981. PAROS, DEDICATION (?) TO PRIAPOS, 2nd - 1st CENT. B.C. Marble block. Ed. pr. A.K. Orlandos, l.c., 33, no. 64 (ph.). Cf. J. and L. Robert, BE (1977) no. 341.

ε̣ ν̣ μ̣ Ἀπολλο[ν--
ι πηστον Πρίαπο̣ν
ἐγὼ δὲ

---

3. So J. and L. Robert, l.c.; ἐπώλε[ι Orlandos.

---

982. PAROS, DEDICATION TO THE GODS, 2nd - 1st CENT. B.C. Marble block, with part of a wreath. Ed. pr. A.K. Orlandos, l.c., 10-11,

no. 8 (ph.).

῎Αρχοντος | κο]ρος Διομήδης
᾿Ισχολείδου | Δ]ιομήδου
3 Δημ]ητρίου ζά- | 6 θεοῖς.

---

983. PAROS, DEDICATION TO ISIS (?), ROMAN PERIOD. Marble block, below rectangular, above an aetoma with three leafs. Ed. pr. A.K. Orlandos, l.c., 27, no. 46 (dr.).

τῇδ' ῎Ισιδι
ΣΚΑΙ

984-1000. PAROS, PAGAN EPITAPHS. A.K. Orlandos, l.c., publishes the following epitaphs:

---

984. P. 15, no. 15; marble block; late Hellenistic period (ph.).

Με]νεστράτου | ἥρωος

---

985. P. 17-18, no. 22; part of a sarcophagus; Roman period (dr.).

Οὐλμίλιο[ν or υ | --ι Φανοκράτου

---

986. P. 18, no. 23; marble block; Roman period (dr.).

Δάφνις | Ζωπύρου

---

987. P. 18-19, no. 24; marble base; 3rd cent. B.C. (dr.).

Αἰσχίνου

---

988. P. 19, no. 25; marble block; late Hellenistic period (dr.).

᾿Αντίοχε | χρηστὲ | χαῖρε

---

989. P. 19, no. 26; marble block; late Hellenistic period (ph.).

᾿Αριστόδημος | ῾Ερμίου χρηστὸς | φιλομήτωρ χαῖρε

3. for φιλομήτωρ cf. J. and L. Robert, BE (1977) no. 344.

---

990. P. 19-20, no. 27; fragment of a funerary relief; late Hellenistic period (ph.).

Παρθενόπη

---

991. P. 20, no. 28; marble base; late Roman period.

Κλεόβουλο[ς] | χρησ̣τὲ χαῖ[ρε]

---

992. P. 20-21, no. 30; base of a grave stele; 2nd - 3rd cent. A.D. (dr.).

Σάρδ[η]το[ς] ᾿Ιδ[αίου]

---

993. P. 21-22, no. 32; part of a sarcophagus with relief; Roman period (ph.).

Δονάτε | [Πάν]ωνος χρη[στὲ] | ---- χαῖρε

Cf. J. and L. Robert, BE (1966) no. 329.

---

994. P. 22, no. 33; part of a sarcophagus with two reliefs and two inscriptions; Roman period (ph.).

A. Πύθεμος | [χ]αῖρε

B. Σώτειρα Η

A. 1. perhaps Πύθε<ρ>μος ? ed. (cf. L. Robert, JS, 1968, 208).

---

995. P. 22-23, no. 34; part of a sarcophagus with a fragmentary grave relief; Roman period (ph.).

Χρυσογό|νη χρησ̣[τὴ χαῖρε]

---

996. P. 23-24, no. 37; fragment of a marble lekane.

Φανοθέμιος | [Σ]ικινήτου

---

997. P. 31, no. 58; marble fragment; Roman period (dr.).

[Κ]λαύδιος | [᾿Α]γ̣αθήμε|[ρ]ος χρηστὲ | χαῖρε

---

998. P. 32, no. 59; marble block; Roman period (dr.).

[Z]ώσιμε χρηστὲ | χαῖρε

---

999. P. 33, no. 63; marble block; Roman period (ph.).

Ἀνδρόν̣|[ικε χ]αῖρε

1000. P. 35-36, no. 74; marble block (dr.).

Σωτάδης | Σώσου χρησ[τὸς or τὲ] | χαῖρε

1001. PAROS, EPITAPH. Base of a classical grave-monument. Ed. D. Schilardi, PAAH (1974) 184 (ph.) (refering to D. Schilardi, JFA 2, 1975, p. 87, ph. 7 - non vidimus).

[Χρ]έμων

1002. PAROS, FUNERARY EPIGRAM FOR SOCHARMOS, 2nd CENT. A.D. IG, XII, 5, no. 306 C (= Peek, GV, 1351). A.K. Orlandos, AE (1975) Chron., 27, no. 47 (ph.) publishes the right half of an epigram, which, as J. Bousquet, BCH 101 (1977) 452-453 shows, belongs to and completes IG, XII, 5, 306 C. The text now runs as follows:

Σωχάρμου παράγ|ων δυερὸν τάφον εἰπὲ τὸ χαίρειν
εἴ τι καὶ ἐς φθιμένο|υς τοῦτ' ἔπος ἡδὺ πέλει·
εἰ γὰρ καὶ παύρας ἐτέ|ω̣ν ἔζησε κελεύθους,
ἄξιος αἰνεῖσθαι τ|έ̣κνα λιπὼν πατρίδι,
ὀρφανὰ μὲν Μοίραις, π|ολιὴν τρίχα δ' ἀνθήσειαν·
κείσθω παισὶ χρόνο|ς πατρὸς ὁ λειπόμενος.

At the right side of the epigram traces of another inscription in different script: ΚΟΔ[-] | ΚΡΑΙ[-] | χρη[στὲ] | χ[αῖρε].

1003. PAROS, EPIGRAM FOR AKRISIOS, IMPERIAL PERIOD. IG, XII, 5, no. 305 (Peek, GV, 1156). R. Merkelbach, ZPE 23 (1976) 235 offers two new readings. In L. 10 he prefers δίκασ[εν κα]ὶ to δικάσ[αι μο]ι; in L. 13 instead of ὧι he suggests ὦι (= ὦ, "mit einem abundierenden Iota"). But cf. IG: "ὧι, non ὦ{ι}".

1004. PAROS, FRAGMENT OF UNKNOWN CHARACTER, HELLENISTIC PERIOD. Marble fragment. Ed. pr. A.K. Orlandos, AE (1975) Chron., 28-29, no. 51 (dr.).

--εο-- |2 --εκγ-- |3 --οισγυο-- |4 --ειγ̣ καὶ πρὸ -- |5 --ηγκα-- |6 --δει--

---

2. ἐκγ[όνοις ?; proxeny-decree ? Orlandos.

1005. PAROS, FRAGMENT OF UNKNOWN CHARACTER, HELLENISTIC PERIOD. Marble fragment. Ed. pr. A.K. Orlandos, l.c., 29-30, no. 53 (dr.).

ἀγ]νώστω[ι ?
ἐνι]αυτῶ[ι ?
ἀγα?]γέτω

1006. PAROS, FRAGMENT OF UNKNOWN CHARACTER, ROMAN PERIOD. Marble fragment of an exedra. Ed. pr. A.K. Orlandos, AE (1960) Chron., 2, no. 15; id., AE (1975) Chron., 21, no. 31 (dr.).

Ἐπαφροδίτου

Perhaps an epitaph J. and L. Robert, BE (1977) no. 344.

1007. PAROS, FRAGMENTS OF UNKNOWN CHARACTER, LATE ROMAN PERIOD. Two fragments of a marble lekane. Ed. pr. A.K. Orlandos, AE (1975) Chron., 23, no. 36 (dr.).

A. αὐτῶ
μιτυ
τιπ̣αν

B. λωίου
ἔ]τους ΝΔ---
ἰου]λ̣ίου νόν[αις

B. 1. Ὁμο]λωίου or Λωίου Orlandos.

1008. PAROS, FRAGMENTARY INSCRIPTIONS, LATER IMPERIAL PERIOD. Two tabulae ansatae on a re-used marble block, found in Oliaros (now Antipatros). Ed. pr. W. Hoepfner - H. Schmidt, JDAI 91 (1976) 299.

A. ---τιων καὶ ---

B. Κλιτομένης Ξ---
νακιος καὶ Χρυ---
α---ηπιωκ---

1009. PAROS, FRAGMENT OF UNKNOWN CHARACTER. Marble fragment. Ed. pr. A.K. Orlandos, AE (1975) Chron., 17, no. 21 (dr.).

Λ̣ΙΕ̣..ι̣ος
Δημό[νό]μου

1010. PAROS, ENIGMATIC FRAGMENT. Marble fragment of a "cube". Ed. pr. A.K. Orlandos, l.c., 35, no. 73 (dr.). Cf. J. and L. Robert, BE (1977) no. 346.

Ἄν[ο]υτον

'Αντ]ύπα ζήσοις

1. 'Ανύγον (= ἀνοίγων) || 2. Ὕπα (= ὕπαγε = "va-t-en")· ζήσοις J. and L. Robert.

1011. PAROS, TABLE OF WEIGHTS, ROMAN PERIOD. Fragment of a marble sekoma. Ed. pr. A.K. Orlandos, l.c., 24, no. 40 (ph.).

Νικίου | Φήλεικος

1012. PAROS, CHRISTIAN INSCRIPTION, IMPERIAL PERIOD. Marble block. Ed. pr. A.K. Orlandos, l.c., 32, no. 60 (dr.).

ενοισ
τοῦ 'Ιω H-H
ρ λγ αο†
που ἅγιε [Θε]όδωρε
ουντος - πεμεαο
ο υδεκαδ
του καλλιδ ω
Δημητρ αριχ

1013. PAROS, CHRISTIAN INSCRIPTION (?), LATE ROMAN PERIOD. Marble fragment with ornaments. Ed. pr. A.K. Orlandos, l.c., 25, no. 41 (ph.).

νεικας ἐν

1014. PAROS, CHRISTIAN FORMULA, LATE ROMAN PERIOD. Marble fragment. Ed. pr. A.K. Orlandos, l.c., 34-35, no. 69 (ph.).

ἀόρατε ἀ[κατάληπτε

Orlandos refers to Joh. Chrysostomos: " Σὺ γὰρ εἶ Θεὸς ἀνέκφραστος, ἀπερινόητος, ἀόρατος, ἀκατάληπτος, ἀεὶ ὤν". J. and L. Robert, BE (1977) no. 345 wonder whether Orlandos' no. 65 (καταλη) and no. 75 (ρασ) do not belong to the same stone: ἀκατάλη[πτε and ἀνέκφ]ρασ[τε.

1015. PAROS, CHRISTIAN INSCRIPTIONS, 5th - 6th CENT. A.D. Four marble fragments. Ed. pr. A.K. Orlandos, l.c., 25, no. 42 (dr.).

(a) τῷ θ(ε)ῷ; (b) 'Ὑ̣λασ̣[ίου; (c) ΕΝΔΟ

(b) Perhaps a reference to Bishop Hylasius Orlandos.

1016. PAROS, CHRISTIAN FORMULA. Cylindrical marble lekane. Ed. pr. A.K. Orlandos, AE (1975) Chron., 24, no. 38.

Νίψον ἀνο|μήματα, μὴ | μόναν ὄψιν.

SYROS

1017. SYROS, EPITAPH FOR THE PRIEST CLEITOPHON, 3rd CENT. B.C. IG, XII, 5, 679; Peek, GV, 553. Cf. D.L. Page, WS 10 (1976) 174 who presents the text (in mixed meter) with commentary.

CHIOS

1018. DELPHI, DECREE OF CHIOS, 245 B.C. F. Delphes, III, 3, 215. Cf. no. 621.

1019. CHIOS, ALEXANDER'S LETTER TO THE CHIANS, 334 B.C. ? $Syll^3$, 283 (Tod, GHI, II, no. 192). H. Hauben, ANCSOC 7 (1976) 84-86 hesitatingly accepts A.J. Heisserer's case for dating this letter to 334 B.C. instead of 332 B.C. (A.J. Heisserer, HISTORIA 22, 1973, p. 191 ff.).

1020. CHIOS, EPIGRAM FOR TYRANNICIDES, HELLENISTIC PERIOD. Ed. pr. C.A. Trypanis, HERMES 88 (1960) 71-72. I. Calabi-Limentani, ACME 29 (1976) 17-18 doubts whether this epigram should be related to the Athenian tyrannicides Harmodios and Aristogeiton (as A.E. Raubitschek, STUDIUM GENERALE 17, 1964, 220 suggested).

1021. CHIOS, HONORARY EPIGRAM FOR MEGAKLES, PRESIDENT OF THE PRESBYTEROI, 1st CENT. B.C. CIG, 2221 (Kaibel, EG, no. 860). W. Peek, ZPE 23 (1976) 87-90 studies this inscription on the basis of a copy in the IG-files. We present the whole text here:

οἱ πρεσβύτεροι
Μεγακλέα Θεογείτονος
γονῆι δὲ Δαμονίκου,
ἄρξαντα τοῦ πρεσβυτικοῦ
εὐσεβείας ἕνεκεν τῆς εἰς τοὺς θεοὺς
καὶ ἀρετῆς καὶ φιλοτιμίας τῆς εἰς ἑαυτούς.
Σοὶ λάμπει μὲν δόξ̣α, καλοῖς δ' ἐσθλὰν̣ χάριν ἔργο<ις>
ὤπασεν ἁ κλεινὰ πρεσβυτέρων σύνοδος
εἰκόν' ἀναστήσασα σέθεν, μορφᾶς τύπον ἔμπνουν,
καί σ' ἐν Ὁμηρείωι γυμνασίωι θεμένα

[Χί]ου σ' [ὕ]ψωσεν, Θεογείτονος υἱέ, Μεγακλέα
[σᾶς], Ν̣ῆτα, καλὸν δεῖγμ' ἀρετᾶς θέμενος.

---

7. Σοῦ λάμ[π]ει μὲν δό[ξ]α, καλοῖς δ' ἐσθλὰ[ν] χάριν ἔργο[ις] CIG, Kaibel; corr. Peek || 8. ξ̣ύνοδος CIG, Kaibel; corr. Peek || 11-12. [πᾶσιν δ' ἔγν]ωσεν Θεογείτονος υἷα Μεγακλέα, | [ἀνδρειάν]τα κα[λ]ὸν δεῖγμ' ἀρετᾶς θεμένα CIG; [πᾶσιν ἐδήλ]ωσεν κτλ. Kaibel; corr. Peek.

SAMOS

1022. SAMOS, HONORARY INSCRIPTION FOR NAUSINIKOS, 324-322 B.C. Ed. pr. C. Habicht, MDAI(A) 72 (1957) 164 ff., no. 2. E. Badian, ZPE 23 (1976) 289-294 offers the following text in L. 8-11:

8 χρησ̣ι̣μ̣[ός τε γε]γένηται περὶ τὸμ π-
[όλεμον τὸμ] πρὸς τοὺς κληρού-
[χους καὶ εἰς] Ἄναια παρέσχετο
11 [Σαμίοις ἡ]μιολίαν κτλ.

8-10. Habicht rejected περὶ τὸμ π|[όλεμον τὸμ] πρὸς τοὺς κληρού-|[χους ...] and opted for περὶ τὸμ π|[αράπλουν (?) τὸμ] πρὸς τοὺς κληρου|[χέοντας τὰ] Ἄναια, κτλ.; J. and L. Robert, BE (1960) no. 318 recommended π|[ορθμόν]; Badian simply has removed the "mental comma" after Ἄναια.

AMORGOS

1023. AMORGOS, FUNERARY EPIGRAM, LATER IMPERIAL PERIOD. Ed. pr. A. Petsetakis, AD 25B, 2 (1970) 453 (ph.). W. Peek, ZPE 21 (1976) 282 improves various readings and offers the following text:

παῖδαν ἀπολλ[ύμενον] | Τέρπνου <ξένε? πέ>τρα ὅμοιο[ν] |
κοσμεῖ ἐνθάδε {τὸν [γῆ]} | τὸν γῆ φθιμένων κατ[έχει], |
ὀκτωκαιδέκατον ζ[ήσαν]|τα βίῳ λυκ[άβ]αντα
Σ[ώφρι]|λον· ἐρχόμενον δ̣ὲ βίο[υ] | μέτρον ἥρπασε δαίμων.

ΠΑΙΔΑΝΑ.....Μ | ΤΕΡΠΝΟ.....ΜΟΙΟ | ΚΟΣΜΕΙ ΕΝΘΑΔΕ ΤΟΝ(Δ) | ΤΟΝ ΓΗ ΦΘΙΜΕΝΩΝ Κ(Α)Τ | ΟΚΤΩΚΑΙΔΕΚΑΤΟΝ Ζ(ΗΣΑΝ) | ΤΑΒΙΩΛΥ(ΚΑΒ)ΑΝΤΑΣ -- | ΛΟΝ ΕΡΧΟΜΕΝΟΝ ΜΕΒΙΟ | ΝΕ(Κ)ΡΟΝΗΡΠΑΣΕΔΑΙΜΩΝ Petsetakis.

IMBROS

1024. IMBROS, INVENTORY OF THE TREASURY OF A GODDESS, 3rd CENT.

B.C. IG, XII, 8, 51 (cf. SEG, XVI, 518). A. Dworakowska, Note on the Greek terminology for abrasive stones, ARCHPOLON 27 (1976) 43-49 comments upon the words καὶ τῶν ζμιρριείων in L. 21 and tries to show that σμύρις from which ζμιρριεῖα is derived, is a general term denoting a "crushed or powdered mineral abrasive substance used in gem-engraving and in stonemasonry" rather than the specific stone, e.g. emery, from which this powder was made.

1025-1026. IMBROS, TWO EPITAPHS. Ed. pr. Cyriacus of Ancona, apud E.W. Bodnar - C. Mitchell, Cyriacus of Ancona's journeys in the Propontis and the Northern Aegean, 1444-1445 (Memoirs Am. Philos. Soc., 112; Philadelphia, 1976) p. 35 ("unpublished"). Cf. J. and L. Robert, BE (1977) no. 8.

1025. Διόδωρος Φιλόφρονος | Πειραεύς
Φιλόφρων Φιλοκλέου Πει|ραεύς

1026. Φιλο<υ>μένη Ἑρμ{ν}ησιάνακτος

ΕΡΜΝΗΣΙΑΝΑΚΤΟΣ Cyriacus

SAMOTHRACE

1027. SAMOTHRACE, DECREE FOR EPINIKIOS, GOVERNOR OF MARONEIA, REIGN OF PTOLEMY EUERGETES (247-223 B.C.). Ed. pr. G.M. Balakis and R.L. Scranton, AJPH 60 (1939) 452-458 (Cf. J. and L. Robert, BE, 1939, no. 298; 1940, no. 105; 1942, no. 139; 1950, no. 25, p. 129; L. Robert, GNOMON, 1963, p. 78). Cf. L. Robert, STUDCLAS 16 (1974) 85-88 who restores in lines 33-34 σι|[τοθ]εσί[αν] instead of σι|[τηρ]έσι[ον] (Balakis - Scranton) or σί[του παράθ]εσι[ν] (Pippidi). Σιτοθεσία is a hapax derived from another hapax (σιτοθέτης) mentioned in P.M. Fraser, Samothrace, II, 1 (London, 1960) no. 5, L. 4. L. Robert thinks that the decrees for Epinikios and for Hippomedon, strategos of the Hellespont and of Thrace (= IG, XII, 8, 156; Syll^3, 502; P.M. Fraser, o.c., p. 39-40. Fraser, l.c., p. 8-9 dates this text to the reign of Euergetes) and perhaps also P.M. Fraser, o.c., no. 5 are contemporary and deal with the same question (but Fraser, o.c., p. 32 dates his no. 5 on paleographical grounds to the early or mid-second century B.C.).

THASOS

1028. RELIGION: THE HERAKLES OF THASOS. J. Pouilloux, REA 76

(1974) 305-316 reviews the studies of D. van Berchem, Sanctuaires d' Hercule-Melquart. Contribution à l' étude de l' expansion phénicienne en Méditerranée: II. Thasos, SYRIA 44 (1967) 88-109 and B. Bergquist, Heracles on Thasos (Uppsala, 1973) and defends against them the view that there was a double aspect (divine and heroic) of Herakles on Thasos. A study of J. Pouilloux about the same subject also appeared in Mélanges A. Bon (Lyon, 1975) - non vidimus.

1029. THASOS, REGULATION CONCERNING THE LEASE OF THE GARDEN OF HERAKLES, CA. 330 B.C. ? Ed. M. Launey, BCH 61 (1937) 380-409. Cf. also BCH 96 (1972) 363-373. Cl. Vatin, BCH 100 (1976) 560-564 restores LL. 4-9 as follows:

4 ... Ὁ μισθωσάμενος τὸν κῆπον τοῦ Ἡρακλέος τὸν
5 [πρὸς τὰς πύλας? ὕδατι χρήσεται τῶι παρὰ τὸν κῆπο]ν ῥέοντι ὅταμ μὴ ἡ πόλις χρῆται· τὸ δὲ χωρίον τὸ ἐξ
6 [ἀριστερᾶς εἰσ(or ἐξ)ιόντι ----]ς ἐπιγνώμοσιν. Τὴν δὲ κόπρον τὴν γινομένην δι' ἐ-
7 [ξοδῶν ---- ἢ ὅσακις ἂν κ]ελεύηι ὁ ἐπιγνώμων· ὅσην δ' ἂν λαμβάνηι ὁ τὸ
8 [χωρίον λαβὼν καταθήσει εἰς κοπρῶνα· ὅπου δὲ πρότε]ρον ἐξεβάλλετο καὶ τὰ πρὸ τῶν πυλέων πάντα
9 [καθαρὰ παρέξει· ἢν δέ τις κοπρώσηι, ἀπαγέτω ὁ λαβὼν τὸν κῆ]πον καὶ τὸν δοῦλον μαστιγῶσας ἀθώϊος ἔστω.

Vatin assumes that in L. 15 there is no question of the payment of the rent but of the delivery of the buildings (mentioned in L. 13-14) by the lessee. In L. 17 the subject of οἰκοδομήσει and παραδώσει is taken by Vatin to be one of the lessors.

6-7. J. and L. Robert, BE (1977) no. 66 remark: "ἔξοδος désigne exactement la sortie, comme εἴσοδος l' entrée, et 'lieu de passage' est une extension abusive: l' emploi de διά surprend dans ce cas".

EUBOIA

1030. EUBOIA (?), DEDICATION OF A SMALL BRONZE STATUE, CA. 450 B.C. Now in the museum of Valencia (Spain). Republished by J. Hoz, ZEPHYRUS 26-27 (1976) 401-404 (ph.) (non vidimus - cf. J. and L. Robert, BE, 1977, no. 29) and assigned to Euboia (instead of Athens).

A. On the shoulder: Ἀπολώνιος
B. Underneath (from the top downwards): ἀνέθεκεν

1031. AIDEPSOS, FRAGMENT OF DIOLETIAN'S EDICT ON MAXIMUM PRICES

301 A.D. Ed. pr. E.J. Doyle, HESPERIA 45 (1976) 85-97. Doyle's manuscript was used by S. Lauffer, Diokletian's Preisedikt (Berlin, 1971) who also re-examined the stone. The tariff is arranged in three parallel columns and covers (in the traditional numbering) in Column I, sections 10.1-11.8; Column II, sections 13.1-14.3; Column III, 15.31a-15.61, with seven new lines following on 15.61. We refer the reader to Lauffer's book for Doyle's contributions to the text.

1032-1033. CHALKIS, STAMPED AMPHORA-HANDLES, 220-180 B.C. Ed. pr. A.K. Andreiomenou, AD 27A (1972) 173 (ph.).

1032. Ἐπὶ Φιλίππο[υ]
Ἀσκληπιόδ-
ωρος Κνίδιο[ν]

1033. Ἀριστοκράτεος

1034-1035. ERETRIA, TWO AGONISTIC INSCRIPTIONS, 2nd CENT. B.C. Texts inscribed on a metope between two triglyphs; under the inscriptions two wreaths. Ed. pr. A.K. Orlandos, EAH (1976) 20-21 (ph.). Cf. AR (1977-78) 17.

1034. At the left: Λευκίου Νομμίου
στάδιον
Βιοττοκλῆς
Βιόττου.

1. Νομμίου (?) J. and L. Robert, BE (1977) no. 364.

1035. At the right: Ἀρτέμιδος
στάδιον
Πύρρος
Ζωβίου

1036. ERETRIA, DEDICATION, 4th CENT. B.C. IG, XII, 9, 273. D. Knoepfler, AK 19 (1976) 57 restores in L. 1 [φυ]λῆς before παισὶ | [χορηγήσας].

1037. ERETRIA, DEDICATION TO KOTHOS. IG, XII, 9, 406. D. Knoepfler, AK 19 (1976) 57 (cf. BCH, 100, 1976, p. 701) points out that, since the name is in the genitive, this is not a funeral stele, but a cippus, marking the place of a temenos, dedicated to Kothos (mythical οἰκιστής of Chalkis).

1038. ERETRIA, EPITAPH OF PANTAUCHOS, CA. 300 B.C. IG, XII, 9, 715. D. Knoepfler, <u>Mélanges Collart</u>, p. 273, note 39 points out that in L. 2 the mason had originally written Θευδώρου (typical of the Thessalian origin of Pantauchos), which he subsequently corrected into Θεοδώρου.

1039. ERETRIA, EPITAPH, 3rd CENT. B.C. Stele. Ed. pr. D. Knoepfler, AK 19 (1976) 57 (cf. BCH, 100, 1976, p. 701).

Κλεονίκη Κωμίου

1040. ERETRIA, EPITAPH, 2nd CENT. B.C. Marble base of a grave-monument. Ed. pr. A.K. Orlandos, EAH (1976) 25 (ph.).

Μενεστράτη | Ἀλεξιμάχου | χρηστὴ χαῖρε

1041. KARYSTOS, REPAYMENT OF PUBLIC LOANS, CA. 370 B.C. IG, XII, 9, 7. Cf. also W.P. Wallace, PHOENIX 16 (1962) 15-28. L. Migeotte, PHOENIX 30 (1976) 26-41 gives a revised edition of the text (with app. crit., translation and commentary); M.B. Wallace, ibid., 42-45 discusses some views of Migeotte. The discussion mainly concerns the restoration of amounts of money (interest-rates), names of creditors and the number of categories of lenders. We give here Migeotte's text (and Wallace's alternatives for Migeotte's restorations):

------Ọ̣Ị̣Ẹ̣Ị------------------------------------
...F̣XXXHͰͰͰͰ⁝σταθμ̣[ὸς τούτων]-------------------------
Θ̣...NO-------------------------------------[Κεφα]-
λή⁝TTTXHͰͰͰͰ⁝παντὸς [δὲ τõ ἀργυρίο?]-----------------
κεφαλή⁝ v Δ̣XXXXHͰͰͰͰ. Ἄρχο[ντος Ἀρχεστράτο τοῖσδε ὁ]
τόκος ἀπεδόθη ἐς Θήβας καὶ Ἱσ[τίαιαν· Βοληκράτης? Καλ]-
λίππωι Θηβαίωι⁝ͰΓ⁝Θεύρων Εὐβ[ολίωνι Θηβαίωι⁝HͰ?⁝]
Θεοζοτίδαι⁝Θηβαίωι⁝ͰͰͰͰΓΓ⁝[Πρόφαντος? Ἀσωποδώρωι?]
Θηβαίωι⁝ͰͰͰͰ⁝Ἀντίμαχος Φιλοκ[ράτει Ἱστιαιεῖ⁝XH?⁝Τιμο?]-
κράτης⁝Φιλοκράτει Ἱστιαιεῖ⁝Ͱ̣ͰΓ̣[Γ?⁝Φερενίκωι? Θηβαίωι]
ἐπόγδοον⁝ͰͰͰͰ⁝Τιμοσθένης Φι[λοκράτει Ἱστιαιεῖ⁝==?⁝κε]-
φαλή⁝XXXHͰͰͰ⁝Τοῖσδε τόκον ἀπέ[δοσαν ἄρχοντος Ἀρχεστ]-
ράτο ταμίαι κατὰ Θεύρωνα ἀπὸ τῆς π[ροσόδο ἣν παρέλα]-
βον παρὰ ταμιῶν τῶν κατὰ Θράσυν⁝Πρ[όφαντος Εὐβολίωνι]
Θηβαίωι⁝Γ⁝Ἀσωποδώρωι Θηβαίωι⁝=-[|̣||OO⁝Ἀντίμαχος?]
Εὐβολίωνι⁝Θηβαίωι⁝Γ⁝Ἀσωποδώρωι [Θηβαίωι⁝=-|||OO⁝]
Βοληκράτης⁝Εὐβολίωνι Θηβαίωι⁝Γ⁝Ἀσω[ποδώρωι Θηβαίωι⁝=-]

|||OO⁝Θεύρων Εὐβολίωνι Θηβαίωι⁝𐅃⁝'Α[σωποδώρωι Θηβαί]-
ωι⁝=-|||OO⁝Τιμοκράτης⁝Εὐβολίωνι Θη[βαίωι⁝𐅃⁝'Ασωποδώ]-
ρωι Θηβαίωι⁝=-|||OO⁝κεφαλή⁝Ⱶ v. Τοῖσδ[ε τόκον οὐκ ἀπέδοσα]-
ν ἐς Θέβας Καρύστιοι ἄρχοντος 'Αρχεστρ[άτο Καλλίππωι?⁝X?⁝]
'Ασ[ω]π[οδώρωι⁝⅂?]⅂⁝Φερενίκωι⁝Ⱶ⅂⅂⅂𐅃==[ἐπόγδοον?⁝Εὐβολίω]-
νι⁝⅂⅂⅂⅂⁝κεφα⁝XX⅂⅂⅂⅂𐅃==⁝τοῦτο τὸ Ε----------------------
ΗΤΟΝ καί ἐστι αὐτοῖς ἐν τῶι κεφαλαίωι ὃ γέγρ̣[απται. Δανεισταί·]
Εὐβολίων, Θεοζοτίδας, Κάλλιππος, 'Ασω[πόδωρος, Φερένικο]-
ς, Φιλοκράτης· τούτοις ἀποδέδοται ὁ τόκ[ος ὃς ὠφείλετο 'Αρχε]-
στράτο ἄρχοντος καὶ ὃς ἐξ̣ελείφθη Κλεομ̣[έδοντος? ἄρχοντος·]
ἐκγμηνοταμίαι δὲ ἀπέδοσαν οἱ κατὰ Βο[ληκράτην ταῦτα καὶ]
παρέδοσαν Βοληκράτης, Θεύρων, 'Αν[τίμαχος, Τιμοκράτης,]
Τιμοσθένης, Πρόφαντος, ταμίαις Εὐκλέγω̣[νι], ---, ---,
Εὐκρίτωι, Χαιρεδήμωι, Νικοξένωι, Τιμηκ---, ----,
Μενεκράτει, Τιμάνθει, Εὐγενεῖ, Κτήσιδι τῆς π̣[ροσόδο ἣν παρέ]-
λαβον παρὰ ταμιῶν τῶν κατ' 'Αριστομέν̣[ην τὰ περιόντα?].
Κεφαλὴ⁝Ⱶ⅂⅂⅂⅂=-Γ|OOO vac.

L. 3 and the beginning of L. 22: erased || M.B. Wallace, l.c., proposes the following alternatives for Migeotte's restorations: 7. ⅂⅂⅂⅂ instead of Ⱶ⅂; 9. Ⱶ⅂⅂ instead of XⱵ; 11. X== instead of ==; 21. Ⱶ⅂ instead of X; 23. Ⱶ⅂ instead of ⅂⅂.

1042. TAMYNAI, FRAGMENT OF DIOCLETIAN'S EDICT ON MAXIMUM PRICES, 301 A.D. Ed. pr. E.J. Doyle, HESPERIA 45 (1976) 79-85. Doyle's manuscript was used by S. Lauffer, Diokletians Preisedikt (Berlin, 1971). The text is arranged in two columns. Column I includes (in the traditional numbering) sections 20.1a to 21.2; column II includes sections 24.13 to 25.2 (with thirteen new lines following on 24.16). We refer the reader to Lauffer's book for Doyle's contributions to the text.

CRETE

1043. ARKADES, HONORARY INSCRIPTION FOR EUKLEIA BY THE Τιβεριοπολιτῶν πόλις, 1st - 2nd CENT. A.D. I. Cret., I, 5, no. 25. H. van Effenterre, Recueil Plassart, p. 205-214 tries to show that "the polis of the Tiberiopolitai" which in this inscription honours Eukleia, daughter (or wife) of Charmistas, is the Cretan city of Arkades in which this inscription has been found (and not the Phrygian city of Tiberiopolis which was supposed to have had mythical links with Arkades, as L. Robert, REG, 1965, p. XXXVIII-XXXIX assumed). Van Effenterre supposes that the city of Arkades was rebuilt in the plain during Tiberius' reign and that as a result of this the city changed its name. His only (rather shaky) evidence is that on archaeological grounds the baths in Arkades date from the time of the Julio-Claudian dynasty. J. and L. Robert, BE (1977) no. 371 rightly express their doubts about this theory.

1044. ARKADES, REGULATION ABOUT THE BATHS, IMPERIAL PERIOD. Ed. pr. P. Ducrey - H. van Effenterre, Κρητικὰ Χρονικά 25 (1973) 281-290. H. van Effenterre, Recueil Plassart, p. 205-210 dates this text, originally assigned to the time of the Principate, to the period of the Julio-Claudian dynasty, on archaeological grounds: the baths of Arkades seem to have been built in Augustus' reign and repaired during the reign of his immediate successor. Though the text does not explicitly refer to building and/or repair-operations and therefore van Effenterre's theory is of dubious value, we present this otherwise interesting text here:

Οἱ σὺμ Πρατομηνίῳ κόσμοι καὶ οἱ οἰκονόμοι
ἐπεμ̣[ελήθ]ην τῶ βαλανε[ίω ἐκ] τῶν [τᾶς] πόλεος δαπαναμ̣[ά]των καὶ
τ-----το---------------μενον. [Ἐ]κό[σμε]ον̣ οἵδε·
Κάραν[ο]ς Σωμένω, Δι̣ν̣[οκλῆ]ς Ἀγεσίππω, Ἱερώνυμος Ἀπολλονίω,
γραμματεὺς Πρατομήνιος Ἐξακέστα· οἰκονόμοι Σωκλῆς Πρατο-
μήδους, Φίλινος Δινοκλέος. ////// Λούειν δὲ τὰς γυναῖκας
[[ ]] ἀπὸ ὥρας //////// μέχρι ὥρας //////// τοὺς δὲ ἄνδρα[ς]
[[ΡΔΑΝΤΑ]] ἀπὸ ὥρας ////////. vac.

7-8. in rasura ΡΔΑΝΤΑ.

1045. CHERSONESOS, EPITAPH, END 3rd CENT. A.D. I. Cret., I, 7, Chersonesos, p. 42-43, no. 24. H. van Effenterre, BCH 100 (1976) 525-553 thinks that there might be a connection between this inscription and an Attic sarcophagus from Mallia. If this supposition is right, also the provenance of this epitaph (as I. Cret., I, 7, Chersonesos, nos. 31 and 32) would be Mallia.

1046. KATO SYME (BIANNOS), DEDICATION OF A TEMPLE TO HERMES KEDRITES, 3rd CENT. A.D. G. Daux, BCH 100 (1976) 211-213 republishes the inscription published in EAH (1973) 122 (cf. also PAAH, 1973, p. 198 and PAAH, 1974, p. 225):

Ἑρμᾶ Κ̣εδρίτᾳ
Νικάνωρ Θεο-
μνάστου τὸν
ναόν.

1. [Δ]ΕΔΡΑ[ΙΤ]Α EAH; Δ̣ΕΔΡΙΤΑ PAAH; Κεδρίτης is related to κεδρία: oil of the cedre Daux.

1047. KNOSSOS, DEDICATION TO DEMETER, LATE 5th CENT. B.C. Boustrophedon inscription on a silver ring bezel. Ed. pr. J.N. Coldstream, Knossos. The Sanctuary of Demeter (ABSA, Suppl. Pap. 8, 1973) p. 131-133, no. 14. Cf. R. Willetts, JHS 95 (1975) 231-232;

H. van Effenterre, JHS 96 (1976) 154, after re-examination of the ring, reads the inscription as follows:

→ Νοθοκάρτης | ← Νικέτα Δ̣ | → αμάτρι.

Νικέτα = patronymic van Effenterre; → Νοθοκάρτης | ← νικέτας F | → Μάτρι Coldstream, Willetts.

1048. KNOSSOS, FRAGMENTARY INSCRIPTION, 2nd CENT. A.D. Large architectural block of poros. Ed. pr. H.W. Catling and D. Smyth, ABSA 71 (1976) 29 (cf. AR, 1973-74, p. 35, fig. 73):

....]ΤΙΩΝ | ....]ΔΙΩΝΟΣ

1049. LATO, TREATY BETWEEN LATO AND HIERAPYTNA, 111-110 B.C. Grey-blue limestone stele, broken in six parts; now in the museum of Haghios Nikolaos. Ed. pr. H. van Effenterre - M. Bougrat, Κρητικὰ Χρονικά 21 (1969) 9-53; L. 52-82 republished by P. Faure, Ἀμάλθεια 13 (1972) 227-240 - non vidimus. Y. Garlan, BCH 100 (1976) 303-304 suggests a number of new readings in various lines. We print the whole text below, with Garlan's new readings:

[᾿Αγα]θᾶ[ι] τύχαι·

[Τάδε συνέθεντο ---- ῾Ιαρα]π̣ύ̣τ̣νιοι κ̣α̣[ὶ Λ]ά̣τιοι. Κοσμιόντων [ἐ]ν̣ μ[ὲ]ν ῾Ιαρα-
[πύτναι ἐπὶ τῶν ------]ν τῶν σὺν [----]κ̣αι τῶ .κε..ο̣[β]ώλω, ἐν [δ]ὲ Λ̣α̣-
[τῶι ἐπὶ τῶν ᾿Εχανορέων τῶν σὺ]ν Αὐτίω̣[νι] τ̣ῶ Ποδ̣αίθ̣ω̣ σ̣υμμαχῆσεν ἀλλ[ά]-
[λοις ἁπλῶς καὶ ἀδόλως καὶ] τὸν [αὐτὸν φίλον κ]αὶ ἐχθ̣[ρὸν ἐ]ξῆν κ̣' α̣ἴ̣ τίς κ' ἐμ̣β̣ά̣[λ]-
[ληι ἐς τὰν τῶν ῾Ιαραπυτνίων χώρα]ν [ἢ ἀπ]οτά̣μ̣νηται χώ[ρας τᾶ]ς ῾Ιαραπυ̣τ̣ν̣ί̣ω̣ν
[ἀπροφασίστως βοαθησῆν τὸς Λατίο]ς̣ κατὰ γᾶν κ̣αὶ κα[τὰ θά]λ̣ασσαν κ̣α̣τ[ὰ τὸ]
[δυνατόν, κ' αἴ τίς κ' ἐμβάλληι ἐς τὰν τ]ῶν Λατίων χώρ[α]ν [ἢ ἀ]ποτ̣ά̣μνηται χ[ώρας]
[τᾶς Λατίων ὡσαύτως βοαθησῆν τὸ]ς̣ ῾Ιαραπυτνίος ἀδ[ό]λ[ω]ς [κἀ-προ]φασίστως π̣α̣ν̣τ̣[ὶ]
[σθένει ἐς τὸ δυνατόν. ᾿Εξέστω δὲ κ]α[ὶ] τ̣ῶ̣ι̣ ῾Ιαραπυτν[ίωι Λατοῖ καὶ τῶι Λατίωι ἐν]
[῾Ιαραπύτναι μετέχεν θίνων καὶ ἀνθρωπ]ι̣νων, δικα̣[ιοπραγήσαντι τοῖς ἰδίοις, ἤ]-
[μεν δὲ καὶ ἐπιγαμίαν καὶ ἔγκτησιν Λ]α̣τίων (?) [θυ]α̣τῶν [καὶ ἀθανάτων κατὰ τὸς ἰ]-
[δίος νόμος] ῾Ιαραπυτνίωι καὶ Λ̣α̣τ̣ί̣ω[ι ------------------------]
[----------- Λάτιον ἐ]ν τῶι τεμ̣ένει [τᾶς ᾿Ελευθυίας ----------]
[-----------------῾Ιαρ]απύτνιον ἐν τῶι [Δωδεκαθέωι -----------]

[--------------- Αἰ]δέ τίς κα[----]χω[---------------------]
----------᾿Ιαραπυτν[ι]ο---------
----------ηνεαι..----------
-----------νος ἐν τῶι ἰα[ρῶι ? ----------
[---------π]ερὶ δὲ τῶν ....[----------------------------.᾿Εξ]-
[αγωγὰν δὲ ἦμε]ν τῶι τε ᾿Ιαραπ[υτνίωι ἐγ Λατῶς καὶ τῶι Λατίωι ἐξ ᾿Ιαραπύτναι κατὰ]
[γᾶν μὲν ἀτε]λές, κατὰ θά[λ]α[σσαν δὲ καταβάλλονσι τὰ τέλια κατὰ τὸς νόμος τὸς]
[ἑκατερῆι ὑ]πάρχοντας, ὀμόσαν[σι ἐς ἰδίαν χρηίαν ἐξάγεν. Αἰ δέ τι κοινᾶι ἐξοδώ]-
[σαντες, θε]ῶν βωλομένων, [ἕλοιμεν ἀγαθὸν ἀπὸ πολεμίων, τὰ μέρια λανχάνεν ἑκατέ]-
[ρος κατὰ τ]ὸς ἕρποντας ἄν[δρας -----------------------------]
[------ τ]αῖς καταγραφαῖς .....ν[---------. Αἰ δέ κα πολεμίωντι ἑκατέραι αἱ]
[πόλιε]ς ἀπὸ χώρας, μὴ ἐξέστω [μ]η[δατέρωι μήτε σπονδὰς ἄγεν μήτε εἰράναν τίθεσθαι]
[αἴ]κα μὴ ἀμφότεραι αἱ πόλιες [β]ωλε[ύσωνται. ᾿Εξορκιξάντων δὲ τὰς ἀγέλας, ἐπ]ε[ί κ᾿ ἐγ]-
[δρ]άμωντι ἐν ἑκατέραι τᾶι πόλι, [οἱ κόσμοι ἐπ᾿ αὐτῶν κοσμιόντων, παριόντων ἐν μὲν]
[᾿Ιαρ]απύτναι Λατίων [πρειγηίας, ἐν δὲ Λατοῖ ᾿Ιαραπυτνίων πρειγηίας. ᾿Αναγινωσκόντων]
[δὲ κ]αὶ τὸν ὅρκον ἐν [μὲν ᾿Ιαραπύτναι ἐν τοῖς ῾Υπερβωίοις, ἐν δὲ Λατοῖ ἐν τοῖς Θιοδαισί]-
[οις π]αραγγελλόντω[ν ἐπὶ τὰν ἀνάγνωσιν οἵ τε ᾿Ιαραπύτνιοι κόσμοι τοῖς Λατίοις καὶ οἱ]
[Λάτ]ιοι τοῖς ᾿Ιαραπυτν[ίοις πρὸ ἀμερᾶν δέκα ἐπεί κα μέλλωντι ἀναγινώσκεν ἢ τὰς ἀγέ]-
[λας] ἐξορκίζεν. Αἰ δέ [μὴ ἐξορκίξαιεν τὰς ἀγέλας οἱ ᾿Ιαραπύτνιοι κόσμοι ἢ μὴ παρα]-
[γ]γήλαιεν ἐπὶ τὰν ἀνάγ[νωσιν ἢ μὴ ἀναγνοῖεν τὰν συνθήκαν καθὼς προγέγρ]απτ[αι]
[ἀπ]οτεισάτω ὁ κόσμος ἕ[κα]σ[τ]ο[ς τοῖς Λατίοις ἀλεξανδρείω ἀργυρίω στατῆραν]ς ἑκατ[όν].
[Αἰ δὲ] μὴ ἐξορκίξαιεν τ[ὰ]ς ἀγέλα[ς οἱ Λάτιοι κόσμοι ἢ μὴ ἀναγνοῖεν τὰν σ]υνθήκ[αν],
[παριόν]των ᾿Ιαραπυτνίων, [ὡσαύτως ἀποτεισάτω ὁ κόσμος ἕκαστος τοῖς ᾿Ι]αραπ[υτνί]-
[οις στατῆ]ρανς ἑκατό[ν. Αἰ δὲ κά τις κοσμίων ἔλθηι ᾿Ιαραπύτνιος ἐς Λατῶ]ν, ἔ[χων]
[τὸ ἱμ]άτιον ἀ[φφ]ανῶ ἑρπέτω [ἐς πρυτανήιον ἐς Λατῶν, ὡσαύτως δὲ κα]ὶ ὁ [Λά]τιο[ς]
[κόσμος] ἔχων τὸ [ἡμ]ά[τι]ον ἀφ[φανῶ, ἑρπέτω ἐς πρυτανήιον ἐς ᾿Ιαράπυτνα]ν κα[θὼς]
[κοί κόσμο]ι ἑρπ[ῶντι Λάτιοι καὶ ᾿Ιαραπύτνιοι ἐς ἑορτὰν ἢ πομπά]ν. ῞Ο[τ]ι
[δέ κα] δόξη[ι] ταῖς πόλεσι [βωλευσαμέναις ἐξελὲν ἢ ἐγγράψαι, ὅτι μὲν κ᾿ ἐξέλ]οιμεν, [τοῦ]-

ṭο μήτε ἔṿθ̣ι̣ṿον [μή]ṭ[ε ἔνορκον ἦμεν, ὅτι δὲ κ' ἐγγράψαιμεν, ἔνθινον καὶ] ἔṿορ[κον].
["Ορ]ḳον δ̣ὲ καὶ στάλας ἀ̣ṿ[αγραψάντων καὶ στασάντων ἑκάτεροι, ἐ]ṇ μὲν Ἱαρα[πύτ]-
[ναι] ἐν τῶι Δωδεκαθέωι, Λ̣α̣[τοῖ δὲ ἐν τῶι τᾶς Ἐλευθυίας, κοινᾶι δὲ στ]α̣σ̣άντων Ἱ[αρα]-
[πύτνιοι] καὶ Λάτιοι [Λυττοῖ ἐν τῶι ἱαρῶι τᾶς Ἀθαναίας Πολιάδος], ἕρπεν δὲ κα[ὶ]
[Ἱαρ]απύτνιο̣ν ἐς [Λατῶν ἐς ---------------------------]αιδ̣ε..
[Λάτιον] ἕρπεν ἐ̣ς̣ Ἱ̣α̣ρ̣ά̣[πυτ]ν̣α̣ν̣ [ἐς -------------] ἐν τᾶι ..α.
[....] παραγγελλό̣[ντων -----------------------------]αγώγιον ..
...σ..σθων τῶ̣ν ἀ̣ρ.[---------------------------------]σ̣πε..ε..
["Ορ]οι [τᾶ]ς̣ [χώ̣ρ]ας Ἱαρα̣[πυτνίων καὶ Λατίων· ἀπὸ θαλάσσας ἅ]μ π[οταμ]ὸν τὸ[ν]
[Κυ]μ̣αῖο[ν] ἆι [ὕδωρ ρ]εῖ κα[ὶ ἐπὶ τὸς Ε------ἐπὶ τὰν Ἱππάγρα]ν καὶ ἄνω ἐπὶ τ[ὸν]
[Β]έγκασον καὶ ἐς τὰ̣ς [-------------------------]η̣ι̣ μακρὰν καὶ ἐπ[ὶ]
[τ]ὸν θῖνον ἄρον καὶ ἐ̣π̣ὶ̣ [--------------------------]ηιον κ̣[α]ὶ ἐς τ̣ὰ̣ṿ χαρά-
[δ]ρω καὶ ἐ<ς> τὰν κ[ε]φ̣α[λὰν ---]το[---------]ν τὰς στεφάνας τῶν
.ΑΝΑΡΩ[ν] καὶ [------]α̣χ̣[-------------]ΝΜ(or Υ)Ε̣(or Ρ)ΛΗΤΙΩΕΣ ΤΟΝΚ.-
ωποιον καὶ ...[-------------------------]ε̣νει καὶ ἀπὸ τᾶς Ἀλω-
[..]ς ὀρθὰν ἐς τὸ ὀξὺ [----------]ω καὶ [ἐς] τὸ ἄ[κ]ρον τᾶς εὐ-
[----] ἆι ὕδωρ ῥεῖ τᾶς [---------] ἇς ἔστων οἱ ὦρο[ι] Λατίοι[ς]
[κα]θὼς καὶ̣ π̣[ά]λαι ἐπιγέ[γραπται Λατοῖ ἐπὶ τῶν σὺν ------ Λ]ατίοις ποτὶ Λυττίος, Λυ[τ]-
[τοῖ] δὲ ἐ̣π̣ὶ τ̣[ῶ]ν [σ]ὺ̣ν Σωκλ̣[----. Ἔντων δὲ καὶ οἱ ὧροι ποτὶ τὰς ἀποδε]δομ[ένας χ]ώ̣ρας κα[ὶ]
[Ὀλο]ντίος ο[ἵ]δε [ἀ]πὸ θαλά[σσας ἐς Πλυμ]ῶν ἀ[ρράχι]ṇ ἐπ]ὶ τὸ ἀρχαῖον [Ἀφ]ροδίσιο[ν]
[καὶ] τούτω ὡς [τῶ Δ]έραι θ[ί]ν[ω τῶ] τεμένω τὸς ὅρος οἱ ἐς τὸν βορέ[α]ν [ἔ]χοντεν
[κή]ς τὰν Αἰρ[επῶ κὴς τὰν Προμε]νήτ[ισσαν] κ[ὴς] Καλολάκα ἐς τὰν περί[β]α̣σιν καὶ ἐς Ἀρχ[έ]-
[λα]ρχον ἐς τὰν Δηράδα πὰρ τῶν πρί[νων κὴς τ]ὸν [Ἀκά]μαντα. vac.
[----]..[----].. δ̣ὲ̣ καὶ οἱ Ἱαραπύτνιοι τοῖς Λατίοις χώραν καθὼς παρεκάλεσ[αν]
[Λά]τιοι, ἐ[μμε]ν[όν]των Λατίων ἐν τᾶ̣ι Γ[ορ]τ[υ]ṿ̣ίων καὶ Ἱαραπυτνίων φιλίαι καὶ συμμαχία̣ι̣
ἇς ἔντι οἱ ὑ̣π[ογε]γραμμένοι ὅροι· ἀπὸ τᾶς τῶ [Β]εγκάσω ἐς τᾶς πέτρας περιαμπέ-
τις ἐς [τ]ὰν [ἆι ἁ]τ̣α̣ι̣ν̣ί̣α̣ π̣α̣ρ̣α̣τ̣ρέχει καὶ τούτω [περιαμ]πέτις [ἐ]ς [ἄ]κ̣ραν τὰν Μίτοις καὶ
ἐς ὀρθὸν [ἐς τ]ὰν κεφαλὰν τῶ πάλαι χέρσ̣ω̣ [τὰν] ἐπέχο[νσαν] ἐπὶ τὰν Ἐξάκωṇτ[ος]
ἀφαμία̣ṿ̣ [καὶ] τ̣ο̣ύ̣τ̣ω̣ ἐπὶ τὰς κεφαλὰς τᾶν ναπᾶν περὶ τὸς Ἐ̣ρ[ειπιώ]νας μέστα ἐς τὰ̣[ν κεφα]-

λὰν τὰν κατάνω τῶ Ἑρμᾶ καὶ περιαμπέτις ὑποκάτω τῶ ἀ[ντ]ροσείδιος καὶ ἐς τ[ὰν ὁδὸν]
τὰν διὰ Λάξον ἄγονσαν καὶ ἐπὶ τ[ὸν] θῖνον ἄρον καὶ ἐς τὰν κεφαλὰν τὰν ὑποκάτω [τῶ Γνά]-
φω καὶ τού[τ]ω ἐς τὸ πέ[ρ]α[ν] ἐς τὸν παχὺν λόφον ὑποκ[άτ]ω τᾶς σκοπᾶς κἀπὸ [τούτω ἐς τὸ]
ἐξέδριον τὸ [κ]ατάνω ἧ αἱ θῆκαι ἔντι καὶ ἐς τὰν ἄνω ἀλικὰν καὶ ἐς τὰν κά[τω ὤιαν τᾶς πέ]-
τρας καὶ ἐς τὸν Βοίνωπα καὶ ἐς τὰν Ἱππάγραν καὶ ἐς τὰν ὁδὸν τὰν ἄγονσαν ἐ[πὶ] Ἄκ[ιμον]
ἐς Ἰαλκέτ[ας κἠ]πὶ τὸς Κωρήτας καὶ ἐς τὸν Κόλον ἇι ὕδωρ ρεῖ καὶ ἐς Κυμνήτ[αλ]λαν ἇι ὕδωρ
ῥεῖ καὶ ἐς [κ]άτω Σοράσσαν κἠς τὰν ὁδὸν κἠπ' Ἐλάφω λίμναν καὶ ἐς τὰν Δηράδα κἠς τὸν Ἀχερ-
δόεν[τα κἠπὶ Δ]ιὸς ἄκρον κἠπὶ Δορηίαν κἠς Κυρταίραξον κἠπὶ τὸν Καταβ[α]θ[μ]ὸν καὶ περιαμ-
πέτις [ἐς τὸν] Σπηνόεντα. Ἐπὶ δὲ τῶ ἱερῶ τῶ Ἑρμᾶ τῶ Κορνισσαίω, ...ίοντι οἱ Ἱαραπύ-
τνι[οι κατὰ τὸς ἰ]δίος νόμος. ὍΡΚΟΣ· ὀμνύω τὸν Ζῆνα τὸν Κρητα[γ]ενία καὶ τὰν Ἥ-
[ραν καὶ Ζῆνα] Δι[κ]ταῖον καὶ Ζῆνα Ὀράτρι[ον] καὶ Ποτειδᾶν καὶ Ἀμφ[ιτρ]ίταν καὶ Ἀθαναίαν
[Ὠλερίαν καὶ Ἐ]λευθυίαν καὶ Ἀπόλ[λων]α Πύτιον καὶ Λατὼν καὶ Ἄρτεμιν καὶ Ἄρεα καὶ Ἀ-
[φ]ροδ[ίταν καὶ] Ἑ[ρ]μᾶν καὶ [τὸ]ς Κωρήτας [κ]αὶ τὰς νύμφας καὶ τὸς ἄλλος θιὸς πάντας καὶ
[π]άνσας· ἦ μὰν ἐγὼ [τοῖς] Λατίοις ἐμμένωσι ἐν τᾶι φιλίαι καὶ συμμαχίαι καὶ τοῖς ὅρκοις
[καὶ β]οαθη[σ]ίω ἀπλῶς καὶ ἀδόλως καὶ κ[α]τὰ γᾶ[ν] καὶ κατὰ θάλασσαν [κ]αἴ τίς κα [τ]οῖ[ς]
[Λ]ατίοις ἢ ἐφ[έρπ]ηι ἢ ἐπὶ πόλιν ἢ ἐ[πὶ χ]ώ[ρα]ν ἴηι, οὐ προλιψίω οὔτ' ἐμ πολέμωι οὔτ' ἐν εἰράν[αι]
[ἀ]λλ' ἐμμενίω ἐν τοῖς ὅρκοις καὶ φιλίαι τᾶι σ[υ]γκειμέναι. Εὐορκίονσι μὲν [ἦμεν]
[π]ολ[λ]ὰ κἀγαθὰ, ἐφιορκίονσι δὲ [τὸ] ἐναντί[ο]ν. vac.

---

12. ἔγκτησιν] πάντων v. E.-B. || 26-27. for the expression πολεμεῖν ἀπὸ τῆς χώρας, cf. Y. Garlan, BCH 100 (1976) 305-308: "Mener une guerre offensive" (instead of: "en cas de guerre sur terre" v. E.-B.) || 52. [---]σ....σ..ρο.[Ὅροι τᾶς Λατίων χώρας· ἀπὸ θαλάσσας ἄ]μ π[οταμ]ὸν τὸ[ν] v.E.-B; [..] ὅρος Λα[τίων πάρος ποτὶ τὸς Ἱαραπυτνίος· ἀπὸ θαλάσσας κτλ.] Faure || 55.]ηιον v.E.-B., confirmed by Garlan; ὀρθὸν Faure || 56. καὶ ἐς τὰν κ[εφαλὰν? ---] v.E.-B.; καὶ ἐς τὰν κ[26 L.] Faure] || 57. αν.ρω[ν] v.E.- B.; Αναρω[ν] Faure ||]τίω ἐς τὸν Κ.- v.E.-B.;]ν Μελητίω ἐς τὸν Κα- Faure || 58. --]τας Ἀλω v.E.-B.; [ἇι ὕδωρ] ῥεῖ, κἠπὶ τὰς Ἀλω- Faure || 59. [α]ς ὀρθὰν v.E.-B., Faure ||]ω καὶ [---]ὸ ἄ[ντ]ρον τᾶς εὐ- v.E.-B;]ω, καὶ [ἐς] τὸ ἄντρον τᾶς εὐ- Faure || 60. ἔντων v.E.-B; ἔστων Faure, confirmed by Garlan || 68. Λατίων ἐν τᾶι Λυττίων v.E.-B., Faure || 70. [περια]μπέτις ....αν τὰ[ν] Μίτοις v.E.-B.; [περιαμ]πέτις [ἐς]

ἄκραν τὰν Μίτοις Faure || 73. ἀ̣ν̣[τρ]ο̣ειδιος v.E.-B.; ἀ̣[ντ]ροσείδιος Faure, Garlan || 74. ἄγονσαν ἐπ̣ὶ̣ v.E.-B., Faure || 75. ἐς τὸ ἕ[ρμ]α v.E.-B.; ἐς τὸ πέ[ρ]α̣[ν] Faure, confirmed by Garlan || 76. [κ]ατάνω v.E.-B.; [Κ]α̣ρ̣ά̣[ν]ω Faure || 78. [κή]πὶ v.E.-B., Garlan; [ἐ]πὶ Faure || 81. τῶ Κ̣ὸρ̣..σαίω v.E.-B.; τῶ Κορνισαίω Faure, confirmed by Garlan || 89. καὶ φιλίαι ταῖς ἐγκειμέναι[ς] v.E.-B.

1050. PHAISTOS, INSCRIPTION ON A PITHOS, CA. 700 B.C. Ed. pr. D. Levi, Κρητικὰ Χρονικά 21 (1969) 153-176. O. Masson, *Studies L.R. Palmer*, 169-172 discusses the text, which has been engraved on a large pithos, and opts for the translation: "this (pithos) belongs to Erpetidamos, son of Paidophila". He adduces supporting evidence for the use of the metronymic in the archaic period. The text runs as follows:

Ἑρπετιδάμο Παιδοπίλας ὅδε.

SICILY

1051. ARCHAIC SCRIPT. M.T. Manni Piraino, KOKALOS 21 (1975) 121-137 studies the origin and the development of the alphabet of Megara Hyblaia and its connection with those of Megara Nisaia, Syracuse and Selinous. In an appendix (p. 137-153) she gives a catalogue of 19 inscriptions from Megara Hyblaia.

1052. RELIGION. E. Manni, KOKALOS 21 (1975) 174-195 studies (with the help of inscriptions) the deities of Megara Hyblaia and Selinous.

1053. SLAVERY AND INSCRIPTIONS IN SICILY. M.T. Manni Piraino, Contribution épigraphique à l' étude de l' esclavage en Sicile, *Actes du Colloque 1973 sur l' esclavage* (Paris, 1976) 385-399, discusses several Greek inscriptions (IG, XIV, 28, 38, 315, 485, 492, 581, 582).

1054. ARCHAIC GRAVE-INSCRIPTIONS FROM SICILY. C. Gallavotti, HELIKON 15-16 (1975-76) 96-99 studies several archaic grave-inscriptions with "οἴμοι" from Sicily (Selinous, Megara Hyblaia).

1055. AKRAGAS, DEDICATION OF A BENCH TO HERMES AND HERAKLES BY A GYMNASIARCH. Inscription on the back of a long bench (20 metres, 16 blocks). Ed. pr. P. Griffo, KOKALOS 9 (1963) 179-184 (ph.). Cf. J.A. de Waele, *Acragas Graeca. Die historische Topographie des griechischen Akragas auf Sizilien* (The Hague, 1971) 38-39 (ph.) and L.

Moretti, RFIC 104 (1976) 182-186. Moretti presents the text as follows:

Λούκιος [......]ς, Λουκίου υἱὸ[ς ...]ο[... γυμνασίαρχος τῶν τε ἐφήβων καὶ νε]ωτέρων τοὺς ἀν̣[κ]λ[ί]τ̣ας ἐκ τῶν ἰδίων Ἑρμᾶι καὶ Ἡρακλε[ῖ].

Date: 1st - 2nd cent. A.D. Griffo; Roman period De Waele; 1st half 1st cent. B.C. Moretti || Λούκιος [.......]ς, Λουκίου Πο[τιαν]ὸ[ς --ca. 32 L.--]ω Ἱέρων τοὺς ἀν[κ]λίτας κτλ. Griffo (ἀν[κ]λίτας suggested by M. Guarducci); Λούκιος [---]ς Πο[....]ο["versuchsweise": γυμνασιάρχος τῶν (τε) ἐφήβων καὶ τῶν νε]ωτέρων τοὺς ἀ[....]τας κτλ. De Waele.

1056. AKRAGAS (RAVANUSA), GRAVESTONE OF SAKON AND MYLOS, CA. 500-490 ? Jeffery, LSAG, p. 274, no. 58. Cf. M.T. Manni Piraino, KOKALOS 10-11 (1964-65) 482 and C. Gallavotti, HELIKON 15-16 (1975-76) 103-104. Gallavotti interprets in line 1 and 2 το as τὸ (and not τοῦ: Piraino).

1057. AKRAGAS (RAVANUSA), EPITAPH, CA. 475 ? Jeffery, LSAG, p. 274, no. 63. Cf. M.T. Manni Piraino, KOKALOS 10-11 (1964-65) 483 and C. Gallavotti, HELIKON 15-16 (1975-76) 105. Gallavotti reads this text as follows:

ͱ̣αγιάδα or Fασιάδα or Π̣ασ̣ιάδα ἐμί

[---]α̣δα εμι Jeffery; Fαγιάδα ἐμί Piraino.

1058. AKRAGAS, EPITAPH, 2nd - 3rd CENT. A.D. Ed. pr. P. Griffo, KOKALOS 9 (1963) 174-175, no. 6 (ph.). Cf. L. Moretti, RFIC 104 (1976) 183, note 1 who discusses the meaning of the final formula of this inscription (Ἀέρι μὴ φόβι) and translates it as "Aerio, non aver paura" (instead of: "Non aver paura delle tenebre - o: degli Inferi" Piraino).

1059. AKRAGAS, EPITAPHS, 2nd - 3rd CENT. A.D. M.T. Manni Piraino, IGLP, nos. 1, 2, 3 (ph.). G. Alföldy, GNOMON 48 (1976) 511 proposes in no. 1, L. 1 Ἀγρ[ία Ἐ]λπίς instead of Ἀγρ[---]λπις; in no. 2, L. 1 he finds [ἐ]τελ[εύτησεν] just as possible as [---]τελ[ευτᾷ]; in no. 3, L. 1 he considers [--- (name) Ν]εικάνδρου (υἱός) to be more correct than [ὁ δεῖνα Ν]εικάνδρου.

1060. ALOUNTION, AGONISTIC INSCRIPTION, 2nd CENT. B.C. Ed. pr. G. Manganaro, ARCHCLASS 17 (1965) 202 (ph.). Cf. L. Moretti, RFIC

104 (1976) 182, note 2 who corrects in line 4 Λαμιάδι τοῦ Α[--- into λαμπάδι τοῦ Ἀ[πόλλωνος?], preceded by νεανίσκοι.

1061. ALOUNTION, HONORARY INSCRIPTION FOR CN. POLLIENUS. M.T. Manni Piraino, IGLP, no. 44 (ph.). G. Alföldy, GNOMON 48 (1976) 512 points out that on onomastic grounds this text cannot be later than ca. 50 A.D. (Piraino: 1st half 2nd cent. A.D.). J. and L. Robert, BE (1976) no. 58 expect in L. 4-5 εὐεργέτην ἀπὸ [προγό]νων instead of εὐεργέτην ἀπό|γονον.

1062. ENNA, INSCRIPTIONS ON BULLETS, HELLENISTIC PERIOD. E. Manni, Mélanges Heurgon, p. 606-607 doubts whether the letters φα ἐκγυ, interpreted by G. Manganaro, SICGYMN 17, 2 (1964) 251 ff. as meaning φα(τρία) Ἐκγυ(ίνων) and refering to the city of Ἔγγυον (which had become a phratria of Enna), can bear this construction; he suggests φα(...) ἐκ Γυ(...) as another possibility and finds it improbable that Eggyon was a phratry of Enna.

1063. GELA, ARCHAIC EPITAPH, 525 B.C. C. Gallavotti, HELIKON 15-16 (1975-76) 106-107 studies Jeffery, LSAG, p. 278, no. 49.

1064. HIMERA, EPITAPHS OF MEVIA AND MUNATIUS, 3rd - 4th (?) CENT. A.D. M.T. Manni Piraino, IGLP, nos. 119 and 120 (ph.). G. Alföldy, GNOMON 48 (1976) 511 points out that in no. 119, L. 1 one should read Μεβία and not Μηβία. He holds no. 120 not to be later than the 2nd cent. A.D.

1065. HYBLA HERAIA, GRAVE-INSCRIPTION, LATE 6th CENT. B.C. (?) Jeffery, LSAG, p. 269, no. 21. C. Gallavotti, HELIKON 15-16 (1975-76) 98-99 studies this inscription and reads it as follows:

	οἴμ[οι ὦ]		ο τõ Σαν[ί]-
2	Ἔπαλβ[ι, *h*]-	4	qō.

οιμ[οι] | Επαλυ̣[q ?]|ο το Σαν|qο Jeffery.

1066-1072. IAITAS (MONTE IATO), STAMPED TILES. P. Müller, Studia Ietina, I (ed. by H. Bloesch and H.P. Isler, Zürich, 1976) p. 49-77 (ph.) publishes the inscribed tiles found in Iaitas during the first four campaigns (plus two tiles of the fifth campaign). He divides them into seven groups, bearing the following stamped inscriptions:

1066. I. Ἰαιτου (49 fragments). Date: early hellenistic period - middle 1st cent. A.D. Müller remarks that the only parallel we have, is a tile of Pella (Πέλλης). Normally one uses the genitive plural of the ethnic of the town, or words like δημόσιον, δημοσία etc.

1067. II. Θεάτρου (137 fragments). Date: 200 B.C. - middle 1st cent. A.D. Cf. the inscription "σκανᾶς" on bricks from Sparta (Müller).

1068. III. Ἱεραί (97 fragments). Date: early hellenistic period - middle 1st cent. A.D. Three fragments bear also the name of an eponymous official (1 ἐπὶ Ταμμαρου and 2 ἐπὶ Διονυσίου).

1069. IV. ΑΤ· ἱεραί (35 fragments). Date: 2nd cent. B.C. - late hellenistic period. Müller discusses the first part of the stamp: abbreviation for Ἰαιτου (less probable) or abbreviation of the name of the manufacturer (more probable) ?

1070. V. Names of eponymous officials:

1. Ἐπὶ Συμμάχου (19 fragments). Date: 3rd cent. B.C. - middle 1st cent. A.D.
2. Ἐπὶ Ταμμαρου (20 fragments). Date: 2nd cent. B.C.- middle 1st cent. A.D.
3. Ἐπὶ Διονυσίου (16 fragments). Date: 2nd cent. B.C. middle 1st cent. A.D.
4. Ἐπὶ Νικία Δεινία (11 fragments). Date: 2nd cent. B.C. - middle 1st cent. A.D.
5. Ἐπὶ Λάκωνος (24 fragments). Date: 2nd cent. B.C. - middle 1st cent. A.D. The name Lakon appears here for the first time in Sicily (Müller).
6. Ἐπὶ Φίλωνος (5 fragments). Date: 2nd cent. B.C. - middle 1st cent. A.D.
7. Ἐπὶ Τίτου (12 fragments). Date: 3rd cent. B.C. - middle 1st cent. A.D.
8. Ἐπὶ Ζωπύρου (2 fragments). Date: middle 3rd cent. B.C. - middle 1st cent. A.D.
9. Ἐπὶ Πασίωνος (6 fragments). Date: 2nd cent. B.C. or later.
10. Incomplete names of officials and fragmentary stamps: a) --ο]ụκολοβου A tile fragment found in 1976 and bearing the stamp ἐπὶ Δι]ọνυσίου Κολό[βου (cf. H. Bloesch - H.P. Isler, SICILIA ARCHEOLOGICA 32, 1976, p. 18, ph.) now permits the restoration of the stamp: Διονυσίο]υ Κολόβου; b) --]ọụδ̣ịọ[-- or --]ọυ Δ̣ịọ[--: name or name + patronymic; c) -]σσ

1071. VI. Five fragments: a) Ὀνασο[. in tabula ansata, and three similar fragments; b) --?]ọυνασọ[--? (in tabula ansata?). Date: 1st cent. B.C. - middle 1st cent. A.D. (but also 2nd cent. B.C. is possible). Müller supposes that the tiles bear the same name Ὀνάσου (in b. for some reason written as Οὐνάσου), and that we have here the stamps of a manufacturer.

1072. VII. Latin stamps (26 fragments).

1073. KATANE, EPITAPH, 2nd - 3rd CENT. A.D. M.T. Manni Piraino, IGLP, no. 6 (ph.). G. Alföldy, GNOMON 48 (1976) 511 suggests in L. 5 Εὔπλ[ους] or Εὐπλ[ία] as the name of the dedicator. However, the inscription is not a dedication, but an epitaph.

1074. KENTORIPA, EPITAPH OF KALE, 4th - 5th CENT. A.D. M.T. Manni Piraino, IGLP, no. 13 (ph.). G. Alföldy, GNOMON 48 (1976) 511 points out that in L. 1 πρε(σ)β(ῦτις) is uncertain in view of what the photo shows.

1075. LILYBAION, EPITAPH ON A NAÏSKOS, END 3rd CENT. B.C. Poros block. Ed. pr. M.T. Manni Piraino, Studi E. Manni, p. 213-215, no. 1 (ph.).

	Δάματρι		μακαρῖτα
2	Ποπλείου	4	χαῖρη

1076. LILYBAION, EPITAPH, CA. 150 B.C. Partly preserved funerary cippus. Ed. pr. M.T. Manni Piraino, Studi E. Manni, p. 215-217, no. 2 (ph.).

	Γάιος [----]		Ἀρτ[----]
2	Ῥουμα[----]	4	χα[...]

Γάιος [Σήιος] | Ῥουμα[----] (= τοῦ δεῖνα) | Ἀρτ[αφᾶν] | χα[ῖρε] M.T. Manni Piraino.

1077. LILYBAION, EPITAPH OF IASON, 1st HALF 3rd CENT. A.D. M. T. Manni Piraino, IGLP, no. 26 (ph.). J. and L. Robert, BE (1976) no. 58 (cf. no. 783) doubt whether the names Ἰάσων Ἀρταφᾶντος are Jewish. Ἀρταφᾶν is Libyan.

1078. LILYBAION, INSCRIPTION ON A MEDICINE BOTTLE, CA. 200 B.C. Inscription in a seal on a small pot. Ed. pr. M.T. Manni Piraino,

Studi E. Manni, p. 217-219, no. 3 (ph.).

Ἰάσονος | Λυκίου

1. Propably the name of a φαρμακοπώλης Piraino || 2. patronymic Piraino (who rejects a reading λύκιο<ν> (a medicine); but a reading λυκίου does not seem to be impossible (a bottle filled with "lykion of Iason"), though the nominative λύκιον appears more frequently on such bottles.

1079. LILYBAION, IVORY HOSPITALITY-TESSERA, 2nd CENT. B.C. IG, XIV, 279. O. Masson, SEMITICA 26 (1976) 93-96 (ph.) studies the names Ιμυλχ ("brother of the king"; Franz, CIG, 5496 incorrectly corrected this name into Ιμ<ι>λχ<ων>), Ιμιλχων ("brother of the queen") and Ινιβαλος. The Punic author of the inscription made in lines 3 and 4 errors in the declension of the Greek.

1080. LILYBAION, GRAFFITO, END 1st - 2nd CENT. A.D. Remnants of three lines in cursive writing on a fragment of stucco. M.T. Manni Piraino, Studi E. Manni, p. 219-220, no. 1 offers two interpretations (ph.):

a) ε[--]ϑ[--]|[--]σαι ἀνφότερ[αι --]|[--]τ
b) ε[--]ϑ̣[--]|[--]σαε ἀνφότερ[αι --]|[--ν]τ

In b. --σαε and --ν]τ are endings of a Latin fem. plural (--sae) and of a verbal form (-nt) respectively.

1081. LILYBAION, WRITING-EXERCISE (?), BYZANTINE PERIOD (?) Disconnected letters on a fragment of stucco. Ed. pr. M.T. Manni Piraino, Studi E. Manni, p. 221-222, no. 3 (ph.). Among these letters a koppa, a digamma, a lunar epsilon.

1082. LILYBAION, NAME. Graffito on a fragment of stucco. The letters represent a stage between capitals and cursive writing. Ed. pr. M.T. Manni Piraino, Studi E. Manni, p. 220-221, no. 2 (ph.).

Ὀκταυ[---]

Ὀκτάυ[ιος vel sim. Piraino.

1083. LYKODIA (NOW VIZZINI), EPITAPH OF LANTHANOUSA, 3rd - 4th CENT. A.D. M.T. Manni Piraino, IGLP, no. 18 (ph.). G. Alföldy, GNOMON 48 (1976) 511 suggests to read in L. 4 εὐσεβῆ instead of εὐσεβή<ς>; εὐσεβῆ properly goes with ἰδίᾳ μητρί, the deceased (cf.

e.g. L. Robert, Hellenica, II, p. 81 - ed.).

1084. MEGARA HYBLAIA, SACRIFICIAL LAW, 1st HALF 6th CENT. B.C. Limestone block; the boustrophedon inscription runs on the front side (a) and continues on the left side (b) of the block. Ed. pr. M.T. Manni Piraino, KOKALOS 21 (1975) 141-143, no. 5 (ph.).

a) Γασαράτ- →
ō hάδε : hός κ- ←
α(τὰ) τὸ ἄρχōμ- →
α ὀ̄ θύε, ὀγδ- ←
όαν ἀποτε̣[ι- →
σάτō : αἰ δὲ[-- ←
-Ν -----Α ---- →
----ΑΘ -------ΔΕ- ←
b) κα λιτρὰς : ἀ- ←
ποτεισάτō →

1085. MEGARA HYBLAIA, EPITAPH. Ed. pr. M. Guarducci, KOKALOS 10-11 (1964-65) 474. Cf. M.T. Manni Piraino, KOKALOS 21 (1975) 139-140, no. 3 (ph.).

ερατο ←

'Ερατώ ? Guarducci; (σᾶμα ἐμὶ) [--]εράτō or (σᾶμα τō δεῖνα τō) [--]εράτō Piraino.

1086. MEGARA HYBLAIA, EPITAPH, 1st HALF 6th CENT. B.C. Limestone block. Ed. pr. M.T. Manni Piraino, KOKALOS 21 (1975) 140-141, no. 4 (ph.).

'Αριστίōνο[ς] | Νίσιος

1087. MEGARA HYBLAIA, EPITAPH, CA. 550 B.C. Funeral stele with boustrophedon inscription. Ed. pr. M.T. Manni Piraino, KOKALOS 21 (1975) 144-145, no. 8 (ph.).

Μαρύλō τόδε σᾶμ̣|α ←

1088. MEGARA HYBLAIA, EPITAPH, END 6th CENT. B.C. IG, XIV, 590; Jeffery, LSAG, p. 270, no. 26. Cf. M.T. Manni Piraino, KOKALOS 21 (1975) 145-146, no. 9 (ph.) who reads the inscription as follows:

Καλ(λ)ιστέōς : ἐιμί

ΚΑΛΙΣ͵ΕΟΣ ⁝ ΕΙΜΙ IG; Καλισ<τ>εος ⁝ ειμι Jeffery.

1089. MEGARA HYBLAIA, FUNERARY INSCRIPTION, END 6th - BEGINNING 5th CENT. B.C. Jeffery, LSAG, p. 270, no. 29; M. Guarducci, EG, I, p. 316, no. 7; M. Lejeune, KOKALOS 16 (1970) 22 ff; M.T. Manni Piraino, KOKALOS 21 (1975) 146-147, no. 10 (ph.). C. Gallavotti, HELIKON 15-16 (1975-76) 111-113 studies this inscription and suggests that it contains the name of a woman in the nominative, followed by the ethnicon Κυβοῖτις:

---]τωι Κυβοῖ[τις

Κύβος: "localita africana, vicina ad Utica". For the name of the woman, Gallavotti suggests: Μυρτώι, Κιττώι, Καλλιστώι, Τιτώι etc.

Date: 1st half 6th cent. B.C. Guarducci || [---]οι Κλεοι[---] or [---]οι Κυβοι[---] Jeffery; -τõι Κύβõι--- Guarducci; [datif d' anthroponyme] + τõι Κυβοί[ο] Lejeune; [---]τ̣οικυβοι[---] Piraino.

1090. MEGARA HYBLAIA, EPITAPH, END 6th - BEGINNING 5th CENT. B.C. Ed. pr. M. Guarducci, KOKALOS 10-11 (1964-65) 479 f.; ead. EG, I, p. 317, no. 8. Cf. M.T. Manni Piraino, KOKALOS 21 (1975) 147, no. 11 (ph.):

Καλ(λ)ιοψ[--] | εἰμί

1. Καλιοψ[ίō] ? Guarducci.

1091. MEGARA HYBLAIA, EPITAPH, BEGINNING 5th CENT. B.C. SEG, IV, 65; Jeffery, LSAG, p. 270, no. 28; M. Guarducci, EG, I, 315-316, no. 6. Cf. M.T. Manni Piraino, KOKALOS 21 (1975) 148, no. 12 (ph.).

τᾶς ℎαγία θ|υγατρὸς εἰμί | Καπρογόνō

Date: end 6th cent. B.C. Guarducci || 2. εἰμ[ι] Guarducci.

1092. MEGARA HYBLAIA, EPITAPH, BEGINNING 5th CENT. B.C. Jeffery, LSAG, p. 270, no. 27; L. Agostiniani, SE 41 (1973) 394, no. 13. Cf. M.T. Manni Piraino, KOKALOS 21 (1976) 148-149, no. 13 (ph.

Κλεομέδεος

1093. MEGARA HYBLAIA, EPITAPH, BEGINNING 5th CENT. B.C. Limestone block. Ed. pr. M.T. Manni Piraino, KOKALOS 21 (1975) 149, no. 14 (ph.).

Ἀγ̣α̣θ̣άρχō τõ Πολι̣[--]||[--]α

1094. MEGARA HYBLAIA, EPITAPH, BEGINNING 5th CENT. B.C. Part of a funeral stele. Ed. pr. M.T. Manni Piraino, KOKALOS 21 (1975) 150, no. 15 (ph.).

Θεσ(σ)αλõ τόδε σᾶμα τõ [δεῖνα] | *h*υιõ

1095. MEGARA HYBLAIA, EPITAPH, END 4th - BEGINNING 3rd CENT. B.C. Ed. pr. G. Vallet - F. Villard, Mégara Hyblaea 4 (Paris, 1966) p. 65. Cf. M.T. Manni Piraino, KOKALOS 21 (1975) 151-152, no. 17 (ph.).

Δημήτριος | Κηφισοδώρου | Ἀθηναῖος

1096. MEGARA HYBLAIA, EPITAPH (?), 3rd CENT. A.D. (?) Limestone block. Ed. pr. M.T. Manni Piraino, KOKALOS 21 (1975) 152-153, no. 19 (ph.).

ΞΕΝ[--] | ◻̣ẠΚΛ̣[--] | --Η.[--] | [------]

Probably a sepulchral inscription with the formula ὁ δεῖνα τοῦ δεῖνα ἔζησεν ἔτη ... Piraino.

1097. MEGARA HYBLAIA, GRAFFITO ON A VASE. Ed. pr. M. Guarducci, KOKALOS 10-11 (1964-65) 474; ead., EG, I, p. 312-314. Cf. M. T. Manni Piraino, KOKALOS 21 (1975) 139, no. 2 and E. Manni, ibid., 191-192; C. Gallavotti, HELIKON 15-16 (1975-76) 89-90 reads the text as follows:

].εροισι θεο.[
----].λ.[-------

He suggests in line 1: *ḥ*ε̄ρο̄ΐσι (form of ἡρωΐς), or *h*υπερ]-,*h*υψι]-, ἀνφο]ṭέροισι θεοῖ[σι, or ...*h*]ịεροῖσι θεõṿ (vel sim.); in line 2 a form of *h*υ]β̣λα̣[ῖος, or the name of the place.

Date: 650 B.C. or a little later Guarducci, Gallavotti; end 7th cent. B.C. Piraino || *h*]ἔ̄ρο̄ισι θεοῖ[ς | --.λ.-- | ---- Guarducci; *h*]ἔ̄ρο̄ισι θεοῖ[σι | --]γ̣υ̣.[-- Piraino.

1098. MEGARA HYBLAIA, DIPINTO ON A VASE (SIGNATURE OF THE ARTIST), 625-600 B.C. Ed. pr. G. Vallet - F. Villard, Mégara Hyblaea 2 (Paris, 1964) 176 ff. Cf. M.T. Manni Piraino, KOKALOS 21 (1975) 137-138, no. 1 (ph.) who reads the text as follows:

[----]αγμα *h*ο ϙορυνθιος

ϙορυνθιος Vallet - Villard.

1099. MEGARA HYBLAIA, GRAFFITO ON A VASE, 1st HALF 6th CENT. B.C. Ed. pr. M. Guarducci, KOKALOS 10-11 (1964-65) 476 f. Cf. M. T. Manni Piraino, KOKALOS 21 (1975) 143, no. 6 (ph.) who presents the graffito as follows:

ʼΑψα[---

ʼΑχα-- Guarducci; Piraino, l.c., p. 132 f. restores e.g. ἄψα[υστον.

1100. MEGARA HYBLAIA, GRAFFITO ON A SKYPHOS, ± 450 B.C. Ed. pr. G. Vallet - F. Villard, Mégara Hyblaea 4 (Paris, 1966) p. 61 f. Cf. M.T. Manni Piraino, KOKALOS 21 (1975) 150-151, no. 16 (ph.) who reads the graffito as follows:

---]ται ἀνέθε̄κε

ʼΑφροδί]ται ἀνέθεκε Vallet-Villard; apart from ʼΑφροδίτα, the dedication can also be to ʽΕκάτα or, less probably, to Πασικράτα Piraino.

1101. MEGARA HYBLAIA, INSCRIPTION ON A KOUROS, ± 550 B.C. SEG, XIV, 599; Jeffery, LSAG, p. 270, no. 25; M. Guarducci, EG, I, p. 314 f., no. 5. Cf. now also M.T. Manni Piraino, KOKALOS 21 (1975) 143-144, no. 7 (ph.).

1102. MEGARA HYBLAIA, NAME, 2nd CENT. B.C. Inscription on a floor mosaic. Ed. pr. M.T. Manni Piraino, KOKALOS 21 (1975) 152, no. 18 (ph.).

Γναΐου Μοδίου

"La nostra iscrizione sembra costituire una specie di biglietto da visita del proprietario ai visitatori della casa". Piraino.

1103. "CONTRADA VECCHIA" (NEIGBOURHOOD OF PAESTUM), SIGNATURE ON A HYDRIA, CA. 350 B.C. Ed. pr. A. Bottini - E. Greco, DARCH 8 (1974-75) 252:

ʼΑ[στέ]α[ς] | ἔγ[ραφε]

1104. SALAPARUTA, DEDICATION, EARLY 6th CENT. B.C. Ed. pr. M.T Manni Piraino, KOKALOS 5 (1959) 159-162. C. Gallavotti, HELIKON 15-16 (1975-76) 95-96 reads the inscription as follows:

← τõ *h*[ε]ρακλέος *h*ιαρόν ἐμι, *h*ε̣-
→ ῖ̣σ̣[ε] δέ με ʼΑρίστυλο[ς *h*ο] *h*-
← ε̣ρ̣[μ]ί̣α *h*υιός.

1-2. *h*ε̣ῖ̣σ̣[ε] or *h*ε̄[σ]α̣τ̣[ο] Gallavotti; *h*έ̣ρ̣ξ̣[ε] Piraino.

1105. SELINOUS, CULT OF MEILICHIOS. C. Gallavotti, HELIKON 15-16 (1975-76) 99-103 studies several inscriptions from Selinous concerning the cult of Meilichios.

1106. SELINOUS, VOTIVE-STELE, 2nd HALF 6th CENT. B.C. Ed. pr. M.T. Manni Piraino, KOKALOS 16 (1970) 281. Cf. C. Gallavotti, HELIKON 15-16 (1975-76) 102-103. Piraino read the text as follows:

← τō̃ Μιλ[ιχίō ἐμὶ]
→ [προτὰ Μύλō τ]ọ̄̃ [Σ]άϙōνος

Gallavotti suggests: τō̃ Μιλ[ιχί]ọ̄ [Σ]άϙōνος or τō̃ Μιλ[ιχίō ἐμὶ προτ]ὸ̣ [Σ]άϙōνος but remarks that also other names as Σάκων are possible, e.g. Μάκων.

1107. SELINOUS, CIPPUS OF ZEUS MEILICHIOS, CA. 525 B.C. ? Jeffery, LSAG, p. 270, no. 31. C. Gallavotti, HELIKON 15-16 (1975-76) 101-102 studies this inscription and explains in line 3 προτα as πρὸ-τά (with the meaning of πρὸς τά).

1108. SELINOUS, EPITAPH, END 7th CENT. B.C. Ed. pr. M.T. Manni Piraino, KOKALOS 9 (1963) 145; M. Guarducci, KOKALOS 12 (1966) 183. C. Gallavotti, HELIKON 15-16 (1975-76) 90-93 studies this boustrophedon inscription and presents it as follows:

→ Εὐκρίτου τόδ[ε σᾶ-
← μ' Εὐ]άνδρου *h*υιοῦ

Or, in a longer form: Εὐκρίτου τόδ[ε σᾶ|μα Ϝαναξιμ]άνδρου *h*υιοῦ

Εὐκρίτου τοῦ [Εὐ]α̣νδρου *h*υιοῦ Piraino; Εὐκρίτου τόδ[ε σᾶμα τοῦ --]άνδρου *h*υιοῦ Guarducci.

1109. SELINOUS, EPITAPH, END 7th CENT. B.C. Ed. M.T. Manni Piraino, KOKALOS 12 (1966) 200-201, no. 1; M. Guarducci, EG, I, p. 317-319, no. 9. C. Gallavotti, HELIKON 15-16 (1975-76) 93-95 studies this inscription and reads it as follows:

	→	[σᾶ]μα εἰμ-		→	Μενεπτό-
2	←	ι Μύσϙō τō̃	4	←	[λιος?]

4. [λέμō] Piraino, Guarducci.

1110. SELINOUS, EPITAPH OF THEOXENOS, 2nd HALF 6th CENT. B.C. M.T. Manni Piraino, IGLP, no. 85 (ph.). Cf. J. and L. Robert, BE (1976) no. 58 who point out that Ν[ι]ϙόλας is the genitive of the feminine Νιϙόλα and that consequently we have a case of "metronymie".

1111. SELINOUS, FUNERARY EPIGRAM, CA. 450 B.C. Ed. pr. M.T. Manni Piraino, KOKALOS 12 (1966) 202 ff. (ph.). W. Peek, ZPE 23 (1976) 93-94 tries the following restoration:

[*h*ίλο π]αῖδ' οἴκτιρ' Ἐ[ρασίστρατον, ὄντα γάμοιο] |
[ἄμ]μορον *h*[όντε Ἀίδας *h*άρπασε | δακ]ρυόες.

[---------- μοίρ]αι δ' οἰκτίρε|[τε ὦ παροδεῖται ἄμ]μορον *h*|[ε̄βε̄-τε̄́ν κεῖται ἐκεῖ κ]ρυόες Piraino.

1112. SELINOUS, DEFIXIO, 2nd HALF 6th CENT. B.C. Lead tablet broken into three parts. Ed. pr. A. Brugnone, Studi E. Manni, p. 68-73, no. 1 (ph.).

← --]κοίνο̄<ι> καλεῖ εἶ ἀτέλε-
→ στα καὶ ἔργ̣α καὶ ἔπεα ε[ἶ-
← να]ι καὶ Σικανᾶι ἀτέλε-
→ στα v. καὶ ἔργ̣α καὶ ἔπε[α εἶ-
← να]ι καλεῖ εἶ.

1. --]κοίνο̄<ι>: end of a proper name in the dative ? Brugnone.

1113. SELINOUS, CURSE, END 6th CENT. B.C. Lead tablet, inscri-ked on two sides, broken into three parts. Ed. pr. A. Brugnone, tudi E. Manni, p. 73-79, no. 2 (ph.).

Recto

→ τὰν Ε[ὐ]κλέος γλõ(σ)σαν κ-
← αὶ τὰν Ἀριστοφάνιος
→ καὶ τὰ̣ν Ἀνγείλιος κα-
← ὶ τ[ὰν] Ἀλκ[ί]φρο̣νο[ς] κ-
→ αὶ τὰν *h*αγεστράτο̄· τõ-
← ν συνδίϙο̄ν τ̣õν [.]υ[.]λι-
→ ος κα[ὶ τ]õν̣ Ἀριστοφάνε-
← ος [τὰς γ]λõ[(σ)σ]ας· κα[ὶ τ]ὰν
→ [....]λ[.]ονος [γλõ(σ)σαν]

Verso

→ καὶ τὰν Ο[ἰ]νο̣[θ]ε̣ο̄ καὶ τ-

→ ἀν α̣[... γ]λõ[(σ)σ]αν.

6-7. [Α]ὐ[κ]λί|ος ? Brugnone.

1114. SELINOUS, DEFIXIO, END 6th CENT. B.C. Fragment of a lead tablet. Ed. pr. A. Brugnone, Studi E. Manni, p. 80-81, no. 3 (ph.).

ϙυλίχα | Ξενοκλε͂ς | Γλαυκίας

1115. SELINOUS, DEFIXIO, BEGINNING 5th CENT. B.C. Rectangular lead tablet. Ed. pr. A. Brugnone, Studi E. Manni, p. 81-83, no. 4 (ph.).

Χαμ<α>ὶ σ' ἐπέχō
κά(ν) νόσσō ροπᾶι
ἐπ' ἀτελείαι *h*ο
ε̣[.]κσ[..]ε̣[..]ο̣ντι.

1116. SELINOUS, DEFIXIO, FIRST HALF 5th CENT. B.C. Fragment of a lead tablet, broken on all sides. Ed. pr. A. Brugnone, Studi E. Manni, p. 83-84, no. 5 (ph.).

ϑ.
ς δαγυ or δαγο

2. δαγύς = wax-figure Brugnone.

1117. STAFENNA (NEAR ROSOLINI), EPITAPH, LATER IMPERIAL PERIOD. Limestone cippus, damaged at the left. Ed. pr. S.L. Agnello, ASSIR 2 (1972-73) 99-102 (ph.).

["Α]μ̣πλις [ἔ]ζησ-
[χ]ρ̣ηστὸς [ε]ν ἔτη̣
[κ]α̣ὶ ἄμ̣ε- 7 γ'.
4 ν̣πτος

1. ["Α]μ̣πλις: first epigraphic attestation of this name Agnello.

1118. SYRACUSE, INSCRIPTION ON THE STEP OF THE TEMPLE OF APOLLO, 2nd HALF 6th CENT. B.C. ? IG, XIV, no. 1; SEG, XII, 406; Jeffery, LSAG, p. 265, no. 3. C. Gallavotti, HELIKON 15-16 (1975-76) 112-117 studies this inscription and proposes the following restorations:

Κλεο[μέν]ε͂ς (or Κλεο[κράτ]ε͂ς) : ἐποίε͂σε τὀ͂πέλō͂νι : *h*ο Κ̣υ̣ι̣β̣ε̣[ί]δ̣α (or Κ̣υ̣ι̣δ̣ι̣[ά]δ̣α) : κ' 'Επικ̣[λ]ε͂ς τυλεῖ̣α : κα[τ]ὰ̣ Ϝέργα.

1119. SYRACUSE, EPITAPH OF Q. CORNIFICIUS. M.T. Manni Piraino, IGLP, no. 108 (ph.). According to G. Alföldy, GNOMON 48 (1976) 512 this text is earlier than the 3rd cent. A.D.

1120. SYRACUSE (?), EPITAPH OF KALLITYCHE, 4th CENT. A.D. M.T. Manni Piraino, IGLP, no. 111 (ph.). G. Alföldy, GNOMON 48 (1976) 511 reads in L. 1-2 κῖτε ἡ (visible on the photo) μακαρία μνήμης Καλλιτύχη instead of κῖτε μακαρία<ς> μνήμης Καλλιτύχη.

1121. SYRACUSE, EPITAPH OF EULIBA. IG, XIV, 535. Anna Maria Marchese, ASSIR 2 (1972-73) 103-108 studies the provenance of this inscription with the help of 18th cent.- sources and concludes that it was found in 1722 in the crypt of St. Marcianus in Syracuse (and not in Catania). The text of the inscription (as restored by A. Ferrua, ASS 4-5, 1938-39, p. 29-30) runs as follows:

Ἐνθάδε κατάκιτε
ἡ τῆς μακαρίας μν-
ήμης Εὐλίβα. Μνήσ<θ>[η]-
τ[ί] σ[υ] ὦ θ(ε)ὲ εἰς
[αἰῶνα αὐτῆς].

1122. SYRACUSE, INSCRIPTION ON A PYXIS FRAGMENT, 700-675 B.C. Jeffery, LSAG, p. 125, no. 3; M. Guarducci, EG, I, p. 341-342, no. 1. Cf. M.T. Manni Piraino, KOKALOS 21 (1975) 127-128 and C. Gallavotti, HELIKON 15-16 (1975-76) 86-88. Gallavotti presents the text as follows:

παρβ[---
---]ανκλασε.[---

He proposes to restore (e.g.): πὰρ Β[ίονός ἐ͂μι δõρον,]| [ἄγε δ' Ἄλεξις ἐκ Δ]άνκλας ἐμ̣[έ] or [hὸς δ'] ἂν κλάσε̄ μ̣[ε, τυφλὸς ἔσται] or [ἔσται δὲ τυφλός, hὸς] ἂν κλάσε̄ι̣

[---]παρε̣[---]|[---]ανκλασε̣[--- Jeffery; παρβ[---]| [Δ]άνκλας ε.[-- Guarducci (who suggests in line 1 a name as Παρβάλλων vel sim.); 1. ΓΑƳ̣Ḍ̣Α̣ Piraino.

1123. TAUROMENION, CATALOGUE OF HISTORICAL AUTHORS COLLECTED IN THE LIBRARY OF THE TOWN GYMNASIUM, 2nd CENT. B.C. (± 130 B.C. ?) Inscriptions on three fragments of wall-plastering. Ed. pr. G. Manganaro, PP 29 (1974) 389-409 (ph.); id., apud A. Alföldi, Römische Frühgeschichte (Heidelberg, 1976) p. 83-96 (ph.). Cf. N. Horsfall, LCM 1 (1976) 18 who argues that, since this inscription (fragment III) confirms the praenomen given by Dionysus of Halicarnassus (1.6.2), it is hardly possible any longer to ascribe the Greek annals of Fabius Pictor to any other member of the gens but the conventional Hannibalic Quintus. Cf. also J. and L. Robert, BE

(1976) no. 820. The text of the inscriptions runs as follows:

Fragment I:

Καλλισθένης 'Ολύν[θιος·]
'Εγένετο μὲν κ[αὶ 'Α]-
λεξάνδρου ἐπισ[το]-
λαγράφος· ἀπ' οὗ ἡ[μ]-
πεδεκὼς πράξε[ις]
διαγράφειν τῶν [-
------]ως ἐ[-------

Fragment II:

Παραβάλλ?]ων 'Ηλεῖος
---------------Σ
-------------ΛΓ---

Fragment III:

Col. A (at the left):

[Κόι]ντος Φάβι[ο]ς ὁ Πι-
[κτω]ρῖνος ἐπικαλού-
[μεν]ος, 'Ρωμαῖος, Γαΐου
[υἱό]ς· vac.
[ὃ]ς ἱστόρηκεν τὴν
['Η]ρακλέους ἄφιξιν
[εἰ]ς 'Ιταλίαν καὶ δ' ἔτι
[νόσ]τον Λανοΐου συμ-
[μάχ]ου τε Αἰνεία καὶ
['Ασκα]νίου· πολὶ ὕστε-
[ρον ἐγ]ένοντο 'Ρωμύλος
[καὶ 'Ρ]έμος καὶ 'Ρώμης
[κτίσις ὑ]πὸ 'Ρωμύλου, [ὃς]
[πρῶτο]ς βεβασί[λευκεν --]

Col. B (at the right):

Φίλιστος Συρακόσ[ιος·]
τοῦτον Εὐήνου σο[φοῦ?]
φασὶ γενέσθαι μαθη-
τὴν τοῦ τὰς ἐλεγείας
[γ]ράψαντος· πρῶτον ἄσ-
τυ στήσασθαι τὸν νῦν
εὐημεροῦντα τρόπον
μερίσασθαί τε τὸν δή-
μον ὁμῶς καὶ πρότε-
[ρον ἐχθ]έσθαι τ[ὰ δι]αγράμ-
[ματα περὶ τῶν τυράν]-
[νων, ἔπειτα δέ ---?]

A. 10. πολί = πολύ Manganaro.

ITALY

1124. ALTINON, BIBLICAL CITATION. Marble vase found in Altinon, date and origin uncertain. IG, XIV, 2320. The IG-text runs as follows: ΕΥΦΡΩΣΥΝΗΖ ΦΩΝΗ ΚΝ· ΕΠΙΤΩΝ. Kaibel noted about this fragmentary text: "Nihil apparet praeter Εὐφρ<ο>σύνη nomen". Republished by D. Feissel, AN 47 (1976) 169-170. Feissel presents the text as follows: ['Αντλήσατε ὕδωρ μετὰ] εὐφρωσύνη<ς>, φωνὴ Κ(υρίο)<υ> ἐπὶ τῶν [ὑδάτων]. Cf. no. 792.

1125-1132. ANCONA, EPITAPHS. Liliana Mercando, L' ellenismo nel

Piceno (in Hellenismus in Mittelitalien, I, Abh. Akad. Wiss. Göttingen, 97; Göttingen, 1976, p. 160-218) (re)publishes on p. 168-169 several steles from Ancona.

1125. White marble stele representing the deceased and his servant who holds a horse by its bridle; Museo Naz. Ancona. Ed. pr. L. Mercando, l.c., 168 (ph.).

Σύμμαχε Σωπάτρου | χρηστὲ χαῖρε

The patronymic is the same as in no. 1129.

1126. Stele representing a togatus and a child; late 2nd cent. B.C.; Museo Naz. Ancona. Ed. pr. B. Andreae, AA (1959) 177 (ph.). Cf. L. Mercando, l.c., 169, note 75 (ph.) who republishes the inscription.

Ἀπολλώνιε Πασίωνος | χρηστὲ χαῖρε

1. ΑΠΟΛΛΩΝΙ ΕΠΑΣΙΩΝΟΣ Andreae.

1127. Stele representing the deceased and a child; Museo Naz. Ancona. Ed. N. Alfieri, Topografia storica di Ancona antica (1938) 76, no. 7. Cf. L. Mercando, l.c., 169, note 75 (ph.) who republishes the inscription.

Γαυλίων Διοπόμπου | χαῖρε

1128. Stele representing the deceased with two children; Museo Naz. Ancona. Ed. N. Alfieri, l.c., 74, no. 4. Cf. L. Mercando, l.c., 169, note 75 (ph.) who republishes the inscription.

Ἀνφηρίστε Ἀνφηρίστου | χρηστὲ χαῖρε

1129. Stele representing a farewell scene; Museo Naz. Ancona. Ed. N. Alfieri, l.c., 75, no. 5. Cf. L. Mercando, l.c., 169, note 76 (ph.) who republishes the inscription.

Ἀρβέντα Σωπάτρου | χαῖρε

The patronymic is the same as in no. 1125.

1130. Stele representing a veiled woman and a girl holding a basket (?) in her left hand; 1st cent. B.C.; Museo Naz. Ancona. Ed. pr. L. Mercando, l.c., 169, note 77 (ph.).

[...]ε̣τία Γαΐου | [---] χαῖρε

1131. Stele representing a veiled woman and a girl holding a basket in her left hand; Museo Naz. Ancona. Ed. N. Alfieri, l.c., 74, no. 2. Cf. L. Mercando, l.c., 169, note 78 (ph.) who republishes the inscription.

Δάμω χρησ|τῆι χαῖρε

1132. Stele representing a banquet; now in the Bibliotheca Oliveriana di Pesaro (and not lost as Alfieri thought). Ed. N. Alfieri, l.c., 77, no. 10. Cf. L. Mercando, l.c., 169, note 79 (ph.) who republishes this inscription.

Ἀπολλώνιε Ἀπολλω[.]	Ἡράκλειε Ἡράκλειε
2 Ἀπολλωνίου Νικολάου̣	4 χρηστοὶ χαίρετε

1133. ANCONA, STAMPS ON A RHODIAN AMPHORA, 1st HALF 2nd CENT. B.C. Ed. pr. Liliana Mercando, in Hellenismus in Mittelitalien, I (Abh. Akad. Wiss. Göttingen 97; Göttingen, 1976) p. 163-164 (ph.).

a) Δαμοκράτευς
b) Ἐπὶ Νικασαγόρα Θεσμο[φορίου]

1134. ANCONA, STAMPS ON THE HANDLE OF A RHODIAN AMPHORA. Ed. pr. Liliana Mercando, l.c., p. 165 (ph.).

a) Ἐπὶ Ἀστυμήδευς | Ὑακινθίου
b) M... caduceus and bunch of grapes

1135. ANCONA, STAMP ON THE HANDLES OF A KNIDIAN AMPHORA. Ed. pr. Liliana Mercando, l.c., p. 165 (ph.).

Ἐπὶ Φρουράρχου Ἐπιγένους Ἀριοτ

1136. CAPUA, EPITAPH OF IULIA MARCELLA, 2nd CENT. A.D. CIG, III, 5875 d; IG, XIV, 885. P. Cavuoto, STUDI PUBBLICATI DALL' ISTITUTO ITALIANO PER LA STORIA ANTICA, QUARTA MISCELLANEA (1975) 207-214 makes the very unlikely suggestion that in this inscription (Ἰουλία Μάρκελλα | Ἰουλίου Βάσσου | θυγάτηρ | Κομμαγηνὴ ἄλυπε | χαῖρε) the father of the deceased was the early 2nd cent. A.D. governor of Syria-Kommagene C. Iulius Quadratus Bassus and that this explains her ethnicon Κομμαγηνή.

1137. GRAVISCA, DEDICATION TO APOLLO, CA. 500 B.C. Marble cippus. Ed. pr. M. Torelli, PP 26 (1971) 55-60 (ph.). Cf. F.D. Harvey, PP 31 (1976) 206-214 who discusses the possible identity of the dedicator with the Herodotean Sostratos (4.152.3), his career as trader, the time of the dedication (high date: ca. 505, or low date: 495-475 B.C.) and draws some conclusions from this inscription about trade in antiquity. The text runs as follows:

Ἀπό|λο̄ν|ος Αἰ|γινά̄|τᾱ ἐ̄μ|ί. Σόστ|ρατος | ἐποίε̄|σε *h*ο | [---]

1138. HERCULANEUM, GRAFFITO ABOUT DIOGENES THE CYNIC, 1st CENT. A.D. CIL, IV, Suppl. 3, fasc. 4, no. 10529. W.D. Lebek, ZPE 22 (1976) 293-296 proposes the following text:

Διογένης ὁ κυνικὸς φιλόσοφος
ἰδὼν γυναῖκα ὑπὸ ποταμοῦ φε-
ρομένην, εἶπεν· ἄφες φέρεσθαι
τὸ κακ<ὸν> ὑπὸ κακοῦ κακῶς.

4. τὸ κακὴν ὑπὸ κα$^{κοῦ}_{κιυς}$ CIL.

1139. HIPPONION, ORPHIC TEXT, CA. 400 B.C. Gold leaf. Ed. pr. G. Pugliese Carratelli, PP 29 (1974) 108-126 (ph.). Cf. R. Merkelbach , ZPE 17 (1975) 8-9; M.L. West, ZPE 18 (1975) 229-236; M. Guarducci, EPIGRAPHICA 37 (1975) 19-24; M. Marcovich, ZPE 23 (1976) 221-224; G. Zuntz, WS 10 (1976) 129-151; G. Pugliese Carratelli, PP 31 (1976) 458-466.

Μναμοσύνας τόδε ἠρίον. Ἐπεὶ ἂμ μέλληισι θανεῖσθαι,
εἰς Ἀΐδαο δόμους εὐήρεας ἔστ' ἐπὶ δ<ε>ξιὰ κρήνα,
πὰρ δ' αὐτὰν ἑστακῦα λευκὰ κυπάρι<σ>σος·
ἔνθα κατερχόμεναι ψυχ{κ}αὶ νεκύων ψύχονται.
ταύτας τᾶς κράνας μηδὲ σχεδὸν ἐνγύθεν ἔλθῃς·
πρόσθεν δὲ *h*ευρήσεις τᾶς Μναμοσύνας ἀπὸ λίμνας
ψυχρὸν ὕδωρ προρέον· φύλακες δὲ ἐπύπερθεν ἔασι,
[*h*]οἳ δέ σε εἰρήσονται ἐν φρασὶ πευκαλίμαισι
[*h*]ότι δὴ ἐξερέεις Ἄϊδος σκότους ὀλοέεντος.
Εἶπον· ὑὸς Βαρέας καὶ Οὐράνοῦ ἀστερόεντος,
δίψαι δ' εἰμὶ αὖος καὶ ἀπόλλυμαι· ἀλλὰ δότ' ὦ[κα]
ψυχρὸν ὕδωρ π[ρο]ρέον τῆς Μνημοσύνης ἀπὸ λίμ[νης]·
καὶ δή τοι ἐλεοῦσιν <*h*>υπὸ χθονίωι βασιλῆϊ·
καὶ δὴ τοι δώσουσι πιεῖν τᾶς Μναμοσύνας ἀπ[ὸ] λίμνας·
καὶ δὴ καὶ συχνῶν *h*οδὸν ἔρχεα<ι>, *h*άν τε καὶ ἄλλοι
μύσται καὶ βάχχοι *h*ιερὰν στείχουσι κλεινοί.

1. <θ>ρῖον West; σρῖον (i.e. θρῖον) Marcovich || 2. εἶς P. Carratelli; εἶσ' Zuntz || As to punctuation, Merkelbach and Marcovich print a comma after ἠρίον and a full stop at the end of L. 1; P.

Carratelli, Guarducci and Zuntz print a full stop after ἠρίον in line 1; in L. 2 P. Carratelli puts a full stop after εὐήρεας, Zuntz a comma. We print Guarducci's text. || Marcovich adds one line which is supposed to be missing and reads Εἰς 'Αΐδαο δόμους εὐήρεας <e.g. *h*ως ἀφικάνεις, | *h*ευρήσεις μελάνυδρον ἐκεῖθ'> {ἐστ'} ἐπὶ δ<ε>ξιὰ κρήνα<ν> || 3. πὰρ δ' αὐτᾶι λευκὰ<ν> ἐστακυ<ῖ>α<ν> κυπάρισ<σ>ον Marcovich || 7. *h*ύδωρ Merkelbach || ἐπ' ὕπερθεν ἔασι<ν> Marcovich || 8. ἐν<ὶ> Merkelbach, Marcovich || 9. ὅττι P. Carratelli; ὅτ<τ>ι Merkelbach; ὅτ<τ>ι Marcovich; †...]ι Zuntz || ΔΕ (δέ vel δή) Zuntz || σκότος οὐλοέεντος Merkelbach, Guarducci, Marcovich; σκότΟΣ (σκότος vel σκότους) Ο[..]ΕΕΝΤΟΣ † Zuntz || 10. ὑὸς Γαίας Zuntz || 11. εἰμ' αὖος Guarducci, Marcovich || δότ[ω τις] West || 13. <τ>ελέουσι or <στ>ελέουσι, perhaps <τ>ελέουσί σ' ὑποχθονίωι βασιλεί<αι> West; ὑποχθονίοι βασιλῆες Lloyd-Jones apud West; <*h*>υποχθονίωι Merkelbach, Marcovich; ΗΥΠΟΧΘΟΝΙΟΙ ΒΑΣΙΛΕΙ Zuntz || 14. Μναμοσύνας λίμνας P. Carratelli, Merkelbach; πιεῖν <ταύτας ἀπὸ> {τᾶς Μναμοσύνας} λίμνας Marcovich; Μναμοσύνας [ἀπὸ λίμνας] Zuntz || 15. συχνόν P. Carratelli; συχν<ά>ν Burkert apud West; συχνάν Zuntz || 16. βά<κ>χοι P. Carratelli; βάκχοι Zuntz || κλ<ε>εινοί Merkelbach, Marcovich; ΚΛ.[... Zuntz.

1140. LOKROI EPIZEPHYRIOI, DIALECT. J. Blomqvist, OATH 11 (1975) 17-35 studies the dialect of Lokroi Epizephyrioi. His study is mainly based on 26 bronze tablets of the archive found in the temple of Zeus (the complete edition by A. de Franciscis, Stato e Societa in Locri Epizefiri, Naples, 1972 was not yet available to Blomqvist).

1141. LOKROI EPIZEPHYRIOI, ARCHIVE OF THE OLYMPIEION, 350-250 B.C. J. Blomqvist, OATH 11 (1975) 17-35 presents, prior to his study of the dialect based on the bronze tablets found in the temple of Zeus (cf. no. 1140), a list of nine previously known inscriptions (cf. J. and L. Robert, BE, 1976, no. 817 who add Coll. Froehner, no. 82, pp. 127-128) and suggests some corrections in the bronze tablets. After the complete edition by A. de Franciscis, Stato e Societa in Locri Epizefiri, Naples, 1972 (not yet available to Blomqvist) the following corrections are still valid: II, L. 8 and 10. κὰτ ταὐτά instead of κατταῦτα; VII, L. 9. ἔχρησαν το<ὶ> ἱερομνάμονες instead of ἐχρήσαντο ἱερομνάμονες; IX, L. 10. τοῦτα δὲ instead of τοῦ τάδε; XII, L. 2. [[ι]] Ἡρία (genitive of Ἡρίας = Ἡρέας) instead of Ἰηρία; XV, L. 9-10. ἄλλ<αν> χρῆστιν τὸ ποιθεθὲν ποὶ τοῖς καταβόλοις instead of ἄλλο τὸ ποὶ χρῆστιν θεθὲν ποὶ τοῖς καταβόλοις; 15. τραχέος: "a fraction of a stater" instead of "luogo aspro, petroso" (A. de Franciscis, l.c., p. 121); XXIII, L. 10. *h*ιαρᾶν μίστωμα: "rent of holy lands" instead of "mercede delle sacerdotesse" (A. de Franciscis, l.c., p. 151); on this problem cf. also J. and L. Robert, BE (1969) no. 634, (1970) no. 677, p. 487 and no. 677a, (1972) no. 643, D. Musti, PP 29 (1974) 8 and R. v. Compernolle (cf. infra); 11. δωρεᾶν τᾶν ἐπίτηνα τῶ ℎάληκος instead of δωρεὰν τὰν ἐπὶ Τῆνα τῶ ℎάληκος (cf. D. Musti, PP 29, 1974, p. 5-9 who also suggests ἐπίτηνα and M. Gigante, PP 31, 1976, p. 421 who accepts this reading). Blomqvist also studies the (relative) chronology of the bronze tablets (p. 20-23). M. Gigante, PP 31 (1976) 417-432 makes a stylistic study of the bronze tablets and tries on this basis to group them. He also corrects in II, L. 1, VII, L. 1, XII, L. 1, XV, L. 1, XVII, L. 1, XXVI, L. 1 ἱερομναμονώντων into ἱερομναμόνων τῶν. R. v. Compernolle, ASNP (1976) 329-400 deals with several problems pertaining to documents from this archive; he rejects matriarchate (p. 361-364), denies the relation between temple prostitution and ℎιαρᾶν μίστωμα (p. 377-381).

1142. NAPLES, ERECTION OF A STATUE FOR QUEEN ARSINOE. IG, XIV, 727; OGIS, 14. R.S. Bagnall, PHILOLOGUS 120 (1976) 202 assigns this text to the period 279-270 B.C., together with OGIS 27 (and not to 280-278 B.C. as L. Moretti, RFIC 93, 1965, 177 suggested).

1143. PISA, DEDICATION TO Θεοὶ ἐπήκοοι, 1st HALF 2nd CENT. A.D. Votive relief with above the inscription three pairs of ears surmounted by symbols (in which Cristofani recognizes the head-coverings of the Alexandrian triad). Ed. pr. M. Cristofani, SCO 19-20 (1970-71) 343-346 (ph.). Cf. W. Swinnen, ORIENTALIA LOVANIENSIA PERIODICA 6-7 (1975-76) 531-534 who comments upon the name of the dedicant.

Θεοῖς ἐπηκόοις ἀνέ-
θηκεν Τ. Φλάουιους
Φαρνουτιάνους ʽΡούφους

1. On the basis of the symbols Cristofani identifies the Θεοὶ ἐπήκοοι as the Alexandrian triad Harpokrates, Sarapis, Isis || 3. Φαρνουτιάνους: cognomen formed on the name Φαρνοῦτις (stream in Bithynia) Cristofani; the name is Egyptian Swinnen.

1144. PITHEKOUSSAI, INSCRIPTION ON "NESTOR'S CUP". SEG, XIV, 604. Cf. P.A. Hansen, GLOTTA 54 (1976) 25-43 who discusses the date of this inscription (pressing the early date), the state of preservation (correcting some current errors), the restorations in lines 1 and 2 (pressing the case for ε̣[ἰμ]ι̣ and ποτερί[ο]), and the interpretation of the text whereby Hansen explains this construction as a παρὰ προσδοκίαν joke. Cf. also C. Watkins, HSPH 80 (1976) 25-40 who studies this inscription from the point of view of linguistics and comparative metrics, suggests that Νέστορος in line 1 refers not to a resident of Pithekoussai but to the Homeric hero, restores in line 1 ἔ̣[στ]ι̣ and assumes that ποτέριον in lines 1 and 2 refers to two different cups. The text of the inscription runs as follows:

Νέστορός : ε̣[ca.2]ι̣ : εὔποτ[ον] : ποτέριον.
hὸς δ' ἂ̣ν τõδε πίεσ̣ι : ποτερί[ο] : αὐτίκα κε͂νον
hίμερος hαιρέσει : καλλιστε̣[φά]ν̣ο : Ἀφροδίτες.

Date: early 7th cent. B.C. SEG; 8th cent. B.C. Hansen || 1. ε̣...ι̣ SEG; ε̣[ίμ]ι̣ Hansen; ἐ̣[στ]ι̣ Watkins || 2. ἄ<ν> SEG, Watkins; ἄν Hansen || 3. hί̣μερ[ος : hαιρ]έσει SEG; hίμερος hαιρέσει Hansen, Watkins.

1145. ROCCAGIONE, SEPULCHRAL INSCRIPTION FOR A FREEDWOMAN. SEG, IV, 104. Cf. Robert E.A. Palmer, PHOENIX 30 (1976) 159-173 who gives a commentary on this text which he reads as follows:

C[l]odia P(ubli) l(iberta)---
Compitalia tu totidem [qui concelebrasti] | hoc
perfer. ut aequa mih[i fuerint Fata aspi]ce. t[um] | dum
tempus et hora [mihi, dum suppeditat] quo[que vita],
concordes animae duo vix[imus anno]s cas[tos].
Tempora cunta vides. hoc, hospe[s, te monet hora]
quae tulit hoc. aliquo te tempor[e terra tenebit].
εὐφροσύνη, πόθος, οἶνος, ὕπν[ος ταῦτ' ἐστὶ βροτοῖσι]
πλοῦτος· ἀνευφράντων Ταντάλ[ου ἐστὶ βίος].

---

2. totide[m] te --- | hoc SEG || 3. perfer, ut aequa mihi quo ----- | dum SEG || 4. tempus et hora [e...]ga s--- SEG || 5. vix[imus atque perimus] SEG || 6. hospe[s, te monet annus] SEG.

1146. ROME, RELATIONS WITH LITERATURE. IGUR, I, 223 and 229. Cf. no. 226.

1147. ROME, THRACO-GETIAN ELEMENTS IN GREEK INSCRIPTIONS. I.I. Russu, SCIV 27 (1976) 35-44 discusses four inscriptions dedicated by Thracians (IGUR, I, nos. 132, 134, 135, 205) and discovers two Thracian names in a list of mystae of a Roman dionysiac thiasos (IGUR, I, no. 160, II, C, 33: Dekibalos and III, C, 6: Trallis).

1148. ROME, SUCCESSOR OF POSEIDONIOS, 2nd CENT. A.D. Marble slab broken on all sides, except (partly) at the right and (perhaps) at the bottom. Ed. pr. L. Moretti, RFIC 104 (1976) 191-194.

[---] ἀπ̣ὸ τ̣ῆ[ς]
[στ]ο̣ᾶς διάδοχος
[τοῦ] Ποσειδωνίου

The inscription has probably been engraved either on a base of a statue, or under a bust of a person in a gallery of famous men.

This successor of Poseidonios can perhaps be identified with Iason, the leader of the school in Rhodes, or with Athenodorus ("Calvus") from Tarsos, teacher of philosophy of the future emperor Augustus and his sister Octavia. Moretti.

1149. ROME (OSTIA), DEDICATION TO ZEUS HELIOS SARAPIS, REIGN OF HADRIAN. Marble stone with "cornice". Ed. pr. L. Moretti, RPAA 48 (1975-76) 315-319 (ph.).

Διὶ ῾Ηλίῳ μεγάλῳ ἐπη[κόῳ Σα]ράπ[ιδι]
Τ. Αἴλιος Φηλικίσσιμος συ[--------- τὰς]
ἀηττήτους αὐτοῦ ἐνεργίας τὸν [ναὸν ἀνέθηκεν]

2. συ[νεγνωκώς, συ[νειδώς, συ[γκεκρικώς etc. Moretti.

1150. ROME, DEDICATION TO SARAPIS AND OTHER GODS, BETWEEN 185-192 A.D. Marble stone, broken into four fragments, built into the catacomb of Callistus. Ed. pr. L. Moretti, RPAA 48 (1975-76) 319-323 (ph.).

Σαράπιδι καὶ θ[εοῖς ---]
οἱ οἶκοι καθιερώθ[ησαν -]
Εὐσεβοῦς Εὐτυ[χοῦς --]

Moretti combines this fragment with the fragment IGUR, I, 177 and presents the following text:

Σαράπιδι καὶ θ[εοῖς συν]ναίοις καὶ συμβώμοις
οἱ οἶκοι καθιερώθ[ησαν ὑπὲρ αὐτ]οκ. Κομμόδου ᾽Αντωνείνου
Εὐσεβοῦς Εὐτυ[χοῦς Σεβαστοῦ] ὑπὸ Κ. Τεινείου ῾Ρούφου.

1151. ROME, EPITAPH FOR GEMINIA, 2nd CENT. A.D. ICUR, V, 12901. H. Solin, ZPE 22 (1976) 75-76 (cf. also GGA 229, 1977, p. 97-98) convincingly proposes to read in L. 6-8 κεῖται τῷ θανάτῳ μηκέτι ὀφιλομένη (a pentameter after the hexameter in L. 2-4), instead of κεῖται τῷ θανάτῳ Μηκετίο φιλουμένη (ICUR: "Megethius as brother or next of kin of Geminia"). Solin further points out that the inscription seems to be pagan rather than Christian; but cf. D. Feissel, BCH 102 (1978) 550, note 27 who hesitates.

1152. ROME, EPITAPH OF POTETAS, 5th CENT. A.D. (?) M.T. Manni Piraino, IGLP, no. 132 (ph.). G. Alföldy, GNOMON 48 (1976) 511 reads in L. 4-7: <ό>κτὼ μηνὶ ᾽Αγόστ(ῳ) | (ἡμέρᾳ) τεσ(σαρακαι)δεκά-(τῃ) καὶ ς (= ἑβδόμῃ) Σε|λήνῃ ἐν(ν)εακε|δεκάτῃ, instead of <ό>κτὼ μηνὶ ᾽Αγόστῳ | τ<ῆ>ς δεκά(της) καὶ Ζό<η> [῾Ε]|λ<έ>νη ἐν<ν>εακε|δεκάτη(ς). Potetas died on August 14th, i.e. on Saturday (7th day), i.e. " am 19. Mondtag"; such luna-inscriptions are common in Rome.

1153. ROME, CHRISTIAN EPITAPH. G. Mennella, EPIGRAPHICA 38 (1976) 126-128 discovered on the reverse of ICUR, I, 3122 the following inscription (ph.):

Φιλικίσσιμος τρι
καὶ ἑπτὰ μημη

Mennella assumes that originally the stone-cutter meant to inscribe ICUR, I, 3122 on this side of the stone but that various reasons (lack of space, mistakes) forced him to re-engrave the text on the other side || 1. τρι<ῶν ἐτῶν> || 2. μη<νῶν> Mennella.

1154. ROME, EPITAPH. CIL, VI, pars 4, fasc. 2, no. 33680; IGUR, II, 2, 803. Cf. A. Ferrua, RPAA 48 (1975-76) 368, fig. 1, b and 376 who studied a squeeze of this inscription (made by De Rossi) and presents the following text:

Νέαρχος καὶ
Φιλίη ὧδε
3 ἀναπα<ύ>ον-
ται·
5 ὁδοιπόρε, μή μου παρῇ.

Νεαρχὶς καὶ | Φιλίη ὧδε | ἀναπάον|ται· | [γρ]ήγωρε· μὴ μ[ῦ]ρε L. Moretti, IGUR, II, 2, 803 || 2. ΦΙΛΙΗ or ΦΙΛΙ<Τ>Η ? Ferrua.

1155. ROME, FRAGMENT OF A CHRISTIAN EPITAPH. Ed. pr. A. Ferrua, RAC 52 (1976) 208, fig. 5, e. Ferrua publishes among several Latin fragments also this minor Greek fragment:

ΚΥΜΗ | ΕΔΥ

1. κύμησις or ἐκυμήθη (pro κοίμησις or ἐκοιμήθη) Ferrua.

1156. ROME, EPITAPH, AFTER 465 A.D. ? CIG, IV, 9770. H. Solin, ARCTOS 10 (1976) 95, no. 6 prefers in general the interpretation of CIG (Christian) to A. Ferrua's view (EPIGRAPHICA 3, 1941, p. 42: Jewish).

1157-1202. ROME, ROMAN IMPERIAL PERIOD, JEWISH EPITAPHS. Ed. pr. U.M. Fasola, RAC 52 (1976) 7-62. Fasola publishes several Jewish epitaphs, some of them with representations on the stone, found in the two Jewish catacombs of the Villa Torlonia. Below we give the texts, as engraved on the stone, and a brief description of the representations. The precise chronology of these texts is uncertain, cf. Fasola, l.c., 61-62 (3rd-4th cent. A.D.).

1157. P. 12-13; marble slab; above the inscription an axe; ph.

Ἐνθάδε κεῖται ζήσας ἔτη τριάκοντα
2 Φίλιππος ὁ φιλάδελφος 4 τρία.

1158. P. 14; painted inscription; at the left a menorah.

Ἐνθάδε κ[εῖται] | Ζώσιμο[ς] | ΕΥΔ..... | C N

1159. P. 18; marble fragment.

...ΑΤΡΟ...ΧΕΡΑΙΑC... (?)
[Ἐν εἰρ]ή[ν]ῃ ἡ κοίμισις α[ὐτοῦ or -ῆς]

1160. P. 18; two marble fragments.

ΟΝΕΙC..... | ΡCIC ΥΙΟΕ.... (sic) | ΕΥΛΟΓΗΩ... | ΑΥΙΛΝΛ ΠΕ...

1. [γ]ονεῖς ? Fasola || 3. Εὐλογή(=ι)ῳ ed.

1161. P. 18-19; inscription painted on a fragment of stucco.

[Ῥ]ουφῖ[νος] | [ἐ]ν εἰρήν[ῃ] | [ἐτ]ῶν .....

Traces of the letters ΙΟC | ΟΝΟ are also visible; they belong to a text which preceded Rufinus' epitaph.

1162. P. 19-20; marble slab; above the text a shofar, oil-vase, aron, menorah and ethrog; ph.

Ἐνθάδε κῖτε Γαϊα-
νὸς γραμματέους
3 ψαλμῳδὸς φιλό-
νομος. Ἐν ἰρήνῃ ἡ
5 κοίμισις αὐτοῦ.

2. For γραμματέους instead of γραμματεύς, cf. L. Robert, Ét. Anat., p. 516, note 3 (ed.).

1163. P. 20; inscription painted on a plastered tile of a loculus.

Ἐνθάδε κῖτε Ι[....... ἀπὸ τῆς]
Ἀχαΐας. Ἐν ἰρή[νῃ ἡ κοίμισις αὐτοῦ or -ῆς]

1164. P. 21; inscription painted on a loculus.

'Ενθάδε κῖτε Εὐμένις

1165. P. 21; graffito on the loculus of a child; under the inscription a menorah with five arms.

ΒΛΕΡΙΝΟϹ

I.e. Verinus Fasola.

1166. P. 21; marble slab; at the end of the text a menorah; ph.

Σινπλιχ[ί]- δέκα {α}ἐν εἰ-
2 ως {α}ἐτῶν 4 ρένῃ.

3-4. ΗΡΕΝΗ corrected on the stone into ΕΙΡΕΝΗ Fasola.

1167. P. 21-22; small slab; ph.

Μάξιμος | Θαβρακενός

Thabraca: in Numidia Fasola.

1168. P. 23; inscription painted on the grave of an adult.

'Ενθάδε κῖ[ται] 'Εν ἰρήν[ῃ ἡ]
2 Σπουδέος. 4 κοίμ[ησις αὐτοῦ].

1169. P. 23-24; two fragments of an inscription painted on the edge of a tomb.

a) [Πομ]πωνία Θε[....]
b) ['Ενθάδ]ε κ[εῖται]

1170. P. 24; fragmentary inscription painted on a tile.

ΤΕΟ..... | ἐτῶν .....

1171. P. 24; inscription painted on a tile closing a loculus; at the right side a small glass vessel was found.

υκος εἰρήνης ἐν ἰρή-
Κερδῶν μετὰ εὐλογίας νῃ

υκος = οἶκος Fasola.

1172. P. 24; inscription painted on a tile.

...HNOC

Perhaps the ending of a name Fasola.

1173. P. 25-26; marble slab; above the inscription a shofar, ethrog, aron, oil-vase, menorah; ph.

'Ενθάδε κῖτε 'Ιοῦσ-
τος, υἱὸς 'Αμαχίου
τοῦ Κατανέου,
ἐτῶν κβ'. 'Εν ἰρήνῃ
ἡ κοίμισις αὐτοῦ.

1174. P. 27; fragment of an inscription painted on a tile. Of the two lines only [νή]πιο[ς] is legible.

1175. P. 27; fragmentary painted inscriptions.

a) ..NA
b) ...ΥΠΟΙ...
c) .....HC |.....O εὐλο[γία?] | .....ΝΔΕ..... | K.....

1176. P. 35; inscription on a loculus; next to it a menorah.

ἐν[θ]άδε κῖτε

1177. P. 35; graffito on a loculus.

[ἐν εἰρήν]ῃ ἡ κί[μη]σι[ς αὐτοῦ or -ῆς]

1178. P. 36-37; marble slab; next to the inscription a menorah and an ethrog; ph.

'Ενθάδε κῖτε
'Αναστασίους
ἀρχιγερουσιάρ-
χης υἱὸς 'Αν[ασ]-
τασίου ΟΙ.....

5. <ἔ>τ[ῶν]...? Fasola.

1179. P. 37; marble fragment.

['Ενθάδε] κεῖτε | [....]ενος | [....]ος ἐτῶ[ν]

1180. P. 45; painted inscription.

[῎Ε]νθα κῖτ[αι]...| Κ · ΤΗϹ Ζ...

2. κ(αὶ) τῆς Ζ... Fasola.

1181. P. 45; painted inscription.

Σεβήρο[ς] | .....ϹΕΑ.....

There were four lines but of lines 3 and 4 only a M and a P remain.

1182. P. 45; painted inscription.

......ΜΕΤΟϹ | ΔΙϹ ΑΡ[χων](?)

Four letters of this inscription (MET and P) are in J.-B. Frey, CIJ, 66; probably a δὶς ἄρχων is mentioned. Fasola.

1183. P. 46; marble slab; ph.

῾Ρουφεῖνος φι-
λογονέους.
῎Εζησεν ἔτη
δέκα δύω.

For φιλογονέους instead of φιλογονεύς, cf. L. Robert, Et. Anat., 516, note 3 (ed.).

1184. P. 46; marble slab; ph.

ΑΒΙΒΟ[---]
ΑΠΟΛΙΝ̣[--]
ου ἐνθ̣άδε
κεῖται. ῎Εζη-
σεν ἔτη λʹ.

1-2. ῾Αβῖβος ... ἀπὸ Λίν[δ]ου Fasola; ἀπὸ Λίν[δ]ου is impossible in this period. Certainly one has to restore ᾿Απολιν[αρί]ου Moretti.

1185. P. 46; marble slab; ph.

Iulius [---]
Iuliae F[--- coniu]-
gi cum [-----]
XVIII vixi[t ---]
᾿Εν ἰρήνῃ ἡ̣ [κοίμησις αὐτῆς].

3-4. [coniu]gi cum q[ua vixit annis] XVIII. Vixit [annis ...] Fasola; perhaps: cum [qua annis] XVIII vixit ed.

1186. P. 46; marble fragment.

ἐνθάδε [κεῖται]

1187. P. 47; inscription on a tile.

Ἰούδ[ας]... | MEN·Γ

The name of the deceased (perhaps a child of three months: μεν(ῶν) γ') could also be read Ἰούλ[ιος] or Ἰουλ[ία] Fasola.

1188. P. 48; painted inscription; at the right a menorah.

[Εὐ]πρέπιος

1189. P. 49.

Ὀκ[λα]τία Πία γυνή ... | ἐν[θάδε κεῖται]... (?)

1190. P. 49.

[Ἐ]νθάδε κ[εῖται] ¦ [Φιλόδ]οξο[ς] (?)

1191. P. 49.

[Ἐ]νθάδε κ[εῖται] | παιδιν Ἰουλία

παιδιν pro παιδίον Fasola.

1192. P. 49.

Ἐνθάδε [κεῖται] | πεδιν Ἀπ[ελλῆς] (?)

πεδιν pro παιδίον Fasola.

1193. P. 49; marble slab.

Ἐνθάδε κῖτε
2 Γέροντις
ζήσας ἔτη δύο
4 παρὰ ἡμέρας ι'.

1194. P. 50; inscription painted on a tile.

Ἐνθ[άδε κεῖται] ¦ ΓΕΓΟ... [ἐν εἰρήνῃ] | [ἡ κοίμησ]ις αὐ[τοῦ or ·

1195. P. 56; inscription painted on a loculus.

'Αθη[ναῖος (?).... ἐν εἰρή]¦νῃ ἐτῶ[ν] ...

1196. P. 56; painted inscription.

[Λ]έοντις

1197. P. 56; graffito.

Αὔια νεπία

Avia: Latin name; for νέπιος pro νήπιος, cf. J.-B. Frey, CIJ, 97 and 138 Fasola.

1198. P. 56; painted inscription.

['Ενθάδε κ]εῖτε | ....ΥΤΑ Σάρα

1199. P. 56; painted inscription.

--- | --- | ἐτῶν .... ἐν εἰρήνῃ | [ἡ κοίμησις] αὐτοῦ

1200. P. 57; painted inscription.

...ΟϹ δὶς [ἄρχων?] | ἐν εἰρήν[ῃ ἡ κοίμησις] | [α]ὐτοῦ

1201. P. 57; painted inscription.

'Ενθά[δε] .... καὶ ΕΠΑ....
Τ......ΘΕΙΑ [εὔ]τεκνος ἐν ἐρή[νῃ ἡ κοίμη]-
σ[ις] αὐτοῦ μετὰ τῶν ὁσίων.

1202. P. 57; painted inscription with at the left a menorah.

ΕΙ | ἐν ε[ἰρήνῃ ἡ κοίμησις α]ὐτο[ῦ]

1203-1206. ROME, JEWISH EPITAPHS. U.M. Fasola, RAC 52 (1976) 57-59 corrects the following texts from J.-B. Frey, CIJ:

1203. CIJ, no. 12.

'Ενθάδε κῖται Βηριά[νη μήτηρ Μ]αρίες καὶ
'Ιούδατος καὶ Σάρες κα[ὶ 'Ιώσ]ητος καὶ
Εὐφραντικοῦ κ[αὶ ....] τῶν ὁσίων.

3. καὶ Εὐφραντικοῦ κ[αὶ ... ἐ]τῶν [.. μην]ῶν CIJ.

1204. CIJ, no. 16. In the final third line Fasola reads 'Εν εἰρήνῃ ἡ κοίμη[σις] σου (Frey's reading was ἡ κοίμη[σις σου]).

1205. CIJ, no. 25.

[Ε]ὐσεβὶς ὧδε [κεῖται γυ]νὴ Γηλασίου
τοῦ Κεσαρέως ἐτῶν λε'. Εὐλογί
α πᾶσιν.

2. εὐλογί(α) Frey.

1206. CIJ, no. 44. Next to the text as given by Frey, there is at the left side of a menorah the word εὐλ|ογί|α; at the right the Latin stamp Sap|ri|ci; representations of loulab, shofar and ethrog.

1207. ROME, EPITAPH. Inscription on the lid of a sarcophagus, broken into several parts. Ed. pr. A. Ferrua, RPAA 48 (1975-76) 373, fig. 3 c and 375.

[ἡ δεῖνα τῷ ἀνδρὶ] ἀειμνήστῳ· τοῦτο σοι μόνον, Καλλίκλης.

1208. ROME, NAME ON THE BASE OF A STATUE. Ed. pr. A. Ferrua, RPAA 48 (1975-76) 369.

Καλλιόπη

1209. ROME, STAMPED AMPHORA-HANDLE. Handle of a Rhodian amphora, with a rectangular seal. Ed. pr. Elisa Lissi Caronna, NSA 30 (1976) 261 (dr.).

['Επὶ] | ['Αγεσ]τράτου | [Θεσμοφ]ορίου

1210. ROME, GRAFFITO ON THE TOMB OF ST. PETER. G. Pugliese Carratelli, PP 31 (1976) 466-467 defends his restoration Πέτρ[ος οὐκ] | ἔνι (PP 25, 1970, p. 348-351; cf. also PP 27, 1972, p. 350-353) against the objections of M. Guarducci, ARCHCLASS 24 (1972) 117-126 (cf. also ARCHCLASS 19, 1967, p. 53-65; ibid., 20, 1968, p. 354, 366 and note 25; ibid., 23, 1971, p. 130-141) who reads herself Πέτρ[ος] | ἔνι. Cf. J. and L. Robert, BE (1973) no. 549.

1211. VELIA, TWO "HOROS"-INSCRIPTIONS, 5th and 4th CENT. B.C. Ed. pr. M. Guarducci, PP 21 (1966) 287-294, no. 4 and PP 25 (1970) 256-259, no. 3. The texts concerned run as follows: Ὀλυμπίō Καιρō̃ and Ἥρης Θελξίνης. G. Pugliese Carratelli, PP 31 (1976) 467-468 discusses the interpretations of M. Guarducci: Ὀλύμπιος is not an ethnic (as Ὀλυμπιακός) refering to Olympia ("from Olympia") (cf. also for this interpretation M. Guarducci, ARCHCLASS 23, 1971, p. 124-130 and ibid., 24, 1972, p. 112-117) but an adjective meaning that Kairos was the son of Zeus participating in the θειότης of the Ὀλύμπιοι ("Olympian") (cf. also Pugliese Carratelli, PP 25, 1970, p. 248 ff. and ibid., 27, 1972, p. 347-350). Hera Θελξίνη is not "benigna (eufemisticamente)", but "incantatrice, ammaliatrice".

GAUL

1212. GAUL, GRAFFITI ON ATTIC VASES. J.-J. Jully, DHA (1976) 53-71 gives a survey of 98 graffiti on Attic vases found in the southern part of the Languedoc.

1213. AUGUSTODUNUM (AUTUN), ANAKREON-MOSAIC, 2nd CENT. A.D. Ed. pr. Michèle and Alain Blanchard, REA 75 (1973) 268-279 (ph.). Cf. R. Führer, ZPE 20 (1976) 54 who restores vs. 3 of the second Anakreon-fragment as follows: ἐ[γὼ θέλω] | προ[πίνειν], instead of ἐ[μοὶ δὲ δὸς] | προ[πίνειν] (M. and A. Blanchard, e.g.).

1214. LUGDUNUM (LYON), METRICAL EPITAPH FOR THE SYRIAN IOULIANOS, END 2nd - 3rd CENT. A.D. Ed. pr. J.-F. Reynaud - A. Audin - J. Pouilloux, JS (1975) 47-75 (p. 58-75: Le texte, par J. Pouilloux; ph.). M. Guarducci, MEFR 88-II (1976) 843-852 (ph.) tries to put forward evidence for the view (already suggested by Pouilloux) that Ioulianos was a Christian. Cf. also C.P. Jones, AJPH 99 (1978) 336-353 who contributes several new readings, incorporated by us in the text below, and correctly distrusts the view that Ioulianos was a Christian missionary; Jones prefers a date in the 3rd cent. A.D. to Pouilloux's 2nd half of the 2nd cent. A.D. Cf. also J. and L. Robert, BE (1977) no. 599 bis.

Col. I εἰ γνῶναι ποθέεις ὅστις βροτὸς ἐνθάδε κεῖται,
οὐδὲν σειγήσει τάδε γράμματα, πάντα δὲ λέξει·
Εὐτέκνιος ἐπικλήν, Ἰουλιανὸς τοὔνομα τῷδε,
Λαοδίκια πατρίς, Συρίης περίβλεπτον ἄγαλμα·
ἔντιμος πατρόθεν, μήτηρ δ' ἔχε δόξαν ὁμοίην,
χρηστὸς καὶ δίκαιος, πᾶσιν πεφιλημένος ἀνήρ,
οὗ Κελτοῖς λαλέοντος ἀπὸ γλώσσης ῥέε πειθώ·
ποικίλα μὲν περιῆλθεν ἔθνη, πολλοὺς δέ δήμους
ἔγνω καὶ ψυχῆς ἀρετὴν ἤσκησεν ἐ<ν> αὐτοῖς·

κύμασιν καὶ πελάγει συνεχῶς ἐπέδωκεν ἑαυτόν,
δῶρα τὰ πάντα φέρων εἰς Κελτοὺς καὶ Δύσεως γῆν
[ὅ]σ̣σ̣α̣ θεὸς προσέταξε φέρειν χθόνα πάνφορον Ἠοῦς·
[τοὔνε]κα τὸν φιλέ[ε]σ̣κ̣ε̣ βροτὸν τριπλὰ φῦλα τὰ Κελτῶν.

Col. II ἤλασεν εἰς ΒΑΘ
ἀντὶ τρόπων Α.
τῷ πάντων ΚΡ
ἐν δόξῃ ΚΑΤΕ
ὑεῖ ΠΑΝΜΑΚ
καὶ πᾶσιν ΤΟ
τοὔνεκα ΤΟ
υἱὸς Η.ΕΚ
ΑΙΤΗΤΟΣΙ
ψυχῆς ΤΕ.
δοίη ΤΕΘ.

----

2. Jones, accepted by Pouilloux per ep. (cf. also J. and L. Robert, BE, 1977, no. 599 bis and G. Daux, REG 90, 1977, p. 475); οὐδὲν σειγῆς, ἔργα δὲ γράμματα πᾶν τάδε λέξει Pouilloux || 6. in fine Jones; cf. also G. Daux, REG 90 (1977) 475-476; ἀντί Pouilloux || 8. δέ <τε> δήμους Jones || 9. in fine Jones and Guarducci; ἤσκησ' ἐν ἑαυτοῖς or ἤσκησεν ἑαυτοῖς Pouilloux || 12-13. Jones; Ἠοῦς, | [οὕνε]κα τὸν φιλέεσκε (sc. θεός) βροτόν· τριπλᾶ φῦλα τὰ Κελτῶν | ἤλασεν κτλ. Pouilloux, Guarducci || 14. βαθ[μούς or βάθ[ος Pouilloux; βαθ[μούς Guarducci; βάθ[εα Jones || 15. in fine Jones; ΑΚ Pouilloux || 16. initio Jones; τῶν πάντων Pouilloux and Guarducci || 18. πανμάκ[αρι or -αρίστῳ Guarducci; cf. however Jones who rightly distrusts Guarducci's view that these epithets "are of exclusively Christian usage" || 21. in fine Jones, who suggests something like ἠδὲ κ[άσις or -ασίγνητος; ΗΛΕΚΤ Pouilloux; ἠλέκτ[ωρ Guarducci || 22. Jones; αἰτητός . Pouilloux || 23. in fine Jones; ΤΕΜ Pouilloux || 24. in fine Jones; τε θε Pouilloux.

SPAIN

1215. CORDOBA, DEDICATION OF A POEM TO ARTEMIS BY THE PROCONSUL ARRIANUS. Ed. pr. A. Tovar, Estudios sobre la obra de Americo Castro (Madrid, 1971) 401-412 (ph.). Cf. M.F. Galiano, EMERITA 40 (1972) 47-50; M. Marcovich, ZPE 12 (1972) 207-209; W. Burkert, ZPE 17 (1975) 167-169; A.B. Bosworth, GRBS 17 (1976) 55-64; M. Marcovich, ZPE 20 (1976) 41-43; W. Peek, ZPE 22 (1976) 87-88; G. Giangrande, EMERITA 44 (1976) 349-355 (ph.); L. Koenen, ZPE 24 (1977) 35-40. This poem has been interpreted in very different ways. All the authors cited, except Marcovich, identify the proconsul Arrianus with the famous historian and philosopher. L. Koenen seems to hesitate. Cf. also J. and L. Robert, BE (1973) no. 539 and W. Eck, RE, Suppl. 14 (1974) 120, s.v. Flavius. Bosworth dates the poem to ± 125 A.D.

Κρέσσονά σοι χρυσοῖο καὶ | ἀργύ̣ρου ἄμβροτα δῶρα |
Ἄρτεμι, καὶ θήρης πολλὸν | ἀ̣ρειότ[ερα] |
Μουσάων .[ ]θρων̣ δ̣ὲ καρήατι | δῶρα κομί[ζ]ειν |
είς θεὸν οὐχ ὁ̣σ̣ίη δαίστορας | ἀλλοτρίων. |
Ἀρριανὸς ἀνθύπατος |

---

3. ἐ[χ]θρῶ<ι> με Tovar; ἐ[χ]θρῶι̣ γε Galiano; [Σα]θρῶ<ι> δ̣έ Marcovich (ZPE 12, 1972, p. 207-209); [ῥ̣εί]θρων̣ δ̣έ Burkert, Bosworth, Koenen; Μουσάων, [ἄν]θρωπ̣ε, καρήατι Peek; [λ̣ύ]θρων̣ δ̣έ Marcovich (ZPE 20, 1976, p. 42); Ἐ̣[χ]θρῶν δὲ Giangrande.

1216. HISPALIS, INSCRIPTION IN HONOUR OF HERAKLES, 2nd CENT. A.D. Marble stone, now in the Archaeological Museum of Sevilla. Ed. pr. J. Gil, REVISTA DE LA UNIVERSIDAD COMPLUTENSE (Homenaje a Garcia Bellido II) 25 (1976) 195-199 (ph.).

Ἑνδέκατον κύνα Κ[έρβερον ἤγαγεν ἐξ Ἀΐδαο]
ἔνθα σιδήρειαί τε πύλ[αι καὶ χάλκεος οὐδός]

The inscription probably was an explanatory text belonging to a series of reliefs which represented Herakles' labours. Gil.

1217. TARRACO, FUNERARY EPIGRAM FOR VALERIA MOUSA, 3rd CENT. A.D. G. Alföldy, Die römischen Inschriften aus Tarraco (Madrider Forschungen, vol. 10; Berlin, 1975) no. 684. W.D. Lebek, ZPE 22 (1976) 297-300 returns to the text, comments on the implications of vs. 4 ("Kuss und Seelenhauch") and gives a translation. We present his text:

Λυπηρὸν μὲν ἔχει γόον αἴλινον ἐνθάδε τύμβος,
ἀγνῆς ἐρατῆς καλῆς δέμας Οὐαλερίης Μούσης,
ἧς γαμέτης παίδων τε πατὴρ γλυκερὸς Θησεύς
4 πότμον ἐποιχομένης ἐπί τε στόματι στόμα πήξας
ὕστερον ἐκ στέρνων ψυχῆς διεδέξατο δῶρον.

---

4. ἐπί τε στόματι στοματήξας Alföldy.

NORICUM

1218. AGUNTUM, INSCRIPTION ON THE HANDLE OF AN IMPORTED VASE. Ed. pr. R. Noll, AAWW 113 (1976) 35.

ΘΕΟΙC

CARIA

1219. APHRODISIAS, HONORARY INSCRIPTION FOR TI. CLAUDIUS ZELOS, 2nd HALF 2nd CENT. A.D. Inscription engraved on a pediment block in the theatre, in two lines. Ed. pr. D.J. MacDonald, Greek and Roman Coins from Aphrodisias (BAR, Suppl.Ser. 9; 1976) p. 20. Cf. J. and L. Robert, BE (1977) no. 459.

῾Η βουλὴ καὶ ὁ δῆμος καὶ ἡ γερουσία καὶ οἱ νέοι ἐτείμησαν Τιβέριον Κλαύδιον Ζῆλον ἀρχιερέα καὶ ἱερέα διὰ βίου θεᾶς ᾿Αφροδείτης καὶ τοῦ Δήμου, κτίστην καὶ εὐεργέτην ἐν πᾶσιν τῆς πατρίδος, ἐπιμεληθέντος Ποπλίου Αἰλίου Καλλικράτους τοῦ προτολόγου ἄρχοντος.

1. ἀρχιερέα: high priest, sc. of the cult of the emperors J. and L. Robert, BE (1977) no. 459 || 2. δήμου MacDonald; Δήμου J. and L. Robert, ibidem || προτολόγου (or πρωτολόγου ?): cf. J. and L. Robert, BE (1967) no. 645.

1220. APHRODISIAS, DEDICATION TO ANTONINUS PIUS BY TI. CLAUDIUS ZELOS, 139-161 A.D. Inscription engraved across the pulpitum of the theatre in a single line. Ed. pr. D.J. MacDonald, l.c., p. 20. Cf. J. and L. Robert, BE (1977) no. 459.

[[Θεᾶι ᾿Αφροδείτηι]] καὶ Αὐτοκράτορι Καίσαρι Τ[[ίτῳ Αἰλίῳ ῾Αδριανῷ ᾿Α]]ντωνείνῳ Σεβαστῷ Εὐσεβεῖ καὶ Μ̣άρκῳ Αὐρηλίῳ Οὐήρῳ Καίσαρι καὶ τῷ σύμπαντι οἴκῳ τῶν Σεβαστῶν καὶ τῇ γλυκυτάτῃ πατρίδι· Τι. Κλ. Ζῆλος ἀρχιερεὺς καὶ ἱερεὺς διὰ βίου θεᾶς [[[᾿Αφροδείτης]]] τοὺς κείονας καὶ τὸν κατ᾿ αὐτῶν κόσμον καὶ τὴν σκούτλωσιν τοῦ τοίχου καὶ τοῦ ἐδάφους ἐκ τῶν ἰδίων κατεσσκεύασεν <καὶ?> ἀνέθηκεν.

βίου: probably forgotten by MacDonald, corr. J. and L. Robert || <καί?> J. and L. Robert.

1221. HALIKARNASSOS, LIST OF VOTIVE-GIFTS TO ATHENA, 1st HALF 4th CENT. B.C. (?). Two joining pieces of marble. Ed. pr. M.Ç. Şahin, ZPE 20 (1976) 21-22, no. 4 (ph.). Cf. J. and L. Robert, BE (1977) no. 466, p. 411.

᾿Εξετασταὶ οἱ ἐπὶ Ζηνοδώρου ἱερ[έως]
ἀνέγραψαν τὰ τῆς ᾿Αθηνᾶς τῆς̣ [ ]
ἀναθήματα·
φιάλη χρυσῆ πόλεως ἰτεόφυ̣[λλος]
κατ᾿ ᾿Αφροδίτης· σταθμὸς δρα̣[(χμαὶ)]
φιάλη πόλεως ἰτεόφ[υ]λλος [ ]
φιάλη πόλεως ἰτεόφ̣[υλ]λος̣ : ΠΔ
φιάλη πόλεως καρ[υω]τ̣ή : ΡΛΒ
φιάλη πόλεως ἰτε̣ό̣φυλλος : ΠΘ

[φιάλη] π̣όλεως ἰτ̣εόφυλλος : Π[Η
π]ο̣λεὼς : ΠΖ, [
[φιάλη πόλεως ἰτ]εόφυλλος ερ[
[φιάλη πόλεως ἰτε]όφυλλος Ἡρακλ[έους
[φιάλη πόλεως ἰτεό]φυλλος Ἀφροδίτ̣[ης
[φιάλη πόλεως ἰτεόφυ̣λλο]ς̣[

For similar lists, cf. SEG, III, 187 and 188 || 12. probably should be completed as Ἑρ[μοῦ Şahin.

1222. HALIKARNASSOS, PROXENY DECREE, 1st HALF 3rd CENT. B.C. Marble stone. Ed. pr. M.Ç. Şahin, ZPE 20 (1976) 19-20, no. 1 (ph.).

[Ἐπὶ] νεωποιοῦ Μητροδώρου τοῦ Λε[ον]-
[τ]ιάδου, μηνὸς Ἀνθεστηριῶνος δεκάτη[ι ἀ]-
νομένου, ἐπὶ πρυτανείας τῆς μετὰ Πολυκ̣[λεί]-
του τοῦ Πολυκλείτου, γραμματεύοντος
Ἀγοράνακτος τοῦ Χαρμύλου, ἔδοξεν
τῆι βουλῆι καὶ τῶι δήμωι, γνώμη πρυτάνεω[ν·]
ἐπειδὴ Λεοντίσκος Λέοντος Ἀλεξανδρε[ὺς]
εὔνους καὶ πρόθυμος ὢν διατελεῖ ἐμ παντ[ὶ]
καιρῶι περὶ τὴν πόλιν καὶ ἰδίαι τε ἑκάστου[ς]
τῶν πολιτῶν τοῖς ἐντυγχάνουσιν χρε[ί]-
ας παρέχεται καὶ κοινῆι τῆι πόλει τὰ συμφέ-
ροντα πράσσει, δεδόχθαι· ἐπηινῆσθαι τε
αὐτὸν [ἀρε]τ̣ῆς ἕνεκεν καὶ εὐνοίας ἣν ἔχω[ν]
δια[τελεῖ κοι]ν̣ῆι τε περὶ τὴν πόλιν καὶ ἰδίαι̣
[πρὸς τοὺς ἐντυ]χ̣άνοντας αὐτῶι τῶ[ν πολι]-
[τῶν· εἶναι πρόξενον καὶ ε]ὐεργέτη̣ν̣, [δεδόσ]-
[θαι δὲ αὐτῶι καὶ πολιτείαν] κ̣α̣ὶ ἔγ̣[κτησιν]
[γῆς καὶ οἰκίας·]

9. ἑκάστου[ς]: one expects ἑκάστοις Şahin || 14-15. ἰδίαι̣ | [τοὺς ἐντυγ]χ̣άνοντας Şahin, corr. Herrmann.

1223. HALIKARNASSOS, DECREE CONCERNING THE DONATION TO A FOREIGNER OF THE RIGHT OF OWNING LAND AND HOUSING, 3rd CENT. B.C. Marble stone; upper and lower parts broken. Ed. pr. M.Ç. Şahin, ZPE 20 (1976) 20-21, no. 3 (ph.).

[τῆι π]όλει πο[λλοῖς]
[τῶ]ν πολιτῶν χρείας παρεισχ̣[ημέ]-
νος ἐπελθὼν ἐπὶ τὴν βουλὴν κ̣α[ὶ]
τὸν δῆμον αἰτεῖται δοθῆναι αὐτ[ῶι]
καὶ ἐκγόνοις γῆς καὶ οἰκίας ἔγ-
κτησιν, δεδόχθαι· δεδόσθαι αὐτῶι̣
καθ' ἃ αἰτεῖται καὶ τῶι δήμωι περ̣[ὶ]
τούτων ἐψήφισται. Τοὺς δὲ

ἐξεταστὰς τοὺς ἐπ' Ἀθηνίωνος
ἀναγράψαι τόδε τὸ ψήφισμα ἐν στή-
ληι λιθίνηι καὶ στῆσ[α]ι ἐν τῶι ἱερῶ[ι]
τ[οῦ Ἀπό]λ̣λωνος [εἰ̣ς τὸν δεδογμ]ε̣ένον τό-
[πον].εκ[ ]εν

1224. HALIKARNASSOS, FRAGMENT OF A PROXENY DECREE, 1st CENT. B.C. (?) Marble stone; top, bottom and left side broken. Ed. pr. M.Ç. Şahin, ZPE 20 (1976) 20, no. 2 (ph.).

[ ] Ἁλικαρνα̣[σσ-- ·]
[ἀναγράψαι αὐτ]ὸ̣ν πρόξενο̣ν κ-
[αὶ εὐεργέτην] τῆς πόλεως, ε[ἶ]-
[ναι δὲ αὐτῶ]ι καὶ πολιτείαν
[μετέχοντ]ι̣ πάντων ὧγ καὶ
[οἱ ἄλλοι Ἁλι]καρνασσεῖς μετ-
[έχουσι καὶ π]ροεδρίαν ἐν τ[ο]-
[ῖς ἀγῶσι κα]ὶ πρόσοδον πρό[ς]
[τε τὴν βου]λ̣ὴν καὶ τὸν δῆμ̣[ον]
[ ]ᾳ πρώτωι .[ ]

6. [οἱ δ' Ἁλι]καρνασσεῖς Şahin, corr. Herrmann || 10. perhaps [μετὰ τὰ ἱερ]ὰ πρώτωι .[---] Şahin.

1225. HALIKARNASSOS, BOUNDARY STONE OF A SANCTUARY OF APOLLO, HELLENISTIC PERIOD. Oblong rectangular slab of marble. Ed. pr. M.Ç. Şahin, ZPE 20 (1976) 22-23, no. 5 (ph.)

Ο[ὗ]ρος ἱ[εροῦ]
Ἀπόλλωνος·
μηθένα προσ-
πορεύεσθαι
πρὸς τὴν
ἄκραν, ὧι μὴ πρᾶ-
γμα· ὃς δ' ἂν πα-
ρὰ ταῦτα ποιῆι,
αὐτὸν αἰτιάσε-
ται.

9-10. αὐτὸν αἰτιάσεται: for other examples, cf. J. and L. Robert, BE (1977) no. 466.

1226. IASOS, THE RELATIONS BETWEEN ANTIOCHOS III AND IASOS. A. Mastrocinque, PP 31 (1976) 311-315 studies the relations between Iasos and Antiochos III on the basis of the following inscriptions: the letter of Laodike III and the decree in honour of Antiochos III (ed. G. Pugliese Carratelli, ASAA 29-30, 1967-68, p. 445-453, no. II, with important interpretations, improvements and new readings by J. and L. Robert and others; cf. BE, 1971, no. 621; ibid., 1972, no. 423; ibid., 1973, nos. 432 and 436-438; ibid., 1974, no. 544; ibid., 1977, no. 465) and GIBM 442 = OGIS, 237 (which forms part of the same monument, cf. J. and L. Robert, BE, 1971, no. 621,

p. 507-508).

1227. KNIDOS/DELPHI, "PIRACY LAW", 101-100 B.C. Delphi: SEG, III, 378 (G. Colin, F. Delphes, III, 4, no. 37); Knidos: M. Hassall - M. Crawford - J. Reynolds, JRS 64 (1974) 195-220 (ph.). Cf. A.N. Sherwin-White, JRS 66 (1976) 6-8 who discusses some aspects of this law. He dates it to the end of 101 B.C. but adds that it may still be one of the first promulgations of the tribunes of 100 (against Hassall - Crawford - Reynolds, l.c., p. 215, note 16 and p. 218). He also discusses the meaning of ἐπαρχεία στρατηγική (Knidos, III, 37) and thinks that it means something like "provincia militaris" (and not "praetorian province": Hassall - Crawford - Reynolds). Cf. also A.W. Lintott, ZPE 20 (1976) 65-82 who, considering ἐπαρχεία στρατηγική as the translation of provincia praetoria, thinks that "the passage should not be taken to mean that Cilicia was to be permanently a provincia praetoria; it need only refer to the coming year" (p. 81-82). Lintott, being sure that the texts of Delphi and Knidos are different Greek versions of the same Roman law, also studies the dating (he prefers a date in late 101 B.C.) and character of the law, the nature of the provisions on Knidos V and the discrepancies between this text and Delphi C. He proposes the following text for Knidos, V, lines 14-45:

τεσσαράκοντα πέν[τε ἐλεῖν ἐκ τῶν]
τριακοσίων, ἐκείνου, ὧι τούτου κατ[ηγορεῖται, ἔστω κρ]-
ατ[ό]ς. Ἵν[α τοῦ γ]έρατ[ος ἐκστῶσ]ι τ[ρι]άκον[τα ἐκ τῶν τεσ]-
σαράκοντα πέντε, [πρὸς τοῦτο] ἕκαστος [τῶν ἀγόντων ἡ]-
μέρα[ι] δ[ίκης ἀν'] ἕνα ἕκαστος ἐκ τούτ[ων κρίτων ἀπολεγέτω],
ἕως οἱ δεκαπέντε λοιποὶ [ἐκλεκτ]οὶ [ἂν ὦσιν. Ἐάν τις νοσῆι],
ὑπὲρ ἐκείνου ἄρχων, ὃν ἀντὶ αὐτοῦ ἕκασ[τος ἂν ἕληι, εἰσέτω]
μέχρι τούτου, ἕως [[τ]]<δ>έκ[α α]ἱρ[εθῶσιν ἄν, οἷς περὶ τούτου τοῦ]
πράγματος εἰς ἐκεί[[λ]]<ν>ους δέδωκεν [ε]ἰσ[ιέναι. Ἄρχων, ὅπως]
ἐκεῖνοι κρείνωσιν, ὀμωμοκό[τ]ες [περὶ τῆς ζημίας ἀπαιτη]-
τεοῦ ὡς τοῦτο τὸ πρᾶγμα ἐ[ξέ]μ[αθον], δ[έλτοις κήρι]-
ναις πρὸς αὐτὸν περὶ τούτου τοῦ πράγματος, ἵ[να κρυφῆ]
κριθῆι, καί, καθὼς ἐκείνωι τὸ πλέον μέρος περ[ὶ τούτου]
τοῦ πράγματος γνώμην ἀπεφήνατο [ἢ κατακρῖναι ἢ λῦ]-
σαι, ποιείτω. Εἷς τε τοῦτο <τὸ> πρᾶγμα [τῶι ἄγ]ον[τι μάρτυ]-
σιν προσαγγεῖλαι μέχρ<ι> εἴκοσι δοθήτω ἐξου[σία. Ἐπαι]-
νὸν μὴ ἄλλως, οἷς τοῦτο τὸ πρᾶγμα μαρτυ[ρεῖν ἂν γένηται],
λέγειν ἢ ὡς, καθὼς ἄν, εἰ ἐκείνου ὄνομα πε[ρὶ τοῦθ', ὅ ἐστι με]-
ταπορευθησόμενον προσπεφωνημένον, [καταφέροι, ἐξ ἐπιπέ]-
δου μαρτυρίαν τε ἐξῆι λέγει<ν>. Ὅστις κατὰ τοῦτ[ον τὸν νόμον]
λελυμένος ἔσται ὥστε προκρίματος ἀδικ[ίας ἄλλης μὴ ὑπεῖ]-
ναι περὶ τούτου τοῦ πράγματος, ἐφ' οὗ οὕτω[ς κατηγορία]
ἔσται, κατὰ τοῦτον τὸν νόμον μὴ ἔνοχος ἔστ[ω μηδ' εἰς αὐτὸν]
περὶ τούτου τοῦ πράγματος κατὰ τοῦτον τ[ὸ]ν ν[όμον ἔστω ἀφορ]-
μή. Ἔστω δὲ κατὰ τοῦτον τὸν νόμον [μ]ὴ κ[ατάχ]ρ[εος ὁ λελυμένος]

ἕκαστος αὐτῶν χρημ̣ά̣των ὅθε̣ν [ἀπητίτηται. Ὅστις κατὰ τοῦ]-
τον τὸν νόμον κατάκ̣ρ̣ι̣τ̣ος ἔσται, τ̣ὸ τού̣το<υ> χρῆ[μα ἄρχων, παρ' ὧι τοῦτο]
τὸ κριτήριον διήκ̣ο̣υ̣σεν, ἐκ τῶν ὑπ̣α̣ρ̣χ̣ό̣ντω̣ν [τῶι κατακρίτω]ι
εἰσοδιασάτω ἀποκαταστησάτω [ποιείτω τε ὅπως, ἐπειδὰν] οὕ-
τως εἰσοδιάσηι ἢ ἀποκαταστήσηι, τὸ ἥμι[συ τούτου τοῦ χρή]ματος
εἰς τὸ δημόσιον πρὸς τὸν ταμίαν ἀποκα[τασταθήσεται], τὸ δὲ ἥ-
μισυ, [ἄγ]ειν ὧι δόθηται, ἀποδόθητα[ι ...

1228. LAGINA (KORANZA), HONORARY DECREE FOR KONON, SON OF POSEIDIPPOS, 318 B.C. Limestone block. Ed. pr. M.Ç. Şahin, ANADOLU 17 (1973) 177-179 (Turkish) and 187-189 (English), no. 1 (ph.).

Ἕκτου ἔτους Φιλίππου βασιλεύο[ν]τος,
μηνὸς Δίου, Ἀσάνδρου σατραπεύοντος,
ἐπὶ ἀρχόντων Υσσώλλου Αρρισσιος
καὶ Οβροκα Μαλοσώου, ἔδοξε Κοαραν-
ζεῦσιν, ἐκκλησίας κυρίας γε̣ν̣ο̣μέ-
νης σὺν τοῖς ἱεροκήρυξιν. Ἐπειδὴ
Κόνων Ποσειδίππου καλὸς κά̣γ̣α̣-
θὸς καὶ εὔνους γεγένηται εἰς τ[ὴν]
πόλιν τὴν Κοαρανζέων, δεδόσθ̣αι
αὐτῶι καὶ ἐγγόνοις πολιτείαν
καὶ ἔγκτ̣[ησιν γῆς] T⌒NIM⌐T[ ]
ιερω̣

On Lagina and Koranza, cf. Şahin, l.c., 182-185 (Turkish) and 192-195 (English).

1229. LAGINA (KORANZA), DEDICATION OF A FIELD TO APOLLO AND ARTEMIS BY SKOARANOS AND HIS WIFE, MIDDLE 4th CENT. B.C. Limestone stele; upper part broken. Ed. pr. M.Ç. Şahin, ANADOLU 17 (1973) 179-182 (Turkish) and 189-192 (English), no. 2 (ph.).

]ωσι τῶι Ἀπόλλωνι καὶ τῆ̣[ι Ἀρτέμιδι]
Κωρανζεῖς. Σκοάρανος δὲ κ̣αὶ Τε[ ]
ἡ γυνὴ αὐτοῦ ἀνέθηκαν Ἀπόλλωνι
καὶ Ἀρτέμιδι γῆν ἔνδενδρον τὴν
καλουμένην ἐγ Κοαρβωνδοις ἐλα-
ιτιν, ἀριθμῶι δένδρη τεσσαράκοντα,
σπόρου μεδίμνων εἴκοσι, ἣν ὁμουρεῖ
τὰ ἱερὰ χωρία τῆς Ἀρτέμιδος, ὅπως
διαμένη αὐτοῖς τὸν ἀεὶ χρόνον. Ἐπι-
μεληθῆναι δὲ Ἑκατόμνων Οβορκα,
Υσσωλλον Αρτ̣αου ἐξ Υθυβιρων, Μάνη̣ν
Ἀρτίμου, Παον Πακτύου ἐκ Παταρουσων,
Πακτύην Μανέω, Δερσωμανην Θυσσου
Ἀγγωρέας, Ἑκαταῖον Ἑκατόμνω, Μάνην

῾Εκατόμνω Λαγινέας, Ιδβελαν Μυός,
Υργοσων Υσσαλδομου Ωνδρέας, ὅπως
ἂν τὸ δόγμα ἀναγραφῆι ἐν στήληι λιθί-
νηι καὶ σταθῆι ἐν τῶι τεμένει τõ ᾿Απόλλω-
νος καὶ τῆς ᾿Αρτέμιδος. ῎Εδωκαν δὲ Κω-
ρανζεῖς. Καὶ ὃς ἂν τοῦ μνήματος τοῦ
Σκωράνου ἐπιμελῆται, τῶν δούλων ἀτε-
[λῆ εἶναι καὶ πάντω]ν πλὴμ φόρωμ βασιλικῶν.

21-22. ἀτε|[λῆ εἶναι καὶ πάντω]ν or ἀτε|[λῆ εἶναι καὶ ἄλλω]ν; the available space is not enough for καὶ τῶν ἄλλων Şahin.

1230. STRATONIKEIA, SALE OF A VINEYARD, 276 B.C. SEG, XV, 652. M.Ç. Şahin, The Political and Religious Structure in the Territory of Stratonikeia in Caria (Ankara, 1976) 4-5 makes the following remarks: L. 11. the name may have been Δεροωμανης ΝΩΤΡΑ..; 13. perhaps ἐν ...σσου ποτ[αμίσκ]ωι (but cf. J. and L. Robert, Mélanges Isidore Lévy, Brussels, 1955, p. 566, n. 2 who find the word ποταμίσκος too risky); 14. the reading in SEG is .ΩΙΟΙ ὁμ[ο]ρεῖ Λεωνίδ̣η̣[ς]. Şahin opts for ὃν ὁμ[ο]ρεῖ Λεωνίδ̣η̣[ν] (but one cannot accomodate two accusatives ed.).

1231. STRATONIKEIA, DEDICATION OF LAND TO HEKATE SOTEIRA, CA. 39 B.C. Ed. C.T. Newton, A History of Discoveries at Halicarnassus, Cnidus and Branchidae II (London, 1863) 793, no. 98; G. Cousin - G. Deschamps, BCH 11 (1887) 238. Cf. M.Ç. Şahin, The Political and Religious Structure in the Territory of Stratonikeia in Caria (Ankara, 1976) 40-41 who holds that in line 8 and 10 respectively $\overline{ΕΟ}$ and $\overline{ΚΘ}$ were copied incorrectly and were both $\overline{ΚΟ}$, the abbreviated form of the demotic Koliorgeus. He further argues that in line 9 both demotics (Hierokometes and Koliorgeus) refer to the prytanis Artemidoros.

1232. TRALLES, EPITAPH. Ed. pr. M. Pappakonstantinou, Αἱ Τράλλεις (Athens, 1895) no. 53 (dr.). Cf. R. Merkelbach, ZPE 21 (1976) 156 who republishes the inscription with some restorations.

᾿Ακέσω[ν ...]σιμει-
νους ὠ[νησά]μενος
παρὰ Τ[....]ξωσθι
ωρητ[.....]ριτου
[.]ερα[.....]αργου
[κ]ατε[σκεύα]σεν ἐκ
τῶν ἰ[δίων] <σ>ὺν τῷ
παντ[ὶ]αὐτοῦ
κόσμ[φ]τῷ λευ-
κολίθ[φ]πρὸς ὃ
θωρα[κεῖον] αὐτῷ
[ ]ς καὶ

1. e.g. ᾿Ακε]σιμέ{ι}νους Merkelbach || 4. πε]ρί? Merkelbach || 12. e.g. [εἴσοδο]ς καὶ [γυναικὶ κτλ. Merkelbach.

1233. TRAPEZOPOLIS, EPIGRAM FOR THE WRESTLER HERMES, (BEGINNING?) 3rd CENT. A.D. MAMA, VI, 61 (ph.). After R. Merkelbach, ZPE 19 (1975) 301-302, J.E. Ebert - W. Luppe, ZPE 23 (1976) 49-56 return to this text and offer a facsimile-drawing based on the photo of the squeeze in MAMA. We present the following text:

].ων αὐτοκρατόρων ..[
].ιων τὸν ἀγῶνα vac.
ẹ̓νθάδε παρὰ ἀθλοθετῆρι μακαρτῷ | Ζευξιθέῳ β΄(=δὶς)
εὐπατρίδῃ τῇδε Τραπεζοπόλει |
χαλκοῦν ἀνδριάντα τὰ Πύθια τοῦτον ὁ|ρᾶται·
νεικῶ τούσδε πάλην, ἐστὶ δέ μοι τοὔ|ν[ο]μα Ἑρμῆς·
οὐκ οἶτ΄, εἴτε ἀλκῇ τόσσον σθένι | ἠέ τις ἡμεῖν
ἀθάνατος δαίμων ὤπασαι κῦδος | ἔχειν.

1-2. Prose lines, Ebert - Luppe; Ebert tentatively proposes: -- τῶν κυρίων ἡ]μ̣ῶν αὐτοκρατόρων [ἐ]ν̣[ι]|[κα τῶν ἀγεν]ε̣ίων τὸν ἀγῶνα; [τίς ποθ΄ ὁ νεικήσας λίθινον κατὰ βαθρικὸν οὗτος̣]| τ̣ῶν αὐτοκρατόρων Ἐπ̣[ινεικε]ίων τὸν ἀγῶνα MAMA; [Name des Siegers im Genitiv, τοῦ νικήσαντος ---] | τῶν αὐτοκρατόρων ἐπ[ινεικε]ίων τὸν ἀγῶνα Merkelbach; MAMA and Merkelbach connect the Epinikia with the Severi || 3. ἔνθα{δε} Merkelbach and Luppe || Ζευξιθέῳ (τῷ) (Ζευξιθέου) Merkelbach || 4. Ebert considers but rejects the possibility of εὐπατρίδῃ <κόσμον> or <κόσμῳ> τῇδε κτλ.; Luppe plays with εὐπατρίδῃ, <ταμίᾳ> and above all with εὐπατρίδῃ <προκαθηγη>τῆι δὲ Τραπεζοπολει[τῶν], which seems rather rash || 6. ἐστὶ<ν> δέ μοι {τ}οὔνομα Merkelbach and Luppe || 7. οὐκ | οἶδ΄ εἴτ΄ ἀλκῇ<ς> σθέν(ε) Merkelbach. On coins from Trapezopolis, dating from Iulia Domna's time, an archon Zeuxitheos is mentioned (MAMA).

IONIA

1234. DIDYMA, HONORARY DECREE FOR APAME, 299 B.C. SEG, IV, 442; I. Didyma, no. 480. H. Müller, Milesische Volksbeschlüsse. Eine Untersuchung zur Verfassungsgeschichte der Stadt Milet in hellenistischer Zeit (Hypomnemata 14; Göttingen 1976), p. 21, note 8 proposes to read in L. 27 f. Ἀριστ[οφῶμ] Μιννίωνος instead of Ἀριστ[είδης] Μιννίωνος.

1235. DIDYMA, BUILDING INSCRIPTION, 165-164 B.C. Ed. pr. W. Günther, MDAI(I) 19-20 (1969-1970) 237 ff. J. Ebert, PHILOLOGUS 120 (1976) 126-127 proposes the following text for the prescript:

[Ἐπὶ στεφανηφόρου Λυσήους τοῦ ca.5-6]
[.ου, προφητεύον]τ̣ος Θράσυ̣[ο]ς̣ [τοῦ Ἀρκε]-
[σιλάου], ταμιευόντων δὲ καὶ παρεδρευ-
όντων ἐν τῶ<ι> ἱερῶι κτλ.

---

1. Cf. I. Didyma, no. 469 || 2. [ου, προφητεύον]τ̣ος <δὲ> Θρασ[ύου]ς̣ Günther || 4. ἐν τῷ Günther.

1236. EPHESOS, AWARD OF CITIZENSHIP TO A CITIZEN OF KYRENE (PROBABLY AN EQUESTRIAN VICTOR), 4th CENT. B.C. Ed. pr. D. Knibbe, JÖAI 49 (BEIBLATT, 1968-1971) 50, no. 20. H. Engelmann, ZPE 22 (1976) 84 restores in L. 2 of the prescript [εἰς πολιτεία]ν or [πολιτείας ἐ]ν ἴσωι νόμωι and in L. 4 [Θαργηλιῶ]νος. The formula in L. 2 refers to the subject-matter of the decree. Cf. J. and L. Robert, BE (1977) no. 434.

1237. EPHESOS, INSCRIPTION OF A DIONYSIAN SANCTUARY, 4th - 3rd CENT. B.C. Limestone block. Ed. pr. D. Knibbe, JÖAI 50 (BEIBLATT, 1972-75) 21-26, no. 8 (ph.).

ἱερὸν Διονύσου καὶ ΕΝΕΔΡΑ[.]
2 ὀρειογυάδων 4 εἶναι. vac.

3. Ἐνέδρα[ς]: personification of ἐνέδρα ("ambush") Knibbe || 2-4. "Syllabes énigmatiques" J. and L. Robert, BE (1977) no. 416.

1238. EPHESOS, HONORARY INSCRIPTION FOR A HIGH PERGAMENE OFFICIAL, CA. 150 B.C. White marble block. Ed. pr. D. Knibbe, l.c., 12-14, no. 4 (ph.).

[Δημ]ήτριον Ἀπολλων[ίο]υ
[τὸν γ]ενόμενον ἐπὶ τ[ῆ]ς
3 [σφρα]γῖδος τοῦ βασιλέως Θεοῦ
[Εὐμέ]νου Σωτῆρος καὶ στρατη-
[γὸν ἐ]πί τε Ἐφέσου καὶ τῶν κατ᾽ Ἔ-
6 [φεσο]ν τόπων καὶ Καΰστρου πε-
[δίον] καὶ τὸ Κιλβιανὸν ΔΗΜΗ-
[..]Σ̣

6-7. πε|[δίου] Knibbe, corr. Herrmann.

1239. EPHESOS, LETTER OF ATTALOS II, PRAISING THE TUTOR OF HIS NEPHEW (= ATTALOS III), CA. 150-140 B.C. Ed. pr. D. Knibbe, JÖAI 47 (BEIBLATT, 1964-65) 3-4 (with J. and L. Robert, BE, 1968, no. 464). Cf. also H. Engelmann, ZPE 19 (1975) 224 and P. Herrmann, ZPE 22 (1976) 233-234. We present the following text:

[Βασιλεὺς Ἄτταλος Ἐ]φεσίων τῆι βουλῆι καὶ τῶι δήμωι χαίρειν· Ἀριστο[......]
[.........] πολίτης θ᾽ ὑμῶν κριθεὶς ἄξιος ὑφ᾽ ἡμῶν εἶναι τῆς Ἀττάλου τάδελ[φοῦ]

[υἱοῦ ἐπιμε]λ̣είας μετεπέμφθη καὶ συσταθεὶς αὐτῶι τῆς καθη[κ]ούσης παιδείας
[προενόη]σ̣ε, πολὺ δὲ μᾶλλον ὑφ' ἡμῶν ἀπεδέχθη διὰ τὸ μὴ μόνον ἐν τῆι τῶν λόγων ἐνπει-
[ρίᾳ καὶ π]αραδόσει προέχειν πολλῶν ἀλλ' ὅτι καὶ τῶι ἤθει τοῦ παντὸς ἐφαίνετ' ἄξιος
[ἐπαίν]ου καὶ ἐπιτηδειότατος νέωι συναναστρέφεσθαι, ὅτι γὰρ ζηλοῦσι τὰς ἀγωγὰς
[τῶν ἐ]πιστάτων οἱ ἐκ φύσεως καλοκάγαθικοὶ τῶν νέων, παντὶ πρόδηλόν ἐστιν, δι' ὃ
[δὴ] οὗτος οὐ μόνον ὑφ' ἡμῶν ἀλλὰ καὶ ὑπ' αὐτοῦ τοῦ Ἀττάλου σφόδρα προσηνῶς
[ἀ]ποδεχθεὶς δικαίας παρ' ἡμῖν καὶ παρὰ τούτωι ἐτύγχανεν ἐπισημασίας.

2-3. Herrmann; Ἀττάλου<υ> ἀδελ[φι]|[δοῦ μου] Knibbe, Robert || 3. παιδεί]ας Knibbe, Robert; ἐπιμε]λείας Herrmann || 4. [ἕνεκα] πολύ Knibbe; [προέστη] Robert; [προενόη]σ̣ε Herrmann || 5. we print Robert's restorations; [ρίας π]αραδόσει προέχειν πολλῶν ἄλλο τι Knibbe || 6. Engelmann's restoration; [τοῦ Ἀττάλ]ου Knibbe || 8. [δή] added by Herrmann ("aus Raumgründen").

1240. EPHESOS, HONORARY INSCRIPTION FOR AN ATHLETE, CA. 50 B.C. White marble block. Ed. pr. D. Knibbe, JÖAI 50 (BEIBLATT, 1972-75) 14-15, no. 5 (ph.).

[Ἡ βουλὴ καὶ ὁ δῆ]μος
[Μόσχο]ν Ταυρέου τοῦ
[Χαροπίνο]υ, νικήσαντα
[τοὺς ὑπο]γεγραμμένους
[ἀ]γῶνας· vac.

1241. EPHESOS, DECREE ABOUT THE PROTECTION OF THE ALTAR OF ARTEMIS, 40-39 B.C. Marble statue-base, broken below. Ed. pr. D. Knibbe, l.c., 2-6, no. 1 (ph.).

Ἔτους δεκάτου τῆς Γαίου Ἰουλίου Καίσα-
ρος νίκης, ἐπὶ πρυτάνεως Ἀράτου
τοῦ Ἀράτου τοῦ Ἀρτέμωνος, μηνὸς Μαι-
μακτῆρος ἐνάτῃ ἱσταμένου,
Ἡρόφιλος Μηνοδώρου τοῦ Σώτου Πάννη-
ος ὁ γραμματεὺς τοῦ δήμου καὶ οἱ στρα-
τηγοὶ τῆς πόλεως Ἀπολλωνίδης Διομ[έ]-
δοντος, Ἡρακλείδης Ἡρακλείδου τοῦ Ἡρ[α]-
κλείδου, Ἀπολλώνιος Ἀπολλωνίου τοῦ
[Δημ]ητρίου, Τίμων Ἀρτεμιδώρου νεώ-
[τερος, Μ]ηνότιμος Μηνοτίμου τοῦ [Δι]ονυσίου,
[ἐνεφάνισαν?] οἵδε καὶ περὶ τοῦ εἰσενεγ-
[κεῖν ψήφισμα περὶ] τῆς βωμοφυλακίας

[τῆς --------'Αρτέ]μιδος καὶ τῶν παρẹ-
[δρευόντων ---------] δειάταξιν
[ca. 27] 'Αρτέμ[ι]-
[δ..

This text clarifies the chronology of Forschungen in Ephesos, 2, 155 ff. (list of agonothetai); cf. also J. and L. Robert, BE (1972) no. 388 || 13-14. for εἰσφέρειν ψήφισμα cf. L. Robert, Le Sanctuaire de Sinuri, I, p. 32 || 15. [τῆς ἀρχηγετίδος 'Αρτέ]μιδος Knibbe || 15-16. τῶν παρη|[δρευομένων θεῶν κατὰ τὴν] Knibbe; τῶν παρẹ|[δρευόντων ---] ("gens détachés dans le sanctuaire") J. and L. Robert, BE (1977) no. 414.

1242. EPHESOS, SENATUS CONSULTUM, END OF THE ROMAN REPUBLICAN PERIOD. Right half of a white marble base. Ed. pr. D. Knibbe, JÖAI 50 (BEIBLATT, 1972-75) 6-9, no. 2 (ph.).

[ca. 43]ων ἐν κομετίωι. Γραφομένῳ παρῆσαν· vacat
[ca. 43] Μᾶρκος Αἰμύλιος Μάρκου υἱὸς Μάρκου υἱ[ωνὸς ....]
3 [-- περὶ τούτου τοῦ πράγματο]ς οὕτως ἔδοξεν· οἵτινες δῆμοι ἔθνη τε[...........]

1243. EPHESOS, PART OF A LARGE CATALOGUE OF NAMES, 27-26 B.C. (L. 1-11) AND (AFTER?) 26-25 B.C. (L. 12-16). White marble block. Ed. pr. D. Knibbe, l.c., 15-20, no. 6 (ph.).

'Απολλώνιος 'Ηρακλείδου τοῦ — (='Ηρακλείδου)
Πασσαλᾶς, ὃς καὶ προενοήθη τῆς
καθιδρύσεως τοῦ Σεβαστοῦ
καὶ τῆς καθιερώσεως
τοῦ τεμένους,
Πρέσβων 'Ανταίου, ἱερεὺς Διονύσου α'
Φλέω Ποιμαντρίου,
Περικλῆς 'Ηρακλείδου φύσει δὲ Χα-
ροπίνου Χαροπῖνος, ἱερονείκης ἀπ[ὸ]
συνόδου,
'Ηρακλείδης 'Απολλᾶ τοῦ Ζηνοδ[ότου],
'Αριστώναξ Εὔφρονος,
'Ισίδωρος 'Απολλωνίδου τοῦ 'Απο[λ]-
λωνίδου ὁ ἱερεὺς Καρποφόρου Γῆ[ς],
Πρέσβων 'Ανταίου, ἱερεὺς Διο-
[νύσ]ου τὸ β' καὶ π̣[..

6. α'= not τὸ πρῶτον (Knibbe) but πρῶτος: "premier prêtre de Dionysos adoré sous les épithètes de Phleus et Poimantrios" J. and L. Robert, BE (1977) no. 415, p. 393 || 9-10. ἱερονείκης ἀπ[ὸ] | συνόδου: cf. the parallels given by J. and L. Robert, BE (1977) no. 415, p. 393 || 16. καὶ π̣[ρυ]|[τανεύσας (Knibbe, l.c., 19, note 61) or per-

haps π̣[ρύ]|[τανις ...; in the latter case L. 12-16 date from 26-25 B.C., the year of Presboon's prytany.

1244. EPHESOS, HONORARY INSCRIPTION FOR C. IULIUS KLEON, 54-59 A.D. Ed. pr. D. Knibbe, JÖAI 47 (BEIBLATT, 1964-65) 18-19 (ph.). Cf. H. Engelmann, ZPE 20 (1976) 86 who finds Iulius Kleon also mentioned on coins from his native town Eumeneia. His father Epigonos is identical with the Eumeneian Ἐπίγονος φιλόπατρις on coins from the reign of Tiberius.

1245. EPHESOS, HONORARY DECREE, END 1st CENT. A.D. Fragments of a large marble stone. Ed. pr. D. Knibbe, JÖAI 50 (BEIBLATT, 1972-75) 33-36, no. 3 (ph.).

A.
[Ἀγα]θῇ · Τύχη̣.
[Ἔ]δοξεν τῇ βο[υλῇ]
[κ]αὶ τῷ νεωκόρ[ῳ δήμῳ]
φιλοσεβάστοι[ς· περὶ ὧν]
ἐνεφάνισ[α]ν – Μᾶρκος
Τιγέλλ[ιος Μ]άρκου υἱὸς
Μάρκ[ου (υἱωνὸς)] Λ[οῦπος] φιλοκαῖσαρ
ὁ γρ[αμ]ματεὺ[ς τ]οῦ δήμου
[καὶ] οἱ στρατηγοὶ τῆς πόλε-
ως φιλ[ο]σέβαστοι·
ἐπεὶ τοῖς νέοις τῶν Σεβασ-
τείων ἔ[ρ]γων μεγεθέσιν
καὶ ἡ τῶν παλαιῶν κτισμά-
[τω]ν ἀν[α]νέωσις ἔπρεπεν
[..]ν̣τα[.]ωρούντων τῶν εὐ-
[τυχ]εστ[ά]των καιρῶν τοῦ
[θεῶν ἐμφ]ανεστάτου Αὐτο-
[κράτορος ? ------------]

B.
[ἐπ]ανορθ[ω ---- γενέσ]-
θαι χρόνω[ν ---------]
πῳ προσ[------------]
χείας· ΤΑ[-----------]
μεγε[θ---------------]

C.
ẠΚΥΑΣ[------------------ μέγε]-
θος ἀπο[------------------ με]-
γαλοπρεπ[εσ------------------]
-τῶν [---------------]
δεδόχ[θαι τῇ βουλῇ καὶ τῷ δήμῳ]·
ἐξεῖν[αι ---------------------]
[.]ΥΡ̣Ε[------------------------]

D.
[--------]ΤΑΧΕ[------------------]

[--------]δοῦναι ΤΑ[-------]
[--------]ρον διὰ τ[--------]
[----------]ΟΥΣΩ[------------]
[-------------]Ν[-----------]

E.

[----------]ΣΙ[-------------]
[-----------]ΣΕ[------------]
[----------]ΣΩ[-------------]
[----------]ΩΝΕΔ̣[-----------]
[----------]ἀπο[------------]

A 11-12. For Σεβάστεια ἔργα cf. the expression Σεβάστεια χρήματα, JÖAI 11 (1908) 101 (money given by the Emperor or money destined for the imperial cult) || 15-16. εὐ|[πρεπ]εστ[ά]των Knibbe; εὐ|[τυχ]εστ[ά]των L. Robert, RPH 51 (1977) 13-14 || 17. [? ἐπιφ]ανεστάτου Knibbe; [θεῶν ἐμφ]ανεστάτου G. Petzl, ZPE 31 (1978) 227-228.

1246. EPHESOS, HONORARY INSCRIPTION FOR L. VIBIUS LENTULUS, BETWEEN 98-106 A.D. Fragment of a white marble base. Ed. pr. D. Knibbe, JÖAI 50 (BEIBLATT, 1972-75) 57-58, no. 1 (ph.). For lines 1-5, cf. H. Engelmann, ZPE 24 (1977) 204, no. 5 (ph.).

[Λ.] Οὐείβιον Γ[αίου υἱόν],
[Αἰ]μιλία Λέντ[ουλον],
[ἐ]πίτροπον Α[ὐτοκράτορος]
Νέρβα Τραι[ανοῦ Καίσαρος]
[Σ]εβαστοῦ ἀπὸ τῶ[ν] λό[γων],
[λωρ]εικάτης, Ἀσίας, Π[αννο]-
[ν]ίας, Δαλματίας, μο[νήτης],
ἔπαρχον εἴλης Φλ[αουίας]
πολειτῶν Ῥωμαίω[ν, χειλίαρ]-
χον·λεγιῶνος·ζ'·π[είας]
φιδήλεως, ἔπαρχ[ον τεκτόνων],
βοηθῷ·Λ·Πομπ[ηίου Οὐοπίσ]-
κου·Κατελλίου [Κέλερος ὁδῶν]
ναῶν ἱερῶν τό[πων τε δημοσίων].
Τιβέριος Ἰού[....]
Κον[----------]

1-5. H. Engelmann thinks that a fragment of five lines (copy of Benndorf and mentioned by Heberdey and Keil) forms the upper part of the inscription. Knibbe had restored these lines as follows: [Λ. Οὐείβιον Γαίου υἱὸν] | [Λέντουλον, ἐπίτροπον] | [Αὐτοκράτορος Νέρουα] | [Τραιανοῦ Καίσαρος Σε]|[βαστο]ῦ κτλ.; the text of Knibbe begins with the Y of Σεβαστοῦ || 6. [Λωρ]εικάτης Knibbe || 13. [Κέλερος ἐπὶ] Knibbe, but cf. Année Épigraphique (1924) 81 ed.

1247. EPHESOS, HONORARY INSCRIPTION FOR TI. CLAUDIUS TUENDIANUS

JR., 1st - 2nd CENT. A.D. Marble base. Ed. pr. D. Knibbe, l.c., 59-63, no. 3 (ph.). Cf. J. and L. Robert, BE (1977) no. 420.

῾Η βουλὴ καὶ ὁ
δῆμος ἐτείμ[ησαν]
Τι·Κλαύδιον, Τιβ[ερίου]
Κλαυδίου Τουενδ[ια]-
νοῦ Μάγνου τρὶς χει[λι]-
άρχου καὶ πρυτάνεω[ς]
καὶ Κλαυδίας, Τιβερίου
θυγατρός, Χαριδημίδος
υἱόν, θυγρατριδοῦν ᾿Ιουλίου
Κάρου·δὶς πρυτάνεως·, Κυρεί-
να·Τουενδιανὸν·νεώτερον
τὸν πρύτανιν·καὶ ἀγωνοθέ-
την τῶν πρὸ πόλεως·ἱερέων
καὶ ἱερονεικῶν·πρυτανεύσαν-
τα·ἀξίως τοῦ γένους·καὶ τῆς πατρίδος.
Ποιησαμένης τὴν ἀνάστασιν τοῦ
ἀνδριάντος·Κλαυδίας Χαριδημίδος
τῆς μητρὸς αὐτοῦ, ἥτις καὶ τὴν πρυτα-
νείαν ὑπὲρ τοῦ υἱοῦ ἐκ τῶν ἰδίων·ἐποιή-
σατο.

4-5. Τουενδ[ια]|νοῦ: probably a Latin name Tuendianus J. and L. Robert, l.c., no. 420, p. 397- 398 || 12-14. for these lines, cf. J. and L. Robert, l.c., no. 420, p. 398-399.

1248. EPHESOS, LIST OF NAMES, CA. 120 A.D. Lower part of a white marble base, broken into two joining parts and inscribed on two sides. Ed. pr. D. Knibbe, l.c., 46-48, no. 14 (ph.).

A. Front:

[Μᾶρ]κος [Οὔλ]πιος
῎Αλυπος σὺν Μάρκῳ
Οὐλπίῳ Μάρκου υἱῷ
Σεργία Πείῳ ᾿Ολυμπίῳ
υἱῷ.
Νεοκοροῦντος Γ. Κασκελλίου
Γαίου υἱοῦ Κολ(λίνα)·Πολιτικοῦ.

B. Right side:

[....Κα]ρπο[φό]ρου
[....γέ]νης ῎Ερωτος
[....]γένης — τοῦ ῎Ερ[ωτος]
[...]κλῆς Μητρ[οδώρου]
[᾿Απ]ολ[λ]ώνιος — τοῦ — το[ῦ —]
[῎Α]τταλος — Φωτεῖν[ος]
᾿Αθηναγόρας — τοῦ Συ[.....]
῾Ερμογένης ᾿Απολλω[νίου]
Διονύσιος Τρύφων[ος]

Εἰσίδωρος Ἀγαθοκ[λέους]
Τρόφιμος Ἡρακλείδ[ους]
Νεικομήδης·γ'·[--------]
Πλουτίων·β'·τοῦ·Μ[-----]
τοῦ Ἑρμίου.

A. 5. υἱῷ seems an unnecessary repetition || 6-7. perhaps identical with Κασκέλλιος [Πον]τικός in GIBM, III, no. 486 (27 Sept. 120 A.D.) Knibbe || B. In lines 3, 5, 6, 7 the patronymics are indicated on the stone by —.

1249. EPHESOS, HONORARY INSCRIPTION FOR THE HIGH PRIEST TIMAEUS, BETWEEN 170-184/5 A.D. Fragments of a statue base. Ed. pr. D. Knibbe, JÖAI 50 (1972-75) 30-33, no. 2 (ph.). Cf. J. and L. Robert, BE (1977) no. 417.

[Τῆς πρώτης καὶ μεγ]ίστης μητροπ[όλε]ως τῆς Ἀσίας καὶ δὶ[ς νεωκό]-
[ρου τῶν Σεβαστῶ]ν Ἐφεσίων πόλεως [ἡ βο]υλὴ καὶ ὁ δῆμος ἐτ[είμησαν]
Τείμαιον Ἀττ[άλ]ου, ἀρχιερέα Ἀσίας ν[αῶν] τῶ[ν ἐ]ν Ἐφέ[σ]ῳ κα[ὶ γυν]αῖκα
αὐτοῦ Ἀπφίλλαν Μενάνδρου συν[αρχ]ιερασ[αμ]ένην αὐτῷ [καὶ υἱὸ]ν αὐ-
τ[οῦ Ἀκ]ύλαν, φιλοτείμως καὶ ἐκτ[ε]νῶς ἐ[κτε]λέσ[α]ντα τὴ[ν ἀρχ]ιερω-
σύνην, δόντα δὲ καὶ εἰς τὸν ΤΟ̣[ca.5-6]ΤΟ[.]ΚΑΙΣ[.]ΡΟΣΝΕ̣[----]ΕΡ τῶν
κυνηγεσίων ἀργυρίου δηναρίω[ν μ]υριά[δα]ς ἑπτά, ἀγων[οθετ]ήσαντα
τῶν τε μεγάλων Ἐπιν[εικίων] καὶ τοῦ [Κ]οινοῦ τῆς Ἀ[σίας] ἐν [Ἐφέσ]ῳ.
[.ca.7.. Π]αυλεῖνο[ς ....ca.15......] ἀνέσ[τ]ησεν [τῇ γλυ]-
[κυτά]τῃ πατ[ρίδι καθὼς ὑπέσ]χ[ετο τῷ δήμῳ ? -----------].

5-6. τή[ν τε] ἱερω|σύνην Knibbe; τὴ[ν ἀρχ]ιερω|σύνην J. and L. Robert || 6. εἰς τὸν τό[πον τῆς] το[ῦ] Καίσ[α]ρος νε[ίκης ὑπ]ὲρ Knibbe, who interprets these words as follows: "Wie oben ἔτος δέκατον τῆς Γαίου Ἰουλίου Καίσαρος νίκης (cf. no. 1241, L. 1-2) möchten wir auch τόπος τῆς τοῦ Καίσαρος νίκης auf den Sieg Caesars bei Pharsalos beziehen, doch käme auch der Sieg Octavians bei Aktium durchaus in Frage"; for a more probable interpretation cf. J. and L. Robert, l.c. || 7. μ]υριάκ[ι]ς Knibbe; μ]υριά[δα]ς J. and L. Robert || 11. ὑπέσ]χ[ετο ἐν τῷ δήμῳ ? ------] Knibbe.

1250. EPHESOS, HONORARY INSCRIPTION FOR T. FL. LOLLIANUS ARISTOBOULOS, CA. 175-200 A.D. White marble base. Ed. pr. D. Knibbe, l.c., 63-65, no. 4 (ph.).

Τ·Φλ·Λολλιανὸν
Ἀριστόβουλον
συνκλητικόν,
υἱὸν Γαίου·Φλ·
Φουρίου Ἄπτου.
Γ·Φλ·Διονύσιος
Πρωρεσιανὸς
τὸν ἴδιον
εὐεργέτην.

1251. EPHESOS, HONORARY INSCRIPTION FOR P. VEDIUS ANTONINUS, 2nd CENT. A.D. White marble base. Ed. pr. D. Knibbe, l.c., 71-72, no. 3 (ph.).

[Ἡ βουλὴ καὶ ὁ δῆμος τῆς πρώτης καὶ]
μεγίστης μητροπόλεως·τῆς Ἀσίας [καὶ]
δὶς νεοκόρου·τῶν Σεβαστῶν Ἐφεσίων
πόλεως·ἐτείμησαν·Πόπλιον·
Οὐήδιον·Ἀντωνεῖνον, χειλίαρχον
λεγιῶνος πρώτης·Ἰταλικῆς.

1252. EPHESOS, HONORARY INSCRIPTION FOR TI. CLAUDIUS ZENON, 2nd CENT. A.D. Three fragments of a white marble base. Ed. pr. D. Knibbe, l.c., 37-39, no. 6 (ph.).

Τιβ. Κλ·Ζήνωνα [-------------------]
δὶς ἀσιάρχη[ν ναῶν τῶν ἐν Ἐφέσῳ]
αὐθαίρετον δι[---------------------]
καὶ γυμνασί]αρ[χον? ---------------]

3. For αὐθαίρετος cf. L. Robert, OMS, I, 288.

1253. EPHESOS, HONORARY INSCRIPTION FOR GAVIUS IUNIOR, 2nd HALF 2nd CENT. A.D. Right half of a white marble base. Ed. pr. D. Knibbe, l.c., 40, no. 10 (ph.).

[Ψηφίσματι τῆ]ς βουλῆς καὶ
[τοῦ δήμου ..] Γαουίῳ
[........... υἱ]ῷ Ἰουνιόρι

1254. EPHESOS, HONORARY INSCRIPTION, CA. 200 A.D. Fragments of a white marble base. Ed. pr. D. Knibbe, l.c., 35-36, no. 4 (ph.).

[--------- ἀδελφι]δῆν
[Λ. Κοσσωνίου Ἐγγί]ου
[Μ]αρύλ[λου τ]οῦ
ἀνθυ[πάτου Ἀφρι]κῆς,
θεω[ρὸν τῶν Ὀ]λυμπίων.
Προν[οη]σαμ[έν]ου τῆς
ἀνασ[τ]άσεως [Φο]υρίου
Ἑσπ[έρ]ου φιλ[οσεβ]άστο[υ].

5. Cf. L. Robert, CRAI (1974) 176-181.

1255. EPHESOS, HONORARY INSCRIPTION FOR THE GOVERNOR M. CLAUDIUS PUPIENUS MAXIMUS, EARLY THIRD CENT. A.D. Fragments of a white marble base. Ed. pr. D. Knibbe, JÖAI 50 (BEIBLATT, 1972-75) 39, no. 7 (ph.).

Ἀγαθῆι Τύχηι.
[Μ.] Κλώδιον·Πουπιῆνον
Μάξιμον
τὸν λαμπρότ[ατον ἀν]θύπατον

For the chronology of Pupienus' career, cf. K. Dietz, CHIRON 6 (1976) 394-395.

1256. EPHESOS, HONORARY INSCRIPTION FOR CARACALLA. Left half of a white marble base. Ed. pr. D. Knibbe, l.c., 40, no. 9 (ph.).

Ἀγαθῇ [Τύχῃ].
Αὐτοκράτ[ορα Καίσαρα]
τὸν τῆς οἰκ[ουμένης σωτῆρα?]
Μ. Αὐ[ρήλιον Ἀντωνῖνον]

1257. EPHESOS, HONORARY INSCRIPTION, BETWEEN 213-217 A.D. Two fragments of a white marble base. Ed. pr. D. Knibbe, l.c., 36-37, no. 5 (ph.).

[Αὐτοκράτορα Καίσαρα]
[Μ. Αὐρήλιον Ἀντωνῖνον]
[εὐσ]εβῆ ε[ὐτυχῆ Σεβασ]-
[τὸν Πα]ρθικὸ[ν μέγιστον]
[Βρι]ταννι[κὸν μέγιστον]
[Γε]ρμανικὸν [μέγιστον]
τὸν τῆς πα[τρίδος]
εὐεργέ[την καὶ]
ἑαυτο[ῦ σωτῆρα]
[Τι. Κ]λ·Κλεό[βουλος ....]

1258-1261. EPHESOS, FOUR HONORARY INSCRIPTIONS FOR ATHLETES, CA. 225 A.D. ? (1258-1260) AND 235-238 A.D. (1261). Four small white marble columns, re-used in the so-called Bath of Varius. Ed. pr. D. Knibbe, l.c., 48-56, no. 15 (ph.). Cf. W. Eck, ZPE 25 (1977) 231-233 (especially on the chronology of Lollianus Avitus' proconsulship of Asia Minor: ca. 225 A.D.) and J. and L. Robert, BE (1977) no. 419.

1258. Μάριος Σεπτίμιος
Μαρίων φιλοσέβ(αστος)
ἀθλοθέτης διὰ βίου
τῶν μ[ε]γάλων Μαριανῶ[ν]
Ἰσθμίων
Μ·Αὐρ. [Ἀ]σκληπιάδην
Ἐφέσιον καὶ Ἠλεῖον
καὶ Ἀθη[ν]αῖον παλαιστὴ[ν],

νεική[σα]ντα ἐνδόξως τὸν
ἀγῶνα τῶν Μαριανῶν νέω[ν]
Ἰσθμίων [ὑ]πὸ ἐπιστάτην Αὐ(ρ).
Νεικίαν [Ἐ]φέσιον. Ἐπετελέσθ[η]
ὁ ἀγὼν ἀνθ[υπάτῳ] Λολλιανῷ Ἀουίτῳ,
καὶ μετὰ τοῦτο νεικήσαν[τα]
Ὀλύμπια ἐμ Πείσῃ τὸν πρῶτο[ν]
τῆς περιόδου κριθέντα, Ἁδριάνει[α]
ἐν Ἀθήναις, Ἐλευσείνια ἐν Ἀθήν[αις]·
ὑπὸ ἀλείπτην Αὐρ. Λεωνίδαν.

---

6. For M. Aurelius Asklepiades, cf. IG, V, 1, 666 || 11. for ὑπὸ ἐπιστάτην cf. e.g. L. Robert, Et. Anat., 139, note 2 || 15-16. for the interpretation of these lines, cf. J. and L. Robert, l.c., no. 419, p. 395-396.

1259. Μάριος Σε[πτίμι]ος
Μαρίων φ[ιλοσέ]βαστος
ἀθλοθέτ[ης διὰ] βίου τῶν
μεγ[άλων Μαρια]νῶν
Ἰσθμίων [Μᾶρκος] Αὐρ.
Ζωτικὸς [ὁ καὶ ..]π̣ιννης,
Καισαρεὺ[ς Τραλ]λιανὸς
[κ]αὶ Ἐφέσι[ος πα]λαιστὴς,
νεικήσας ἐ[νδόξ]ως τὸν
[ἀ]γῶναν τ[ῆς πάλ]ης τῶν
μεγάλων Μ[αριανῶ]ν
[Ἰσθμίων].
[Ἐ]πετελέσθ[η ὁ ἀγ]ὼν
[ἀ]νθυπατ[εύοντ]ος
Λολλιανο[ῦ Ἀουί]του·
ὑπὸ ἐπισ[τάτη]ν
Τρο[φιμί]ωνα
γʹ.

1260. Ἀγ[αθῆ]ι Τύχῃ.
Μάριο[ς Σε]πτίμιος
Μαρ[ίων φι]λοσέβαστος
ἀθλο[θέτη]ς διὰ βίου
τῶν με[γάλω]ν Μαριανῶν
Ἰσθμί[ων. Μ]ᾶρκος Αὐρ.
Χρήσ[ιμος ὁ] καὶ Γρηγόρις,
Καισαρ[εὺς Τ]ραλλιανὸς
καὶ Ἐφέ[σιος] πανκρατιά-
στης ν[εικήσ]ας ἐνδόξως
τὸν ἀγῶ[να τοῦ] πανκρατί-
ου τῶν μ[εγάλ]ων Μαριανῶν
[Ἰσθμίων].
Ἐπετελέ[σθη ὁ] ἀγὼν ἀν-
θυπατ[εύον]τος Λολ-
λιανο[ῦ Ἀου]ίτου· ὑπὸ
ἐπιστ[άτη]ν Τροφι-
μίω[να] γʹ.

1261. ------------------------------
[Αὐτοκράτορος Καίσαρος Γ. Ἰουλ.]
Ο[[ὐήρου Μαξιμί]]νου Σεβαστο[ῦ]
κα[ὶ υἱ]οῦ αὐτοῦ Καίσαρος Γ. Ἰουλ.
Μ[[αξιμίν]]ου Σεβαστοῦ Ἐπινείκια.
Αὐ[ρ. Β]ασιλέα Κεδ̣ά̣χ̣ου Ἐφέσιον
ν[εική]σαντα ἐνδόξως τὰ μεγάλα
Πύθια ἐν Ἐφέσῳ.
Μ[άριο]ς Σεπτίμιος Μαρίων
ὁ [φιλο]σέβ(αστος) γραμματεὺς δήμου
[καὶ ἀγω]νοθέτης διὰ αἰῶνος καὶ

[Μάρι]ος Σεπτίμιος Μαριανὸς
[ἐκ φ]υσεωμάτων ἀγωνοθέτης
[διὰ αἰ]ῶνος τῶν μεγάλω<ν> Πυθίω<ν>
τὴν τειμὴν ἀνέστησ<αν>·
ἀνθυπατεύοντος
[Οὐ]αλερίου Μεσσάλα·
ἀγωνοθεσία ε'.
[Ν]εικήσας δὲ καὶ ἐν Ὑπαίποις
Ἀρτεμ[ί]σια [------------]

4. On Ἐπινείκια in general, cf. L. Robert, OMS, II, 1140-1141 and CRAI (1970) 11 f. || 6-7 and 13. for μεγάλα Πύθια cf. GIBM, III, 618; for Πύθια in general in Asia Minor, cf. L. Robert, Laodicée du Lycos, p. 291, note 2; perhaps one should read in Forschungen in Ephesos, 2, 73 τὰ μεγάλα [Πύ]θια Μαριάνεια (and not Ἀ̣δ̣ριάνεια as M. Lämmer, Olympien und Hadrianeen von Antiken Ephesos, 1967, p. 47 suggested); cf. J. and L. Robert, l.c., no. 419, p. 396-397 || 17. ἀγωνοθεσία ε' = fifth agonothesia and not a reference to pentaeteric Pythia (as Knibbe thinks) J. and L. Robert, l.c., p. 396.

1262. EPHESOS, HONORARY INSCRIPTION FOR AN ATHLETE, CA. 225 A.D. Marble column. Ed. pr. D. Knibbe, JÖAI 50 (BEIBLATT, 1972-75) 54, note 71. For the chronology of Avitus' governorship, cf. W. Eck, ZPE 25 (1977) 231-233.

[νεική]σαντ[α ἐνδόξως]
[τὸν ἀγ]ῶνα τῆς [......]
[τῶν με]γάλων Μαριανῶν.
[Ἐπετε]λέσθη ὁ ἀγὼν ἀνθ(υπατεύοντος)
[Λολλια]νοῦ Ἀουίτου
[ὑπὸ ἐ]πισ{σ}τάτην
[.....]ΠΓΗΝ

1263. EPHESOS, HONORARY INSCRIPTION FOR L. NESENNIUS APOLLINARIS, 1st HALF 3rd CENT. A.D. White marble base. Ed. pr. D. Knibbe, l.c., 43-45, no. 11 (ph.).

Ἀγαθῆι Τύχηι.
Λ. Νεσσήνιον Ἀπολλινάριον

1264. EPHESOS, LIST OF AGORANOMOI, ROMAN IMPERIAL PERIOD. White marble corner-block with two sides inscribed. Ed. pr. D. Knibbe, l.c., 69-71, no. 2 (ph.).

A. (left side): [Ἀγαθῇ]·Τύχῃ.
[....... Διο]νύσιος
[φιλοσέβασ]τος·ἠγορα-

[νόμησεν] ἁγνῶς
[καὶ εὐσ]ταθῶς.
vacat
[Ἀγαθῇ]·Τύχῃ.
[......]λεστος·
[.......]νος φιλοσέ-
[βαστος] ἠγορανό-
[μησεν] ἁγνῶς
[καὶ εὐ]σταθῶς.
[Ἀγαθῇ]·Τύχῃ.
[.......]Ῥουφεῖνος
[φιλοσέβ]ασ{σ}τος·ἠγο-
[ρανόμησεν] ἁγνῶς καὶ
[εὐσταθ]ῶς·οὗ καὶ τ[..]
[..........]ος ἐν

B. (front):

Ἀγαθῇ·Τύχῃ.
Ἐπὶ ἀγορανόμου·Α[ὔλου?]
Ἰουλίου·Διογένους [Μητρο]-
δωριανοῦ·πατρὸς π[ρυτάνεως?]
θείου ἀγορανόμ[ου ἐφ' οὗ]
κόρος·ἁ[γνεία].
vacat
Ἀγαθ[ῇ Τύχῃ].
Ἐπὶ ἀγο[ρανόμου .....]
Σαλβ[ίου ....]

For ἁγνῶς cf. e.g. L. Robert, Hellenica, XIII, 42, note 2; for εὐσταθῶς id., Hellenica, XI-XII, 269, note 2.

1265. EPHESOS, INSCRIPTION OF DIONYSIAC MYSTES, ROMAN IMPERIAL PERIOD. White marble block. Ed. pr. D. Knibbe, l.c., 72-73, no. 4 (ph.).

Οἱ σακηφόρọι μύσ[ται]

1266. EPHESOS, HONORARY INSCRIPTION FOR AN ATHLETE. White marble base. Ed. pr. D. Knibbe, l.c., 58-59, no. 2 (ph.).

νεικήσαντα Ὀλύμπι-
α·ἱερὰ·ἰσελαστικὰ·ἀν-
δρῶν·πάλην·Τιβ·Κλ·
Νύσιο[ς]·ὁ δι' αἰῶνος·ἀ-
[γω]νοθέτη[ς ἀν]έθηκεν·
[ἀ]λυταρχοῦν[τ]ος·Μ·Πομ-
[π]ηίου·Ἀπολλω[νί]ου
[Κ]λαυδιανο[ῦ, ἐπιμελη]-
[θ]έντος τῆς Ὀλυμπιά-
[δο]ς·Μ·Πομπηίου·
[Δη]μέου·Καικιλιανοῦ
τοῦ υ(ἱ)οῦ αὐτοῦ.

1267-1268. EPHESOS, ERECTION OF STATUES OF SEXTILIUS POLLIO AND HIS WIFE OFILLIA BASSA, BETWEEN 4-14 A.D. Two bases of statues.

Ed. pr. W. Alzinger, JÖAI 50 (BEIBLATT, 1972-75) 269 (ph.).

1267. BASE I: C(aio) Sextilio Pollioni
C(aius) Ofillius Proculus patri
Γάιον Σεξτίλιον Πωλλιῶνα
Γάιος Ὀφέλλιος Πρόκλος τὸν πατέρα

1268. BASE II: Ofilliae Bassae
C(aius) Ofillius Proculus matri
Ὀφελλίαν Βάσσαν
Γαίος Ὀφέλλιος Πρόκλος τὴν μητέρα

1269. EPHESOS, DEDICATION OF A BASILICA TO AUGUSTUS AND TIBERIUS, BETWEEN 4-14 A.D. Fragment of a building-inscription. Ed. pr. W. Alzinger, l.c., 266-279 (ph.).

Basili[cam Dianae Ephesiae et imperatori Caesari Divi f(ilio) Augusto et Tiberio C]aesa[ri A]u[gusti f(ilio) et] civitati Eph[esiorum C(aius) Sextilius P(ublii) f(ilius) Pollio cum Ofillia A(uli) f(ilia) Bassa] uxor[e sua] e[t C(aio) Ofillio] Pro[culo f(ilio) suo ceterisque liberis suis] d(e) s(ua) [p(ecunia) f(aciendam) curavit. Βασ]ιλ[ικὴν στοὰν Ἀρτ]έμι[δι Ἐφεσίαι καὶ αὐτοκράτορι Καίσαρι θεοῦ] υἱῶ[ι Σεβαστῶι καὶ Τιβερίωι] Καίσαρι Σεβασ[τοῦ υἱῶι καὶ τῶ]ι δήμ[ωι Ἐφεσίων. Γάιος Σεξτίλιος Ποπλίου υἱὸς Πολλίων σὺν Ὀφελλίαι Αὔλου θυγατρὶ Βάσσηι τῆι γυναικὶ καὶ Γαίωι Ὀφελλίωι Πρόκλ]ωι τῶι υἱῶι [καὶ τοῖς λοίποις τέκνοις ἐκ τῶν ἰδίων ἀνέθηκεν].

Cf. JÖAI 50 (BEIBLATT, 1972-75) 87-89 (fig. a+b): a recently found fragment of the building-inscription (with the Latin letters OFI) confirms the restoration of it made by W. Alzinger.

1270. EPHESOS, DEDICATION OF A BUILDING TO NERO, BETWEEN 55-68 A.D. Block of a building-inscription. Ed. pr. A. Bammer, JÖAI 50 (BEIBLATT, 1972-75) 385 (ph.).

----δίωι Καίσαρι Σε[βαστῶι] Γερμανι[κ]ῶι ἱερεῖ μ[εγίστωι] ---

Cf. JÖAI 50 (HAUPTBLATT, 1972-73) 222, Nachtrag || ἱερεῖ μ[εγίστωι] seems very doubtful (not contained on photograph fig. 8) Herrmann.

1271. EPHESOS, DEDICATION TO ARTEMIS, TRAJAN AND THE EPHESIAN DEMOS, EARLY 2nd CENT. A.D. Blocks of a white marble architrave. Ed. pr. D. Knibbe, JÖAI 50 (BEIBLATT, 1972-75) 27-30, no. 1 (ph.).

Ἀρτέ[μιδι καὶ Αὐτοκράτορι Νέρουᾳ Τραιαν]ῷ Καίσ[αρι Σ]εβαστῷ [Γερ-

μ]ανικῷ Δακικῷ [καὶ τῷ νεωκόρῳ Ἐφεσίων δήμῳ] Μᾶρκος Ἰούλιος [..
..]εριανὸς ΣΥ[----------το]ῦ δήμ[ου ----] τ̣ρ̣ία ἐργαστή[ρια ---- ἀν-
έθηκεν].

συ[γκλητικὸς ὁ γραμματεὺς το]ῦ δήμ[ου ----]τ̣ρ̣ια ἔργα στή[σας -- Knibbe; τρία ἐργαστή[ρια ("restitution évidente") J. and L. Robert, BE (1977) no. 417, p. 393-394.

1272. EPHESOS, DEDICATION OF AN ALTAR TO HADRIAN, BETWEEN 119-129 A.D. Small white marble altar. Ed. pr. D. Knibbe, l.c., 75-77, no. 6 (ph.).

Αὐτοκράτορα Καίσαρα
Θεοῦ Τραιανοῦ Παρθικοῦ
υἱόν, Θεοῦ Νέρουα υἱωνόν,
[Τ]ραιανὸν Ἁδριανὸν Σε-
[β]αστόν, ἀρχιερέα μέγιστον, δη-
[μ]αρχικῆς ἐξουσίας, ὕπατον
τὸ γ΄, οἱ πρὸ πόλεως μύσται σύ[ν]-
θρονον τῷ Διονύσῳ· ἱερεύοντ[ος]
Κλ. Ῥωμύλου, ἱεροφαντοῦντος
Κλ. Εὐβίου, ἐπιμελητοῦ Ἀντωνίο[υ]
Δρόσου. Ἀναθέντος τὴν τειμὴν
ἐκ τῶν ἰδίων Θεοδότου — (= Θεοδότου) Προκλ[ί]-
ωνος μυσταγωγοῦ μετὰ τῶν τέκν[ων]
Πρόκλου ὑμνῳδοῦ καὶ Ἀθηνοδώρου.

1273. EPHESOS, DEDICATION TO HADRIAN, BETWEEN 129-138 A.D. White marble altar; lower part of the surface of the stone erased. Ed. pr. D. Knibbe, l.c., 78-80, no. 7 (ph.).

Ἀγαθῇ·Τύχῃ.
Αὐτοκράτορι
Καίσαρι Ἁδριανῷ
Σεβαστῷ Διὶ
Ὀλυμπίῳ.

1274. EPHESOS, DEDICATION OF A STATUE OF TYCHE SOTEIRA, 2nd HALF 2nd CENT. A.D. White marble base. Ed. pr. D. Knibbe, l.c., 67-70, no. 1 (ph.).

Τύχης Σωτείρας.
Ὑπὲρ τῆς πρώτης καὶ
μεγίστης μητροπόλε-
ως τῆς Ἀσίας καὶ δὶς νεω-
κόρου τῶν Σεβ(αστῶν) καὶ φιλοσε-
βάστου Ἐφεσίων πόλεως,
ἡ Ἀντιοχέων κολώνων
Καισαρέων πόλις τὸν

ἀνδριάντα ἀνέστησε,
εἰσηγησαμένου Γαίου
Φλαουωνίου Ἀνικιανοῦ
Σάνκτου πάτρωνος τῆς
κολωνείας·
διὰ πρεσβευτῶν·Μ·Ἰουλί-
ου Οὐειβιανοῦ Παυλεί-
νου·καὶ·Λ·Ἰουλίου Μετ-
τιανοῦ Πρόκλου·
Γραμματεύοντος·
τοῦ·δήμου·
Γν·Πομπήιου Κουαρ-
τείνου νεωκόρου.

Cf. B. Levick, Roman Colonies in Southern Asia Minor (Oxford, 1967) 100-101, 114, 127; H. Engelmann, ZPE 26 (1977) 155-156.

1275. EPHESOS, DEDICATION OF AN ARCHITRAVE OF A BAKCHEION. Three joining fragments of a white marble architrave. Ed. pr. D. Knibbe, JÖAI 50 (1972-75) 45-46, no. 12 (ph.).

Φίλιππος·δὶς·Μαζαῖς νεοποιὸς τὸ ἐπιστύλιν
τῷ Βαχχείῳ ἀνέθηκεν.

1276. EPHESOS, EPITAPH, 7th - 6th CENT. B.C. White marble block. Ed. pr. D. Knibbe, l.c., 20-21, no. 7 (ph.).

Ἀρτεμõς τὸ σῆμα
τῆς Θεόχō.

1277. EPHESOS, EPITAPH, 7th - 6th CENT. B.C. White marble block. Ed. pr. D. Knibbe, l.c., 46, no. 13 (ph.).

Πυθαγόρεω | τõ Θάλεω | Σαμίō.

1278. EPHESOS, EPITAPH FOR AURELIUS POPAEUS AND AURELIUS RUFUS, 3rd CENT. A.D. Sarcophagus of white marble. Ed. pr. D. Knibbe, l.c., 65-66, no. 5 (ph.).

Ὁ βωμὸς καὶ ἡ κατ' <αὐτ>οῦ σορὸς καὶ αἱ δύο
ὀστοθῆκαί εἰσιν Αὐρ(ηλίου) Ποπαίου καὶ
Αὐρ(ηλίου) Ῥούφου {καὶ τε} καὶ τέκνων αὐτῶν.
[Ἐάν τις θελήση ἐκ]κόψαι τὰ γράμματα ἢ πωλῆσαι, δώσει τῷ
[φίσκῳ? ..ca. 10... καὶ τῷ τα]μείῳ ∗ φ'. Ζῶσιν.

1279. EPHESOS, EPITAPH FOR AEMILIA VERA IUVENTIANE. White marble lid of a sarcophagus. Ed. pr. D. Knibbe, l.c., 79-80, no. 8 (ph.).

[Τοῦτο τὸ ....]ον μόνα ἐστὶν Αἰμιλίας Βήρας Ἰουβεν-
τιανῆς
[........................]λίαν Δημητρίαν.
[Ἐάν τις θελήσῃ ....]εσθαι ἢ σκυβαλίσαι τι τῶν ἐνόντων
[δώσει τῷ φίσκῳ ? ....]

3. σκυβαλίσαι: cf. J. and L. Robert, BE (1977) no. 423.

1280. EPHESOS, EPITAPH. Blue-greyish marble grave-relief with inscription. The relief shows a woman on a seat (a kind of throne) with a small box in her left hand; between the woman and a dog (on the right side of the representation) a small burning altar. Ed. pr. D. Knibbe - R. Merkelbach, ZPE 21 (1976) 191-192 (ph.). Cf. W. Peek, ZPE 28 (1978) 178-179.

Τύμβος ὧδε κατέχει καλὸν
δέμας αἲ βιόμοι<ρ>ον. |
῾Ηλικίην γὰρ ἔχουσαν ἐτ[ῶ]ν
ἓξ·ἢ ἔ{ι}τι πλῖον σε | Κούρη [Π]λο[υ]-
τῆος ἤγαγεν εἰς Ἀίδην. Ἀ[λλ]ὰ
θεοὶ μάκα[ρε]ς οἰκτείραντες |
ψυχὴν οὐ πρόλιπαν δῦν[αι]
δόμον Ἄϊδος ἴσω· | ἠέρι δ' ἐμ̣[πεπό]-
τηται κατ' οὐρανόν· ἐν δὲ̣ [θεοῖ]-
σιν | εἴσην μοῖραν ἔχει ἠ̣ρ[ωίσι δὴ ?]
Στρατονείκη. | Εἰ δέ τις ἤ[ν κ]ατέ-
χει τύμβος ζῶσάν ποτ' ἔ[βλεψεν], |
οὐκ ἂν ἀδακρυτεὶ τόν[δε]
διῆλθε τόπον.

1. Read ὅδε Knibbe - Merkelbach || 2. βιόμοι<ρ>ον = βιαιόμοιρον Knibbe - Merkelbach; cf. W. Peek, l.c., 179 || 4. ΗΕΙΤΙΠΛΙΟΝΣΕ is an error for ΚΟΥΤΙΠΛΙΟΝΓΕ = κοὔτι πλῖον (= πλεῖον) γε Peek || 6. in this verse some syllables are missing: <⏑⏑–⏑⏑> οἰκτείραντες Knibbe - Merkelbach || 8. read εἴσω Knibbe - Merkelbach || 8-9. δὲ πεπό|τηται Peek || 10. read ἴσην Knibbe - Merkelbach || ἠρ[ωίσι], ἠ̣ρ̣[φ̣ν̣η̣] or ἠρ[ωίνῃ] Peek || 12. ἐσ̣ε̣ῖ̣δ̣ε̣ν̣ Peek.

1281. EPHESOS, ACCLAMATION, EARLY 5th CENT. A.D. Mosaic inscription. Photo in H. Vetters, ÖSTERR. ARCH. INSTITUT, GRABUNGEN 1971-72 (ed. 1976) p. 36 (cf. p. 38). For the transcription and dating, cf. J. and L. Robert, BE (1977) no. 425.

† Αὔξι Ἀσκλή|[2]πις ὁ μεγαλοπρε|πέστατος ἀν|[4]θύπατος.

1282. ERYTHRAI, ATTIC DECREE, CA. 387 B.C. Fragment of blue-grey marble found in Erythrai; now in the Izmir museum. Ed. pr. S. Şahin, BELLETEN 40 (1976) 565-571 (ph.).

.ΛΗΣ................
ντων ἐν [Ἐρ]υθρα[ῖ]ς, [δεδόχθ]-
αι τῶι δήμωι· μὴ ἐξεῖνα[ι τ]-
ῶν στρατηγῶν διαλλάξαι
μηθενὶ πρὸς τοὺς ἐν τῇ πό-
λει ἄνευ τοῦ δήμου τõ Ἀθη-
ναίων· μηδὲ τῶμ φυγάδων, ο-
ὓς ἂν ἐξελάσωσιν Ἐρυθρα-
ῖοι, μηδενὶ ἐξεῖναι κατά-
γειν ἐς Ἐρυθρὰς ἄνευ τοῦ
δήμου τοῦ Ἐρυθραίων· περ-
ὶ δὲ τοῦ μὴ ἐκδίδοσθαι Ἐρ-
υθραίους τοῖς βαρβάροι-
ς, ἀποκρίνασθαι τοῖς Ἐρυ-
θραίοις, ὅτι δέδοκται [τῶ]-
ι δήμωι τῶι Ἀθηναίων ...
....

1283. ERYTHRAI, HONORARY INSCRIPTION FOR AN EMPEROR ?, 1st CENT. A.D. Ed. pr. H. Engelmann - R. Merkelbach, Die Inschriften von Erythrai und Klazomenai, I (Bonn, 1972) no. 136. W. Peek, ZPE 23 (1976) 85-86 used an old (and very good) photograph of this stone (unfortunately he does not publish it) and restores the text as follows:

Ἀγαθῇ Τύχῃ.
[[ ]]
[[ ]]
4 [.ca.10-11.. ἡ] λαμπροτάτη Ἐ[ρυθραί]-
ων πόλις, καθὰ ἐψηφίσατο [..ca.10...]
[ἀπ]ὸ τῶν τῆς πόλεως χρημ[άτων, ἀνα]-
[σ]τήσαντος Τιβερίου Κλαυ[δίου .ca.7?.]
8 δίου τοῦ ἱεροποιοῦ.

5. [παμψηφεί] (e.g.) or a verb Peek || 7-8. Κλαυ[δίου Καλοπο]|δίου e.g. Peek || The text of Engelmann - Merkelbach runs as follows (L. 4 ff.): ἡ] λαμπροτάτη .[---] |5[--].αις καθ' [ἃ] ἐψηφίσατο |6 [ἐκ τ]ῶν τῆς πόλεως χρημ[άτων] |7 [ἀναστ]ήσαντος Τιβερίου Κλα[υ] |8δίου τοῦ ἱερο[ποι]οῦ.

1284. ERYTHRAI, EPITAPH FOR A CITIZEN OF ERYTHRAI WHO DIED IN KLAROS, 1st CENT. A.D. H. Engelmann - R. Merkelbach, Die Inschriften von Erythrai und Klazomenai, II (Bonn, 1973) no. 307. Cf. W. Peek, ZPE 23 (1976) 82-83 (ph.), who offers some quisquiliae for this text. We present the inscription as follows:

[-⏑⏑-]ειναὶ καὶ ἐναύλια μακρὰ Κλάροιο
    [ ]τ̣ο καὶ μητρὸς γηραλέης στοναχαί·
3 [ἔν]θ᾽ ἄρα τῆι φθονερῆι φλογὶ κάππεσον, ἐγ δ<έ> μευ ὤ[ρη]
    ὤλετο καὶ πρώτην ἣν ἀνέτινα γένυν·
κεῖθέν με πάτρης ἐπεβήσετε· τί πλέον, αἰαῖ,
6   τίς χάρις εἰς κωφὴν <σ>πεισαμένοις σποδιήν;

---

1. [-⏑⏑ με κλ]ειναί Engelmann - Merkelbach; [ἄκραι με κλ]ειναί Peek, who, however, finds this too long and opts for P. Maas' [ἄκριες αἰπ]ειναί, which seems hardly shorter || 2. [μύρε]τ̣ο Engelmann - Merkelbach; [δέξ̣α]τ̣ο Peek || 5-6. τί πλέον αἰαῖ, | τ̣ίς χάρις εἰς κωφὴν <σπ>εισαμένοις σποδιήν Engelmann - Merkelbach; τί πλέον, αἰαῖ, | τίς χάρις εἰς κωφὴν <σ>πευσαμένοις σποδίην Peek.

1285. ERYTHRAI, EPITAPH FOR A YOUNG WOMAN WHO DIED IN CHILDBIRTH, 1st CENT. A.D. H. Engelmann - R. Merkelbach, o.c., no. 308. Cf. W. Peek, ZPE 23 (1976) 83-84 who suggests for L. 3 Ἐλ[ειθυῖαι μιν ἀνῆγον] |, defends his supplement [τέτυκτο] in L. 5 (GV, no. 1269), accepts in L. 6 Engelmann - Merkelbach's reading ἦ ... ἦ ("einerseits ... andererseits") but prefers παρέχον (participle) to Engelmann - Merkelbach's παρέχον (imperf.).

1286. ERYTHRAI, FUNERAL EPIGRAMS. W. Peek, ZPE 23 (1976) 84-85 restores e.g. three mutilated epigrams from H. Engelmann - R. Merkelbach, o.c., nos. 309, 312, 313. We refer the reader to ZPE for these restorations.

1287. ERYTHRAI, EPITAPH. H. Engelmann - R. Merkelbach, o.c., no. 399. Cf. H. Engelmann, ZPE 20 (1976) 156 who remarks that this inscription has to be excluded from the Pontic corpus (Studia Pontica, III, no. 207 a, under the heading: "Euchaïta and the Galatian border") since its provenance is certain: Erythrai.

1288. KLAROS, DELEGATION-LIST OF PERINTHOS, BEGINNING 2nd CENT. A.D. (BEFORE 115). White marble stele. Ed. pr. L. Robert, STUDCLAS 16 (1974) 74-80 (ph.).

Περίνθιοι μ᾽ ἀνευρόντες ἔσ-
τησαν διὰ Λ. Ἀγιδίου Ῥούφου ἀρχι-
ερέος καὶ Ἐπιγένους Ἥδυος, Νεικίου Νεικίου,
4 Ἀπολλοδώρου Ποπλίου, Λατεινίου Βάσσου
vacat

Ἐπὶ πρυτάνεος Κοσκωνίας Μύρτου, ἱερέος δὲ Γ. Ἰουλίου
Ἀγαθοκλέους διὰ βίου καὶ προφήτου κατ' ἔτος, γραμματευ-
όντων Ἀλεξάνδρου τοῦ Ἀλεξάνδρου καὶ Οὐαλερίου Ἀσιατι-
κοῦ v. οἱ πεμφθέντες ὑπὸ Περινθίων κατὰ χρησμὸν
Ἀπόλλωνος Κλαρίου ὑμνήσοντες τὸν θεὸν v.
Λ. Ἀγίδιος Ῥοῦφος νέος, Π. Ἀγίδιος Καπίτων, Μίκκαλος
Διογένου, Φιλήμων Ἐπιγένους, Ἀσκλᾶς Ἰουλιανοῦ,
Ἑρμογένης Νεικίου, Βάσσος Ἀπολλοδώρου, Ἀντωνεῖ-
νος Συμμάχου, Μᾶρκος Λατείνιος· v. γράψαντος
τὸν ὕμνον μελοποιοῦ Κοίντου Ἀππατιώνος.

---

1. με: unknown object; "quelque vieille idole archaïque retrouvée ?" Robert || 2. for the epitaph of Agidius (or his elder son, L. 9), cf. E. Kalinka, JÖAI 1 (BEIBLATT, 1898) 115, no. 13 where the name Agidius is correct Robert || 5. Cosconia Myrton appears also in an inscription of the city of Bargasa (eastern Caria; cf. no. 1289) and probably also in CIG, 3173 (Smyrna, 83 A.D.) and on coins of Domitian from Smyrna Robert || 10. these two Agidii are the sons of the archiereus (L. 2) || 11. Φιλήμων Ἐπιγένους: son of Ἐπιγένης Ἥδυος (L. 3) || 12. Ἑρμογένης Νεικίου: son of Νεικίας Νεικίου (L. 3) || Βάσσος Ἀπολλοδώρου: son of Ἀπολλόδωρος Ποπλίου (L. 4) || 13. Μᾶρκος Λατείνιος: son of Λατείνιος Βάσσου (L. 4). For all these relations, cf. L. Robert, l.c., 78-79.

1289. KLAROS, DELEGATION-LIST OF BARGASA, BEGINNING 2nd CENT. A.D. (BEFORE 115). Ed. pr. L. Robert, STUDCLAS 16 (1974) 75 (Robert gives lines 1-8 of the inscription; lines 9-13 are read by H. W. Pleket on the photo in L. Robert, La Carie, II, Paris, 1954, pl. 34, 2).

Βαργασηνῶν.
[Ἐπὶ] πρυτάνεως Κοσκωνίας
[Μύρ]του, ἱερέως δὲ καὶ προ-
[φήτ]ου Γ(αίου) Ἰ(ουλίου) Ἀγαθοκλέους,
[γραμ]ματέων δὲ Ἀλεξάνδρου
[τοῦ] Ἀλεξάνδρου καὶ Λ(ουκίου) Β(αλερίου) Ἀσιατι-
[κοῦ]. Κατὰ χρησμὸν τοῦ θεοῦ παῖ-
[δε]ς οἱ ὑμνήσαντες τοὺς θεοὺς
τὸ ε'· Φλ. Ἀπολλώνιος Φιλόπαππος,
Ἀρτεμιδώρος Μόλων, Ζωΐλος σὺν
Ζωΐλῳ τῷ πατρί, Σώπατρος Φλ. Εὐ-
άρχου, Ἀριστίδης Ἀριστίδου τοῦ
Μοσχίωνος, Ἑρμόφαντος Θυσσου.

2-3. For Cosconia Myrton, cf. no. 1288 || 13. Θυσσος: for this Carian name, cf. L. Robert, l.c., 75, note 2.

1290. KLAROS, THE ORACLE OF APOLLO. M. Euzennat, ANTAFR 10 (1976) 63 discusses six Latin inscriptions from the Western part of the Roman Empire, all dedicated "dis deabusque secundum interpretationem oraculi Clarii Apollinis" (= κατὰ χρησμόν). The oracle was given in reply to Caracalla's request for help, against his illness; Euzennat suggests that both these dedications and the Constitutio Antoniniana should be dated at the end of 213 A.D.

1291. MAGNESIA (ON THE MAEANDER), THE LETTER OF DARIUS TO GADATAS, AFTER 494 B.C. Syll^{3}, 22; I. von Magnesia, no. 115. E. Marinoni, ACME 29 (1976) 227-228 discusses the identity of the god mentioned in LL. 26-29 (Apollo or Ahura Mazda); for the ἱεροὶ φυτουργοί in this text, cf. L. Robert, BCH 101 (1977) 84-85.

1292. MILETOS, CONSTITUTIONAL HISTORY OF MILETOS IN THE HELLENISTIC PERIOD. H. Müller, <u>Milesische Volksbeschlüsse. Eine Untersuchung zur Verfassungsgeschichte der Stadt Milet in hellenistischer Zeit</u> (Hypomnemata 14; Göttingen, 1976) investigates the extant Milesian decrees in order to establish which possibilities existed for political initiative. His over-all conclusion is that from the early 3rd cent. B.C. an increasing predominance of small groups of magistrates (prytaneis, epistatai) developed who controlled all political initiative on the part of individual members of the assembly and of the council.

1293. MILETOS, FRAGMENT OF A DEDICATION, CA. 500 B.C. Now in the museum of Izmir. SEG, XVI, 727. Cf. P.A. Hansen, ZPE 21 (1976) 37-38. Hansen had given in "<u>A List of Greek Verse Inscriptions down to 400 B.C.</u>" (Opuscula Graecolatina, III; Copenhagen, 1975) no. 443a a text, quite different from the SEG-text, and indicates in ZPE briefly his interpretation. He supposes that the inscription will have consisted of four hexameters and reads it as follows:

[ ] Θεοκύδ{ρ}ης [ ]
[–⏓⏑ –⏓⏑ –⏓⏑̣ –⏓⏑ –⏑⏑ –]εος·
Μόλπις δ' αὐτα̣[⏑–⏓⏑ –⏓⏑ –⏑⏑ ––]
[–⏓⏑–σὺ δ' ἄ̣ν]ασσα δίδο χαρίεσ[σαν ἀμοιβήν].

W. Peek, ZPE 31 (1978) 262-264 does not agree with Hansen: he thinks that the epigram consisted of three hexameters, and proposes "versuchsweise" the following reconstruction:

["Αρτεμι, σοί με καλὸν] Θεοκύδ{ρ}ης [ἄνθετ' ἄγαλμα]
[καὶ παῖς Μνησίθ]εος· Μόλπις δ' Αὐτά[νδρο ἐποίει]
[αἷς χερσίν. Σὺ δ' ἄν]ασσα δίδο χαρίεσ[σαν ἀμοιβήν].

---

1. Because Peek suspects the name Θεοκύδης, he thinks that also the following reconstructions are possible: [τὤγαλμ', "Αρτεμι, Σωσι]θέο Κυδρῆς [σοι ἔθηκεν] or [τὤγαλμ' 'Αρτέμιδ' 'Ηρο]θέο Κυδρῆς

[ἀνέθηκεν] || 2. also [καὶ κάσις Εὐξίθ]εος or [Νηλέος ἐκ γέν]εος is possible Peek.

1294. MILETOS, DEDICATION OF AN ALTAR (TO ARTEMIS BOULAIA ?), 1st HALF 2nd CENT. A.D. Marble altar. Ed. pr. H. Hommel, CHIRON 6 (1976) 319-327 (ph.).

Σέξτ. [Καίλιος ?]
ἀπόγ[ονος βα]-
3 σιλεώ[ς Τιμ]ά̣ρ̣-
χου καὶ ἡ γυνὴ
αὐτοῦ Ἰουλία
6 πρόπ̣ο̣[λος θεᾶς ?]

1. Cf. the stemma on p. 327 || 3-4. Timarchos: "Gegenkönig" of the Seleucid King Demetrios I (after 162 B.C.) Hommel.

1295. SMYRNA, A DOCUMENT OF THE SMYRNAEAN TECHNITAI, 150 A.D. Ed. pr. H.W. Pleket, The Greek Inscriptions in the Rijksmuseum van Oudheden at Leyden (Leyden, 1958) no. 58; G. Petzl, ZPE 14 (1974) 77-87. W. Williams, ZPE 22 (1976) 235-240 tries to show that (a) the fragments are part of a petition in Greek to which a Latin subscript has been added and (b) a copy of this petition has been made at Rome when the original petition (and subscript) were on public display in the temple of Apollo. He restores LL. 1-4 as follows:

[----------- ἐκγεγ]ραμμέν[ον] καὶ ἀντιβεβλημ[ένον]
[e.g. ἐκ τεύχους βιβλειδίων προτεθέντων ἐν Ῥώμῃ ἐν τῷ] ἐ̣ν τῷ Παλατ̣[ί]ῳ ἱερῷ Ἀπόλλω̣ν[ος]
[------------------------------ τὰ ὑ̣πο]γεγραμμένα. v. Τῷ
4 [e.g. φιλοθεωτάτῳ αὐτοκράτορι Καίσαρι Τίτῳ Αἰλίῳ Ἀδριανῷ Ἀντω]νείνῳ Σεβαστῷ Εὐ-
[σεβεῖ.

1-4. [--- ἀπογεγ]ραμμέν[ων] κ̣αὶ ἀντιβεβλημ̣[ένων] |² [--- ἐν τῷ] ἐν τῷ Παλατ̣[ί]ῳ ἱερῷ Ἀπόλλων[ος] |³ [---]γεγρ̣αμμένα v. Τῳ̣[--] |⁴ [̣---- Ἀντω̣]νείνῳ Σεβαστῷ Εὐ|[σεβεῖ Petzl. Cf. SEG, XVIII, 491.

1296. SMYRNA, ORACLE, 2nd CENT. A.D. SEG, XVIII, 495. Cf. W. Peek, ZPE 21 (1976) 145 who suggests some restorations in the following lines: L. 1. [21-22]ΠΗΡΧΕ ΧΡ[max. 8]. E.g.: [-⏑⏑, ἐκ μακροῦ χρησμὸς δ᾽ ὅδ᾽ (respectively γὰρ) ὑ]πῆρχε χρ[όνοιο]; 4. before [τῆς βουλῆ]ς 9-10 letters are missing. Perhaps [κατὰ δόγμα τῆς βουλῆ]ς or [ἐκ δόγματος τῆς βουλῆ]ς; 5. before Ἀρτεμιδώρου ca. 22 letters are missing, so [ἐπειδή + name] (G. Dunst) cannot fill up the lacuna.

1297-1298. SMYRNA, TWO GREEK INSCRIPTIONS ON A MILESTONE, 3rd CENT. A.D. CIG, 3179; CIL, III, 471 and 472. M. Yenim, TÜRK AR-

KEOLOJI DERGISI 23, 2 (1976) 167-172 (ph.) republishes the six inscriptions, engraved on a large column which once stood in a cemetery two hours east of Smyrna (in Hadjilar) but now is in the Izmir Museum; four of the inscriptions are in Latin, the other two are Greek. Combination of the majuscule facsimiles in CIG/CIL and Yenim's drawning gives the following texts:

1297. Ἡ λαμπροτάτη [καὶ πρώτη]
τῆς Ἀσίας καὶ τ[ρὶ]ς νεωκόρος
τῶν Σεβαστῶν Σμυρναίων
πόλις ἀνέστησεν ἐπ' ἀνθυπάτου
Λολλιανοῦ Γεντιανοῦ.

2. καὶ ΤΗΣ CIG, corrected by Boeckh into τ[ρί]ς; δίς CIL; τ(ρί)ς Yenim || 4. πόλις ἀνέστησεν ἐπὶ ἀνθυπάτ[ου] CIL; πόλις ἀνέστ(η)σεν ἐπ(ὶ) ἀνθυπάτ(ου) Yenim.

1298. [Αὐ]τοκράτωρ
[Κα]ῖσαρ Λούκ(ιος)
[Δομίτιος Αὐ]-
[ρηλιανὸς] Εὐσε-
βής, Εὐτυχής, Σεβ(αστὸς)
[καὶ Οὐ]λπ(ία) Σεβηρεῖνα Σεβ(αστή)
[ἀπὸ Σ]μύρνης
M.

8. ΜΕ CIG; Mϛϛ CIL; ML (ΕΚΤΟΝ) Yenim, who prints μι(λιάριον) ἕκτον.

1299. SMYRNA, DEDICATION OF AN ALTAR, 2nd CENT. A.D. CIG, 3170; IGR, IV, 1436. H.W. Pleket, ZPE 20 (1976) 9-15 discusses this inscription and the function of C. Claudius Valerianus Licinnianus, alytarches in Olympia.

1300. SMYRNA, EPITAPH FOR THE GIRL NIKOPOLIS, 1st HALF 2nd CENT. B.C. Peek, GV, I, 1512. Cf. D.L. Page, WS 10 (1976) 174-176 who presents the text (in mixed meter) with commentary.

1301. SMYRNA, HONORARY EPIGRAM FOR TELLON, LATE HELLENISTIC PERIOD. Ed. pr. T. Drew-Bear, GRBS 16 (1975) 281-293 (ph.). W. Peek, ZPE 23 (1976) 91-92 puts forward the following text:

[γόνον ἐ]κ Πρ[οτίμου? τύμβος ὅδε κατα|κρύφ]ε̣ι v.
Τέλλω̣[ν' ἄριστον ἄνδρα, π]ρ̣ῶτ[ον γνω|ρίμω]ν· v.

τιμαῖς τ[ὸν ηὔξ]ε δόξα κάρ[ε|τή, ξέ]ν[ε]· v.
ὃς πολλὰ πάτρᾳ δῶρ' ἔτευχεν ἀ[γλα|ά] v.
[ἦρξε]ν τ' ἐφήβων καὶ νέων ἐπαξίως v.v.v. |
[ἀγῶν]α τ' ἐβράβευσεν, ὃν δῆμος τελεῖ. v.v. |
[ἔφυσε] γῆ τούς, καὶ πάλιν κομίζ[ε]ται. v.v.v. |
[υἱὸς δ' ἀ]γασθεὶς Μαιάδος διάκτορο[ς] v.v. |
[ἔνθ' εὐ]σεβεῖς ναίουσιν, αὐτὸν σῶ[σ' ἄ|γων]. v.
[σὺ] δ' ὃς κέλευθον τὴν παρ' ἠρίον | [πατεῖς], v.
τὸν πᾶσιν ἀστ[οῖ]ς καὶ ξένοις | [ποθούμενο]ν v.
χαίρειν προσείπας v.v.v. | [ἀβλα]βὴς ὁδοιπόρει. vac.

1-5. [---]Γ[---------------------] |[2] [--]ΚΠΡ[------------------] |[3] [--]ΔΩΤΕΛΛΩ[--------]ΩΤ[---] |[4] [--]Ν. τιμαῖς Τ[.ca.8...] δόξα κατ[-] |[5] [-- ὅ]ς πολλὰ πάτρᾳ δῶρ' ἔτευχεν α[--] Drew-Bear || 7. τε[λεῖ] Drew-Bear || 8. [φύει δὲ] γῆ Drew-Bear || 9. [υἱὸς δ' ἀγ]ασθεὶς Μαιάδος δια[⏑ -]| Drew-Bear || 10. ναίουσιν αὐτὸν σω[⏑ -]| Drew-Bear. Cf. J. and L. Robert, BE (1977) no. 40 for the Smyrnaean provenance.

1302. SMYRNA, EPIGRAM FOR THE GOVERNOR EUSTHATIOS, LATER IMPERIAL PERIOD. Ed. pr. L. Robert, Laodicée du Lycos, Le Nymphée (Quebec/Paris, 1969) 342-343 (ph.). Robert reads the first line of this epigram as follows: Εἰκὼν Εὐσταθίοιο πέλω φίλος· εἰμὶ δὲ μάρτυς κτλ. and he defends this punctuation in BE (1974) no. 476 and BE (1977) no. 400. Cf. W. Peek, PHILOLOGUS 116 (1972) 260 who proposes Εἰκὼν Εὐσταθίοιο πέλω· φίλος εἰμὶ δὲ μάρτυς κτλ. and R. Merkelbach, ZPE 14 (1974) 88 and ZPE 20 (1976) 276-277 who punctuates Εἰκὼν Εὐσταθίοιο πέλω, φίλος· εἰμὶ δὲ μάρτυς κτλ.

1303. SMYRNA, EPIGRAM ON A STATUE-BASE IN HONOUR OF HERMODOROS, ADVANCED IMPERIAL PERIOD. Ed. L. Robert, Hellenica, II (Paris, 1946) 109-113 with references to earlier publications by A. Fontrier (cf. L. Robert, Hellenica, XI-XII, Paris, 1960, p. 558-560); H.W. Pleket, Epigraphica II (Textus Minores 41; Leiden, 1969) no. 59, p. 57-58. Cf. G. Petzl, ZPE 18 (1975) 315-316 (ph.); W. Peek, ZPE 21 (1976) 146; J. and L. Robert, BE (1977) no. 399.

Ἑρμόδωρον καθορᾶ[τ']
ἐμὲ χάλκιον ὧδε,
φίλοι, γύμνιχον, ἐν παι-
δὶ κυνηγε<τ>ῶν τὸν ἄρι-
στον, αὐτὸν θηρεύσαν-
τα Εὐχρωτίῳ τόνδε λα-
γωόν· δεσποίνῃ τε φέρω
τοῦτο τὸ δῶρον ἐγώ. Εἴ
τίς τοι μετάθοι με ἢ ἐν-
τεῦθεν μετενέγκῃ, δώ-
[σ]ει Μητρὶ Θεῶν Σμυρ-
[ν]αϊκῇ τελέτω χρυσοῦς κβ'.

1-2. καθορᾶ|τε Fontrier; καθορᾶ[τ'] | ἐμέ (but also καθορᾶ|τε με is possible) Petzl || 2. ἐμὲ χάλκιον, <ὦ φίλοι, ὧδε> Merkelbach (apud Petzl); ἐμὲ χαλκῖον (= εἶον) φίλοι ὧδε Peek || 3-4. παί|δ<εσσ>ι Merkelbach, Peek (but cf. L. Robert, Hellenica, XI-XII,

p. 560 and note 1 who rejects this reading || 4. ΚΥΝΗΓΕΣΙΩΝ lapis; κυνηγεσίων Fontrier, Petzl, Peek. Petzl translates: "den Besten von der Jagd(mannschaft)". But cf. L. Robert, who prefers κυνηγετῶν (l.c. and BE, 1976, no. 586) || 4-5. τὸν ἄριστον αὐτόν, κτλ. Fontrier || 6. εὐχρωτίῳ sive ἔυχρωτ' ιῷ Fontrier || 7. Δεσποίνῃ Fontrier || 10-11. δῶ[ρον] Merkelbach, but cf. J. and L. Robert, BE (1976) no. 586 || 12. τελέτω: L. Robert, Hellenica, II, p. 109, note 3: "Il y a une grosse difficulté, que je ne sais résoudre, dans le pentamètre. Le verbe signifiant 'payer' y est exprimé deux fois... Y a-t-il une correction à introduire ? ou le souci de faire un vers a-t-il entraîné cette répétition anti-grammaticale ?"; Klaffenbach (cf. Petzl) rejects τελέτω = τελείτω and suggests that it is an epithet of the Mother of the Gods or that one has to separate the words as follows: Σμυρναϊκῆ τε + λετῳ; R. Keydell (apud Peek): τελετῶ<ν> (or perhaps with the pronunciation τελετῶγ and disappearance of the nasal): genitive of relation.

1304. TEOS, CURSES, AFTER 479 B.C. Syll^3, no. 38. On the meaning of the word ἀγών in this inscription (L. 32) cf. J.D. Ellsworth, GLOTTA 54 (1976) 232 who rejects the meaning "assembly" and suggests "contest" or rather "the people gathering for a contest".

1305. TEOS, EXEMPTION FROM TAXES FOR NEW CITIZENS, 2nd HALF 4th CENT. B.C. SEG, II, 579; H.W. Pleket, Epigraphica I (Textus Minores 31; Leiden, 1964) no. 22, p. 35-36. J. and L. Robert, JS (1976) 175-188 (ph.) restudy this text, adding an exhaustive commentary, and make the following changes in Pleket's text: L. 1. [-- ῶν κ]αί; 2-3. καὶ χορηγ[ιῶν] | [καὶ ..ca.6..]οχιῶν; 8-9. καὶ προβάτω[ν] | [....ca.8.. ἐ]ξεῖναι; 11-12. ὅσα δ' ἂν τῶν ἀνδραπόδων | [ἄνθρακας] ἢ ἄλλο τι; 13-14. ἐργάζωνται ἢ α---|---- ἢ ἄλλο τι; 14-15. ἢ μα[λακῶν] | ---- τούτων; 17-18. εἶναι δὲ αὐτοῖς τὴν ἀτέλειαν [τούτων]· | ------ καὶ κήπων; 20. [---- εἶν]αι δὲ αὐτοῖς.

1306. TEOS, TREATY ABOUT A SYMPOLITEIA BETWEEN TEOS AND KYRBISSOS, 3rd CENT. B.C. Marble stone, broken at the top. Ed. pr. J. and L. Robert, JS (1976) 153-235 (ph.) (with a detailed commentary).

2 ....ca.16-17.......ΙΗΙ συμφερόντως, ὀμ[όσ]αι [τ]οὺς ἐν τῆι πόλε[ι πο]-
[λίτας μὴ κα]τασκάψειν Κυρβισσὸν μηδ' ἑτέρω[ι] ἐπιτρέψειν κα[τὰ]
[δύναμιν μη]δ' ἐγκαταλίψειν μηθένα τῶν πολιτῶν τῶν ἐγ Κυρβισσῶ[ι]
[κατοικούν]των· ὀμόσαι δὲ καὶ τοὺς ἐγ Κυρβισσῶι κατοικοῦντας [μὴ]
6 [ἐγκαταλείψ]ειν τὸν φρούραρχον τὸν ὑπὸ τοῦ δήμου ἀποστελλόμενον
[καὶ διαφ]υλάξειν τὸ χωρίον τῇ πόλει· ἐὰν δέ τις μὴ ὀμόσηι, ...
[..... κα]τ' (?) αὐτοῦ τὸν δῆμον ὡς ἀδικοῦντος· ἀποδείκνυσθαι δὲ καὶ φ[ρού]-
[ραρχο]ν εἰς Κυρβισσὸν μὴ νεώτερον τριήκοντα ἐτέων κατὰ τετρά[μη]-

[νον ὧι] ἔστι τίμημα γῆς καὶ οἰκίας ἐλεύθερον τεσσέρων ταλάν-
[των· κατά]ρχειν δὲ τὸμ βουλόμενον τῶμ πολιτῶν ὀμνύντα ἐν τῆι ἐκκλη-
[σίαι· ὁ] δὲ ὅρκος ἔστω· κατάρξω φρούραρχον εἰς Κυρβισσὸν ὅστις μο[ι]
[ἂν δόξηι] ἄριστα καὶ δικαιότατα ἐπιμελέσε[σ]θαι τῆς φυλακῆς τοῦ χωρί-
[ου] καὶ διαφυλάξειν τὸ χωρίον τῆι πόλει ναὶ μὰ τὸν Ἀπόλλ[ω ..ca. 8....]
[1-2] καί μοι εὐορκ[οῦν]τι [μ]ὲν εὖ [εἴη], ἐπιορκοῦντι δὲ κακῶς· τὸν δὲ αὐτ[ὸν]
φρούραρχον μὴ ἀποδείκνυσθαι ἐφ' ἔτη πέντε· ὅπως δ' ἂν εἰδῶμεν τοὺς φρου-
ραρχήσαντας καὶ ....ca. 25............, ἀναγράψαι τοὺς
τιμούχους εἰς [λ]εύκω[μα .....] Τ........ ἐς τὸ βουλευτήριον· φρ[ου]-
ροὺς δ' ἔχειν τὸ[μ] φρο[ύραρχον μ]ὴ ἐλάττους ἢ εἴκοσι τῶμ πολιτῶν καὶ
κυνὰς τρεῖς· τοὺς δὲ κυνὰς [π]ριαμένην παραδοῦναι τῶι φρουράρχω[ι]
τὴμ πόλιν· τρέφειν [δὲ] τοὺς κυνὰς τὸμ [φ]ρούραρχον· ὃς δ' ἂν παραλαβὼν
τὸ χωρίον μὴ παραδῶ[ι τ]ῶι φρουράρχω[ι] τῶ[ι] ὑπὸ τῆς πόλεως ἀποσ[τελ]-
λομένωι ἀεὶ καθ' ἑκάστην τετράμη[νο]ν, φ[ε]ύγειν τε αὐτὸν ἀραιὸν
ἐκ Τέω καὶ ἐξ Ἀβδήρων καὶ ἐκ τῆς χώρας καὶ τῆς Τηίων καὶ τῆς Ἀβδηρ[ι]-
τῶν καὶ τὰ ὄντα αὐτοῦ δη[μό]σια ε[ἶ]ναι, καὶ ὃς ἂν ἀποκτείνηι αὐτὸν μ[ὴ]
μιαρὸς ἔστω· ἐὰν δὲ μαχόμενος [ἀποθάνηι, ὑπάρχ]ε[ι]ν αὐτοῦ δημόσια τὰ ὄν-
τα· τῶι δὲ καταρχθέντι φ[ρο]υρ[άρχωι μὴ ἔστω] ἀποσπᾶσθαι· διδόναι
δὲ αὐτῶι τὸμ μισθὸν τὸν [--------- τε]τραμήνου τοὺς ταμ[ίας ἐ]-
πάναγκον ὅταν πορεύηται [εἰ]ς τὸ [χωρίον· μ]ισθὸν δὲ εἶναι τῶ[ι μὲν]
φρουράρχωι τεσσέρας δραχμ[ὰς] ἀ[λεξ]ανδρε[ίας], τῶν δὲ φρουρῶ[ν]
ἑκάστωι δραχμὴν ἀλε[ξ]ανδρ[είαν] μίαν· ἐὰν δ]έ τις [ἀ]τάκτηι ἢ μὴ πε[ι]-
[θ]άρχηι τοῦ φρουράρχο[υ], ἐ[ξε]ῖναι [τῶι φρ]ουράρχωι καὶ καταδεῖν κα[ὶ]
ἀπόμισθον ποιῆσαι· ἐχέτω δὲ τῶν φρ[ου]ρῶν [ἕκα]στος ἀσπίδα κα[ὶ]
δορὺ καὶ μάχαιραν καὶ περικεφαλαίαν· [τὸν] δὲ φρούραρχον [καὶ]
τοὺς φρουροὺς πρὶ[ν] ἀποστέλλ[ε]σθαι ὀ[μνύν]αι [ἐν] τῆι ἀγορᾶι
ἦ μὴν ἀποδώσειν καὶ δ[ι]αφυλάξειν τῆι π[όλει] τὸ χωρίον· ἐπομνύναι δ[ὲ]
[τ]ὸν νόμιμον ὅρκον· ὁρκισάντων δὲ αὐτ[οὺς οἵ τε σ]τρατηγοὶ καὶ οἱ τιμ[οῦ]-
[χ]οι· ὀμνύτωσαν δὲ καὶ ὅσοι Α.ΤΩΝ ...ca. 14......ΙΟΝΤΙ ἀρεστ.
.Σ. τῶν φρουρῶν τῶν ὑπαρχόντ[ων]..ca. 4..ΛΥ..ca. 8-10..ὡς (?) δὲ καὶ οἱ ἐν τ[ῆι]
[πό]λει ὤμοσαν· παρέχεσθαι δὲ καὶ ..ΡΑ..ca. 7...ΤΕ ἐν τῶι χωρίωι·

τὸ[ν δὲ]
[ὅ]ρκον εἶναι τῶμ μὲν ἐ[ν] τῆ[ι] πόλει οἰκούντων τόνδε· οὐ κατα-
σκάψω
42 [Κυρ]βισσὸν οὐδ' ἑτέρωι ἐπιτρέ[ψ]ω [κ]α[τ]ὰ δύναμιν τὴν ἐμὴν οὐδ' ἐγ[κ]α-
[ταλ]είψω τῶμ πολιτῶν τῶν ἐγ Κ[υρβισσῶι κ]ατοικούντων οὐθένα· ταῦ-
[τα οὖ]ν ἀληθῆ ναὶ μὰ Δία κ[αὶ Ἥλιογ καὶ Ποσειδῶ κ]αὶ Ἀπόλλω
καὶ Ἀθηνᾶ[ν]
[καὶ θεο]ὺς πάντας καὶ πάσας καί [μ]ο[ι εὐ]ο[ρκ]οῦντι μὲν εὖ
εἴη, ἐ[πι]-
46 [ορκοῦντι] δὲ κακῶς· τῶν δὲ ἐγ Κυρβ[ι]σσ[ῶι] κατοικούντων· οὐ[κ]
[ἐγ]καταλί[ψω τ]ὸμ φρούραρχο[ν] τὸν ἐκ τῆς πόλεως ὑπὸ τοῦ δήμου ἀ-
[ποστελ]λόμενον καὶ διαφυλάξω [τ]ὸ χω[ρί]ον τῆι πόλει καὶ ἄν
[εἰδῶ]
[τινα] ἐπιβουλεύοντα τῶι χωρίωι ἢ τῶι φρου[ρ]άρχωι δηλώσω τῆ[ι]
50 [πόλει] καὶ τῶι φρουράρχ[ω]ι καὶ οὐκ [ἐπ]ιτρέψω κατὰ δύναμιν
τὴν [ἐ]-
[μὴν] καὶ ὅ τι ἂν ὁ φρούραρχος παραγ[γε]ίληι ποιήσω ὅσα εἰς φυ-
λ[ακ]ὴ[ν]
[τοῦ χω]ρίου καὶ τῆς χώρας [ναὶ μὰ Δί]α καὶ Ἥλιογ καὶ Ποσειδῶ
καὶ [Ἀ]-
[πόλλω κ]αὶ Ἀθηνᾶν καὶ θεοὺς π[ά]ντας καὶ π[άσ]ας καί [μοι ε]ὐ-
ορκοῦ[ντι]
54 [μὲν ε]ὖ εἴη, ἐπιορκοῦντι δὲ κακ[ῶ]ς· ὁρκισάτωσαν δὲ [ο]ἱ στρα-
τη[γοὶ]
[καὶ οἱ τι]μοῦχοι τοὺς πολίτας ἐν τῆι ἀγορᾶι ταύρωι καὶ κρίωι
[καὶ κά]-
[πρωι· ὁρκί]σαι δὲ καὶ τοὺς ἐγ Κυρβισσῶι κατοικοῦντας ..ca.8..
.....ΣΤΑ· τὰ δὲ ὅρκια παρασχέσθαι τοὺς ταμίας· τοὺ[ς] δὲ ὀμό-
58 [σαντας τῶμ] πολιτῶν τῶν ἐγ Κυρβισσῶι ἀναγράψαι εἰς λεύκω[μα ...]
[..ca.9... κ]αὶ εἰς τὸ βουλευτήριον· ἀναγράψαι δὲ καὶ τὸ ψήφισ-
μα [τόδε]
[τοὺς τιμούχ]ους εἰσ[τή]λας δύο καὶ ἀνα[θ]εῖναι τὴμ μὲ[ν μίαν
ca.4-5]
[..ca.10...]ν. ἐν τῆ ἀγορᾶι, τὴν δὲ εἰς [τὸ ἱ]ερὸν τ.ca.9-10..
62 traces of letters, after a lacuna of ca. 12 letters

J. and L. Robert make the following remarks: 2-3. perhaps οἰκοῦντας instead of πολίτας || 7-8. the sense seems to be φάσιν (e.g.) εἶναι κατ' αὐτοῦ || 14. Ἀπόλλ[ω] Α...ΚΑ..; before kappa "deux lettres si évanides qu' il ne suffit pas de pointer ce tau et cet omicron" || 17. perhaps φρουράρχῆσαι, ἀναγράψαι || 28. in the lacuna of ca. 20 letters one could insert the following words, which must correspond with the sense: τὸν [ἑαυ]τ[οῦ καὶ τ]ῶ[ν φρουρῶν] || 38. Α.ΤΩΝΦΡΟΥ[Ρ]ΑΡΧΑΙΖ...ΙΟΝΤΙΑΡΕΣΤ. || 39. "S' agirait-il de gardes autres que ceux qui ont prêté serment sur l' agora ?" || 40. δὲ καί ..ΡΑΣΑΣ3-4.ΤΕ ἐν τῶι χωρίωι: "S' agirait-il de la fourniture des victimes pour le serment, les ἱερά ou les ὁρκωμόσια ?" || 56. κατοικοῦντας ..Ε(or Ρ)ΙΠ.1-2: before epsilon (or rho) and after pi perhaps a round letter || 57. ....ΥΣΤΑ || 58. after λεύκωμα there is space for three letters which might have been written or not || 59. "On pourrait penser avant εἰς τὸ βουλευτήριον à une généralité comme [ἐν τῆι ἀγορ]ᾶι".

1307. TEOS, HONORARY DECREE FOR ANTIOCHOS III, CA. 204-203 B.C. Ed. pr. P. Herrmann, ANADOLU 9 (1965) 29-259. G. Daux, BCH 100 (1976) 201-202 (see already ZPE 12, 1973, p. 235-236) reads in LL. 77-78: ὅσοι ἂν ἱερεῖς ἢ ὅσαι ἱέρειαι πρὸ πόλεως θυσίαν συντελῶσιν, χ[ρῆσ]|θαι πρὸς τὰς θυσίας ἐν οἷς δεῖ ὕδατι τούτωι κτλ. He translates: "dans toutes les opérations qui exigent de l' eau" (and not "bei allen Opfern, bei denen es nötig ist" as P. Herrmann, and ἐν αἷς δεῖ as J. and L. Robert, BE, 1969, no. 495, p. 504 per errorem).

1308. TEOS, EPITAPH, HELLENISTIC PERIOD. The stele from the Berlin Museum, Conze, Beschr. ant. Skulpt. (1891) no. 771 (with above the relief the inscription ὁ δῆμος | [--κ]λεί̈δου), attributed to Halikarnassos, has been referred on iconographical grounds to the area of Smyrna (especially to Magnesia on the Sipylos or Teos) by L. Robert, Hellenica XI-XII (1960) p. 217, note 5. H. Engelmann, ZPE 20 (1976) 24 supposes now that the museum was misled by the modern Turkish name Bodrum, denoting the ancient Halikarnassos as well as Teos. Cf. J. and L. Robert, BE (1977) no. 407.

1309. TEOS, EPITAPH. SEG, II, 628. Cf. H. Engelmann, ZPE 20 (1976) 156 who mentions that when Ruge saw this stone in 1890, the damaged lower part of the inscription was still better preserved. Ruge read it as follows: Πελοπίδης Οὐενούστῃ γυναικὶ χρηστῇ μνείας χάριν (BERLINER PHILOL. WOCHENSCHRIFT, 1892, 707, no. 7).

SEG: Πελοπίδη[ς] | Οὐενούστῃ | γυναικὶ χρησ|τῇ .α...ιας | χαῖρε. G. Crönert proposed in L. 4 ("e.g. filiae s. amicae nomen") [κ]α[ὶ Ἀμ]ιάς.

LYDIA

1310. MAIONIA (AYAZÖREN), DEDICATION TO THE METER ANATIDOS. Stele with a representation of Kybele in relief; now in the museum of Bodrum. Ed. pr. E.N. Lane, AS 20 (1970) 52-53, no. 3 (ph.). Cf. G. Petzl, ZPE 20 (1976) 223-224 and J. and L. Robert, BE (1977) no. 451. Petzl reads the inscription from the photo as follows:

Ἄδμητος Ἀδμήτου	τρὶ Ἀνάτιδος χα-
2 καὶ Γλυκέα ἡ γυνὴ Μη-	4 ριστήριον.

2-3. ἡ γυνὴ ὑπ|ὲρ 'Ιανάτιδος Lane; G. Petzl refers to the dedication Μητρὶ 'Ανάτιδος from Gürneit (10 km. south-western of Kula), ed. J. Keil - A. v. Premerstein, Bericht über eine zweite Reise in Lydien (Denkschr. Ak. Wien 54; 1911) p. 89, no. 178.

1311. MERMERE, HONORARY INSCRIPTION FOR MENEKRATES, 1st - 2nd CENT. A.D. J. Keil - A. v. Premerstein, Bericht über eine Reise in Lydien und der südlichen Aiolis (Denkschr. Ak. Wien 53; 1908-1909) p. 62, no. 126; IGR, IV, 1359. V. Nutton, ZPE 22 (1976) 93-96 rejects L. Moretti's restoration μ[ουλο]|[ι]ατρόν in L. 2-3 (RFIC 103, 1975, p. 189 f.), because the term is unattested (and the common ἱππιατρός to hand) and because the social status of the veterinary is not compatible with Menekrates' other high distinctions. J. Benedum, ZPE 29 (1978) 115-121 argues for Keil - Premerstein's restoration of L. 2-3 and for an identification of our Menekrates with Ti. Claudius Menekrates, founder of a medical school and on record in IGUR, II, 1, no. 686.

Μενεκράτ[ην]
Πολυ[ε]ίδου μ[....]
[ἰ]ατρὸν καὶ φιλ[...]
4 [.]ον, ἥρωα, λό[γιον],
στρατηγόν, γ[υμνα]-
[σ]ίαρχον, πρύτ[ανιν],
[ἀ]γωνοθέτ[ην ἡ]
8 [πόλ]ις ἐτ[ε]ί[μησεν]

2-3. μ[έγαν] | [ἰ]ατρὸν καὶ φιλ[όσο]|[φ]ον Keil - Premerstein; μ[ουλο]|[ι]ατρόν καὶ φιλ[όσο]|[φ]ον Moretti; μ[έγαν] ?? Nutton, who prefers to consider the mu as the beginning of the third part of the man's name, a further patronymic or an ethnic, and suggests φιλ[όσο]|[φ]ον or φιλ[όλο]|[γ]ον || 4. λο[γιστήν] IGR.

1312. PHILADELPHIA, HONORARY INSCRIPTION FOR THE ATHLETE M. AURELIUS PIUS FROM DALDIS, REIGN OF GALLIENUS. CIG, 3427. L. Robert, RPH 50 (1976) 181-192 points out that this inscription, assigned by G. Laminger-Pascher, Index grammaticus zu den griechischen Inschriften Kilikiens und Isauriens, II (SAWW, 298; 1974) 133-135 to Korykos, in fact belongs to Philadelphia in Lydia, and that the correct readings are to be found already in CIG, 3427, Le Bas - Waddington, no. 645 and in his article in RA (1934) I, 54 sqq. (OM, II, 1018 sqq.).

1313. PHILADELPHIA, INSCRIPTION ON A STATUE-BASE, 3rd CENT. A.D. Ed. pr. L. Robert, RPH 50 (1976) 186 (ph. of the squeeze).

Βασιλεὺς | ῎Ατταλος

I.e. Attalos II Philadelphos, founder of the town and in later times still honoured Robert.

1314-1320. SARDIS. C. Foss, Byzantine and Turkish Sardis (Arch. Expl. Sardis, Monograph 4; Cambridge Mass. and London, 1976) gives the text of several unpublished Sardis inscriptions in an appendix, entitled "The Sources". Though he does not give descriptions of the stones and a definitive publication has been entrusted to L. Robert, we give the texts here (all dated to the 4th - 6th cent. A.D.). Cf. also J. and L. Robert, BE (1977) no. 453 (with still another unpublished epitaph).

1314. P. 106, no. 2; tombstone.

Λεκτὶς διαφέρων [e.g. Π]ανίονος φαβρικησίου καὶ δουκηναρίου.

1315. P. 113, no. 15; building inscription.

Ἐπὶ Σεου(ή)ρ(ου) Σιμπλικίου τοῦ λαμπ(ροτάτου) κόμ(ητος) πρώτ'(ου) βαθμ'(οῦ) διέπ(οντος) τὴν ἔπαρχ(ον) ἐξουσίαν καὶ τοῦτο τὸ ἔργον τῆς ἀ[λει]πτηρίας ἀνενεώθη.

1316. P. 114, no. 16; epigram.

Θαῦμα μ' ἔχει πόθεν ἔργον ... γαῖα
δώματος ὑψορόφου χρυσαυγέος ἀπλέτ[ου ...]
... τὸ γῆρας ...
...νονιος πάτρης γενέτη[ς ...]
Ὡς ἴδεν ὡς κόσμ[ησε ... αὐ]τίκα τεῦξεν
κόσμον ἀεὶ ζώοντα τὸν οὐ φθόνος οἶδεν ...
ὤπασε δ' εὐρὺ θέμιλον ἀναπτύξας ...
αἰὲν ὀπιπευ[...]
Ἀνανεώθη χρυσοροφ[...] τῆς πόλεως ἰνδ. η' μηνὸς Ἰουλίῳ σκούτλωσιν [...] στρώσεις δὲ τοῦ ἐδ[άφους ...] δίχα τοῦ μουσίου καὶ τῶν ἄλλων

1317. P. 114-115, no. 17; epigram.

Οἱ κρήνης ποτ' ὕπερθε μέσην κατ' ἄγυιαν ὁδοῖο
πᾶσι παρερχομένοισιν ὁρώμενοι εἰσὶ δράκοντες
οὗτοι χαλκείησιν ἑλισσόμενοι φολίδεσσιν
οὓς Βασιλίσκος ἔθηκε δικασπόλος ἔνθα κομίσσας
χρυσῷ ἐρευθομένους ὑπὸ δε<ι>ράδα μέχρι καρήνων
νέρθεν ἄνω πέμποντας ἐπὶ στόμα χεύματα πηγῆς.

1318. P. 115, no. 18; building inscription.

Ἐκτίσθη ὁ ἔμβολος ἀπὸ τοῦ Ὑπεπηνοῦ ἐνβόλου ἄχρι τοῦ τετραπύλου ἐκκοπίσης τῆς πίλης καὶ παντὸς τοῦ τόπου.

1319. P. 115, no. 19; building inscription.

Ἐκχωσθέντος χωρὶς πόρων πολιτικῶν.

1320. J. and L. Robert, l.c.

Θ(ε)ὲ βοήθει αὐτοῖς, Φλ(αβίῳ) Χρυσανθίῳ δουκηναρίῳ φαβρικησίῳ καὶ τῷ οἴκῳ αὐτοῦ· κατεσκεύασεν τὸν λεκτείκα σὺν τῇ γοινεκὶ αὐτοῦ καὶ τέκνοις.

1321. AREA OF THYATEIRA AND LORA (HACIOSMANLAR), ACTIVITIES OF HEAD MEN OF A VILLAGE, 3rd CENT. A.D. (AFTER 212 A.D.). White marble block, broken at the right and the left side; found in Haciosmanlar, 20 km s.e. of Thyateira. Ed. pr. G. Petzl, ZPE 23 (1976) 243-244, no. 1 (ph.).

]Α̣Ϲ̣ΟΩΠΑΡΙ' ¯ΙΡΗΝΩ̣Κ..[
]Αὐρή̣[λι]οι Ἰουλιανὸς[
]ΙΟΔ.ΟΙ κωμάρχ̣[οῦν]τες[
4]τὸ ὕδωρ εἰσήγ̣αγ[ο]ν ἐπὶ ΤΟΓ̣.Α[
? ἐργαστ]ή̣ριον [ἐ]πόησαν ἐν τῇ στοᾷ Τ̇ΗϹ[
? ἐκ τῶν κω]μ̣ητικῶν πόρων, λογιστεύοντος [Praenomen, Nomen gentile ?
Ε̣Τατια-
8 νοῦϹ[

---

1. -τιρηνῷ (or -τιρηνῶ̣ν ?) Petzl ("Herkunftsbezeichnung") || 5. οἰκητ]ή̣ριον Petzl, who adds in his commentary: "auch ἐργαστ]ή̣ριον möglich" (cf. J. and L. Robert, BE, 1977, no. 450) || 7-8. "Das Zeichen vor ΤΑΤΙΑΝΟΥ (anscheinend kein Ε; eine Kürzel ?) und das lunare Sigma danach weiss ich nicht zu deuten (heteroklitischer Gen. in -οῦς ?)". Petzl.

1322. AREA OF THYATEIRA AND LORA (HACIOSMANLAR), HONORARY INSCRIPTION FOR DOKIMOS, IMPERIAL PERIOD. Marble stele, with a wreath and within it a star; found in Haciosmanlar, 20 km s.e. of Thyateira. Ed. pr. G. Petzl, ZPE 23 (1976) 244-249, no. 2 (ph.). Cf. J. and L. Robert, BE (1977) no. 450 (especially on the Λορηνοί of L. 2).

Ὁ δῆμος ἐτείμησεν
ὁ Λορηνῶν καὶ ὁ Θυα-
τ<ε>{τ}ιρηνῶν Δόκιμον
4 Διοκλέος Λεύκου Λεῦ-
κον· Σπένδουσα ἐτ<ε>ίμησε
Δόκιμον τὸν ἑαυτῆς

ἄνδρα· Ἀρτεμίδωρος
καὶ Διοκλῆς Ἡφαιστίωνος
ἐτείμησαν Δόκιμον.
Μή με μακροῖς ἐπέεσσιν ἐπὶ στήλῃ πο-
τὶ τύμβῳ, ὦ τέκνα, κοσμήσητε̣ ἐν δολίχοις
ἐλέγοις· ἀλλὰ μόνον τ̣όπερ̣ ἦ̣ν ὄνο-
μ', αὐτό μοι ἐνγράψαιτε· ὠ̣ς̣ ἄρ' ἐκλή-
ζετ̣[ε] μ' ἦν ἐν βι[ό]τῳ· δόκιμος.
Λού̣κιε̣ ΜΛΛΡΟΕΤΙ.Ο...Ε
ΗΛΥΕ̣ΤΑ̣ Δοκίμου.

---

3. ΤCΤ lapis || 5. ΤCΙΜ lapis || 13. ΩΣΑΡΕΚΛΗ¦ΖΕΤ[Ε] lapis; "stimmt meine Wiederherstellung des Gedankengangs, passte ὡς <γ>ὰρ ἐκλή|ζετε besser" Petzl || 15-16. Λούκι' ἐμ(ὰ) αἶθε τι ... | ἀλλ' ἀρετὰ Δοκίμου Merkelbach apud Petzl ("versuchsweise") || 16. μετά Herrmann apud Petzl.

1323. AREA OF THYATEIRA AND LORA (AKCAALAN), HONORARY INSCRIPTION FOR APOLLODOTOS, IMPERIAL PERIOD. White marble stele, with in the tympanon a star in a circle and under it a wreath with ribbons; found in Akcaalan, 5 km s. of Haciosmanlar. Ed. pr. G. Petzl, ZPE 23 (1976) 249-250, no. 3 (ph.).

Πρυτάνεων, δήμου Θυατει-
ρηνῶν μηνὸς Δαισίου ζ'.
Ὁ δῆμος ἐτίμησεν
Ἀπολλό (wreath) δοτον
Ἀπολλο δότου·
καὶ Ἀπολ λόδοτος τὸν
ἑαυτοῦ πατέρα· καὶ <Ἰ>γνατία τὸν ἄν-
δρα· καὶ Γάιος τὸν ἀδελφόν· καὶ Δ<α>-
μ<ᾶ>ς καὶ [Γ]έμελλος τὸν μήτρω· καὶ οἱ συν-
γενεῖς πάντες καὶ τὰ θρέμματα τὸν
θρέψαντα.

---

7. ΚΑΙΓΝΑΤΙΑ lapis || 8. ΔΛΜΛΣ lapis.

1324. AREA OF THYATEIRA AND LORA (AKCAALAN), HONORARY INSCRIPTION FOR APOLLONIOS (?), IMPERIAL PERIOD. White marble stele with two wreaths above the inscription; found in Akcaalan, 5 km s. of Haciosmanlar. Ed. pr. G. Petzl, ZPE 23 (1976) 250, no. 4 (ph.).

[Ὁ] δῆμος ἐτείμησεν Ἀπολλώ-
[νιον ?]ω Διόφαντος
[ ]Στρατο-
[τὸ]ν πατέρα
[Ἀπ]ολλώνιο[ ]
[ ]ω̣ν̣[ ]
[ ]ου[ ]

AIOLIS

1325. KYME, CORPUS. H. Engelmann, Die Inschriften von Kyme (Inschriften Griechischer Städte aus Kleinasien, 5; Bonn, 1976) presents a corpus of Kymaean inscriptions with full commentaries and with occasional translations. An exhaustive list of testimonies about Kymaean history and citizens and full indices conclude this volume. Cf. J. and L. Robert, BE (1978) no. 401-406.

1326. KYME, EPITAPH, ROMAN PERIOD. White marble stele, in the museum of Smyrna since 1930. Ed. pr. M. Yenim - G. Petzl, ZPE 20 (1976) 278 (ph.). Cf. O. Masson, ZPE 23 (1976) 263.

Ἱεροκλῆς καὶ
Μοῦσα τῆς ἰδί-
3 ας θυγατρὸς
Χωταρίου
μνείας ἕνε-
6 κεν.

4. Χωτάριον: Carian name Yenim - Petzl; vulgar pronunciation of Χρωτάριον (from χροῦς) Masson.

TROAS

1327. ALEXANDREIA TROAS, DEDICATION TO DIONYSOS, HELLENISTIC PERIOD. Ed. pr. G.E. Bean, apud J.M. Cook, The Troad (Oxford, 1973) p. 404, no. 27. Cf. G. Daux, BCH 100 (1976) 226 who restores in L. 2 [Κ]αλλιστῆς instead of [Φ?]αλλιστῆς (Bean).

1328. ALEXANDREIA TROAS (KEMALLI), EPIGRAM FOR THE GLADIATOR LUKAS, IMPERIAL PERIOD. Ed. pr. G.E. Bean, apud J.M. Cook, The Troad (Oxford, 1973) p. 404, no. 28 (ph.). Cf. P. Frisch, ZPE 13 (1974) 111 and W. Peek, ZPE 21 (1976) 259. We present the following text:

[Τὸ]ν σθεναρόν με Λυ-
[κ]ᾶν καθορᾷς, ὢ παρο-
[δ]εῖτα, πᾶλον πρῶτον
4 [Θρ]αικῶν, μονομα-
[χῶ]ν δέκατον ΚΑΝ
6 [...]ΛΥ'' ....ΤΩΝ

4-6. [Γαλ]λικῶν μονομά|[χω]ν, δέκατον ΚΑΝ̣ | ..λυ......των Bean; [Θρ]αικῶν μονομά|χων, δέκα τὸν (= ὃν) κἀν|[ν̣έα] λυγρα[βάν]των (= λυκαβ.) | [ὄντα ἥρπασε Μοῖρα] vel sim. Peek; but see J. and L. Robert, BE (1974) no. 459 where Frisch's text printed above, is supported and in vs. 6 λυτ̣ρα is suggested hesitatingly; cf. also BE (1977) no. 387.

1329. ASSOS, CORPUS. R. Merkelbach, Die Inschriften von Assos (Inschriften Griechischer Städte aus Kleinasien, 4; Bonn, 1976).

1330. ASSOS, HONORARY INSCRIPTION FOR AN AGONOTHETES. R. Merkelbach, Die Inschriften von Assos (Bonn, 1976) no. 43. Four fragments of a trachyte block, now in the museum of Fine Arts at Boston. C. Naour, ZPE 23 (1976) 236-239 (ph.) re-arranges the fragments and presents the following text:

[ἡ βουλὴ]
κα̣[ὶ ὁ δῆμος] ἐτεί-
μ[ησαν Ἀν]τ̣ί̣π̣ατρον
Ἀτ̣[τά]λου τὸν
[δι̣ὰ βί̣ο]υ ἀγωνο-
[θέ]τη̣ν.

1331. ILION, FUNERARY EPIGRAM, 1st - 2nd CENT. A.D. CIG, 3627; P. Frisch, Die Inschriften von Ilion (Bonn, 1975) no. 176. W. Peek, ZPE 22 (1976) 76-78 republishes this epigram with many new readings (on the basis of photographs of squeezes in Frisch, Pl. 23), gives translations of vv. 4, 7, 11, 15 and 17, and assigns the text to the 1st cent. A.D. (Frisch: 2nd cent. A.D.).

[Τ]ὴν στήλλην, παροδῖτα, παρέρ̣χ̣ε̣[ο, τὸν κατὰ γαῖαν]
   εὐφήμῳ γλόσσῃ χέρε προσειπά̣μ̣[ενος]
Κεῖντον{ι} τὸν τριπόθητον ἀεὶ γονέ[εσ]σι περ ὄντα{ν}·
εἰ δὲ μαθὼν τὸν ἐμὸν μόρον, ὦ ξένε, καὶ σύ με κλαύσις,
λέξο· καὶ θνήσκων γὰρ ἔχο νόον οὔ τινα βαιόν·
κουρῆα τὴν τέχνην ἐσορᾷς ἐμὲ τὸν παρὰ μοῖραν
   ῥήγματι δυσστήνῳ πνεῦμα βίᾳ θέμενον·
ἐξόπιθεν χεὶρ γάρ μαι ἔβαλεν δύστηνον ἐς Ἄδην
   κἤλυθον ἐξ ζοῆς ἐν δυσὶν ἑβδομάσιν,
[μέ]τ̣ρον δ' οὐκ ἴασε Τύχη δαίμων ται ἀλόγισστος
   [αἰ]ξανύσαι, πῖς δ' ὢν ἀρτιφυὴς ἔθανον{ι}·
[ἐνὰ] δ̣ὲ καὶ μάτηρ με ὀδύρετε ὃν κατὰ οἶκον{ι}
μάτηρ δ̣υσπενθής, [τὸ φίλον τέκο]|ς οὐκέθ' ὁρῶσα{ι}
οἰκτίσζουσά τε | ἐμὰς φρονίμους φρένας οἷ{ε}ά | τε παιδὸς
   σὺν πατρὶ δυσστή|νῳ βαλλομένῳ πολειὴν |
   δέμοσιν· ὦ μοίρης πικρὰ λογισ|ζομένης·
οὓς γὰρ ἐδεῖτο εὐ|[[χ...]]χαῖς τέκνου ὕπο τυμ|βεύεσσθαι
   οὗτοι νῦν τέκνου | σῆμα{ι} ἐπέθεντο τάφωι.

---

3. γονέ[ται]ς ἐόνταν{ι} Frisch || 11. [ἐ]ξανύσαι πιέσδων Frisch (as to Peek's text, [αἰ]ξανύσαι stands for [ἐ]ξανύσαι (αι = ε), πῖς for παῖς || 12. [πολλὰ δ]έ Frisch (as to Peek's text, [ἐνά] = [αἰνά]) || 13. [.]αιηΙδΙΙενθη[ ]|ς Frisch || 14. οἷ{ε}ά τε Frisch || 17. ἐδεῖτο εὐχαῖς Frisch.

1332. ILION, EPITAPH FOR PAUSIEPES, ROMAN PERIOD. CIG, 3628; P. Frisch, Die Inschriften von Ilion (Bonn, 1975) no. 169. W. Peek,

ZPE 22 (1976) 76-77 proposes (exempli gratia) the following restorations in Frisch's text:

[Υἱέα Π]αυσιέ[πην, ξένε, ¦ θάψε] ὁ πατὴρ [Διόδωρος?] |·
[τοῦ]το μνημεῖον [δὲ κάσις | ποί]ησε δακρύων |
Γάιος.

1. [Π]αυσίπ[που] ? Peek.

1333. SARIDÜZÜ, EPIGRAM FOR KRATIOS (?), IMPERIAL PERIOD. Ed. pr. G.E. Bean, apud J.M. Cook, The Troad (Oxford, 1973) p. 397, no. 7 (ph.). W. Peek, ZPE 21 (1976) 259 restores the text as follows:

[Σῆμα τόδε] Κρατ̣ίο[υ τεῦξαν] | Πρόκλος ἠδ' Ἀπόλαυστος, |
παῖδες πατρὶ φίλ̣ῳ, | γαμετὴ καὶ Ὄνησις ἀκοίτη̣.

1. [τῷ δεῖνι --]κρατ̣ίο[υ] or Κρατ̣ίο[υ] Bean.

1334. SKEPSIS, REGULATION FOR THE PRIEST OF DIONYSOS BAMBYLEIOS (?), 2nd CENT. B.C. (?). Ed. pr. Z. Taşliklioğlu - P. Frisch, ZPE 17 (1975) 106-109 (ph.). F. Sokolowski, ZPE 22 (1976) 185-188 proposes some new readings. Cf. J. and L. Robert, BE (1976) no. 572 and BE (1977) no. 382.

['Επὶ]'Αριστογένου τοῦ Σφοδριάδου, μ[ηνὸς]
['Αγαθ]ῆι τύχηι. 'Ο πριάμενος τὴν ἱερητείαν τοῦ Δ̣[ι]-
[ονύσ]ο̣υ τ̣[ο]ῦ̣ Β̣αμβυλείου ἀτελὴς ἔσται [..]λα
[... σ]τρατείας, ἐπικεφαλίου, σταθμοῦ καὶ δικα̣ι̣
[...]α ἐν δικαστηρίῳ ἐπάναγκες, τὰς δὲ επ[..]
[....]ΜΑΙΑΣΔΙΚΛΑΝ[..]Κ̣Ε̣Ι̣, ἀτελῆ δὲ εἶναι καὶ τὸν
[νε]ωκόρον τῶν αὐτῶν· ὁ̣ δὲ γενόμενος ἱερεὺς ἐ-
[στε]φαν[ώ]σθω κισσοῦ στεφάνῳ ἐν τῷ μηνὶ τῷ Ληναιῶ-
[νι] ἐν ταῖς νουμηνίαις [κ]αὶ ἐν ταῖς δημοτελέσιν ἑορταῖς πάσα̣[ις
[ἐν] τῷ ἄλλῳ δὲ χρόνῳ παντὶ ἐὰν αὐτῷ φαίνηται· ἐξέστω [δ]ὲ̣ α̣[ὐ]-
[τ]ῷ καὶ στέφανομ φορεῖν χρυσοῦν καὶ χιτῶνας ἀλουργ[ο]ὺς κα[ὶ]
[ὑ]πόδεσιν ἀκόλουθον τῇ ἐσθῆτι· καλεῖσθαι δὲ αὐτὸν καὶ εἰ[ς]
[τ]ὸ πρυτανεῖον ἐπὶ τὰς θυσίας ἃς συντελεῖ ἡ πόλις καὶ επ[.]
[..]ο̣ν ἐπ[ὶ] τὰς θυσίας τὰς συντελουμένας· τίθεσθαι δ[ὲ]
[αὐ]τ̣ῷ καὶ θρόνον ἐν τῷ θεάτρῳ καὶ καθῆσθαι αὐτὸν ἐν
[προεδ]ρ̣ί̣α̣ ἔν τε ταῖς τριετηρίσιν καὶ ἐν τῇ πανηγύρει ᾗ σ[υν]-
[τελεῖ]ιο[...]ω̣[.] π̣ά̣ντας θ[ ]

3. Β̣αμβυλείου: possibly also could be read Κ̣αμβυλείου Taşliklioğlu - Frisch || 4-5. καὶ δικᾷ [μη]|[δέν]α Sokolowski || 5-6. τὰς δὲ ἐπ[ικρίσεις] | [μὴ νο- or ἀναβολι]μαίας δικᾷ αν..κ̣ε̣ι̣ Sokolowski, who translates ἐπίκρισις as "judgment in cases of appeal" and notes that J. Bousquet (per litt.) read on the photo in L. 6 Λ̣Ο̣Ι̣ΜΑΙΑΣ.

However, on the photo there is hardly space for 2-3 letters after ΕΠ (ed.) || 7-8. ὁ δὲ γενόμενος ἱερεὺς ἐ[ξ ὠνῆς] | [στε]φαν[ού]σθω Sokolowski; but is there room for ἐ[ξ ὠνῆς]| ? ed. || 11. φέρειν Taşliklioğlu - Frisch || 13-14. καὶ ἐπ' [αὔ]|[ρι]ọν̣ Sokolowski (from J. Bousquet), but cf. J. and L. Robert, BE (1977) no. 382.

MYSIA

1335. AREA OF DASKYLEION (KÖSERESUL), MILESTONE, 168-169 A.D. Milestone, now in the garden of the Istanbul Archaeological Museum, with at least three texts: (I) Marcus Aurelius (in Latin and in Greek), (II) Constantinus and sons (in Latin), (III) Iulianus (in Latin). D. French, ZPE 21 (1976) 77-78 publishes text I:

Imp(erator) Caesar M(arcus) Aurelius
Antoninus Aug(ustus) Armeni-
acus Parthicus Medicus
pontifici maximi XXIII
imp(erator) V co(n)s(ul) III p(ater) p(atriae) proco(n)s(ulis)
Sexti Quintili Maximi
XVIII

Αὐτοκράτωρ Καῖσαρ
Μ(ᾶρκος) Αὐρήλιος Ἀντωνῖνος
Σεβαστὸς Ἀρμενιακὸς
Παρθικὸς Μηδικὸς ἀρ-
χιερεὺς μέγιστος δημαρ-
χικῆς ἐξουσίας τὸ κγ'
αὐτοκράτωρ τὸ ε' ὕπατος
τὸ γ' πατὴρ πατρίδος
ἐπὶ ἀνθυπάτου Σέξτου
Κυιντιλίου Μαξίμου
ιη'

Date: possibly 2nd half 169 A.D. French; on the find-spot Köseresul, cf. J. and L. Robert, BE (1977) no. 380 || 4. sic ! (error of the stonecutter or copyist ?) Herrmann.

1336. DASKYLEION, DEDICATION BY A PHROURARCH TO APOLLO AND ASKLEPIOS, HELLENISTIC PERIOD. White marble stele with relief, representing a sacrificial scene. Ed. pr. J. and L. Robert, JS (1976) 232-235 (ph.).

Πρωταγορίδ[η]ς Ἑκαταίου
φρουραρχήσα[ς ἐ]πὶ Διὸς ἱππαρ[χέω]
Ἀπόλλωνι καὶ Ἀσκληπιῶι
χαριστήριον.

1337. KYZIKOS, DEDICATION FOR A PRISONER OF WAR, 46 B.C. Syll[3], no. 763. H. Heinen, ANCSOC 7 (1976) 141 points out that E.P. Golubcova (apud T.V. Blavatskaja - E.P. Golubcova - A.I. Pavlovskaja, *Die Sklaverei in hellenistischen Staaten im 3-1 Jahrh. v. Chr.*, Wiesbaden, 1972, p. 129) incorrectly uses this text as evidence for slavery and slave trade in Kyzikos. The text clearly refers to the enslavement of a Kyzikene prisoner of war in Libya.

1338. PERGAMON, INSCRIPTIONS ABOUT QUEEN APOLLONIS. H. van Looy, ANCSOC 7 (1976) 151-165 uses various inscriptions for his study of the Attalid queen Apollonis.

1339. PERGAMON, LAW OF THE ASTYNOMOI, 2nd CENT. B.C. (BEFORE 133 B.C.). OGIS, 483; SEG, XIII, 521. C. Vatin, BCH 100 (1976) 558-559 questions the restoration [δέκα] in L. 34.

1340. PERGAMON, SENATUS CONSULTUM ABOUT PERGAMON, 133 B.C. OGIS, 435. B. Schleuszner, CHIRON 6 (1976) 97 ff. dates this text to 133 B.C. (and not to 129 B.C. as D. Magie, *Roman Rule in Asia Minor*, 2, Princeton, 1950, 1033 f., A 1 did) and suggests that the στρατηγοί in L. 6/7 are the future governors of Asia, against J. Vogt, *Sklaverei und Humanität* (Studien zur antiken Sklaverei und ihrer Erforschung; Wiesbaden, 1972) 65 ff. who sees in them legati pro praetore, i.e. ambassadors with special powers.

1341. PERGAMON, INSCRIPTIONS ABOUT HADRIAN. M. Le Glay, Hadrien et l' Asklépieion de Pergame, BCH 100 (1976) 347-372 argues with the help of inscriptions that the heyday of the Asklepieion of Pergamon began under the emperor Hadrian. He discusses the main inscriptions from Pergamon about Hadrian, and gives a long list of cities (a) named after Hadrian in Asia Minor, (b) celebrating a cult of Hadrian (temple, agoon). Cf. J. and L. Robert, BE (1977) no. 392 for some critical observations.

1342. PERGAMON, RESCRIPT OF HADRIAN ABOUT BANKING, 123/124 OR 129-131 A.D. OGIS, 484. A.D. Macro, GRBS 17 (1976) 169-179 gives a bibliography, translation and commentary of this text. He also suggests or makes the following corrections: L. 2. ἐπεσκε]ψάμην instead of μετεπεμ]ψάμην; 3-4. if the restoration of Dittenberger is correct, τῶν ἐργαζομένων refers not to the exchange dealers (Dittenberger) but to the tradesmen; 6. ὡς νόμιμ]ον or δίκαι]ον or καθῆκ]ον ἦν instead of ἵνα δῆλ]ον ἦν; 6-7. οἱ οὖν τῆς ἀ¦[μειπτικῆς κεκοινωνηκότες πο]λ<λ>ά instead of ὁ οὖν τῆς ἀ|[μείψεως τρόπος οὐ νόμιμος ἦν, ἀ]λ<λ>ά; 10. τοῦ δη]ναρ̣[ίου] (with W.K. Prentice) instead of [τὸ δη]νάρ̣[ιον]; 49. καθ]ὡ̣ς instead of ὅπως; 49-50. [δούλου μὴ ἄ]με|τρον (J.H. Oliver, per litt.) instead of [δούλου μὴ σύ]ṃμε|τρον.

1343. PERGAMON, SIGNATURE OF THE SCULPTOR MYRON OF THEBES. Altertümer von Pergamon, VIII, 1, no. 136. P. Mingazzini, JÖAI 50 (HAUPTBLATT, 1972-73) 13-22 dates this inscription to the period 200-ca. 160 B.C. and on the basis of stylistic arguments she dates the akme of Myron to 200-170 B.C.

1344. PROKONNESOS (PALATIA), DEDICATION TO ZEUS ORNEOS, IMPERIAL PERIOD. Ed. pr. M.J. Gédéon, Προικόννησος, ἐκκλησιαστικὴ παροικία, ναοὶ καὶ μοναί, μητροπολῖται καὶ ἐπίσκοποι (Constantinople, 1895) pl. IV, 30 and p. 139; F.W. Hasluck, Cyzicus (Cambridge, 1910) 272, no. 24. Cf. L. Robert, STUDCLAS 16 (1974) 80-85 who presents with a commentary the following text:

Διὶ Ὀρνέῳ εὐχα-
2 ριστοῦμεν να-
ῦται Ἡρακλ[ε]-
4 ῶτα[ι].

1. Δι(ὶ) Hasluck || Zeus Orneos = Zeus of Ornoi, on the coast of the area of Bisanthe and of Tekir Dağ-Rodosto Robert || 3-4. Ἡρακλ[ε]|ῶτα[ι]: M. Gédéon thinks that Herakleia was Perinthos, L. Robert rather thinks of Herakleia of Pontus.

1345. PROKONNESOS, INSCRIPTION ON A CAVE. Ed. pr. Cyriacus of Ancona, apud E.W. Bodnar - C. Mitchell, Cyriacus of Ancona's journeys in the Propontis and the Northern Aegean, 1444-1445 (Memoirs Am. Philos. Soc., 112; Philadelphia, 1976) p. 34 ('unpublished'). Cf. J. and L. Robert, BE (1977) no. 8.

Ἰουλιανὸς γραμματεύς

BITHYNIA

1346. BITHYNION-CLAUDIOPOLIS, SUN-DIAL, 134 A.D. Bronze medaillon with Greek inscriptions. Ed. pr. E. Buchner, CHIRON 6 (1976) 329-336 (ph.).

a) Ἡ πατρὶς Ἀντίνοον θεόν
b) Ἰούλιος ΠΟΙΕΙ (= ποιεῖ or ἐποίει)
c) A list of Bithynian names of the months: Διον(ύσιος), Ἡράκ(λειος), Δῖος, Βενδ(ίδαιος), Στρά(τειος), Πρά(στιος), Ἄρει(ος), Ἀφρ(οδίσιος), Δημ(ήτριος), Ἡραῖ(ος), Ἑρμ(αῖος), Μη(τρῷος) (= from January - December).

1347. NIKOMEDEIA, ORACLE FROM KLAROS, IMPERIAL PERIOD. Ed. pr. CIG, 3769; Kaibel, EG, no. 1036; now TAM, IV, 1, 92. Cf. R. Merkelbach, ZPE 18 (1975) 100 and W. Peek, ZPE 21 (1976) 260 (with reconstruction sketch) who both deal with vv. 1-2. We present both versions:

I. Merkelbach:

ἀμφὶ̣ π̣ολ<ε>[ι]τραφίης γεοθ<α>λπέος, ὦ πτολι<ά>ρ<χ>α,
[ε]ἰ̣ῆναι κέλομαί σε σ[ε]λώπυρον ὠρ[ο]μέ<δ>οντα

II. Peek:

ἀμφὶ̣ π̣ολυτραφίης γεοθα̣λπέος, ὦ πτολιάρ[χ]α,
[κρ]η̣ῆναι κέλομαί σε σα̣ώπυρον ὠρ[ο]μέδοντα

1. Ἀμφίπολ' [ε]ὐτραφίης Boeckh, Kaibel || 2. [ε]ἰῆναι Boeckh, Kaibel; as to κραίνειν Peek refers to Hesychios (κραίνειν = τιμᾶν) || σ[α]ω[τῆ]ρ' [ὑψι]μέ[δ]οντα Boeckh; ...... ὠρ[ο]μέ[δ]οντα Kaibel.

1348. AREA OF NIKOMEDEIA (KARAYAKUPLU), EPITAPH FOR STRATON AND IOLE. Ed. pr. S. Şahin, ZPE 18 (1975) 42, no. 125; now TAM, IV, 1, 303. C.P. Jones, ZPE 21 (1976) 189 and W. Peek, ZPE 21 (1976) 288 independently restored vv. 1-2 (vv. 1-4 are in iambics). We present the whole text here:

Ἄμπαυμα μόχθων καὶ φύλαγμα σωμ̣[άτων]
ἔθεντο κοινὸν ἐς τὸ τοῦ βίου [τέλος]
Στράτων Ἱέρωνος καὶ Ἰόλη τούτου δάμαρ
στοργὴν βεβαίαν κἀν φθιτοῖς αἱρούμενοι.
Ὃς ἂν δὲ μετὰ τὸ τεθῆναι τὸν Στράτωνα
καὶ τὴν Ἰόλην ἕτερον βάλῃ τινα, δότω
προστείμου τῷ φίσκῳ καὶ τῇ πόλει *,α--.
[Χαίρε]τ[ε]

1. φύλαγμα σων...... Şahin || 2. βίου .... Şahin.

1349. NIKOMEDEIA, EPITAPH. Ed. pr. S. Şahin, ZPE 18 (1975) 34-35, no. 103 (ph.); now TAM, IV, 1, 132. Cf. C.P. Jones, ZPE 21 (1976) 190-191 who corrects vs. 3 and explains the violations of the meter in vs. 9 and 10.

Μνήμης χάριν γλυκίας σῆς, ἐπισ|τάτα,
στήλην ἔγρ<α>ψα τήνδε κὲ ἐθ|έμην τάφῳ
Εὐφρᾶς ποθῶν Βεστᾶ|λιν, κὲ ἂν κεῖτε νέκυς·
ὁ γὰρ κα|λῶς παθών τις λήθην οὐκ ἔχει· |
τέχνην διδάξ̣ας τῆς πάσης μετ' [ε]|ὐνοίας
ἔδωκεν ἀφορμὴν τῆς [ζ]|ωῆς κὲ τῆς τροφῆς

ῥάπτην τεχν|είτην παρὰ πᾶσιν φίλοις φίλον·|
ὅτα<ν> ἐξέθρεψε κὲ ἐδιδάξετο τέ|χνην,
ἐλπίζων παρ' ἐμοῦ χάριτ|ας v.v. τὰς αὐτὰς ἀμοιβὰ[ς] | λαβεῖν,
οὐκ ἔτυχεν, ἀλλ' ἔ[θ]|ανε πέντε κὲ τρειάντα ἐτ|ῶν.

3. Βεπάλιν, κὲ ἄνκειτε νέκυς Şahin || 9. ἀμοιβάς: superfluous to sense and meter; it is an "interpolation" Jones || 10. the violation of the meter is due to the difficulty of fitting in the numeral Jones.

1350. PROUSIAS, UPPER-CLASS FAMILIES. On some important families (Titii, Ulpii, Statilii) in the honorary inscriptions of Prousias, cf. Maija Väisänen, ARCTOS 10 (1976) 125-132, with special reference to IGR, III, 55, 58 (date: end 2nd cent. - beginning 3rd cent. A.D., against H.G. Pflaum, Les carrières procuratoriennes équestres sous le Haut-Empire romain, III, p. 1102 who preferred ca. 250 A.D), 63, 69, 1420, and F.K. Dörner, Bericht über eine Reise in Bithynien (Denkschr. Ak. Wien 75, 1; Wien, 1952) p. 17, no. 11 and p. 21, no. 19.

PONTOS

1351. INSCRIPTION EXCLUDED FROM THE PONTIC CORPUS. Studia Pontica, III, no. 207 a. Cf. no. 1287.

PHRYGIA

1352. AIZANOI, HONORARY INSCRIPTION FOR A. CLAUDIUS LEPIDUS, 2nd CENT. A.D. Marble statue base. Ed. pr. W. Günther, MDAI(I) 26 (1976) 111-115 (ph.).

Ἡ Ἀδρι[ανὴ φυλὴ Ἀ.]
Κλ. [Λ]έ[πιδον, τὸν]
ἀρχινεώκο[ρον]
καὶ ἱερέα τοῦ αὐ[το]-
κράτορος διὰ β[ίου],
ἀρχιερέα Ἀσίας [ναῶν]
τῶν τῆς λαμπ[ροτά]-
της Σμυρν[αίων πό]-
[λ]εως, στεφ[ανηφό]-
ρον καὶ ἀγ[ωνοθέ]-
την ἀπο[δεδειγμέ]-
νον τῆς π[ατρίδος]
τὸν εὐεργέ[την],
ἐπιμεληθέντο[ς]
Φιλίππου Ἀγαθίωνο[ς]
τοῦ φυλάρχου. vacat

1. Ἀδριανίς seems too long Günther || 1-2. the honorand is attested in IGR, IV, 586 Günther.

1353. AIZANOI, EDICT OF THE GOVERNOR FULVIUS ASTICUS (PROMULGA-

TING THE PRICES EDICT OF DIOCLETIAN), 301 A.D. Ed. pr. M.H. Crawford - J. Reynolds, JRS 65 (1975) 160-163 (ph.). Cf. J. Reynolds, JRS 66 (1976) 183, note 119 who proposes some new readings in LL. 4-6 after re-examination of the stone, and J.H. Oliver, AJP 97 (1976) 174-175. We present Reynolds' text:

Φούλβιος Ἄστικος ὁ διασημότατος ἡγεμὼν v. λέγ[ει v.]
Καὶ τοῦτο τῆς θείας προμηθείας, λεγόντων <τῶν> ἀηττήτων
καὶ πάντα νεικώντων δεσπότων ἡμῶν βασιλέων τε
καὶ Καισάρων εὐχέρειαν βίου τῆς τῶν ὠνίων [.5-6..]ίας κα-
ταστάσης ἐν τειμαῖς δικαίας v. χορηγεῖσθαι [ca.3]ΙΑΤΟ τὸ αὐτὸ ἢ ἀν-
θρώποις ἅπασιν, καὶ δι' ὑπερβάλλουσαν [2-3]μην καὶ φιλαργυρίαν
τινῶν ἀπορεῖν τῶν πρὸς τὴν χρείαν ἀναγκαίων μηδένα, ἀ-
πάσης περικοπείσης ἐνθυμήσεως πανούργου, ἴσην καὶ ὡ-
ρισμ v. ένην τὴν ἐφ' ἑκάστοις τετάχθαι τειμήν· ὅπερ ἵνα πα-
ραφυλ v. {λ}άττηται καὶ δι' ἅπαντος α<ἰ>ῶν{ν}ος μένῃ τῇ θειότητι
αὐτῶν προνενοεῖται, ἀλλ' ἵνα καὶ ὑμεῖ{ι}ν δῆλον καταστῇ σὺν
{σὺν} ἐπιμελείᾳ{ς} πάσῃ τοῦ θείου διατάγματος τοῦ ἐπὶ τῆι τειμῇ
τῶν τε ὠνίων καὶ συναλλαγμάτων δοθέντος νόμου τὸ ἀντί-
γραφον μετὰ τοῦ προσήκοντος σεβάσματος τοῦδέ μου τοῦ δια-
τάγματος προτεταγμένον φαίνεται. Proponatur.

2. Καὶ τοῦτο τῆς θείας προμηθεία<ς> ἔλεγον τῶν ἀηττήτων Oliver || 4. [εὐων]ίας or [εὐπορ]ίας Reynolds; [κανό]νας Oliver || 5-6. ἐν τειμαῖς δι[κ]αίαις κα[ὶ] ῥηταῖς [συμβόλ]αιο<ν> τὸ αὐτὸ ἢ ἀν|θρώποις ἅπασιν <ὥστε> καὶ Oliver || 6. [τολ]μήν or [ὁρ]μὴν Reynolds.

1354. AKMONIA, HONORARY INSCRIPTION FOR THE CAESAR GALLUS, 351-354 A.D. Marble slab. Ed. pr. T. Drew-Bear - W. Eck, CHIRON 6 (1976) 293-294, no. 4 (ph.).

Ἀγαθῆι Τύχηι
τὸν γῆς καὶ θαλάσσης
δεσπότην
4 Φλ. Κλαύδιον
Κωστάντιον hedera
τὸν ἀήττητον βασιλέα
7 ἡ Ἀκμονέων πόλις.

1355. AKMONIA, DEDICATION TO THE THEOS HYPSISTOS. Inscription on a small altar decorated by a tendril with three leaves. Ed. pr. T. Drew-Bear, GRBS 17 (1976) 247-248, no. 1 (ph.).

Ἐβίκτητος
ἐπύησε-
3 ν Θεῷ
Ὑψίστῳ
5 εὐχήν.

1356. AKMONIA, DEDICATION TO THE THEOS HYPSISTOS. Inscribed rectangular block. Ed. pr. T. Drew-Bear, GRBS 17 (1976) 248-249, no. 2 (ph.).

Ἀγαθῇ Τύχ[ῃ]·
Αὐρ. Τατις Ὀ-
νησίμου χαλ̣-
κέος σύνβιος
σὺν τῷ συμβί-
ῳ Ὀνησίμῳ Θε-
ῷ Ὑψίστῳ ἐκ τ-
ῶν ἰδίων ἀνέ-
[θ]ῆσαν.

1357. AKMONIA, DEDICATION TO SOZON. Inscription known only from a copy made by a resident of Banaz. Ed. pr. T. Drew-Bear, GRBS 17 (1976) 249-250, no. 3.

Αὐξάνων Κ-
οΐντου ὑπὲ-
ρ σωτηρίας Σώ-
ζοντι εὐχήν.

It cannot be excluded that this is a dedication to Apollo Sozon Drew-Bear.

1358. AKMONIA, DEDICATION BY A VILLAGE TO APOLLO ALSENOS. Inscription known only from a copy made by a resident of Banaz. Ed. pr. T. Drew-Bear, GRBS 17 (1976) 250, no. 4.

Κταηνῶν κώμ-
η κατ' ἐπιταγὴ-
ν Ἀπόλλωνι
Ἀλσηνῷ.

1359. AKMONIA, DEDICATION TO APOLLO. Inscription known only from a copy made by a resident of Banaz. Ed. pr. T. Drew-Bear, GRBS 17 (1976) 250, no. 5.

Ἀπελλᾶς Ὀ|νησίμου Ἀπό|λλωνι εὐχήν.

1360. AKMONIA, DEDICATION TO APOLLO. Inscription known only from a copy made by a resident of Banaz. Ed. pr. T. Drew-Bear, GRBS 17 (1976) 251, no. 6.

Ἐλαϊνὸς εὐ|χὴν Ἀπόλ|λωνι.

1361. AKMONIA, DEDICATION. Inscription known only from a copy made by a resident of Banaz. Ed. pr. T. Drew-Bear, GRBS 17 (1976) 251, no. 7.

Ἀρτεμίδωρος
παρ' ἑαυτοῦ
Γλύκωνος
ἀνέθηκεν.

1362. AMORION, DEDICATION TO ASKLEPIOS, AFTER 212 A.D. Inscribed base of a statue of Asklepios, with patera and serpent. Ed. pr. T. Drew-Bear, GRBS 17 (1976) 257-259, no. 13 (ph.).

Αὐρ. Ουαναξος Μανου
ἐποίησε τὸν ναὸν σὺν
τοῖς ἀγάλμασι.

The group of names Ουαναξος, Ουαναξιων is concentrated in a small area between Amorion and Philomelion Drew-Bear.

1363. ANKYRA SIDERA, ERECTION OF A STATUE OF CONSTANTINUS II, AFTER 324 A.D. Base of a statue. Ed. pr. T. Drew-Bear - W. Eck, CHIRON 6 (1976) 290-293, no. 2 (ph.).

Φλάβ. Κλαύδ. Κωσταν-
τεῖνον ἐπιφανέστα-
τον Καίσαρα υεἱὸν
βασιλέως.

1364. ANKYRA SIDERA, ERECTION OF A STATUE OF CONSTANS, AFTER 334 A.D. Base of a statue. Ed. pr. T. Drew-Bear - W. Eck, CHIRON 6 (1976) 291-293, no. 3 (ph.).

[Φλάβ. Ἰούλ.]
Κώνσ̣τ̣α[ντα]
ἐπιφανέστα-
τον Καίσαρα
υεἱὸν βασιλαίος.

1365. APPIA, MILE-STONE WITH TWO VERSIONS, I) BETWEEN 198 AND 209 A.D., II) PROBABLY REIGN OF CONSTANTINUS I. Mile-stone, twice inscribed; first text erased (with exception of lines 1, 2, 9, part of 10, part of 12-13) under the first tetrarchy or later. Ed. pr. T. Drew-Bear - W. Eck, CHIRON 6 (1976) 296-297, no. 6 (ph.).

I (in rasura)

Αὐτοκράτο-
ρι Καίσαρι Λου-
[[κίῳ Σεπτιμί]]-
[[ῳ Σεουήρῳ]]
[[Περτίνακι Σεβασ]]-
[[τῷ Ἀραβικῷ Ἀδι]]-
[[αβηνικῷ Παρθι]]-
[[κῷ μεγίστῳ καὶ]]
Αὐτοκράτορι Κ-
αίσαρι [[Μάρκῳ]]
[[Αὐρηλίῳ Ἀντ]]-
[[ωνείνῳ]] Σεβασ-
τῷ [[καὶ Π. Σεπτι]]-
[[μίῳ Γέτα̣ Καίσαρι]]

II

Αὐτοκράτο-
ρι Καίσαρι Λου-
//////////////
//////////////
//////////////
//////////////
//////////////
//////////////
Αὐτοκράτορι Κ-
αίσαρι ///////
//////////////
///////Σεβασ-
τῷ///////////
Φλαβίῳ

καὶ [[Ἰουλίᾳ Δόμ]]-
16 [[νῃ Σεβαστῇ]]
[[μητρὶ κά]]-
[[στρων]]
μ(ίλια) α'

Κοσταντίνῳ
16 ἀνικήτῳ
Σεβαστῷ
///////
μ(ίλια) α'

1366. APPIA, MILE-STONE WITH THREE VERSIONS, I) (L. 1-10a) 293-305 A.D., II) (L. 10b-14a) 305-306 A.D., III) (L. 14b-17) 313-317 A.D. Ed. pr. T. Drew-Bear - W. Eck, CHIRON 6 (1976) 298-300, no. 8 (ph.).

I [Τοῖς] κυ[ρίοις]
[ἡμ]ῶν Γ. Α[ὐρ.]
[Διοκ]λητια[νῷ]
4 [κὲ Μ]αξιμιαν[ῷ κὲ]
τοῖς ἐ v.v. [πι]-
φανεστάτο[ις]
Κέσαρσι Μαρ. Αὐ[ρ.]
8 Κωσταντίῳ
κὲ Μαξιμιανῷ
10a μ(ίλια) α'

II 10b κὲ τοῖς ἐπιφα-Σεβα[στ]-
νεστάτ οις
12 Κέσαρσ[ι]ν
Σεβήρῳ
14a [[κὲ Μαξιμίνῳ]]
III 14b [ὑπὲ]ρ τῶν δεσποτῶν ἡμ[ῶν]
Κωνσταντίνου [κὲ Λικιν]-
16 [νίου] τῶν ἀωνίω[ν]
αὐτω̣κ̣ρ[ατόρων]

1367. APPIA, DEDICATION TO ZEUS ANDREAS. Stele with the bust of Zeus, right hand spread across his chest, a garland and two ox-heads. Ed. pr. T. Drew-Bear, GRBS 17 (1976) 252-253, no. 9 (ph.).

[Ἐπι]τύν v. χανος λατύπος ὑπὲρ τῆς
[κώμ]ης σωτηρίας Διὶ Ἀνδρέᾳ εὐχὴν
τὴν είστήλην.

1368. APPIA, DEDICATION TO ZEUS ANDREAS. Stele with the bust of Zeus, right hand spread across his chest, a garland and two ox-heads. Ed. pr. T. Drew-Bear, GRBS 17 (1976) 253-254, no. 10 (ph.).

Αππης Τείμωνος σύνβιο[ς]
Δεὶ Ἀνδρέᾳ εὐχή.

For more dedications to the same divinity, cf. J. and L. Robert, BE (1977) no. 495.

1369. APPIA, DEDICATION TO ZEUS BENNIOS. Stele broken at the top. Ed. pr. T. Drew-Bear, GRBS 17 (1976) 254-255, no. 11 (ph.).

[----]η̣ς̣ ὑ̣π̣ὲ̣[ρ ἑαυτ]-
ῶν καὶ τέκνων καὶ συν-
βίου καὶ Πριάμου καὶ

4 συνβίου αὐτοῦ καὶ
Μοσσυνέων Διὶ Βεν-
νίῳ εὐχήν
Ζηλᾶς καὶ Ἐπιτύν-
8 χανος λατύποι.

5-6. For Zeus Bennios, cf. S. Şahin, Zeus Bennios, in Studien zur Religion und Kultur Kleinasiens (Festschrift F.K. Dörner, Leiden, 1978) II. Band, p. 771-790 || 7-8. Ἐπιτύνχανος: cf. no. 1367.

1370. APPIA, DEDICATION TO ZEUS BENNIOS. Round altar, with the inscription in a tabula ansata; above the text a garland, an eagle, ox-heads. Copied by W.M. Ramsay, JHS 5 (1885) 259, no. 11. Re-edited by T. Drew-Bear, GRBS 17 (1976) 255-257, no. 12 (ph.); S. Şahin, in <u>Studien zur Religion und Kultur Kleinasiens</u> (Festschrift F.K. Dörner, Leiden, 1978) II. Band, p. 782.

Διὶ·Βεννίῳ
Διογένης ὑπὲρ
Διογένους πάππου
καὶ Κλ. Χρυσίου
5 μάμμης καὶ τῶν
κατοικούντων
ἐν Ἰσκόμῃ καθιέρω-
σεν.
9 Ἀπολλώνιος Ἰσγερεανὸς ἐποίει.

1. For Zeus Bennios, cf. note in no. 1369.

1371. CAY (= IULIA ?), MILE-STONE WITH THREE VERSIONS, I) 293-305 A.D., II) CA. 317 A.D., III) (in Latin) 18 Sept. 335 - 22 May 337 A.D. Ed. pr. T. Drew-Bear - W. Eck, CHIRON 6 (1976) 301-304, no. 10 (ph.).

I
Τοῖς κυρίοις ἡμῶν
Γ^{V} Οὐαλ^{V} Διοκλητιανῷ
καὶ Μ Οὐαλ^{V} Μαξιμιανῷ
4 Σεβ^{V}β^{V} καὶ
Φλα^{V} Οὐαλ^{V} Κωσταντίῳ
καὶ Γ^{V} Οὐαλ^{V} Μαξιμιανῷ
ἐπιφανεστάτοις Καίσαρσιν
8 μι
ƎI

II
[[Φλ. Κρίσπος]]
[[καὶ]] Κωνστ[αν]-
τεῖνος [[Λικίν]]-
4 νιος κ[αὶ] Φλ. Κων-
σταντεῖνος οἱ
ἐπιφανέστατοι
7 Καίσαρες

III
dd.nn. Fl. V<a>l. Constanṭịṇ[o]
max. vict. ac triumf.
senper (sic) Aug. et Fl. Cl.
4 Constantino et
{Fl. Iul. Constantino et}
Fl. Iul. Constantio et
Fl. Iul. Constante
8 fortiss. ac nobb. Caess.

et Fl. Dalmatio fortis.
ac nob. Caes{s}
μι ιε'

1. After each abbreviation, there is a small sign in the form of a v; in L. 3 this sign stands above the M; in L. 4 also a v after the first β.

1372. DIONYSOUPOLIS ?, DEDICATION TO ZEUS TROOSSOU. Stele with inscription below an ox-head; found in Bekilli and said to have been brought from the village of Üçkuyu. Ed. pr. T. Drew-Bear, GRBS 17 (1976) 261-262, no. 16 (ph.).

Μανης
Ἀπολλω-
3 νίου Διὶ
Τρωσσου
ἀνάθε-
6 μα.

1373. DORYLAION, DEDICATION OF A MONUMENT (A HEROON ?) FOR ULP. FL. CLAUDIANUS PONTICUS, REIGN OF COMMODUS - MIDDLE 3rd CENT. A.D. Fragment of an architrave block. Ed. pr. T. Drew-Bear - W. Eck, CHIRON 6 (1976) 304-305, no. 11 (ph.)

[. Οὔλ]πιον Φλάουιον Κλαυδιανὸν Πόντικον τὸν
χειλίαρχον πλατύσημον ἡ πό[λις].

1374. DORYLAION, EPITAPH, 5th - 6th CENT. A.D. Grave-stele. Ed. pr. T. Drew-Bear - W. Eck, CHIRON 6 (1976) 305-307, no. 12 (ph.).

†
† Ἐνθάδε
κατάκιται
3 Θεόδουλος
κόμ(ης) σχολῆς
γεντιλίων
6 ἰωνιόρων

4. σχολῆ<ς> ("statt eines Σ ein O") Drew-Bear - Eck; G. Daux, REG 90 (1977) 477, note 26 reads a lunar sigma on the photo.

1375. EMIR DAGH, VOTIVE EPIGRAM. Ed. pr. L. Tuğrul, ANNUAL ARCH. MUS. ISTANBUL 13-14 (1967) 184 f., no. 23 (ph.). Cf. W. Peek, ZPE 21 (1976) 151 who reads the inscription as follows:

[× – ∪ – × – ∪ – | ·ω]ν εἵνεκα, |
θεῶν ἄναξ, | ἔθηκα σοὶ τοῦ|τ'· ἀλλά μιν
κα|λῶς ὁρᾶν θεί|ης, ἄριστε δαι|μόνων Ὀλύμ|πιε.

---ΕΙΝΕΚΑ | θεῶν ἄναξ, | ἔθηκα σοί τ' οὐ | τ' ἀλλά μιν κα|λῶ σοι Ἀνθεί|ης, ἄριστε δαι|μόνων Ὀλύμπιε Tuğrul; in vs. 1-2 Peek accepts the reading of J. and L. Robert, BE (1968) no. 526.

1376. EUMENEIA, DEDICATION TO APOLLO PROPYLAIOS. Stele bearing a double-axe. Ed. pr. T. Drew-Bear, GRBS 17 (1976) 260-261, no. 15 (ph.).

[᾿Απόλλω]-
[νι Προ]-
[πυ]λαίῳ
4 [᾿Επ]ιτύν-
[χ]ανος κολα-
ζόμενος
7 [ἀ]νέθηκεν.

1377. EUMENEIA, TWO EPITAPHS, 3rd CENT. A.D. I) SEG, VI, 210; L. Robert, Hellenica XI-XII, p. 414 ff. II) L. Robert, Hellenica XI-XII, 429 ff. N.G. Cohen, JSJ 7 (1976) 125-128 discusses the identity of a person, named Roube, in these two epitaphs. He thinks that this name makes it highly likely that Roube stemmed from the semi-Jewish, semi-Christian, oriental urban milieu of one of the Graeco-Roman centres of the Levant (and was not a local Jewish convert to Christianity: L. Robert).

1378. HIERAPOLIS, ORACLE OF APOLLO KAREIOS, 2nd - 1st CENT. B.C. Ed. pr. G. Pugliese Carratelli, ASAA 41-42 (1963-64) 353-370 (ph.). M. Gigante, PP 31 (1976) 323 defends, with G. Nenci, ASNP, s. III, vol. V, 1 (1975) 99-101 in I, 13 the reading φωσφόρος ἀκτή (against Cazzaniga and West who proposed φωσφόρος ἀκτίς). He explains it, with Nenci, as "i promontori scogliosi biancheggianti ... dotati di una propria luminosità" (and not, as M. Guarducci, RFIC, 102, 1974, p. 201, as a "riva portatrice di un faro").

1379. HIERAPOLIS, HONORARY EPIGRAM FOR AN ATHLETE, 2nd CENT. A.D. Altertümer von Hierapolis, no. 46 (non vidimus). After R. Merkelbach, ZPE 7 (1971) 43-44 (cf. also J. and L. Robert, BE, 1971, no. 640), W. Peek, ZPE 22 (1976) 246-247 returns to this text.

[---------------]|λην ἔπι Λήναιος | εἰκόνα χαλκῆν |
μαρτύριον προφέ|ρει τῶν ἰδίων κα|μάτων
3 ἄθλων | Ἡρακλέους κρατε|ρόφρονος, ὧν διέθ[η]|κεν
Ζωτικὸς εὐπα|τρίδης κλεινὸς | ἀγωνοθέτης·
τεῦ|ξαι δὲ τὴν κεφα|λὴν Γλαβρίων | κὲ θήκατο κόσ|μον
6 ῥάβδῳ τειμη|[θε]ὶς ΗΝΙΑΛΗΣΥΠΑ

---

1. [? μαρμαρέην στή]|λην ἔπι Λήναιος Merkelbach; [τὴνδε τιθεὶς στή]|λην ἔπι or [νικήσας με πά]|λην ᾿Επιλήναιος ("singuläre Name") Peek || 3. ἄθλων [θ᾿]| Judeich, Merkelbach || 5-6. κόσ|μον ῥάβδῳ τειμη|[θε]ὶς <Εἵτ>αλ<ί>ης ὑπά[τῳ] Merkelbach, who identifies Glabrio with the legatus Asiae Acilius Glabrio and interprets ῥάβδος as the

Greek equivalent of the fasces ("geehrt mit den Konsular-Fasces Italiens"); rightly rejected by J. and L. Robert (and Peek) who identify Glabrio as one of the ῥαβδοφόροι of the agonothetes Zotikos; κόσ|μον ῥάβδῳ τειμη|[θε]ὶς <Σ>ημ̣ιά̣δης Ὑπά[του] or <Σ>ημ̣ιά̣δης· ὕπα[γε] Peek.

1380. KOTIAEION OR NAKOLEIA, DEDICATION TO ZEUS SYREANOS BY THE VILLAGERS OF Εἰσκώμη. Altar with the bust of Zeus, right hand across his chest, a chalice and two ox-heads; now in the museum at Kütahya. Ed. pr. T. Drew-Bear, GRBS 17 (1976) 251-252, no. 8 (ph.)

'Αγαθῇ Τύχῃ·
2 Ε̣ἰσκωμῆται
Διὶ Συρεανῷ
4 εὐχήν.

1381. BETWEEN KOTIAEION AND APPIA (ASLANAPA), MILE-STONE, 293-305 A.D. The stone has been inscribed twice: the first text, of unknown date, has been erased almost entirely. Ed. pr. T. Drew-Bear - W. Eck, CHIRON 6 (1976) 300-301, no. 9 (ph.).

Αὐτοκράτορσ[ι]
[[---------------]]
3 Γ. Οὐαλερ.
Διοκλητιανῷ κὲ
Μαξιμιανῷ
6 κὲ τοῖς ἐπιφανεστάτοις
6a Σεββ.
[Κέσαρσιν]

2. ---Ω (rest of the erased text) Drew-Bear - Eck || 3. incomprehensible sign at the end of the line; perhaps KE in ligature from the erased inscription ? Drew-Bear - Eck.

1382. METROPOLIS, DEDICATION TO AGDISTIS. Poros stone altar with at front a serpent, at right an amphora, on the left side the inscription. Ed. pr. T. Drew-Bear, GRBS 17 (1976) 259-260, no. 14 (ph.).

Ανγδισι | εὐχήν.

1383. (PROBABLY) PRYMNESSOS, ERECTION OF A STATUE OF THE EMPEROR L. SEPTIMIUS SEVERUS. Base of a statue, now in Afyonkarahisar. Ed. pr. T. Drew-Bear - W. Eck, CHIRON 6 (1976) 289-290, no. 1 (ph.).

Αὐτοκράτορ̣[α]
Καίσαρα Λ̣. Σε-
πτίμιον Σεουή-
ρον Περτίνακα
5 Σεβαστὸν
Π. Αἴλιος Φι-
λότιμος Μα-
τιδιανὸς στε-
9 φανηφόρος.

1384. SOA, NUMBERS ON QUARRY BLOCKS. T. Drew-Bear - W. Eck, CHI-

RON 6 (1976) 316, no. 19 and 20 publish two quarry blocks with Latin and Greek numbers (ph.): a) οζʹ | LXXVII; b) CXIIX | ριηʹ (cf. also J. Röder, JDAI 86, 1971, 312).

1385. SYNNADA, EPIGRAM FOR DEMETRIOS, HIGH PRIEST OF ASIA, CA. 240-250 A.D. IGR, IV, 707. R. Merkelbach, ZPE 23 (1976) 74 suggests that the ἀρχιερεὺς Ἀσίας Demetrios, on record in IGR, IV, 707, is to be identified with the Asiarch Aurelius Demetrios, mentioned on coins of the neighbouring city of Stektorion.

1386. UNCERTAIN PROVENANCE, DEDICATION TO HOSION AND DIKAION. Inscribed altar with two figures, one holding a pair of scales, the other a measuring rod; now in the museum at Afyonkarahisar. Ed. pr. T. Drew-Bear, GRBS 17 (1976) 262-266, no. 17 (ph.).

[Τελ]έσφορος καὶ Ἑ[ρμ]-
ογένης Σταλλα-
ηνοὶ παρορκή-
σαντες ἀνέθη-
καν.

3-4. παρορκή|σαντες: this inscription confirms T. Wiegand's reading "παρορκίας" in L. 3 of an inscription found in Emet, northwest of Aizanoi (MDAI(A) 29, 1904, p. 331) Drew-Bear.

1387. UNCERTAIN PROVENANCE, DEDICATION TO DEMETER. Relief broken at top, depicting a veiled goddess seated on a sort of bench; now in the museum at Afyonkarahisar. Ed. pr. T. Drew-Bear, GRBS 17 (1976) 266, no. 18 (ph.).

[ὁ δεῖνα καὶ ἡ] | γυ̣νὴ Μ.α.ια κυ|ρίᾳ Δήμητρι

1388. UNCERTAIN PROVENANCE, DEDICATION TO SOZON. Altar with the bust of a radiate god; now in the museum at Afyonkarahisar. Ed. pr. T. Drew-Bear, GRBS 17 (1976) 266-267, no. 19 (ph.).

[----------] ον τι
σις εὐχ<ὴ>ν [ἀ]ν ἐθη-
Σώ ζ- κ̣εν.

Provenance: province of Burdur ? Drew-Bear.

1389. UNCERTAIN PROVENANCE, DEDICATION TO APOLLO. Altar with on the shaft at front a female bust, surrounded by an inscription; now in the museum at Afyonkarahisar. Ed. pr. T. Drew-Bear, GRBS 17 (1976) 267-268, no. 20 (ph.).

"Αττα-
λος
3 Νέωννος Του-
<α>ντος
ἐ̣πη-
6 κόῳ
θεῷ
Ἀπό-
9 λωνι
εὐχὴ-
[ν] ἀ̣νέθηκε

Provenance: "... the name Τουης, abundantly attested on the southern coast of Asia Minor from Pamphylia to Rough Cilicia, a fact which suggests a general provenience for this altar" Drew-Bear; "Vient-il d' aussi loin que la Cilicie Trachée ?" J. and L. Robert, BE (1977) no. 485.

PISIDIA

1390. AKÇAVIRAN, FUNERARY EPIGRAMS FOR A DOCTOR, 2nd CENT. A.D. SEG, XIX, 794. W. Peek, ZPE 21 (1976) 244 supposes that we have two epigrams here (vv. 1-3 and 4-7) and offers the following text:

[Ἐν ζωοῖς ἐγὼ ἦν ἰητρ]ῶν ἔξοχ' ἄριστος,
εὔκαρπος γενεὴ[ν Ἡ|ρακλῆς -∪∪- πα]ῖς.
3 Ἀλλά με Μοῖρ' ἐπέδησε κατοικεῖν ἐν [φθι]|μένοισιν.
[-∪∪-] φίλος υἱὸς ἀπώλετο πασιμ̣έ̣λ̣ητος, |
[ὥστε ἰητρὸς κλυτὸ]ς ἦν, Ἡρακλῆ̣ο̣ς̣ δ' ὄνομα εἶχεν.
6 Νῦν δ' Ἀ[ί]|[δην καταβὰς κεῖτα]ι φιλίῳ παρὰ παιδί.
Εὐτυχεῖτ' εὖ ζῶντε[ς αἰεὶ] | καὶ ἰητροὺς διδάσκετε.

1391. OLBASA, DEDICATION TO HERAKLES. SEG, XIX, 787. R.S. Bagnall, *The Florida Ostraka. Documents from the Roman army in Upper Egypt* (Gr. Roman Byz. Monogr. 7; 1976) p. 18, note 33 points out that in this inscription γαλεάριος means "soldier's servant" (and not "helmet-maker"). Cf. also J. and L. Robert, BE (1977) no. 513.

1392. SAGALASSOS, EDICT OF SEXTUS SOTIDIUS STRABO LIBUSCIDIANUS ON REQUISITIONED TRANSPORT, BEGINNING OF THE REIGN OF TIBERIUS. Grey marble stone, found near Burdur railway station. Ed. pr. S. Mitchell, JRS 66 (1976) 106-131 (ph.). Cf. J. and L. Robert, BE (1977) no. 510.

Sex. Sotidius Strabo Libuscidianus leg.
Ti. Caesaris Augusti pro pr. v. dic.
Est quidem omnium iniquissimum me edicto meo adstringere id quod
Augusti alter deorum alter principum
maximus diligentissime caverunt, ne quis gratuitis vehiculis uta-
tur, sed quoniam licentia quorundam

praesentem vindictam desiderat, formulam eorum quaẹ [pra]ẹstari
iudico oportere in singulis civitatibus
et vicis proposui servaturus eam aut si neglecta erit vindicatu-
rus non mea tantum potestate sed
principis optimi a quo .D....VMEN mandatis accepi maiestate. v.
Sagalassenos {o} ministerium carrorum decem et mulorum totidem
praestare debent ad usus neces-
sarios transeuntium, et accipere in singula carra et in singulos
schoenos ab iis qui utentur aeris denos, in mulos autem singulos
et schoenos singulos aeris quaternos, quod si asinos malent eodem
pretio duos pro uno mulo dent.
Aut, si malent, in singulos mulos et in singula carra id quod ac-
cepturi erant si ipsi praeberent v.
dare praestent iis qui alterius civitatis aut vici munẹre fungen-
tur, ut idem procedant.
Praestare autem debebunt vehicula usque Cormasa et Conanaṃ. Neque
tamen omnibu
s huius rei ius erit, sed procuratori principis optimi filioque
eius, usu dạ[to us]que ad carra decem aut
pro singulis carris mulorum trium aut pro singulis mulis asinorum
ḅinorum quibus eodem te
mpore utentur soluturi pretium a me constitutum; praeterea milita
tibus, et iis qui diplomum h
ebunt, et iis qui ex alis provincis militantes commeabunt ita ut
senatori populi Romani non plus quam
decem carra aut pro singulis carris muli terni aut pro singulis
mulis asini bini praestentur soluturis id quod
praescripsi; equiti Romano cuius officịo princeps optimus utitur
ter carra aut in singula terni muli aut
in singulos [mu]ḷos bini asini dari debebunt eadem condicione, s
amplius quis desiderabit conduc
arbitrio locantis; centurioni carrum aut tres muli aut asini sex
eadem condicione. Iis qui frume
tum aut aliudq<u>id tale vel quaestus sui caussa vel usus portan
praestari nihil volo, neque cuiquam
ro sụọ aut suorum libertorum aut servorum iumentu. Mansionem omn
bus qui erunt e
comitatu nostro eṭ militantibus ex omnibus provincis et principi
optimi libertis et servis et iumenti
eorum g̣ratuitam p̣ṛạẹṣtari oportet, ita ut reliqua ab invitis gra
tuita non e<x>sigant. v
Σέξτος Σωτίδιος Στράβων Λιβουσκιδιανὸς πρεσβευτὴς Τιβερίου Καίσα
ρος Σεβαστοῦ ἀντιστρα
τηγὸς λέγει· ἔστιν μὲν ἄδικον τὸ ἀκρειβέστατα ἠσφαλισμένον ὑπὸ
τῶν Σεβαστῶν τοῦ μὲν
θεῶν τοῦ δὲ αὐτοκρατόρων μεγείστου ἐμὲ διατάγματι ἐπισφείνγειν·
ἐπεὶ δὲ ἡ τινῶν πλεο-
νεξία τὴν παραυτίκα ἐκδικίαν αἰτεῖ, κατὰ πόλιν καὶ κώμην ἔταξα
κανόνα τῶν ὑπηρεσιῶν ὃν τη-
ρήσω οὐ μόνον δι' ἐμαυτοῦ ἀλλὰ ἐὰν δεῇ καὶ τὴν τοῦ σωτῆρος Σεβα

τοῦ δεδωκότος μοι
περὶ τούτων ἐντολ[ὰς] προσπαραλαβὼν θειότητα. Σαγαλασσεῖς λειτουργεῖν δεῖ μέχρι δέκα κάρ-
ρων ἕως Κορμάσων καὶ Κονάνης, νωτοφόροις δὲ ἴσοις· ἐπὶ τῷ λαμβάνειν ὑπὲρ μὲν κάρρου
v. κατὰ σχοῖνον ἀσσάρια δέκα, ὑπὲρ δὲ νωτοφόρου κατὰ σχοῖνον ἀσσάρια τέσσαρα, ὑπὲρ δὲ
ὄνου κατὰ σχοῖνον ἀσσάρια δύο· ἢ εἰ προκρείνουσιν χαλκὸν διδόναι τοῖς ὑπηρετοῦσιν ἐξ ἄλ-
λων τόπων προσθέτωσαν αὐτοῖς ὅσον αὐτοὶ ὑπηρετοῦντες ἔμελλον λ<α>μβάνειν· οὐ πᾶ-
σιν δὲ τοῖς βουλομένοις τὴν τοιαύτην ὑπηρεσίαν παρέχεσθαι δίκαι<όν> ἐστιν, ἀλλὰ τῷ τοῦ
Σεβαστοῦ ἐπιτρόπῳ καὶ τῷ υἱῶι αὐτοῦ μέχρι κάρρων δέκα ἢ νωτοφόρων ε̣ἰς λόγον
ἑνὸς κάρρου τριῶν ἢ ὄνων εἰς ἑν̣ὸ̣ς ἡμιόνου λόγον δυεῖν οἷς ὑπὸ τὸν αὐτὸν
καιρὸν χρήσ{εσ}ονται ἀποδιδόντες τὸν ὡρισμένον μισθόν· ἐπὶ τούτοις καὶ τοῖς
στρατευομένοις, καὶ τοῖς διπλώματα ἔχουσιν, καὶ τοῖς ἐξ ἄλλων ἐπαρχειῶν διοδεύου-
σιν, ἐξ ὧν τοῖς μὲν συνκλητικοῖς οὐ πλείονα τῶν δέκα ζευκτῶν, ἢ ὑπὲρ ἑνὸς τρεῖς ἡμι-
όνους, ἢ ὑπὲρ ἑνὸς ἡμιόνου δύο ὄνους, ἀποδιδοῦσιν τὸν ὡρισμένον μισθὸν
παραστῆσαι ἀνάνκην ἕξουσιν· τοῖς δὲ ἱππικῆς τάξεως ἐάν τις ἐν ταῖς τοῦ
Σεβαστοῦ χρή[αις] ἢ̣ κάρρων τριῶν, ἢ εἰς τὸν ἑκάστου λόγον ἡμιόνων τριῶν,
ἢ ὄνων ἓξ ἐπὶ τῇ ἰδί[α]ι αἱρέσει· ἑκατοντάρχῃ̣ κάρρον ἢ νωτοφόρους τρῖς, ἢ ὑπὲρ ἑκάσ-
του ὄνους δύο, [τοῖς] τὸν μισθὸν διδοῦσιν, ἐὰν δέ τις τούτοις μὴ ἀρκῆται τὰ λοι-
πὰ μισθώσε[ται παρ]ὰ̣ τῶν βουλομένων. Τοῖς σεῖτον ἢ ἄλλο τι τοιοῦτο ἐπ' ἐμπορίᾳ
ἢ χρήσει διακομίζουσιν ὑπηρετεῖσ[θ]<αι> οὐ βούλομαι· ὑπὲρ ἰδίων ἢ ἀπελευθερικῶν ἢ
δουλικῶν κτηνῶν λαμβάνεσθαί τι ἀποδοκιμάζω. Σταθμὸν πᾶσιν τοῖς τε με-
θ' ἡμῶν καὶ τοῖς στρατευομένοις ἐν πάσαις ἐπαρχείαις καὶ τοῖς τοῦ Σεβαστοῦ ἀπε-
λευθέροις καὶ δούλοις καὶ τοῖς κτήνεσιν αὐτῶν ἄμισθον παρασχεθῆναι δεῖ, τἄλ-
v. λα δὲ ...Ρ̣Ν.ca. 5.\Ν̣ΠΑΡΑϹ̣..ΟΝΤΩΝ v.

1-2. Sex. Sotidius Strabo Libuscidianus: governor of Galatia ca. 13-15 A.D Mitchell || 14. filioque eius: error for filiique eius Mitchell || 25. the final eight letters can be read as EASIGANT or FASIGANT Mitchell; e<x>sigant Brunt || 39. ΧΡΗϹΕϹ̣ΟΝΤΑΙ lapis; "this is presumably a mistake for χρήσονται, but there is a possibility that the passive χρησθήσονται, which can perhaps be reconciled with the traces, was originally inscribed here" Mitchell || 52. "the last word of the text should perhaps be read as παρασ[χό]ντων, referring to the provision of payment for additional services" Mitchell.

PAMPHYLIA

1393. THE DIALECT OF PAMPHYLIAN INSCRIPTIONS. Cl. Brixhe, *Le dialecte grec de Pamphylie. Documents et grammaire* (Bibl. Inst. Fr. Ét. Anatoliennes Istanbul, 26; Paris, 1976) gives an elaborate discussion of the Pamphylian dialect, followed by a corpus of Pamphylian documents from Perge (coins), Sillyon (coins and inscriptions), Aspendos (coins and inscriptions) and Selge (coins). The inscriptions from Aspendos (nos. 17-169) are copious and partly new (nos. 107-166). The volume is concluded with Pamphylian texts from Egypt (nos. 171-174; known before), with Pamphylian amphora stamps (nos. 175-177) and with a dikastic tablet of unknown provenance, all published before. Elaborate indices and 48 plates enlarge the value of the book. For the sake of convenience we give a comparatio numerorum of SEG XII and XVII with Brixhe: SEG, XII, 485 = Brixhe, no. 60, 486 = 62, 487 = 63, 488 = 65, 490 = 66, 491 = 67, 492 = 68, 494 = 74, 495 = 75, 496 = 78, 497 = 79; SEG, XVII, 642 = Brixhe, no. 85, 643 = 81, 644 = 82, 645 = 83, 646 = 84, 651 = 76, 652 = 77, 653 = 69, 654 = 70, 655 = 86, 656 = 87, 657 = 88, 658 = 89.

1394-1407. ASPENDOS, EPITAPHS. In ETUDES D'ARCHÉOLOGIE CLASSIQUE 5 (1976) 9-16 Cl. Brixhe publishes 14 new Pamphylian inscriptions from the vicinity of Aspendos (with photos). This supplement continues the numbering of Brixhe's above mentioned corpus (cf. no. 1393). Since these stelai are architecturally hardly interesting, we restrict ourselves to a mention of the Greek text. Unless indicated otherwise, they date from the 2nd cent. B.C.

1394. P. 9, no. 179; 1st half 2nd cent. B.C. ?

Τιμόθεμις | Ἀπελονίιυ

1395. P. 9-10, no. 180.

[...]ο̣υλις | [e.g. Μάν]ιτους | [...]ρ̣ί̣α̣ | [---------]

1396. P. 10, no. 181.

[Κ]οπερίνα | [Μ]ạ́νιτụς̣

1397. P. 10-11, no. 182 (all letters in rasura).

Πελᾶς
Πελλαδώρου
3 Κουδ[ραμου]αυ (?)
Πελλαδώρ[ου]
5 [----------]

1398. P. 11, no. 183.

Δαμάτρεις |2 Μεννέαυ | Fαρνόπα |4 Μάνιτους

1399. P. 11, no. 184.

ΔειFείδωρος | ΚεδαιFειου

1400. P. 11-12, no. 185.

Δα | Ατᾶτυς

1401. P. 12, no. 186.

ΖόFις | Ἀρτεμιδόρ[υ]

1402. P. 12, no. 187.

[e.g. Ἐπιγ]ẹ́νις | [e.g. Α]τᾶτυς

1403. P. 12-13, no. 188.

Μανία Fάρνιτους
Ἀρτιμίδωρυς
3 Ἀρτιμιδώρου
Χορεῖνα
5 ῞ΕρμαF

L. 1 has been added later Brixhe.

1404. P. 13-14, no. 189; 2nd half 2nd cent. B.C.

Δαμάτρεις |2 ΟρουμνῖFους | ΣFαρδιạ |4 Φιλίσκου

1405. P. 14, no. 190.

[-------] |² [-------] | ΔιFίδωρ[ο?]υς |⁴ Δαμάρχου

1406. P. 14, no. 191.

Μειναδόρας | ʽΙαρεῖFους

1407. P. 14-16, no. 192.

ΚεδαιFεις |² ΟυFραβρᾶτους | Μινόπα |⁴ ΖόFιτους

1408. PERGE, THE ROMAN FAMILY OF THE PLANCII. C.P. Jones, HSPH 80 (1976) 231-237 studies, with the help of inscriptions, some aspects of the history of this family.

1409. PERGE, HONORARY INSCRIPTION FOR PLANCIA MAGNA, 1st HALF 2nd CENT. A.D. Ed. pr. A.M. Mansel, AA 71 (1956) 119 (ph.); S. Jameson, JRS 55 (1965) 55. C.P. Jones HSPH 80 (1976) 233 reads in L. 9 (with J. and L. Robert, BE, 1958, no. 496 and ANNÉE ÉPIGRAPHIQUE, 1958, no. 78) μόνην instead of μόν[ο]ν.

ISAURIA

1410. DAMLA, ACCLAMATION. Ed. pr. J. Keil - H. Swoboda, Denkmäler aus Lykaonien, Pamphylien und Isaurien (Vienna, 1935) no. 1. Cf. G. Laminger-Pascher, ZPE 10 (1973) 193 and B. Lifshitz, EUPHROSYNE 6 (1974) 47. Laminger-Pascher had read the beginning of the inscription as follows: Κ(ύρι)ε βοήθι τῶν δύλον Θ(εοῦ) Γεοργῆς κτλ. (βοήθι + names in the genitive). Lifshitz corrects this and reads: Κ(ύρι)ε βοήθι τὼν δῦλον (pro τὸν δοῦλον = accusative) Θ(εοῦ) Γεόργης (= nominative used instead of an accusative).

LYCIA

1411. LYCIAN DYNASTS IN THE 5th - 4th CENT. B.C. D. Morkholm, AARCH 47 (1976) 47-90 deals with the coinages of these dynasts and on p. 87-89 he tries to make a stemma of them, for which he uses the coins and the recent inscriptions from Xanthos (CRAI, 1974, p. 82-149 and ibid., 1975, p. 138-150).

1412. BURIAL FEES IN LYCIAN EPITAPHS. T.R. Bryce, AS 26 (1976) 175-190 studies the mention of burial fees in Lycian epitaphs and occasionally discusses bilingual (Lycian-Greek) and Greek inscriptions.

1413. BALBOURA, EPITAPH FOR MOLESIS, LATE HELLENISTIC PERIOD. Limestone block. Ed. pr. Ch. Naour, ZPE 22 (1976) 127-128, no. 19 (ph.).

[ca. 5.]οσ[----------------]
καὶ Τρώιλος καὶ [ὁ δεῖνα]
καὶ Μολης καὶ Κρ̣[-----------]
Μολεσιν Ἑρμαίου [----------]
τὸν ἑαυτῶν πα̣[τέρα φιλοσ]-
τοργίας ἕνεκ[εν].

---

3. Perhaps Κρ[άτερος] Naour.

1414. BETWEEN BALBOURA AND TYRIAION (ÇIVGALAR), EPITAPH FOR THOAS AND ARTEMIS, 2nd - 3rd CENT. A.D. Inscription on a sarcophagus. Ed. pr. Ch. Naour, ZPE 22 (1976) 131-132, no. 26 (ph.). Cf. J. and L. Robert, BE (1977) no. 479.

Κα[τεσκεύασεν] τὴν σωματοθήκην Θόας Θόαντος Ὀρέστου ἑαυτῷ
καὶ τῇ γυναικὶ αὐτοῦ Αρτεμει καὶ τῦς{ς} ἑαυτῶν ἅπασιν τέκνοις
καὶ τῇ μητρί μου Αρτεμει καὶ ἱς δοχεῖον Διογένους Ἱλάρου.

---

3. δοχεῖον: "urne funéraire" Naour; εἰσδοχεῖον ? J. and L. Robert.

1415. AREA OF BOUBON (KIRAZLI YAYLA), EPITAPH FOR ACHILLEUS AND ONOBASIS, 4th CENT. A.D. Inscription on the wall of a Lycian rock-tomb. Ed. pr. Ch. Naour, ZPE 22 (1976) 124-126, no. 15 (dr.).

Τὸ μνῆμα τοῦτο ἐργά-
σαντο· Ἀχιλλεὺς καὶ Ονοβ-
ασις [οἱ] Ὀνεσᾶδος υἱοὶ
ἄνδρες εὐδαίμονες ἑαυ-
[τοῖς] καὶ γυναιξὶ καὶ ἐγγόνο-
ις [ca. 5.] vacat

1416. BOUBON-KIBYRA (HEKIMLER), EPITAPH (?) FOR DIODOROS, LATE HELLENISTIC PERIOD. Limestone block. Ed. pr. Ch. Naour, ZPE 22 (1976) 118-119, no. 10.

Διόδωρος | Ἀπολλωνίου

1417. BOUBON-KIBYRA (ÇAMELI), EPITAPH FOR APOLLONIOS AND KADOUAS, 2nd - 3rd CENT. A.D. Round marble base. Ed. pr. Ch. Naour, ZPE 22 (1976) 112, no. 1 (ph.).

Ἀπο<λλ>όνις
καὶ Καδαουας
Κα<δ>αουᾳ <τ>ῷ πα-
τρὶ μνίας ἕνε-
κον.

1. ΔΔ lapis || 3. Λ and Σ (square) lapis.

1418. BOUBON-KIBYRA (ÇAMELI), EPITAPH FOR KADAAS, 2nd - 3rd CENT. A.D. Funerary altar with relief representing a young child. Ed. pr. Ch. Naour, ZPE 22 (1976) 113-114, no. 2 (ph.).

Καδαας Καδααδι
τῷ τέκνῳ τὸν βωμὸν
μνείας χάριν.
2 leafs

1419. BOUBON-KIBYRA (ÇAMELI), EPITAPH FOR SOKRATES, 2nd - 3rd CENT. A.D. Round marble base. Ed. pr. Ch. Naour, ZPE 22 (1976) 114, no. 3 (ph.).

Καδαουας
Σωκράτει
τῷ ἀδελφῷ
μνήμης
ἕνε<κ>ε<ν>.
2 leafs

5. ΕΝΕΙΛΕ⅂ lapis; "les erreurs du graveur furent sans doute corrigées à la peinture" Naour.

1420. BOUBON-KIBYRA (ÇAMELI), EPITAPH ERECTED BY MASAS, 2nd - 3rd CENT. A.D. Round marble base, with relief representing two heads. Ed. pr. Ch. Naour, ZPE 22 (1976) 114-115, no. 4 (ph.).

Μασας ἐπέστησεν
μητρὶ καὶ <ἰ>δίῳ ἀ<δ>ελ-
relief
φῷ μνήμης χάριν.

2. ΚΑΙΔΙΩΑΚΕΛ lapis.

1421. BOUBON-KIBYRA (ÇAMELI), EPITAPH FOR NANAS AND MENIS, 2nd - 3rd CENT. A.D. Round marble base. Ed. pr. Ch. Naour, ZPE 22 (1976) 115, no. 5 (ph.).

Τατας Μήνιδος
Νανᾳ τῇ μητρὶ
καὶ Μήνιδι τῷ πα-
τρὶ ζῶντι μνείας
χάριν.

1422. BOUBON-KIBYRA (ÇAMELI), EPITAPH FOR PAPES AND NANA, 2nd - 3rd CENT. A.D. Round marble base. Ed. pr. Ch. Naour, ZPE 22 (1976)

115-116, no. 6 (ph.).

Παπης
Παπῃ τῷ
πατρὶ
μνήμης
ἕνεκα
καὶ Νανạ
τῇ μητρὶ
ζώσῃ

1423. BOUBON-KIBYRA (ÇAMELI), EPITAPH FOR NANAS, 2nd - 3rd CENT. A.D. Round marble base, with relief representing a man and a woman. Ed. pr. Ch. Naour, ZPE 22 (1976) 116, no. 7 (ph.).

Μῆνις
[καὶ ..]ας ἀνέσ-
[τησαν] τὸν
[βωμὸν] Ναναδι
[τῇ ἀδε]λφῇ καὶ
[c̣ạ.3] τῷ ἀνδρὶ
μνήμης χά-
[ρι]ν.

1424. BOUBON-KIBYRA (ÇAMELI), EPITAPH FOR SIMONIS, LATER IMPERIAL PERIOD. Limestone block, with a cross. Ed. pr. Ch. Naour, ZPE 22 (1976) 116-117, no. 8 (ph.).

Ἔνθα κατά-
χιτε ὠ τῆς μα(κα)-
ρίας μνήμης Σιμ-
ῶνις.

1425. BOUBON-KIBYRA (BIÇAKÇI KÖYÜ), EPITAPH FOR ATTES, 2nd - 3rd CENT. A.D. Round limestone base, with relief representing a woman and two children. Ed. pr. Ch. Naour, ZPE 22 (1976) 117-118, no. 9 (ph.).

Μολης καὶ Δύδ[υ]-
μος ἐπιστά-
νουσιν τῷ
πατρὶ Αττῃ
χάριν μνή-
μνης συναγω-
νισαμένης τῆς
γυνεκὸς Νανας

1426. BOUBON-KIBYRA (TAŞAVLU), EPITAPH FOR MENIS AND KRATEROS, 2nd - 3rd CENT. A.D. Round limestone base. Ed. pr. Ch. Naour, ZPE 22 (1976) 119-120, no. 11 (ph.).

Μῆνις Κρατέρου ἐπί-
κλη Σέργιος Μήνιδι τ-
ῷ τέκ<ν>ῳ καὶ τῷ ἀ-
δελφῷ Κρατέρ[ῳ]
[μνεί]ας χάριν.

3. triangular letter after the K lapis.

1427. BOUBON-KIBYRA (KIZILYAKA KÖYÜ), EPITAPH FOR HIEREIA, 2nd - 3rd CENT. A.D. Round limestone base, with relief representing a man (with a lance in his hand) and a veiled woman. Ed. pr. Ch.

Naour, ZPE 22 (1976) 120-121, no. 12 (ph.).

'Αρτεμεις
ἐπὶ <'I>ερεία
καὶ τοῖς τέκ[ν]-
4 ο<ι>ς ἐπέστησ-
εν στήλην
εἰς μνήμης
7 κάριν.

2. ΕΠΙΕΡΕΙΑ lapis || 4. ΟΣ lapis.

1428. BOUBON-KIBYRA (KIZILYAKA KÖYÜ), EPITAPH. Round limestone base. Ed. pr. Ch. Naour, ZPE 22 (1976) 120-121.

[-------]λ̣ης καὶ Με|^{2}[------ ἐ]π̣ὶ̣ ? τῷ πα|^{3}[τρὶ --------------]

1429. BOUBON-KIBYRA (IBECIKDERE KÖYÜ), EPITAPH OF SILLEAS, 2nd - 3rd CENT. A.D. Round limestone base. Ed. pr. Ch. Naour, ZPE 22 (1976) 121, no. 13 (ph.).

Σιλλέας Νώ-
νιος Κιβυράτης
3 ἀνέστησεν ἀ-
τῷ μνήμης
5 χάριν.

1430. BOUBON-KIBYRA (SOFULAR), EPITAPH FOR HERMAIOS, 2nd - 3rd CENT. A.D. Round limestone base; under the inscription two raised hands. Ed. pr. Ch. Naour, ZPE 22 (1976) 122, no. 14 (ph.).

Μολη<ς> Μ(άρκου)'Ιου-
λίου δὶς τοῦ Πυ-
3 <θ>ᾶ τῷ ἀδελφῷ
'Ερμαίῳ μνήμης
5 χάριν.

1. ΜΟΛΗΛ lapis || 3. ΟΑ lapis.

1431. KIBYRA (YUSUFÇA), EPITAPH FOR MELEAGROS, 1st CENT. A.D. Round marble base. Ed. pr. Ch. Naour, ZPE 22 (1976) 126, no. 16 (ph.).

Δημήτριος
Δημητρίου
3 Μελεάγρῳ τῷ υἱῷ
φιλοστοργίας
5 ἕννεκεν.

1432. KIBYRA (YUSUFÇA), EPITAPH FOR MOLES, 2nd - 3rd CENT. A.D. Round marble base. Ed. pr. Ch. Naour, ZPE 22 (1976) 127, no. 17 (ph.).

Καλλικλῆς
καὶ Μολης Μολ-
3 ητι τῷ πατρὶ καὶ
τοῖς ἀ<δ>ελφοῖς
5 μνίας ἕνεκον.

4. ΤΟΙΣΑΛ lapis.

1433. KIBYRA (YUSUFÇA), EPITAPH FOR DEMETRIOS, 2nd - 3rd CENT. A.D. Round marble base. Ed. pr. Ch. Naour, ZPE 22 (1976) 127, no. 18 (ph.).

Δημήτρις κατεσ-
κεύασεν τὸν
βωμὸν Δημητρίῳ
τῷ πατρὶ μνίας
leaf χάριν. leaf

1434. KORYDALLA, SEPULCHRAL INSCRIPTION, 4th CENT. B.C. Bilingual stoichedon inscription; line 1 is in Greek, lines 2-4 are in Lycian; the stone is broken at the right. Ed. pr. F.J. Tritsch, KADMOS 15 (1976) 158-167 (ph.).

Σαπια Μαναπίμιος [κατεσκευάσατο]

Translation of the Lycian text: "Sapia (Sepie) the son of Manapimis (Mahanepiyemi) built this Heroon for himself and his wife (name) and his son Tahñ and his grandchildren" Tritsch.

1435. MYRA, DECREE ABOUT SHIPPING, 2nd - 3rd CENT. A.D. OGIS, 572. K.A. Worp, Miscellanea Tragica in honorem J.C. Kamerbeek (Amsterdam, 1976) 501-504 interprets the words ἐὰν δέ τις αὐτόστολον ναυλώσῃ (L. 40 ff.) as meaning "if a person leases a vessel without a pilot / skipper, i.e. bypassing the official ferryman". But would a translation "a vessel with a skipper of its own" not be closer to the Greek ? (ed.)

1436. MYRA, EPITAPH. Stone with relief representing mother and daughter; on both sides of the relief a supinate hand. Ed. pr. G. Dunst, ZPE 21 (1976) 90 (who received photos of the stone from a traveller).

[..]χη Θεοδώ-
[ρα]ν τὴν θυγα-
[τ]έραν μνή-
α̣ς χ̣ά̣ριν.

Date: on archaeological grounds, one would date the relief to the Hellenistic period, but on the ground of the letter forms, Dunst does not exclude the Imperial period. || 1. [Τύ]χη or [Ἀρ]χή or [Εὐ]χή Dunst.

1437. OINOANDA, DIOGENES-INSCRIPTION, CA. 200 A.D. Ed. C.W. Chilton, Diogenes Oenoandensis Fragmenta (Leipzig, 1967) p. 24, frg. 11, col. III. Fernanda Decleva Caizzi, RFIC 104 (1976) 435-

442 compares the editions of Heberdey-Kalinka, J. William, C.W. Chilton and A. Grilli of this part of the inscription and proposes the following text:

εἰ μὲν
γὰρ ἀντιτεθήκει τῇ
πρώτῃ φωνῇ "οὐ μὴν
Col. III ὅτι μή εἰσιν", [δῆλος ἂν ἦν]
σχεδὸν ἐγχει[ρῶν πρόφα]-
σίν τινα πρὸς [τὸ μὴ δο]-
κεῖν τελέως [ἀναιρεῖν]
τοὺς θεούς. Ἔ[φησε δὲ τὸ]
"εἶναι αὐτοὺς" [ἄνευ τοῦ]
"μὴ εἶναι", τὸ ἀ[ληθὲς]
ποιῶν ἴσον Δ[ιαγόρᾳ, καὶ]
εἰπὼν τὸ μὴ [εἰδέναι]
ὅτι εἰσὶν αὐ[τῶν δὴ ἐ]-
παύσατο. Τ[οῦτον δέ, ὅν]-
περ λέγω κτλ.

M.F. Smith, Denkschr. Ak. Wien, 117 (Vienna, 1974) published thirteen new fragments of Diogenes of Oinoanda. D. Clay, AJPH 97 (1976) 308-309 points out the following: (1) In Smith, NF 19, 11 he prefers διακαθαίρειν to διακαθαιρεῖν; (2) he doubts that NF 24 belongs to the Letter to Mother; (3) in NF 27, 8 he restores [ἐστιν] and not [εἰσίν]; (4) in NF 13, 8 he suggests τοὺς περὶ ἐν[υπνίων] λόγους instead of περὶ ἐν[πτώσεων].

1438. NEIGHBOURHOOD OF OINOANDA (CALTILLAR), DEDICATION TO THE GODS. Ed. pr. G. Cousin, BCH 24 (1900) 338. Cf. G. Daux, BCH 100 (1976) 225-226 who maintains that in this text Νενας (L. 1-2) is a nominative and not the genitive of Νενα. The text of the inscription runs as follows:

Αὐρ. Ἀθηνοδωριανὴ Νε-
νας Σιδῆτις [γ]υ[ν]ὴ Ἀρτέμω-
3 νος Γιδλάσιος — θεοῖς εὐχαριστήριον.

1-2. Νενασσίδητις Cousin, corr. W. Ruge, RE, XVI, 2, col. 2390 and L. Robert, Villes d' Asie Mineure[1] (1935) p. 168.

1439. TLOS, SACRED LAW, 2nd CENT. B.C. SEG, VI, 775; F. Sokolowski, Lois Sacrées de l' Asie Mineure (Paris, 1955) no. 77. F. Kolb, ZPE 22 (1976) 228-230 tries to show that in this text a specific group of men, viz. those dressed in woman's dress (στολὴ ἀνθινή), gets permission to participate in a woman's cult (for Dionysos ?). He restores L. 1-2 as follows: [---] ἔχων στολὴν ἀνθινήν· ἄλλος μὴ ἀγειρέτω μ[ήτε εἰς τὸ ἱερὸν ἐλθέτω χωρὶ]ς τούτων ἐν γυναικείαι στολῆι κτλ.

1440. TYRIAION (KOZAĞAÇ), HONORARY INSCRIPTION FOR COMMODUS, 180-192 A.D. Large marble base. Ed. pr. Ch. Naour, ZPE 22 (1976) 133, no. 28 (ph.).

Αὐτοκράτορα Καίσα-
ρα Μᾶρκον Αὐρήλιον
3 [[Κόμμοδον Ἀντων]]-
[[εῖνο]]ν Εὐσεβῆν Εὐ-
τυχῆ Σεβαστὸν
6 Τυριαειτῶν ὁ δῆμος.

1441. TYRIAION (KOZAĞAÇ), EPITAPH OF KANNIS, ATTAS AND ARMONANIS, 2nd - 3rd CENT. A.D. Round marble base, with relief representing a standing person and a person reclining on a couch. Ed. pr. Ch. Naour, ZPE 22 (1976) 133-135, no. 29 (ph.).

Καννις Κλέωνος εἰκοσ-
τώνου ἀνέστησεν
ἑαυτὴν ζῶσα καὶ τὸν
4 γενόμενον αὐτῆς
ἄνδρα Ατταν Αρμονα-
{να}νιος καπήλου καὶ τὸν
7 πενθερὸν Αρμονανιν.

1-2. εἰκοστώνου: "fermier du vingtième" Naour; Naour's view that the "vingtième" is the vicesima libertatum (cf. also J. and L. Robert, BE, 1977, no. 480) should be reconsidered in the light of W. Eck, ZPE 27 (1977) 201-209.

1442. TYRIAION (KOZAĞAÇ), EPITAPH OF TROILOS, 2nd - 3rd CENT. A.D. Round marble base, with relief representing four standing persons. Ed. pr. Ch. Naour, ZPE 22 (1976) 136, no. 32 (ph.).

Τρώιλος Ἡρακλέ-
ου{ου} ὁ ἐκλογιστὴς
ἀνέστησεν ἑα[υ]-
4 τὸν καὶ τὴν [γ]υ[ναῖκ]-
[α] αὐτοῦ καὶ υ̣[ἱὸν ?]
αὐτοῦ καὶ [-------]
αὐτοῦ [----------]
8 [..]Ν[-----------]

1443. TYRIAION (KOZAĞAÇ), DEDICATION TO THE DIOSKOUROI, 2nd - 3rd CENT. A.D. Small limestone votive stele, with relief representing a horseman and traces of a standing female. Ed. pr. Ch. Naour, ZPE 22 (1976) 135, no. 30 (ph.).

Ἑρμαῖο[ς patronymic] | Διοσκόρ[οις εὐχήν]

For the Dioskouroi, cf. also Ch. Naour, l.c., 129-130.

1444. TYRIAION (KOZAĞAÇ), DEDICATION TO THE DIOSKOUROI, 2nd - 3rd CENT. A.D. Relief on a rock, with two pilei and an indistinct object, perhaps the five pointed star. Ed. pr. G.E. Bean, ABSA 51 (1956) 155, no. 56. Ch. Naour, ZPE 22 (1976) 135-136, no. 31 republishes the text (ph.).

Ζώιλος Ζήνωνος
Αἰγύπτιος Διοσκόροις εὐχήν.

---

2. Αἰγυπτίο[υ] Bean.

1445. XANTHOS, DEDICATION TO LETO, 2nd CENT. B.C. Inscription on a fragment of a small round marble altar. Ed. pr. E. Hansen - C. Le Roy, RA (1976) 317-318 (ph.).

-]ρεύς Λητοῖ

This inscription proves that the largest temple of the sanctuary (temple A) was dedicated to Leto; the first word is an ethnikon [Λιμυ]ρεύς, [Πατα]ρεύς, [Μυ]ρεύς Hansen - Le Roy.

1446-1447. XANTHOS, TWO GRAFFITI, BEFORE THE 7th CENT. A.D. Two graffiti on the floor of the northern peristyle of the temple and on a block from the door of the cella of the temple respectively. Ed. pr. E. Hansen - C. Le Roy, RA (1976) 336.

1446. Κ(ύρι)ε βοήθι Παύλω.

1447. Νικᾶ ἡ τυχὴ τῶν Μαριανῶν.

CILICIA

1448. CILICIAN CITIES IN THE FIRST PERIOD OF THE ROMAN OCCUPATION. Cf. no. 1870.

1449. ANEMURION, COMMEMORATION OF THE DONATION OF A MOSAIC ALONG WITH A BUILDING, GATEWAY AND STAIRCASE. Mosaic inscription set inside a tabula ansata of which the right hand edge is lost. Ed. pr. J. Russell, CLASSICAL NEWS AND VIEWS 20, 1 (January, 1976) 22.

----------------	σὺν τῷ οἰκήματ[ι]
----------------	καὶ τῷ πυλῶνι [κ(αὶ)]
3 τὴν ψηφοθεσ[ίαν]	6 τῇ ἀποκλιμακώσ[ι]

C.P. Jones thinks it's possible that there was more space to the right, and that one might read in L. 4 οἰκηματ[ίῳ], 5. [καὶ], 6. ἀποκλιμακώσ[ει] (information by letter).

1450. ANEMURION, FUNERARY INSCRIPTIONS, EARLY 3rd CENT. A.D. Painted decorations in a tomb: (a) upper part of a male draped in red tunic, (b) deceased and his wife reclining side by side, (c) winged genius representing Autumn. Ad (a): Ἑρμῆς and [Ψυ]χή, ad (b) ὁ βίος ταῦτα, ad (c) Ἔρως. Ed. AS 26 (1976) 22-23 and AJA 80 (1976) 286 (reports contributed by J. Russell).

1451. DIOKAISAREIA, HONORARY INSCRIPTION FOR ZENAS, HIGH PRIEST OF ZEUS, EARLY 1st CENT. B.C. Limestone base, broken at the left and at the right-hand bottom corner. Ed. pr. A.M. Vérilhac - G. Dagron, REA 76 (1974) 237-242 (ph.) who also study related inscriptions (MAMA, III, 63-65, 67, 68; cf. nos. 1452-1455) and provide a stemma of Zenas' family.

[Ὀ]λ̣βέων ὁ δῆμος καὶ
[Κα]ν̣νᾶται ἀρχιερέα
[μ]έ̣γαν Ζην̣ᾶν Ζηνοφά-
4 [ν]ο̣υ τοῦ Ζ̣ηνοφάνου
τὸν ἀδελφὸν τῶν βα-
[σ]ιλέων, ἀρετῆς ἕνε-
[κ]ε̣ν καὶ εὐνοίας ἧς ἔχω[ν]
8 [εἰ]ς̣ αὐτοὺς διετ̣[έ]λ̣[ει].

5-6. βασιλέων: Philip I and Philip II, the last Seleucids Vérilhac - Dagron.

1452-1455. DIOKAISAREIA, HONORARY INSCRIPTIONS FROM AND FOR HIGH PRIESTS OF ZEUS, EARLY 1st CENT. B.C. MAMA, III, 63, 64, 65 and 67. A.M. Vérilhac - G. Dagron, REA 76 (1974) 237-242 propose, on the basis of a new inscription (cf. no. 1451), the following corrections to these inscriptions:

1452. MAMA, III, no. 63, L. 1: [Ζηνᾶς] instead of [Ζηνοφάνης]; 3-4. τὸν [τῶν βασιλέων ἀδελ]|φόν instead of τὸν [ἑαυτοῦ ἐξάδελ?]|φον. This inscription is older than MAMA, III, no. 64 and the new inscription (our no. 1451).

1453. MAMA, III, no. 64, L. 1: [Ζηνᾶς] instead of [Ζηνοφάνης]; 2-3. [ὁ ἀδελφὸς τῶν] | βασιλέων instead of [ὁ φίλος τῶν (?)] | βασιλέων.

1454. MAMA, III, no. 65, L. 2: perhaps [Ζηνᾶν] instead of [Ζηνοφάνην].

1455. MAMA, III, no. 67: the dedicator of this inscription is perhaps the same as the honorand of no. 68. In that case one has to restore: [Ἀρχιερεὺς μέγας] |[2] [Ζηνοφά]νης |[3] [Τεύκρου] τ̣οῦ Ζην[ο]|[4] [φάνου κτλ.

1456. KOLYBRASSOS, EPITAPH FOR THE JURIST KONON, 4th CENT. A.D. Ed. pr. G.E. Bean - T.D. Mitford, *Journeys in Rough Cilicia* (Denkschr. Ak. Wien, 102; Vienna, 1970) p. 74-76, no. 49. Cf. also J. and L. Robert, BE (1972) no. 504; J.F. Gilliam, ZPE 13 (1974) 147-150. W.D. Lebek, ZPE 21 (1976) 39-41 comments upon LL. 1-4 and 17-19. For the sake of convenience we present the whole text here, with in LL. 17-20 Lebek's readings:

Βηρυτὸν τὸ πάροιθεν ὅτε πτόλιν ἦλθον ἐς ἐ̣[σθλὴν]
  Ῥωμαϊκῆς μούσης εἵνεκα καὶ νομίμων,
ἐλπωρὴν γελόωσαν ἔχων καὶ δαίμονα πικρό̣[ν],
  οὐκέτ᾽ ἐπὶ πάτρην ἤλυθον ἡμετέρην.
Ἀλλά με πρῶτον ἔδεκτο δικασπολίῃσι μέ̣λ̣οντα
  ἄστυ Παλαιστίνης ὄρχαμος ἀμφιέπων·
κεῖθεν δ᾽ Ἀντιόχοιο φίλη πόλις, ἐκ δέ μ᾽ ἐκείνης
  Βειθυνῶν ἀγαθὴ δέξατο μητρόπολις·
ἔνθεν ἐμὸν στήθ̣ε̣σ̣σι νόον καὶ ἐπίφρονα μῆτιν
  Κέρτος ὁμηλικίης πολλὸν ἀγασσάμενος
συνκάθεδρον Θήβης Νειλώϊδος ἡγεμονῆος
  θῆκεν. Ὁ δ᾽ ἁρπάκτης, πρὶν χρόνον ἐκτελέσαι
πρὶν πάτρην ἰδέειν με τὸ δεύτερον ἠδὲ γονῆας,
  ἥρπασεν ἐξαπίνης εἰς Ἀχέροντ᾽ Ἀίδης.
Τ̣η̣λ̣[όθε? δ᾽] ἐ̣ρ̣χ̣ό̣μ̣ενός? με πατὴρ προσπτύξατο χερσί,
  νεκρὸν ἐπὶ ξεινῆς κείμενον εἰσορόων.
Ἀλλὰ καὶ ὣς Νεῖλόν τε μέγαν καὶ πόντον ἀνύσσα[ς]
  ἀντὶ γάμων στοναχῶν τοῦτον ἔδειμε τάφο[ν].
Μήτηρ δ᾽ αὖτ᾽ ὀδύνῃσι πεπαρμένη ἐν χθονὶ κῖται
  <– ⏑⏑ – ⏑⏑ – – ⏑⏑ – ⏑⏑ –>
κεῖμε δ᾽ ὧδε Κόνων ἀνὴρ Μούσῃσι μεμηλώς,
  ψυχὴν ἐς μακάρων ν̣ῆσσον ἔχων ἀγαθήν.
Ἀλλά, πάτερ Τρώϊλε, μὴ τόσσον ὀδύρεο· καὶ γὰρ ἄριστοι
  παῖδες ἐπουρανίων ἤλυθον εἰς Ἀίδην.

3-4. ἐλπωρὴν γελόωσαν ἔχον καὶ – δαίμονα πικρό̣[ν], | οὐκέτ᾽ ἐπ(ε)ὶ πάτρην ἤλυθον ἡμετέρην Lebek || 17. ἄνυσσα Bean - Mitford; ἀνύσσα[ς] restored by R. Merkelbach, ZPE 13 (1974) 147, Anm. 1 || 18. τοῦτον ἔχει<ν>? με τάφο[ν] Bean - Mitford || 20. inserted by Lebek, not by Bean - Mitford. For LL. 15-18, cf. also BE (1978) no. 491.

1457. TARSOS, HONORARY EPIGRAM FOR HEMERIOS. Ed. L. Robert, *Hellenica* VII (1949) 197-205 (ph.). G. Daux, ZPE 20 (1976) 249-252 supports (and gives the history of) the reading μέγ᾽ ἔξο|χον in L. 2-3; in L. 10 he reads Παπειν (proper name). In EPIGRAPHICA 39 (1977) 51-70 he gives a survey of the entire bibliography of the text and repeats his suggestions made in ZPE.

Εὐτύχι Ἡμέρι.
Ῥωμαίων ὕπατον, μέγ᾽ ἔξο-
χον ἐν Κιλίκεσσιν, εἵνεκα

καὶ παιδὸς πανυπέρτατον ἐν
πολιήταις, τούτῳ γὰρ βασιλῆς
δῶκαν γέρας ὄφρα οἱ υἱὸς συνκλή-
του βουλῆς μετέχοι πολυκυδέα
τειμὴν, τρεῖς στεφάνους ἑξῆς
[ἀ]ναδησάμενον παναρίστους
δημιουργὸν ΠΑΠΕΙΝ Κιλικάρχην
γυμνασίαρχον σύνδικον ἀγνότα-
τον, βουλῆς στέφος, εὐγενὲς αἷμα
Δήμητρος θεράποντες ἀγακλέα τόνδ' ἀνέ-
θηκαν· ἐπὶ γραμματέων τῶν περὶ Νέω-
να τὸ β' καὶ Λούκιον τὸ β' καὶ Ἀλέξανδρον
τὸ β' καὶ Μυραγένην τὸ β'· οἱ αὐτοὶ γραμμα-
τεῖς τὴν στατίωνα ἐκ τῶν ἰδίων τῷ ἱερῷ συνεργίῳ.

Date: L. Robert, l.c., 198: "Certaines lettres dépassent largement la ligne; ... c' est une élégance que l' on constate, semble-t-il, souvent dans les documents de la fin du IIe siècle et du IIIe siècle"; G. Daux, EPIGRAPHICA 39 (1977) 69: "La forme des lettres oriente vers la fin du IIe siècle de notre ère" || 2. in rasura one reads ἱππῆα (under ὕπατον), cf. T. Drew-Bear, HSPH 71 (1975) 301-303 || μεγέξο|χον Robert || 10. either παπειν (office: L. Robert) or Παπειν (proper name: G. Daux); for the name Παπεις, cf. also G. Daux, BCH 101 (1977) 346-347; but see also L. Robert, BCH 101 (1977) 92-93, note 17 ("a moins que παπειν ne se rapporte étroitement à 'démiurge'") and BE (1978) no. 510.

CYPRUS

1458. PROSOPOGRAPHY. I. Michaelidou-Nicolaou, Prosopography of Ptolemaic Cyprus (Studies in Mediterranean archaeology, 44; Göteborg, 1976).

1459. PROSOPOGRAPHY. Cypriots attested by inscriptions and literary texts in Delphi, cf. no. 619.

1460. THE POPULATION OF CYPRUS. J. Seibert, Zur Bevölkerungsstruktur Zyperns, ANCSOC 7 (1976) 1-28 uses copious epigraphic evidence in a study of the Hellenisation of urban life in Cyprus.

1461. INDICES. I. Nicolaou, RDAC (1976) 256-259 gives indices to Inscriptiones Cypriae alphabeticae XI-XV (published in RDAC 1972, 1973, 1974, 1975, 1976).

1462. AMATHOUS, EPITAPH, 2nd CENT. B.C. (?) Inscribed funerary stele in sandstone. Ed. pr. K. Nicolaou, AJA 80 (1976) 366 (ph.).

Βιάνωρ Κόνωνος
Ἀδαδεὺς
3 ΤΩ.$^{5-6}$..ΡΩΝ
Κόμων ΤΡΟΚ.....
5 Ἀδαδεὺς χρ[ηστοὶ χαίρετε ?]

5. χρ[ηστοὶ χαίρετε ?] J. and L. Robert, BE (1977) no. 553.

1463. ANOGYRA (LIMASSOL DISTRICT), VOW FOR THEODOROS, 5th CENT. A.D. Sandstone block. Ed. pr. I. Nicolaou, RDAC (1976) 245-246, no. 6 (ph.).

Ὑπὲρ --------
τοῦ δούλου τοῦ
Θεοῦ Θεωδώρο̣[υ] (sic)
4 κὲ τῆς δούλης τ̣[οῦ]
Θεο[ῦ] Μ[αρ]τυρία̣-
ς κ[ὲ τῶν] τ[έ]κ<ν>ων
7 α̣ὐ̣τ̣ῶ̣ν̣.

1464. EPISKOPI (LIMASSOL DISTRICT), EPITAPH OF DEMETRIOS, 2nd - 3rd CENT. A.D. Limestone cippus. Ed. pr. I. Nicolaou, RDAC (1976) 246, no. 8 (ph.).

Δημήτριε | χρηστέ, χαῖρε.

1465. GERASA (LIMASSOL DISTRICT), EPITAPH OF TIMAGORAS, 2nd - 3rd CENT. A.D. Limestone funerary cippus. Ed. pr. I. Nicolaou, RDAC (1976) 245, no. 4 (ph.).

Τιμαγώρ[α] (sic) | χρηστέ, | χε͂ρε (sic).

The chi is cross-shaped Nicolaou.

1466. GERASA (LIMASSOL DISTRICT), EPITAPH OF ELPIS, 2nd - 3rd CENT. A.D. Funerary cippus. Ed. pr. I. Nicolaou, RDAC (1976) 245, no. 5 (ph.).

Ἐλπὶς | χρη<σ>τή, | χαῖρε.

2. The sigma was omitted by the cutter.

1467. HAGHIOS ATHANASIOS (LIMASSOL DISTRICT), EPITAPH OF SAMBON, 2nd - 3rd CENT. A.D. Limestone funerary cippus. Ed. pr. I. Nicolaou, RDAC (1976) 244, no. 3 (ph.).

Σάμβων | χρηστέ, | χαῖ v. ρ v. ε.

1468. KATO PAPHOS (PAPHOS DISTRICT), HONORARY INSCRIPTION (?), HADRIANIC PERIOD (?) Fragment of a slab of whitish marble broken on all sides. Ed. pr. I. Nicolaou, RDAC (1976) 250, no. 12 (ph.).

---ων τ̣------- ---- Κ̣λέωνος ---
2 [ἡ βουλὴ] καὶ ὁ δῆ̣[μος]--- 4 ---- τ̇ὸ ιϑ' ˙L τọ----

3. "The genitive Κλέωνος, if the name of an archon, then: ἄρχοντος Κλέωνος; if the patronymic of the archon, then τοῦ δεῖνα Κλέωνος ἄρχοντος" Nicolaou || 4. τὸ ιϑ' L usually denotes annual magistracy Nicolaou || the τọ at the end of the line may refer to the magistracy of previous years, for instance: τọ[ῦ καὶ τὸ ιη' L ἄρξαντος] Nicolaou.

1469. KHLORAKA (PAPHOS DISTRICT), INSCRIBED MORTARIUM, 4th CENT. A.D. (?) Fragment of red gritty clay belonging to the rim of a mortarium. Ed. pr. I. Nicolaou, RDAC (1976) 252, no. 16 (ph.).

Γεμε|λῖν<ε>

This manufacturer's name is already known in Cyprus (cf. HESPERIA 36, 1967, p. 346, no. 162) Nicolaou.

1470. KITION (LARNAKA DISTRICT), ERECTION AND DEDICATION OF A COLUMN, 1st CENT. A.D. Lower part of a white marble column. Ed. pr. I. Nicolaou, RDAC (1975) 155, no. 4; K. Nicolaou, AJA 80 (1976) 365-366 (ph.).

Κιτιέων ἡ πόλις
Τίτος Μάνλιος Σούρας Σεπτικιανὸς
ταμίας v. καὶ ἀντιστράτηγος καθιέρωσεν.

Cf. T. Drew-Bear - R.S. Bagnall, PHOENIX 24 (1970) 220-221 and W. Eck, RE, Suppl. XV, col. 29, no. 67 aa.

1471. KOUKLIA (PALAIPAPHOS, PAPHOS DISTRICT), FRAGMENT OF AN INSCRIBED STELE, EARLY 3rd CENT. B.C. Upper part of a sandstone stele, broken on both sides and below, and found in the debris of a demolished house near Aphrodite's temple. Ed. pr. I. Nicolaou, RDAC (1976) 251, no. 14 (ph.).

[Στ]ạσίοικο[ς or υ]

1472. KOUKLIA (PALAIPAPHOS, PAPHOS DISTRICT), METRIC EPITAPH, EARLY 3rd CENT. B.C. Fragmentary stele of whitish marble, broken on all sides and found under the same circumstances as no. 1471. Ed. pr. I. Nicolaou, RDAC (1976) 251, no. 15 (ph.).

---σικ̣------
---ς̣ πάτρη[ν] δ' ca.4 σῆμ̣[α ?] --
--ομενοις·

1473. KOURION (LIMASSOL DISTRICT), INSCRIBED MARBLE FRAGMENT, 1st CENT. A.D. (?) Fragment of a grey marble slab broken on all sides. Ed. pr. I. Nicolaou, RDAC (1976) 246, no. 7 (ph.).

ἔτο[υς or ἔτος]

1474. KOURION (LIMASSOL DISTRICT), MOSAIC-INSCRIPTION OF EUSTOLIOS, LATE 4th CENT. A.D. (?) Ed. pr. T.B. Mitford, The Inscriptions of Kourion (Philadelphia, 1971) no. 204. W. Peek, ZPE 23 (1976) 97-98 presents the following text:

[Κουριέας] τ̣ὸ πάρο̣ι̣θ̣ε̣ ἐ̣ν̣ [ὄλβ]ῳ παντὶ πέλοντας
[νῦν ἐν δίῃ ἰδ]ῶν ἐκ ποδὸς Εὐστόλιος
[οὐ πατρίης χώ]ρης ἐπελήσατο, ἀλλ' ἄρα καὶ τῆς
[ἐμνήσθη φιλί]ως, λουτρὰ χαρισσάμενος·
[ἧ ῥ' αὐτὸς δὴ] δίζετο Κούριον, ὥς ποτε Φοῖβος,
[γαίην δὲ β]ρυχίην θῆκεν ὑπηνεμίην.

1. τ̣ὸ πάροιθεν [ἐν ὄλβ]ῳ Mitford || 2. [δυστήνους ἐσιδ]ῶν Mitford || 3. [οὐ πατέρων χώ]ρης Mitford || 4. [ἡμετέρας πόλε]ως Mitford || 5. [αὐτὸς δὴ τότ' ἐ]δίζετο Mitford || 6. [ἤρχετο, καὶ] ψ̣υχ[ρ]ὴν θῆκεν ὑπηνεμίην Mitford.

1475. LARNAKA, HONORARY INSCRIPTION FOR TIBERIOS KLAUDIOS NIKOPOLINOS HIPPARCHOS, 1st CENT. A.D. Statue-base of greyish local marble. Ed. pr. T.B. Mitford, OPUSCULA ARCHAEOLOGICA 6 (1950) 72-76, no. 43 (ph.). Cf. I. Nicolaou, RDAC (1976) 247-250, no. 11 (ph.) who revised the inscription and presents it as follows:

Τιβέριον Κλαύδιον Νικοπολινὸν Ἵππαρχ[ον ἱερο]μ̣νήμονα,
ἀρχιερέα διὰ βίου τῶν Σεβαστῶν καὶ τῆς ἱερᾶς Συ[γκλήτ]ου, τὸν φιλόπατριν,
πανάρετον υἱὸν τῆς πόλεως, ἀγωνοθετήσαντα τετράκις,
γραμματεύσαντα βουλῆς καὶ δήμου, ἄρχοντα τῆς πόλεως,
Γάιος Γερελλανὸς Ῥοῦφος ἄρχων τῆς πόλεως καὶ οἱ
τούτου υἱοὶ Γάιος Γερελλανὸς Καπίτων καὶ Γάιος
Γερελλανὸς Ῥο̣[ῦφος (?) καὶ Γάιο]ς Γερελλανὸς Γελλιανός,
[τιμῆς] χάριν.

1. Νικοπο̣λ̣ι̣ν̣ὸν ? ἵππαρ̣[χον ? ca.4]ΝΙ̣[ca.5.] Mitford || 2. τῆς ἱερᾶς σ[υ̣ν̣ό̣δ]ου Κ̣[ύπρου ?] Mitford || 3. [ἐξ]αίρετον Mitford; [αὐθ]αίρετον J. and L. Robert, BE (1951) no. 236 || 5-6. καὶ ο[ἱ τρ]|[εῖς α]ὐ̣[τ]ο̣ῦ̣ υἱοὶ Mitford || 7. [Γερελλανὸς ..ca.7.. καὶ Γάϊο]ς Mitford ||

8. not read by Mitford.

1476. LARNAKA, EPITAPH OF HERMIONE, 2nd - 3rd CENT. A.D. Upper half of a limestone cippus. Ed. pr. I. Nicolaou, RDAC (1976) 247, no. 9 (ph.).

Ἑρμι[όνη] | χρηστή, | χαῖρε.

1477. LARNAKA, EPITAPH OF AGATHANGELOS, 2nd - 3rd CENT. A.D. Limestone cippus. Ed. pr. I. Nicolaou, RDAC (1976) 247, no. 10 (ph.).

Ἀγαθάγγελε | χρηστέ, | χαῖρε.

1478. LIMASSOL, EPITAPH, ROMAN PERIOD. Limestone cippus. Ed. pr. K. Nicolaou, AJA 80 (1976) 366.

Ἐπαφρόδειτε | χρηστέ, | χαῖρε.

1479. LIMASSOL, EPITAPH, ROMAN PERIOD. Limestone cippus. Ed. pr. K. Nicolaou, AJA 80 (1976) 366.

Ἐλαφεία | χρηστή, | χαῖρε.

1480. NEA PAPHOS, NAME. Inscription on a small altar (for burning perfume). Ed. pr. W.A. Daszewski, RDAC (1976) 218.

Ἑρμαγόρου

1481. NIKOSIA DISTRICT, EPITAPH OF GORIANE, 2nd - 3rd CENT. A.D. Limestone cippus, now in the Cyprus Museum (purchased from a person in Idalion). Ed. pr. I. Nicolaou, RDAC (1976) 243-244, no. 1 (ph.).

Γοριανὴ | χρηστή, | χαῖρε.

1482. NIKOSIA DISTRICT, EPITAPH OF ASKLEPIAS, 2nd - 3rd CENT. A.D. Limestone cippus, now in the Cyprus Museum (purchased from a person in Idalion). Ed. pr. I. Nicolaou, RDAC (1976) 244, no. 2 (ph.).

Ἀσκληπιὰς | χα[ῖρε].

1483. OVGOROS (FAMAGUSTA DISTRICT), INSCRIBED BREAD STAMP, 5th CENT. A.D. Fragmentary circular bread stamp of limestone. Ed. pr. I. Nicolaou, RDAC (1976) 252-253, no. 17 (ph.).

Τῆς Ἁγ-ί̣ας Θ̣-εοτό-κου

1484. PAPHOS, HONORARY INSCRIPTION FOR T. CLODIUS EPRIUS MARCELLUS, PROCONSUL OF CYPRUS, 59 A.D. (?) SEG, XVIII, 587. J. Devreker, EPIGRAPHICA 38 (1976) 180 restores in L. 3 Κλαυδ]ίου Καίσαρος Σεβαστοῦ instead of Γα]ΐου Καίσαρος Σεβαστοῦ.

1485. PAPHOS, INSCRIBED MORTARIUM, 4th CENT. A.D. Fragment belonging to the rim of a mortarium, found in Paphos; exact provenance unknown. Ed. pr. I. Nicolaou, RDAC (1976) 251, no. 13 (ph.).

Ἑρμογ|ένους

The name of this manufacturer is also attested in Egypt, Palestine, Syria, Greece Nicolaou.

1486. SALAMIS, CAREER OF AN UNKNOWN ROMAN KNIGHT, 1st HALF 2nd CENT. A.D. Ed. pr. I. Michaelidou-Nicolaou, Πρακτικά τοῦ πρώτου διέθνους κυπρολογικοῦ συνεδρίου I (Leukosia, 1972) p. 125-127 (ph.). After S. Demougin, ZPE 21 (1976) 135-145, who restored the inscription on the assumption that in the first two preserved lines remnants of the name of the honorand had been preserved ([praenomen] Φλ̣[--- tribus ?] | [---]εα Βοήθου κτλ.), W. Eck, ZPE 25 (1977) 227-231 returns to this text and convincingly shows that in LL. 1-2 the militiae equestres of the honorand were mentioned. We print Eck's restoration below:

[------------------- ἔπαρχον]
[σπείρης --] Φλ[αυίας, ---, χειλίαρχον]
[λεγεῶνο]ς α' Βοηθοῦ, ἔπ[αρχον εἴλης ---],
4 [ἐπίτρο]πον ἐπαρχείας Π[αννονίας τῆς ἄνω or τῆς κάτω, ἐπίτροπον κ'?
[κληρο]νομιῶν, ἐπίτρ[οπον ἐπαρχείας ---]
[ἐπὶ τ]ῶν λόγων τῶν κ[αθόλου ... Αὐτοκράτορος]
[Καίσ]αρος Τραιανοῦ Ἁδρι[ανοῦ Σεβαστοῦ]
[---]ιος Ἀττικός, βοηθὸ[ς γενόμενος, τὸν]
8 ἑαυτοῦ εὐεργέ[την].

2. [Τίτον] Φλ[αύιον υἱὸν] Michaelidou-Nicolaou || 3. [..8.....]εα Βοήθου, ἐπ[ίτρ̣οπον Κύπρου ?] Michaelidou-Nicolaou; [---]εα Βοήθου, ἐπ[ίτροπον ἐπαρχείας Ἠπείρου ? vel Ἀραβίας ? vel Ἰουδαίας ?] Demougin || 4. Π[όντου καὶ Βιθυνίας ?] Michaelidou-Nicolaou; Π[όντου Βιθυνίας, ἐπίτροπον] Demougin; in fine Eck restored [ἔπαρχον κ'?] which is an error for [ἐπίτροπον κ'?] || 5. ἐπίτρ[οπον κράτιστον] Michaelidou-Nicolaou; ἐπίτρ[οπον ἐπαρχείας Ἀσίας ?] Demougin || 7. [Φλαύ]ιος Ἀττικός, Βοήθο[ν τὸν] Michaelidou-Nicolaou; [---]ιος Ἀττικός, βοηθὸ[ς ἐν Ῥώμῃ τὸν] Demougin.

1487. UNKNOWN PROVENANCE, STAMPED AMPHORA-HANDLES. Rhodian wine amphora, now in the Cyprus Museum. Ed. pr. I. Nicolaou, RDAC (1976) 253, no. 18 (ph.).

A. Left handle: Ἐπὶ Συμμά|χου | Ὑακινθίου
B. Right handle: Ἀριστάρχου

KOMMAGENE

1488. APAMEIA ON THE EUPHRATES, EPITAPH, 138 A.D. White limestone sepulchral stele; under the inscription, representation of an eagle. Ed. pr. J. Wagner, Seleukeia am Euphrat/Zeugma (Wiesbaden, 1976) 84, no. 1 (ph.).

Ἀβίνεος Διονυσίου | ἔτους νυ'.

2. νυ' = 450 (era of the Seleucids) = 138 A.D.

1489. APAMEIA ON THE EUPHRATES, EPITAPH. Small limestone sepulchral stele, with the inscription in a tabula ansata. Ed. pr. J. Wagner, l.c., 84, no. 2 (dr.).

Ζήνων | χαῖρε.

1490. ARSAMEIA ON THE NYMPHAIOS, EPITAPH ON A "HIEROTHESION" FOR ISIAS. Grave-tumulus (Karakuş) southwest of Arsameia on the Nymphaios. OGIS, 403. Cf. J. Wagner - G. Petzl, ZPE 20 (1976) 211-212 who identify the βασιλεὺς μέγας Μιθραδάτης in L. 2-3 with Mithradates II (34-31 B.C.), successor of Antiochos I (and not with Mithradates I, father of Antiochos I). Isias (L. 1) would then be the wife of Antiochos I.

1491. AŞAGI ÇARDAK (NORTH OF HORUM HÜYÜK, NEAR SELEUKEIA ON THE EUPHRATES), BUILDING INSCRIPTION. Mosaic inscription in tabula ansata; above the inscription a peacock. Ed. pr. J. Wagner, Seleukeia am Euphrat/Zeugma (Wiesbaden, 1976) 111 (ph.).

Ἐπὶ Σαβίνου ἐπισκό-
που ἐκτείσθη τοῦ-
3 το τὸ μαρτύρειν ἐν κ(ύρι)ε.

1492-1493. AŞAGI ÇARDAK (NORTH OF HORUM HÜYÜK, NEAR SELEUKEIA ON THE EUPHRATES), FRAGMENTARY BUILDING INSCRIPTIONS. Two mosaic-inscriptions; under the inscriptions a pigeon with a twig. Ed. pr.

J. Wagner, l.c., 111.

1492. At the left:

---Υ
---ἔκτισε]ν· κ(ύρι)ε·
μνησθήτει] αὐτοῦ.

1493. At the right:

λημου [..]νειου
ἔκτισεν· κ(ύρι)ε· μνησ-
θήτει αὐτοῦ.

1494-1496. NISIBIS (NEAR SELEUKEIA ON THE EUPHRATES), EPITAPHS. J. Wagner, Seleukeia am Euphrat/Zeugma (Wiesbaden, 1976) 111-113 publishes four sepulchral stelai; three of them bear an inscription:

1494. P. 112, no. 1 (ph.).

Κύριλλε | ἄλυπε | χέρε.

1495. P. 112, no. 2.

Ἡράκλιτε ἄλυπε | χέρε.

1496. P. 112-113, no. 3 (ph.).

Σ̣ύνα[γ]γος Κόϊντος | [ἄ]λυπε χέρε.

---

1. Cf. J. and L. Robert, BE (1977) no. 531, p. 430: "Il n'y a pas place pour un second gamma; n'a-t-on pas ici le nom macédonien Κύναγος, attesté en Syrie (cf. L. Robert, Nouv. Inscr. Sardes, 11, n. 4) ?"

1497. SELEUKEIA ON THE EUPHRATES/ZEUGMA, LOCATION OF THE CITY. Cf. no. 1876.

1498. SELEUKEIA ON THE EUPHRATES/ZEUGMA, HONORARY INSCRIPTION. Limestone block. Ed. pr. J. Wagner, Seleukeia am Euphrat/Zeugma (Wiesbaden, 1976) 130 (ph.).

Ὁ δῆμο̣[ς]
[..]Σ τοῦ ναοῦ θεῶν

[πα]τρώων v. Ἀντίο̣[χος]
Κ̣λεινίου τ̅ὸ̅ν̅ ἑαυτ[οῦ]
φ̣ίλον. hedera

1. Illegible on the photograph; there are other letters J. and L. Robert, BE (1977) no. 531, p. 429 || 3. Ἀντίο̣[χον ?] Wagner, corrected by J. and L. Robert, l.c.

1499. SELEUKEIA ON THE EUPHRATES, DEDICATION. Small dedicatory altar; on the front an eagle and inscription (a); on the left a jumping bull and fragmentary inscription (b); on the back a garland and an illegible inscription (c); on the right a garland. Ed. pr. J. Wagner, Seleukeia am Euphrat/Zeugma (Wiesbaden, 1976) 130-131 (ph.).

(a) κατ' εὐ|χὴ|ν | ἀνέθηκεν.
(b) ---ΕΥΣ
(c) ---Ν---

1500-1609. SELEUKEIA ON THE EUPHRATES, EPITAPHS. J. Wagner, Seleukeia am Euphrat/Zeugma (Wiesbaden, 1976) 175-254 presents a catalogue of sepulchral stelai from Seleukeia on the Euphrates, most of them with inscriptions (with photographs and/or drawings). He classifies these sepulchral stelai according to the architectural form (a. "Aedicula" = no. 1-71; b. "Aedicula mit Segmentgiebel" = no. 72; c. "Aedicula ohne Architrav mit Nische" = no. 73-76; d. "Nische in architektonischer Ausgestaltung" = no. 77-87; e. "Nische ohne architektonische Ausgestaltung" = no. 88-131; f. "Stelenfragmente" = no. 132-139) and according to the representations of the stelai (eagle, basket, eagle and basket etc. We indicate these representations in the separate lemmata). Most of the stelai are unpublished. They are (probably) all from Belkis; we also indicate where they are now.

1500. P. 175-176, no. 1; in the wall of a house in Belkis.

Σενταῖε |² Φοράκου | ἄλυπε |⁴ χαῖρε.

1501. P. 176, no. 2; eagle; Museum Gaziantep.

Σπόρος ἄλυ|πε χαῖρε.

1502. P. 176-177, no. 4; eagle; Museum Adana.

Εὔδημε Διο|φάνους ἄλυπε | χα[ῖ]ρε.

The catalogue of the Museum in Adana mentions Carablus (Europos) as find-spot for this stele and for Wagner's nos. 7, 8, 12, 22, 31, 42, 71, 72, 81, 94, 105, 109, 115, 125, 128, 129, and 135. Nevertheless Wagner assigns them to Zeugma (cf. Wagner, l.c., 173-175).

1503. P. 177, no. 5; eagle; Museum Gaziantep.

Ἀγαθοκλῆς | Γλαύκου.

1504. P. 177-178, no. 6; eagle; Museum Gaziantep.

Βοῖος Πρόκλος | ἄλυπε χαῖρε.

1505. P. 178-179, no. 7; eagle; Museum Adana.

Μάτερνος Πό|πλου ἄωρε χαῖ|ρε.

For the find-spot of this stele, cf. no. 1502.

1506. P. 179, no. 8; eagle; Museum Adana.

Λούκιος Μερκού|ρι<ο>ς ἄλυπε χα[ῖρε].

For the find-spot of this stele, cf. no. 1502.

1507. P. 179, no. 9; eagle; Museum Urfa.

Λούκιος Φάβιος | Τραϊανὸς ἄλυπαι (sic) | χε͂ρε.

1508. P. 180-181, no. 11; eagle; Museum Gaziantep.

Αὔγουρος Ἀθηνο|δώρου ἄ[λυ]πε χαῖρε.

1509. P. 181, no. 12; eagle; Museum Adana.

Δροῦσε ἄλυπε | χε͂ρε.

For the find-spot of this stele, cf. no. 1502

1510. P. 181-182, no. 13; Ed. Jalabert - Mouterde, I. Syrie, I, no. 108; eagle; Museum Gaziantep.

Ἀθηνόδωρος Γερ|μανοῦ.

1511. P. 182, no. 14; eagle; Museum Gaziantep.

Γάϊος ᾽Ιούλιος ᾽Ιουλιανὸς | ἄλυπε χαῖρε.

1512. P. 183, no. 15; eagle; Museum Urfa.

Γ̣ρᾶτος ῾Ρούφου ἄ|[λυπ]ε χαῖρε.

1513. P. 183, no. 16; eagle; Museum Gaziantep.

Στάσιμος | ἄ̣λυπε χε͂ρε.

1514. P. 183-184, no. 17; eagle; Museum Adana.

᾽Αβάσκαντο[ς] | [ἄ]λυπε χαῖρ[ε].

1515. P. 184-185, no. 19; eagle; in the court of a house in Belkis.

Δω̣σ̣ᾶ̣ ἄ|λυπε χαῖρε.

1516. P. 185, no. 20; eagle; Museum Urfa.

Κλαύδιος

1517. P. 185-186, no. 21; eagle; Museum Urfa.

--σ̣ε ἄω̣ρε χα[ῖρε].

1518. P. 186-187, no. 22; eagle and inscription on front and back of the stele; Museum Adana.

a) (front) Εὐδαίμων | ἄλυπε χαῖρε.
b) (back) Τυράννι | ἄωρε εὐ|θύμει.

For the find-spot of this stele, cf. no. 1502 || Inscription on the back, L. 1: One does not have to correct into Τυραννί<α> (as Wagner does); Τυράννι could be the vocative of Τυράννις = Τυράννιος J. and L. Robert, BE (1977) no. 531, p. 429.

1519. P. 187, no. 23; eagle; Museum Adana.

Ζήνων ἄλυ|πε χαῖρε.

1520. P. 188, no. 25; eagle; Museum Urfa.

ΣΑΣΜΟΥΚΑΙ ἄλ|υπε χαῖρε.

1521. P. 188, no. 26; eagle; in a house in Belkis.

Οὔλιος βλʹ ἔ(τη) | ἄλυπε̣ χαῖρε.

1522. P. 188-189, no. 27; eagle; in a house in Belkis.

Βαρλάα ἄ̣[λυ]|π̣αι (sic) χαῖ[ρε].

1523. P. 189, no. 29; eagle; Museum Gaziantep.

---ΟΣΡΟΓΑ--ΤΟΣ

1524. P. 190-191, no. 31; eagles in the upper and in the lower half of the relief; Museum Adana.

a) Πουπαῖο͜ς Πουπαίου ἄ<λ>υπ̣[ε χ]α̣ῖ̣ρε.
b) Πουπαῖο͜ς ἄω͜ρε χαῖρε.
c) Ζώσιμο͜ς Πο͝υπαίου ἄλυ|π͜ε χαῖρε.

For the find-spot of this stele, cf. no. 1502 || a. ΑΑΥΠ̣[Ε Χ]Α̣Ι̣ΡΕ lapis.

1525. P. 191-192, no. 32; in the upper half of the relief: eagle, in the lower half: supinate hands; in the house of the burgomaster of Belkis.

Ἡράκλειτε̣ | Ἀρτεμιδώρο[υ] | χαῖρε.

1526. P. 192, no. 33; eagle and basket; Museum Gaziantep.

Οὐαλέρι̣[ος] ---ιων | Δομνῖνα̣ ---οντος | ἄλ̣υπε χα̣ῖ̣ρε.

1527. P. 192-193, no. 34; eagle and basket; Western necropolis of Belkis.

Γάϊ<ο>ς Ἰούλι<ο>ς Ἀπουλι|νάρι<ο>ς ἄωρε | χε͂ρε.

1528. P. 193, no. 35; eagle and basket; Museum Adana.

Διονύσιος | ἄλυπε χε͂ρε.

1529. P. 193-194, no. 36; eagle and basket; in a house in Belkis.

Διονύσιος ¦ ἄλυπε χε͂ρε

1530. P. 194, no. 37; Ed. Jalabert - Mouterde, I. Syrie, I, no. 109; eagle and basket; Museum Gaziantep.

Ζέ<α> ἀγ<α>θὴ ἄ[λυ]-
πε χε͂ρε καὶ ʼΟλυ-
3 [μ]πιὰς ἄλυπε χαῖρε.

1. ΖΕΔΑΓΔΘΗ lapis.

1531. P. 194-195, no. 38; eagle and basket; Museum Urfa.

Δομ-
νῖνα
3 Θησέως ἄω-
ρε χαῖρε.
Κομίνιος Θησέως
6 ἄωρε χαῖρε.

1532. P. 195-196, no. 40; eagle and basket; Museum Gaziantep.

ʼΑ̣ρτεμίδωρος | [ἄλυπ]ε̣ χα̣ῖ̣ρε.

1533. P. 196-197, no. 41; eagle and basket; Museum Urfa.

Λουκείλ̣|^{2}λη φίλα|νδρος ἄλυ|^{4}πε χαῖρε.

1534. P. 197, no. 42; on the front: eagle and basket, on the back: bust of a woman with inscription; ca. 150 A.D.; Museum Adana.

ʼΟβθᾶς Γερμαν|οῦ | χαῖρε.

For the find-spot of this stele, cf. no. 1502.

1535. P. 198, no. 44; basket; Museum Gaziantep.

ʽΕρμαί<α> ʽΕρμοῦ ἄωρε | χαῖρε.

1536. P. 198-199, no. 45; basket; Museum Gaziantep.

Μάρτα Τηλεμά|χου ἄλυπε χαῖρε.

1537. P. 199, no. 46; basket; Museum Gaziantep.

Πῶλα Ἑρ-
2 μέ<ο>υς ἔτων θ'
ἡμέρων μϛ' ἄωρε
4 χαῖρε.

1538. P. 199-200, no. 47; basket; Museum Gaziantep.

Μαρκία
Μάρκου
3 Ἀλεξάνδρου
γυνὴ
φίλανδρε εὐ-
6 σεβῆς ἄλυπε χὲρε.

1539. P. 200, no. 48; basket; Museum Adana.

Ἀγέλη ἄλυπε | χαῖρε.

1540. P. 200-201, no. 49; basket; Eastern necropolis of Belkis.

Δημαία Ζαρδαί|ου ἄλυπε χαῖρε.

1541. P. 200-201, no. 50; basket; Museum Urfa.

Φλαουΐα | Μαλχί<ου>.

2. Μαλχί<ου> or Μαλχί<ωνος> Wagner.

1542. P. 202, no. 51; basket; Museum Gaziantep.

Ἀσία Δεκμία Εὐ|καρπία ἄλυπε | χὲρε.

1543. P. 202-203, no. 53; basket; in the court of a house in Belkis.

Οὐαλερία | Μάρκελα | ἄλυπε χαῖρε.

1544. P. 204, no. 54; basket; in a house of Belkis.

Δομνῖνα | ἄωρε χαῖρε.

1545. P. 204-205, no. 55; Ed. Jalabert - Mouterde, I. Syrie, I, no. 111; basket; Museum Gaziantep.

Μάρθας ἄλυ|πε χαῖρε.

1. Μάρθας: so far only known as name of a man, but in this case, in connection with the basket on the relief, probably the name of a woman Wagner.

1546. P. 205, no. 56; basket; Museum Adana.

Σεμήραμις | ἄλυπε χαῖρε.

1547. P. 205, no. 57; basket; in a house in Belkis.

Μαρκία Οὐα<λ>ερί|α Φαδανάθ<α> ἄ|λυπε χαῖρε.

---

2. Φαδανᾶ: place in Syria Wagner.

1548. P. 206, no. 58; basket; Museum Urfa.

Ἰουλία Ἀκυλῖνα | ἄλυπε χε̃ρε.

1549. P. 206-207, no. 59; basket; at the foot of the Western necropolis of Belkis.

Ἀντων[ί]|α σώφρων | κὲ φίλαν|δρος.

1550. P. 207, no. 60; basket; in a house in Belkis.

Λουκία Πείσω|νος ἄλυπε. hedera

1551. P. 207-209, no. 61; Ed. pr. N. Altan, BELLETEN 34 (1970) 211-215; on the front: basket with inscription, on the back: bust of a woman and inscription; Museum Ankara.

a) (front) Γαβινία Ὑ̣γία | ἄλυπε χε̃ρε.
b) (back) Πριμίλλα ἄ̣|λυπε χε̃[ρ]ε.

Chronology: the grave-relief of Gabinia (3rd cent. A.D.) is older than the relief of Primilla (end 3rd - early 4th cent. A.D.) Wagner (against Altan who thought that the grave-relief of Primilla was the oldest)

1552. P. 210, no. 64; basket; in a house of Belkis.

Σεκοῦνδα Γράτου | ἄλυπε χαῖρε.

1553. P. 210-211, no. 65; basket; in the court of a house in Belkis.

Καμάθα <ἄ>λυπε | χαῖρε.

1554. P. 211, no. 66; basket; in the court of a house in Belkis.

Φορτο[ῦνα] | ἀταρά[κτα] | ἄλυπε χ̣[αῖρε].

1-2. J. and L. Robert, BE (1977) no. 531, p. 430 suggest: Φορτο[υν]|ᾶτα ʽΡα[--.

1555. P. 212, no. 67; basket and pair of supinate hands; Museum Urfa.

Μαρθών[η] ἄωρε χẽρε. | Καταμ̣[εῖται ἔ]τη α'.

2. "Est-ce sûr ?" J. and L. Robert, BE (1977) no. 531, p. 429-430; this line has been added later Wagner.

1556. P. 212, no. 68; basket and pair of hands; Museum Urfa.

ΕΥ---

1557. P. 212-213, no. 69; representation of a man in chiton and himation; 64 A.D.; Museum Gaziantep.

ʼΑπολλᾶ ἄωρε χαῖρε | ϛοτ'.

2. ϛοτ' = 376 (era of the Seleucids) = 64 A.D.

1558. P. 215, no. 72; eagle; Museum Adana.

ʽΗλιάδης | ἄλυπε χẽ|ρε.

For the find-spot of this stele, cf. no. 1502.

1559. P. 215-216, no. 73; eagle; Museum Gaziantep.

Λοῦκι | εὔψυχι.

Some traces are visible of an erased inscription of three lines Wagner.

1560. P. 217-218, no. 77; Ed. Jalabert - Mouterde, I. Syrie, I, no. 113; eagle; Museum Istanbul.

Ἀνείκ[ητ]ε ἄλυπε | χαῖρε.

1561. P. 218, no. 78; eagle; Museum Gaziantep.

Βαράδαδος | ἄωρε χαῖρε.

1562. P. 218-219, no. 79; eagle; Museum Urfa.

Φάλαδ<ος> ἄλυ|πε.

1563. P. 219, no. 80; eagles; Museum Urfa.

Μάῤῥος — Μάξιμ[ος] | Λαῖτος | [ἄλυ]π̣ε̣ χαῖρε.

1564. P. 219, no. 81; basket; Museum Adana.

[Ἰ]ουστίλλα Πρῖ|μου ἄωρε χαῖρε.

For the find-spot, cf. no. 1502.

1565. P. 220, no. 82; basket; Museum Adana.

Ἀπολλωνί<α> | Ἀγαταία

1566. P. 220-221, no. 83; Ed. H.F. Mussche, BCH 83 (1959) 543-548 and L. Robert, OM II, 862-867; representation of a boy carrying a bird, probably a pigeon; 2nd half 2nd cent. A.D.; Museum Adana.

Βρούτ(τιος) Κοσκώνιος ἄωρε | χαῖρε.

The stele was located at Doliche by Mussche (and Robert); they thought that the bird on the relief was a "porphyrion ou poule sultane" || 1. The reading of Mussche "βίου ι´" was corrected by L. Robert, l.c., into Βρούτ(τιος).

1567. P. 221-222, no. 84; representation of a boy with a kind of staff; 2nd half 2nd cent. A.D.; Museum Gaziantep.

Κύριλλος Ἀπο̣|λιναρίου ἄω|ρε χαῖρε. hedera

1568. P. 222-223, no. 85; bust of a young man; period of the tetrarchy; Museum Adana.

Κα<λ>λῖν(ος) Σικε|λ<ι>ώτου | Ὠκίμου χαῖρε.

1-2. ΚΑΑΛΙΝΣΙΚΕ|ΛΩΤΟΥ lapis; cf. J. and L. Robert, BE (1977) no. 531, p. 430 who suggest: "nous dégagerions Καλλίνεικε, mais ne savons que faire de la suite".

1569. P. 223-224, no. 87; bust of a woman with chiton and himation; period of the Antonini; Museum Gaziantep.

Γαΐα ἄλυπε χαῖρε.

1570. P. 224, no. 88; eagle; Museum Urfa.

Βάσσε ἄλυπε χαῖρε.

1571. P. 224, no. 89; eagle; Museum Urfa.

Κωστᾶ

1572. P. 225, no. 90; eagle; in a house in Belkis.

Ἑρμῆς ἄλυ|πε χαῖρε.

1573. P. 225-226, no. 92; Ed. Jalabert - Mouterde, I. Syrie, I, no. 114; eagle and pair of hands; Museum Aleppo.

Εὐθύμι, Μάρ|ρι· οὐδὶς ἀθάνα|τος.

1574. P. 226, no. 93; eagle and basket; in a house in Belkis.

Ματρώνα | ἄλυπε χαῖρε.

1575. P. 226-227, no. 94; in the upper half of the relief: two eagles, in the lower half: a basket; Museum Adana.

Φρῦμε ἄλυ|πε χέρε.

For the find-spot of this stele, cf. no. 1502 || 1. ΦΦΡΥΜΕ lapis; "das erste Φ ist nur vorgeritzt" Wagner.

1576. P. 227, no. 95; in the upper half of the relief: two eagles, in the lower half: a basket; Museum Adana.

Γαϊανὲ ἄλυπε χαῖρε.

1577. P. 227, no. 96; in the upper half of the relief: a basket, in the lower half: an eagle; in a house in Belkis.

Ἑρμιόν|η ἄλυπε | χαῖρε.

1578. P. 227-228, no. 97; basket; Museum Gaziantep.

Μαρκία | ἄλυπε χαῖρε.

1579. P. 228, no. 98; basket; Museum Gaziantep.

Δ̣ωρείθ|[2]α ἄλυπ|ε χαῖ|[4]ρε.

1580. P. 228-229, no. 99; basket; Museum Gaziantep.

Δημέα | ἄλυπε | χε͂ρε.

1581. P. 229-230, no. 101; bust of a man in chiton and himation; reign of Trajan; Museum Adana.

Μικαλῖνε Θε|οφίλου ἄλυ̣πε̣ | χα[ῖρ]ε.

1582. P. 230-231, no. 102; Ed. Jalabert - Mouterde, I. Syrie, I, no. 125; bust of a man; reign of the Flavii; Museum Dresden.

Κ̣αλὲ ἄνθρωπ̣ε | [χ]αῖρε.

---

1. Ἄνθρωπος: a proper name which is attested for a winner in the 81st Olympian games Wagner; rather a greeting-formula J. and L. Robert, BE (1977) no. 531, p. 429.

1583. P. 232, no. 104; bust of a man in chiton and himation; reign of the Antonini; Museum Gaziantep.

Διονύσιος Χαιραφάν[ης] | ἄ̣λ̣υ̣πε χα[ῖρε].

1584. P. 232, no. 105; bust of a man in chiton and himation;

reign of the Antonini; Museum Adana.

Σεύθη ἄλυπε χαῖ|ρε.

For the find-spot of this stele, cf. no. 1502.

1585. P. 233, no. 107; Ed. Jalabert - Mouterde, I. Syrie, I, no. 110; bust of a woman in chiton and himation; reign of the Antonini; Museum Gaziantep.

Μάμμη ἄλ|[υ]πε χαῖρε.

1586. P. 233-234, no. 108; bust of a woman in chiton and himation; reign of the Antonini; Museum Adana.

Ἡραεῒς ἄλυπε | χε͂ρε.

1587. P. 234, no. 109; bust of a woman in chiton and himation; reign of the Antonini; Museum Adana.

Δημήτρεις | ἄλυπε χαῖρε.

For the origin of this stele, cf. no. 1502.

1588. P. 234-235, nc. 110; bust of a woman in chiton and himation; later period of the Antonini; Museum Adana.

Σωσιπάτρα ἄ|λυπε χα<ῖ>ρε.

---

2. XA PE lapis.

1589. P. 235, no. 111; bust of a woman in chiton and himation; Museum Adana.

Θεκί|μη | ἄλυπ|ε χαῖρε.

1590. P. 236, no. 113; bust of a young man; period of the tetrarchy; Museum Adana.

Ἀδίακις | χαῖρε.

1591. P. 236-237, no. 114; bust of a man in chiton and himation; reign of the Severi; Museum Gaziantep.

Ἄλυπε χε͂ρε.

1592. P. 237, no. 115; bust of a man in chiton and himation; reign of the Severi; Museum Adana.

Ζέβιννε ἄ̣[λυπε χα]ῖρε.

For the find-spot of this stele, cf. no. 1502.

1593. P. 237-238, no. 116; bust of a woman; Museum Adana.

Μάρθα Διογέν|ο<υ>ς ἄ̣λυπα (sic) χε͂ρε.

1594. P. 238, no. 117; bust of a woman; Museum Gaziantep.

Εὐθύμ̣ε̣ι, Ἀσία· | οὐδ̣εὶς ἀθά̣να̣το[ς]

1595. P. 239-240, no. 119; bust of a person in chiton and himation; in the court of a house in Belkis.

Μαρᾶ Θάβου ἄ|λυπε χαῖρε.

1. Μαρᾶ: nominative or vocative of the masculine name Μαρᾶς (voc. Μαρᾶ) or the feminine name Μάρα (= also the vocative form) Wagner.

1596. P. 240, no. 120; Ed. Jalabert - Mouterde, I. Syrie, I, no. 112; bust of a woman in chiton and himation; Museum Adana.

Γαΐα | Μάρκου | ἄλυπε χαῖρε.

1597. P. 240-241, no. 121; bust of a woman between two men; reign of Claudius; Museum Gaziantep.

a) Μα̣ρκία <ἄ>λυπε | χαῖρε.
b) ---E---IPỊ

1598. P. 245, no. 126a; bust of a woman; Museum Istanbul.

Ἀθθαία ἄλυπε | χαῖρε.

N. Altan, BELLETEN 34 (1970) 214 thinks that this and the following number are part of one sepulchral stele; but since the two fragments do not fit together, J. Wagner disagrees.

1599. P. 245, no. 126b; bust of a man in chiton and himation; Museum Istanbul.

Μόνιμε ἄλυπε χαῖ|ρε.

Cf. no. 1598.

1600. P. 246-247, no. 127; in the upper half of the relief: busts of a man and woman, in the lower half: bust of a young man — their son ?; reign of the Severi; Museum Adana.

Φλά(ουιος) Τηλέγονος | λειβράρις | χαῖρε.

1601. P. 247-248, no. 128; in the upper half of the relief: busts of a man and woman with under them the inscriptions; in the lower part: bust of a woman; reign of the Antonini; Museum Adana.

a) At the left: Ὀχχουμία <ἄ>λυ|πε χαῖρε.
b) At the right: Οὐαλεντῖνε | ἄλυπε χαῖρε.

For the find-spot of this stele, cf. no. 1502.

1602. P. 248, no. 129; Ed. pr. H.F. Mussche, GENTSE BIJDRAGEN TOT DE KUNSTGESCHIEDENIS EN DE OUDHEIDSKUNDE 18 (1959-1960) 33-34, fig. 2; in the upper half of the relief: bust of a young man, in the lower half: two eagles; early period of the Antonini; Museum Adana.

Θεο|[2]τέκ|νοε |[4] Δεί|ου ἄ|[6]ωρε | χαῖ|[8]ρε.

For the find-spot of this stele, cf. no. 1502 || 1-3. on the name Θεότεκνος cf. Wagner, l.c., p. 167.

1603. P. 249-250, no. 130; in the upper half of the relief: bust of a woman, in the lower half: an eagle with next to it the inscription; reign of the Antonini; Eastern necropolis of Belkis.

Μάξι|με ἄ|ωρα (sic) | χαῖρε.

1604. P. 250-251, no. 131; Ed. pr. H.F. Mussche, GENTSE BIJDRAGEN TOT DE KUNSTGESCHIEDENIS EN DE OUDHEIDSKUNDE 18 (1959-1960) 33-34, fig. 1; on the front of the stele: in the upper half bust of a man with inscription and in the lower half eagle with inscription, on the left side of the stele: eagle with inscription; reign of the Antonini; Museum Adana.

a) (front side): I. Πόπλιε | ἄλυπε | χαῖρε.

II. ʼΑετωρῖνε | ἄλυπε χέρε.

b) (left side): Εὔσροχε ἄ|λυπε χέρε.

---

a, I. Initially the stone-cutter had written Πόπλιος, but he corrected it into Πόπλιε Wagner || b. Is it not Εὔστοχε ? J. and L. Robert, BE (1977) no. 531, p. 430.

1605. P. 251, no. 133; eagle; in the inner court of a house in Belkis.

Εὐδέμων ἄ|[λ]υπε χαῖρε.

1606. P. 252, no. 135; eagle; Museum Adana.

a) (under the eagle): ---ΚΩΝ---
b) (at the left, above the eagle): --------ΙΝΜΟ | [---ἄλυπ]ε χέρε.

For the find-spot of this stele, cf. no. 1502.

1607. P. 252-253, no. 136; Ed. Jalabert - Mouterde, I. Syrie, I, no. 84; 125 A.D.; eagle; now lost.

Βαρλάα | (eagle) |² ἄλυπε χαῖ|ρε· |⁴ ἔτους ζλυʹ.

---

1. Βαρλάας = the Syrian name Barʼalâhâ, translated into Greek as Θεότεκνος (cf. no. 1602) || 4. ζλυʹ = 437 (era of the Seleucids) = 125 A.D.

1608. P. 253, no. 137; in the upper half of the relief a basket, in the lower half (later added) at the right an eagle (with under it rasura of a text) and at the left a basket, with next to it the inscription; Museum Urfa.

Ἄλυπε | χαῖρε.

1609. P. 254, no. 139; three baskets, with under them three inscriptions; Museum Gaziantep.

a) Κυρίλ|²λα ἄ|λυπε |⁴ χαῖρε.
b) Ἔσθ<α> | ἄωρα | χαῖρε.
c) Δημητροῦ | χέρε.

1610-1616. SELEUKEIA ON THE EUPHRATES, EPITAPHS. J. Wagner,

Seleukeia am Euphrat / Zeugma (Wiesbaden, 1976) 254-261 presents a catalogue of the reliefs and inscriptions in the sepulchral chambers in Belkis (with photographs and drawings).

1610. P. 255-259, no. 140a-o; Ed. Jalabert - Mouterde, I. Syrie, I, no. 94-105; grave of Zenon and his family; Western necropolis of Belkis.

I. P. 255, no. 140a:

Τὸ μνῆμα
Ζήνωνος
3 χωρὶς τοῦ
ἀριστεροῦ
5 μέρ{σ}ου<ς>

II. P. 255-256, no. 140c (relief with eagle):

Λιριποζ|[2]<α>ία | ἄλ|[4]υπ|ε χ|[6]ε͂|ρ|[8]ε.

III. P. 256, no. 140d (eagle):

Αὐγ--------- | ἄλ[υπε χε͂ρε].

IV. P. 256, no. 140e (basket):

'Αζυρία | [ἄ]λυπαι (sic) χε͂ρε.

V. P. 256, no. 140f (eagle):

Βάσσε | ἄλυπαι (sic) χε͂ρε.

VI. P. 256, no. 140g (bust of a man):

Δᾶμι χαῖρε.

VII. P. 257, no. 140h (bust of a man):

Ζήνων χαῖρε.

VIII. P. 257, no. 140i (bust of a woman):

Φαλαδωνία | ἄλυπε χαῖρε.

IX. P. 257, no. 140j (bust of a woman):

'Αθθαία μή|τηρ Δαμί(ου).

X. P. 257, no. 140m (two eagles):

Φάλαδος Ζοώρας | ἀδελφοί.

XI. P. 257-259, no. 140n (bust of a woman):

Σουμαία ἀμμὴ | αὐτῶν.

XII. P. 259, no. 140, o (basket):

Ζεβιννοῦ ἀδελ|φὴ | αὐτῶν.

II, 1-2. ΛΙΡΙΠΟΖΛΙΑ lapis; corrected into Λιριποζ<α>ία by Wagner (who follows Cumont); Σ<α>ιριποζ<α>ία Jalabert - Mouterde, I. Syrie, I, no. 105 || XI, 1. ἀμμή: transcription of the Semitic word for "mother" Wagner; but cf. J. and L. Robert, BE (1977) no. 531, p. 429 who think that ἀμμή rather indicates the nurse of the two brothers named in X || XII, 1. Ζεβιννοῦς: daughter of Σουμαία (XI; but cf. J. and L. Robert, l.c.) and sister of Φάλαδος and Ζοώρας (X) Wagner.

1611. P. 259, no. 141; Ed. Jalabert - Mouterde, I. Syrie, I, no. 106; bust of a woman in chiton, under it the inscription in a tabula ansata; grave in the Western necropolis of Belkis.

Μαρκια|^{2}νὴ ἄω|ρε χαῖρε· |^{4} φιλ̣ου|μ̣έν|^{6}η̣.

1612. P. 260, no. 142; Ed. Jalabert - Mouterde, I. Syrie, I, no. 107; bust of a woman in himation and chiton; grave in the Western necropolis of Belkis.

Ἀ̣ρτεμιδώρα | χαῖρε.

1613. P. 260, no. 143; bust of a woman in chiton and himation; grave in the Western necropolis of Belkis.

Ἡλιοδώρα | Ἀπολλοδότου | ἄωρε χαῖρε.

1614. P. 260, no. 144; eagle and basket; grave in the Western necropolis of Belkis.

Αὐρηλία <ἄ>λ|[[υπ]]ε χε̃ραι (sic).

1615. P. 261, no. 146; eagle; grave in the Eastern necropolis of Belkis.

Φιλόθεος | Δάνου ἄλ|[υπε] χαῖρε.

1616. P. 261, no. 147; inscription in a tabula ansata; grave in the Western necropolis of Belkis.

Λονγεῖ-
να ἄωρε
χἔρε·
ζήσασα ἔτη ε'
μῆν(α) α' καὶ ἡμ(έρας) κη'.

1617. SELEUKEIA ON THE EUPHRATES, EPITAPH, 325 A.D. Grave titulus from Belkis, seen and read by H. Seyrig in 1931 in Aleppo. Ed. R. Mouterde - A. Poidebard, Le limes de Chalcis I (Paris, 1945) p. 212 f., no. 47 (fig. 33, II pl. CXVIII 5). Republished by J. Wagner, Seleukeia am Euphrat / Zeugma (Wiesbaden, 1976) 261-262, no. 148.

Ἔτους ϛλχ', λ'
Δύστρου, σπηλεο-
κοινονίας Μ[ι]γ-
δέου καὶ Βαγράθ-
θου, μεριτίας ἀνα-
τολικῆς Μιγδέου
καὶ δυτικῆς τῶι
Βαγράθθου ΛΧ-
ΜΩ πεποίητε·
Εἷς Θεὸς ὁ δύναη
τὰ πάντα.

1. ϛλχ' = 636 (era of the Seleucids) = 325 A.D.

1618-1622. SELEUKEIA ON THE EUPHRATES, EPITAPHS. J. Wagner, Seleukeia am Euphrat / Zeugma (Wiesbaden, 1976) 263-271 publishes the grave-statues (some of them with inscriptions) from Belkis (with photographs).

1618. P. 263, no. 150; statue of a sitting woman; 2nd half 2nd cent. A.D.; Museum Gaziantep.

Ἀματραία Θηδησιφαία
Ἀμβηγαρμεία <ἄ>λυπε χαῖρε.

1619. P. 263-264, no. 151; statue of a sitting woman; 1st cent. A.D.; Museum Adana.

Κορνηλία ἄ[λυ]|πε χἔρε.

1620. P. 264-265, no. 153; statue of a sitting mother with child; Museum Gaziantep.

Θεοθαία | ἄλυπε χαῖρε.

1621. P. 270, no. 163; statue of a woman; Museum Gaziantep.

Θεκίμα ἄωρε χαῖρε.

1622. P. 271, no. 165; statue-base; Museum Gaziantep.

Ὑέα πρωθήβην, ὃν ἀνέτρεφε[ν] | ἐλπίδα γήρους,
Μαινιανὸς [γε]|νέτης τὸν ὁμώνυμον εἰκ[όνι] | τῇ<ι>δ̣ε̣.

1623. SOFRAZ KÖY, TEMENOS-STELE OF KING ANTIOCHOS I OF KOMMAGENE, 66-64 B.C. Relief stele made of basaltlava; the relief represents a dexiosis between Antiochos I and Apollo-Helios; lines 1-6a of the inscription are on the back of the stele, lines 6b-33 on the right, back and left sides of it. Ed. pr. J. Wagner - G. Petzl, ZPE 20 (1976) 201-223 (ph.). Cf. W. Clarysse, ZPE 23 (1976) 264.

Βασιλεὺς Ἀντίοχος Θεὸς Δί-
καιος Ἐπιφανὴς Φιλορώμαιος
καὶ Φιλέλλην ὁ ἐγ βασιλέως Μι-
θραδάτου Καλλινίκου, ὁ κτίστης
καὶ εὐερ<γ>έτης καὶ πρῶτος ἀναλα-
βὼν τὴν κίταριν, Ἀπόλλωνι ἐπηκόῳ καὶ Ἀρτ[έμι]-
[δι] Δικτύννῃ τὸν τόπον τοῦτον ἀφιέρωσα καὶ τάς τε τῶν θεῶ[ν εἰ]-
[κό]νας τὰς ἐνγεγλυμμένας ἐν ταῖς στήλαις καὶ τὰς ἐμὰς τ[ὰς]
[σ]υνκαθιδρυμένας ταύταις ἀναστήσας κατέστησα ἱερεῖ[ς ἔν]
[τ]ε τῷ ἱερῷ τούτῳ καὶ ἐν τοῖς λοιποῖς τοῖς τῆς βασιλείας ἱερο[ῖς καὶ]
[ἀ]φώρισα χώρας τοῖς ἱεροῖς πᾶσι, ὅπως οἱ ἱερεῖς ἐκ τῶν γινομένω[ν προσ]-
όδων τῆς αὐτῆς χώρας ποιῶνται τὰς ἐπιθύσεις καὶ τὰς θυσίας [κατὰ]
[μ]ῆνα τῇ ἑκκαιδεκάτῃ γενεθλίῳ μου ἡμέρᾳ καὶ ἑορτάζωσιν καὶ ε̣[ὐω]-
[χ]ῶνται οἱ κατὰ μέρος. v. Διεταξάμην δὲ ἵνα καὶ πάντες οἱ ἐκ τῆς β-
ασιλείας πανδημεὶ κατ' ἐνιαυτὸν συνέ̣ρ̣χωνται, ἕκα[σ]τοι εἰς τὰ <ἐ>[γ]-
[γ]ὺς αὐτοῖς ἱερά, ἔν τε τῇ ἑκκαιδεκάτῃ τοῦ Αὐδναίου οὔσῃ ἐνιαυσίῳ [γενε]θλίῳ μου ἡμέρᾳ καὶ τῇ δε[κάτῃ]
τοῦ Λῴου μηνός, ἐν ᾗ τὸ διάδημα ἀνέλαβον, [κ]αὶ ἐπιθύοντες ἐν τοῖς ἱεροῖς εὐωχῶ[νται]
[τ]αύτας τὰς δύο ἡμέρας· ὁμοίως δὲ καὶ ἱεροδού<λ>ους ἀφιέρωσα, ἵ̣ν̣α̣ προ[σκαρτε]-
[ροῦ]ντες τοῖς ἱεροῖς παρέχωνται τὰς χρείας. Ἐὰν δὲ καὶ οἱ υἱοί μου καὶ [οἱ]
[ἔγ]γονοι αὐτῶν οἱ τὴν βασιλείαν διαδεχόμενοι ἄγωσιν τὴν ἔμμηνόν μου [γενέθλι]-
ο̣ν̣ ἑκκαιδεκάτην, ὁμοίως δὲ καὶ ἐν τοῖς λοιποῖς ἱεροῖς ἅπασιν τοῖς κ̣[ατὰ τὴν]
[ἐμ]ὴ̣ν βασιλείαν διατάξωνται ἄγεσθαι τὴν αὐτὴν ἡμέραν καθὼς καὶ [πρὸ]
[τῶ]ν ἐμῶν χρόνων ἤγετο, εὐμενεῖς εἴησαν αὐτοῖς οἱ θεοὶ καὶ ἵλεῳ

[αὐτοῖς]
24 [συ]ντυγχανέτωσαν. Ὅσοι δ' ἂν τῶν βασιλέων ἢ δυναστῶν ἢ στρα-
[τηγῶν]
[ἢ] ἐθναρχῶν ἢ ἄλλοι τινὲς παραγένωνται εἰς τοῦτο τὸ ἱερὸν καὶ
β[ούλωνται]
ἐπιθύειν καὶ σπενδοποιεῖσθαι ἐπὶ τῶν βωμῶν τῶν καθιδρυμένω[ν ἐν]
[το]ύτῳ τῷ ἱερῷ, ὁμοίως δὲ καὶ τῇ ἐμῇ εἰκόνι τῇ καθιδρυμένῃ σὺν
τ[αῖς τῶν]
28 [θ]εῶν εἰκόσιν, κατὰ ταὐτὰ δὲ καὶ ἐν τοῖς ἄλλοις τοῖς ἐν τῇ βα-
σιλε[ίᾳ ἱε]-
[ρ]οῖς, ἐν οἷς καθίδρυνται καὶ αἱ ἐμαὶ εἰκόνες σὺν ταῖς τῶν θεῶν
εἰκ[όσιν],
[συν]αύξουσι[ν αὐ]τοῖς τῶν τε θεῶν καὶ τὰς ἐ[μὰς εἰκό]νας καὶ
τὸ[ν πρέ]-
[ποντ]α <σ>ẹ[βασμ]ὸν ἀπομερίζουσιν εὐμε[νεῖς εἴησα]ν οἱ θεοὶ
κ[αὶ παρ']
32 [ὅλον αὐτοῖς τὸν χ]ρόνον τὰ παρὰ τούτων ἀ[παντάσθω] ἀγαθά· ο[ἳ]
[δ' ἂν παραγενόμενοι] ẹịṣ ṭọụṭọ ṭ[ὸ ἱερόν, ὁμοίως δὲ καὶ εἰς τὰ
λοιπὰ ἱε]-
[ρὰ, τοῖς τῆς βασιλείας τόποις, ἐν οἷς συνκαθίδρυνται τοῖς θεοῖς
καὶ αἱ]
[ἐμαὶ εἰκόνες, μὴ τὸν πρέποντα σεβασμὸν ἀπομερίσωσιν, ἀλλ' ἐκ
τῶν]
36 [ἐναντίων βλάψωσίν τι ἢ λυμήνωνται τὰ ἱερὰ ἢ τὰς ἐμὰς εἰκόνας],
[συμβαίνοι αὐτοῖς τὰ ἐναντία τούτων καὶ γίνεσθαι (or γινέσθω)
αὐτοῖς]
[ἃ τοῖς ἀσεβοῦσι περὶ τοὺς θεοὺς γίνεται].

5 ΕΥΕΡΓΕΤΗΣ lapis || 5-6. πρῶτος ἀναλα|βὼν τὴν κίταριν: cf. Wagner - Petzl, l.c., 206-208 || 13-14. ΚΑΙΣ[|]ΩΝΤΑΙ lapis; σ[υνέρ-χ]ωνται is possible, but ẹ[ὔω|χ]ῶνται seems preferable Wagner - Petzl || 14. ΔΙΕΤΑΞΑΜΗΝΔΕ lapis; Διέταξα μῆνα<ς> Wagner - Petzl; Διεταξάμην δέ Clarysse || 16-17. rasura; the original text of the inscription was afterwards enlarged in the spot where the dates for the yearly holidays were mentioned (in the text underlined), to make clear the meaning of 16 Audnaios and 10 Loos in Antiochos' life Wagner - Petzl || 17. [κ]αὶ ἐπιθύοντες: in the enlarged text, καὶ is considered as erased Wagner - Petzl || 18. ΙΕΡΟΔΟΥΔΟΥΣ lapis || 23. ἵλεῳ: perhaps ἵλεω[ς] Wagner - Petzl || 28-29. [ἱε]|[ρ]οῖς: also [τό]|[π]οις is possible Wagner - Petzl || 31. ΕΓ....ΟΝ lapis || 34-38. the restoration of these lines is confirmed by paralleltexts Wagner - Petzl.

BABYLONIA

1624. BABYLON, DEDICATION TO ANTIOCHOS IV EPIPHANES, SEPT./ OCT. 166 B.C. OGIS, 253; M. Zambelli, RFIC 38 (1960) 374 ff. After a long discussion of the inscription and its meaning, J.G. Bunge,

CHIRON 6 (1976) 63, note 60 presents the following text (with a complete bibliography, cf. p. 58, note 26):

Βασιλεύοντος Ἀντιόχου Θ[εοῦ Ἐπιφανοῦς]
σωτῆρος τῆς Ἀσίας καὶ κτίσ[του καὶ εὐεργέτου]
τῆς πόλεως ἔτους ϛμ' κα[ὶ ρ' τῆι θυσίαι καὶ τῶι]
ἀγῶνι χαριστηρίοις ὑπὸ [Δάφνηι ἀγομένοις ϛ']
ἀπιόντος Ὑπερβερεταίου [Βασιλεῖ Ἀντιόχωι]
Θεῶι Ἐπιφαν[εῖ βωμὸ]ν ἀνέ[θηκεν ἐν τῆι ἀγορᾶι]
Φίλιππος Δι[.................................]
ἐν τῶι δμ' [καὶ ρ' ἔτει ....]

The text of Zambelli runs as follows: Βασιλεύοντος Ἀντιόχου θ[εοῦ Ἐπιφανοῦς] | σωτῆρος τῆς Ἀσίας καὶ κτίσ[του καὶ εὐεργέτου] | τῆς πόλεως ἔτους ϛμ' καὶ [ρ'... θυσίαι? καὶ] |[4] ἀγῶνι χαριστηρίοις ὑπο[..............] | ἀπιόντος Ὑπερβερεταίου [βασιλεῖ Ἀντιόχωι] | θεῶι Ἐπιφαν[εῖ ...].αν.[.............] | Φίλιππος Δια[.......... ....] |[8] ἐν τῶι δμ' [καὶ ρ' ἔτει ....]

SYRIA

1625. CHRONOLOGY. J.-P. Rey-Coquais, MUB 47 (1972) 94-105 studies the dating of inscriptions of North-Lebanon and explains when, where, and why the era of the Seleucids, the local era of a town, or the regnal years of the emperors were used for that purpose.

1626. ANTIOCHEIA ON THE ORONTES, INSCRIPTION ON MOSAIC, 5th CENT. A.D. Cf. no. 1884.

1627. APAMEIA, MAKING OF A PAVEMENT IN HONOUR OF THE DECEASED ZACCHAEUS, 533 A.D. Marble block (found in the Eastern cathedral). Ed. pr. J. Ch. Balty, Mélanges Collart, p. 32 (ph.).

† Ἐπὶ τοῦ ὁσιωτ(άτου) κ(αὶ) ἁγιωτ(άτου) Παύ-
λου ἐπισκ(όπου) ἐγένετο τὸ πλα-
κοτὸν ὑπὲρ ἀναπαυσέο·
Ζαχχεου πρεσβ(υτέρου) κ(αὶ) πατ̣..
τεν.ο̣ν τοῦ ἁγιοτ(άτου)...
σπουδῇ Δομετίου ταμί-
ν̣ου ἔτου εμω' ἰν̣δ(ικτίωνος)...

4-5. κ(αὶ) παρ̣αμ̣|{τ}ο̣ναρίου τοῦ ἁγιοτ(άτου) ν̣α̣[οῦ] ? Balty || 6-7. ταμί|νου for ταμίου Balty.

1628-1630. APAMEIA, GIFTS OF BISHOP PAUL TO THE CATHEDRAL, 533-

540 A.D. Ed. pr. J.Ch. Balty, Mélanges Collart, p. 33-34 (ph.).

1628. P. 33; inscription in a medallion in a mosaic (in iambic trimeters: p. 40).

Τὴν ποικί-
λην ψηφῖδα
3 Παῦλος εἰσάγει
ὁ ποικιλόφρων
τῶν ἄνωθεν
6 δογμάτων.

1629. P. 34; inscription on a round marble plaque in an opus sectile pavement (in iambic trimeters: p. 40).

Πολλῶν μετ᾽ ἄλ-
λων κ(αὶ) τόπον τὸν
3 ἐνθάδ᾽ ἐκόσμησε
Παῦλος τῆι πολυ-
5 μόρφωι συνθέσει.

1630. P. 34; inscription in a medallion on the head of a column.

† Παύλ|ου ἁγιωτ|άτου μη|τρο{λο}πολ(ίτου) | Ἀπαμ(είων).

1631. DJEBEL AKRUM, FUNERARY INSCRIPTION, 309 A.D. Above a sepulchral cavern a "Nephesh"; at the left of the Nephesh: A, on it: B, lower: C. Ed. pr. Ch. Ghadban, MUB 49 (1975-76) 573-578 (ph).

A. Ἀβεδ|λαα | πάτ|ερ ζοή | σου ἔ|τη ο᾽.
B. Ἔτου|ς σκχ᾽ | μήνος | Δαίσιου | κ᾽. Θάρσει.
C. [[Οὐδεὶς ἀθάνατος ?]]

Probably pagan Ghadban.

1632. DJEBEL AKRUM, FORMULA FROM THE HOLY SCRIPTURE, 541 A.D. Inscription on a block placed above the entrance of a church. Ed. pr. Ch. Ghadban, MUB 49 (1975-76) 566-573 (ph.).

[Κύριος φυλάξει τὴν εἴσοδόν σου καὶ] τὴν ἔξοδόν
[σου ἀπὸ τοῦ νῦν καὶ ἕως] τοῦ αἰῶνος.
[Ἔτο]υς βνω᾽ ἰνδ[ικτιῶνος δ᾽]

The formula is borrowed from Psalm CXX, 8 Ghadban.

1633. HELIOPOLIS (BAALBEK), BUILDING-INSCRIPTION, 3rd CENT. A.D. Mosaic-inscription in a building. Ed. pr. R. Mouterde, BMB 14 (1958) 44-46 (photo in vol. 15, 1959, pl. 21, 3). Cf. W. Peek, ZPE

21 (1976) 188 who proposes corrections in lines 2 and 4.

Οἶκον Ὀλυμπίοιο πάις τεκτήνατο τοῦτον
2 Πατρίκιος, σοφίης ἄξιο[ς] Εὐδοξίου
τοῦ Πλατωνιάδαο σαόφρονος· <ά>λλὰ καὶ αὐτὸς
4 ἄξια τῆς προ[γ]η̣νῶν εὐσεβίης φρονέε̣[ι].

2. ἄξιο[ς] Mouterde; ἄξιον Peek || Εὐδοξίου: probably Eudoxos of Knidos Mouterde || 4. ΠΡΟ[.]Η̣ΝΩΝ lapis; προ[γη]νῶν (pro προγενῶν) Mouterde; προ[φ]<α>νῶν Peek || φρόνε[ε] Mouterde; φρονέε̣[ι] Peek.

1634. HIERAPOLIS (MEMBIJ), HONORARY INSCRIPTION FOR THE HIGH PRIEST ALEXANDROS, MIDDLE 1st CENT. A.D. Ed. pr. R.A. Stucky, SYRIA 53 (1976) 127-130 (ph.) who has seen in a shop a basalt relief fragment found in 1924 in Membij (now in the National Museum of Damas). The relief represents a high priest from Hierapolis. At the left of the head the following inscription of eleven lines, forming two epic disticha:

[.]ΕΙ̣[.]ΕΝΟϹ ἀρχιερῆα | πανέξοχον ἐνθάδ' Ἀχαῖ|ος
2 στᾶσεν Ἀλέξαν|δρον γνήσιον ἐν | φιλία̣ι̣
σ̣πένδων | ὄφρα θεοῖσιν ἐ|πεύχηται μα|κάρεσσιν
4 πατρί|δ' ὅπως σώ|ζωσι α<ἶ>εν ἐν | εὐνομίαι.

1. ΕΙ[.]ΕΝΟϹ Stucky, corr. Bingen || 4. σωζωσία<ι>εν ἐν εὐνομίᾳ Stucky, corr. Bingen who remarks: α<ἶ>εν nisi ἄεν.

1635-1639. IBN HANI, STAMPED AMPHORA-HANDLES. Ed. pr. A. Bounni, E. and J. Lagarce, N. Saliby, SYRIA 53 (1976) 253-254 (ph.).

1635. Δαμοκράτευς (with rose)

Stamp of a Rhodian manufacturer; late 3rd - early 2nd cent. B.C.

1636. [Εὐφρ]άν[ω][ρος] (with head of Helios)

Rhodian manufacturer; after 175 B.C.

1637. Ἐπὶ Κλεάρχο[υ] Ἀρταμιτίου

Ἀρταμίτιος = name of a month in Rhodes; after 240 B.C.

1638. Μενεκράτευς

Perhaps a Rhodian manufacturer of the 2nd half 3rd - 1st half 2nd cent. B.C.

1639. 'Επὶ Τιμοκλείδα

An undated eponymous Timokleidas is attested on Rhodes.

1640. MAAD, TWO DEDICATIONS TO THE GOD Σατράπης, 8 B.C. AND 3rd - 4th CENT. A.D. Ed. E. Renan, Mission de Phénicie (Paris, 1864) 241-242 (the second inscription was re-edited by R. Mouterde, SYRIA, 26, 1949, p. 69). A. Dupont-Sommer, CRAI (1976) 648-662 identifies the God Satrapes (cf. also Pausanias, VI, 25, 5-6) as the syncretic God Apollo-Mithras. Study of the diffusion of this cult.

1641. PALMYRA, HONORARY INSCRIPTION FOR MARCUS AURELIUS AND LUCIUS VERUS, 166 A.D. Hard limestone block which served as a lintel to support the statues of the two emperors; the stone is from Palmyra but was found in Qasr el Heir el sharqi. Ed. pr. G.W. Bowersock, CHIRON 6 (1976) 349-355 (ph.).

vacat τοῦ ηο̣[υ' ἔτους μηνὶ 'Υπερβερεταίῳ]
Αὐτοκράτορα Καίσαρα [Μᾶρκον Αὐρήλιον 'Αντωνεῖνον Σεβαστὸν καὶ]
Αὐτοκράτορα Καίσαρα Λ[ούκιον Αὐρήλιον Οὐῆρον Σεβαστὸν]
4 θεοῦ 'Αντωνείνου υἱοὺς [θεοῦ 'Αδριανοῦ υἱωνοὺς θεοῦ Τραιανοῦ]
Παρθικοῦ ἐκγόνο[υ]ς θε[οῦ Νέρουα ἀπογόνους ἀρχιερέας μεγίστους]
'Αρμενιακοὺς Μηδικοὺς [Παρθικοὺς μεγίστους ----------------]
Συμωνου ἀρχιερεὺς κα[ὶ συμποσίαρχος ἱερέων μεγίστου θεοῦ Διὸς]
8 Βήλου, ἱερεὺς δὲ καὶ τῶν [Σεβαστῶν ἐξ ἰδίων ἀνέστησε --------]
πρὸς τοὺς Σεβαστοὺς Κα[ίσαρας ------------------------------]
καὶ τὴν ἐν τῷ <τ>ῆς συμ[ποσιαρχίας αὐτοῦ καιρῷ -------------]
ἐπιστολὴν τῶν αὐτῶ[ν Σεβαστῶν ------------------------------]
12 προσθέσεος θυμ<ι>ατόρων περ[ὶ -----------------------------]
τοῖς αὐτοῖς [[π̣ρ̣ε̣.....ο̣...]]------------------------------------

---

1642. PALMYRA, DEDICATION OF A STATUE OF SALAMALLAT, 64 A.D. Ed. J.T. Milik, Dédicaces faites par les dieux (Paris, 1972) p. 82-83. J.P. Rey-Coquais, apud M. Gawlikowski, Mélanges Collart, p. 200 restores L. 1-2 as follows: [Κατὰ χρηματ]ισμὸν ['Αθήνας θεᾶς] | [ἡ φυλ]ὴ πᾶσ[α ---. Milik's text was: [Θεὰ Νέμεσ]ις, Μεζ[ι] α[νηνῶν τε φυλὴ] | [καὶ σύ]μπας δῆμο[ς ---.

1643. PALMYRA, DEDICATION OF STATUES BY THE GODDESS ATHENA AND OTHERS, END 1st CENT. A.D. Part of a column. Ed. pr. M. Gawlikowski, Mélanges Collart, p. 200 (ph.).

Μαλιχον Νασσουμ[ου]
τοῦ Σαμψιγεραμου
καὶ Νασσουμον τὸν υἱὸ[ν]
αὐτοῦ Ἀθ[ήν]α θεᾷ καὶ
......Ỵ̱Ị̱Ọ̱------------

Malichos and the others are well-known members of the Palmyrene aristocracy Gawlikowski.

1644. PALMYRA, DEDICATION BY THE TOWN, 171 A.D. Ed. M. Gawlikowski, Le temple palmyrénien. Étude d' épigraphie et de topographie historique (Warsaw, 1973) p. 26, no. 1. G.W. Bowersock, CHIRON 6 (1976) 353, note 14 reads in L. 3 ἔφιππον instead of ἐφ' ἵππον

1645. PHILADELPHEIA (AMMAN), DEDICATION OF A BUILDING, REIGN OF M. AURELIUS. Ed. E. Littmann, Greek and Latin Inscriptions — Section A, Southern Syria Part I, Ammonites (Publication of the Princeton University Archaeological Expedition to Syria in 1904-1905, Division III; Leyden, 1907) p. 10-11. Cf. F. el Fakharani, WZRostock 24 (1975) 533-554. Fakharani suggests that the dedicated building (on the acropolis of the city of Philadelpheia), usually considered as a temple, could be a library.

1646. SIDON, DEDICATION BY A VICTOR IN THE ASKLEPIEIA, 44-43 B.C. Inscription on a limestone urn. Ed. pr. B. Soyez, MUB 47 (1972) 167-168 (ph.).

("Ετους) ηξ
Σωσᾶς
Ζήνωνος
νικήσας
ἀνέθηκεν
Ἀσκληπιῷ.

1647-1650. TELL EL HAJJ, GRAFFITI. Fragment of a white limestone column; probably the graffiti were cut by soldiers who garrisoned Tell el Hajj. Ed. pr. R.A. Stucky, AARCHSYR 25 (1975) 168-169 (ph.).

1647. On the left side:

Μνησθῇ
Κ̣ορνηλιανός
ζοή
Χαρίδημος
μνησθῇ
Ἀντι<ο>χιανός
ζοή
Παυ<σ>α<νί>ας
ζοή
Θεσσ<α>λ<ό>ς
ζọή.

1648. On the right side, at the top: Κάστω̣<ρ>

1649. Under no. 1648: Μνησθῇ ὁ γράψας | Φρόντων.

1650. Between no. 1648 and no. 1649 has later been added:

Δημοσθένης ὁ [....]
2 τῷ κατηγορ[.....]
κλέπτου τ[.....]
4 εἶπεν ὅτι [......]

At the bottom of the column a Greek alphabet.

1651. TELL EL HAJJ, GRAFFITO, 4th - 5th CENT. A.D. Graffito on the wall of a subterranean sepulchral chamber. Ed. pr. R.A. Stucky, AARCHSYR 25 (1975) 170 (ph.).

Τρυκλίνι(ον) Βηλης

1652. VALLEY OF WADI ABOU MOUSSA (NORTH-LEBANON), DEDICATION OF A BUILDING, 184 A.D. Inscription engraved on a rock, northeast of Tripoli, near the remains of a Roman temple. Ed. pr. J.P. Rey-Coquais, MUB 47 (1972) 87-105 (ph.).

Ὑπὲρ σωτηρίας Καίσαρος
Μάρκου Αὐρηλίου Ἀντωνείνου
Σεβαστοῦ τοῦ κυρίου Διογένης Χορ[η]γίου
4 [ἅ]μα Διοδότᾳ συμβίῳ εὐξάμενοι ὑπὲρ ὑ-
γείας τοῦ κυρίου καὶ ἑαυτῶν τὴν βαίτην
τὴν σὺν τῇ ἐν αὐτῇ στιβάδι καὶ τῇ πρὸς ταύ-
τῃ κειμένῃ στοᾷ καὶ τῷ λάκκῳ κατεσκεύ[α]-
8 σαν ἐκτεμόντες τὴν πέτραν ταύτην
διεχούσαν μέχρι τοῦ ἕρκους τοῦ ἱεροῦ
καὶ ἀφιέρωσαν ὀγδόῃ Δύστρου τοῦ
πέμπτου Ϙ̅Υ̅ ἔτους.

1653. UNKNOWN PROVENANCE, INSCRIPTION ON THE STATUE OF A SYRIAN PRIEST, 101 A.D. Now in the National Museum of Alep. Ed. pr. R. A. Stucky, SYRIA 53 (1976) 130-131 (ph.).

ιγυ
Νικαφῶν Βηδανου
3 ὁ καὶ Σεν<ε>κᾶς.

1. ιγυ = year 413 of the Seleucid era (=101 A.D.) Stucky || 2. Βηδανος: "forme hellénisée de Byd῾nw ('dans la main du dieu ANU')" Stucky.

1654. UNKNOWN PROVENANCE, DEDICATION TO SARAPIS, ROMAN PERIOD. Ed. L. Vidman, Sylloge Inscriptionum Religionis Isiacae et Sarapiacae (Berlin, 1969) p. 184, no. 364. W. Peek, ZPE 21 (1976) 281 proposes the following text (engraved on a foot, on which an eagle is sitting):

῞Ιχνος ἔχων, |² πόδ᾽ ἂν ἴχνος | ἔχων ἀνέθηκα |⁴ Σεράπει.

2. ἀν᾽ ἴχνος Vidman || 3. ἔχ<οντ᾽> ? R. Keydell apud Peek.

1655. UNKNOWN PROVENANCE, EPITAPH, 91 A.D. Inscription on a white limestone column; now in the National Museum of Alep. Ed. pr. R.A. Stucky, SYRIA 53 (1976) 130 (ph.). Under the inscription the representation of a Syrian priest.

ἔτους |² γυ Δ<ί>ου ϑ | Διογένη |⁴ χρηστέ | Π

The inscription, dated to the year 403 of the Seleucid era (= 91 A.D.), is older than the relief (early 2nd cent. A.D. or later) Stucky || 2. ΓΥΔΟΓΘ Stucky, corr. Bingen.

PALAESTINA

1656. AREA OF AÏLA/EILATH (SINAÏ), ACCLAMATION, 6th - 7th CENT. A.D. Inscription on a rock, of pilgrims crossing the desert to Mt. Sinaï. Ed. pr. B. Lifshitz, EUPHROSYNE 6 (1974) 39-41 (from a photo published in 1972 in a journal of the Hebrew University of Jerusalem).

† Κ(ύρι)ε εὐλόγησον τὸν δοῦλον (σου)
Θεώδορον καὶ Κασσία καὶ Αὔξον καὶ Νόνν(αν)
3 καὶ Στέφανον καὶ ᾽Ιωάννην.

1. (σου) and 2. (αν): not visible on the photo Lifshitz.

1657-1664. AREA OF AÏLA/EILATH (SINAÏ), GRAFFITI. B. Lifshitz, EUPHROSYNE 6 (1974) 41-44 republishes several inscriptions found ± 100 km south-west of Aïla/Eilath and first published by A. Negev, ERETZ-ISRAEL 10 (1971) 180-187 (in Hebrew, English summary). These inscriptions are important for the study of the history of the Christianity and its diffusion in the south of Palaestina. They confirm that the first Christians in the Sinaï and the south of Palaestina were Egyptians.

1657. P. 41-42, no. 1; cf. also D. Feissel, BCH 100 (1976) 275-276 who presents the following text:

† Κ(ύρι)ε βοήθι τὸν δοῦλόν
σου Τιμόθεον καὶ
τῆς αὐτοῦ ὀρμασ-
τρίδος Ολεφαθης.

3-4. ΟΡΜΑΣ|ΤΡΙΔΟΣΟΛΕΦΑΘΗΣ Negev; (γυναικὸς) Ὁρμᾶς | Τρι<ά>δος ὀλεφα<ν>θῆς Lifshitz; ὀρμασ|τρίδος Ολεφαθης Feissel (ὀρμαστρίς = "fiancée").

1658. P. 42, no. 2.

† Πεττήρις †

Abbreviated form of the Egyptian name Πεττήριος (and not a form of Πέτρος as Negev suggested) Lifshitz.

1659. P. 42, no. 3.

† Κ(ύρι)ε βοήθησον τὸν δοῦ(λόν) σου Ἐπιφάνις
2 καὶ Σουαιρος καὶ Μουσῆς καὶ Ἰωάννις

---

2. Σουαιρος (= Σουαιροῦς): Egyptian name Lifshitz.

1660. P. 42, no. 4.

Ἴσοις Χασέτου | Μουσῆ

---

1. Ἴσοις: the woman's name Ἶσις, fairly frequent in Egypt (and not a transcription of a Nabataean name as Negev thought) Lifshitz | Χασετος: Greek form of a Nabataean name Negev - Lifshitz.

1661. P. 43, no. 5.

† Κ(ύρι)ε Ἰ(ησο)ῦ Χ(ριστ)έ· Μνέσθετι καὶ βωήθεσον τὸν
δοῦλόν σου Σαμμασας Ἀβραμ(ίου) κ(αὶ) Πέτρος
Ἀναστασίας.

---

2. Σαμμασας: Nabataean name Lifshitz.

1662. P. 43, no. 6.

Εἷς Θεὸς
ὠ βοηθῶν
† τὸν δοῦλός (sic) †
4 σου Θεωνῆ
μητὰ γυνη-
κὸς καὶ τή-
7 {καὶ τη}κνον.

---

4. Θεωνῆ: name very frequent in Egypt Lifshitz.

1663. P. 43, no. 7.

† Κ(ύρι)ε βωήθι τῶν δοῦλῶ σου
Λέωνος Καλλινίκου Ζαδακα-
3 θων κ(αὶ) τὸυς φίλους αὐτοῦ. Ἀμέν.

2-3. Ζαδακα|θων: Zadakatha, on the limes, south-western of Petra Lifshitz.

1664. P. 43-44, no. 8.

Κ(ύρι)ε Ἰ(εσο)ῦ Χ(ριστ)ὲ Μ(αρίᾳ) γ(εννηθείς).

Μ(έγισ)τ(ε) Negev.

1665. AZOTOS (ASHDOD), LEAD WEIGHT WITH INSCRIPTION, 69-70 A.D. The inscription is published by B. Lifshitz, EUPHROSYNE 6 (1974) 34, no. 2.

Ἀγορανο[μ]ο[ῦ]-
ντ[ος] Ἡρω-
3 δου ἔ[τ]ους
β' Οὐησπαση-
5 αν(οῦ) Καίσ(αρος).

1666. AZOTOS (ASHDOD), LEAD WEIGHT WITH INSCRIPTION, LATE 3rd - MIDDLE 4th CENT. A.D. The inscription is published by B. Lifshitz, EUPHROSYNE 6 (1974) 33, no. 1.

Ἀγορα-
νομοῦν-
3 το[ς] Ὤμ-
βρ[ου ἔ]τ(ους) αρ' (or αο')
μητρο-
6 πολη(τείας).

3-4. Ὤμ|βρ[ου]: Greek transcription of the Latin name Umber or Umbrius Lifshitz || 5-6. μητρο|πολη(τείας): Kaisareia (= also the provenance of the weight) Lifshitz.

1667. DIOKAISAREIA, BUILDING-INSCRIPTION, 517-518 A.D. SEG, XX, 417. J. Gascou, BIAO 76 (1976) 202, note 5 completes in L. 9 πατ(ρός) (instead of πατρ(ιάρχου): SEG).

1668. AREA OF HEBRON (KHIRBET ZIF), EPITAPH, 3rd CENT. A.D. Bilingual (Greek-Aramaic) inscription on a sarcophagus. Ed. pr. L.Y. Rahmani, IEJ 22 (1972) 113-116 (ph.). Republished by B. Lifshitz, EUPHROSYNE 6 (1974) 44-46:

Κύνωρος Διο-
2 δό[τ]ου πρω-
τοπολείτη-
4 ς.

1. Κύνωρος (accentuated Κυνωρός by Rahmani): form of the name Κύλλαρος and formed on the adjective κυλλός ("crooked, crippled") Lifshitz || 2-4. for the title πρωτοπολείτης, cf. also a Jewish inscription of Volubilis (Ed. E. Frézouls, Acta 5th International Congress of Greek and Latin Epigraphy, Cambridge 1967 (Oxford, 1971) p. 287-292).

1669. JAFFA, JEWISH EPITAPH. Ed. pr. B. Lifshitz, EUPHROSYNE 6 (1974) 29-31.

Μνῆμα διαφέροντ-
2 α Βαβαειν καὶ Ἐξικί-
αν ἀνεψιοῖς Εἰσὰκ Κ-
4 ωζωμος.

2. For the name Βαβαειν, cf. Lifshitz, l.c., 30-31 ("Lallname") || 3-4. Κωζωμος: form of the name Κόσμος or Κοσμᾶς Lifshitz.

1670. JAFFA, JEWISH EPITAPH. J.B. Frey, CIJ, II, 916. Cf. B. Lifshitz, EUPHROSYNE 6 (1974) 31-32 who republishes this inscription as follows:

Ζαχ-
χάη-
3 ς υἱὸς
Ἀστε-
5 ρίου.

1-3. Ζαχ|χαμ|ίς Frey; Ζαχχάης is an abbreviated form of Ζαχχαῖος, the Greek transcription of a Hebrew name Lifshitz.

1671. JAFFA, JEWISH EPITAPH. SEG, VIII, 143; J.B. Frey, CIJ, II, 929. Cf. B. Lifshitz, EUPHROSYNE 6 (1974) 32 who discusses the formula at the end of the inscription (διὰ σαλώ) and thinks that we have here "une abbréviation du participe διαφέρον ou du verbe διαφέρει; ... σαλώ est la transcription du mot hébreu 'shalom', paix" (instead of "un hébraîsme qui essaie de rendre la formule grecque 'ἐν εἰρήνῃ'" = interpretation of H. Vincent, adopted by Frey).

1672. AREA OF JERUSALEM (BETH SAFAFA), DEDICATION ON A MOSAIC OF A MARTYRION AND FAMILY-GRAVE, 490 A.D. ? SEG, XVI, no. 850. D. Feissel, BCH 100 (1976) 277-281 presents the following text:

† Ἐγένετο τὼ πᾶν ἔργ<ο>ν τῆς ἀνεγέρσεως τοῦ οἴκ-
2 ου τῶν ἁγίων μαρτύρων ὑπὲρ σωτηρίας κ(αὶ) ἀντηλή-
μψ<ε>ως Σαμουήλου κ(αὶ) τῶν αὐτοῦ δι<α>φερόντων κ(αὶ) ὑπὲρ ἀν-
4 απαύσ<ε>ως τῶν π<ρ>ολαβότων ἐν μη(νὶ) Ἰουνίῳ ἰνδ(ικτιῶνος) ιδ'

ἔτους ςσ'.

4. π<ρ>ολαβότων = προλαβόντων = "de ceux qui m'ont devancé dans la tombe"; Feissel's solution is supported by convincing parallels; other restorations in SEG, XVI, 850: πολ<υ>βοτῶν, πολ<υ>β<ώ>των, πολ<υε>τῶν, <ά>πολ<ωλ>ότων.

1673. JERUSALEM, EPITAPH, 4th CENT. A.D. ? SEG, XVII, 785. Cf. B. Bagatti - J.T. Milik, Gli scavi del Dominus flevit. I. La necropoli del periodo romano (Jerusalem, 1958) 84, no. 13 (fig. 23, 4, pp. 35, 112) who republished the inscription and B. Lifshitz, EUPHROSYNE 6 (1974) 46-47. Bagatti - Milik read τυρᾶ (genitive of τυρᾶς, popular form of τυροποποιός = "cheese-maker") instead of Τύρου and B. Lifshitz reads Ἰούδαν instead of Ἰούδα ν(εώτερος).

1674. KAISAREIA, HONORARY INSCRIPTION FOR AURELIUS MARON, PROCURATOR AUGUSTI AGENS VICE PRAESIDIS OF SYRIA PALESTINE, 260-282 A.D. Ed. pr. B. Lifshitz, Hommages M. Renard (Coll. Latomus, 102; 1969) 467 (ph.). M. Christol, ZPE 22 (1976) 170-176 republishes the text with full commentary; we present this text here:

Αὐ[ρ(ήλιον) Μ]άρωνα ἐπίτρ(οπον)
τ̣[ο]ῦ̣ Σεβ(αστοῦ) διέποντα
τ̣ὰ [μέ]ρ̣η τῆς ἡγεμον(ίας)
ΝΟ̣[...] Ἀλέξανδρος
[.̣.....]αρχος τὸν φίλον.

Date: 5th cent. A.D Lifshitz || 2-3. [ε]ὐσεβ(ῶς) διέποντα | πα[λαι(στίνης)] τρίτης ἡγεμον(ίαν) Lifshitz || 5. [.... ἔπ]αρχος Lifshitz; [ἑκατόντ]αρχος ? Christol.

1675. KAISAREIA, JEWISH EPITAPH. Marble slab, ornamented with the seven branched menorah design, flanked by lulab and shofar. Ed. pr. J.H. Landau, ʿATIQ̣OT 11 (1976) 91 (ph.).

Θήκη Ἠλ|^{2}ίας Ἐντ|ουλίου Κρ|^{4}ουν(ί)ου

1-2. ΗΛΙΑΣ: the abbreviation symbol S, here inverted, seems to be used here as a rather general indication of the genitive; a less likely interpretation of S would be to consider it as the sign standing for καί Landau || 2-3. Ἐντ|ουλίου: this name, found in Jewish and Christian inscriptions means "observing the (religious) commandments" Landau || 3-4. Κρ|ουν(ί)ου: this word could refer to the father of two brothers (cf. the note ad 1-2); a more probable interpretation is "a native of ..." (Κρουνοί in Mysia near the Pontus, or, more likely, Κρουν(ί)ου = Κουρν(ί)ου (metathesis) = Κυρνίου (i.e. a Corsican) or more convincing, a place north of Beth-Shean) Landau.

1676. KHISFIN (SOUTHERN GOLAN), DEDICATORY MOSAIC INSCRIPTION, 561 or 618 A.D. Ed. pr. V. Tzaferis - S. Bar-Lev, ʿATIQOT 11 (1976) 114-115 (ph.).

† Προσφορὰ Ὀλυμπίου κ(αὶ) ὑ[πὲρ σωτηρίας Λ]εοντίου
[κ(αὶ)] Εὐγενίου υἱῶ<ν>. Κ(αὶ) ὑπὲρ μνήμης καὶ ἀναπα[ύσ]εως
Οὐάρου πατρ(ὸς) κ(αὶ) Βασι[λί]ο[υ κ(αὶ)] Εὐγενίου ἀδελφῶν καὶ
[Οὐ]άρου υἱοῦ. Εὐχαριστῶν ἀνενέωσεν τὸν ἅγιον Οἶκ(ον)
[διὰ σ]πουδῆς Θωμᾶ Πρε(σβυτέρου) κ(αὶ) Ἡγουμέ(νου), ἐν μη(νὶ)
Ἰουλ(ίῳ), Ἰνδ(ικτιῶνος) ζ, ἔτ(ους) ζξχ. †

5. The secular era used in Khisfin may be either the era of the Provincia Arabia, beginning in 106 B.C., or the Syrian era, beginning in 49 B.C.; the year 667 mentioned in the inscription may thus be either 561 or 618.; however, 618 seems more likely. Tzaferis - Bar-Lev.

1677. KHORSIA (EASTERN COAST OF THE LAKE OF TIBERIAS, AREA OF DEKAPOLIS HIPPOS), MOSAIC INSCRIPTION, DECEMBER 585 A.D. Ed. pr. B. Lifshitz, EUPHROSYNE 6 (1974) 37-39.

[†] Ἐπὶ τοῦ θεοφιλ(εστάτου) Στε-
[φ]άνου πρεσβ(υτέρου) καὶ ἡγου-
μένου ἐγένετο ἡ ψή-
φωσις τοῦ φωτιστη-
ρίου ἐν μη(νὶ) δεκεμβρίῳ
ἰνδ(ικτίωνι) τετάρτῃ ἐπὶ το(ῦ)
εὐσεβ(εστάτου) καὶ φιλοχ(ρίστο)υ ἡ-
μῶν βασιλέως Μαυρικίου
ὑπατίας πρώτης.

In line 1, 2, 6, 7: the abbreviation symbol S.

1678. MT. SINAÏ (MONASTERY OF ST. CATHERINE), INSCRIPTION AT THE RELICS OF SINAÏ'S HOLY FATHERS, 6th CENT. A.D. ? Ed. pr. I. Sevcenko, DOP 20 (1966) 258 and 263. Ph. Mayerson, DOP 30 (1976) 375-379 proposes a new solution for the abbreviated numeral in L. 1: it indicates the 14th of January (of a year between 373 and 410) when an unknown number of monks and solitaries on and around the Holy Mountain were killed by Bedouins (against Sevcenko, l.c., who translates it as "four times ten" and relates this number to forty martyrs cited in a literary fabrication of the 6th cent. A.D.).

1679. PTOLEMAIS (AKKO), EPITAPH FOR A CRETAN MERCENARY, 2nd CENT. B.C. Funerary stele. Ed. pr. Y. Landau, BASO 224 (1976) 39-40 (ph.).

'Υπεργένης
Εὐρ[υ]μήδ[ο]υς [Κ]ρῆς
3 Δητ̣[ό]ννιος [χ]αῖρ[ε].

1680. SHIQMONA, STAMPED AMPHORA HANDLE, 133-132 B.C. Apparently local amphora. Ed. pr. J. Elgavish, IEJ 26 (1976) 67 (ph.).

("Ετους) πρ' 'Αριστοκ[ράτους] | ἀγορανό[μου]

1681. SHIQMONA, STAMPED HANDLES OF A RHODIAN AMPHORA, HELLENISTIC PERIOD. Ed. pr. J. Elgavish, IEJ 26 (1976) 74 (ph.).

a) 'Επὶ Τιμο|θέου, | 'Αρταμιτίου
b) Εὐκ[λεί]του

1682. SKYTHOPOLIS (BETH-SHEAN), GREEK CULTS IN THE HELLENISTIC AND ROMAN PERIODS. Cf. no. 1906.

1683. SKYTHOPOLIS (BETH-SHEAN), DEDICATORY MOSAIC INSCRIPTION. Mosaic inscription, flanked by two pheasants; found in the synagogue of Skythopolis. Ed. pr. B. Lifshitz, EUPHROSYNE 6 (1974) 27-29.

Π(ροσ)φ(ορὰ) ὧν Κ(ύριο)ς γ-
ινόσκι τὰ
3 ὀνόματ-
α· αὐτὸς
φυλάξι ἐν
6 χρό(νῳ).

1. Π and Φ in ligature: 

1684. TEL DAN, VOTIVE INSCRIPTION TO THE "GOD WHO IS IN DAN", LATE 3rd/EARLY 2nd CENT. B.C. Limestone slab with a bilingual (Greek-Aramaic) inscription. Mentioned by A. Biran, IEJ 26 (1976) 204 (ph.). A photo also appeared in THE BIBLICAL ARCHAEOLOGIST 39, 3 (1976) 89 and in ARCHEOLOGIA (Paris), fasc. 107 (1977) 81. Cf. J. and L. Robert, BE (1977) no. 542.

Θεῶι | τῶι ἐν Δανοις | Ζώϊλος εὐχήν.

1685. TIBERIAS, JEWISH EPITAPH. Ed. pr. M. Schwabe, in Sepher Johanan Lewy (Jerusalem, 1949) 208-211 (in Hebrew). Republished by B. Lifshitz, EUPHROSYNE 6 (1974) 23-24, no. 1.

[Μνημῖον ?]
[Οὐίτ ?]ου τοῦ
3 ['Ελ]ιάβου τοῦ
[Ο]ὐίτου ἀπὸ
5 ['Αλε]ξαδρίας.

1686. TIBERIAS, JEWISH EPITAPH. Ed. pr. M. Schwabe, in *Sepher Johanan Lewy* (Jerusalem, 1949) 211-216. Republished by B. Lifshitz, EUPHROSYNE 6 (1974) 24-25, no. 2.

Θαλεθθι Μαρα
θυγάτηρ Σαμ-
ουήλ, γυνὴ Λε-
[οντίου ?].

1. Θαλεθθι: Greek transcription of the Aramaic word "talitha" = κοράσιον; proper name or simply meaning "young woman" Lifshitz.

1687. TIBERIAS, JEWISH EPITAPH. Ed. pr. M. Schwabe, in *Sepher Johanan Lewy* (Jerusalem, 1949) 216-221. Republished by B. Lifshitz, EUPHROSYNE 6 (1974) 25-26, no. 3, who presents the text as follows:

[? Ἐνθάδε κῖτα]ι Λεοντίνα
[θυγάττηρ ? Σαμ]ουήλου γε-
[ρουσιάρ]χ(ου), Θαυμασίου
[ἀρχισυναγώγ(ου) ?] Ἀντιοχ(έων)
[γυνὴ ? ἐτῶν] ο'.

3-5. [ρουσιάρχου γυν]ὴ Θαυμασίου | [ἀρχισυναγώγου] Ἀντιοχ(έων) | [ἐτῶν] ο' Schwabe.

1688. TIBERIAS, JEWISH EPITAPH. IGR, III, 1204. Republished by B. Lifshitz, EUPHROSYNE 6 (1974) 26-27, no. 4. Lifshitz compares also his text to earlier publications (of L. Oliphant, A. Schumacher and M. Schwabe). His text runs as follows:

Αὐρ(ηλίῳ) <Μ>αρκελ<λ>είνῳ
Χα<ρ>ίτ<ω>νι βιώ<σ>αντ[ι ἔ]τη
οδ' μ<ῆ>νες ἡμέρας ιε'
Αὐρ(ηλία) Βάσσα σύμβιος
καὶ κληρονόμος
τῷ ἀσυνκρίτῳ μν-
v. ήμης χάριν v.

2-3. ἑκατοντάρχῳ λεγ(εῶνος) ι' Φρετ(ένσις) βιώσαντι ἔτη | ο' (vel π') μηνὲς ε' ἡμέρας ιε' IGR.

1689-1697. WADI HAGGAG (SINAÏ), RELIGIOUS ACCLAMATIONS AND FORMULAE, CA. 299-300 A.D. A. Negev, ERETZ-ISRAEL 12 (1975) 132-141 (Hebrew Section) publishes the following inscriptions, all engraved on a rock:

1689. P. 132, no. 1.

Μνησθῇ ...

1690. P. 134, no. 2.

Μνησθῇ ΟΥΑΒΟ..ΑΛ..ΝΟΥ
Εἷς Θεὸς ὁ βοηθῶν.

1691. P. 134, no. 3.

Μνησθῇ τὸν δοῦλόν σου | ΗΝΟ...

1692. P. 134, no. 4.

Σῶ|σον | τ̣ὸν ...

1693. P. 134, no. 5.

Εἷς Θεὸς ἐμο(ῦ) | ὁ βοηθῶν Δ̣...

1694. P. 134, no. 6.

Οὖρος

1695. P. 134, no. 7.

Χάρις. Μν|ησθῇ Σ...

1696. P. 134, no. 8.

Χάρις. Μνη|σθῇ Θεόδοτος | ὁ ἔπαρχος Κλ|αυδίου.

1697. P. 136, no. 9.

Εἷς Θεὸς Υ ד Θ
ὁ βοηθῶν
Οὐαλέριος Ἀντι-
γούνου στρα-
τηγός. γʹ ἰνδικτι(ῶνος)

---

1. At the end, two Greek letters Υ and Θ with a Hebrew dalet between: Θ(εὸς) Ὕ(ψιστος); dalet = ʾḥ̣d = "one" || 2. at the end of this line: a symbol representing a seven-branched menorah or a palm branch || below the inscription: a nine-leaf palm branch Negev.

EGYPT

1698. PTOLEMAIC IMPERIALISM. Cf. no. 1878.

1699. FOREIGN POLICY AND POSSESSIONS OF THE PTOLEMIES. W. Huss, Untersuchungen zur Aussenpolitik Ptolemaios' IV (Münch. Beiträge Pap. Rechtsgesch., 69; München, 1976) uses many inscriptions in his discussions. For some criticism, cf. J. and L. Robert, BE (1977) no. 69.

1700. USE OF THE IOTA ADSCRIPTUM IN EGYPT IN THE 3rd CENT. B.C. W. Clarysse, CE 51 (1976) 150-166 proves that disappearance of the iota adscriptum remained very exceptional in Egypt until the end of the 3rd cent. B.C.

1701. THE MACEDONIAN CALENDAR IN EGYPT. U. Hagedorn, ZPE 23 (1976) 143-167 discusses the use of Macedonian (and, in an appendix, of Milesian) months in Roman Egypt.

1702. FUNERARY EPITHETS IN EGYPT. B. Boyaval, ZPE 23 (1976) 225-230 studies the funerary epithets used in epitaphs of five Egyptian sites (Alexandria, Tell el Yahoudijeh, Kom Abou Billou, Tehneh and Akhmim). He shows that χρηστός was very popular at the first, φιλότεκνος at the third, πασίφιλος and χρηστός at the second site. He focusses on ἄωρος which is popular everywhere, tries to correlate this adjective to the ages mentioned in the epitaph and concludes that this epithet "signifiait réellement qu'un défunt, quel que soit son âge, est toujours arraché trop tôt à l'affection des siennes".

1703. EPITAPHS AND DEMOGRAPHY IN EGYPT. On the basis of the epitaphs found in the five sites mentioned in no. 1702 B. Boyaval, ZPE 21 (1976) 217-243 studies various demographic problems (sex-ratio, the rounding off of ages, age-groups in epitaphs, the average length of life). His conclusion deserves to be quoted: "... chaque site donne une image différente de la mortalité. Il y a toutes raisons de penser que la multiplicité de ces images correspond à des variations locales, non de la mortalité mais de pratiques funéraires. Raison supplémentaire de ne pas chercher dans l'épigraphie funéraire la démographie du passé".

1704. CORPORA OF INSCRIPTIONS. G. Geraci, AEGYPTUS 56 (1976) 329-353 reviews three books of A. Bernand (Le Delta Égyptien d'après les textes grecs, vol. 1: Les confins Libyques; De Koptos à

<u>Kosseir; Le Paneion d'El-Kanaīs: Les Inscriptions Grecques</u>). His remarks mainly pertain to chronological and onomastic problems. He quotes other reviews extensively so that the reader gets a reasonable survey of the reception of Bernand's works in the scholarly world.

1705. GREEK INSCRIPTIONS FROM EGYPT, REIGN OF AUGUSTUS. C. Bolconi, AEGYPTUS 56 (1976) 269-280 provides a list of Greek (and Latin) inscriptions from Egypt, dating from the reign of Augustus.

1706. FALSIFICATION: SB, III, 6697. K. Parlasca, AA (1976) 83 proves this inscription to be a falsification, copied from a marble-inscription from Egypt, now in the museum of Bologna.

1707. ABOUSIR, EPITAPH. SB, I, 5121 a-b. O. Masson, ZPE 23 (1976) 262 points out that this epitaph, which has been read (with varying readings) as a Greek text, in fact is a Carian text.

1708. ABYDOS (TEMPLE OF RAMSES II), GRAFFITO, EARLY 5th CENT. B.C. Ed. pr. O. Masson, CE 51 (1976) 305-306, no. 1 (ph.).

Δᾱμόκριτος εὐρύπρο̄κτος.

Damokritos probably was a Cretan mercenary Masson.

1709. ABYDOS (TEMPLE OF RAMSES II), GRAFFITO, EARLY 5th CENT. B.C. Ed. pr. O. Masson, CE 51 (1976) 307-308, no. 2.

῾Υπερβάλλο̄ν.

Hyperballon probably was a Cretan mercenary Masson.

1710. ABYDOS (TEMPLE OF SETI I), GRAFFITO, HELLENISTIC PERIOD. Mentioned by A.H. Sayce, TRANS. SOC. BIBL. ARCH. 9, 1 (1887) 148. O. Masson, CE 51 (1976) 309, no. 3 publishes this inscription on the basis of a copy made in 1955 by J. Yoyotte.

Ποτάμω̣[ν].

1711. ABYDOS (TEMPLE OF SETI I), GRAFFITO, HELLENISTIC PERIOD. O. Masson, CE 51 (1976) 309, no. 4 publishes this inscription on the basis of a copy made in 1955 by J. Yoyotte.

Νέων Φασηλίτ[ης].

1712. ALEXANDRIA, HONORARY INSCRIPTION FOR T. FURIUS VICTORINUS, 159-160 A.D. OGIS, 707; IGR, III, 1103; ILS, 8846. P.R.C. Weaver, EPIGRAFISCHE STUDIEN 11 (1976) 222 prefers, as Dittenberger and Cagnat, in L. 5 Σεβασ[τοῦ] instead of Σεβασ[τῶν], given by Dessau and Pflaum (H.G. Pflaum, Les carrières procuratoriennes équestres sous le Haut-Empire romain, Paris, 1960, I, no. 139, p. 327). The discussion is superfluous because on the stone, which is in the museum at Leyden, one can easily read Σεβαστ[ο]ῦ: cf. H.W. Pleket, The Greek Inscriptions in the 'Rijksmuseum van Oudheden' at Leyden (Leyden, 1958) no. 55. Cf. also L. Robert, BERYTUS (1966) 35-36 for the provenance "Alexandria" (and not "Tyrus" as Weaver has it). S. Daris, AEGYPTUS 56 (1976) 50 discusses the date of this text. He rejects a date after 23 November 162 and opts for 160 A.D.

1713. ALEXANDRIA, DEDICATION TO SARAPIS AND ISIS BY ARCHAGATHOS, EPISTATES OF LIBYA, AND HIS WIFE STRATONIKE, 283-278 B.C. SEG, XVIII, 636. On Archagathos, his wife Stratonike, his function and his place in the political context of the early 3rd cent. B.C., see now R.S. Bagnall, PHILOLOGUS 120 (1976) 195-209.

1714. ALEXANDRIA, DEDICATION. SB, I, 4528. W. Clarysse, CE 51 (1976) 154 dates this text later than the 3rd cent. B.C. (SB). He assigns it to the post-Ptolemaic period, on palaeographical grounds.

1715. ALEXANDRIA, ROMAN GAME COUNTERS WITH ALEXANDRIAN MOTIFS, 45 B.C. - 68 A.D. Elisabeth Alföldi-Rosenbaum, CHIRON 6 (1976) 205 ff. provides a catalogue of numerous Alexandrian tesserae: she interprets them as objects "used for a game and not as admission 'tickets' to the theatre or gladiatorial performances" and dates them to the period 45 B.C. - 68 A.D. She discusses the inscriptions on, and the typology of the tesserae.

1716. ANIBAH, CHRISTIAN EPITAPH. SEG, VIII, 864; SB, III, 7190. Cf. B. Boyaval, ZPE 20 (1976) 23 who reads in L. 6 Ταναστασία (compound of the Coptic feminine definite article and the Greek name Ἀναστασία) instead of τ' Ἀναστασία (SEG, SB).

1717. AREA OF ANTINOOUPOLIS, LOVE-CHARM, 3rd - 4th CENT. A.D. Lead tablet, now in the Louvre. Ed. pr. S. Kambitsis, BIAO 76 (1976) 213-223 (ph.). Kambitsis also compares this inscription with other similar texts.

Παρακατατίθεμαι ὑμῖν τοῦτον τὸν κατάδεσμον θεο[ῖ]ς καταχθονίοις, Πλούτωνι καὶ Κόρῃ Φερσεφόνῃ Ἐρεσχιγαλ καὶ Ἀδώνδιι τῷ καὶ Βαρβαριθα καὶ Ἑρμῇ καταχθονίῳ Θωουθ φωκενσεψευ ερεκταθου μισονκταικ καὶ Ἀνούβιδι κραταιῷ ψηριφθα, τῷ τὰς κλεῖδας ἔχοντι τῶν κατὰ Ἅδους, καὶ δαίμοσι καταχθονίοις θεοῖς, ἀώροις τε καὶ ἀώραις, μέλλαξι καὶ παρθένοις, ἐνιαυτοῖς ἐξ ἐνιαυτῶν, μήνασι ἐκ μηνῶν, ἡμέραις ἐκ ἡμερῶν, ὥρασι ὡρῶν, νύκτες ἐκ νυκτῶν· ὁρκίζω πάντας τοὺς δαίμονας τοὺς ἐν τῷ τόπῳ τούτῳ συνπαραστῆναι τῷ δαίμονι τούτῳ Ἀντινόῳ. Διέγειραί μοι σεαυτὸν καὶ ὕπαγε εἰς πᾶν τ[όπο]ν, εἰς πᾶν ἄμφοδον, εἰς πᾶσαν οἰκείαν καὶ κατάδησον Πτολεμαίδα, ἣν ἔτεκεν Ἀϊᾶς, τὴν θυγατέρα Ὡριγένους, ὅπως μὴ βινηθῇ, μὴ πυγισθῇ, μηδὲν πρὸς ἡδονὴν ποιήσῃ ἑταίρῳ ἀνδρὶ εἰ μὴ ἐμοὶ μόνῳ τῷ Σαραπάμμωνι, ὃν ἔτεκεν Ἀρέα, καὶ μὴ ἀφῇς αὐτὴν φαγεῖν, μὴ πεῖν, μὴ στέ<ρ>γειν μήτε ἐξελθεῖν μήτε ὕπνου τυχεῖν ἐκτὸς ἐμοῦ τοῦ Σαραπάμμωνος, οὗ ἔτεκεν Ἀρέα. Ἐξορκίζω σε, νεκύδαιμον Ἀντίνοε, κατὰ τοῦ ὀνόματος [τοῦ] τρομεροῦ καὶ φοβεροῦ, οὗ ἡ γῆ ἀκούσασα τοῦ ὀνόματος ἀνυγήσεται, οὗ οἱ δαίμονες ἀκούσαντες τοῦ ὀνόματος ἐνφόβως φοβοῦνται, οὗ οἱ ποταμοὶ καὶ πέτραι ἀκούσαντες ῥήσσ[οντα]ι· ὁρκίζω σε, νεκύδαιμον Ἀντίνοε, κατὰ τοῦ Βαρβαραθαμ χελουμβρα βαρου[χ] Ἀδωναὶ καὶ κατὰ τοῦ Ἀβρασὰξ καὶ κατὰ τοῦ Ἰαὼ πακεπτωθ πακεβραωθ σαβαρβαραει καὶ κατὰ τοῦ Μαρμαραουωθ καὶ κατὰ τοῦ Μαρμαραχθα μαμαζαγαρ. Μὴ παρακούσῃς, νεκύδαιμον Ἀντίνοε, ἀλλ' ἔγειραί μοι σεαυτὸν καὶ ὕπαγε εἰς πᾶν τόπον, εἰς πᾶν ἄμφοδον, εἰς πᾶσαν οἰκείαν καὶ ἄγαγέ μοι τὴν Πτολεμαίδα, ἣν ἔτεκεν Ἀϊᾶς, τὴν θυγατέρα Ὡριγένους· κατάσχες αὐτῆς τὸ βρωτόν, τὸ ποτόν, ἕως ἔλθῃ πρὸς ἐμὲ τὸν Σαραπάμμωνα, ὃν ἔτεκεν Ἀρέα, καὶ μὴ ἐάσῃς αὐτὴν ἄλλου ἀνδρὸς πεῖραν λαβεῖν εἰ μὴ ἐμοῦ μόνου τοῦ Σαραπάμμωνος. Ἕλκε αὐτὴν τῶν τριχῶν, τῶν σπλάγχνων, ἕως μὴ ἀποστῇ μου τοῦ Σαραπάμμωνος, οὗ ἔτεκεν Ἀρέα, καὶ ἔχω αὐτὴν τὴν Πτολεμαίδα, ἣν ἔτεκεν Ἀϊᾶς, τὴν θυγατέρα Ὡριγένους, ὑποτεταγμένην εἰς τὸν ἅπαντα χρόνον τῆς ζωῆς μου, φιλοῦσάν με, ἐρῶσ[ά]ν μου, λέγουσάν μοι ἃ ἔχει ἐν νόῳ. Ἐὰν τοῦτο ποιήσῃς, ἀπολύσω σε.

4-5. Read ἐνιαυτοὺς ἐξ ἐνιαυτῶν, μῆνας ἐκ μηνῶν, ἡμέρας ἐξ ἡμερῶν, ὥρας <ἐξ> ὡρῶν, νύκτας ἐκ νυκτῶν || 6. read διέγειρέ, cf. L. 18 || 7. read οἰκίαν, also in L. 19 || 9. read ἑτέρῳ || 11. read ὃν;

also in L. 24 || 13. read ἀνοιγήσεται || 18. read ἔγειρέ Kambitsis.

1718. BACCHIAS, DEDICATION TO THE GOD SYKNYKYNEUS/-IS, 1st CENT. A.D. (?) Circular inscription on the upper rim of a ritual basin. Ed. pr. G. Wagner, ZPE 20 (1976) 225-227 (ph.).

?] ὑ̣π̣ὲ̣ρ Συ̣κνυκυνίος θε̣ο̣ῦ μεγάλου μεγάλου. Πετ̣ε̣σοῦχος Ὥρ̣ο̣υ̣ κ̣α̣ὶ̣
τ̣ὰ τ̣έκνα γ̣υ̣ναῖκα (sic) vacat

The end of the inscription is incoherent: the normal order would be: name of the dedicator, his wife, and finally the children. Further, the cutter seems to have engraved ΓΑ ΓΕΚΝΑ. These errors perhaps permit us to explain ΓΥ̣ΝΑΙΚΑ. Do we have to understand καὶ ἡ γυνή or, on the contrary, γυναικός ? Wagner.

1719. BOUHEN (SOUTH TEMPLE), MUTILATED ARCHAIC INSCRIPTION. Sandstone block. Ed. pr. O. Masson, CE 51 (1976) 310-311, no. 5 (dr.).

--]ΝΟ̣ΡΙΔΑϟΕΛ.[--

-ᾱ]νο̄ρίδᾱς ΕΛ.[-- Masson.

1720. BOUHEN (SOUTH TEMPLE), SIGNATURE OF A PAINTER, 3rd CENT. B.C. Sandstone block; under the inscription a painted scene, showing a black Pharaoh (Taharqa ?) harpooning his enemies before the goddess Isis. Ed. pr. O. Masson, CE 51 (1976) 311-313, no. 6 (ph.).

Μελά̣γ̣ι̣ππος | Νουμηνίου | Βαρκαῖος

---

3. For the ethnikon Βαρκαῖος and its chronological implications, cf. our no. 1838.

1721-1722. OASIS OF DAKLEH (AMHEDA), ACCLAMATION FOR THE BASILIKOGRAMMATES OF THE OASIS AND LITERARY TEXT. Painted inscriptions on the cornice of a ceiling. Ed. pr. G. Wagner, BIAO 76 (1976) 287-288.

1721. Εὐτυχῶς τῷ καλῷ βασιλικῷ
Εὐτυχῶς τῷ καλῷ βασιλικῷ

....

ΕΡ.........α καὶ χρυσοδότην Ἄμμωνα	Εὐτυχῶς Ἀριστέᾳ Τίτῳ ἀπε-
ἀσίλῳ μάκαρες χώρης ......δος ἁγνῆς	λευτέρῳ Ἀριστονίκῳ βασιλι

1722. (On another fragment of the same piece):

--]ας δάπεδον καὶ οσι.[--
--].ρεων καὶ γαῖαν ικ.[--
--] ἀγλαὰ δῶρα .ασ[--
--].σμον ......[--

1723. OASIS OF DAKLEH (GARA MEZZAWAGA), GRAFFITO. Engraved on the plastering of a grave. Ed. pr. G. Wagner, BIAO 76 (1976) 288.

Ἀτρῆς Παησ[ίο]υ ΚΟΡΥΦ.[--

1724. OASIS OF DAKLEH (MOUT EL-KHARAB), INVOCATION OF THE LORD FOR AN EMPEROR. Inscription on a fragment of a lintel or architrave. Ed. pr. G. Wagner, BIAO 76 (1976) 288.

Ὁ Θεὸς φύλαξαι τῷ κυρ[ίῳ --

1725-1760. FAYOUM, CORPUS OF INSCRIPTIONS. We briefly summarize the comments of J. Bingen, CE 51 (1976) 213-219, E. Will, RH 256 (1976) 443-445 and A.M. Vérilhac, AC 46 (1977) 318-321 on E. Bernand, Recueil des Inscriptions grecques du Fayoum, I: La "méris" d'Hérakleidès (Leiden, 1975). Unless otherwise indicated, the comments are Bingen's.

1725. No. 2, L. 10. ἐκ Θασῖτος does not refer to the dedicator's mother but to a deme or village of Kyrene. (Vérilhac)

1726. No. 3, L. 1-2. One should print iota adscriptum.

1727. No. 6. From Soknopaiou Nesos (and not from Krokodilopolis).

1728. No. 9. At the end of L. 1 no [καί].

1729. No. 10, L. 7. Διόδωρο[ς] ἡγε̣[μών] instead of Διόδωρο[ν] ἡ π[όλις].

1730. No. 14, L. 5. The name of the dedicator has been erased and subsequently replaced by the graffito Ἀρτεμίδωρ̣[ος].

1731. No. 15. Date: final quarter 2nd cent. B.C. (instead of 3rd - 2nd cent. B.C.).

1732. No. 18, L. 1. ΑΘ instead of ΛΟ; 7-9. the restorations are too short; there is no tenth line.

1733. No. 35. Date: ca. 1st cent. B.C. (instead of Ptolemaic period).

1734. No. 39. Date: 1st cent. A.D. (instead of Imperial period).

1735. No. 42, L. 2. ζ<ώ>ντων (instead of ζõντε̣ς̣); Vérilhac reads on the stone ZONTΩN and suggests ζõντ<ες ἐτ>ῶν.

1736. Nos. 44 and 45. Date: 1st cent. A.D. (instead of Imperial period).

1737. No. 50. Date: 1st - 2nd cent. A.D. (instead of Imperial period); L. 3. the upper part of the siglum of (ἐτῶν) is visible.

1738. No. 51. Date: end of the Hellenistic period (instead of Imperial period).

1739. No. 54, L. 3. Κύλινδρος (instead of Κύλινθρος).

1740. Nos. 55, 56, 57. Date: 1st cent. A.D. (instead of Imperial period).

1741. No. 58. Date: 1st cent. A.D. (instead of Imperial period); L. 4. ἀλύπως (instead of ἄλυπο̣ς).

1742. No. 59. Date: 1st cent. A.D. (instead of early Imperial period).

1743. No. 60. Date: 39th year either of Ptolemy VIII or of Augustus (the reign of Ptolemy II being excluded).

1744. No. 61. Date: 1st - 2nd cent. A.D. (instead of "unknown date").

1745. No. 66. Date: 1st - 2nd cent. A.D. (instead of "unknown date"); L. 3. τ̣ένεται (instead of Ṭ̣ENETA); 4.]ωλεσαν ὼς ἂν (instead of ΛΕΣΑΝΩΣΑΝ); 6. θα]νάτου σε π.[- (instead of ΝΑΤΟΥΣΕΠΙ); 7. -]..στοθαν.[- (instead of Ι̣Σ̣ΤΟΘΑΝ).

1746. No. 67. Date: 1st - 2nd cent. A.D. (instead of "unknown date"); L. 1. ΟΕΥΡ̣Ι̣ (instead of Θ̣εϋη[ς ?]); 2. a reading δεκάπ̣[ρωτος] is anachronistic, moreover Bernand's reading ΔΕΚΑΤ is correct.

1747. No. 69, L. 12. (ἔτους) ιγ τὸ (instead of το(ῦ))

1748. No. 71, L. 14. ἀρτά(βας): on top of the tau an "Hakenalpha" as a sign of abbreviation (and not as the siglum of ἥμισυ). On the relation between nos. 70-71 see the comments of E. Will.

1749. No. 72. There can be no question of the dedication of two statues.

1750. No. 73, L. 6-7. τέκν|ων (instead of τέκ|νων).

1751. No. 76. Date: 1st cent. A.D. (instead of early Imperial period); L. 3. ΥΜΟΥΙ (instead of Π̣μοῦϊ) (Vérilhac); 3-4. Παραφε[--- (name)] (instead of παρὰ Φε[μ]|[ν̇εῆ]σις) (Vérilhac).

1752. No. 78, L. 4. (ἔτους) θ (instead of ιθ).

1753. No. 79. Date: beginning of the Imperial period (instead of "Roman period").

1754. No. 85, L. 4. (ἔτους) ζ ἱεροῦ [[Ν[έρωνος]]]| Κλαυδίου Καίσαρος (as in SEG, XX, 650); cf. also W. van Rengen, CE 53 (1978) 162-163 who, after a study of the inscription in situ, has read [[Ν̣έ̣ρ̣[ωνος]]] and confirms the views of J. Bingen.

1755. No. 86, L. 9-10. The genitive τῶν συννά[ων θεῶν], which should replace τοῖς συννά|[οις θεοῖ]ς, depends on ἱεροῦ (and not on καθίδρυσις).

1756. No. 91. Date: uncertain (instead of "after 212 A.D.");

L. 9. ἐπ' ἀγαθῶι (instead of ἐπ' ἀγαθῷ).

1757. No. 92. Date: uncertain (instead of "after 212 A.D.").

1758. No. 95. No trace of a Marcus Aurelius in this fragment.

1759. No. 97. Date: 2nd half 1st cent. B.C. or 1st cent. A.D. (instead of "unknown date"); L. 2-3. Bingen doubts whether Ἀσκλη-πι|οῦ denotes the patronymic of the honorand Herodes.

1760. No. 99, L. 3. [Εὐ]δ̣ή̣μων is a hazardous restoration.

1761. HADRA, TWO INSCRIBED VASES. Ed. B.F. Cook, Inscribed Hadra Vases in the Metropolitan Museum of Art (New York, 1966) p. 24-25, nos. 9 and 10. G. Nachtergael, HISTORIA 25 (1976) 68-71 dates these two vases in the 9th year of Philopator, i.e. 26 Sept. 214-12 Oct. 213 B.C.

1762. KANOPOS AND ROSETTA, DECREES OF THE EGYPTIAN PRIESTS IN HONOUR OF PTOLEMY III AND V, 239-238 and 196 B.C. OGIS, 56 and 90. On the royal ideology of the Ptolemies in these two decrees, cf. Chr. Onasch, APF 24-25 (1976) 137-155.

1763-1773. OASIS OF KHARGEH (TEMPLE OF QASR EL-GHOUEITA), GRAFFITI, PTOLEMAIC PERIOD. Graffiti on the walls of the temple. Ed. pr. G. Wagner, BIAO 76 (1976) 283-285.

1763. Western wall, right of the door:

Ζήνων Μ.δ.[-

1764. Western wall, right of the door; 1st cent. B.C.

Θεόφιλος Σατυρίωνος
Μεγαρεὺς ἥκω πρὸς τὸν Ἄμμωνα
τὸν χρηστόν.

1765. Western wall, right of the door:

Εὔμηλος Δίωνος | Χαλκιδεὺς ἥκω.

1766. Western wall, right of the door:

Ξένων Εὐμήλου | Χαλκιδεὺς ἥκω.

1767. Western wall, right of the door; 3rd - 2nd cent. B.C.

[(.)..]όλυκος | [Εὐ]τυχίδου | Ξάνθιος ἥκω.

1. [Ἑρμ]όλυκος J. and L. Robert, BE (1977) no. 576.

1768. Western wall, right of the door:

Λύκων | Λύκιο̣[ς].

1769. Western wall, right of the door:

Ἱε[ρ]οκλῆς | Φιλοξένου | Λ̣Υ̣..[.]...[

1770. Western wall, right of the door; 3rd - 2nd cent. B.C.

Ἀλέξανδρο[ς] | Περιγένους | Μακεδών.

1771. Western wall, left of the door:

ΙΕΡΟΝ and (above it) ΠΥΛΗΣ

1772. Northern wall:

Τιμόδαμος | ἥκω Ἀμενῆβ̣[ι].

1773. Northern wall (under no. 1772):

Φιλόξενος

1774-1782. OASIS OF KHARGEH (GEBEL TEIR), GRAFFITI, ROMAN AND BYZANTINE PERIOD. Ed. pr. G. Wagner, BIAO 76 (1976) 285. No. 1774-1781: Roman period; no. 1782: Byzantine period.

1774. Τὸ προσκύνημα Α̣μ̣μ̣ω̣ν̣ί̣ο̣υ̣
Ἡρακλείου καὶ Μακρῖνος
υἱός.

1775. Πολλὰ |[2] εὐχαριστῶ | τῇ Τύχῃ |[4] τῶν ὧδε.

1776. Ἀμμωνοῦσα (?) | Ψεν̣νῆσις.

1777. Εἰς τὸ Ἰσῖον.

1778. Τὸ πρ(οσκύνημα) Εμιτσοκλ-
έους (sic! = Θεμιστοκλέους) Ἡρα( )
άκταρίου.

1779. Εὐτυχῶς | Μάρων | Μαρίν[ου].

1780. Πετεχῶ(ν) | Ὠριγένης.

1781. Isolated names: Ἀμάνιος, Ψάις, Ἡράκλειος, Μαικιαν̣[ός], Ἡρᾶς, Ψενατε[ ], Πηλεύς, Σεμφθεύς.

1782. Ἰ(ησοῦ)ς Χ(ριστό)ς,
Ἔσδρα πρ(εσβύτερος).
Ἄπα Παπνουθίου,
βοήθιε (sic) Ἔσδρᾳ πρ(εσβυτέρῳ).

1783-1791. OASIS OF KHARGEH (CHAMS EL-DIN), CHRISTIAN INSCRIPTIONS AND GRAFFITI, 6th CENT. A.D. Inscriptions and graffiti in a church and its annexes. Ed. pr. G. Wagner, BIAO 76 (1976) 285-286.

1783. Εὔτηχὸς (sic) Βίκτωρ
υἱὸς Παῦλος Ἀιῶν
κὲ Δῖος Τανευ στρα-
διώτης λεγιῶνος
Ἀπόλλωνος Ἄνο.

1784. Εἷς θεὸς ὁ βοηθός,
ὁ Χ(ριστὸ)ς αὐτοῦ συντήρησο̣[ν] κ̣α̣ὶ̣
διαφύλαξαι τοῖς Λατωπολ[ίταις]
μετὰ καὶ τῶν ζῴων ἑαυτῶν.

1785. End of an inscription:

... Παῦλον
Φλωρεντίου
ὁ δοῦλος τοῦ θεοῦ
ὁ γράψας ....[

1786. Μιμνήσθη τοῦ
τόπῳ (sic) ἐν τῇ
εὐσκίστῃ (sic = εὐσκιάστῃ) ο-
ικίᾳ τοῦ θεοῦ
Ἡράκλειος.

1787. Εὔτυχος . βọθων | Στράτης Παχοῦμις | τῆς Ἀπόλλων(ος).

1788. Εὔτυχος Παῦλος Ἀπολλ[ῶ]ς.

1789. Εὐτυχῶς Κλάρος | Ἰωάννης.

1790. Παῦλος στρ( ) τῆς Ἀπολ( ) Ἄνω
Κλάρος
Ἰσάκ
δοῦλος
Ἰη(σοῦ) Χρ(ιστοῦ).

1791. Isolated names: Φλ(άουιος) Μακάριος, Φλ(άουιος) Ψενόριος, Μαξιμῖνος, Φίρμος, Ῥοῦφος, Κλάρος, Μακάριος Θεοδ(ώρου), Δίδυμος, Ὀρνίθων, Σεβάσμιος, Παλάμων, Ψῶχις.

1792-1795. OASIS OF KHARGEH (TEMPLE OF DOUSH), PAINTED INSCRIPTIONS, 3rd CENT. A.D. Inscriptions painted on the outer wall. Ed. pr. G. Wagner, BIAO 76 (1976) 287.

1792. Τὸ προσκύνημα
Ψεννῆσις Πελήβιος
ἱεροῦ
ἱερεὺς Ἴσιδι καὶ Σάραπις
θεῶν μεγίστων Κύσεως
Θῶθ κ'.

1793. Πλουτογένης.

1794. Τὸ <προσκύνημα> Ψενπνούθης ...
ἱερέως ἱεροῦ Ἴσιδι Σαράπιδι θεῶν .....

1795. Αὔξι Τύχη.

1796. KOM ABOU BILLOU - TERENOUTHIS (?), EPITAPH, 3rd CENT. A.D. Funerary stele with standing orans (shawl ? over the head and down both sides), hawk, jackal in bas-relief. Ed. pr. M. Rassart-Debergh, Antiquités romaines et chrétiennes d'Égypte. Musées Royaux d'Art et d'Histoire (Bruxelles, 1976) p. 19, fig. 4.

Χαιρημονὶς (ἐτῶν) κη, (ἔτους) ιε Ἁθὺρ ιθ. εὐψύχι.

1797. KOM EL-DIKKA, EULOGIA OF ST. MENAS, 480-560 A.D. Inscription on an ampulla (around the representation of a fruit-basket). Ed. pr. Zsolt Kiss, ETUDES ET TRAVAUX (Centre d'archéologie méditerranéenne de l'académie Polonaise des sciences) 9 (1976) 215-216, no. 5 (ph.).

Εὐλ(ογία) τοῦ ἁγίου [Μη]νᾶ.

1798. KOM EL-DIKKA, EULOGIA OF ST. MENAS, 560-610 A.D. Inscription on an ampulla, in a laurel-wreath. Menas is represented between two crouching camels. Ed. pr. Zsolt Kiss, ETUDES ET TRAVAUX (Centre d'archéologie méditerranéenne de l'académie Polonaise des sciences) 9 (1976) 214-215, no. 3 (ph.).

Ἁγίο(υ) | Μην(ᾶ) | εὐλ(ογία).

1799. KOM OMBO, FRAGMENT OF A LAW OR EDICT ABOUT TAXES AND PUBLICANI, AFTER 79 A.D. Ed. pr. J.G. Milne, Greek Inscriptions (Catalogue générale du Musée du Caire; 1909) p. 11-12, no. 9302; R. Cagnat, IGR, I, 1285; republished by Preisigke, SB, I, 676. Cf. J.D. Thomas, ZPE 21 (1976) 153-156. Thomas finds in this text a new reference to Πεδούκαιος Κόλων as prefect of Egypt: in L. 38 he reads: --]ο Πεδουκαίου Κόλωνος [-- (with Milne, against Cagnat who had read οἰκ]οπέδου καὶ συκοδωνος (?)). He establishes with the help of this stele a little more clearly the dates during which Colo(nus) was prefect: Colo(nus) was still functioning in the early part of A.D. 72. Thomas dates the inscription itself after A.D. 79.

1800. KOPTOS, DEDICATION TO THE GREAT SAMOTHRACIAN GODS. OGIS, 69. W. Clarysse, CE 51 (1976) 152 prefers to date this text on palaeographical grounds to the late third or early second cent. B.C., and not under Ptolemy III Euergetes, hesitatingly suggested by OGIS.

1801. KOPTOS, DEDICATION TO ISIS AND HERA, AUGUST 70 A.D. Limestone block. Ed. pr. G. Wagner, BIAO 76 (1976) 277-281 (ph.).

Ὑπὲρ Αὐτοκράτορος Καίσαρος
Οὐεσπασιανοῦ Σεβαστοῦ
3 καὶ τοῦ οἴκου αὐτοῦ Ἴσιδι καὶ
Ἥραι θεαῖς μεγίσταις Ἑρμερῶς
Ἀθηνίωνος Ἀδανείτης Ἐρυθραῖος
6 ἔμπορος (ἔτους) β μηνὸς Καισαρείου Μεσορὴ ι̅ϛ̅

4-5. For Ἑρμερῶς Ἀθηνίωνος, cf. P. O.Tait, 287 (57 A.D.) Wagner || 5. Ἀδανείτης: refers to Ἄδανα in Arabia (and not to the Cilician Adana which has Ἀδανεύς) Wagner.

1802. KROKODILOPOLIS, DEDICATION TO SOKONICHONNEUS, 101 B.C. E. Bernand, Recueil des Inscriptions grecques du Fayoum, I: La "méris" d'Hérakleidès (Leiden, 1975) no. 7. Cf. G. Wagner, ZPE 20 (1976) 226-227 who prefers in L. 8-9 the reading Σοκον̣ιχων|[ει] (instead of Σοκοπιχῶν|σ̣ει: Bernand).

1803. PHILAI, DEDICATION BY A STRATEGOS AND HIS SONS. Ed. pr. C.C. Edgar, ASAE 15 (1915) 105-106, no. 1; SB, III, 6116; A. Bernand, Inscriptions de Philae I (Paris, 1969) no. 64. Cf. L. Mooren, ORIENTALIA LOVANIENSIA PERIODICA 6-7 (1975-76) 411-417 who identifies the strategos with an Ἀπολλώνιος, possibly the father of the well-known strategos of the Thebaïs Platon (101-88 B.C.), and describes his career from 134-117 B.C. Subsequently Mooren restores the inscription as follows:

[Ὑπὲρ βασιλέως Πτολεμαίου καὶ βασιλίσσης Κλεο]-
[πάτρας τῆς ἀδελφῆς καὶ βασιλίσσης Κλεοπάτρας]
[τῆς γυν]α̣ι̣κὸς θ[εῶν Εὐεργετῶν καὶ τῶν]
4 τούτων τέκ̣ν̣[ων τῆι μεγίστηι θεᾶι Ἴσιδι]
καὶ τοῖς ἐν τῶι Ἀ[βάτωι θεοῖς Ἀπολλώνιος]
Πλάτωνος Ζήνε[ιος τῶν ὁμοτίμων τοῖς συγγενέσι]
καὶ στρατηγὸς κ̣[αὶ e.g. νομάρχης καὶ]
8 οἱ τούτου υἱοὶ̣ [Πλάτων καὶ Φιλόξενος καὶ]
Ἀ̣γαθῖνος τῶν π̣[ρώτων φίλων ἐπ' ἀγαθῶι].

Date: 2nd - 1st cent. B.C. Edgar; 2nd cent. B.C. SB; impossible to give a more exact date Bernand; 119-116 A.D. Mooren.

1804. PHILAI, THE DEDICATION OF C. CORNELIUS GALLUS, 29 B.C. CIL, III, 14147; E. Bernand, Inscriptions de Philae II (Paris, 1969) no. 128. H. Hauben, ZPE 22 (1976) 189-190 reflects upon the Greek and Latin version of LL. 5-7 and 15-16 and in particular upon the propagandistic function of these lines.

1805. SAÏ, EPITAPH FOR THE BISHOP LEON, AFTER THE 7th - 8th CENT.

A.D. Ed. pr. B. Boyaval, REGYPT 24 (1972) 20-24 (ph.). Cf. B. Boyaval, ZPE 21 (1976) 42 (post-scriptum), who reads in L. 7 now επισ̓ͅ = ἐπισ`κ´(όπου) instead of ἐπισ(κόπου). For this abbreviation, cf. our no. 1806.

1806. SAÏ, GRAFFITO. SB, I, 3897. Cf. B. Boyaval, ZPE 21 (1976) 42 (ph.), who revised this graffito with the help of a photo. He reads it as follows:

("Ετους) λ̄β Στέφανος β(ασι)λ(εὺ)ς — ῑῡ
θεοῦ λω ἀμάν. "Αννω † ἐπίσ`κ´(οπος) Ζαή
Κίρ̣ῶ̣να.

1. ("Ετους) λ̄β omitted in SB || Βτενῖνος β(ασι)λ(εὺ)ς ĪV̄ SB || ιυ: abbreviated name, perhaps Ἰ(ησο)ῦ Boyaval || 2. θε̣ω̣ or θω̣ are not impossible Boyaval || "Αννου † ἐπἰͅ β(ασι)λ(εὺ)ς δ̄ SB || 3. Κίρωνος SB.

1807. SAÏ, GRAFFITO. SB, I, 3896. Cf. B. Boyaval, ZPE 21 (1976) 62 (ph.) who points out that this graffito has been engraved twice on the rock. Supra: ιωυ βσλ; infra: ιωυ βλσ. So the supposed abbreviation of βασιλεύς has not the same form and Ιωυ is the abbreviation of a name: Ἰω(άννο)υ or Ἰ(ησ)ωῦ ? In any case one has to remove the name Ἰωΰ from the Namenbuch, col. 156. The reading of SB was: Ἰωὺ β(ασι)λ(εύ)ς.

1808. UNKNOWN PROVENANCE, FUNERARY EPIGRAM, HELLENISTIC PERIOD. Ed. pr. R. Koerner, Festschrift zum 150-jährigen Bestehen des Berliner Ägyptischen Museums (Berlin, 1974) 356-358, no. 4 (ph.). Cf. W. Peek, ZPE 21 (1976) 133-134 and ZPE 28 (1978) 40. We print here the text with Peek's restorations:

Εἰς Ἀίδαν ἀμέριμνον ἐλήλυθα [–⏑⏑ –⏑]
πληρώσας ἐτέων τρεῖς ἱλάρας δεκά[δας],
ἐντάφιον δ᾽ ἔσχον πολλὴν χάριν· οὐ γὰρ ἐλύπουν
οὐδένα, βέλτισ<τος> πᾶσι δ᾽ ἔλαμψα φίλος·
ὃς συνέλεξα βίον καλοκάγαθίαν μεθοδεύων,
οὐθὲν ὀνησιφόρον δ᾽ ἔσχον ἔγωγε βίον.
Ὑῶν θ᾽ ἕξ̣ειν τέκνα ποτ᾽ ἤλπισα, νῦν δὲ λέλοιπα
ὄρφανα τῆς φιλίας πατρὸς ἐμειρόμενα.
Οἷς εἴη μετὰ μητρὸς ἔτη γηραιὰ β[ι]ῶ̣ναι·
[μ]ὴ κείσθω παρ᾽ ἐμεῦ πένθιμος ἁλικία.

1. Perhaps Κ̣ν̣[ήμ]ο̣υ̣ Ὀ̣ρ[όν]τ̣[ας ?] Peek || 3. οὐ γὰρ Ε....ΥΝ Koerner || 7. θ᾽ = aspirated δ᾽ Peek || 8. ἐμ᾽ εἰρόμενα Koerner || 9. μητρὸς ΓΗΡΑΣΛ.Β[..]ΝΑΙ Koerner || 10. [παρ]κείσθω Koerner.

1809. UNKNOWN PROVENANCE, FUNERARY EPIGRAM, LATER IMPERIAL PERIOD. Ed. pr. R. Koerner, Festschrift zum 150-jährigen Bestehen des Berliner Ägyptischen Museums (Berlin, 1974) 358, no. 5 (ph.). W. Peek, ZPE 21 (1976) 273-274 and ZPE 28 (1978) 40 offers the following text:

[Πρὶν κλυτὸς ἰητ]ὴρ λεγόμην μ[όχθων τ' ἐπίκουρος],
[σῆμα δὲ νῦν] ἐπόνει ἐκβίῳ [–⏑⏑–]·
[καὶ φέρε δ' ἔν]τομα μοι Σοφία φ[ιλάδελφος ἅμ' αὐτῇ]
[καὶ Βιττοῦ]ς ἁγνὴ ψυχὴ πιστ[όν τε φρόνημα]
[Ἡδείης, ἧ]ς καὶ γαμέτης με πο[θεῖ Φιλόδημος]·
[καλὰ μεθ'] ὧν κε βιῶν ἤνυσ[α τοὖργον ἐμόν].
[Δὶς δεκ]ά[δω]ν δισσοὺς ἐκτελ[έσας δὲ δρόμους],
[ὦ ξένε, σὺν τρι]σί περ λυκαβαν[τίσι κάτθανον ὥραις].

---

1. ηρ δὲ νομὴν με Koerner || 2. ΕΠΟ.ΕΙΕΚΒΙΩ Koerner; [σῆμα δ' ἔτευξ]ε πόσει Εὐβίῳ [Ἡδέα νῦν] Peek (ZPE, 1976) || 3. σ]τόμα [μ]οι σοφία Koerner || 4. Σ ἁγνὴ τύχη ΠΙΣ Koerner || 5. Σ καὶ γαμέτης μετιο Koerner || 8. ΤΙ περ λυκαβαν[τ Koerner.

1810. UNKNOWN PROVENANCE, CHRISTIAN EPITAPH. Inscription on a sandstone grave stele with low relief. Ed. pr. P.J. Sijpesteijn, ZPE 20 (1976) 166.

† Εἷς θεὸς ὁ βοεθὸς Μαρί-
Ϛ αμ.

1811. UNKNOWN PROVENANCE, EULOGIA OF ST. MENAS, 400-600 A.D. Inscription on a two-handled terracotta ampulla; obverse: encircled by three concentric circles a head of a man (probably St. Menas) facing right; reverse: inscription in relief and encircled by three concentric circles. Ed. pr. P.J. Sijpesteijn, ZPE 20 (1976) 166.

Εὐλ|[2]ογία το|ῦ ἁγίου |[4] Μηνᾶ.

NUBIA

1812. ABUSIMBEL, INSCRIPTION OF A GREEK MERCENARY (?), 591 B.C. Meiggs - Lewis, SGHI, 7, (g), p. 13. P. Tozzi, ATHENAEUM 54 (1976) 482-483 proposes to read in L. 1: Ἀναχσάνορ ἔ[γραφέ με] or ἔ[γραφεν ἐμέ] or ἔ[γραψέ με] or ἔ[γραψεν ἐμέ] *h*ο Ἰαλύσιος *h*όκα βασιλ|εὺς κτλ. (against A. Bernard - O. Masson, REG 70, 1957, p. 13 who suggested: Ἀναχσάνορ ἐ[βάδισ'] etc.). P. Tozzi remarks that, if this restoration is correct, Anaxanor must be considered as a Greek mercenary soldier and not as an "officier commandant peut-être un corps d'infanterie" (A. Bernard - O. Masson, l.c., p. 14).

1813. AXUM, INSCRIPTION OF EZANA, KING OF AXUM, 4th - 5th CENT. A.D. Ed. pr. F. Anfray - A. Caquot - P. Nautin, JS (1970) 260-274 (ph.). Cf. E. Dinkler, ETUDES ET TRAVAUX (Centre d'archéologie Méditerranéenne de l'académie Polonaise des sciences) 9 (1976) 6-15 and F. Altheim - R. Stiehl, KLIO 58 (1976) 471-479.

Ἐν τῇ πίστι τοῦ θ[εοῦ καὶ] τῇ δυνάμι τοῦ [πα]-
τρὸς καὶ υἱοῦ καὶ [ἁ]γί[ο]υ [π]νεύματος, τ[ῷ]
[σ]ώσαντί μοι τὸ βασ[ίλ]ιον τῇ πίστι τοῦ υἱ[οῦ]
αὐτοῦ Ἰησοῦ χριστοῦ, τῷ βοηθήσαντί μο[ι]
τῷ καὶ πάντοταί μοι βοηθοῦντι ἐγὼ
Ἀζανᾶς βασιλεὺς Ἀξωμιτῶν καὶ Ὁμηρι-
[τῶν κ]αὶ τοῦ ΡΕΕΙΔΑΝ καὶ Σαβαειτῶν καὶ
τοῦ Σ[ΙΛ]ΕΗΛ καὶ τοῦ ΧΑΣΩ καὶ Βουγαειτῶν
[κ]αὶ τοῦ Τιαμῶ, ΒΙΣΙ ΑΛΗΝΕ, υἱὸς τοῦ ΕΛΛΕ-
ΑΜΙΔΑ, δοῦλος Χριστοῦ, εὐχαριστῶ Κυρίῳ
τῷ [θεῷ] μου καὶ οὐ δύναμαι εἰπῖν πλίρης
τὰς εὐχαριστίας αὐτοῦ, ὅτι οὐ δύναται
τὸ στό[μ]α μου καὶ ἡ διάνοιά μου πάσας
τὰς εὐχαριστίας ἅσπερ ἐποίησεν μετ' ἐ-
μοῦ, ὅτι ἐπ[οί]ησεν ἐμοὶ ἠσχὺν καὶ δύναμιν
καὶ ἐχαρίσ[α]τό μοι ὄ[ν]ομα μέγα διὰ τοῦ υἱοῦ
[α]ὐτοῦ εἰς ὃν ἐπ[ί]στευσα [κα]ὶ ἐποίησεν μαι ὁ-
[δ]ηγὸν πάσης τῆς βασιλίας μου διὰ τὴν πί-
στ[ι]ν τοῦ χριστοῦ τ[ῷ] θελήματι [αὐ]τοῦ καὶ
δυνάμι τοῦ χριστοῦ, ὅτι αὐτὸς ὁδήγησέν
μαι καὶ εἰς α[ὐ]τὸν πιστεύω καὶ αὐτὸς ἐγέ-
νετό μοι ὁδηγός. Ἐξῆλθα πολεμῆσαι
τοὺς ΝΩΒΑ, ὅτι κατέκραξαν κατ' αὐτῶν
οἱ ΜΑΝΓΑΡΘΩ καὶ ΧΑΣΑ καὶ ΑΤΙΑΔΙΤΑΙ
καὶ ΒΑΡΕΩΤΑΙ λέγοντες ὅτι κατεπόνη-
σαν ἡμᾶς οἱ ΝΩΒΑ, βοηθήσατε ἡμῖν, ὅτι ἔ-
θληψαν ἡμᾶς ἀποκτένοντες. Καὶ ἀνέστην
ἐν τῇ δυνάμι τοῦ θεοῦ χριστοῦ, εἰς ὃν ἐπί-
στευσα, καὶ ὁδήγησέν με. Καὶ ἀνέστην ἀ-
πὸ Ἀξώμεος ἐν μινὶ κατὰ Ἀξωμιτὰς ΜΑΓΑ-
ΒΙΘΕ η' ἡμέρᾳ σαμβάτῳ πίστι τοῦ θεοῦ καὶ
ἔφθασα εἰς ΜΑΜΒΑΡΙΑΝ καὶ ἐκῖθεν ἐσιτάρχησα.

Date: 349, 355 or 360 A.D. A. Caquot - P. Nautin, l.c., 268-269; "also other dates, namely the last third of the 4th or the beginning of the 5th cent. should be considered" E. Dinkler, l.c., 11; Dinkler thinks of an even later date: "Did perhaps King Ezana only become the founder of the Christian Church in Axum during the 5th century and should the new inscription of 1969 as well as the Christian Ezana coins only be evaluated as reflections of this process ?"; at the earliest 451 or some years later Altheim - Stiehl || 8. Σ[ιλ]εην Altheim - Stiehl || 12 and 14. εὐχαριστία = "faveur" Caquot - Nautin; "Danksagungen" Altheim - Stiehl || 32. ἐσιτάρχησα: "je me suis ravitaillé" Caquot - Nautin, "to pay an army" Altheim - Stiehl.

KYRENAIKA

1814. KYRENAIC ONOMASTICS. Cf. nos. 1888-1889.

1815. GYMNASTIC INSTITUTIONS AND ATHLETICS IN KYRENAIKA. M. Luni, QAL 8 (1976) 223-284 studies the gymnastic institutions and athletics in Kyrenaika (against the background of those of Greece). On pp. 235-259 he presents a collection of epigraphic documents (with photographs; nearly all of them are published before) which give information about these subjects (outside Kyrenaika: 5 numbers, Kyrene: 22, Tokra: 4, Ptolemaïs: 4, Apollonia: 1). He also refers to three inedita (Kyrene: no. 9bis, 13, 14bis).

1816. APOLLONIA, BOUNDARY STONE FROM THE PUBLIC LAND OF THE ROMAN PEOPLE. Part of a brown limestone stele, inscribed on two of the three surviving faces (= a and b); re-used in a modern house near the Extra-Mural Basilica; now in the Apollonia Museum. Ed. pr. J. Reynolds, LIBANT 8 (1971) 50-51.

A. Left face, broken above and sliced away on the right side (ph.); 54-55 A.D.

...]
Τ̣ι̣βερίου [Καί]-
σαρος Σε[βα]-
στοῦ κα[ὶ]
Θεοῦ Σε[βα]-
στ v. οὗ ἔ̣[κγ]-
[ο]νος [vac.]
Σεβασ[τὸς]
Γερμα̣[ν(ικὸς)]
αὐτοκ[ρά]-
τωρ [διὰ]
Λουκ[ίου]
Ἀκιλί[ου Στρά]-
βων̣[ος τοῦ]
[ἰδίου πρεσ]-
[βευτοῦ]
[...

B. To the left of A, on what must originally have been the reverse face of the stele (ph.).

...]E
...]ESẠ[..?..]E
...]AV[..?..]N
...]ESṬ[..?..]ṾỌ
...]N
...]TAI[..?..]AẸ
...]ḷọc̣ạṿịṭ
...]Apoḷḷonio
...qu]adringenis
...]s et
...] ob un-
[?um ..?..] medi-
[mnia ..?..] vac.

1817. ARSINOE (TOKRA), HONORARY DECREE FOR ALEXIMACHOS, SON OF

SOSISTRATOS, END 2nd - 1st HALF 1st CENT. B.C. Ed. pr. J. Reynolds, ARCHCLASS 25-26 (1973-74) 623-630 (ph.). Cf. L. Moretti, RFIC 104 (1976) 385-398 who studies L. 5-57 of the inscription; we present here his text (and punctuation) of these lines. Lines 58-80 are Reynold's text:

[..?..]
[..?..]
[... ?Δη]μ̣ητρι-
[ca. 5]Ρ̣Ο̣[..?..]!̣ γερο!̣-
[ca. 5]Μ̣Ο̣[..?..]ΑΙΑΔΕ
[ἐπειδὴ] Ἀλεξ[ίμαχος Σωσιστ]ρ̣άτω τῶν [ἀ]-
[με]τέρων πολ̣ιτᾶ[ν ἀε]ὶ διατελ̣εῖ τὰν̣
[μ]εγίσταν πρόνοιαν ποιείμενος ὑπὲρ
[τ]ᾶς πόλιος ἁμῶν, πολλῶν δὲ καὶ μεγά-
λων ἀγαθ̣ῶν αἴτιος καθέστακε καὶ κοι-
[ν̣]ᾶι̣ κ̣αὶ καθ' ἰδίαν ἑκάστωι, ἐπιεικῆ μὲν
[κα̣ὶ̣] φιλάνθρωπον τὰν ποτὶ τὸς ὄχλος
[κ]α̣ὶ̣ πόλιας ποιείμενος συναναστρο-
[φ]ή̣ν, ἐμφαίνει δὲ ποιῶν τὰν τῶ ἰδίω γ[έ]-
[νο]υ̣ς ἐξ ἀρχᾶς κάλοκα̣γαθίαν, ἐν παν-
τ̣[ὶ κ̣]αιρῶι ἄξια πράσσ̣ων τ̣ᾶς τῶν προγόνων
α̣[ἱρ]έσεω̣ς, καὶ λόγωι καὶ ἔ̣ργωι τὰν καλλίσταν
π[ρ]ο̣νοιά̣ν ποιείμενος· συνεπιδιδοὺς ἑ-
αυτὸν̣ ἐς τὰ συμφέροντα τᾶι πόλει, οὔ-
[..]ς ἁμῶν ἀρχὰν ποιησάμενος ἐπέ-
δωκε χρήματα κατὰ τὰν τῶ πολέ-
μω περίστασιν ἐς τὰν παραφυλα-
κὰν τᾶς πόλιος, οὐθενὸς τῶν πολ[ι]-
τᾶν δεύτερος γινόμενος κατ̣[ὰ]
τὰν τᾶς πατρίδος ἐπανόρθω̣σ̣[ι]ν,
καθὼς αἱ ἐν τοῖς ἐπιφανεσ̣τάτοις
τόποις τιμαὶ αὐτῶ προδιασάφει-
σ̣ι̣ν̣ α̣ἱ̣τέ[ντων] τῶν στραταγῶν· κ̣α̣ὶ̣ φ̣ι̣-
[λοδ]αμίας οὐθὲν ἐνλείπων ὅσον
[ἐπ' α]ὐ̣τῶι δυνατόν ἐστι, συνεγβο-
[ηθ]ῶν τ̣ᾶι τε ἰδίαι πατρίδι κ̣α̣ὶ̣ τ̣οῖς
[πολ]ίταις ἀποδείκνυται τὰν ἐς
[πά]ντας εὔ̣νοι̣αν· καὶ ἐν τῶι πο-
[τὶ Λι]β̣ύ̣α̣ς κ̣α̣ιρῶι τῶ σίτω σπανί-
[ζο]ντο̣ς κ̣αὶ τ̣ᾶς πόλιος προθυ-
[μ]ειμένα̣ς ἀποστῆλαι σιτῶνας
ἰ̣ς Λέπτιν, θεωρῶν καὶ ἐν τούτοις
τ̣ὰ̣ν̣ τ̣ῶν ἰ̣δίων συνπολιτᾶν θλῖψιν̣
διὰ τὰν τῶ κ̣α̣ι̣ρ̣ῶ περίστασιν, οὐ-
θὲν ἧσσον συ̣ν̣α̣ντιλαμβάνεσθαι
τῶν πραγμάτων ζηλόμενος, φιλό-
πατρις ὑ̣π̣ε̣ρ̣φυῶ̣ς καὶ φιλάγαθος ἀ-
[ξίως ?] δ̣ό̣ξας τε καὶ ἀρετᾶς, διάφορον
μὲν ὂν ὀ[λί]γ̣ο̣ν̣ ὁρῶν, ἀκόλουθα δὲ

πράσσων ταῖς ἐν τοῖς νόμοις ἀρε-
ταῖς καταγεγραμμέναις, θεωρῶν
τὰν τῶ σίτω τιμὰν ἀνατεινομέναν,
ἐχοράγησε [τ]ὸν ἴ[δι]ον ὥστε πραθῆμεν
κατὰ μέτ[ρ]ο[ν] ἀξίας δ(ραχμῶν)·Λ· προθυμεί-
μενος δὲ [αὐτ]όθεν [κα]τάξαι τὸν σῖ-
τον ὑπέ[σ]τη μεγαλομερῶς τὰν τῶν ἰ-
δίων χρημάτων αὔξησιν πρὸ πολ-
λῶ λειτουργεῖν τᾶι τῶν ὄχλων σω-
τηρίαι· [δίκ]α[ιον δέ] ἐστι καὶ καλῶς ἔ-
χον τὸς ἀγα[θ]ὸς τῶν ἀνδρῶν προ-
τιμ[ᾶς καταξί]ω καὶ ἀποδοχᾶς μέ-
ζονος τυγχάνειν ὅπως καὶ οἱ λοιποὶ,
[θ]εώρεντες τὰν τᾶς πόλιος ἀνυπό[σ]-
τολον εὐχαριστίαν ὑπαρχοίσαν ἑαυ-
τὸς ἐπιδίδοντες ἐς τὰ συνφέροντα
τᾶι πόλει, τυγχάνωντι τῶν αὐτῶν
φιλανθρώπων v. Δέδοχθαι τοῖς γέ-
ροισι καὶ τᾶι [β]ω[λ]ᾶι ἐπαινέσαι Ἀλε-
ξίμαχον Σωσιστράτω χάριν τῶν
γεγονότων εὐεργετημάτων τῶν ὑ-
π' αὐτῶ, πρός τε ταῖς ὑπαρχοίσαις τι-
μαῖς ἀνθέμεν αὐτῷ τὰν πόλιν ἀνδρι-
άντα χαλκήιον ἐν τᾶι τῶν θεῶν ἀγορᾶι
ἐς ὃν κα αὐτὸς ποταίρηται τόπον, ἔχον-
τα ἐπιγραφὰν τάνδε· v. Ἀλεξίμαχον
Σωσιστράτω Ἀρσινοῆ ἀρετᾶς ἕνεκ[ε]
καὶ εὐνοίας ἇς ἔχων διατελεῖ εἰς v.
τὰν πόλιν Ἀρσινοές v. Οἱ δὲ ἔφοροι
τόν τε ἀνδριάντα ἀναθέντων
καὶ στάλαν λυγδίναν παρ' αὐτῷ[ι]
ἔχοισαν ἀντίγραφον τῶδε [τῶ ψα]-
[φίσμα]τος. [Τ]ὸ δὲ γενηθὲν ἀν[άλω]-
[μ]α ἐς [τ]ὰν στ[άλ]αν δόντων ἐ[κ]
δαμ[οσί]ων ταμίαι [? vac.]
vac. λευκαί v. ρθ' vac.

3. Presumably from the name Δημήτριος, with reference to a civic official Reynolds || 4-5. the final ! may be a scratch; possibly τᾶ]ι γερου|[σίαι, ο]ὶ γέρο|[ντες or τῶ]ν γερό|[ντων Reynolds || 5. perhaps a formula as ἐφόρων καὶ γερόντων ἐπαγόντων τᾶι βωλ]ᾶι ἅδε (Reynolds) or ἐψάφισαν κατ]ὰ τάδε (or an analogous formula) Moretti || 12. τὸς ὄχλος: the non-citizen population in Arsinoe Reynolds; "popolazione indigene stanziate nella chora" Moretti || 13. πόλιας: Reynolds suggests πολί<τ>ας; Moretti rejects this correction and thinks that other cities of Kyrenaika are meant || 14-15. ἤ|[θο]υς Reynolds || 16-17. καὶ τῶν προγόνων | α[ἵρ]εσει Reynolds || 19-20. οὔ|κως ἀμῶν ἀρχὰν ποιησάμενος Reynolds; Moretti wants to restore a word meaning "fortification" and proposes a hapax οὐρία (οὐ|[ρία]ς ἀμῶν ἀρχὰν ποιησάμενος) || 24-25. καὶ εὖ | τὰν τᾶς πατρίδος ἐπανώρθει

γᾶν Reynolds || 27-29. προδιασάφει|σ̣ι ἔ̣ν̣ τε [ταῖς] τῶν στραταγῶν παρε|[πιδ]αμίαις οὐθὲν ἐνλείπων Reynolds || 29-30. ὅσον | [ἐν α]ὐ̣-τῶι Reynolds || 33-34. καὶ ἐν τῶι πο|[...]Ι̣Π̣Ι̣Λ̣Β̣Λ̣Ι̣Α̣Ι̣Ι̣Ω̣Ι Reynolds, who suggests ἐν τῶι πο[λέμω] κ̣α̣ι̣ρῶι or ἐν τῶι πο[λέμω]ι̣ π̣α̣[ρ]α̣κ̣α̣ι̣ρ̣ῶι and adds: "but if πο[λέμω] is right there may have been an ethnic referring to the enemy, though the traces do not suggest to me any likely name" || 37. Ι̣Σ̣Λ̣ΕΠΤΙ̣Ν̣ Reynolds, who gives also Dr. Chadwick's conjecture "ἐς Λέπτιν" || 41. ζηλόμενος or better δ̣ηλόμενος (= βουλόμενος) Reynolds || 42-43. φιλάγαθος α|[..]ι̣ Reynolds, who proposes ἀ|ν̣τ̣ί̣ or ἀ|μ̣φ̣ί̣ || 43-44. ΔΙΑΦΟΡΟΙ̣|ΜΕΝΟΝΩ[..]Τ̣Ο̣ π̣ο̣ι̣ῶν Reynolds (who thinks of a form of διαφορέω) || 45-46. ἀρε|ταῖς καταγεγενημέναις Reynolds || 47-50. ἐ̣χ̣ορ̣άγησε [.]ΟΝΙ̣Ι̣Ι̣[..]Ο̣Ν ὥστε πραθῆμεν | κατα ΜΕΙ̣[.]Ο̣[.]Τ̣Α̣Ζ̣Ι̣Λ̣Χ̣ππ ·Λ· πρόθυμεί|μενος ΛΓΓ̣[.5-6..]ΠΑΞΑΙ τὸν σί|τον κτλ. Reynolds || 52-57. αὐξήειν πρὸ πολ|λῶ λειτουργίαν ἐ̣π̣ὶ̣ τῶν ὄχ-λων σω|τηρίαν Λ̣[...]Ο̣[.]Λ̣[...] ἐ̣σ̣τ̣ι̣ καὶ καλῶς ἔ|χ̣ο̣ν τὸς ἀγα[θ]ὸ̣ς̣ τῶν ἀνδρῶν προ|τιμ[ῶ]ν [.ca.7-8.]ω̣ καὶ ἀποδοχὰς μέ|ζονος τ̣υ̣γ̣χ̣ά̣ν̣ε̣ν̣ ὅπως καὶ κτλ. Reynolds || 54. [ἐπεὶ δίκ]α[ιόν] ἐ̣σ̣τ̣ι̣ Moretti, corr. J. and L. Robert, BE (1978) no. 561.

1818. BALAGRAI, DEDICATION OF A SILVER SNAKE TO ASKLEPIOS BY A PROCURATOR, EARLY 3rd CENT. A.D. Re-used block of white marble, broken away at the left side; relief of a female bust within a medallion to the right of the text (perhaps a representation of Hygieia). Ed. pr. J. Reynolds, LIBANT 8 (1971) 43-45 (ph.).

[Ἀσκληπ]ίωι·Βαλαγρείτηι·Ἰητρῶι·
...Λο]ύκουλλος·ἐπίτροπος·τοῦ Σεβαστοῦ
...]ν ὑγείας·καὶ εἰς ὑπόμνησιν·τῆς πρὸς
[?ἑαυτὸν] φιλίας·δράκοντα·ἀργύρεον leaf

The dedicator was an equestrian procurator, presumably the procurator of the province of Crete and Kyrene. It is possible that he should be identified with Iulius Lucullus (PIR[2] I, no. 387), epistrategus Heptanomiae in A.D. 173 Reynolds.

1819. BEIT THAMIR, BOUNDARY STONE FROM THE PUBLIC LAND OF THE ROMAN PEOPLE, 53 A.D. Brown limestone stele, reconstructed from several pieces, inscribed on two faces (= a and b); now in the Kyrene museum. Ed. pr. J. Reynolds, LIBANT 8 (1971) 47-49, no. 1 (ph.).

A. Front face:

[Τι(βέριος)] Κλαύδιος vac.
[? vac. Κ]α̣ῖσαρ Σεβαστὸς
[? vac.]Γερμαν[ι]κὸς vac.
[? vac. ἀρχ]ι̣ερεὺς μέγιστος
vac. δημαρ[χικῆ]ς ἐξου-
σ[ία]ς τὸ ιγ´ αὐτοκρά-
τ̣[ω]ρ̣ τὸ κζ´ π̣α̣τ̣[ὴρ]

π̣α̣τρ v̲. ἴδος τιμητὴς
[? vac. ὕπα]τ̣ος [τὸ ε']
διὰ Λ(ευκίου) Ἀκ̣[ιλίο]υ vac.
Σ̣τ̣ρ̣ά̣β̣- vac.
ω̣ν̣ο̣ς τοῦ [vac.]
ἰ̣δ̣ί̣ου πρεσβευτοῦ vac.
Χωρία ὑπὸ ἰδιώτων vac.
vac. κατεχόμενα δήμ̣ῳ
vac. Ῥωμαίων ἀπο- vac.
vac. κατέστησε vac.

B. Reverse face:

[Ti(berius) Claudius]
C̣aesa[r Augustus]
Geṛ[manicus]
[5 lines quite illegible]
per L(ucium) Ac[ili]um Str[a]-
bọnem ḷ[e]g̣ạṭụm suum
p̣ṛaeḍịạ [a] p̣ṛịṿạṭịṣ
poss v̲. es[sa p(opulo) R(omano)] res v̲. ti-
vac. tuit vac.

1820. AREA OF HADRIANOPOLIS, TOMB INSCRIPTION. Inscription above the doorway to Tomb I in a quarry ca. 1 km from the city. Ed. pr. G.D.B. Jones - J.H. Little, LIBANT 8 (1971) 62 (ph.).

Ἐλευθέρων | ἐκ τῆς πόλεως.

1821. AREA OF HADRIANOPOLIS, TOMB INSCRIPTION. Inscription above the doorway to Tomb II in a quarry ca. 1 km from the city. Ed. pr. G.D.B. Jones - J.H. Little, LIBANT 8 (1971) 63 (ph.).

Ἀπελευθέρων Εὐ|γένους̣ καὶ δού|λων αὐτοῦ.

1822. AREA OF HADRIANOPOLIS, TOMB INSCRIPTION. Inscription above the doorway to Tomb III in a quarry ca. 1 km from the city. Ed. pr. G.D.B. Jones - J.H. Little, LIBANT 8 (1971) 63 (ph.).

[Κλα]ύδια Κράτεια | αὐτῆι καὶ τοῖς ἰδίοις.

1823. AREA OF HADRIANOPOLIS, FOUR LETTERS. Inscription cut on part of the rock face on the northern side of a quarry ca. 1 km from the city. Ed. pr. G.D.B. Jones - J.H. Little, LIBANT 8 (1971) 64 (ph.).

ΛΥΚΥ

1824. KYRENE (DEMETER SANCTUARY), HONORARY INSCRIPTION FOR OCTAVIA, THE SISTER OF AUGUSTUS. White marble statue base, with base and crown mouldings. Ed. pr. D. White, LIBANT 9-10 (1972-73) 185 (ph.).

'Οκταίαν τὰν Καίσαρος
τῶ Σεβαστῶ ἀδελφὰν
Κυραναῖοι.

1825. KYRENE (DEMETER SANCTUARY), HONORARY INSCRIPTION. Marble block. Ed. pr. D. White, LIBANT 9-10 (1972-73) 185 (ph.).

[...]ίαν Λευκίω τὰν Λε[υκίω]
Φονταίω Λευκίω υἱῶ 'Ρούφω
πάτρωνος καὶ εὐεργέτα ματέρα
Κυραναῖοι
Ἄριστις Ταβάλβιος ἐποίησε.

None of the names mentioned seems immediately familiar within the local setting White.

1826-1827. KYRENE, A BENEFACTION OF ANTONIA MEGO, 106 A.D. J. Reynolds, SOC. FOR LIBYAN STUDIES, 7th Annual Report (1975-76), 11-18 (ph.) republishes the four fragments GIBM, IV, 1057-1058 (cf. IGR, I, 1037) with various new readings, firmly dates the text to July 30th, 106 A.D., and interprets the feast as a celebration of the fall of Sarmizegethusa in Trajan's Dacian war. We present her text below and in the app. crit. we indicate only the variae lectiones of earlier editions in the important lines:

1826. P. 11-14, A.

[Ὑπὲρ Αὐτοκρά]-
[τορος Καίσαρ]-
[ος Νέρουα Τρα]-
[ιανοῦ Γ]ερμα̣-
[νικοῦ] Δα̣κικο̣[ῦ]
[νίκη]ς̣ (?) καὶ δια- v.
[μο]νῆς̣ καὶ τοῦ
[σύ]νπαντος [αὐ]-
[τοῦ] οἴκου καὶ v.
[τῆς] ἱερᾶς συν- v.
[κ]λήτου καὶ δή- v.
μου 'Ρωμαίων v.
'Αντωνία Μεγὼ
Μ(άρκου) 'Αντωνίο̣υ̣ [Ηγι]-
σαντος [. ca. 6 .]
[θ]υ̣γατ[ca. 3 Μ(άρκου) 'Αντω]-
νίο̣υ Σω![. ca. 6 .]
καὶ Ηγισ̣αντ̣[ος v.]
τοῦ Βωλακλέ̣ος ἱ-
έρεια 'Αρτέμιδος
ἀριστιεῖ τὰς τὴν
πόλιν καὶ τὴν χώραν̣
[κα]τοικούσας παρ̣-
[θένους ...

14-16. 'Αντωνίο[υ ἱερατ|εύ]σαντος [...] | [κ]αὶ ... IGR; 'Αντωνίο[υ θύ]|σαντος [...] | ..(κ)αὶ ... GIBM || 18. καὶ 'Ηγησάν(δ)[ρου ? GIBM || 14-19. Reynolds suggests two restorations (she prefers A):

A. M(άρκου) ᾽Αντωνίο̣υ [Ηγι]|σαντος [θυγάτηρ] | [θ]υ̣γατ[ριδῆ M(άρκου) ᾽Αντω]|νίου Σωκ̣̇[λέος (?) v.] | καὶ Ηγισαντ̣[ος v.] | τοῦ Βωλακλέος; B. M(άρκου) ᾽Αντωνίου [Ηγι]|σαντος [γυνὴ] | [θ]υ̣γάτ[ηρ M(άρκου) ᾽Αντω]|νίου Σωκ̣[λέος τοῦ] | καὶ Ηγισαντ̣[ος v.] | τοῦ Βωλακλέος || 20. Cf. A. Wilhelm, AAWW (1948) 313; L. Robert, Hellenica XI-XII (1960) 573 f.

1827. P. 14-16, B.

...]
Ε̣[...
Λ̣ΑΣΙ̣[...
ΧΕΡΙ̣ΩΝ[...
ΜΟΙΗΑΔ̣[...
τῆ ἕκ̣(τῃ) τοῦ Μ[εσορὴ μη]-
νὸς ἕτου[ς ρλς´ τοῦ]
καὶ θ´ Αὐτ[οκράτορος]
Νέρο̣[υα Τραιανοῦ Σε]-
β[ά̣]σ̣[τοῦ ...
[̣...

5. τιβ(ε)κ τοῦ (μ)[... GIBM (25th of the month Tiberios) || 6-7. νος ἕτο(υ)[ς ρλε´ τοῦ] | καὶ (η) Αὐ(τ)[οκράτορος] GIBM || 8-9. Νέρ[ουα Καίσαρος] | (Τ)[ραιανοῦ Σεβαστοῦ] GIBM.

1828. KYRENE, INSCRIPTION IN THE CHAMBER OF THE PRIESTS OF APOLLO, LATE 2nd - 3rd CENT. A.D. Inscription on a pillar. Ed. pr. R.L. Gordon, JOURNAL OF MITHRAIC STUDIES 1 (1976) 214.

Π Δ
ΚΑΝΑΠΡΗΔΣ
Δ Γ Φ
ΦΙΛΑΡΑΔΗΣ

1829. KYRENE, ACCLAMATIONS FOR PRIESTS OF APOLLO, 3rd CENT. A.D. SEG, XVIII, 750. R.L. Gordon, JOURNAL OF MITHRAIC STUDIES 1 (1976) 213-214 (ph.) discusses these three inscriptions (with reference to L. Robert, Hellenica XI-XII, 1960, p. 547-555) to prove that the chamber wherein they were found had around 200 A.D. or later some close connection with the priests of Apollo. The chamber was always connected with Apollo and was never a Mithraeum (against S. Stucchi, Architettura Cirenaica (Monografie di Archeologia Libica, IX; Rome, 1975) p. 266-267).

1830. KYRENE, RECORD OF THE RECONSTRUCTION OF A CULT-CHAMBER OF APOLLO, 3rd CENT. A.D. Inscribed block, broken at the right.

Ed. pr. R.L. Gordon, JOURNAL OF MITHRAIC STUDIES 1 (1976) 215-217 (ph.).

Δε̣[.3̣.]ν Ἀντίπατρος ἱερώμενος [--
ἐκ̣ πρ̣οσόδων ἱερῶν νήους μ[1̣-2]Ι Α̣[--
εὐτυχῶς Ι̣[...?
κορακιω [...?

---

4. κορακιω: probably a cult-title of Apollo at Kyrene Gordon.

1831. KYRENE, DEDICATION TO APOLLO, CA. 330 B.C. SEG, IX, 77. O. Masson, ANTAFR 10 (1976) 50, note 10 attributes this text to the 4th cent. B.C. (ca. 330 B.C), against Hondius who dated it to the 3rd cent. B.C.

1832. KYRENE, DEDICATION TO APOLLO, END 4th CENT. B.C. SEG, IX, 81; SEG, XVII, 794. For a new description of the stone and a study of the inscription (form of the dedication, onomastics, dating), cf. L. Gasperini, QAL 8 (1976) 156-157 (ph.; no new conclusions).

1833. KYRENE, DEDICATION TO DEMETER, 4th - 3rd CENT. B.C. Marble plinth; one long face inscribed with two lines of text set between a simple crown and base moulding. Ed. pr. D. White, AJA 80 (1976) 172, note 21 (ph.).

Ἀριστοπάτρα Θαλίννω
τᾶι Δάματρι ἀνέθηκε.

1834. KYRENE (DEMETER SANCTUARY), DEDICATION TO DEMETER AND KORE, 2nd CENT. B.C. ? White marble statue base. Ed. pr. D. White, LIBANT 9-10 (1972-73) 208, note 26.

[Διο]νύσι[ος ..?..]
[vac.] Δάματ[ρι καὶ κόραι]

1835. KYRENE, DEDICATION OF L. ORBIUS, 2 A.D. SEG, IX, 63; SEG, XVII, 810. F. Chamoux, Recueil Plassart, p. 47-57 (ph.) has reexamined the stone and offers a new reading and interpretation of L. 6 ("Pausanias qui n'a pris de repos qu'au moment opportun"). On p. 47, note 1 he gives a full bibliography of this text:

("Ετους) λγ'. Ἐπὶ ἱερέως Παυσανία Φιλίσκω, φύσει δὲ Εὐφάνους, παυσαμένων πάντων τῆς ἀνείας, Λούκιος Ὄρβιος Λουκίου πυλοκλείστης τὸν λυσιπόλεμον.
Ἡνίκα Μαρμαρικοῦ λῆξεν πολέμοιο κυδοιμός,

γήθησεν Βάττου πολλὰ πόλις μερόπων·
3 τῆμος ἀναγλύψας κατακείμενον ἡδυπο{πο}τοῦντα
Λεύκιος εἰνοδίωι θῆκε παρὰ προθύρωι
κλεῖ[δα] πύλης διέπων, Ὧραι φίλαι, οὗ χάλις ἔσχεν
6 Παυσανίαν ἱερῆ καιρ̣ό̣[φι] παυσάμεν[ον].

6. καιρόθ̣ι παυσάμενον Oliverio; καιρ̣ῶ[ν] Robert; καιρ̣ο̣[ύς] Wilhelm ("ayant mis fin aux malheurs"); καιρὸς ὁ παυσάμενο[ς] Reynolds, who subsequently opts for οὐχ ἅλις ἔσχεν Παυσανίαν ἱερῆ; Chamoux reads on the stone καιρ̣ο̣[..] παυσάμεν̣[ον]; at any rate between ρ and π there is room for max. 3 letters.

1836. KYRENE (DEMETER SANCTUARY), EPITAPH, 1st CENT. A.D. ? Limestone base. Ed. pr. D. White, LIBANT 9-10 (1972-73) 205, note 16.

Δημητρία |² Ἀρρωνίω (ἐτῶν) ι´ | Ἀρρία τὰν |⁴ θυγατέρα.

1837. LEPTIS MAGNA, CURSE ON FOUR HORSES AND THEIR DRIVER, 4th CENT. A.D. Lead curse tablet. Ed. pr. J. Rea, LIBANT 9-10 (1972-73) 92-97 (ph.).

twelve magic symbols
στραβαυ (vac.) αλωθι ταξα (vac.)
ωννυθηρ (vac.) αχουηρ (vac.) δαξαρ αχαω
ιαωυ (vac.) α̣ωυωι (vac.) αεοιαι̣ (vac.) υο̣ι̣ιαωο̣
5 ιαυωο (vac.) Βεντίκ̣ολαν, Γαμέτην,
Βίκτο̣ρα, .οπ..λατ̣..α, καὶ
Ἠβέντ{ντ}ιν τὸν ἡνίοχον
αὐτῶν.

2-5. Twelve incantatory "words", written in Greek letters, but not intelligible as Greek Rea || 5-8. the names occuring first are those of four horses after which comes the name of their charioteer Rea || 6. Rea suggests to restore Π̣οπο̣υ̣λάτ̣ο̣ρα.

1838. PTOLEMAIS, FOUNDATION OF THE POLIS. L. Moretti, RFIC 104 (1976) 186-191 studies the foundation of Ptolemais in Kyrenaika; he holds the date of the honorary inscription for Queen Arsinoe (SEG, IX, 357; two possibilities: Arsinoe II or III) to be irrelevant for the problem of the origin of the new polis. He proceeds to collect in chronological order the epigraphical and papyrological testimonies of people named Βαρκαῖος (cf. also our no. 1720), Βαρκαιεύς, Πτολεμαιεὺς ἀπὸ Βάρκης and concludes that 267 B.C. is the terminus post quem non for the foundation of Ptolemais. So the polis was founded under Ptolemy II Philadelphos.

1839. PTOLEMAIS, LIST OF EPHEBES, 1st CENT. B.C. - EARLY 1st CENT. A.D. White marble stele; now in the museum of Tolmeita. Ed. pr. J. Reynolds - O. Masson, ZPE 20 (1976) 87-100 (ph.) (J. Reynolds is responsible for the epigraphic and historical comment, while O. Masson presents an onomastic study of the text). Cf. id., ZPE 23 (1976) 210.

("Ετους) κη' · ἐφ' ἱερέως Ἐπινίκου τοῦ Σωτέχνου, ἐφηβαρχούντων Τιμώνακτο[ς] τοῦ Νικά<ϑ>λου, Δημητρίου τοῦ Νείκωνος, Σίμου τοῦ Ξένωνος, γυμνασιαρχούντων Θεοδώρου τοῦ Ν[ι]καίου, Δεξικράτους τοῦ Πολυκλέους, Τιμούχου τοῦ Φιλοκώμου, ὑπ[η]ρετοῦντος Δημητρίου τοῦ Ζηνο̣δότου· τοὺς ὑπ' αὐτοὺς ἐφηβε̣ύσαντ[ας].

Ἀρσάκης Ἰάσονος	Ποτάμων Ποτάμωνο̣[ς]
Δημήτριος Δημητρ<ί>ου	Νίκων Θεογένου[ς̣]
Θεόδωρος Φιλοστράτου	Ἐράτων Στράτιος
Σ̣ῶσις Φίλωνος	Ἀμμώνιος Φιλάμμον[ος]
Ἀ̣νδρικὸς Ἀνδρικοῦ	Ἀμμώνιος Αλδαμωνο[ς]
Τ̣ιμόθεος Ὀνασίωνος	Θεόξενος Ἀριστάρχου̣
Τ̣ιμαίνετος Φίλωνος	Ανυσσαν Ιαλος
Λ̣έσχις Ἀμμωνίου	Αισαγυς Δαχιος
Λ̣εύκ̣ιπ<π>ος Ακέσωνος	Εὔτυχος Βρόσωνο[ς]
Ἐ̣πίν̣ικος Ἐπινίκου	Μητρόδωρος Μητρο[δώρου]
Κ̣υρηναῖος Καλλισθένο<υ>ς	Ἀγάθαρχος Δα̣[--
Ὑ̣περβάσσας Ιαλος	Νίκα<ϑ>λος Ν̣<ι>κάθλο[υ]
[Ιτθ]αλαμμων Ἀπελλᾶ	Ἀστυάναξ Ἀριστονάο[υ]
[....]πίων Αωϊνίκου	Διογένης Διο<γ>ένου[ς]
[Καρ]νεάδης Πιθάκου	Σεραπίων Σεραπίωνος
[....]νης Τίμωνος	Δαμόκριτος Δαμοκρί(του)
[---]ος Ἀντιγένο<υ>ς	Δωρ<ό>θεος Σωστράτο[υ]
[-----Θ]εοχρήστου	Ἀμμώνιος Πρατομή(δους)
[------]αντος	Κλεογένης Πισικλέο[υς]
[-------]υ̣	Ἀρίμμαν vac.
[-------]ν̣ος	Δωρίωνος
[-------]α	Σωσίστ[ρ]ατος
[-------]ιος	Ὑπερ[---
[-------]ου	

(on the base)

[..ca.11....]Ρ̣Τ̣Ρ̣Ι̣Ε̣ΔΙΚΛ̣Ι·

Date: ("Ετους) κη' = the year 28, i.e. 68/67 (reckoned from the death of the last king: 96 B.C.) or 4/3 B.C. (era of Actium) || 3. ΝΙΚΑΟΛΟΥ lapis || 5-6. in ZPE 20 Reynolds - Masson had read Νο̣|βάτου, in ZPE 23 they corrected it to read Ν[ι]|καίου || 11, A. ΔΗΜΤΡΟΥ lapis || 18, A. ΛΕΥΚΙΠΡΟΣ lapis || 20, A. ΣΘΕΝΟΣ lapis || 21, B. ΝΙΚΑΟΛΟΣ ΝΚΑΘΛΟ lapis || 23, B. ΔΙΟΕΕΝΟΥ lapis || 26, A. ΓΕΝΟΣ lapis || B. ΔΩΡΘΕΟΣ lapis || Base: Ρ̣ or Β̣, Τ̣ or Γ̣, Ρ̣Ι̣ or Π̣.

1840. RAS EL HILAL, BOUNDARY STONE FROM THE PUBLIC LAND OF THE ROMAN PEOPLE. Brown limestone stele, inscribed on three faces (= A, B and C); now in the Apollonia museum. Ed. pr. J.M. Reynolds, LIBANT 8 (1971) 49-50, no. 2.

A. Front face; the surface is almost completely lost and the only legible letter is an isolated Σ.

B. To the left of A:

... αὐ]-
[τ]οκ[ρ]άτωρ [.]
[πατ]ὴρ πατρί-
[δο]ς ὕπατος ε'
[δ]ιὰ Κ(ουΐντου) Πακωνί-
[ου] Ἀγριππείνου
vac.

C. To the right of A; two inscriptions, the lower one erased (ph.):

I. [το]ῦ ἰδίου πρ[εσ]-
vac. βευτοῦ ἀ̣[γ]-
[ρ]ῶν βασιλ[ι̇]-
κῶν v. δ(ήμῳ) Ῥ(ωμαίκων)
ἀποκ v. ατέσ̣-
v. τη v. σεν
vac.

II. ...]
ἰ̣δ̣ι̣ω̣τ[ῶ]ν̣
δήμῳ Ῥω̣-
μαίων ἀ̣π̣ο̣-
κατέστησ-
[εν].

Date: the fragmentary text on B-C belongs probably to the 1st half of A.D. 74; the erased text II on face C seems to be the remaining fragment of an otherwise erased Neronian text erected by L. Acilius Strabo Reynolds.

1841. RUUS EL ASHLAB, BOUNDARY STONE OF THE ROMAN PEOPLE IN KYRENAIKA, 74 A.D. Cippus inscribed on two faces. Ed. pr. C. Frigerio, QAL 8 (1976) 428-429 (ph.).

Face A

Imp(erator) Caisar {Ves}
Vespasianus Aug(ustus),
pont(ifex) max(imus), trib(unicia) po[t](estate)
V, imp(erator) X, p(ater) p(atriae), co(n)s(ul) V, pẹṛ

Q(uintum) Paconium Agripp[i]-
num, leg(atum) suu[m], agrum
regium [P(opulo) R(omano) resti]tuit.
Α[ὐτοκρ]άτωρ
(one line not inscribed)
Καῖσαρ Οὐεσπασια-
[ν]ός, ἀρχιερεὺς μέγισ-
[το]ς, δημαρχικῆς
[ἐξ]ουσίας ε', αὐτοκρά-
[τω]ρ ι', πατὴρ vac.

Face B

πα[τρίδος, ὕπα]-
τ[ος τὸ ε', διὰ]
Κ(οΐντου) Πακωνίου
Ἀγριππεΐνου
[ἰ]δίου πρεσβ-
ευτοῦ ἀγροὺς
βασιλικοὺς
δ(ήμῳ) Ῥ(ωμαίων) ἀποκα-
τέστησεν.

1842. RUUS EL ASHLAB, CHRISTIAN DEDICATION, NOT BEFORE THE 5th CENT. A.D. Cippus. Ed. pr. C. Frigerio, QAL 8 (1976) 428 (ph.).

N I O
Φ Ο Γ Α Τ [Ο] C +
Α Ν Ε Θ [Η] Κ Ε +
· · Ε Ι · Ε Κ Ν

1843-1853. ZAWIET MSUS, GRAFFITI (NAMES OF SOLDIERS), 1st CENT. A.D. During two visits to the Roman Fort of Zawiet Msus in Kyrenaika, J.M. Reynolds noted ca. 60 graffiti, cut by soldiers of the unit which garrisoned the Fort (cf. also SEG, XIII, 620: graffiti noted by R.G. Goodchild in 1950). In LIBANT 8 (1971) 39-42 Reynolds gives a representative selection of them (No. 1843-1846: graffiti dated by regnal years of Roman emperors; no. 1847-1850: graffiti with Libyan names; no. 1851-1853: graffiti with military terms).

1843. P. 39, no. 1; on the West wall of the Enclosure.

Γ(άϊος) Ἰούλιος Καπίτων
ὃς καὶ Ὀδύσ[σ]ευς ἧκ(ω)
στρατιώτης [..]κων
vac. (ἔτους) γι'

---

2. ἧκ(ω): "this seems a possible explanation of the abbreviation HK in ligature; it is a formula commonly used by ancient visitors

to shrines" Reynolds || 3. the last three letters may be part of another text Reynolds || 4. year 13.

1844. P. 40, no. 2; on the North wall of the Enclosure.

("Ετους) ιη' Πάχων κδ' Βιβι[.]ο[...

Year 18, month of Pachon, 24.

1845. P. 40, no. 3; on the North wall of the Enclosure.

("Ετους) ι' Ἀριστοτέλης [...

Year 10.

1846. P. 40, no. 4; on the East wall of the Enclosure.

...] (ἔτους) δι'

Year 14; the date is probably to be associated with a group of names in which the only legible items are Ἀλέξανδρος and Ἀρίμμας Reynolds.

1847. P. 40, no. 5; on the North wall of the Enclosure.

Μαλλύλας στρατιώτης

1848. P. 40, no. 6; on the North wall of the Enclosure.

Ἰτθαννύρας

1849. P. 41, no. 7; on the East wall of the Enclosure.

Ἀ̣ριπ̣αχθ[ίς] Ν[...

Cf. J. and L. Robert, BE (1976) 794, who have some doubts about this and the following number.

1850. P. 41, no. 8; on the East wall of the Enclosure; SEG, XIII, 620e (incomplete).

Δάχις Χαλδάις Ἑρμαῖος
2 [Ἀ]πολλών[ιος]

Ε[...
4 Δ̣έγμος Δέγ[μου]

Cf. no. 1849 (note).

1851. P. 41, no. 9; on the West wall of the Tower.

...] Ἰούλιος ἱππεύς το[...

1852. P. 41, no. 10; on the North wall of the Enclosure.

...] Λουκιανὸς | vac. ἱππεύς

1853. P. 41, no. 11; on a block re-used inside the Enclosure; SEG, XIII, 620b.

Ἐπίγο|νος τεσ|σεράρις

2-3. τεσ|σεράρι[ος] SEG.

UNKNOWN PROVENANCE

1854. UNKNOWN PROVENANCE, ADVERTISEMENT OF A LETTERING-MASON'S ESTABLISHMENT. M.T. Manni Piraino, IGLP, no. 139 (ph.). According to G. Alföldy, GNOMON 48 (1976) 512 this text dates from the late Republican period (and not from the 2nd cent. A.D); cf. also A.G. Woodhead, JHS 97 (1977) 232 who points out that according to M. Guarducci, EG, III, 550-551 the date is the 1st cent. A.D.

1855. UNKNOWN PROVENANCE, EPITAPH, 1st CENT. B.C - 1st CENT. A.D. Right half of a small marble grave-slab; collection F. Zucker. Ed. pr. R. Koerner, APF 24-25 (1976) 135-136.

[Χα]ίρετε
2 [Διοφαν]τὶ Φιλοκλέους
[χρησ]τ̣ὴ καὶ ἄμεμπτε
4 [καὶ ? ....]ε ἀνὴρ Διοφαντίδος

Provenance: Egypt or Sicily-Italy ? Koerner.

1856. UNKNOWN PROVENANCE, EPITAPH OF VITTILIA DOMNINA, 3rd CENT. A.D. M.T. Manni Piraino, IGLP, no. 141 (ph.). G. Alföldy, GNOMON 48 (1976) 511 suggests in L. 1 [Βι]ττειλία Δομ[νῖ]|[ν]α instead of

[᾿Α]ττειλία Δόμ|[ν]α.

1857. UNKNOWN PROVENANCE, EPITAPH, LATER ROMAN IMPERIAL PERIOD. Round marble tablet; now in the National Museum at Prague. Ed. pr. L. Vidman, ZPRÁVY JEDNOTY KLASICHÝCH FILOLOGU 18 (1976) 99-104 (ph.).

Θ(εοῖς) κ(ατα)-
χθονίοις.
Καλύκη Φιλου-
4 μενῷ χάριν μνή-
μης ἀνέθηκε
συνβίῳ Φιλου-
μεν<ῷ> συνζήσαν-
8 τι ἔτη κ'.

Provenance: Rome ? Vidman.

1858-1859. UNKNOWN PROVENANCE, TWO RINGS WITH INSCRIPTIONS, 1st CENT. B.C. - 2nd CENT. A.D. Ed. pr. M. Ruxer - J. Kubczak, ARCHPOLON 27 (1976) 114 (ph.).

1858. Εὐ|τύχι | ΑΛΑ|ΦΟΝ

1859. ᾿Επ᾿ ἀγ|<α>θῷ

ΑΓ|ΛΘΩ ring.

VARIA

1860. ACCLAMATIONS IN THEATRE AND CIRCUS. A. Cameron, *Circus Factions. Blues and Greens at Rome and Byzantium* (Oxford, 1976) 314-317 discusses various acclamations for the Βένετοι and the Πράσινοι (cf. also p. 76, 79, 147-149, 198-199, 300).

1861. ACCULTURATION: GREEKS, ROMANS AND NATIVES IN DACIA. D.M. Pippidi, Gètes, Grecs et Romains en Scythie Mineure: coexistence politique et interférences culturelles, in *Assimilation et Résistance à la Culture Gréco-Romaine dans le Monde Ancien* (Bucharest - Paris, 1976) 446-453 uses various inscriptions in his discussion of the relation between the Greco-Roman and the native world.

1862. ACTORS IN ANCIENT GREECE. See now P. Ghiron-Bistagne, *Recherches sur les acteurs dans la Grèce antique*, Paris, 1976.

1863. (STAMPED) AMPHORA-HANDLES. Y.S. Badaliantz, SA (1976, 4)

32-41 publishes (in Russian) the chronologically corresponding names of eponymous officials and manufacturers, occuring on the handles of Rhodian amphorae. He gives 163 pairs of names (of which 112 are certain, 51 very probable).

1864. ASIARCHS AND HIGH PRIESTS. Margarete Rossner, STUDCLAS 16 (1974) 101-142 studies whether the Ἀσίαρχοι and Ἀρχιερεῖς τῆς Ἀσίας are identical or not, why and when in their title temple and town are added, and why only five towns were the places of office of these dignitaries. P. 112-142: prosopography in chronological order.

1865. ASSOCIATIONS. L.C. Ruggini, La vita associativa nelle città dell' Oriente greco: tradizione locali e influenze romane, in Assimilation et Résistance à la Culture Gréco-Romaine dans le Monde Ancien (Bucharest - Paris, 1976) 462-491 uses copious epigraphic evidence concerning the many associations of craftsmen in Asia Minor.

1866. GREEK BANKS. R. Bogaert, Texts on Bankers, Bankings and Credit in the Greek World, Epigraphica III (Textus Minores, 47; Leiden, 1976) gives a representative selection of inscriptions on this subject.

1867. BENEFACTORS: THE TERM εὐεργέτης. A. Passoni Dell' Acqua, AEGYPTUS 56 (1976) 177-191, especially 177-184 discusses the evolution of the meaning of εὐεργέτης in epigraphic documents. For euergetism as a socio-political phenomenon, cf. now P. Veyne, Le Pain et le Cirque. Sociologie historique d'un pluralisme politique (Paris, 1976), especially chap. 2 (with the copious notes).

1868. BENEFACTORS IN OLYMPIA. H.W. Pleket, ZPE 20 (1976) 1-18 discusses epigraphic (PP 5, 1970, p. 76, no. 1; CIG, 3170) and literary (Fl. Jos., BJ, I, 426-427; Malalas, X, 248, 286) evidence pertaining to benefactors who assumed an honorary function at the Olympic games and paid for it; in the process he also discusses the function of the alytarches.

1869. CITIES AND COINS OF LYKAONIA. See now H. von Aulock, Münzen und Städte Lykaoniens (Istanbuler Mitteilungen, Beiheft 16; 1976).

1870. CITIES IN CILICIA TRACHEIA. R. Righini uses epigraphical, archaeological and numismatic sources in his article "Cilicia Tracheia. Aspetti di alcune citta di recente scoperta nel primo periodo della dominazione romana", RSC 24 (1976) 126-138.

1871. THE EMPRESS AND HER TITLES IN THE BYZANTINE PERIOD. Cf. E. Bensammar, La titulature de l' impératrice et sa signification. Recherches sur les sources byzantines [including epigraphic sources] de la fin du VIIIe siècle à la fin du XIIe siècle, BYZANTION 46 (1976) 243-291.

1872. EPIGRAMS AND THE PHILOSOPHY OF LIFE. N. Bruyère-Demoulin, AC 45 (1976) 446-463 deals with the topos of "La vie est une course". Within this context she discusses Peek, GV, 945 (Chios) and 1331 (Smyrna).

1873. THE FUNERARY EPIGRAM. B. Lifshitz, EUPHROSYNE 6 (1974) 34-36 discusses the thesis of A.E. Raubitschek, who recently studied the Greek archaic epigram in its relations with the monument and refered to Ilias, VII, 81-91 (A.E. Raubitschek, Das Denkmal-Epigram, in L'Épigramme grecque, Entretiens Hardt, XIV, 1967, p. 3-26). Lifshitz rejects the thesis of Raubitschek.

1874. THE EQUESTRIAN ORDER IN THE ROMAN EMPIRE. For a prosopography of the equestrian officers, see now H. Devijver, Prosopographia militiarum equestrium quae fuerunt ab Augusto ad Gallienum, I, Litterae A-I (Leuven, 1976); II, Litterae L-V (Leuven, 1977).

1875. GEOGRAPHY OF ANATOLIA. Cf. F.J. Carmody, L'Anatolie des géographes classiques, étude philologique, Berkeley, 1976.

1876. GEOGRAPHY OF EASTERN ANATOLIA. J. Wagner, Seleukeia am Euphrat / Zeugma (Beihefte zum Tübinger Atlas des vorderen Orients; Reihe B (Geisteswissenschaften) No. 10; Wiesbaden, 1976) locates Seleukeia on the Euphrates / Zeugma near Belkis (with on the opposite bank of the Euphrates Apameia). He also presents the results of the archaeological survey in the city area. For the inscriptions in this book, cf. no. 1488-1623.

1877. GOVERNORS OF THE PROVINCES IN THE AUGUSTEAN PERIOD. Cf. R. Szramkiewicz, Les gouverneurs de province à l' époque Augustéenne: contribution à l' histoire administrative et sociale du principat, 2 vol., Paris, 1975-76.

1878. THE IMPERIALISM OF THE PTOLEMIES. R.S. Bagnall, The Administration of the Ptolemaic Possessions outside Egypt (Leiden, 1976) extensively uses epigraphic evidence for this theme: see his index on p. 280-285. He discusses the following texts in some detail: SEG, I, 343 (Thera) = B., p. 124-126; SEG, I, 364 (Samos) = B., p. 83-84 and 252-253; SEG, VII, 326 (Syria) = B., p. 16, note 26; SEG, XVI, 786 (Cyprus) = B., p. 75-78 (especially on δεκατηφόρος); SEG, XVII, 639 (Pamphylia) = B., p. 111-113; SEG, XXIII, 617 (Cyprus) = B., p. 59, note 90; OGIS, 41 (Samos) = B., p. 85-87 (especially on παραβολή); IG, XII, 2, 533 (Lesbos) = B., p. 163-164 (cf. IG, XII, Suppl., p. 38); IG, XII, 3, 1291 (Thera) = B., p. 132-133.

1879. ISOPOLITEIA. See now W. Gawantka, Isopolitie. Ein Beitrag zur Geschichte der zwischenstaatlichen Beziehungen in der griechischen Antike (Vestigia, 22; München, 1975).

1880. JEWS AND ATHLETICS. See now H.A. Harris, Greek Athletics and the Jews (1976).

1881. KYRENE. Cf. S. Stucchi, Cirene e la Grecia (QAL, 8, 1976).

1882. LEGAL FORMULA. For the legal formula "καθάπερ ἐκ δίκης", cf. Festschrift M. Kaser (München, 1976) p. 629-634.

1883. MILESTONES OF THE VIA EGNATIA. Cf. P. Collart, Les milliaires de la Via Egnatia, BCH 100 (1976) 177-200. Discussion of the 16 milestones mentioning the Via Egnatia. P. 197-200 chronological inventory of these milliaria.

1884. MOSAICS AND INSCRIPTIONS. M.W. Haslam, ZPE 23 (1976) 48 draws attention to mosaics from Argos and Antiocheia on the Orontes which both show personifications of Ἀπόλαυσις (with Σωτηρία in Antiocheia): "people bathe for pleasure and for health".

1885. Q. MUCIUS SCAEVOLA: THE DATE OF HIS GOVERNORSHIP OF ASIA. B.A. Marshall, ATHENAEUM 54 (1976) 117-130 discusses the two possible dates (ca. 98 or 94 B.C.) and prefers the first one. This view affects the date of OGIS, 437 (Pergamon), OGIS, 439 (Olympia) and W.H. Buckler - D.M. Robinson, Sardis, VII, 1, nos. 91, 122 and possibly 22.

1886. NUMISMATICS. Cf. R. Bogaert, L'essai des monnaies dans l'antiquité, RBN 122 (1976) 5-34 (with epigraphic evidence).

1887. NUMISMATICS. Cf. P. Marchetti, Le cours du Cyzicène au IVe siècle, RBN 122 (1976) 35-58.

1888. ONOMASTICS. O. Masson, RPH 50 (1976) 24-31 studies, on the basis of inscriptions, two Dorian names: Ἀρίμμας ("appartenant au vieux fonds onomastique cyrénéen, qui a connu dans cette région une diffusion particulière") and Ἐχέμμας ("moins localisé et moins fréquent"), and some names in -μμας (Εὐρύμμας, Κλεόμμας, Ὑβρίμμας, Φιλόμμας, Κερδίμμας and Κερτίμμας).

1889. ONOMASTICS. O. Masson, Grecs et Libyens en Cyrénaique, d'après les témoignages de l'épigraphie, ANTAFR 10 (1976) 49-62 (cf. also his contribution under the same title to Assimilation et Résistance à la culture Gréco-Romaine dans le Monde Ancien, Bucharest - Paris, 1976, p. 377-387) describes the conflicts of the Libyan people with the Greek settlers, discusses several indigenous Libyan names, and draws up an inventory of Libyan names, mainly derived from Cyrenaic inscriptions. In GLOTTA 54 (1976) 84-98 Masson deals with the name Battos (and related words).

1890. ONOMASTICS. W. Clarysse - O. Masson, ZPE 20 (1976) 231 discuss the word χηνᾶς, a new example of a name of a profession (as it is in SB, I, 5377, against Preisigke) which can also become a surname and anthroponym (as it is in SB, III, 7365; O. Edfou, 215; L. Robert, Hellenica VI, 1948, p. 114). For a parallel of χηνᾶς as name of a profession, cf. χηνότροφος (SB, I, 5380) and χηνότροπος (CIG, III, 4866, against Pape - Benseler).

1891. ONOMASTICS. E. Marinoni, ACME 29 (1976) 214, note 118 suggests that the name Φαναγόρης in CIRB, no. 971 (4th cent. B.C.) is evidence for genealogical continuity between the founder of Phanagoria and the 4th cent. B.C. descendant.

1892. ONOMASTICS. O. Masson, ZPE 23 (1976) 263 suggests that the names Χωτάριον (cf. no. 1326), Χῆμα (SEG, XXIV, 704) and Χηματῖνος (IOSPE, I^2, 359) are a "prononciation vulgaire, avec simplification du groupe consonantique initial" of Χρωτάριον, Χρῆμα and Χρηματῖνος.

1893. ONOMASTICS. O. Masson, ZPE 20 (1976) 232 adds some notes to his study of the names Aristis and Elpis (cf. ZPE 14, 1974, p. 179-183 and ZPE 16, 1975, p. 36): next to the masculine name Ἄριστις, also a feminine form Ἀρίστις is attested, and next to the feminine Ἐλπίς, there are also traces of a masculine Ἔλπις (but the reference of Foraboschi, Onomasticon, to SB, III, 6178, 6 is wrong).

1894. ONOMASTICS. O. Masson, ZPE 21 (1976) 157-158 studies the name Μαχάτας: he rejects two supposed variants (in Pape - Benseler) of the name: Μαχαίτας (Plutarch) and Μαχετᾶς, misprint for Μαχατᾶς (Polybios). He also remarks that the nominative of the non-Greek patronymic Σαβατταρα of Machatas in Syll^3, 269, 1 is Σαβατταρας

1895. ONOMASTICS AND THE JEWS. N.G. Cohen, JSJ 7 (1976) 97-128 tries "to show that in Antiquity at least, the vogue for certain Jewish names ... not only reflects a Jewish identification on the part of the name-giver, but provides an indication of the specific non-Jewish cultural milieu to which the name-giver wished to belong". He deals with three names: Abraham, Reuben and Shimeʻon. Frequent use of epigraphic sources. Cf. also no. 1377.

1896. ONOMASTICS: THE SECOND NAME IN GREEK ONOMASTICS. R. Merkelbach, ZPE 22 (1976) 200-202 defends the view, supported by Klaffenbach (Gr. Epigraphik, p. 55) that the registration of a second name in Greek inscriptions took place under the influence of the Roman name-system (contra J. and L. Robert, BE, 1958, no. 16 on p. 179). However, in our view one should make a list of relevant cases, arranged chronologically and geographically, before one can attribute this phenomenon to Roman influence. Cf. C.P. Jones, AJPH 99 (1978) 339, note 7.

1897. PHILOLOGY. A. Morpurgo-Davis, The -εσσι datives, Aeolic -SS-, and the Lesbian poets, Studies L.R. Palmer, p. 181-187 discusses copious epigraphic evidence for the grammatical phenomenon indicated in the title.

1898. PHILOLOGY: DEVELOPMENT OF VOWEL SYSTEM. R. Gusmani, Zum Alter des ionischen Wandels α > η, Studies L.R. Palmer, p. 77-82 refers on p. 80 to the epigraphic evidence for this phenomenon in 7th cent. B.C. archaic inscriptions.

1899. PHILOLOGY: PROBLEMS OF VOCABULARY. J. Dennis Ellsworth, TAPHA 106 (1976) 101-111 examines the words ἀγώνιος, ἀγώναρχος and ἀγωνιστήριον and attempts to prove that they do not contain an archaic meaning of ἀγών: "assembly". In his discussion of the word ἀγώναρχος in the Boiotian dialect, Ellsworth uses two inscriptions from Thespiai (IG, VII, 1817 - cf. SEG, XXIII, 275 - and SEG, XXIII, 271) and demonstrates that an ἀγώναρχος cannot be equated with an ἀγορανόμος (cf. Schol. T (Eust.) on Hom., Il., 24, 1) but was an officer concerned with sports and contents.

1900. PROXENOI. Cf. no. 622.

1901. RELIGION AND DELPHI. Cf. G. Roux, Delphes, son oracle et ses dieux, Paris, 1976.

1902. RELIGION: RELIEFS AND INSCRIPTIONS DEDICATED BY DREAMERS. F.T. van Straten, BVAB 51 (1976) 1-38 discusses various inscriptions and reliefs pertaining to people who dedicated something to a deity on the basis of a dream. On p. 12-14, 21-27 he discusses and lists epigraphic terminology relating to dreams (κατ' ὄναρ etc.) and to the behaviour of the Gods.

1903. RELIGION: DIVINE EPITHETS. In a discussion about the relation between poetic language and cult terminology A. Henrichs, HSPH 80 (1976) 253-286 studies various divine epithets (δέσποινα / δεσπότης; κύριος / κυρία; πότνια; ἄναξ / ἄνασσα) and a series of deities bearing these epithets, on the basis of copious epigraphic evidence from various parts of the Greco-Roman world.

1904. RELIGION: DINING-ROOMS IN GREEK SANCTUARIES. For Thasos, cf. no. 1028 above. More in general one should consult E. Will, Banquets et Salles de Banquet dans les cultes de la Grèce et de l'Empire romain, Mélanges Collart, p. 353-362.

1905. RELIGION: THE CULT OF MEN. Cf. E.N. Lane, Corpus monumentorum religionis Dei Menis (Études prél. aux rel. orientales dans l'emp. romain, 19) 4 vol., Leiden, 1971-78.

1906. RELIGION: CULTS IN PALESTINIAN SKYTHOPOLIS. A. Ovadiah, (Greek cults in Beth-Shean / Skythopolis in the Hellenistic and Roman periods, in Hebrew) ERETZ-ISRAEL 12 (1975) 116-124 seeks, mainly on the basis of inscriptions, to determine which Greek cults were common at Skythopolis in the Hellenistic and Roman periods. Six Greek inscriptions (SEG, VIII, 32,33 and 34; ZPALV 77, 1961, p. 186 and 189; ZPE 6, 1970, p. 62) were found to reflect typical Greek cults of several deities in various periods. In these texts the cults of Zeus Olympios, Zeus Akraios, Zeus Bakchos, the Dioskouroi,

Demeter, Ares Hoplophoros and Dionysos are attested.

1907. RELIGION: THE CULT OF ROMA. After R. Mellor, ΘΕΑ ΡΩΜΗ. The Worship of the Goddess Roma in the Greek World (Hypomnemata, 42; Göttingen, 1975), C. Feyer, Il culto della dea Roma. Origine e diffusione nell' Imperio, Chieti, 1976 deals with the same subject (non vidimus).

1908. RELIGION: ORIENTAL CULTS IN DACIA. Cf. I. Berciu and C.C. Petolescu, Les cultes orientaux dans la Dacie méridionale (Études prél. aux rel. orientales dans l' emp. romain, 54) Leiden, 1976.

1909. RELIGION: ORIENTAL DIVINITIES ON THE NORTH SHORE OF THE BLACK SEA. Cf. M.M. Kobylina, Divinités orientales sur le littoral nord de la Mer Noire (Études prél. aux rel. orientales dans l' emp. romain, 52) Leiden, 1976.

1910. RELIGION: THE CULT OF THE DANUBIAN RIDER-GODS. Cf. D. Tudor, Corpus monumentorum religionis equitum danuvinorum (Études prél. aux rel. orientales dans l'emp. romain, 13) Leiden, 1976.

1911. RELIGION: SYMBOLS ON CHRISTIAN INSCRIPTIONS. On the significance of the hammer and other tools depicted on Christian funeral inscriptions, cf. I. Kajanto, ARCTOS 10 (1976) 49-58.

1912. ROMAN ROADS. E. Dabrowa, ÉTUDES ET TRAVAUX (Centre d' archéologie méditerranéenne de l'académie Polonaise des sciences) 9 (1976) 130-141 studies, on the basis of various mile-stones, the development of the Roman road system in Asia Minor.

1913. SENATORIAL CAREERS. I. Piso, REVUE ROUMAINE D'HISTOIRE 15 (1976) 465-481 studies, with the help of Greek and Latin inscriptions, the careers of C. Arrius Antoninus (p. 465-478), and Pollienus Auspex Senior and Iunior (p. 478-481; Piso defends the theory that is was Pollienus Auspex Senior who was governor of Moesia Inferior between 194-196 A.D., and not Pollienus Auspex Iunior).

1914. SLAVES AND FREEDMEN OF THE EMPEROR. P.R.C. Weaver, EPIGRAFISCHE STUDIEN 11 (1976) 215-227 gives corrections and additions to the list of dated inscriptions and papyri relevant to imperial freedmen and slaves, composed by H. Chantraine, Freigelassene und Sklaven im Dienst der römischen Kaiser, Wiesbaden, 1967, p. 56 ff.

1915. SYNOIKISMOS. Cf. M. Moggi, I Sinecismi Interstatali Greci. Introduzione, edizione critica, traduzione, commento e indici, vol. I. Dalle Origini al 338 a.C. (Pisa, 1976).

1916. TABELLAE DEFIXIONUM. D.R. Jordan, PHILOLOGUS 120 (1976) 127-132 discusses several Latin and Greek curse tablets in which the accursed and the curser are identified by their maternal lineage, and reckons with the possibility of influence from the East.

INDICES

I. NAMES OF MEN AND WOMEN

PATRONYMIC ADJECTIVES

LATIN NAMES

II. KINGS, DYNASTS AND THEIR FAMILIES

III. ROMAN EMPERORS AND THEIR FAMILIES

IV. A. GEOGRAPHICAL NAMES (EXCEPT ATTICA)

IV. B. ATTIC TRIBES, DEMES ETC.

IV. C. TRIBES, DEMES OUTSIDE ATTICA

IV. D. LATIN GEOGRAPHICAL NAMES

V. RELIGIOUS TERMS

VI. MILITARY (AND PARA-MILITARY) TERMS

A. GREEK WORLD

B. ROMAN WORLD

VII. IMPORTANT GREEK WORDS

VIII. SELECTED TOPICS

CONCORDANCE

IG I^2	SEG XXVI
1	39
4	1
6	2
10/13	3
14/15	9
18	4
19/20	8
22	5
39	10
47	26
50	11
51/52	12
53	25
54	15
57	17
66	7
71	14
77	15
84	20
85	19
87	18
91/92	16
101	22
113	23
122	21
146	24
156	21
160	15
192	28
205	29
304	30
324	31
325-334	32
354-362	33
370/1	20:34
379	20
392	37
394	38
410	40
461	39
463	35
465	36
475	35
476	36
484	42
672	41
673	43
730	69
770	45
771	44
830	49
850	43
919	60
997	54

IG I^3	SEG XXVI
4	1
6	2
11/12	8
14/15	3
21	5
32	6
34	7
37	9
38	4
40	10
48	11
49	15
52	16
53/54	12
58	15
61	17
67	25
75	18
82	20
89	14
90	13
96	22
113	23
123	26
130	15
131	15
158	15
165	19
181	24
182	21
225	28
236	27
369	31
375	30
377	30
472	20:34

IG II	SEG XXVI
3851	238
3871	235
3899	212

IG II^2	SEG XXVI
11	71
33	70
141	73
212	74
244	142
339	75
348	76
350	85
358	87
360	79
367	81
380	84
392	83
416	78
429	77
448	82
490	90
558	89
561	86
586	83
598	91
734	90
773	88
791	94
845	99:100
848	95
850	102
851	96:97
889	108
904	108
921	113
933	112
973	99:100
977	113
999	135
1003	116
1009	124
1027	111
1035	121
1055	118
1069	121
1077	123
1097	125
1108	127
1109	128
1132	92
1186	132
1202	133
1252	135
1358	138
1363	138
1582	296
1631	141
1666	142
1670	142
1685A	142
1706	143
1713	144
1714	144
1723	121:166
1763	153
1767	145
1792	154:246
1797	146
1803	158
1804	156
1820	159
1825	160
1924	165

1990	166
2037	167
2039	185
2045	175
2050	169
2052	172
2059	170
2069	175
2076	185
2078	168
2081	181
2086	174
2091/2	198
2093	175
2099	173
2100	173
2101	177
2102	176
2105	177
2107	177
2108	191
2110	178
2113	174
2121	173
2133	178
2134	176
2138	175
2139	185
2140	185
2141	185
2145	187
2148	177
2149	187
2151	185
2152	171
2154	173
2157	173
2161	193
2162	175
2164	177
2166	175
2171	175
2174	177
2193	246
2198	185:189
2200	187
2202	181
2203	180
2206	187
2208	182
2210	187
2212	176
2218	186:196
2219	186:196
2226	184
2228	187
2229	183
2230	192
2231	193
2232	188
2233	190
2235	194
2236	190
2242	195
2243	186:193
2249	187
2251	193
2253	184
2254	181
2255	178
2256	183
2259	190
2260	186
2263	197
2267	170
2276	177
2291	179
2311	200
2318	202
2319	203
2320	204
2323	205
2323A	206
2325	207
2409	165
2418	211
2419	209
2472	149
2479	184
2486	195
2487	193
2771	128
2907/8	269
3029	216
3038	214
3067	219
3070	217
3073	222
3075	210
3077	222
3081	223
3082	223
3091	226
3111	210
3194	231
3395	171
3405	265
3412	128
3571	236
3614	237
3662	240
3663	239
3673	232
3709	241
3734	243
3749	244
3760	244
3765	248
3767	249
3781	250
3801	251
3802	252
3968	254
3969	255
3970	254
3971	254
3972	254
3973	254
3974	254
3975	254
3998	256
4200	260
4201	260
4216	258
4256	199:263
4774	254
4843	271
5167	272
5204	273
5212	265
5236	276
5240	276
5633	278
5746	282
5789	283
5935	284
6133	285
6626	287
6768	291
6994	294
7239	298
7341	299
7344	301
7711	296
7942	314
7945	315
9112	325
9233	329
9717	332
10051	336
10385	337
10490	338
10574	339
10575	339
10807	331
11103	346
11205	355
11249	357
11283	314
11407/8	360
11551	362
11557	375
11697	365
12159	369
12162	369
12754	315
13194	254
IG IV	SEG XXVI
204/5	411
348	398

IG IV^2.1	SEG XXVI
5-24	452
94	427:447
95	427:447
255	450
742	451

IG V.1	SEG XXVI
213	463
298	465
515	454
1235	467
1390	469

IG V.2	SEG XXVI
75	472
343	471

IG VII	SEG XXVI
323	603
359	605
360	606
361	607
367	604
370	601
371	601
389	604
390	601
441	609
1714	611
1773	616
1817	1899
2808	527
2809	501
2810	502
2811	503
2812	504
2813	505
2814	506
2815	507
2816	508
2817	509
2818	510
2819	511
2820	512
2821	513
2822	514
2823	515
2824	516
2825	517
2826	518
2827	519
2828	520
2830	521
2831	522
2832	523
2833	526
2834	526
2835	530
2837	549
2838	549
2839	549
2841	549
2842	549
2844	549
2845	533
2846	532
2873	568
2917	568
3003	568
3183	579
3184	580
3185	581
3286	599
3372	493
3515	615
4165	549
4166	549
4167	549
4168	549
4169	549
4170	549
4171	549

IG IX.1	SEG XXVI
163	636
292	549
334	639
658	642

IG IX.1^2	SEG XXVI
717	640

IG IX.2	SEG XXVI
251	643
255	643
270	643
420	643
427	643
729	678
731	681
1014	674
1209	643
1252	682
1290	689
1296	644

IG X.2.1	SEG XXVI
1	733-770
2	733-770
11	733-770
14	733-770
16	733-770
23	776
32	733
37	734
41	733-770
42	733-770
43	733-770
44	780:823
46	733-770
55	733-770
59	733-770: 735
60	733-770
61	733-770
63	733-770
64	736
65	733-770
66	733-770
67	733-770
68	733-770
72	733-770
100	733-770
107	733-770
108	733-770
109	733-770
126	733-770
132	737
133	733-770: 738
137	733-770
138	733-770
140	733-770: 775
150	733-770
151	733-770
152	733-770
160	739
173	733-770
176	733-770
180	733-770
181	733-770
191	740
200	733-770
207	733-770
209	733-770: 741
217	733-770
243	733-770
245	742
255	733-770
256	733-770
259	733-770
260	733-770
267	733-770
269	733-770
271	733-770
280	733-770
284	733-770
291	733-770
296	733-770

300	743
351	733-770
357	733-770
368	733-770: 777
384	733-770
390	733-770
418	733-770
429	733-770
443	733-770
451	733-770
463	733-770
467	733-770
486	733-770
490	733-770
494	733-770: 744
500	745
515	733-770
516	733-770
523	746
539	733-770
557	747
564	733-770
565	733-770: 748
572	733-770: 749
573	733-770
582	750
583	751
607	733-770
608	733-770
618	733-770: 752
623	733-770
628	753
640	733-770
666	733-770
686	733-770: 754
691	733-770
692	755
700	756
710	757
711	733-770: 758
712	733-770
732	733-770
745	759
746	760
763	761
768	733-770
771	762
772	763
774	733-770
789	733-770
796	733-770
804	778
819	764
822	733-770
824	765
838	766
839	733-770
842	733-770
856	733-770: 767
857	733-770
858	733-770
859	768
864	733-770
865	733-770
866	733-770
896	733-770
901	733-770
911	733-770
920	733-770
926	733-770
930	733-770
996	733-770
1008	733-770
1009	774
1010	733-770
1018	771-773
1021	769
1040	733-770

IG XI.2	SEG XXVI
144	857

IG XII.1	SEG XXVI
709	867
719	870
737	865
779-783	872

IG XII.2	SEG XXVI
1	873
4	874
5	875
6	876
7	877
14	878
18	879
19	880
26	881
30	882
34	883
37	884
68	885
74	886
81	887
86	888
88	889
106	890
108	891
109	891
143	892
183	893
210	894
243	895
257	896
273	897
294	898
297	899
335	900
338	901
357	902
449	903
451	903
465	904
503	905
504	906
528	907
533	1878
534	908

S.Charitonidis. Symplērōma	SEG XXVI
2	921
3	922
4	923
6	924
13	925
14	926
15	927
19	928
22	929
30	930
84	931
101	932
104	933
111	934
118	935
119	936
122	937
125	938
133	939
134	940

IG XII.3	SEG XXVI
522	943-944
545	946
1291	1878

IG XII.5	SEG XXVI
305	1003
306C	1002
679	1017

IG XII.8	SEG XXVI
51	1024
156	1027

IG XII.9	SEG XXVI
7	1041
273	1036
406	1037
715	1038

IG XII Suppl.	SEG XXVI
2	909
p.38	1878
50	910
63	911
66	912
72	913
105	914
109	915
114	916
115	917
125	918
127	919
693	920

IG XIV	SEG XXVI
1	1118
28	1053
38	1053
279	1079
315	1053
485	1053
492	1053
535	1121
581	1053
582	1053
590	1088
727	1142
885	1136
2320	1124

SEG I	SEG XXVI
69	426
143	1671
343	1878
364	1878

SEG II	SEG XXVI
358	643
579	1305
628	1309

SEG III	SEG XXVI
17	16
51	60
226	125
369	569
371	581
372	582
373	578
378	1227
421	525

SEG IV	SEG XXVI
65	1091
104	1145
442	1234

SEG VI	SEG XXVI
210	1377
775	1439

SEG VII	SEG XXVI
326	1878

SEG VIII	SEG XXVI
32	1906
33	1906
44	1906
143	1671
864	1716

SEG IX	SEG XXVI
63	1835
77	1831
81	1832
357	1838

SEG X	SEG XXVI
5	1
6	2
7	8
8	4
11	11
13	20
14	5
15	4
17	9
25	6
31	7
36	10
39	11
45	16
46	25
48	12
53	15
60	15
66	17
79	21
80	18
86	14
87	6:13
113	22
127	23
131	21
136	26
142	27
147	28
160	29
227	31
234	30
237-242	32
257-263	33
267	34
309	40
316	39
321	46
323	44
329	50
399	60

SEG XI	SEG XXVI
52	411
188	402
316	424
410/1	447
433	450
650	463
652	464
978	469
1065	472
1101	471
1217	477
1226	478

SEG XII	SEG XXVI
6	8
8	3
12	6
13	7
16	14
18	16
20	12
36	24
38	23
44	31
54	186
67	60
85	73
105	160
113	175
120	177
122	175
124	193
125	175
128	175
133	193
134	191

138	183
314	726
406	1118
485-488	1393
490-492	1393
494-497	1393

SEG XIII	SEG XXVI
5	16
9	25
12-22	32
36	57
37	48
40	79
56	207
107	365
128	301
182	171
394	676
395	675
521	1339
620	1843-1853

SEG XIV	SEG XXVI
1	8
2	4
4	5
5	16
8	18
9	22
10	26
34	70
73	119
78	121
82	135
87	143
90	166
95	160
303	399
307	402
330	463
353	477
384	696
599	1101
604	1144

SEG XV	SEG XXVI
2	2
4	6
5	7
29	32
32	38
76	57
87	70
104	114
200	424
216	463
228	472

353	639
411	719
652	1230

SEG XVI	SEG XXVI
4	14
7	25
12	31
13	32
18	49
29	57
38	63
54	75
71	99
81	107
98	111
136	165
140	80
141	205
145	165
201	298
298	600
336	641
380	643
384	706
385	707
518	1024
727	1293
786	1878
850	1672

SEG XVII	SEG XXVI
2	2
8	34
9	35:36:37
22	74
32	111
41	142
137	399
203	479
287	684
639	1878
642-646	1393
651-658	1393
785	1673
794	1832
810	1835

SEG XVIII	SEG XXVI
3	6
7	32
59	179
65	180
71	231
141	408
153	444
491	1295

495	1296
587	1484
636	1713
750	1829

SEG XIX	SEG XXVI
4	5
8	7
11	14
23-25	32
102	112
127	138
156	155
163	191
167	80
168	202
169	203
170	207
319	444
476	833
621	1144
787	1391
794	1390

SEG XX	SEG XXVI
417	1667
650	1754
787	726

SEG XXI	SEG XXVI
2	1
5	2
7	4
8	3
10	8
17	5
18	6
21	7
22	9
24	10
28	11
30	14
35	12
37	15
40	17
44	18
45	13
56	26
75	31
79	30
82	33
137	54
166	57
168	113
277	75
282	76
295	81
297	82

307	84
317	82
320	85
326	87
370	93
402	95
422	105
441	109
457	111
469	224
470	114
473	116
508	126
509	127
541	138
542	138
608	154
615	150
622	174
629	80
674	213
694	224
703	230
747	259
847	284

SEG XXII	SEG XXVI
2	1
3	8
5	6
6	10
7	16
10	13
18	49
47	31
49	30
50	34
54	38
68	55
76	57
77	58
83	60
92	74
95	82
98	85
102	106
108	114
109	101
131	138
132	138
140	150
142	80
143	206
144	205
229	399
231	392
264	424
274	444

284	450
319	471
434-439	548
437	547

SEG XXIII	SEG XXVI
4	4
7	5
8	6
9	7
10	9
12	10
15	16
20	21
27	32
33	31
36	30
37	33
54	76
59	82
68	106:108: 109
78	131
80	138
84	143
102	225
103	215
114	230
120	262
116	257
189	427
191	444
271	1899
275	1899
410	643
433	643
434	643
453	643
462	670
471	697
478	720
479	721
617	1878

SEG XXIV	SEG XXVI
2	6
3	16
42	31
43	30
46	32
48-53	33
59	36
66	44
71	60
72	380
101	79
144	123

183	152
191	169
192	80
269	399
276	444
280	450
393	640
412	694
446	697
704	1892
1065	839

SEG XXV	SEG XXVI
2	1
3	8
13	9
18	14
21	16
22	12
27	17
33	13
35	20
46	31
48	32
49	34
95	93
113	106
115	105
127	138
130	114
163	138
165	138
168	138
189	101
194	205
324	408
339	400
360	424
376	444
415	450
434	469
448	470
480	488
503	611
653	688
664	623:624: 686
667	643
668	643
711	727

CIG	SEG XXVI
1585	616
1755	549
2025	827
2221	1021
2462	943-944
2463	943-944

3170	1299:1868
3173	1288
3179	1297
3427	1312
3627	1331
3628	1332
3769	1347
4866	1890
5875d	1136
9770	1156

Syll.^{3}	SEG XXVI
22	1291
38	1304
218	848
269	1894
283	1019
502	1027
548	622
684	481
763	1337
1000	951
1112	527

OGIS	SEG XXVI
14	1142
41	1878
56	1762
69	1800
90	1762
237	1226
253	1624
403	1490
435	1340
437	1885
439	1885
483	1339
484	1342
572	1435
707	1712
773	955

GIBM	SEG XXVI
442	1226
486	1248
618	1261
1057	1826-1827
1058	1826-1827

SGDI	SEG XXVI
1338	702
1339	703
1348	708
1352	709
1354	710
1358	711
1359	705
1360	712
1361	713
1362	705
1365	715
2961	627

Agora XV	SEG XXVI
129	95
163	105
173	107
207	105
232	113
246	113
249	115
250	116
259	101
329	153
340	145
372	151
374	151
375	152
410	146
414	157
423	154
440	159
442	148
444	156
455	150
447/8	158
449	158
460	123
476	160
481	155

Raubitschek, DAA	SEG XXVI
168	38
173	38
310	42
323	43
326	35
327	36
328	37
376	41

Inschr.v. Ol.	SEG XXVI
243	479
271	478
717	477

Corinth 8.1	SEG XXVI
1	393
14	394

Corinth 8.3	SEG XXVI
42	402
109	395
199/201	410
306	410
486	396
508	411

F.de Delphes	SEG XXVI
III.1	
396	619
426	619
444	619
497	619
547	619
576	626
III.2	
68	92
III.3	
215	621
III.4	
37	1227
277	628
287	629
288	630
298	631
302	620:632
303	633
304	634
350	635

IGBR	SEG XXVI
II 695	828
IV 1902	829
2257	818
2289	820

IOSPE I^2	SEG XXVI
359	1892

CIRB	SEG XXVI
838	846
971	1891

Inscr. Délos	SEG XXVI
104	855:856
313	858
1408	854
1416	854
1419	854
1497	854
1510	854
2420	859

2535-2539	853
2542	853
2543	853
2545	853
2691	853
2852	853

Blinkenberg, Lindos II	SEG XXVI
430	872
498	872

Inscr.Cret. I	SEG XXVI
5,no 25	1043
7,no 24	1045

IGUR	SEG XXVI
I 132	1147
134	1147
135	1147
160	1147
177	1150
205	1147
223	1146
229	1146
II.1	
686	1311
II.2	
803	1154

TAM IV.1	SEG XXVI
92	1347
132	1349
303	1348

MAMA III	SEG XXVI
63-65	1452-1455
67	1455
68	1451
MAMA VI	
61	1233

IGR I	SEG XXVI
623	838
797	825
1037	1826-1827
1285	1799
IGR III	
55	1350
58	1350
63	1350
69	1350
1103	1712
1204	1688
1420	1350
IGR IV	
707	1385
1359	1311
1436	1299
586	1352

Inschr. Didyma	SEG XXVI
480	1234

Buckler-Robinson, Sardis,vol. VII	SEG XXVI
22	1885
91	1885
122	1885

Studia Pontica	SEG XXVI
III 207a	1287

IGLS I	SEG XXVI
84	1607
94-105	1610
106	1611
107	1612
108	1510
109	1530
110	1585
111	1545
112	1596
113	1560
114	1573
125	1582

Sammel-buch	SEG XXVI
676	1799
3896	1807
3897	1806
4528	1714
5121a-b	1707
5377	1890
5380	1890
6116	1803
6697	1706
7190	1716
7365	1890

E.Bernand, Fayoum,I	SEG XXVI
2	1725
3	1726
6	1727
7	1802
9	1728
10	1729
14	1730
15	1731
18	1732
35	1733
39	1734
42	1735
44	1736
45	1736
50	1737
51	1738
54	1739
55	1740
56	1740
57	1740
58	1741
59	1742
60	1743
61	1744
66	1745
67	1746
69	1747
71	1748
72	1749
73	1750
76	1751
78	1752
79	1753
85	1754
86	1755
91	1756
92	1757
95	1758
97	1759
99	1760

A.Bernand, Paneion	SEG XXVI
general	1704
Delta	
general	1704
Koptos-Kosseir	
general	1704
Inscr.de Philae	
I 64	1803
II 128	1804

J.-B.Frey, CIJud.	SEG XXVI
12	1203
16	1204
25	1205
44	1206
66	1182
97	1197

916	1670
929	1671

ICUR	SEG XXVI
I 3122	1153
V 12901	1151

Jeffery, LSAG	SEG XXVI
p. 97,no 2	684
p. 125,no 3	1122
p. 265,no 3	1118
p. 269,no 21	1065
p. 270,no 25	1101
no 26	1088
no 27	1092
no 28	1091
no 29	1089
no 31	1107
p. 274,no 58	1056
no 63	1057
p. 278,no 49	1063

p. 347,no 1	863
p. 348,no 5	865
p. 349,no 9	866
no 13	869
no 15	867
p. 350,no 30	864
p. 375,no 17	641

Peek, GV	SEG XXVI
77	643
102	642
168	643
176	643
418	643
553	1017
651	832
942	643
945	1872
1020	827
1156	1003
1230	643
1252	643

1269	1285
1331	1872
1351	1002
1501	617
1502	636
1512	1300

CIL	SEG XXVI
III	
471	1297
472	1297
13811	832
14147	1804
IV,Suppl.3, fasc. 4	
10529	1138
VI,pars 4,fasc.2	
33680	1154

ILS	SEG XXVI
8846	1712